Readings in Canadian History
Post-Confederation

Readings in Canadian History
Post-Confederation

R. Douglas Francis
Donald B. Smith

Holt, Rinehart and Winston of Canada, Limited

Canadian Cataloguing in Publication Data

Main entry under title:
Readings in Canadian history

Contents: [v. 1] Pre-Confederation – [v. 2]
Post-Confederation
ISBN 0-03-921106-1 (v. 1). – ISBN 0-03-921107-X (v. 2)

1. Canada - History - Addresses, essays, lectures.
I. Francis, R. D. (R. Douglas), 1944-
II. Smith, Donald B., 1946-

FC164.R42   971   C82-094012-7
F1026.R42

Acquisitions Editor: Beth Burgess
Production Editor: Elizabeth Reid
Cover Design: Cliff Smith
Interior Design: Dreadnaught
Typesetting and Assembly: Compeer Typographic Services Limited

Printed in the United States of America

2 3 4 5 86 85 84

Contents

Preface

This reader has been prepared for use in tutorials for introductory courses in Canadian history. It follows the same format as most universities, which divide survey courses into "pre" and "post" Confederation sections. Our objectives in each volume have been first to select topics relating to the major issues that are dealt with in most such courses, and then to choose readings of a general nature that will be useful to students beginning a study of Canadian history. We have been conscious of the need to include material that deals with the various regions of the country. In addition we have included, wherever possible, readings that reflect new research interests among Canadian historians.

Each volume includes two or three selections on each of fifteen topics; this gives instructors flexibility in choosing readings. Short introductions to each topic set the readings in an historical context and offer suggestions for further readings. It is our hope that this reader will contribute to increased discussion in tutorials as well as complement course lectures and, where applicable, textbooks.

In preparing the reader, we and the publisher have both sought advice from a number of Canadian historians. Their comments have been generously given and have greatly improved the original outline. In particular we wish to thank Douglas Baldwin of the University of Prince Edward Island, who offered numerous helpful suggestions leading to our final selection of topics and readings, and Neil Semple, who provided many useful comments. We also wish to thank Joe McKeon, Beth O'Shaughnessy, and Val Daigen of Holt, Rinehart and Winston for their initial acceptance of the proposal and their constant encouragement in the course of its development. Finally our thanks go to those Canadian historians who consented to let their writings be included in this reader. Their ideas and viewpoints will greatly enrich the study and appreciation of Canadian history among first- and second-year university students.

Douglas Francis
Donald Smith
Department of History
University of Calgary

Topic One
Consolidation of Confederation

The new nation of Canada had just come into existence when it faced some critical challenges. Nova Scotia, one of the original partners, protested what it claimed was its inequitable position in Confederation, while the colony of British Columbia debated whether it wanted to join.

Nova Scotians had consistently opposed Confederation and had been brought into the union largely through the efforts of the premier, Charles Tupper, who refused even to put the question of joining to a vote in the Legislature. They revealed the extent of their dissatisfaction at their first opportunity in the federal and provincial elections of September 1867. Eighteen of the nineteen seats for the federal Parliament went to the separatists, with only Tupper retaining his seat for the pro-Confederationists. Provincially Tupper's Conservative Party was almost eliminated, retaining only two of the thirty-eight seats. Underlying this political protest was an annexation movement to join the United States as an alternative to Confederation and as an expression of dissatisfaction with Britain for encouraging Nova Scotia to join the Canadian union. Donald Warner in "The Post-Confederation Annexation Movement in Nova Scotia" explains the reasons behind this dissatisfaction and shows the continuity between the pre- and post-Confederation protest movements. He reveals the deep divisions within the annexation movement both in personalities and principles and analyses the movement along geographical and class lines.

The motto of the new nation was "from sea to sea." To fulfill this dream required bringing British Columbia into Confederation. There was no assurance that British Columbia, an isolated colony on the Pacific Ocean separated from Canada by the vast unsettled territory of the North-West, would join as the sixth province. In fact, as Walter Sage notes, it was "more British and American in outlook than it was Canadian." Yet, despite these odds, British Columbia joined Confederation on 20 July 1871. Walter Sage explains how this change came about in "British Columbia becomes Canadian (1871–1901)."

Students wishing to pursue the topic of Nova Scotian protest further will find useful Colin D. Howell's "Nova Scotia's Protest Tradition and the Search for a Meaningful Federalism" in *Canada and the Burden of Unity*, edited by D. Bercuson (Toronto: Macmillan, 1977), pp. 169–191. Howell sets this early post-Confederation protest movement in the context of later protest movements in the province. R. H. Campbell's "The Repeal Agitation in Nova Scotia, 1867–1869," Nova Scotia Historical Society, *Collections*, XXV (1942), pp. 95–130 is also helpful.

A useful contrast to Sage's interpretation of the British Columbia question is Margaret Ormsby's "Canada and the New British Columbia," Canadian Historical Association *Report* (1948): 74–85. See also her book, *British Columbia: A History* (Toronto: Macmillan, 1958). *British Columbia and Confederation*, edited by W. George Shelton (Victoria: University of Victoria Press, 1967), is a valuable collection of essays.

2

The Post-Confederation Annexation Movement in Nova Scotia*

DONALD F. WARNER

The story of the anti-Confederation movement in Nova Scotia and of Joseph Howe's part in it is an oft-told tale. Historians and biographers have related how this agitation was launched and how it rode out gales of denunciation only to founder on the rocks of adamant imperial opposition after the desertion of its captain, Howe. Thus the major outline of this story is well known. One aspect, however, has received too little attention — the lively annexation movement which grew out of the agitation against Confederation. Some writers gingerly skirt this bog of treason barely acknowledging its existence. A few discuss it but seem by brevity, to dismiss it as unimportant; they leave the impression that it was nothing more than an attempt on the part of a few desperate Nova Scotians to frighten the imperial government into permitting their province to secede from the Canadian Dominion as the price for keeping it in the British Empire. It is the purpose of this article to remedy the neglect by analysing this annexation movement, showing its causes and course, and demonstrating that, for a time, it did achieve some strength. To prove the sincerity of the annexationists is, of course, very difficult, involving as it does the nearly impossible problem of the exact analysis of human motives. It is probably true that most of the annexationists were "running a bluff." Yet contemporary evidence indicates that many of them, with their loyalty to the British Empire temporarily gone, viewed the question of joining the

*From *Canadian Historical Review*, XXVIII (1947): 156–165. Reprinted by permission of University of Toronto Press.

United States as a business proposition and were honestly convinced that they would gain materially from such a move. Certainly the alarm which this movement caused to the loyal elements in the province could not have been produced by an agitation which was entirely insincere.

Since the annexation movement had its origin in the agitation against Confederation, it is necessary, first, to glance at the latter. By 1864–5, the plan to unite British North America in a federation had aroused the opposition of the people of the Maritime colonies for several reasons. They realized that they would be a minority in the proposed union and that their interests might be subverted by the majority in Ontario and Quebec. Economically, the colonies by the sea also stood to lose by Confederation. They were, of necessity, wedded to free trade for they depended upon lumbering, mining, ship-building, and fishing for a livelihood, exporting their produce and importing much of what they consumed. Canada, on the other hand, was protectionist, and it seemed likely that its tariff wall would be stretched around the new Confederation.[1] Nova Scotia particularly disliked the financial terms of the union, fearing that its government would lose half of its income and would lack money to support such essential functions as education and public works.[2] For these and other reasons, most Nova Scotians preferred to remain as they were, a separate colony, rather than to join in the proposed union. A number of these "antis," as the opponents of federation were popularly called, formed the League of the Maritime Provinces to carry on the fight against Confederation. Joseph Howe, one of the greatest figures in the history of British North America, led this organization, partly, according to tradition, from personal motives. Nearly twenty years before, he had won the fight for responsible government in his province, and his victory had established him as the leader of Nova Scotia. Since then, however, he had accomplished little and his arch-enemy, Dr. Charles Tupper, had risen to dominate the province and to be the leader of its government. Howe, like most Nova Scotians, sincerely opposed Confederation; but he also astutely recognized in the "anti" movement an opportunity to regain his former prestige and to pay off old scores against Tupper, who favoured Confederation.

The first action of the "antis" was an attempt to prevent the passage of the British North America Act by the imperial Parliament, or at least to amend the Act so that it would not include Nova Scotia. For this purpose, the League sent Howe and other delegates to London. There the first mention of annexation occurred; for Howe was to hint to the Colonial Office that Confederation might cause "changes which none of us desire . . . and all of us deplore."[3] As instructed, Howe made the most of this weapon in his correspondence with Lord Carnarvon, the secretary of state for the colonies, by pointing out the "range of temptation" which political union with the United States offered to the Maritimes: they would have free trade with a market of 34 million people, access to American capital, and the benefit of American fishing bounties.[4] These broad hints did not impress the imperial government, which pushed the British North America Act through Parliament with little opposition. Thus Nova Scotia became

3

part of the Dominion of Canada, for Tupper had pledged his province to enter Confederation without consulting the voters.

If Tupper expected the "antis" to accept this *fait accompli* without further ado, he was soon wiser. The "antis" turned from the attempt to prevent the formation of the Dominion to an attempt to withdraw Nova Scotia from it. The secession movement, already strong, was steadily gaining new adherents, largely because the formation of the Dominion coincided closely with the beginning of a severe depression. The termination, in 1866, of the Reciprocity Treaty of 1854 had had the immediate effect of halving the trade with the United States and bringing distress to the merchants, commercial cities, and producers of Canada. This depression was most severe in the Maritime Provinces whose staple exports of fish, coal, and lumber were subject to prohibitive duties after the end of the Treaty. To increase the discontent in these provinces, the fisheries of 1866 and 1867 proved to be complete failures, leaving thousands of families to struggle against hunger and privation.[5] At a time when income was declining, the federal government, as expected, extended the higher tariff of the old colony of Canada to the entire Dominion and considerably increased the price of necessaries in the hard-hit Maritime Provinces. This readjustment of the tariff was said to have cost the inhabitants of these provinces $356 000 a year;[6] even the lieutenant-governor and the confederationists in Nova Scotia felt compelled to condemn the tariff because of the hardship that it worked there.[7] A final affliction to the depression-ridden Canadians was the spectacle of the United States which was, at this time, entering a frenzied post-war boom. The contrast was both vivid and suggestive.

It is not strange that the "antis" took advantage of these circumstances to argue that there was a direct connexion between the formation of the Dominion and the coming of the depression. Nor is it strange that some Canadians envied the seeming prosperity of the United States and longed to share in it. The result of these factors was a double trend in the "anti" movement. As stated above, it grew steadily; and, secondly, some of its followers began to consider secession not as an end in itself but as a step toward annexation.

For a time, however, most of the "antis" regarded political union with the United States as a last resort and hoped to relieve their distress by other means. There was some foundation for this expectation. The first election in Nova Scotia under the new Dominion had resulted in an overwhelming victory for the opponents of Confederation. This made them confident that the British government would accede to their desire for secession from Canada and that a return to the status of a separate, self-governing colony would solve their economic and political problems. Nova Scotia could restore its revenue tariff, the income of its government would increase, and other provinces could not undermine its interests. More important, Nova Scotians were certain that the United States would be willing to negotiate a reciprocity treaty with their province if it were not part of the Dominion. This belief was based on the notion that the United States and Nova Scotia were complementary in production while the United States and Canada were competitive.

Thus secession was still the key to prosperity and the "antis" again set out to get it. The provincial assembly passed a series of resolutions urging the British government to release Nova Scotia from the Confederation. Howe embarked for London bearing this appeal, and the "antis" waited confidently for news that the British government had granted it. Talk of annexation almost disappeared.

Howe did not share the confidence of his followers that his mission would succeed. He knew from his previous experience in Great Britain that the home government was determined to have Confederation and would oppose the withdrawal of Nova Scotia, which might wreck the new union. This official British attitude was well expressed by Lord Monck, the governor-general of the Dominion, who pressed the colonial secretary to refuse Howe's request graciously but firmly. If the union broke up, wrote Monck, "I have no hesitation in expressing my opinion that . . . the maintenance of British power or the existence of British institutions in America will soon become impossible."[8] This advice from the man on the spot fortified the determination of the imperial government to deny the repeal of Confederation. Obviously, Howe had good reasons for admitting privately before he sailed that he expected his mission to fail,[9] and he was not mistaken. The colonial secretary, the Duke of Buckingham, proved to be courteous and willing to listen to the complaints of Nova Scotia but unmovable in his refusal to dissolve the Confederation or to permit the secession of any of the provinces. Early in June, he informed Monck that the imperial government "could not consider" this, or any other, request for repeal.[10]

The publication of this dispatch, bringing the frustration of their highest hopes, was a terrible blow to most of the "antis." A storm of protest arose in Nova Scotia, and bitter denunciations rained down upon the Canadian and British governments. One newspaper, typical of the organs that favoured repeal of Confederation, vented its wrath and sorrow in the following terms: "Nova Scotians have been proud of their connection with England. What have they to be proud of now? We feel assured that the people of Nova Scotia will never be loyal to the Dominion of Canada. They never have consented, never will consent to such an alliance. The Union, whilst it lasts, can only be one of force, so far as Nova Scotia is concerned."[11]

Many soon went beyond philippics and vowed that their loyalty to Great Britain was now gone. Prominent men and newspapers in the province came out openly for annexation.[12] These advocates of political union frankly stated that, with their hope of secession now blasted, their only remaining chance of rescue from the undesired federation was to join the United States.

This outburst of disloyalty frightened Howe, who realized how much he

5

had helped to blow up this tempest. Even before leaving on his second mission to London, he had been uneasy over the extreme doctrines held by some of his followers; on his return to Halifax he became alarmed at the treasonable talk in the province. At once, he determined to check it. Calling a convention of the "anti" leaders, he lectured them sternly for their sedition. He pointed out that any attempt by Nova Scotia to secure annexation would be forcibly resisted with the whole power of the British Empire and would end in disaster.[13] This plain speaking seemed to have its effect; the convention resolved that the "antis" must continue to attempt to secure secession by "lawful and constitutional means."[14]

The conversion of some of the repealers to "lawful and constitutional means" proved to be very temporary. Soon they were again using violent language, advocating seditious action, casting strong hints that American aid would be forthcoming, and that annexation would result. Members of the provincial government and prominent newspapers led the way towards the edge of treason.[15] Howe soon realized that his efforts to secure secession and to quiet the extremists in his group had failed and that it would be a waste of time to repeat them. The repeal movement was in a *cul-de-sac*, and he faced the necessity of choosing between two lines of retreat: to abandon opposition to Confederation, or to attempt to bring Nova Scotia into the American union. To Howe, the former was distasteful and the latter abhorrent. Choosing the lesser of the two evils, he reluctantly decided to accept Confederation, the pain of transition being assuaged by the willingness of Macdonald to make concessions that would partially redress the grievances of Nova Scotia.[16] In November, 1868, Howe suddenly announced that he could no longer remain in the "anti" movement, which was becoming merely a cloak for annexationism.

Howe had apparently hoped and planned that his action would be imitated by many, if not most, of the advocates of the repeal of Confederation, and that the extremists would be driven to cover. His expectation was disappointed. The "antis" were stunned by this spectacular and unexpected about-face on the part of their leader. Some of the moderates followed him, but many others refused to do so, irked because he had not consulted or forewarned them. Even the confederationists in the province condemned Howe on the ground that his action would have been effective only if he had notified his moderate associates of his intentions, so that they might have been prepared to withdraw gradually from the secession movement and become confederationists with some show of consistency.[17] Contemporary observers, friendly to Howe, estimated that his action had important effects in only two counties — Queens and Lunenburg — where about half of the "antis" followed him out of the movement.[18] The rest, if anything, became more determined in opposition, and the tendency towards political union seemed to increase. Moreover, the tone of the annexationists was changing. In the beginning, they had been inspired by anger and had been hopeful of alarming the British government by the intemperance of their sentiments. But by this time, their wrath had cooled and so had their loyalty to the British Empire. With the hope of repeal gone and economic distress still prevalent, Nova Scotians began to view their future without sentiment and some of them concluded that annexation was the only cure for the depression from which they were suffering. It became the expression of cold self-interest, not of hot wrath.[19]

It is impossible to determine the extent of this movement with exactness. Contemporary evidence indicates, however, that it had considerable strength in some areas. Howe, who knew the political situation in Nova Scotia better than any other man, informed Macdonald that "a clear unfettered vote of the people might take it [Nova Scotia] into the American Union."[20] Three by-elections to the Dominion Parliament in 1869, in each of which annexation was a major issue, seemed to bear out this statement. Having accepted a post in the Dominion Cabinet, Howe was forced to stand for re-election, which he did in the constituency of Hants. Thereupon, both the annexationists and the confederationists determined to make this electoral contest a test of strength, and both strained every resource to win. The victory went to Howe because his personal prestige was highest in this, his home district, and because the Dominion government supported him with all of its resources in his "Holy War."[21] Even so, the margin of victory was not great.

7

The excitement in Hants partly obscured significant developments in the two other ridings where by-elections were being held. In Richmond a candidate, reputedly an annexationist, was returned after a canvass which seems to have excited almost no outside interest. The campaign in Yarmouth was more closely watched and contested. The confederationists were most anxious to carry this constituency which was known to contain many annexationists; and there, as in Hants, they raised a large campaign fund and secured aid from the Dominion government.[22] The annexationists nominated Frank Killam, a young merchant, and one of the wealthiest men in the province. Both the banks and every man of means in Yarmouth supported him.[23] The confederationists soon lost hope of defeating him at the polls and planned instead to "work on him" after his election.[24] The results of the polling proved the wisdom of this decision.[25]

Their success in two of the three by-elections greatly encouraged the advocates of political union. They were, by this time, numerous enough to control the League of the Maritime Provinces, which had been founded to fight Confederation, and in June, 1869, formally changed it to the Annexation League. This action was accompanied by the issuing of a manifesto which made the motivation of the annexationists clear: "Our only hope of commercial prosperity, material development, and permanent peace lies in closer relations with the United States. Therefore be it resolved that every legitimate means should be used by members of this convention to sever our connections with Canada and to bring about a union on fair and equitable terms with the American Republic."[26]

While these political unionists were fairly numerous, their strength, geographically and socially, was not uniformly distributed throughout the province. The movement apparently was strongest in the southern part of Nova Scotia, particularly about Yarmouth. This area was a centre for the fishing industry which wanted free access to American markets and hoped to attract capital from the United States.[27] The north-eastern portion of the province, including the adjacent counties of Cape Breton Island, also had numerous advocates of annexation. The coal industry of this area wanted duty-free entry into the United States; such a privilege, mine operators estimated, would increase their annual sales in that market from 200 000 to 11 million tons a year.[28] This industry had prospered during the years of the Reciprocity Treaty of 1854; now it was in the depths of depression, with thousands out of work.[29] Reopening of the American market, preferably on a permanent basis, seemed to be the only hope for restoring and maintaining prosperity. Finally, the commercial cities of the province, especially Halifax, contained many advocates of annexation. They were supplied mostly by the trading and shipping industries, which were then in a serious decline and were particularly anxious to qualify for participation in the lucrative American coasting trade, open only to citizens of the United States.[30]

It is also important to note that the movement in all centres was strongest among the more important economic classes in the province: merchants, ship captains, seamen, commission men, coal operators, and miners.[31] The moneyed interests of Nova Scotia, who had invested capital in the enterprises which would benefit from annexation, financed the movement.[32]

This agitation, however, began to decline as early as 1869 and was a thing of the past by 1872. The first defections took place in the coal region where the annexationist tide began to ebb in December, 1869, and soon disappeared.[33] The agitation was more persistent in southern Nova Scotia but there, also, its strength steadily waned. The *Yarmouth Herald*, most intransigent of the annexationist papers, sounded the death knell in December, 1870, when it declared that the time was not ripe for political union with the United States.[34]

The causes for this decline are not far to seek. As distress and depression had built up the annexation movement, so returning prosperity tore out its foundations. Exports from Canada to the United States, which had reached their nadir in 1867, were strongly reviving. The fisheries, after the complete failures of 1866 and 1867, yielded abnormal catches from 1869 to 1873, and the Treaty of Washington brought a new day of prosperity for the Maritime Provinces by admitting Canadian fish duty-free into the United States. At the same time, exports of coal from Nova Scotia increased greatly. The mine operators reaped heavy profits and were able to employ more men.[35] Finally, the annexationists of Nova Scotia realized that the British government would not stand idly by and see that province secede from the Dominion and join the United States. It seemed that an appeal to force would be necessary, and that it would be bound to fail unless the United States strongly assisted it. When it became apparent that there was no hope of such help, the political union agitation received its *coup de grâce*.[36]

Thus disappeared one of the strongest and most interesting of the Canadian annexation movements. Like most of them, it was born of discontent and it died when the conditions which produced that discontent had disappeared. Unlike most of the others, however, it had considerable and outspoken support and some financial backing. Indeed, for a time, it caused genuine alarm to the loyal majority in the province.

Notes

1. Public Archives of Canada, Howe Papers, vol. 26, pt. 1, Miscellaneous Papers on Confederation, 152–4.
2. The normal annual income of the province, $1 500 000, would be reduced to $750 000 according to the *Yarmouth* (Nova Scotia) *Tribune*, June 27, 1866.
3. Howe Papers, vol. 4, Letters to Howe, 1864–1873, Instructions to Howe from the League of the Maritime Provinces, July 5, 1866.
4. British Parliament, *Accounts and Papers, 1867*, n. XLVIII, 14–15, Howe to Lord Carnarvon, London, Jan. 19, 1867.
5. *Yarmouth Tribune*, May 22 and Dec. 11, 1867 and Jan. 5, 1869.
6. *Saint John* (New Brunswick) *Morning Freeman*, Sept. 7, 1868.
7. P.A.C., Macdonald Papers, Nova Scotia Affairs, vol. I, Lieutenant-Governor Hastings-Doyle to Sir John A. Macdonald, Halifax, Dec. 31, 1867, and P.S. Hamilton to Macdonald, Halifax, Feb. 24, 1868.
8. P.A.C., Series G 573 A, Secret and Confidential Despatches, 1867–1869, Lord Monck to the Duke of Buckingham, Feb. 13, 1867.
9. Howe Papers, vol. 37, Howe Letter Book, Howe to A. Musgrove, Halifax, Jan. 17, 1868.
10. Macdonald Papers, Nova Scotia Affairs, vol. III, Buckingham to Monck, London, June 4, 1868.
11. *Yarmouth Herald*, June 18, 1868.
12. Among the papers outspokenly advocating annexation, the most persistent were the *Yarmouth Herald* and the *New Glasgow Eastern Chronicle*. Others, including the *Halifax Morning Chronicle*, were more reserved but discussed annexation favourably. Among the annexationists of whom I have found mention were Marshall, the former chief justice of the province, and Underwood, a member of the Dominion Parliament. Most of the members of the provincial government frequently spoke favourably of annexation, especially Martin Wilkins, the attorney-general and real leader of the Cabinet. His sincerity, however, seems open to some question, for he likewise protested his loyalty to the Empire when questioned by Hastings-Doyle.
13. Howe Papers, vol. 38, Howe Letter Book, Howe to Livingston, Halifax, Aug. 12, 1868.
14. *Saint John Morning Freeman*, Aug. 11, 1868.
15. Macdonald Papers, Nova Scotia Affairs, vol. I, Hastings-Doyle to Macdonald, Halifax, Sept. 4 and 5, 1868.
16. Macdonald addressed a repeal convention in Halifax in August, 1868, and promised that Nova Scotia would have better terms of union. *Ibid.*, vol. III, Macdonald to Lord Monck, Sept. 4, 1868.
17. *Ibid.*, Hastings-Doyle to Macdonald, Halifax, Feb. 25, 1869.
18. Howe Papers, vol. 4, Letters to Howe, 1861–1873, R. Huntington to Howe, Yarmouth, Dec. 24, 1868.
19. For typical expressions of this view, see M. N. Jackson to F. Seward, Halifax, Aug. 29, 1868. National Archives of the United States, Consular Despatches to the Department of State, Halifax, vol. IX. See also *Halifax Morning Chronicle*, Sept. 16, 1868, and *New Glasgow Eastern Chronicle*, Jan. 9, 1869.
20. Macdonald Papers, Nova Scotia Affairs, vol. II, Howe to Macdonald, Halifax, Oct. 29, 1868 and Nov. 16, 1868.
21. The expression, "Holy War" is Macdonald's. The federal government made 400 appointments to aid Howe in this campaign. See Howe Papers, vol. 4, Letters to Howe, 1864–1873, Macdonald to Howe, Ottawa, Jan. 12, Mar. 8, and Mar. 16, 1869. Also Macdonald Papers, Nova Scotia Affairs, vol. I, Hastings-Doyle to Macdonald, Halifax, Mar. 5 and 30, 1869.
22. Macdonald Papers, Nova Scotia Affairs, vol. III, A. W. Savary to Macdonald, Halifax, Dec. 3, 1868. P.A.C., Macdonald Letter Books, XII, Macdonald to Savary, Ottawa, December 14, 1868.
23. Macdonald Papers, Nova Scotia Affairs, vol. III, J. A. McClellan to Macdonald, Halifax, Feb. 23, 1869.

24. Howe Papers, vol. 38, Howe Letter Book, Howe to Macdonald, Halifax, Mar. 30, 1869. Series G 573 A, Secret and Confidential Despatches, 1867–1869, Young to Granville, Apr. 8, 1869.
25. Killam had a majority in every district in the riding and, in Yarmouth County, polled 1220 votes to 598 for his opponent. *Saint John Morning Freeman*, Apr. 22, 1869.
26. *Ibid.*, June 24, 1869.
27. *Yarmouth Herald*, Apr. 15, 1869 and Apr. 14, 21, 26, and 30, 1870.
28. *New Glasgow Eastern Chronicle*, Nov. 25, 1869.
29. *Boston Daily Advertiser*, Oct. 17, 1868.
30. Series G 573 A, Secret and Confidential Despatches 1867–1869, Young to Granville, Apr. 8, 1869.
31. *Ibid*.
32. Macdonald Papers, Nova Scotia Affairs, vol. III, J. McClellan to Macdonald, Halifax, Feb. 23, 1869.
33. The last annexation meeting in the region seems to have taken place in Feb., 1870. *Yarmouth Tribune*, Feb. 9, 1870.
34. *Yarmouth Herald*, Dec. 5, 1870.
35. *Saint John Morning Freeman*, Nov. 13, 1869.
36. There were annexationists in the United States, but they were in the minority and very few of them were willing to fight Great Britain in order to obtain Canada or any part of it. See L. B. Shippee, *Canadian-American Relations 1849–1874* (New Haven, Toronto, and London, 1939).

10

British Columbia Becomes Canadian (1871-1901)*
WALTER N. SAGE

In an impassioned speech against federation delivered in the Legislative Council of British Columbia in March, 1870, Dr. John Sebastian Helmcken uttered these prophetic words:

No union between this Colony and Canada can permanently exist, unless it be to the mutual and pecuniary advantage of this Colony to remain in the union. The sum of the interests of the inhabitants is the interest of the Colony. The people of this Colony have, generally speaking, no love for Canada; they care, as a rule, little or nothing about the creation of another Empire, Kingdom, or Republic; they have but little sentimentality and care little about the distinctions between the forms of Government of Canada and the United States.
    Therefore no union on account of love need be looked for. The only bond of union outside of force — and force the Dominion has not — will be the material advantage of the country and the pecuniary benefit of the inhabitants. Love for Canada has to be acquired by the prosperity of the country, and from our children.[1]

The last four words are more than prophetic. They are a stroke of genius! Probably in his old age the good doctor was fated to hear the school-children of British Columbia singing:

Our fair Dominion now extends
From Cape Race to Nootka Sound.

The children and children's children were in the process of becoming Canadians. It was not a speedy evolution. At Confederation British Columbians were *not* Canadians. By 1901 Canadianism had spread and

* From *Queen's Quarterly*, LII (1945): 168–183. Reprinted by permission of the editors.

penetrated the province. But there were still many in the older age groupings who remembered the colonial period and were still definitely British
Columbians. The youngsters were Canadians, but Canadians with a difference. The barrier of the Rocky Mountains had conditioned them. Their
outlook was towards the Pacific and not towards the Atlantic nor even
towards Hudson Bay. They were not well acquainted with Ontario and
knew little of the prairies or the Maritimes, and probably still less about
Quebec. None the less they were becoming increasingly conscious that
they were a part of Canada.

Dr. Helmcken was right. Love for Canada was at first not a spontaneous
or a natural growth in British Columbia. It did not spring from the native
soil of the provinces as did love for British Columbia. In the colonial days
and even for a time after Confederation 'Canadians' were unpopular. They
were known as 'North American Chinamen' — a tribute to their thrift.
They sent their money home and did not spend it so freely as did the
open-handed Americans. But British Columbia could not thrive without
the aid of the rest of Canada. She was cut off from American markets by
the tariff laws of the United States. Until the completion of the Canadian
Pacific Railway in 1885 there was no direct link through Canadian territory
between the Coast and Eastern Canada. It is true that during the critical
years from 1866 to 1871 British Columbia might have followed 'Manifest
Destiny' and as the Territory of Columbia have become a weaker edition
of Washington Territory — weaker because, in spite of her huge expanse,
she had a smaller and more widespread population. But British Columbia
had made her decision. She would remain British even though it entailed
paying the high price of becoming Canadian. The only other course open
to her was to remain a bankrupt British colony on the edge of nowhere!

11

A glance at the early history of the British colonies on the Northwest
Coast and especially at the so-called critical period between 1866 and 1871
will show that British Columbia was much more British and American in
outlook than it was Canadian. In fur-trading days before 1849 there was
relatively little Canadian influence. There had been some when the North
West Company was operating west of the Rockies, but the union of 1821
left the Hudson's Bay Company in complete control. Very few of the
company's officers were from Canada, although there were many French-
Canadians among the *voyageurs*. The Colony of Vancouver Island was a
British, not a Canadian, venture. The gold-seekers of 1858 were from
California. A few of them were Canadians who had been attracted to the
placer mines of the Golden State and were now following the paystreak
north. The miners' meetings stemmed from California and even 'Ned
McGowan's War' had its roots in the troubles between the Vigilantes and
the Law and Order Group, rival California organizations, members of
which had come north to Fraser River.[2] The United States was omnipresent.
The British Isles were half the world away, and Canada, although
geographically nearer than Great Britain, was even farther away in spirit.
There was a sentimental tie with the Mother Country but as yet practically

none with Canada. Joseph Despard Pemberton, former Colonial Surveyor, in a letter to the Victoria *British Colonist* early in 1870, summed up the situation neatly in verse:

True Loyalty's to Motherland
And not to Canada,
The love we bear is second-hand
To any step-mama.

At first sight it would seem that American influences preponderated in British Columbia. The economic tie was with California, and this tie remained until the completion of the Canadian Pacific Railway. As the late Marcus Lee Hansen has penetratingly observed:

The new province of British Columbia, although firmly attached to the empire by political, naval and military bonds, was in commerce and population a part of the Pacific region which had its center at San Francisco.[3]

12   Hansen also states that

Fully three-fourths of the fifteen thousand miners who in 1864 made up the principal element in the population were Americans, and half of the business houses were branches of American establishments.[4]

The only regular steamship communication which British Columbia possessed with the outside world was by American vessels.[5] The express companies were of American origin, although local express was carried by British Columbian companies which maintained American connections. Postal service was through San Francisco. It was necessary for letters posted in British Columbia, destined for Great Britain, Canada, the United States, or elsewhere, to bear United States stamps in addition to their local postage. Governor Musgrave protested against this practice, but it was found impossible to change it.[6] Telegraph service with San Francisco, by way of Portland, Oregon, was established in 1865. The completion of the Union Pacific Railroad in 1869 provided British Columbia, through San Francisco, with railway connections with the Atlantic seaboard, and put an end to travel by the tedious, and often dangerous, Panama route.

From California the mining frontier spread eastward and northward to Nevada, Utah, Colorado, Wyoming, Montana, Idaho and British Columbia. The gold rushes of 1858 to Fraser River and of 1862 to Cariboo stemmed from San Francisco. Later rushes to Omineca, the Stikine, Cassiar, and finally to Atlin and the Klondike were closely connected with California. Mining methods in British Columbia were similar to those in vogue in California, and the miners who came north were accustomed to 'frontier justice'. In British Columbia, however, they found Judge Begbie, but not 'Judge Lynch'.

American influences were economic, and, to a less degree, social and cultural. British influences were political and institutional and also social and religious. The political and legal structure of British Columbia was entirely British. The colonial governors were all of British origin. Most of the government officials had been born in the British Isles. In the Legislative Council of British Columbia, which in 1870 discussed terms of union with Canada, the majority had come from the Motherland. The Royal Navy was another link with 'Home'. The part played by the Special Detachment of the Royal Engineers in the early development of the Crown Colony of British Columbia is too well known to demand more than a passing reference. The Church of England was also a link with the Mother Country. Bishop Hills, the first Bishop of Columbia, was consecrated in Westminster Abbey and set apart for his work in the far-off colony. In 1860 he arrived in Victoria, where he diligently upheld the traditions and dignity of his Church, but was unable to secure its establishment as the State Church of the colony. The first Presbyterian ministers came from Ireland, but the 'Scottish Kirk' flourished under their ministrations, and for many years retained a close connection with the Established Church of Scotland. The Roman Catholics and the Methodists, on the other hand, had Canadian connections. The first Roman Catholic priests came from Canada to the Columbia in the 1830's, and later in the 1840's came north to Fort Victoria and the Fraser River. The Methodists were sent from Canada, in the late 1850's, to establish a mission in British Columbia. *13*

Canadian influences were at first relatively weak, but they strengthened as the battle for Confederation was fought. The leading Confederationists were chiefly British North Americans: *e.g.*, Amor De Cosmos, John Robson, Dr. R. W. W. Carrall, Francis J. Barnard, and J. Spencer Thompson. Some Englishmen — *e.g.*, Robert Beaven and Alfred Waddington — also joined the cause of federation. George A. Walkem was Irish by birth but Canadian by adoption. Many of the Confederationist leaders had come to British Columbia by way of California. Their sojourn in the United States had, apparently, not dulled their affection for British institutions, but had strengthened rather than weakened their determination that British Columbia should join Canada.

A mining population is notoriously unstable. It is a case of 'Here to-day and gone to-morrow'. As a rule the American gold-seekers returned to the United States when they had 'made their pile' or had become disgusted with the 'Fraser River humbug'. It was the British and the Canadians who remained and settled down in Cariboo, along the lower Fraser River, or on Vancouver Island. Unfortunately it is not possible to make an accurate check of the birthplace of British Columbians before 1871.[7] Some idea of the national origins of British Columbians at that date may, however, be obtained from a study of J. B. Kerr's *Biographical Dictionary of Well-Known British Columbians*, published in Vancouver in 1890. Of the 242 names listed in this publication, 178 were resident in British Columbia in 1871. An analysis of their birthplaces is rather enlightening: *British Isles,* 94, divided as follows: England, 57; Scotland, 21; Ireland, 16. *Dominion of Canada*: 45, — Nova Scotia, 7; New Brunswick, 3; Prince Edward Island, 1; Quebec, 5; Ontario, 29.[8] *British Columbia,* 7; *Other British possessions,* 5; United States, 12; Other Foreign Countries, 14; no birthplace, 1.

These figures clearly show that British Columbia was *British* in the broadest sense of the term. The Americans had come and gone. The British, including the Canadians, remained.

In the Canadianization of British Columbia from 1871 to 1901 three phenomena are clearly observable: political development, the building of the Canadian Pacific Railway, and the arrival as settlers of large numbers of Eastern Canadians. It must not be thought that British and American influences did not continue to be strong. What happened was that Canadian influence strengthened, especially after the completion of the Canadian Pacific Railway. The period divides naturally at 1886. The first regular transcontinental passenger train from Montreal arrived at Port Moody on July 4th of that year. Vancouver came into existence in April, and was burnt to ashes in June. But nothing could daunt the future Canadian metropolis of the West Coast. It arose triumphantly from its ashes and five years later had a population of 13 709 as compared with Victoria's 16 841. The census of 1901 showed that Vancouver had already surpassed Victoria in population — 29 432 as against 20 919.[9] Since Victoria was the centre of the British-born (natives of the British Isles) Vancouver's rapid advance was a sign of Canadianization. The roots of its people strike deep into Eastern Canada.

The political phase of Canadianization is concerned chiefly with the establishment of the provincial government and with the relations existing between the Lieutenant-Governor of British Columbia and the Government of Canada. Before federation British Columbia had possessed representative but not responsible government. Her political education was, therefore, not so far advanced as that of the eastern provinces. On the other hand, British Columbia had been the only Crown Colony west of the Great Lakes, and was rather more experienced than Manitoba in the art of self-government. Yet British Columbians in 1871 were still politically immature.

The Terms of Union with Canada provided for "the introduction of Responsible Government when desired by the Inhabitants of British Columbia".[10]

It was not, however, until after the first provincial elections had been held in October, 1871, that Lieutenant-Governor Joseph William Trutch could claim to have "established a Responsible Cabinet".[11] Actually, it may be doubted whether responsible government was fully established during the régime of John Foster McCreight, the first Premier of British Columbia. McCreight was a distinguished lawyer, Irish by birth, who had no previous political experience. Probably Trutch selected him because he was "a 'safe' man, one whom the Lieutenant-Governor could direct and guide".[12] Trutch virtually ruled British Columbia during the McCreight régime, 1871–1872. When Amor de Cosmos became premier in December, 1872, Trutch found his power challenged. De Cosmos, with his Nova Scotian tradition and his long political experience in British Columbia, was not prepared to yield the reins of power to any Lieutenant-Governor,

14

even though he had once held office in colonial days as Chief Commissioner of Lands and Works.

Trutch was in a unique position as regards Ottawa. He considered himself the accredited representative of the federal government in British Columbia. His letters to Sir John A. Macdonald and Macdonald's replies clearly indicate that he was definitely the *liaison* officer between Ottawa and Victoria during the period from July 20th to November 14th, 1871, that is, until the McCreight ministry was formally constituted. The real difficulty was that Trutch did not hand over full authority to McCreight. In his analysis of the situation R. E. Gosnell saw very clearly:

During the transition from Crown Colony government to Provincial autonomy there was a brief interregnum in which it was necessary for him [Trutch] to administer affairs on his own initiative, but he continued this rule much longer than was necessary, or than was constitutionally defensible.[13]

Part of Trutch's difficulties arose from his selection of McCreight as premier. Neither he nor McCreight had any real acquaintance with responsible government. The leading opponents of Trutch and McCreight — Amor De Cosmos and John Robson — possessed this experience. Either of them could, in all probability, have headed a real responsible ministry. In a rather pathetic passage in a letter to Sir John A. Macdonald Trutch unburdened himself as follows:

15

I am so inexperienced and indeed we all are in this Province in the practice of Responsible Govt. that we are initiating that I step as carefully and guardedly as I can — and whilst teaching others I feel constantly my own extreme need of instruction on this subject — which must account to you — if you please — for the trouble which I have put you to — and which I know I ought not to have imposed on you.[14]

De Cosmos, for his part, roundly denounced the Trutch-McCreight combination in an appeal addressed to "the Liberals of the Province":

To rally round their old leaders — the men who have year after year fought their battles and have in no instance deserted the popular cause. To take any other course is to convict themselves of Treason to manhood, Treason to the Liberal party, that year by year for fourteen years have urged Responsible Government, Union of the Provinces, and Confederation with the Dominion. It is no Treason, no public wrong to ignore the nominees of Governor Trutch.[15]

The reference to the "Liberal party" is extremely interesting. Actually there were no political parties, in the federal sense of the term, in British Columbian provincial politics until 1903, when Richard McBride announced the formation of a Conservative ministry. De Cosmos, in his federal career, supported Macdonald and Mackenzie in turn. It is noteworthy, however, that as early as 1871 he could make his appeal to the 'Liberals'.

By the Terms of Union British Columbia was entitled to three senators and six members of the House of Commons. The senators were Dr. R. W. W. Carrall, Clement F. Cornwall and W. J. Macdonald. Carrall was from Ontario, but the other two senators were born in the British Isles. The six

Members of Parliament were J. Spencer Thompson, Hugh Nelson, Robert Wallace, Henry Nathan, Amor De Cosmos, and Charles F. Houghton. Two of them, Thompson and De Cosmos, both Canadians, had been prominent Confederationists. In Ottawa all six were classed as supporters of the Macdonald administration.

In the federal elections of 1872 Sir Francis Hincks was elected by acclamation for Vancouver Island. Six years later, in the well-known National Policy election, Sir John A. Macdonald, defeated in Kingston, Ontario, was elected for Victoria City. His colleague was Amor De Cosmos.

During the Macdonald régime from 1878 to 1891 the British Columbian Members of Parliament were Conservatives. They gave their political allegiance to the party which had promised to build the transcontinental railway. It must be confessed that, with the exception of Amor De Cosmos, the British Columbians do not seem to have played any large part at Ottawa. But their presence there showed that the Pacific province was part of the Canadian federation.

As has been noted, federal parties as such took no part in provincial politics until 1903. Political divisions in the provincial area were local rather than national. Until the population of the Mainland had surpassed that of Vancouver Island the division was Mainland vs. Island. But local issues in the 1870's and early 1880's were closely intertwined with the all-important railway question.

The greatest single Canadianizing force in British Columbia during the period 1871 to 1901 was the Canadian Pacific Railway. Its construction had been promised in the Terms of Union. Delay in carrying out those terms almost led to the secession of British Columbia from the Canadian federation in 1878. The change of government in 1873 and the attitude of the Mackenzie administration were largely responsible for this delay, but there is no denying that George A. Walkem in British Columbia made political capital out of the difficult situation. The return of Sir John A. Macdonald and the Conservatives to power in 1878 put an end to the secession movement and led to the chartering of the new company which built the railway. Over that railway from 1886 to 1901 came thousands of eastern Canadians who were to become the cement binding British Columbia more closely to the rest of the Dominion.

The well-known story of the building of the Canadian Pacific Railway need not here be retold. Its terminus was fixed at Port Moody, not Esquimalt. The so-called "Island section of the main line" became the Esquimalt and Nanaimo Railway, constructed not by the Canadian Pacific Railway Company, but by Robert Dunsmuir, the 'coal king' of Vancouver Island, and the 'Big Four' of the Southern Pacific Railway — Collis P. Huntingdon, Mark Hopkins, Leland Stanford, and Charles Crocker. The Yellowhead Pass route through the Rocky Mountains was abandoned in favour of the Kicking Horse. In 1887 the 'branch' line from Port Moody to Vancouver was built.

From the vantage-point of nearly three-quarters of a century after the event the real wonder is that the railway was ever built at all. The total population of the Dominion, including Prince Edward Island, in 1871 was 3 689 257. Of this total 25 228 are listed for Manitoba, 36 247 for British Columbia, and 48 000 for the Northwest Territories.[16] The white population of Western Canada was probably short of 25 000. The four 'original provinces' of Eastern Canada had a population of 3 225 761. It was a tremendous undertaking for Canada to build a transcontinental railway, and it is not surprising that others than Edward Blake had misgivings. But Sandford Fleming blazed the trails before the Canadian Pacific Railway Company was formed and that great group of railway builders who made up the new company built the road. James J. Hill withdrew from the directorate in 1883 when it became evident that the company was determined to build the Lake Superior section. Hill then began to plan the Great Northern Railway, which would invade the prairies and southern British Columbia.

The completion of the main line in 1886 did not, however, end the activities of the Canadian Pacific Railway in British Columbia. There was American competition to be faced, especially in the Kootenays and the Boundary country. In the 1880's and early 1890's the chief American competition was the Northern Pacific Railway, but in the late 1890's the Great Northern had seriously invaded the field. The Canadian Pacific Railway began to buy up, or lease, local lines in the Kootenays, especially the Columbia and Kootenay, the Columbia and Western and the British Columbia Southern. Eventually the south line of the Canadian Pacific from Lethbridge, Alberta, through Crowsnest Pass and through the Kootenays and Boundary country was completed in 1916 by the construction of the Kettle Valley Railway. By that time the Great Northern had been worsted. The Trail smelter, which originally had been an American venture, was in the hands of the Consolidated Mining and Smelting Company of Canada, a subsidiary of the Canadian Pacific Railway. Thus did Canadian interests triumph over American in the Kootenays.

17

For many years there was a story current in British Columbia that an old-timer in Victoria addressed a newcomer from Eastern Canada as follows: "Before you Canadians came, you know, we never had to take the shutters down till ten o'clock." Whether apocryphal or not, the tale illustrates the clash between the early settlers, who usually had come from the British Isles, and the rather more hustling and energetic 'Canadians'. On the whole, this clash was more in evidence on Vancouver Island than on the Mainland. Cariboo had never been so 'English' as Victoria and the lower Fraser Valley after 1886 rapidly absorbed the newcomers from 'the East'. Vancouver was, *par excellence*, the Mecca of the men and women from Ontario and the Maritimes.

In a study of this sort there is no accurate yardstick by which the growth of Canadianism can be measured. Still, it is possible to detect certain tendencies. In 1871 Canadians in British Columbia had made their presence felt. Many of them had come from California during the early gold rushes. Others had come direct to British Columbia by way of Panama and San Francisco. One devoted band — 'The Argonauts of 1862' — had come 'the plains across' through British Territory from Fort Garry. But it was not until after the completion of the Canadian Pacific Railway that eastern Canadians came in large numbers to 'the West beyond the West'.

During the decade from 1871 to 1881 the population of British Columbia increased from 36 247 to 49 459. Manitoba's went up from 25 228 to 62 260. The next decade, 1881 to 1891, witnessed an increase in British Columbia from 49 459 to 98 173, but Manitoba shot up from 62 260 to 152 506. British Columbia from 1891 to 1901 increased from 98 173 to 178 657 and Manitoba from 152 506 to 255 211.[17] But even as late as 1901 British Columbia possessed only 3.33 per cent. of Canada's total population. In 1901 only 12.02 per cent. of Canadians lived west of the Ontario-Manitoba border. The proportion in 1941 was 28.30 per cent., roughly 3 250 000 out of 11 500 000.

18   The first Census of Canada contained figures dealing only with the four 'original provinces'. It was not until the 1880–1881 Census that information was published regarding Manitoba, British Columbia and Prince Edward Island. The population of British Columbia is given as 49 459. According to birthplace this number was made up as follows:[18]

Born in British Columbia		32 175
Born in the British Isles		5 783
English	3 294	
Irish	1 285	
Scottish	1 204	
Born in other parts of Canada		2 768
Prince Edward Island	23	
Nova Scotia	379	
New Brunswick	374	
Quebec	396	
Ontario	1 572	
Manitoba	24	
Born in The Territories		14
Born in other British Possessions		211
Born in the United States		2 295
Born in other countries and at sea		5 462
Birthplace not given		751
Total		49 459

The Third Census of Canada, 1890–91, gave the population of British Columbia as 98 173, but apparently gave no statistics as regards the birthplaces of the people. It did, however, provide information regarding the numbers born in Canada and in foreign countries. In British Columbia 37 583 are classed as native, born of a native father; 19 268 as native, born of a foreign father; and 41 322 as foreign-born.[19] In this census, as in the previous one, the native Indians of British Columbia are included in the native-born totals. No attempt has been made to separate white men and Indians.

It is from the Fourth Census of Canada, 1900–1901, that most information is obtained regarding racial origins, nationalities and the birthplaces of the people. The population of British Columbia was now 178 657. According to racial origins 106 403 were of British birth (English, 52 863; Irish, 20 658; Scottish, 31 068), 25 488 were Indians, 532 Negroes, 19 482 Chinese and Japanese and the remainder of continental European origins or "unspecified". On the basis of nationality, 144 989 are classed as Canadian, 10 088 as American, 14 201 as Chinese, 3516 as Japanese and the remainder from the continent of Europe. But it is Table XIII — "Birthplaces of the People" — which best tells the story. Of the 99 612 listed as born in Canada 59 589 were born in British Columbia; 2203 in Manitoba; 2839 in New Brunswick; 4603 in Nova Scotia; 23 642 in Ontario; 1180 in Prince Edward Island; 4329 in Quebec; 991 in the North West Territories and 236 in "Canada not given". The total of those born in the British Isles was 30 630 distributed as follows: English, 19 385; Irish, 3957; Scottish, 6457; Welsh, 710; Lesser Isles, 121. From the other British Possessions had come 1843. The foreign-born totalled 46 110, of whom 17 164 were from the United States.

From the statistics given above it is obvious that by 1901 the Canadianization of British Columbia was fairly well complete. A new generation had grown up west of the Rockies since 1871. No matter where their parents came from these young people were Canadians. To be sure, they were British Columbian Canadians, not quite the same as Canadians from the other provinces, nevertheless Canadians. Many of them were destined to prove their loyalty to Canada and to the British Empire in 1914. By 1901 east and west in Canada were really joined and 'the West beyond the West' had become Canadian.

19

Notes

1. *Debate on the Subject of Confederation with Canada*, Victoria, 1878, p. 13.
2. On this subject see F. W. Howay, *The Early History of the Fraser River Mines*, Victoria, 1926, pp. viii–xvii.
3. Marcus Lee Hansen and J. Bartlet Brebner, *The Mingling of the Canadian and American Peoples*, New Haven, 1940, p. 155.
4. *Ibid*.
5. For a discussion of this topic *cf.* F. W. Howay, W. N. Sage and H. F. Angus, *British Columbia and the United States*. Toronto: Ryerson, 1942, pp. 184–186.
6. *Cf.* A. S. Deaville, *The Colonial Postage Systems and Postage Stamps of Vancouver Island and British Columbia, 1849–1871*. Archives Memoir No. VIII, Victoria, B.C., King's Printer, 1928, pp. 137–143.
7. *The Census of Canada, 1870–1871*, Volume I, does not give figures for British Columbia. In *The Census of Canada, 1880–1881*, the total population of British Columbia, in 1871, whites, Indians, Chinese and coloured is given, however, as 36 247. Of this number 25 661 were Indians. *Cf.* L. T. Marshall, *Vital Statistics of British Columbia*, Victoria, B.C.; Provincial Board of Health u.d. (1932), p. 192.
8. Technically, of course, Prince Edward Island was not part of Canada till 1873, but this seems a hair-splitting distinction.
9. *Canada Year Book 1943–1944* Ottawa: King's Printer, 1944, p. 125.
10. *Journals of the Legislative Council of British Columbia, Session 1871*, Victoria, B.C., 1871, p. 6.
11. J. W. Trutch to Sir John A. Macdonald, Nov. 21, 1871, *Macdonald Papers*, Trutch Correspondence, 1871–1873, p. 98. (Public Archives of Canada.)
12. W. N. Sage, "John Foster McCreight, the first Premier of British Columbia", in the *Transactions of the Royal Society of Canada*, Third Series, Section II, Vol. XXXIV, 1940, p. 177.

13. E. O. S. Scholefield and R. E. Gosnell, *British Columbia, Sixty Years of Progress*, Vancouver and Victoria, 1913, Part II, p. 15, n.1.
14. *Macdonald Papers,* Trutch Correspondence, 1871–73, pp. 101–102.
15. Victoria *Daily Standard*, November 21, 1871.
16. *Canada Year Book, 1943–44*, p. 79.
17. *Canada Year Book, 1943–44*, pp. 79, 80.
18. *Census of Canada, 1880–1881*, Ottawa: McLean, Roger & Co., 1882, Vol. I, pp. 396–7, Table IV.
19. *Census of Canada, 1890–1891*. Ottawa: King's Printer, 1893, Vol. II, p. 228.

Topic Two
The National Policy

The National Policy has been the subject of considerable debate since its inception. Why was it implemented? Was it designed to benefit certain classes or regions at the expense of others? To what extent was the policy truly "national"? Has Canada survived because of or in spite of the National Policy? These and other questions have received considerable attention.

The National Policy was a policy of tariff protection implemented by John A. Macdonald's Conservative government in 1879. It imposed a tariff of more than $17^1/2\%$ on many manufactured goods coming into the country from the United States. The aim of the policy was to direct trade from a north-south to an east-west axis in the hope of stimulating the growth of Canadian industries. It appeared to be a logical solution to the problem of the depressed Canadian economy in the mid-1870s and in the light of declining trade relations with Britain and the United States. Britain had abandoned the mercantile system of trade with her colonies in the late 1840s in favour of free trade, while the United States had adopted its own highly protectionist policy toward Canada after the abrogation of the Reciprocity Treaty in 1866. Canadians were thus forced to look within for a solution to their problems. A policy of high protection to foster Canadian industrial growth seemed one of the few options available.

The National Policy was also seen as one component of a broader "national policy" that included as well the building of a transcontinental railway and large-scale immigration to the West in an effort to create a viable transcontinental nation. The logic went as follows: the railway would enable east-west trade, while the growing population of the West would provide the necessary markets for Canadian manufactured goods and a ready source of raw materials, for the growing industries of Central Canada. The high tariff would force Canadians to buy Canadian products, thus encouraging industrial growth within the nation.

Craig Brown in "The Nationalism of the National Policy" explains the popularity of the National Policy at the time by showing it in a larger historical and international context. In "Some Historical and Theoretical Comment on Canada's National Policies," John Dales questions the logic of the National Policy in terms of its long-range benefits for Canadians.

Craig Brown's views can be examined in greater detail in his book *Canada's National Policy, 1883–1900: A Study in Canadian-American Relations* (Princeton: Princeton University Press, 1964) and John Dales's in his study *The Protective Tariff in Canada's Development* (Toronto: University of Toronto Press, 1966). The traditional defence of the National Policy is presented in Donald Creighton's works, for example, *Canada's First Century* (Toronto: Macmillan, 1970). The negative impact of the National Policy on developments in the hinterlands of the Maritimes and the West can be found in *Canada and the Burden of Unity*, edited by D. Bercuson (Toronto: Macmillan, 1977) and in an article by T. W. Acheson, "The National Policy and the Industrialization of the Maritimes, 1880–1910," *Acadiensis*, I (1972):3–28. A recent issue of the *Journal of Canadian Studies*, 14 (Fall 1979) is devoted to "The National Policy, 1879–1979."

22

The Nationalism of the National Policy*
CRAIG BROWN

Debating nationalism is the great Canadian national pastime. Since Confederation it has been the pre-eminent preoccupation of politicians, journalists, scholars and plain ordinary citizens. All have wrestled diligently with the problem that Canadian nationalism — if such there be — does not fit any of the classic definitions of nationalism. Common language, religion, and ethnic origin must obviously be rejected. Except for the disciples of Harold Adams Innis, geography provided few satisfactory clues to the Canadian identity. And a common historical tradition, in the words of Mill, "the possession of a national history and consequent community of recollections, collective pride and humiliation, pleasure and regret, connected with the same incidents in the past," raises more questions about a Canadian "nationality" than it answers. There is no great national hero who cut down a maple tree, threw a silver dollar across the St. Lawrence and then proceeded to lead a revolution and govern the victorious nation wisely and judiciously. There are no great Canadian charters of freedom or independence expressing the collective will of the people. But the search goes on. Historians and retired Governors General laboriously attempt to define "the Canadian identity" or "being Canadian." Many nations have manifested their nationalism through great public acts; Canada has asserted its nationalism by looking for it.

*From *Nationalism in Canada*, edited by the University League for Social Reform. Copyright 1966 by McGraw-Hill Limited. Reprinted by permission of McGraw-Hill Ryerson Limited.

Yet there is abundant evidence that Canadians have both thought and acted like contemporary nationalists in other countries. Much, though by no means all, of the evidence is provided by the politicians.[1] The evidence is mundane, for seldom have Canadian politicians been political theorists or philosophers. Rather, their concerns have been with everyday problems of government. But within this framework their thoughts and acts have been decidedly nationalist in character. A brief look at the men who implemented and carried out the National Policy may serve to illustrate the point.

Writing to a Conservative editor in 1872, Sir John A. Macdonald noted in a postscript that "the paper must go in for a National policy in Tariff matters, and while avoiding the word 'protection' must advocate a readjustment of the tariff in such a manner as incidentally to aid our manufacturing and industrial interest."[2] In this obvious afterthought at the conclusion of a letter devoted to the necessity for finding an appropriate label for Macdonald's party, is the origin of the National Policy. The context is significant. Macdonald was looking for a policy that would attract, at one and the same time, voters and dollars to his party, and the National Policy would do both. The manufacturers would contribute to the party war-chest and the simplicity of the title and concept of the National Policy would appeal to an electorate looking to fulfill the promise of Confederation. Moreover, as a transcontinental railway, immigration and opening of the Northwest were added to the tariff as items in the National Policy, it took on a strikingly familiar complexion that added to its political attractiveness. It was in most respects a duplication of a similar "national policy" designed for continental expansion in the United States. It was "a materialistic policy of Bigness"[3] in an age when expansionism appealed to nationalist sentiment. Canadians could take pride in their ability to compete with their neighbours in the conquest of the continent.

The National Policy was equally attractive because a policy of tariff protection meant another step in the long path from colony to nation within the Empire. As early as 1859, Galt argued for protection less on its economic merits than on the grounds that tariff autonomy was implicit in responsible government. Referring to Imperial objections to the Cayley-Galt tariff of that year, the crux of Galt's argument was that "self-government would be utterly annihilated if the views of the Imperial Government were to be preferred to those of the people of Canada."[4] With tariff autonomy not only achieved but emphasized by protection, in 1911 the ardent nationalist John S. Ewart proudly summed up the elements of "Canadian Independence" by pointing first to the fact that "we are fiscally independent". "By that I mean that we make our own tariffs; that we frame them as we wish; that we tax British, and other goods as we please; and that neither the Colonial Office nor the British Parliament has any right whatever to interfere."[5]

That the National Policy was politically attractive, is, then, evident. By 1886 the Liberal party had been driven so far into a "me too" position that Blake in essence declared his party's policy to be, to borrow a phrase, the

23

National Policy if necessary, but not necessarily the National Policy. It is true that in 1891, with a new leader and the new policy of Unrestricted Reciprocity with the United States, the Liberals came closer to victory than they had at any time since 1874. But within two years the Liberals had again revised their policy to "freer trade" and in 1897 the Liberal Government admitted the futility of attempting to destroy Macdonald's brainchild. "I not only would not retire from the Government because they refused to eliminate the principle of protection from the tariff, but I would not remain in the Government if they did eliminate the principle of protection entirely from the tariff", wrote Clifford Sifton. He added that "the introduction of a tariff from which the principle of protection would be entirely eliminated would be fraught with results that would be most disastrous to the whole Canadian people."[6] In 1911, Sifton and 17 other "revolting" Liberals issued their manifesto against reciprocity "believing as we do that Canadian nationality is now threatened with a more serious blow than any it has heretofore met with."[7] Robert Borden simply added that "we must decide whether the spirit of Canadianism or of Continentalism shall prevail on the northern half of this continent."[8]

In short, the idea of protection embodied in the tariff became equated with the Canadian nation itself. The National Policy, by stressing that Canadians should no longer be "hewers of wood and drawers of water" for the United States, as Tilley put it, recalled and reinforced that basic impulse of survival as a separate entity on this continent that had been born of the American Revolution, made explicit in Confederation, and remained the primary objective of Canadian nationalists. Protection and the National Policy, then, took on a much larger meaning than mere tinkering with customs schedules.

The same idea was evident in the building of the Canadian Pacific Railway and the opening of the Northwest. The Northwest was the key to the future of both the National Policy and the nation, and an expensive and partially unproductive railway through Canadian territory was the price Canada had to pay to "protect" it from American penetration and absorption. It was to be the great market for Canadian industry and the foundation of a "Canadian economy". Emphasizing that building the railway was "a great national question", Sir Charles Tupper remarked that "under the National Policy that Canada has adopted we must look forward not only to building up thriving centres of industry and enterprises all over this portion of the country, but to obtaining a market for these industries after they have been established; and I say where is there a greater market than that magnificent granary of the North-west?"[9] He added that upon the success of the venture "the rapid progress and prosperity of our common country depends".

The United States played an interesting role in the National Policy that emphasized its nationalistic assumptions. Fundamental to the thinking of the framers of the policy was the idea that the United States was much less a friendly neighbour than an aggressive competitor power waiting for a

24

suitable opportunity to fulfill its destiny of the complete conquest of North America. The National Policy was intended to be the first line of defence against American ambitions. And this, I think, is the reason any Canadian alternative to it was unsuccessful. It was the "national" implications of the National Policy that hindered the Liberals in their attempt to formulate an opposition policy before 1896. They could not accept Commercial Union because it meant the total surrender of tariff autonomy. Unrestricted Reciprocity was adopted as a compromise that retained autonomy. But its distinction from Commercial Union was too subtle for much of the electorate to grasp and left the party open to skillful exploitation by Macdonald's "loyalty" cry. More important, the very indefiniteness of what the Liberals meant by Unrestricted Reciprocity caused confusion and disruption in party ranks and eventually led to the revelation that Unrestricted Reciprocity did not mean the complete free interchange of all Canadian and American products after all. Rather, most Liberals simply wanted a more extensive reciprocity agreement with the United States than the Conservatives. Or, to put it another way, the Liberals were only interested in somewhat less protection from American competition than their opponents. W. S. Fielding's budget speech in 1897 had a very familiar ring to Canadian ears: "If our American friends wish to make a treaty with us, we are willing to meet them and treat on fair and equitable terms. If it shall not please them to do that, we shall in one way regret the fact but shall nevertheless go on our way rejoicing, and find other markets to build up the prosperity of Canada independent of the American people."[10]

25

Other problems in Canadian-American relations in the latter part of the nineteenth century were related to the nationalism of the National Policy. With the abrogation of the fishery articles of the Treaty of Washington by the United States, Canada was forced to adopt what can properly be called a "protectionist" policy for her inshore fisheries. The fisheries and the commercial privileges extended to Americans by the treaty were considered a national asset by Canadians. The object of their Government was to use that asset for the benefit of the whole of Canada, not simply the Maritime Provinces. It was for this reason that from 1871 on the fishery question was always related to reciprocity. On each occasion when Canada participated in negotiations the policy was always the same: Canada's exclusive and undoubted rights in the inshore fisheries would be bargained for the free exchange of natural products.

A different and more complex problem was presented by the Behring Sea dispute arising out of the seizure of Canadian pelagic sealers by United States revenue cruisers. The central problem was one of international law involving the doctrines of freedom of the seas and *mare clausum*. And because the Canadian vessels were of British registry, the British Government assumed a much more active negotiating role than was the case in some other disputes. But Canadian participation was far from negligible, and Sir Charles Hibbert Tupper and Sir Louis Davies made a point of protecting Canadian interests. Significantly, they argued that despite the legal technicalities, it was a Canadian industry that was threatened with destruction by the illegal acts of the United States Government and that the Mother Country had a clear duty to protect that industry.

The Alaska Boundary question also illustrated the relationship between the National Policy and Canada's relations with the United States. All of the evidence available suggests that the Canadian case was hopelessly weak and members of the Canadian Government (Laurier and Sifton) as much as admitted it both privately and in public. Why, then, was the case pressed with such vigour? Part of the answer, it seems to me, is that when the Alaska Boundary question became important for Canadians after the Yukon gold rush began, those responsible for Canadian policy, led by Clifford Sifton, regarded the question less as one of boundary definition than of commercial competition with the United States. Definition of the boundary was important because it was related to control of the growing Yukon trade. The intricate legal details of the boundary dispute were generally ignored by the Canadian Government. Writing during the meetings of the Joint High Commission in 1898, Lord Herschell complained to Lord Salisbury that "I found that the question had not been thoroughly studied or thought out by any Canadian official."[11] The urgent and ill-considered introduction of the Yukon Railway Bill of 1898 providing for a "Canadian" route to the Yukon — a route which was dependent upon trans-shipment privileges at the American customs port at Fort Wrangel and on navigation rights on the American portion of the Stikine River — illustrates the same point. The "imperative reason for immediate action" was that the Yukon trade was at stake, as the Minister of Railways and Canals explained to the House of Commons: "The importance of securing that trade and preserving it to Canada becomes a national question of the greatest interest . . . . It is ours, it is within our own borders and of right belongs to us, if, by any legitimate or proper means we can secure it for the people of our own country."[12]

Again, in the negotiations at the Joint High Commission of 1898–99 the Canadians insisted that if the boundary question went to arbitration, Pyramid Harbour should be reserved for Canada to match American insistence that Dyea and Skagway be reserved for the United States. While both sides thus rejected an unqualified and impartial arbitration, it must be admitted that Dyea and Skagway were established and settled communities under American control; Canada could make no such claim regarding Pyramid Harbour. Pyramid Harbour, as a Canadian outlet to the sea with a corresponding Canadian land corridor to the interior, had not arisen in negotiations until the meetings of the Joint High Commission and, as before, the Canadian claim was based primarily on the desire to secure control of the Yukon trade.

Ultimately, of course, Canadian indignation knew no bounds when Lord Alverstone reportedly suddenly changed his mind and awarded Pearse and Wales Islands to the United States in 1903. The settlement of 1903 was unquestionably diplomatic rather than "judicial". Theodore Roosevelt's pressure tactics before and during the meeting of the so-called "judicial tribunal" were certainly deplorable and these factors, combined with the apparent sacrifice of Canadian interests by Great Britain, have supplied grist for the mills of Canadian nationalists ever since. But too often the emphasis in Canadian historiography on this point has been misplaced by concentrating solely on the alleged British sellout. The more interesting point in all the clamour surrounding the Alaska Boundary decision is that, once again, National Policy interests were considered to be threatened by the decision. Alverstone's agreement with Lodge and Root, that Pearse and Wales Islands belonged to the United States, threatened the Laurier Government's first venture in transcontinental railway building. The projected terminus of the Grand Trunk Pacific, chartered just a few short months before, was Port Simpson on Observatory Inlet; Pearse and Wales Islands, which the Canadians believed could be armed by the United States, commanded the shipping lanes into Port Simpson. Thus, though the Yukon trade had drastically declined in value by 1903, from first serious consideration of the problem to final settlement the National Policy — an "all Canadian" trade route to the Yukon or a secure terminus for a new Pacific railway — dominated Canadian consideration of the Alaska Boundary dispute.

27

I have tried to suggest that the National Policy was a manifestation of Canadian national sentiment. Its basic assumptions, protection against the United States, the need for a "Canadian economy" with a strong industrial base and secure markets, and the implicit assumption of achieving greater autonomy within the Empire all crystallized that ill-defined, but deeply felt, sense of difference that set Canadians apart from both their neighbours to the south and the mother country. But why did this desire to proclaim a national identity take its form in economic terms?

Perhaps a part of the answer rests in the dilemma posed at the beginning of this paper. Appeals to a common language, a common cultural tradition or a common religion were simply impossible for Canadians and when they were attempted they were rightly regarded by French Canadians as a violation of their understanding of Confederation. Most Canadians, especially those who built or paid for the building of the transcontinental railways, argued that the Canadian nation would have to be built in spite of its geography and regarded their efforts as "the price of being Canadian". Appeals to national history could also be a divisive rather than a unifying factor for, as often as not, the two ethnic groups disagreed as to what, in their historical tradition, was a matter of pride or of humiliation. What was necessary, then, as Cartier put it in the Confederation debates, was to "form a political nationality". And it is not at all surprising that the political nationalism of the early decades of Confederation was expressed in terms of railways and tariffs.

It is a commonplace to equate the politics of North America in the latter part of the nineteenth century with self-seeking capitalism. But we might remind ourselves that the age of Darwinism and of industrialism was also a great age of nationalism. The nationalism of the large assertive states of the age, the United States, Germany and Great Britain, was assuredly economic in its emphasis. In the United States, in particular, nationalism was equated with the problems of industrialism and industrial expansion. In keeping with Darwinian assumptions, bigness was a virtue for a nation state, and industrialism was the key to bigness. At the very time their own nation was being born, Canadians reasoned that industrialism was the determining factor in the victory of the North in the Civil War and in the apparent reunification of the United States. Industrialism meant power; power to withstand the pressures from the south and power to expand and consolidate the Canadian nation. And a political programme that emphasized expansion and industrialism had the added advantage of ignoring the potentially divisive issues that would disrupt a "political nationality".

In sum, then, the National Policy, a policy for a "Canadian economy" and a "Big Canada", a materialistic policy for a materialistic age, was the obvious policy to give expression to Canadian national sentiment. That policy was adopted in 1878 and accepted by the Liberal party in 1896. Three years later J. I. Tarte urged Laurier to do more than simply accept the National Policy, to expand upon it with more railways, canals and harbour improvements (and presumably with higher tariffs). "Voilà", he observed, "le programme le plus national et le plus populaire que nous puissons offrir au pays".[13]

Notes

1. Carl Berger, "The True North Strong and Free", in *Nationalism in Canada*, Toronto, 1966, p. 3ff.
2. *Macdonald Papers*, (P.A.C.) Macdonald to T. C. Patteson, February 27, 1872.
3. John Dales, "Protection, Immigration and Canadian Nationalism", in *Nationalism in Canada*, op. cit. pp. 167–170.
4. A. B. Keith, *Selected Speeches and Documents on British Colonial Policy, 1763–1917*, London, 1953, p. 60.
5. J. S. Ewart, *The Kingdom Papers*, Vol. 1, Ottawa, 1912, p. 3.
6. *Sifton Papers*, (P.A.C.) Sifton to James Fleming, March 13, 1897.
7. *Manifesto of Eighteen Toronto Liberals on Reciprocity*, February 20, 1911; cited, *Canadian Annual Review*, Toronto, 1911, p. 49.
8. Henry Borden (ed.) *Robert Laird Borden: His Memoirs*, Vol. 1, Toronto, 1938, p. 327.
9. *House of Commons Debates*, April 15, 1880, pp. 1424–5.
10. *House of Commons Debates*, April 22, 1897.
11. Cited in R. C. Brown, *Canada's National Policy, 1883–1900*, Princeton, 1964, p. 379.
12. *House of Commons Debates*, February 8, 1898, pp. 191–2.
13. *Laurier Papers* (P.A.C.), Tarte to Laurier, April 3, 1899.

28

Some Historical and Theoretical Comment on Canada's National Policies *

JOHN H. DALES

"It is high time that someone should write the history of Canada since Confederation as a triumph of the forces of economic and political development over the policies of Macdonald and his successors."

I

To the infant industry argument for protectionism Canadians have added an infant nation argument. Among Canadian academic historians, journalists, and citizens at large there seems to be a dangerous unanimity of opinion that Canada is a transparently artificial entity whose very existence has always depended on something called a national policy. Canada, in this view, is a denial of geography and a travesty of economics that stands as living proof of the primacy of politics in the affairs of men. Critical comment to the effect that most Canadian manufacturers still depend on protective tariffs is very apt to be greeted first by astonishment that anyone would think the comment worth making, and then by patient explanation that of course many parts of the Canadian economy — not only manufacturing — have *always* depended on government bounty in one form or another, and that Canada simply wouldn't exist as a nation if public support were not continuously made available to key sectors of the economy. Such a policy is necessary, the explanation continues, both in order to overcome the outrageous geography of the country and in order to defend the nation's economy against the formidable efficiency, and thus the natural expansionism, of the American economy. In Canada infant industries are not *expected* to grow up.

I reject this view of Canada. It seems to me to be subversive not only of the nation's wealth but also of the nation's pride. National pride and economic performance I believe to be positively, not negatively, correlated; both efficiency and honour, as the parable of the talents teaches, come from making the most of what one has, not from having the most. And yet Canadian economic policy — and, what is more important, the economic policy of so many developing nations to-day — aims consistently at maximizing the purse. Gross National Product, rather than the performance, Gross National Product per citizen.

Sir John A. Macdonald gave us our first national policy, and our first lessons in the irrelevance of economics. Western lands, he argued, must be controlled by the Dominion because provincial land policies "might be obstructive to immigration", i.e. provinces might try to sell land rather

* From *Queen's Quarterly*, LXXII (1964): 297–316. Copyright 1967 by John H. Dales. Reprinted by permission of the editors.

rather than give it away. Canadian railways, in Macdonald's view, were not to be thought of primarily as business enterprises; they were instruments of national development and served this end by providing both attractive objects of government expenditure and reliable surces of party support. As for the tariff, Macdonald rang all the changes on the protectionist fallacies and promised that *his* tariff would benefit everyone, the teachings of the dismal science notwithstanding. Macdonald was the first great Canadian non-economist; he was also an endearing figure, full of robust good humour, who practised with zest what he preached.

It is hard to believe, though, that Macdonald deserves the whole credit for the low esteem in which economics and economists are held in Canada to-day. Macdonald has in any event had powerful support from Canadian historians, of both the political and economic persuasions, who have rationalized his national policy and have encouraged Canadians to believe that by disregarding economics they could build a nation that would represent a victory over mere materialism. The national policy originally consisted of government support for three main ventures: railway building, Western settlement, and manufacturing development. (We adopt the original convention of using "national policy" for the famous trinity of Canadian nation-building policies, and of reserving "National Policy" for the protective tariff policy.) The mutual consistency of Western settlement and railway building was perhaps fairly obvious; land grants helped to finance railways, and railway companies encouraged settlement. From an economist's point of view, however, the rationalization has been carried a little far. The government has been praised for using valuable lands as a loss-leader, while the C.P.R. has been praised for selling land to immigrants at prices considerably below those charged by other land owners, and for showing great initiative in developing uneconomic irrigation projects.

What was at first difficult for historians to discover was the consistency between Macdonald's tariff policy and the other two prongs of his national policy. The late Professor H. A. Innis seems to have provided the connecting argument. The role of the tariff in the Canadian economy, he taught, was to inhibit Canadian-American trade, to promote East-West trade in Canada, and in this way to provide revenue for Canadian transcontinental railways. Though I cannot resist a long footnote on the subject, I do not want to make a full textual analysis of Innis's writings in order to try to find out whether he believed that his tariff-railway link was (a) the *ex post* result of the two policies — the way things worked out, or (b) the *ex-ante* design — the way things were intended to work out, or (c) either or both of these combined with the opinion that the link was felicitous. (See Appendix). I wish only to suggest that once the Innis link was forged the way was wide open for a full-scale rationalization of the national policy. Thus D. G. Creighton:

[The tariff] was intimately and vitally related to the other national policies. By means of the tariff, the settlement of the west would provide a national market; and this national

30

market would supply east-west traffic for Canadian transcontinental railways and areas of exploitation for eastern Canadian industry. (*Dominion of the North*, 1944, 346).

And J. B. Brebner:

Looking backward from the present, it is easy to see that the very existence of both the Province and the later Dominion of Canada as entities separate from the United States has depended on such expensive transportation services that a large proportion of their cost has had to be met from the public purse . . . it was [in the exuberant 1850's] that Canadians . . . began systematically to adopt the *only* procedure by which they could surmount this handicap, that is, the imposition of quite high tariffs on manufactured goods. (*North Atlantic Triangle*, 1945, 158, my italics).

W. T. Easterbrook and H. G. Aitken:

[The detailed program of Canadian nation building] appeared slowly and in piecemeal fashion but by 1879 . . . the parts of the comprehensive and more or less complete pattern had fallen into place: a transcontinental railway, protective tariffs, land settlement policy, the promotion of immigration. (*Canadian Economic History*, 1956, 383).

31

And the present author, who providentially has written very little on the subject:

The Dominion immediately proceeded to fulfil its purposes. A transcontinental railway system was constructed, an energetic settlement policy was adapted to the needs of the West, and the tariff was designed to develop Canadian industry and stimulate Canadian trade. These policies proved effective in the period of prosperity which began towards the end of the nineteenth century. (J. H. Dales, *Engineering and Society*, Part II, 1946, 246.)

Two features of the historians' stereotype of the national policy should be noted. First, much emphasis is placed on the consistency of the three pillars of the program, while inconsistencies are either ignored or glossed over. Among the authors I have consulted, several mention the regional inconsistency inherent in the policy. V. C. Fowke, in particular, interprets the national policy as a program designed by and for Central Canadians. The national policy is therefore seen not as national at all but rather as a policy of Central Canadian Imperialism. Fowke comes dangerously close to shattering the whole myth of the national policy, yet in the end he refuses to be an iconoclast. Thus his glosses that the national policy was "prerequisite to western development" and that "the groundwork [for western development] . . . was laid . . . by the institution of the 'National Policy' of tariff protection . . . "[1] seem wildly inconsistent with his main position, particularly in view of his insistence that Macdonald's railway policy was *not* prerequisite to western development: "As far as the western provinces are concerned . . . Canadian railways are expensive alternatives to American railways rather than to no railways at all."[2] Brebner and Careless both hint at the logical inconsistency inherent in protectionism, namely, the attempt to build a wealthy nation by lowering the standard of living of its population. Thus Careless notes that "A protective tariff plainly meant that goods would cost more to buy in Canada," yet after a token flirtation with this line of reasoning he surrenders to the stereotype on the following page and concludes that "as far as Canada is concerned the protective tariff system that was adopted under Macdonald . . . did much in the long run to develop the wealth and encourage the industry of the Dominion." (*Canada*, 1953, 277-8). He then goes on to paint the usual picture of the wonderful consistency among Canada's railway, settlement and tariff policies.

None of the authors I have examined has flatly challenged the national stereotype of the beneficence of the national policy. W. A. Mackintosh, however, writes very cautiously about this subject. He outlines the "Basic National Decisions" and their interrelations in Chapter II, of his *The Economic Background of Dominion-Provincial Relations*, but adds at the end of the chapter: "It is not suggested that these national decisions were taken by governments, or still less by electorates, in full consciousness of their implications, nor that the inter-relations among them were fully appreciated. They were in large measure the outcome of conflicts of interest and, to some extent, of political expediency" (p. 21). Later he notes the regional conflicts occasioned by the national policies, and the tendency of these policies to rigidify the economy by creating "vested interests, regional and sectional, which would resist readjustment" (p. 37). Also two other authors, both political historians, have distinguished themselves by refusing to have anything to do with the standard patter. Chester Martin disdains even to mention the tariff in his *Foundations of Canadian Nationhood*; A. R. M. Lower bluntly refers to the National Policy as being a "frank creation of vested manufacturing interests living on the bounty of government," and in exasperation writes that "Macdonald's way of imposing the new tariff was simple: he just invited anyone who wanted a duty to come to Ottawa and ask for it." (*Colony to Nation*, 1946, 373-4).

The stereotype of the national policy is powerful enough not only to bridge logical inconsistencies but also to abridge time. To its defenders the national policy was both a well designed and a powerful engine of nation-building. Yet it refused to function for some twenty or thirty years. Many authors simply ignore this awkward gap in timing, as does Dales in the quotation above. Others mention it and then ignore it, as for example Easterbrook and and Aitken: "The three decades following Confederation . . . seemed to many a prolonged period of marking time . . . Not until the turn of the century did the program of nation-building begin to pay off . . ." (381). After a long account of the Time of Troubles in both its economic and political aspects, Careless finds himself concluding that "conservative nationalism was played out," and thus in imminent danger of rending the stereotype beyond repair. But he draws back at the very brink of the abyss, and proclaims in strident tones that "Macdonald nationalism had not failed. It was the age that had failed . . . " (295).

Why can we not bring ourselves to say quite simply that the national policy was a dismal failure? Everyone admits, for example, that the land settlement policy was a failure before 1900. After 1900 the demand for Western land was so brisk, and the C.P.R. and various land companies so zealous in attracting settlers to the region, that it is hard to believe that the homestead policy was in any sense necessary as a means of settling the West. It was, indeed, probably undesirable. After writing of the efficiency and enterprise of the private land companies, Martin notes that "The general opening of 'Dominion lands,' even- and odd-numbered sections alike, to homestead entry after 1908 brought a deluge of less selective migration to Western Canada. In vain the government had sought to reserve vast areas with marginal rainfall in 'Palliser's triangle' for grazing and other purposes. In the queues which formed up at the land offices prospective settlers, as one observer records, 'held their place in the line day and night for two or three weeks to enable them to file on certain lands,' and places in the queue were frequently bought and sold for 'substantial sums of money.'" Uneconomically low prices inevitably produce queues. No one, I suggest, really believes that without the homestead policy in particular, and the settlement policy in general, the West would not have been settled. These policies were powerless to promote settlement before 1900; after 1900 their chief effect was to promote not settlement but *rapid* settlement, and there is much evidence to suggest that the rapidity of settlement did much short term and long term harm in Western Canada. Martin's trenchant criticism of the homestead system certainly permits one to believe that Canada would have been better off without this member of the national policy trilogy.

33

As with land settlement policy so with tariff policy; later in this paper, when I comment on international trade theory, I shall suggest that we would have been much better off still if we had never tangled with the National Policy. Historically it need only be noted that manufacturing was developing in Canada well before the tariff of 1879; Mackintosh notes that the "Census of 1871 reveals that Canada had made some progress along the path of industrialization," and that "The new protectionist policy intensified, broadly speaking, industrial trends already visible." (*The Economic Background of Dominion Provincial Relations*, 1939, 17 and 20). Moreover Canadian manufacturing grew less rapidly than American manufacturing both before and after the tariff and net emigration from Canada was a feature of the decades both before and after 1879. To the extent that the National Policy was intended to reverse, or even to reduce, the disparity in Canadian and American growth rates it was clearly a failure. After 1900 the Canadian economy, including Canadian manufacturing, grew more rapidly than the American economy for a dozen years, and Canadian historians have not hesitated to attribute this surge to the beneficial, if somewhat delayed, effects of the National Policy. As Careless wrote, it was the "age that had failed" before 1900 and the rise of a prosperous age after 1900 that "spelt success at long last for the National Policy . . . " (295 and 312). In Canadian history it is heads the National Policy wins, and tails the age loses.

There remains the curious case of the C.P.R. While a Canadian transcontinental railway, as Fowke argues, was not prerequisite to Western development, economists and political scientists can agree that as a matter of political economy such a railway was an essential adjunct of nationhood for the new Dominion. The railway had to be built for political reasons, whatever the subsidy involved; sensible economic policy required only that the subsidy be kept as low as possible. The C.P.R. was in fact heavily subsidized. Still, given the lacklustre performance of Canadian settlement and tariff policies before the middle 1890's one might have expected, on the basis of the national policy stereotype in general and the Innis link in particular, that the C.P.R. would have been unable to survive its first bleak decade. Surely no one would wish to argue that the population of Western Canada in 1895 (perhaps a third of a million people, an increase of something over 100 000 since the completion of the C.P.R.) was able to supply either enough wheat or a large enough market for manufactured goods to make a paying proposition out of even so heavily subsidized a transcontinental railway as the C.P.R. Yet the C.P.R. was profitable from the minute it was completed and began to pay dividends on its common stock in 1889. The Wheat Boom that began in the closing years of the century was only the frosting on the cake that allowed the Company to raise dividends from 4% in 1897 to 10% in 1911, despite large decreases in railway rates around the turn of the century. The chronology of C.P.R. earnings thus raises a nagging doubt about whether the C.P.R. ever *needed* to be subsidized indirectly by the tariff as well as directly by grants of money and a kingdom in land. Professor Fogel's conclusion that the Union Pacific Railway would have been profitable *without* subsidies, despite unanimous opinion, before the fact, that it would not be,[3] suggests a need for testing the hypothesis that the C.P.R. would have been profitable with direct subsidies alone, or even, subversive thought, without *any* subsidy! Careful analysis of this matter seems to be an urgent necessity. The core of the national policy has always been the protective tariff, and although today the tariff is more and more often brazenly defended simply on the grounds that we must protect the vested interests we have built up, the argument of last resort is still that the tariff is the defender of the railways, and thus of the East-West economy. The defence retains its appeal since the railways still carry a great deal of freight, if not many passengers, and the Innis link remains persuasive. If it were possible to deny the validity of the Innis argument that without the tariff there would be no C.P.R., it would be much more difficult for present-day nationalists to argue that if there were no tariff there would be no Canada.

There are, therefore, reasonable grounds for questioning the validity of the historians' stereotype of the national policy. To stress the consistency of the national policy as an interrelated whole is to ignore all too cavalierly its inconsistencies. And to write as if the wisdom and power of a nation-building program that is ineffective for two or three decades is somehow "proved" or "demonstrated" by a subsequent period of great prosperity is to mislead the public with a monstrous example of the *post hoc ergo propter hoc* fallacy. Moreover, the whole tortuous exercise is so unnecessary, for a

34

much more reasonable, and very much simpler, explanation of the Great Canadian Boom is also standard fare in our textbooks. This explanation runs in terms of a number of world events and developments in the last decade of the nineteenth century, all of which reacted favourably on the Canadian economy — the "closing" of the American frontier, rising world prices, falling shipping rates, the development of the gradual reduction process for milling wheat, and the development of the technique of making paper from wood pulp are perhaps the principal items in the list. None of these factors owed anything to the national policy.

Why, then, do historians insist on overdetermining their explanation of the Great Boom by trying to fit a perfectly straightforward argument into the national policy stereotype, as Fowke, for example, does when he writes that "This conjuncture of world circumstances created the opportunity for Canadian expansion, but a half-century of foundation work along the lines of the national policy had prepared Canada for the opportunity." (70). Economic man does not need to be prepared by government policy before he reacts to opportunities for making profits. Is it crude hero worship, or an unconscious human predisposition to human explanations of history that leads Canadians to believe that what success they have enjoyed "must" reflect Macdonald's wise nation-building policies? Or are we all of us merely prisoners of our own history — as it has been written? It is very odd that, enjoying one of the highest standards of living in the world, Canadians in all walks of life should nevertheless believe that their economy is a frail, hothouse creation, whose very survival depends on the constant vigilance of a government gardener well provided with props and plant food. Who but historians could have created this chasm between reality and belief? It is high time that someone should write the history of Canada since Confederation as a triumph of the forces of economic and political development over the national policies of Macdonald and his successors.

35

II

We turn, now, on the economic theorists. Was it not Keynes who insisted that we were all of us likely to be prisoners, not of plausible history, but of outmoded economic theory? And what branch of economic theory could be more outmoded than international trade theory, which still hews to the Ricardian line that factors of production never move from one country to another? A theory based on the absurd assumption that men, capital, and knowledge never cross national borders is guaranteed to produce conclusions that are irrelevant to the real world. Did Ricardo imagine that his assumption was the only possible way in which to distinguish international trade from any other trade? Our present-day mathematical ethic enables us to see clearly enough that there is no qualitative difference between international trade, interregional trade, inter-city trade and inter-household trade. The realities of national differences in monetary units and monetary and fiscal policies, in immigration policies and tariff policies, not to mention international differences in tastes and natural resources, surely provide sufficient justification for treating international trade as an institutionally distinct branch of economic theory; it seems a work of supererogation to create an additional unrealistic distinction between domestic trade and international trade.

Be that as it may, the Ricardian assumption has stultified international trade theory in at least one major respect; it has prevented the development of any long run theory of international trade, and thus of any long run theory of protectionism. The long run in economics is defined as the time during which supplies of the factors of production adjust to changes in price; thus the assumption that national supplies of factors of production never change means — to overstate the matter somewhat — that we have no theory of the long run effects of international trade. The theory of international trade is thereby distinguished from all other branches of economic theory by its inability to say anything about changes in capacity to produce.[4] It is no doubt for this reason that the short run theorems of international trade have been so little heeded by politicians, who have always been able to reply, "Ah, yes, but in the long run . . . " infant industries will grow and reap the economies of scale, the labour force will be transformed from low-productivity agriculture to high-productivity manufacturing, G.N.P. will grow, the population will increase, we will be more self-sufficient, and so on and on. International trade theory has failed conspicuously to provide any check on the long run "theorizing" of the man in the street and in government.

In principle it is clearly possible for a protective tariff to create a sustained change in the terms at which domestic goods relative to imported goods are available to domestic consumers. This change in relative prices, consumers' tastes remaining unchanged, will affect the factor supplies available to the domestic economy — just as a sustained change in the prices of two domestic goods will affect the factor supplies available to each of the two industries producing them. But while in a free price system resources will flow *away* from the industry whose product has risen in price, as a result of an increase in the real costs of producing it, artificial distortion of relative prices by government policy may make at least some resources flow up-hill *to* a high-cost industry. Suppose the state were to "protect" the production of hand-made cigars by making illegal the sale of machine-made cigars. The cost of producing cigars, and consequently their price, would rise. If, however, the demand for cigars were inelastic, consumption would fall less than proportionately, the value of output of the industry would rise, and, with the more labour-intensive method of production, at least one factor of production, labour, would flow to the industry. It is not my purpose to develop here a full theory of the effects of a protective tariff on domestic factor supplies, but I do suggest that the tariff case may prove to have certain similarities to the cigar example, including the conclusion of negative economic progress to which the example points. My studies of the Canadian economy have led me to believe that in the long run the Canadian tariff: (1) tends to increase the supplies of labour and capital in the country and thus to raise G.N.P.; (2) tends to keep the standard of living — G.N.P. per capita — lower than it would otherwise be; and (3) may lower the average quality of the Canadian labour force by promoting the immigration of workers with average, or perhaps lower than average, skill levels, and the emigration of those who may, more confidently, be supposed to have above average levels of education and training. I shall not here attempt fully to support these views, but I shall comment briefly on each of them merely in order to suggest that they are sensible hypotheses that merit the attention of international trade theorists.

We must first of all exorcise a widely-held but erroneous assumption. Discussions of the economic effects of tariffs are usually based on the implicit assumption that the tariffs on the law books always produce their intended effects on the economy; in fact, many actual tariffs constitute a species of economic "blue laws" that have no economic effect whatever. Tariffs can have a variety of economic effects, but we are here interested only in their effect on the allocation of resources within a country. We therefore define *an effective tariff* as one that directly affects resource allocation, and refer to all other tariffs as being *ineffective*. Ineffective tariffs are of various kinds: (1) a tariff that is exactly matched by an excise or sales tax on domestic production of the good in question; (2) a tariff on goods that are not domestically produced — the tariff is then just a tax on the consumption of a particular commodity, and has no direct effect on domestic resource allocation; and (3) a tariff on a good that is produced so efficiently at home that even in the absence of the tariff imports could not compete with domestic production — the tariff then has no effect on prices, government revenues or resource allocation and is the sort of "blue law" tariff referred to above.

37

Consideration of the third type of ineffective tariff leads us to a surprising conclusion. If a domestic producer exports regularly and in significant volume we can be sure that he is a low-cost producer by international standards and that he has nothing to fear from import competition; accordingly sustained exports of a good provide *prima facie* proof that a domestic tariff on that good is ineffective. Since the United States during the first half of this century was a large exporter of a very wide range of manufactured goods, we can conclude that, in general, tariff protection of manufacturing in the United States during this period did not exist, and that American tariffs on most manufactured goods were of the "blue law" variety. It is important to note, however, that both the second and third types of ineffective tariffs may, without any change in the law, become effective. If the prospective domestic costs of producing an article that is not now produced domestically fall secularly relative to the costs of producing that article elsewhere, a time will come when domestic costs of production are marginally lower than world costs plus the domestic tariff;

domestic entrepreneurs will then begin to produce the good under the protection of the tariff, and the ineffective "revenue" tariff (type two above) will be transformed into an effectively protective tariff. In the reverse case, when domestic costs of production rise relative to foreign costs of production a "blue law" tariff (type three above) can easily become an effective tariff. In view of the great reduction achieved in the costs of producing manufactured goods in Western Europe and in Japan in recent years, one might hazard the guess that many American tariffs which were "blue laws" a decade ago are now effective, i.e., protective in fact.

This discussion serves to remind us that a given tariff may provide any degree of protection from zero to infinity at a point of time, and a degree of protection that may vary, again from zero to infinity, over time. The upshot is that it is not only very difficult to measure the economic effects of a protectionist policy; it is also very difficult to find out whether it has any effect at all! Generally, it is clear that a protectionist policy with respect to manufacturing will do little harm either to countries with manufacturing capacity that is low cost by world standards, e.g., the United States in the first half of this century, or to countries with such a large comparative disadvantage in manufacturing that even with high tariffs little manufacturing develops in the country. The countries that suffer from protectionism are the countries where tariffs are effective, i.e., countries where manufacturing costs are only moderately above world costs, and thus lie below world costs plus domestic tariff rates. These countries suffer, in brief, because their tariffs really work. On the basis of a considerable amount of statistical work contained in an unpublished study, I am satisfied that the Canadian tariff *has* been effective over the period since 1926, the beginning date for the central part of the statistical study. More generally, it seems very likely that the National Policy has been effective, and probably strongly so, during most of the past eighty-five years.

We return now to our alleged long run effects of protectionism. An effective tariff, we claim, will lead on the one hand to an increase in a country's supplies of labour and capital, and on the other, as traditional theory argues, to a reduction in income per capita. Since it may seem odd to argue that the same force that leads to a decrease in income per head will also lead to a growth of population, we must pause to note the institutional assumptions that make this result possible. In the first place we assume that the major, and normal, mechanism of population adjustment is change in net migration; there is statistical evidence that such has been the case in Canadian development.[5] The second assumption is statistically untested, but I think it gives a fair representation of Canada's historical experience with respect to both immigration and emigration. It is that migration is responsive not only to differences in per capita income levels between countries, but also to differences in the volume of job opportunities between countries. Accordingly, immigration to a country may rise so long as job opportunities in the country are increasing, provided only that the standard of living in the country, though falling, remains above the standard of living in the country of emigration; conversely emigration from a country may fail to rise, even if the standard of living in the country is falling, if employment opportunities are scarce in countries of prospective emigration, i.e., those countries where the standard of living is higher. By creating jobs, even if they be jobs in uneconomic industries, an effective tariff can, under certain conditions, promote net immigration and population growth. Granted that effective protectionism in general, and the Canadian National Policy in particular, actually does tend to raise a country's population and G.N.P., we can see why any proposal to move from protection to free trade is so unattractive politically. Politicians dearly love big populations and big national incomes; the only question seems to be how far they are willing to depress their electorate's standard of living in order to add another thousand people and another two or three millions of dollars to the total magnitudes.

Our third statement about protection alleges, in effect, that an effective tariff policy may lower the average quality of a country's labour force. We have argued that protection is likely to lead to net immigration, the increased labour force being absorbed in the growing manufacturing sector and associated service industries. I shall simply assume that the average skill level required in these employments is the same as the average skill level in the country's labour force before protection. Under this assumption, protection leaves the quality of the labour force unchanged so far as immigration is concerned. But what of emigration?

Let us continue to consider the manufacturing sector of the economy to be the main "beneficiary" of protection. I suggest that protected industries impose a low ceiling on the careers available to their executive personnel, and thus severely cramp the style of ambitious members of the business élite. The reason is that protected industries, which by definition produce at costs above world costs, are thereby prevented from exporting and are confined to the home market. (In passing we should note that it is far closer to the truth to say that the domestic tariff confines industries to the home market than to say that foreign tariffs do so. Tariffs throughout the world restrict trade but they do not reduce it to zero. The market available to any business is always the world market; if a protected manufacturer of widgets in Canada is undersold in third markets by a manufacturer of widgets in Sweden *given existing tariffs*, an abolition of all foreign tariffs will be of no benefit whatever to the Canadian widget producer because he will *still* be undersold in foreign markets by his Swedish competitor.) Home markets have never been large enough to contain the energies of the best businessmen. Having gained experience in a protected industry, and having bumped his head on the ceiling of the home market, the ambitious executive is likely to move to some other country where his industry is not protected, and where he can get into the international swim. Thus there is some reason to expect the average quality of business leadership in protected industries to be below that in

39

non-protected industries. I leave it to other investigators, more courageous than I, to test this hypothesis empirically in Canada, perhaps by comparing the quality of business leadership in Canada's export industries with that in the protected industries. The export of brains from Canada is certainly not to be explained entirely, or even mainly, in terms of protectionism, but I think it probable that the National Policy acts as a selective mechanism tending to increase the proportion of second-grade business executives in Canada, and thus to lower the average quality of business leadership in the country. It might be noted, finally, in view of the current interest in investment in human capital as an attractive avenue to economic development, that there is little point in a society's striving to increase its supply of highly-trained businessmen if it can offer an increased demand for them only by expanding its protected production; top-flight people on the average display high mobility.

40 III

In this paper I have questioned the adequacy of conventional historical interpretations of Canada's nation-building policies, and especially of Canadian protectionism, by reference to simple economic theory; and have questioned the adequacy of conventional tariff theory by reference to the economic history of Canada and to some speculation about the contemporary Canadian economy. If my hunches about the long run costs of protectionism to the Canadian economy turn out on further investigation not to be grossly exaggerated, the probable economic cost of the National Policy to Canada in terms of a general, and perhaps progressive, weakening of economic efficiency and economic morale, will be heavy indeed — of an order of magnitude entirely different from the "cost of the tariff" as conventionally calculated under the Ricardian assumption.[6] Moreover there should be charged to Canada's national policy a heavy cost in terms of political obfuscation, for it is a serious matter in a democracy when the purposes of economic policy are confused. All three Canadian nation building policies have been intended to increase the size of the economy. Whatever political attraction this goal may have it has no economic justification; economics has to do with the maximizing of income from given resources, not with the maximizing of resources. In practice it may very well happen that the size of an economy can only be increased at the expense of the quality of its economic life. In Canada our National Policy leads us to think even today in terms of size rather than quality, greatly to the detriment, in my opinion, of our national life. It is perhaps time for Canadian historians to take economic theory seriously; and for international trade theorists to accept the historical record of large-scale movements of men and capital across international borders as a challenge to develop a theory that will elucidate the long run effects of protectionism on a country's capacity to produce. It is possible that both groups would then have something of value to tell developing nations about the long run dangers of national policies in general, and of the protectionist route to economic salvation in particular.

Appendix

The Innis link was derived from Galt's argument, made in reply to protests from British manufacturers against his raising of the Canadian tariff in the late 1850's, that increased tariff revenue was necessary to help pay for Canadian canals and railways that could not be profitably built by private concerns, and that British manufacturers ought to be pleased with the arrangement because the cheaper cost of transportation would lower the price of British manufactured goods in Canada and thus increase the market for them. Innis accepted as profound this economic doubletalk of a suave politician, though with a certain amount of incredulity about its source: " . . . whether or not [Galt's] explanation was one of rationalization after the fact, or of original theoretical analysis, reliance on the customs was undoubtedly the only solution." Surely it wasn't the only solution; if the canals had been paid for by domestic taxation, or by import duties that were no heavier than domestic excise duties, the British manufacturers would have been at least as well off, and Canadians would have been better off. A subsidy is always to be preferred to a tariff on both economic grounds and political grounds; on economic grounds because direct payments distort resource allocation less than indirect payments, and on political grounds because direct payments involve less deception than indirect payments.

41

Galt was talking *mainly* of revenue tariffs. Innis extended the Galt argument to tariffs that were mainly protective, and thereby compounded Galt's error. "The National Policy was designed not only to increase revenue from customs [as in Galt's argument] but also to increase revenue from traffic from the standpoint of the railways. The increasing importance of railways has tended to emphasize the position of protection rather than revenue." As economic theory this is absurd, not only because the railways, like the canals, could have been financed more efficiently by subsidy than by tariff, but also because a tariff cannot at the same time maximize both protection and revenue; the greater the protective effect of a tariff the less the revenue will provide. The charitable interpretation of this passage is that Innis was indulging in "rationalization after the fact." In the article in which these passages occurred, Innis at any rate doubted the *future* application of his argument: "Dependence on the application of mature technique, especially in transport, to virgin natural resources must steadily recede in importance as a basis for the tariff. It will become increasingly difficult to wield the tariff as the crude but effective weapon by which we have been able to obtain a share of our natural resources."

All of the above quotations are taken from an article by Innis published in 1931, and reprinted in H. A. Innis, *Essays in Canadian Economic History* (Toronto, 1956), pp. 76–7. Two years later Innis was in a deep quandary

about the effect of the Canadian tariff. "Inflexibility of the tariff down-
ward contributed to the difficulties during the period of prosperity which
began . . . in 1896 . . . " (ibid., p. 91). On the following page he wrote
that "During a period of prosperity the tariff should be raised to act as a
brake . . . . If railroad rates are lowered at the beginning of a period of
prosperity tariff rates should be raised accordingly . . . . Lowering the
tariff during the period of a depression and raising the tariff during a
period of prosperity might do much to alleviate the problem of a staple-
producing area" (pp. 92–3). The only way I can see of resolving the
contradiction between these two quotations is to suppose that in the first
Innis was thinking of the combined effect on C.P.R. revenues of the wheat
boom and the continued support of the tariff, and the consequent effect of
swollen railway revenues in promoting a new, and uneconomically large,
railway building program in Canada: had the tariff been lowered, and the
C.P.R.'s profit thereby dampened, the incentive to build *two* new transcontinental railways in Canada would have been reduced; and that in the
second he was thinking of the Western farmer: the wheat boom might have
been dampened by raising farm cost by means of *increased* tariff rates in
order to offset the advantages that farmers gained by lowered railway
rates. Since the final part of the second quotation recommends a counter-
cyclical tariff policy (Innis must have known how politically impracticable
this was!), with no qualification about how railway rates should be changed,
one can only make sense out of this passage by supposing that by 1933
Innis was willing to sacrifice the railways to the farmers during depression
and the farmers to the railways during prosperity; his recommended
policy would be counter-cyclical for farmers and pro-cyclical for railways!
Perhaps the subtlety, or the confusion, was covering a retreat. Realizing
that a high tariff may "become inadequate" during depressions (p. 91),
and suggesting that the period of resource expansion in Canada had ended,
Innis in fact repudiated his linking of the National Policy and railways by
reverting to the lesser economic confusions of Galt's position: "Assuming
relative stability in the production of raw materials as a result of exhaustion of natural resources the tariff must assume to an increasing extent the
position of a toll, as Galt originally planned, and should approximate the
deficit on transportation finance" (p. 93). Unfortunately the damage had
been done, for text book writers cannot spare the time to assess qualifications to, or second thoughts on, powerful generalizations.

Notes

1. V. C. Fowke, *Canadian Agricultural Policy* (Toronto, 1946), 8. Fowke may mean that the National
policy was a prerequisite from Central Canadians' point of view, i.e., that Central Canada would not
have "invested" in the West without it. At the same time he would not argue that Eastern investment
was a *sine qua non* of Western development; see footnote 2.
2. V. C. Fowke, *The National Policy and The Wheat Economy* (Toronto, 1957), 69.
3. R. W. Fogel, *The Union Pacific Railroad* (Baltimore, 1960), Passim.
4. Writings in the field of international trade are not, of course, entirely devoid of discussions of
international factor movements; recent literature on the subject is summarized in R. C. Caves, *Trade and*

Economic Structure (Cambridge, 1960), Ch. V. The literature has concentrated to a large extent on the question of whether, and to what extent, factor movements are substitutes for goods movements in international trade; interest has thus been focussed on the short run effects on trade of the movement of factors, rather than on the long run effects of the factor movements on a country's capacity to produce. This is particularly true of the literature on capital movements which has been concerned largely with the "transfer problem" and thus, as Caves writes, "with the monetary and short run disturbances accompanying the capital transfer." (p. 133). The international trade literature on labour migration comes closer to the problem of long run changes in capacity to produce; see the summary of this work, pp. 139 ff. It remains true, I think, that work on the long run effects of international trade on a country's capacity to produce is still fragmentary and not integrated into the main body of trade theory.

5. In an unpublished paper D. J. Daly has shown that gross immigration has been much more important as a proportion of population change in Canada than in the United States, and that changes in net migration have been more important than changes in natural increase of population in determining changes in total Canadian population. (D. J. Daly "Kuznets Cycles in Canada," paper presented to the Ottawa Chapter, Canadian Political Science Association, March 13, 1962, Charts 2 and 3).

6. J. H. Young, *Canadian Commercial Policy* (Ottawa, 1957), Ch. 7; H. G. Johnson, "The Cost of Protection and the Scientific Tariff" in *Journal of Political Economy*, August, 1960, 327–345.

43

Topic Three

The Métis, Louis Riel, and the Rise of Western Alienation

44

From the beginning, the Canadian West felt exploited by outside interests and dependent on imperial centres beyond its own borders. Incorporation into Confederation intensified this feeling of alienation and aroused a regional consciousness.

The early Canadian West was the scene of rivalry between two competitive fur-trading interests: the Hudson's Bay Company and the French traders in the French Regime and, after the Conquest, the Hudson's Bay Company and the North West Company traders. The French traders intermarried with the Indians, creating on the Plains a new group of seminomadic people known as Métis. Many of the Métis settled in what became known after 1811 as the Red River colony at the junction of the Red and Assiniboine Rivers. By the mid-nineteeth century they had developed their own sense of nationality.

In 1869 the newly formed Canadian government purchased Rupert's Land, the territory administered by the Hudson's Bay Company, for a cash payment of £300 000 plus one-twentieth of the fertile area in the West. It was to be a colony of the Dominion of Canada, and administered by a federally appointed lieutenant governor and council until provincial status was granted. The Canadian government acquired control of the land and natural resources to be used in the means most suited for the expansion of the nation. These transactions were concluded without consulting the local western population. The Canadian government also arranged for the new lieutenant governor and a group of surveyors to go west to prepare the way for settlement and the building of a transcontinental railway.

The Métis resisted under the leadership of Louis Riel, a Métis who had been educated in Quebec. They formed their own provisional government to represent their interests and to present their views. Armed conflict arose between the settlers who had recently arrived in the Red River colony from Ontario (and whose interests were largely those of the federal government) and the Métis. Out of the Riel uprising of 1869 emerged the terms for the incorporation of Manitoba as a province the following year.

Donald Swainson in "Canada Annexes the West: Colonial Status Confirmed" provides an overview of the history of the Canadian West from the beginning to the late nineteenth century from the perspective of western alienation. In "The Myth of the Downtrodden West," a short interpretive article, J. M. S. Careless offers an alternative view. In "Louis Riel: Patriot or Rebel?" George Stanley presents a biographical sketch of the central figure in the drama of Métis resistance to Canadian domination.

On the early history of the Métis, see D. B. Sealey and A. S. Lussier's, *The Métis: Canada's Forgotten People* (Winnipeg: Métis Federation Press, 1975). There is a growing literature on Louis Riel and the Métis uprisings. In particular see G. F. G. Stanley's *The Birth of Western Canada: A History of the Riel Rebellions* (Toronto: University of Toronto Press, 1961; first published 1936); Thomas Flanagan's *Louis 'David' Riel: 'Prophet of the New World'* (Toronto: University of Toronto Press, 1979); and H. Bowsfield's *Louis Riel: The Rebel and the Hero* (Toronto: Oxford University Press, 1971). Douglas Owram presents the Central Canadian view of the West in *The Promise of Eden: The Canadian Expansionist Movement and the Idea of the West, 1856–1900* (Toronto: University of Toronto Press, 1980).

45

Canada Annexes the West:
Colonial Status Confirmed *

DONALD SWAINSON

The early history of the Canadian West[1] is characterized by dependence and exploitation. The area and its resources were controlled from outside, for the benefit of several distant centres, whose relative importance changed from time to time. London, Montreal and Toronto, the major and competing metropolises, were flanked by such lesser competitors as Minneapolis-St. Paul, Benton and Vancouver. A prime result of this pattern of development has been a continuing resistance to outside controls. At the same time, the character of western people and institutions has been heavily influenced by forces outside western control. Even indigenous peoples were largely defined by the forces that controlled the region. The interplay of these factors has played a large part in moulding the character of the West and in determining fundamentally its role in Canadian federalism.

I

The pattern of dependence preceded federal union and for the West is the context within which federalism must be viewed. It began in the seventeenth century when English traders established themselves in posts around Hudson Bay. Chartered in 1670 as the Hudson's Bay Company, this "Company of Adventurers of England tradeing [*sic*] into Hudson Bay"[2] tapped an enormously profitable trade in furs. To this prestigious and powerful firm the Crown delegated vast responsibilities and valuable privileges:

> [T]he Company was granted the "sole Trade and Commerce of all those Seas Streightes Bayes Rivers Lakes Creekes and Soundes in whatsoever Latitude they shall bee that lye within the entrance of the Streightes commonly called Hudsons Streightes together with all the Landes and Territoryes upon the Countryes Coastes and confynes of the Seas Bayes Lakes Rivers Creekes and Soundes aforesaid that are not actually possessed by or granted to any of our Subjects or possessed by the Subjects of any other Christian Prince or State". They were to be the "true and absolute Lordes and Proprietors" of this vast territory, and they were to hold it, as had been envisaged in the grant of October 1669, in free and common socage. . . . These lands were to be reckoned as a plantation or colony, and were to be known as Rupert's Land; and the Company was to own the mineral and fishing rights there as well as the exclusive trade and the land itself.[3]

46

For two hundred years, the Hudson's Bay Company was the (more or less) effective government of Rupert's Land, an enormous territory stretching from Labrador through the shield and the prairies and into the Arctic tundra in the West. It included most of what are now the provinces of Manitoba, Saskatchewan and Alberta. Control over the West was thus vested in a firm centred in London and exercised in the interests of commerce.

Montreal businessmen (whether French before the Conquest, or British after) refused to recognize the HBC's trade monopoly, and wanted to share in the profits. In spite of enormous overhead costs French traders penetrated the West in the middle of the eighteenth century, and entered into competition for the favour of the Indian fur gatherers. After the Conquest Montreal's challenge to the Hudson's Bay Company's monopoly was even more serious. Numerous Montreal-based traders entered the field, but the most famous and effective were organized late in the eighteenth century as the North-West Company. This marvel of capitalist organization exploited the wealth of the shield and the prairies. It opened the rich Athabasca country and its agents penetrated north to the Arctic and west to the Pacific. The Nor'Westers introduced the influence of Montreal into the mainstream of western life. The vicious competition between Montreal and London for the control of the western trade, however, proved too costly; in 1821 the Hudson's Bay Company and the North-West Company amalgamated. But both Montreal and London continued to exercise great influence in the West. And, of course, the officers and men of the reorganized Hudson's Bay Company remained a powerful force in the West until Canada annexed the area in 1870.

Children of mixed white and Indian blood were an inevitable result of the presence of fur traders in the West. By the late eighteenth century these people were a numerous group on the prairies. They can be very roughly divided into two sub-groups: English-speaking half-breeds and French-speaking Métis. The former tended to be relatively settled and to have close ties with the white communities in the Red River Valley. The Métis were more autonomous and distinctive. During this period, they developed into a powerful force.

As a people, the Métis were very much a product of the fur trade. Like many other unsophisticated and indigenous peoples, they were manipulated by the great business firms that exploited the natural resources of their area. The North-West Company employed them first as labourers and hunters. The trade war between the fur trading giants increased their utility, especially after Lord Selkirk established his famous settlement in the Red River Valley in 1811–12. Selkirk's colony and the HBC functioned as interdependent units, and challenged the viability of the NWC opera- *47* tions west of the Red River. The NWC could not declare war on one without fighting the other. Consequently it declared war on both, and the Métis became its prime weapon. The leaders of the NWC encouraged the growth of a primitive nationalism; the Métis were encouraged to believe that the Red River settlers threatened their claim to western lands, a claim inherited from their Cree and Saulteaux mothers. Cuthbert Grant, a Scottish-educated half-breed, was appointed Captain of the Métis by the North-West Company, and his followers became a small private army. They harassed the Selkirk settlers, a process that culminated in 1816 in the battle of Seven Oaks where Grant's men massacred Governor Robert Semple and twenty of his settlers. But in spite of its superior military strength, the NWC, primarily for geographical reasons, could not sustain a protracted campaign against the Red River colonists and the HBC. Consequently, the firms united in 1821; the West was pacified.

The four-year struggle (1812–1816) against the Selkirk settlers was a decisive event in western history. It marked the beginning of the Métis as an organized and self-conscious group. After 1821, they continued to accept Grant's leadership. They founded Grantown on the Assiniboine River west of the restored Selkirk settlement and made that village their capital; for the next seventy years they were at the centre of prairie history.

After the union of the firms, Cuthbert Grant and his people were coopted by the controlling interests. The Métis defended the growing and prosperous community of Selkirk settlers, their former enemies, from the Sioux. In 1828, Grant was made Warden of the Plains of Red River, with responsibility for enforcing the Hudson's Bay Company trade monopoly. During these quiet years of the 1820s and 1830s the Métis of Grantown organized and refined their most important institution, the famous buffalo hunt, which provided important food reserves for settlers and traders alike, and an economic base for the Métis.[4] The implications of the hunt were endless. It was organized along military lines and was easily adaptable to military and political purposes. The Métis, self-confident about their identity and proud of their place in western society, referred to themselves as the "New Nation" but nonetheless they remained dependent on buffalo and fur traders.

The Métis were created as a people only after the arrival of white traders in the West; the Indians had peopled the prairies for several millennia. It might be argued, however, that European influences recreated Indian society; these forces certainly revolutionized Indian history. When white men first came to North America the Indians who inhabited the western plains lacked horses and guns. The acquisition of these items, combined with trade, radically altered Indian society. In some instances, and for a brief period, the result was startling. A recent historian of Alberta illustrates:

> For a few vivid decades Blackfoot culture, based upon horses, guns and unlimited buffalo, rose rapidly into the zenith of the rich, colourful and glamorous life which many regard as the apogee of plains culture. Prior to 1730, during the long era which the Blackfoot called the dog-days they travelled on foot and used dogs for transport. About that year, the acquisition of horses and guns swept them rapidly onward and upward until slightly over a century later they were at the peak of their spectacular horse-based culture. . . . Though horses and guns had made the Blackfoot aggressive, they also provided the leisure which led to the flowering of their social life.[5]

48

Revolutionized Indian societies were highly vulnerable to external forces. They could not manufacture either guns or ammunition; traders could (and did) cause social calamities through the introduction of liquor and a variety of diseases; trading patterns could not be controlled by Indians. More important, the buffalo could be liquidated and settlement could destroy the basis of Indian independence. In the mid-nineteenth century these successful western Indian societies were in a delicately balanced position. European contacts had changed the very character of their society; at the same time they were dependent upon and vulnerable to white society. Further white encroachment in the West could destroy them. That encroachment of course quickly occurred, and in the 1870s the western Indians were swamped. A recent student of Canadian Indians comments: "For the sake of convenience, and recognizing the arbitrariness of the choice, we may use the date 1876, that of the first Indian Act, as the beginning of what we call the "colonial" period. From the point of view of the European, the Indian had become irrelevant."[6]

The full complexity of mid-nineteenth-century prairie society cannot be revealed in a few paragraphs. The main characteristics, however, can be delineated. The West was inhabited by French-speaking Métis, English-speaking half-breeds, officers and men of the Hudson's Bay Company, Selkirk settlers and a handful of missionaries, retired soldiers and free-traders. Except for the Indians, these groups were all centred around the forks of the Red and Assiniboine Rivers, where a pluralistic society emerged. Reasonable amity usually prevailed, although the Métis could not be controlled against their will by the aging and increasingly ineffective HBC regime. This was a civilized society, with its own churches, schools and law courts. Its various components produced their own indig-enous middle-classes, leaders, institutions and traditions. Several religions were sustained within the settlement and promoted amongst the Indians.

At the same time these diverse western societies were fragile and derivative. W. L. Morton describes the Selkirk settlers as "Scottish crofters on the banks of the Red."[7] Indian society had been recreated through European contact and persons of mixed blood were a product of liaisons between fur traders and Saulteaux and Cree women. Employees of the HBC were often of British birth. None of these groups had sufficient cultural integrity or autonomy to retain their distinctiveness and independence without a considerable degree of isolation from the larger North American society. As Bishop Taché observed about immigration into the West: "[T]he movement [of immigration] is an actual fact, and we must cease to be what we have hitherto been, an exceptional people."[8]

They were dependent on more than isolation. Economically they needed the fur trade and the buffalo hunt. Buffalo products were sold to traders, settlers and Americans at Minneapolis-St. Paul. The fur trade supplied cash, employment and markets. Agriculture, "subsistent, riparian, and restricted,"[9] was nonetheless an important enterprise. Markets were obviously extremely limited. The large-scale export of commodities was hardly reasonable and, even within the West, Red River Valley farmers had no monopoly on food production as long as the buffalo survived. The agricultural sector of the western economy thus remained modest.[10]

Within the West some of these groups, particularly HBC officials, Indians and Métis, could exert tremendous authority; their futures, how-ever, were in the hands of forces that could not be contained. They had sufficient group-consciousness to defend collective interests, and to vary-ing degrees they were all willing to resist encroachments from the outside. The Métis revolted against the locally enforced trade monopoly; HBC officials became dissatisfied with the treatment meted out to them by their London superiors. The Scots settlers resented the suggestion that the area could be disposed of without prior consultation. A willingness to resist in spite of dependence and relative weakness was a striking western charac-teristic long before the West was annexed by Canada. It is an important component of the western context of federalism.[11]

II

The Central Canadian context is equally important. French-Canadian explorers penetrated the West in the eighteenth century, and thereafter the West was always a concern of at least some Central Canadians. The connection became somewhat tenuous after the union of the fur companies in 1821, but it was never lost; there was always full cognizance of the fact that Rupert's Land was British territory.

A more pointed interest became evident in the late 1840s, and the nature of that interest illuminates Central Canadian attitudes about what

49

the West was, what it should become and how it should relate to what was then the Province of Canada. This interest, while by no means partisan in nature, centred in the Upper Canadian Reformers. It can be illustrated by an examination of two of its representative manifestations: the campaign of the Toronto *Globe* to annex the West and the organization of the North-West Transportation Company.[12]

The *Globe* was the organ of George Brown, who emerged in the 1850s as the Upper Canadian Reform leader. It was a Toronto newspaper that spoke to the farmers of what became western Ontario, but at the same time represented many of the metropolitan interests of Toronto's business elite. Its interest in the North-West tended to be economic and exploitative. Underlying this early tentative interest in the West was the assumption that the West would become an economic and social adjunct of Upper Canada. On 24 March 1847, for example, Brown reprinted Robert Baldwin Sullivan's lecture, "Emigration and Colonization." While primarily concerned with Upper Canada, Sullivan also discussed settlement possibilities in the North-West. He viewed the West as a potential settlement area for Upper Canadians. In 1848 the *Globe* claimed the West for Canada, and dismissed the rights of the Hudson's Bay Company. The West, it argued, was "capable of supporting a numerous population. This wide region nominally belongs to the Hudson's Bay Company, but in point of fact it does not seem to be theirs."[13] The *Globe's* interest petered out in 1850, but revived after a few years. In 1856 it published a series of revealing articles by an anonymous correspondent, "Huron": "I desire to see Canada for the Canadians and not exclusively for a selfish community of traders, utter strangers to our country; whose only anxiety is to draw all the wealth they can from it, without contributing to its advantages even one farthing."[14] He pronounced the charter of the Hudson's Bay Company "null and void" and declared that "[t]he interest of Canada require that this giant monopoly be swept out of existence. . . ." "Huron" was emphatic on this point:

The formation of a Company in opposition to the Hudson's Bay Company would advance the interests of Canada; it would consolidate and strengthen the British power on the continent. . . . In the organization of [opposition to the HBC], every patriot, every true Canadian, beholds results the most important to his country.

According to the *Globe*, westward expansion was an urgent need because of a shortage of settlement land "south of Lake Huron." "[Canada] is fully entitled to possess whatever parts of the Great British American territory she can safely occupy. . . ."[15]

Interest in westward expansion was by no means confined to the *Globe*. In 1856 the Toronto Board of Trade indicated interest in western trade.[16] Various politicians took up the cause and the matter was aired in both houses of parliament.[17]

In 1858 a Toronto-based group made a "quixotic" and "abortive"[18] attempt to penetrate the West through the incorporation of the North-West Transportation, Navigation and Railway Company (known as the

North-West Transit Co.).[19] The project, designed to link Central Canada and the Red River Valley by a combination of rail and water transport, was premature and unsuccessful, but its promoters' attitudes towards the West were both representative and persistent.[20] The objects were the exploitation of such likely and unlikely western possibilities as buffalo hides, furs, tallow, fish, salt, sarsaparilla and cranberries, "the opening [of] a direct communication between Lake Superior and the Pacific . . ." and the opening of trade with the Orient. "[W]e place before us a mart of 600 000 000 of people [in China] and [our project will] enable us geographically to command them; opening the route, and leaving it to the guidance of commercial interests, Canada will, sooner or later, become the great tollgate for the commerce of the world." By "Canada," of course, was meant Toronto, and these promoters dreamed of controlling a great empire: "Like the Genii in the fable [the East Indian trade] still offers the sceptre to those who, unintimidated by the terms that surround it, are bold enough to adventure to its embrace. In turn Phoenicia, Carthage, Greece, Rome, Venice, Pisa, Genoa, Portugal, Holland and lastly England, has won and worn this ocean diadem; Destiny now offers [the East Indian trade] to us."

51

During the 1850s a dynamic and expansive Upper Canada saw the North-West as its proper hinterland. It was regarded as a huge extractive resource, designed to provide profit for the businessman, land for the farmer and power for Toronto.

While cultural attitudes are sometimes difficult to identify, it was probably assumed that the North-West would be culturally as well as economically dependent on the St. Lawrence Valley. J. M. S. Careless, for example, suggests that "Brown used the North-West agitation to complete the reunification of Upper Canada's liberal party, merging Toronto urban and business leadership with Clear Grit agrarian strength in a dynamic party front."[21] Brown's "party front," which wanted "French Canadianism entirely extinguished,"[22] was dedicated to majoritarianism and the sectional interests of Upper Canada. While the nature of Reform attitudes towards French Canada is debatable, it is hardly likely that the same men who strove to terminate duality in Central Canada sought to extend it to the North-West. Some Lower Canadian leaders (both French- and English-speaking), especially those identified with Montreal business, were interested in westward expansion for economic reasons. There was, however, little French-Canadian enthusiasm for expansion westward.[23] French-Canadian attitudes emanated from the nature of Lower Canadian society, which was profoundly conservative and lacked the buoyant and dynamic qualities of Upper Canada: "Not movement but stasis, enforced by the very nature of the task of 'survival', was the keynote of French-Canadian society."[24] French Canadians lacked confidence in the economic viability of the North-West, in major part because of pre-Confederation missionary propaganda that emphasized difficulties related to the West. It was generally assumed that "western settlement was the sole concern of Ontario"[25] and that large-scale French-Canadian emigration would threaten French Canada's ability to survive. Thus there existed no Lower Canadian force to counterbalance Upper Canada's drive westward or Upper Canadian assumptions about how the West should be used. The only additional British North American region that could have possessed western ambitions consisted of the Atlantic colonies: New Brunswick, Nova Scotia, Prince Edward Island and Newfoundland. Their traditional orientation was towards the Atlantic, not the interior. The Atlantic colonies were not about to launch an imperialistic venture in the 1860s.

Apart from Montreal business ambitions the field was clear for Upper Canada, but little could be done until a new political order was established in Central Canada. The constitutional settlement embodied in the Act of Union of 1840 broke down during the 1850s. The complexities of Central Canadian politics during the 1850s are not germane to this discussion, although it should be noted that a prime reason for the breakdown of Canadian government was the incompatability between the uncontrollable dynamism and expansionism of Upper Canadian society on the one hand, and the conservative and inward-looking society of Lower Canada on the other.

The new order was worked out by the Great Coalition of 1864 that was committed to the introduction of "the federal principle into Canada, coupled with such provision as will permit the Maritime Provinces and the North-West Territory to be incorporated into the same system of government."[26] The solution was Confederation, which was established by the British North America Act of 1867. It created a highly centralized federation that included the Province of Canada (divided into Ontario and Quebec), Nova Scotia and New Brunswick, and that made explicit provision for the inclusion of the remaining British North American territories:

> It should be lawful for the Queen, by and with the Advice of Her Majesty's Most Honourable Privy Council, on Addresses from the Houses of the Parliament of Canada, and from the Houses of the respective Legislatures of the Colonies or Provinces of Newfoundland, Prince Edward Island, and British Columbia, to admit those Colonies or Provinces, or any of them, into the Union, and on Address from the Houses of the Parliament of Canada to admit Rupert's Land and the North-western Territory, or either of them, into the Union. . . .[27]

Confederation was thus the constitutional framework within which the West was destined to relate to Central Canada.

The nature of the new confederation had profound implications for the West. The system was highly centralized, so much so that in conception it hardly qualified as a federation in the classic sense. The Fathers of Confederation wanted a strong state that could withstand American pressure. Heavily influenced by trade considerations, they saw federation in mercantilistic terms. As children of the empire as it existed prior to the repeal of the corn laws, it is not surprising that their federal model was the old colonial system, modified to involve "the citizens of the provinces . . . in the government of the whole entity":[28]

The purpose of the Fathers of Confederation — to found a united and integrated transcontinental Dominion — was comparable with that of the mercantilists: and in both designs there was the same need that the interests of the parts should be made subordinate to the interest of the whole. The Dominion was the heir in direct succession of the old colonial system. It was put in possession of both the economics and political controls of the old regime. On the one hand, it was given the power to regulate trade and commerce, which had been the chief economic prerogative of Great Britain; on the other hand, it was granted the right to nominate provincial governors, to review provincial legislation and to disallow provincial acts, the three powers which had been the chief attributes of Great Britain's political supremacy.[29]

In his more optimistic moments, John A. Macdonald went so far as to predict the demise of the provinces: "If the Confederation goes on, you, if spared the ordinary age of man, will see both local parliaments and governments absorbed in the general power. This is as plain to me as if I saw it accomplished."[30]

It is true that Lower Canada and the Atlantic colonies were part of the new dominion, but the effective pressure for the new settlement came from Upper Canada. French Canada realized the inevitability of change, but generated little enthusiasm for Confederation. She could offer no better alternative and hence acquiesced (not without considerable protest) in the new arrangement.[31] The creative role was played by Upper Canada, and for that section Confederation was a great triumph. The new system was posited on the abandonment of dualism and, through representation by population in the House of Commons, the acceptance of majoritarianism, albeit with limited guarantees for French Canadian culture within the Province of Quebec. Majoritarianism was very much to the advantage of Ontario, which, according to the 1871 census, had 1 600 000 persons — or 46 per cent of Canada's 3 500 000 people. This translated into 82 of 181 seats in the House of Commons. The first prime minister was an Ontarian, as were the leading lights of the opposition — George Brown, Edward Blake and Alexander Mackenzie. In the first cabinet Ontario, the wealthiest province, had 5 of 13 places. Even the capital was an Ontario city.

The Ontario Liberals became the leaders of the nineteenth-century provincial rights agitation and Ontario emerged as the bastion of provincial rights sentiment, but while the federal scheme was being defined most of Ontario's leaders, regardless of party, concurred on the utility of this "quasi federal" scheme.[32] This is hardly surprising. The Reformers or Liberals were the larger of the two Ontario parties, and doubtless looked forward to a great future as the rulers of *both* Ontario and the dominion. Although they realized this aim by 1873 and ruled simultaneously in Toronto and Ottawa for five years, they suffered humiliating defeats in 1867 at both levels. The deep autonomist drives within Ontario society quickly reasserted themselves and Ontario's Liberals began their protracted assault on Macdonald's constitutional edifice. This should not obscure the fact that quasi-federalism met with little Ontario opposition during the mid-1860s.

The acquisition of the North-West would take place within the context of Canadian federalism. The Fathers of Confederation tended to assume that the "'colonial' relationship with the provinces was a natural one. . . . It therefore seems more appropriate to think of the dominion-provincial relationship at that time as similar to the relationship of the imperial government with a colony enjoying limited self-government."[33] Ontario Liberals quickly adopted a different approach to federalism; federal Conservatives did not. The West was to be "annexed as a subordinated territory."[34] Ontario's leaders were anxious that expansion take place quickly, and assumed that Ontarians would benefit through the creation of a miniature Ontario in the West. At the same time the settled portion of the West, shaken by the breakdown of its isolation and possessing a tradition of resistance to outside control, was accustomed to colonial status, exploitation and dependency.

III

54

Canada's first Confederation government was anxious to honour its commitment to annex the West. William McDougall and George Cartier went to London in 1868 to negotiate the transfer to Canada of Rupert's Land and the North-West Territory. Their mission was successful. The Hudson's Bay Company agreed to transfer its territory to Canada; the dominion agreed to compensate the company with one-twentieth of the fertile area in the West, land surrounding HBC posts and a cash payment of £300 000. The initial transfer was to be to the Crown, which would immediately retransfer the area to Canada.

In preparation for the reception of this great domain, Canada passed "An Act for the temporary Government of Rupert's Land and the North-Western Territory when united with Canada."[35] This short act provided that the West, styled "The North-West Territories," would be governed by federal appointees — a lieutenant governor assisted by a council. It also continued existing laws in force and public servants in office until changes were made by either the federal government or the lieutenant governor. The act was to "continue in force until the end of the next Session of Parliament."

It has been suggested that this statute does not reveal much about the intent of the federal authorities because it was preceded by such phrases as: "to make some temporary provision" and "until more permanent arrangements can be made."[36] At the same time P. B. Waite notes that it was not a temporary provision at all. After the creation of Manitoba, "the rest of the vast Northwest Territories remained under the Act of 1869, that 'temporary' arrangement. It was re-enacted in 1871 as permanent without any alteration whatever."[37] There is no reason to assume that in 1869 Macdonald and his colleagues intended any very radical future alteration in the statute, which, with the appointments made thereunder, revealed much about Ottawa's attitude toward the West. The area, not a crown colony in 1869, was to join Confederation as a federally controlled territory — not as a province. It was not assumed that the West was joining a federation; rather, Canada was acquiring a subservient territory. Local leaders were neither consulted nor considered. These assumptions emerge even more clearly when the initial appointments under the act are studied. Ontario's ambitions to control the West were symbolized by the appointment of William McDougall as Lieutenant Governor. He was a former Clear Grit who represented Ontario Reformers in the first Confederation government. An imperious and sanctimonious expansionist, he had neither the ability nor the desire to take local leaders, especially those who were not white, into his confidence. Certainly the federal government's request that he search out westerners for his council[38] would hardly inspire local confidence. McDougall was regarded as anything but impartial.[39] Initial executive appointments were not likely, with the possible exception of J. A. N. Provencher,[40] to inspire local confidence in a regime that was organized in Central Canada. Two appointments were flagrantly political. A. N. Richards was the brother of a minister in Sandfield Macdonald's Ontario government and Captain D. R. Cameron was Charles Tupper's son-in-law. Even if one accepts the argument that the "temporary" act was indeed temporary, it is difficult to argue that Lieutenant Governor McDougall, Attorney General Richards or Chief of Police Cameron were temporary.

These various decisions made in distant capitals caused an upheaval in the Red River settlement, the only really settled part of Rupert's Land. Red River was, in fact, on the verge of explosion — a point forcibly made to federal and imperial authorities by Anglican Bishop Machray, HBC Governor of Assiniboia Mactavish, and Roman Catholic Bishop Taché.[41] The unsettled state of Red River was a product of many factors. By the end of the 1840s the commercial authority of the HBC had been irretrievably eroded. During the 1850s the isolation of the area was just as irretrievably lost. American traders pushed up from St. Paul and by the late 1850s a Canadian party, allied with the anti-HBC agitation in Canada, had emerged in the settlement. These Canadians, whose attitudes had been previewed in the 1840s by Recorder Adam Thom and were later to merge with those of Canada First, were arrogant, threatening and racist. They led a concerted assault on the authority of the company, and were instrumental in producing political chaos at Red River during the 1850s. To the Métis especially they represented a threat to their rights and way of life. These justified fears[42] were confirmed by Canadian government officials who entered the area prior to the transfer and offended local sensibilities. Instability was abetted by a "breakdown of the traditional economy of the Settlement" during the late 1860s. In 1868 Red River "was threatened by famine."[43]

The people of Red River could assess Canadian intentions only on the basis of Canadian activities, appointments, and laws. The response was resistance, spearheaded by the Métis but reluctantly supported to varying degrees (or at least tolerated) by most people at Red River, except the members of the Canadian party: "Riel's authority, although it originated in armed force, came within a few months to be based on the majority will of the community."[44]

The details of the resistance of 1869–1870 are well known and are not germane to this paper. What is important is that Louis Riel's provisional government was in such a strong strategic position that it was able to force the federal authorities to negotiate on terms of entry. The results were embodied in the Manitoba Act that created the Province of Manitoba.

Provincehood was a victory (more, it might be noted, for the Métis than for the other sections of the Red River community), but Manitoba nonetheless entered Confederation as a dependency, not as a full partner with a federal system. Two broad circumstances explain the continuation of "subordinate"[45] status. First, Manitoba was not constitutionally equal to the other provinces. The Métis leaders and their clerical advisors placed great emphasis on cultural problems. Anticipating an influx of Ontarians, they demanded and obtained educational and linguistic guarantees. The federal authorities were concerned primarily with such larger issues as the settlement of the West and the construction of a transcontinental railroad. To facilitate these policies, in the formulation of which Manitoba had no say, Ottawa retained control of Manitoba's public lands and natural resources "for the purposes of the Dominion."[46] Professor Eric Kierans comments:

> The ownership of the land and resources belong [sic] to the people collectively as the sign of their independence and the guarantee of their responsibility. By British law and tradition, the ownership and control of the public domain was always handed over to the political authority designated by a community when the citizens assumed responsibility for the government of their own affairs. . . . During the . . . hearings [related to the *Report of the Royal Commission on the Transfer of the Natural Resources of Manitoba* (Ottawa, 1929)] Professor Chester Martin . . . testified: "The truth is that for 35 years, (i.e., until the creation of the Provinces of Saskatchewan and Alberta), I believe that it will be correct to say, Manitoba was the solitary exception within the British Empire to accepted British practice with regard to control of the crown lands and it still remains in respect of public lands, literally not a province but a colony of the Dominion." . . . In substance, any attempt to grant responsible government to a province or state, while retaining for the Imperial or Federal authority the control of crown lands and revenues, was held to be a "contradiction in terms and impossible."[47]

Just as serious as Manitoba's inferior constitutional position, was her effective status. She was in no way equipped to function as a province with the full paraphernalia of responsible government. She was ridiculously small, limited in 1870 to some 12 000 persons and 13 500 square miles. The province had an extremely limited tradition of representative government and, to complicate matters further, several of her key leaders were fugitives from justice because of their roles in the resistance. As Lieutenant Governor A. G. Archibald explained in 1872: "You can hardly hope to carry on responsible Government by inflicting death penalties on the leaders of a majority of the electors."[48] Perhaps even more important, provincial finances were hopelessly inadequate; the federal government granted "provincial status to an area which was essentially primitive; and it gave financial terms modelled improperly upon those given to the older provinces."[49] Under the Manitoba Act the province received $67 104 per annum in grants. Her own revenue came to only about $10 000. Even by

1875, 88 per cent of provincial revenues were federal subsidies. "During the whole period from 1870 to 1885 Manitoba was little more than a financial ward of the federal government. . . ."[50] The province could not even afford public buildings to house the lieutenant governor and assembly until Ottawa advanced the necessary funds. In 1871 about one-third of provincial expenditures were used to cover legislative expenses.

Thus provincehood was granted prematurely to a jurisdiction that could sustain neither its responsibilities nor the kind of status it ought to have occupied with a federal state. The primary fault lay with the federal leaders: "[T]he Manitoba Act bears on its face evidence both of the inexperience of the delegates from the Red River settlement and of the lack of mature consideration given to the measure by the federal government. The former circumstance was unavoidable; the latter can hardly be condoned."[51] During the early years of Manitoba's history even the outward trappings of real provincehood were absent. For several years the province's immaturity prevented the development of responsible government and the first two lieutenant governors, A. G. Archibald and Alexander Morris, functioned as effective governors rather than as constitutional monarchs. Until 1876 the lieutenant governors even attended cabinet meetings.

57

Early Manitoba was a colony of Central Canada because of constitutional discrimination and because she had neither the maturity nor resources to support provincehood. But that was not all. With the advent of formal provincial status came an influx of settlers from Ontario, a process that started with the arrival of the Anglo-Saxon Ontarian hordes that dominated Colonel Garnett Wolseley's expeditionary force of 1870. That small army had no real military function. It was sent west in 1870 to appease Ontario — to serve as symbolic compensation for the inclusion in the Manitoba Act of cultural guarantees for the Métis. In extreme form, the expeditionary force was a model of what the later Central Canadian influx was to mean. Local traditions were shunted aside as agriculture was commercialized and society revolutionized. The Indians were unable to assimilate themselves; many Métis sold the land they had been granted to unscrupulous speculators and moved into the North-West Territories. In a symbolic action a group of Ontarians who arrived in 1871 seized some Métis land on the Rivière aux Ilets de Bois. In spite of Métis protests they kept the land and sharpened the insult by renaming the river "the Boyne"! Some Scots settlers sympathized with the Canadians, but like the HBC traders they had to watch the old society die. Within a few years Manitoba was a colony of Ontario demographically as well as constitutionally, politically and economically.

The Province of Manitoba was only a miniscule portion of the territory annexed by Canada. The remaining enormous area was organized as the North-West Territories. With virtually no permanent white settlement, it received even shorter shrift than Manitoba. Its initial government was provided under the "temporary Government" act. That statute was "reenacted, extended and continued in force until . . . 1871" by the Manitoba Act.[52] Prior to its second automatic expiry in 1871 it was again reenacted without major change, this time with no expiry date. Until 1875, therefore, government for the North-West Territories was provided under the initial legislation of 1869. During these six years the administration of the territories was somewhat casual. There was no resident governor — that responsibility was simply added to the duties of the Lieutenant Governor of Manitoba. Most of the members of the council were Manitobans who did not live in the territories. The Indians, the largest group of inhabitants, were managed not consulted.

The Mackenzie government overhauled the administration of the North-West in 1875 by securing the passage of "The North-West Territories Act." Although not "fully thought out"[53] it did provide a fairly simple system of government consisting of a separate governor and a council that was initially appointed but that would become elective as a non-Indian population grew. The capital was established at Battleford until 1882 when it was moved to Regina. Mackenzie appointed David Laird, a federal cabinet minister from Prince Edward Island, as the first full-time Lieutenant Governor of the North-West Territories. His first council included neither an Indian nor a Métis who resided in the NWT. There was no elected councillor until 1881.

Prior to 1869 the West was a dependent area, ruled (if at all) in a casual, chaotic but paternalistic manner for the benefit of a huge commercial firm centred in London. Westerners feared that the transfer involved simply a change of masters, not a change of status. The Métis feared that in the process they would lose their life style and culture through an inundation of Ontario settlers. The result was a movement of resistance led by the Métis, but with broad support within the Red River settlement. For the bulk of the West the resistance resulted in no change whatsoever. For a small district on the Red River the result was a tiny, anemic province incapable of functioning as a viable partner within a federal system.

IV

After 1867 Macdonald and his colleagues were not able to maintain "quasi-federalism" over the original components of Confederation, but for the West annexation to Canada involved the confirmation of colonial status. The fifteen years after the transfer was the launching period for the West in Confederation. During those years federal sway on the prairies was virtually unchallengeable.

Ottawa's most powerful instrument was federal possession of the West's public lands "for the purposes of the Dominion." This enabled Ottawa to implement two policies that were crucial to the Canadianization of the West: rapid settlement and the construction of a transcontinental railroad. Extreme difficulties did not prevent the execution of these policies. Public lands were made available to settlers in a variety of ways. Although settlement did not proceed as quickly as the federal authorities desired, Manitoba experienced rapid growth during the 1870s and 1880s. Within a generation of the transfer the territories west of Manitoba had been populated by Ontarians, Americans and Europeans. Consequently the provinces of Saskatchewan and Alberta were established in 1905. The federal authorities had recognized from the outset that a transcontinental railroad was required if the West was to be properly Canadianized. After several false starts, the Canadian Pacific Railway was chartered in 1880. The CPR was heavily subsidized, receiving from the federal government some $38 000 000 worth of track constructed at public expense, $25 000 000 in cash, a railroad monopoly in western Canada for twenty years and 25 000 000 acres of prairie land. The land grant was considered indispensible to the line's success and the success of the railroad was one of the fundamental "purposes of the Dominion." The federal government designed its transportation policies to suit the needs of Central Canadian business, and was not particularly tender towards western interests. As Charles Tupper, Minister of Railroads, put it in 1883: "The interests of this country demand that the Canadian Pacific Railway should be made a success. . . . Are the interests of Manitoba and the North-West to be sacrificed to the interests of Canada? I say, if it is necessary, yes."[54]

59

Federal Conservative strategists, who were in power during 1867–73 and 1878–96, tied tariff policy to settlement and transportation. They saw the West as Central Canada's economic hinterland. The area was to be settled quickly and become an exporter of agricultural products and an importer of manufactured goods. Central Canada was to be the manufacturing centre. The CPR was to haul eastern manufactured goods into the West and western agricultural produce to market. High tariffs were designed to protect the manufacturing industries from foreign competition and at the same time guarantee freight traffic to the CPR by forcing trade patterns to flow along east-west, not north-south, lines. These basic decisions determined the nature of post-1870 western development. They were made by federal leaders to serve Central Canadian interests and they perpetuated the status of the West as a colonial region.

Federal management of the West during these years should be looked at in micro as well as macro terms, although it is clear that federal authorities had little interest in day-to-day western conditions. If settlement was to proceed in orderly and rapid fashion the Indian "problem" had to be solved. That task involved extinguishing Indian rights to the land and rendering the tribes harmless by herding them onto reserves. The instrument used for these purposes was the Indian "treaty." During the 1870s a series of agreements was negotiated between the crown and the prairie tribes. Through these treaties the Indians gave up their rights to their traditional lands in return for reserves and nominal concessions, payments and guarantees. However, they tended to resist being forced onto reserves as long as the buffalo, their traditional source of food, remained plentiful. By 1885 the buffalo were on the verge of extermination and most Indians had been coerced to settle on reservations.

In 1873 Canada founded the North-West Mounted Police, another instrument of federal control.[55] The mounties constituted an effective federal presence on the prairies, chased American traders out of southern Alberta, policed the Indians and Métis, and symbolized the stability and order desired by white settlers. In bringing effective federal rule to southern Alberta they abetted the termination of the international aspect of Blackfoot life. This breakdown of regional international societies was part of the process of Canadianization.

The federal political structure also functioned as a control instrument. Until 1887 Manitoba's handful of MPs constituted the West's entire representation in the House of Commons. These members tended to support the government of the day because of its immense patronage and fiscal authority.

60

Dependent upon federal largesse yet suspicious of eastern dictation, the western attitude towards national politics was often a curious mixture of ministerialism and defiance. Some papers seemed to believe that the electorate should always give a general support to the government, for such support would ensure a continuous supply of federal monies for western projects. At the same time these papers admitted the need to champion regional interests.[56]

During the 1870s and 1880s the West was Canadianized. By the end of the century massive immigration (which incidentally produced a distinctive population mix that helped differentiate the region from Central Canada) combined with basic federal policies had produced a new West, but its status had changed little. The process generated resistance. The government of Manitoba challenged the CPR's monopoly and sought to obtain better financial terms. Farmers in Manitoba and along the Saskatchewan River organized unions and began their long struggle for a host of reforms including lower tariffs and a transportation system sensitive to their needs. Under Louis Riel's leadership a minority of Indians and Métis rose in 1885 in a pathetic and ill-led rebellion. Territorial politicians crusaded for representation in parliament and responsible government for the North-West Territories.

By the end of the century western resistance to federal control and leadership was a well-established tradition. The West, however, was not strong enough to challenge Canada's great national policies successfully. Consequently the West has remained a subordinate region; the Canadian federation retains its imperialistic characteristics. As W. L. Morton suggested: "For Confederation was brought about to increase the wealth of Central Canada, and until that original purpose is altered, and the concentration of wealth and population by national policy in Central Canada ceases, Confederation must remain an instrument of injustice."[57]

Notes

1. In this essay the "West" refers to the territories that became the provinces of Manitoba, Saskatchewan and Alberta. Rupert's Land consisted of the Hudson's Bay Company territories. The North-West

Territory included the other British lands in the northwest. British Columbia was separate and is not considered in this essay.

2. E. E. Rich, *Hudson's Bay Company, 1670–1870,* 3 vols. (Toronto, 1960): 1:53.

3. Cited in ibid., 1:53–54.

4. For a superb account of the buffalo hunt, see Alexander Ross, *The Red River Settlement* (London, 1856), Chap. XVIII.

5. James G. MacGregor, *A History of Alberta* (Edmonton, 1972), pp. 17, 24. For further illustrations see Stanley Norman Murray, *The Valley Comes of Age: A History of Agriculture in the Valley of the Red River of the North, 1812–1920* (Fargo, 1967), p. 13: "By 1800 the Sioux and Chippewa tribes also had acquired horses. Because these animals made it possible for the Indians to hunt the buffalo over great distances, these people soon spent most of the summer and fall roaming the vast prairie west of the Red River. As they became more nomadic, the Indians placed less emphasis upon agriculture, pottery making, weaving, and the idea of a fixed dwelling place. In years when the buffalo were numerous, they could live from the hunt alone. Such was the case between 1800 and 1840 when the Sioux and Chippewa experienced degrees of luxury and leisure they had never known."

6. E. Palmer Patterson, *The Canadian Indian: A History Since 1500* (Don Mills, 1972) pp. 39–40. Different dates apply in different areas: "Thus, by 1865 the plight of the Indians in the Red River Valley was a pathetic one, and for the most part their culture no longer had any effect upon this area" (Murray, *Valley Comes of Age,* p. 15).

7. W. L. Morton, "Introduction to the New Edition" of Alexander Ross. *The Red River Settlement* (Edmonton, 1972), p. xx.

8. Cited in A. I. Silver, "French Canada and the Prairie Frontier, 1870–1890." *CHR* 50 (March 1969): 13.

9. W. L. Morton, "Agriculture in the Red River Colony," *CHR 30* (December 1949): 321.

10. Murray, *Valley Comes of Age,* pp. 44 and 48: "[T]here can be little question that the economy of the Selkirk colonies stagnated soon after they were able to produce a surplus. The major reason for stagnation in Red River agriculture was the limited market for farm produce, and this situation developed primarily out of the economic prerogatives of the Hudson's Bay Company. . . . [I]t continued to rely upon supplies brought from England and pemmican furnished by the métis hunters." In short, "agriculture did not become really commercial under the fur company regime. . . ." Morton points out that Red River agriculture lacked both "an export staple and transportation" ("Agriculture in the Red River Colony," p. 316).

11. There has recently been considerable discussion of western "identity." Debate on this question will doubtless continue. It can be argued that this persistent willingness to resist is one of the most distinctive western characteristics and is certainly a part of any western "identity," and that it long antedates Confederation. P. F. W. Rutherford, however, dismisses Métis influence: "Unlike other regions in the dominion, the western community was essentially a product of events set in motion by Confederation" ("The Western Press and Regionalism, 1870–96," *CHR* 52 [September 1971]: 287). Morton, however, comments: "Louis Riel was a more conventional politician than William Aberhart . . ." and "[t]his was the beginning of the bias of prairie politics. The fears of the Métis had led them to demand equality for the people of the Northwest in Confederation" ("The Bias of Prairie Politics" in *Historical Essays on the Prairie Provinces,* ed., Donald Swainson [Toronto, 1970], pp. 289 and 293). What is more "western" than this recurring "demand" for "equality"?

12. For a more detailed discussion by the present author see *Ontario and Confederation.* Centennial Historical Booklet No. 5 (Ottawa, 1967) and "The North-West Transportation Company: Personnel and Attitudes," Historical and Scientific Society of Manitoba *Transactions,* Series III, No. 26. 1969–70.

13. *Globe* (Toronto), 14 June 1848.

14. Quotations from articles by "Huron" are from *Globe,* 18 and 31 October 1856.

15. Ibid., 10 December 1856.

16. Ibid., 4 December 1856.

17. Province of Canada, *Journals of the Legislative Council of the Province of Canada.* Being the Third Session of the 5th Provincial Parliament, 1857, vol. XV, pp. 60, 80, 184, 195; Province of Canada, *Appendix to the Fifteenth Volume of the Journals of the Legislative Assembly of the Province of Canada.* Being the 3rd Session of the 5th Provincial Parliament, 1857, vol. XV, Appendix 17.

18. Joseph James Hargrave, *Red River* (Montreal, 1871), p. 143.

19. Province of Canada, *Statutes,* 1858, pp. 635ff.

20. Material that follows is from *Memoranda and Prospectus of the North-West Transportation and Land Company* (Toronto, 1858): Allan Macdonnell, *The North-West Transportation, Navigation and Railway Company: Its Objectives* (Toronto, 1858) and *Prospectus of the North-West Transportation, Navigation and Railway Company* (Toronto, 1858).

21. J. M. S. Careless, *The Union of the Canadas: The Growth of Canadian Institutions, 1841-57* (Toronto, 1967), p. 206.

22. PAC, George Brown Papers, George Brown to Anne Brown, 27 October 1864, cited in Donald Creighton, *The Road to Confederation* (Toronto, 1964), p. 182.

23. For an analysis of French-Canadian attitudes see Silver, "French Canada and the Prairie Frontier."
24. Ibid., p. 29.
25. Ibid., p. 15.
26. Cited in Chester Martin, *Foundations of Canadian Nationhood* (Toronto, 1955), p. 314.
27. British North America Act, Section 146.
28. Bruce W. Hodgins, "Disagreement at the Commencement: Divergent Ontarian Views of Federalism, 1867-1871," in *Oliver Mowat's Ontario*, ed., Donald Swainson, Toronto, 1972), p. 55.
29. Donald Creighton, *British North America at Confederation* (Ottawa, 1939), Appendix II, *The Royal Commission on Dominion-Provincial Relations* (Ottawa, 1940), p. 83.
30. PAC, John A. Macdonald Papers, 510. Macdonald to M. C. Cameron, 19 December 1864, cited in Creighton, *The Road to Confederation*, p. 165.
31. See Jean Charles Bonenfant, *The French Canadians and the Birth of Confederation*, Canadian Historical Association booklet No. 10 (Ottawa, 1967).
32. See Hodgins, "Disagreement at the Commencement."
33. J. R. Mallory, "The Five Faces of Federalism," in *The Future of Canadian Federalism*, eds., P.-A. Crepeau and C. B. Macpherson (Toronto, 1965), p. 4.
34. W. L. Morton, "Clio in Canada: The Interpretation of Canadian History," in *Approaches to Canadian History*, ed. Carl Berger, Canadian Historical Readings I (Toronto, 1967), p. 44.
35. This act is reprinted in W. L. Morton, ed., *Manitoba: The Birth of a Province* (Altona, 1965), pp. 1-3.
36. See Ralph Heintzman, "The Spirit of Confederation: Professor Creighton, Biculturalism, and the Use of History," *CHR* 52 (September 1971): 256-58. Heintzman comments: "Now even a cursory examination of the text of this Act of 1869 would cast serious doubt upon the worth of this argument" (p. 256) — i.e., that the act revealed the "real intentions of the federal government" (p. 247). "The purely temporary character of the Act is made clear in the preamble. . . . But all of this informed speculation is quite unnecessary. We have an explicit statement of the intentions of the government from the mouth of John A. Macdonald himself. Macdonald told the House of Commons flatly that the 1869 Act was 'provisional' and 'intended to last only a few months' . . ." (p. 257). Heintzman's chief concerns are educational and linguistic rights.
37. P. B. Waite, *Canada 1874-1896: Arduous Destiny* (Toronto, 1971), p. 65. See also Lewis Herbert Thomas, *The Struggle for Responsible Government in the North-West Territories 1870-97* (Toronto, 1956), p. 48. It is clearly possible to debate the implications of the act, but a document that Macdonald's government made the permanent constitution for the North-West Territories cannot simply be dismissed as meaningless. It is interesting to note that when the statute was made permanent in 1871, with only insignificant modifications, and, of course, the exclusion from its provisions of the new Province of Manitoba, it was justified in its preamble as follows: "whereas, it is expedient to make provision for the government, after the expiration of the Act first above mentioned [i.e., An Act for the temporary government of Rupert's Land], of the North-West Territories, that being the name given . . . to such portion of Rupert's Land the North Western Territory as is not included in . . . Manitoba . . ." (*An Act to make further provision for the government of the North-West Territories*, 34 Vict. Cap. XVI).
38. "Instructions issued to Hon. Wm. McDougall as Lieutenant Governor of the North West Territories, Sept. 28, 1869," in *The Canadian North-West: Its Early Development and Legislative Records*, ed., E. H. Oliver (Ottawa, 1914-15), II: 878-79.
39. For his earlier hopeless insensitivity concerning Red River see W. L. Morton, "Introduction" to *Alexander Begg's Red River Journal* (Toronto, 1956), p. 23.
40. Provencher, a nephew of Bishop J. N. Provencher of St. Boniface (1847-53), was a Central Canadian newspaperman. He had only a minimal contact with the West and was described by Alexander Begg, an intelligent and representative citizen of Red River, as "a pleasant sort of a man who had come up altogether wrongly informed regarding this country . . ." (*Alexander Begg's Red River Journal*, p. 176). Provencher's relationship with the Bishop was his only tie with the West, unless it is assumed that the Métis were French Canadians and therefore identified closely with other French Canadians. The Métis, of course, assumed no such thing, regarding themselves as a New Nation. To assume that the Métis were French Canadian is to commit a sort of historiographical genocide. Heintzman, "Spirit of Confederation," p. 253, for example, comments: "This awareness of the 'canadien' community at Red River was one reason to rejoice in the annexation of the North-West: it meant that the French of the west would be welcomed back into the fold and raised the possibility that colonists from Lower Canada would find themselves 'at home' on the prairies." Presumably, for Heintzman, these 'canadiens' included the Métis. Alexander Begg held the members of McDougall's party in very low esteem. McDougall was characterized as "overbearing," "distant," "unpleasant" and "vindictive." Richards "does not appear to be extraordinarily [sic] clever on Law Subjects although appointed Attorney General." Cameron was "a natural ass" and Dr. Jacques "an unmannerly young fellow" (W. L. Morton, "Introduction," *Alexander Begg's Red River Journal*, p. 176). Is it any wonder that Canada's initial attitude toward the North-West was looked at through a jaundiced eye?

41. George F. G. Stanley, *The Birth of Western Canada: A History of the Riel Rebellions* (Toronto, 1936), pp. 63-64.
42. Morton, "Introduction," *Alexander Begg's Red River Journal*, pp. 29, 40-42, 45.
43. Ibid., p. 17.
44. M. S. Donnelly, *The Government of Manitoba* (Toronto, 1963), p. 10.
45. Morton, "Clio in Canada." p. 44.
46. Manitoba Act, Section 30.
47. Eric Kierans, *Report on Natural Resources Policy in Manitoba* (Winnipeg, 1973), p. 1. The severity of this kind of analysis has been questioned. See, for example, J. A. Maxwell, *Federal Subsidies to the Provincial Governments in Canada* (Cambridge, Mass.: 1937).
48. Cited in Donnelly, *Government of Manitoba*, p. 16.
49. Maxwell, *Federal Subsidies to the Provincial Governments*, p. 37.
50. Donnelly, *Government of Manitoba*, p. 161.
51. Maxwell, *Federal Subsidies to the Provincial Governments*, pp. 37-38.
52. Section 36.
53. R. G. Robertson, "The Evolution of Territorial Government in Canada," in *The Political Process in Canada* (Toronto, 1963), p. 139 note.
54. Cited in Chester Martin, *"Dominion Lands" Policy* (Toronto, 1938), p. 470.
55. See S. W. Horrall, "Sir John A. Macdonald and the Mounted Police Force for the Northwest Territories," *CHR* 53 (June 1972). Horrall notes, pp. 182-83: "To Macdonald the problem of policing the Northwest resembled that faced by the British in India."
56. Rutherford. "Western Press and Regionalism," p. 301.
57. Morton, "Clio in Canada," p. 47.

The Myth of the Downtrodden West *
J. M. S. CARELESS

A recent Toronto *Globe and Mail* article by two western authors contained a crisp synopsis of Canadian history since Confederation: "We take it as a 'given' that . . . the Hinterland (West and Maritimes) has suffered economically, socially and culturally under Central Canada's domination of the country for 113 years." The article was on senate reform, but what was most plain about it was the conviction that the West (not to mention the Maritimes) had been thoroughly and steadily held back by a controlling central Canada. Here was a direct expression of western alienation. What had been an attitude of grievance, grown to be a popular tradition of discontent, was now a comprehensive view of history. In many parts of Canada this is today the conventional wisdom. But how valid is it? To what degree are current western sentiments justified by the historical record, and to what degree are they a regional distortion of memory and experience — half truths selectively kept in mind by a "hinterland" that thinks it has been exploited and isn't going to take it any longer?

Since the nineteenth century, the West has felt exposed to powerful forces beyond its control — not just huge distances, the vagaries of climate and harvests, and the problem of distant market prices, but the power of outside human interests over the West's promised destiny. Nature and the

* First published in *Saturday Night*, 96 (May 1981): 30–37. Copyright 1981 by J. M. S. Careless. Reprinted by permission.

"natural" laws of the market could be lived with, perhaps to some extent offset. But dependence on eastern-controlled transport and business, and on federal government policies, grew much harder to accept.

People and money from outside first built up the West, laying down the vital rail lines from the 1880s, patterning the settlement of land, investing in towns and business enterprises, and subordinating the West to metropolitan centres half a continent away. The same could be said of other regions in Canada, and of North America in general. But even when the West grew (with startling speed), its undiversified economy and its reliance on long traffic routes to far-off markets left it particularly vulnerable. It was unsheltered, and uncertain, and considerably divided. The Pacific West was clearly different from the plains West, not only in terrain and economy but in outlook. And on the plains, Manitoba was not Saskatchewan, and Alberta was different again. Yet, in their comparative newness, their hopes of progress based on rich internal resources, and their frustrations readily blamed on dark external influences, the young western provinces had a good deal in common. They shared the same historical experience and displayed the same collective response. The West was eager and aggressive, prickly and aggrieved. And its mood could change like a chinook.

Developments from the First World War onward consolidated this outlook. Resentment over the wartime conscription of farm labour, the post-war weight of war-inflated farm debt, and the widespread slowdown in the prairie wheat economy through much of the 1920s all left their marks. In the 1930s the Depression made westerners feel even more helplessly subject to outside forces. The Second World War and the booming 1950s brought dramatic recovery and new advances, but bitter memories of the Depression were all but indelible. And then, in the years approaching the present, came the oil, gas, and potash bonanzas in the prairies, and the coal, gas, logging, and electric-power booms in British Columbia. For almost the first time, the West began to think that its dreams were within its grasp, that it could escape its self-seen role as victim.

Recently this buoyant, increasingly diversifying West was confronted by a fresh outside intervention. Federal power (central Canadian Power, in western eyes) sought, it seemed, to seize control of the new western wealth in energy: to draw it off in support of a faltering East and centre. No wonder the West sharply reacted. No wonder western provincial politicians began to raise defensive barriers. No wonder many aroused westerners could ardently agree that the whole history of their region added up to a century of victimization by central Canada.

The reaction is understandable, but not fair. It is grounded in experience, but it sees just one side of history. Western problems have to be judged in the light of the fuller Canadian record: regions are not closed entities, embattled armies of us against them, but interlinked communities in broad national and international frames. At the very least, the historic treatment of the West must be assessed within the wider realm of the Canadian nation. Three of the crucial issues that have affected the West across its history — the tariff, freight rates, and control of natural resources — provide good tests of the West's belief in its past subservience.

Westerners have continually protested that the federal protective tariff, originally created by John A. Macdonald's government, compelled them to buy higher-priced, protected central Canadian goods instead of cheaper alternatives from outside the country, where their own primary products went. Thus they were held subservient. Traditionally they have seen the tariff as imposed to benefit central Canada at the cost of other Canadian regions, diverting part of their incomes to sustain the centre's domination. They have argued that this diversion and imbalance retarded the growth of manufacturing within the West itself, keeping it industrially dependent on the centre.

N. P.

This whole position expresses one-sided judgements. The original National Policy of protection begun in 1879 was part of a larger package aimed at building the Canadian union, including the West, by promoting a more diversified, higher-level economy with a broad home market — one that would not be absorbed piecemeal by the already highly protectionist United States. The very settlement and development of the West, the construction of costly railways to open it, and the amassing of capital to invest in its growth, were seen by Macdonald's government to depend on the revenues and wealth created by industrial advances in the older, settled eastern regions.

65

Yet if the would-be nation-builders of the time mainly considered the West a great new property to be developed under central direction — and they did — it's also true that there was virtually no western regional community *until* that process got under way. Of course, there were a few whites and a long-standing thinly spread community of Indians and Métis in the wilderness West of fur-trade days. And certainly the native peoples were little considered by anyone back East as settlement began to infringe on their ways of life: thus the two western risings of 1869 and 1885. Still, without at all condoning the treatment of Indians and Métis (who in the long run probably suffered as much from local white prejudices as from the patronizing parsimony of distant imperial Ottawa), it is still true that the West as we now know it came into being only under a central, national design — and this included building east-west trade behind a tariff wall. How could the designers think otherwise than in terms of centrally directed purposes, when a western regional society had yet to be created? The imposition of the tariff was not just centralist greed and self-interest, but part of a genuine nation-making effort. The achievement of this design, in fact, was the rapid settling of the West, which then increasingly protested central domination — and the policy which had helped make the modern West possible.

Westerners would still contend that the National Policy did not work out as it should have; that it failed to produce a well-rounded economic unit and left the hinterland thoroughly subject to central metropolitan interests. The centre developed industrial strength because of the gift of protection, and — secure behind the tariff wall — proceeded to exploit the trade of both a weaker Atlantic region and a subordinated West. Central Canada got the fat of the land (this argument runs) at the expense of the rest.

A good deal else can be said against the historic workings of the Canadian tariff: that it fostered powerful vested interests, especially in Ontario, that it promoted unhealthy alliances between governments and businessmen (who quite liked state support), that it shored up inefficient industries, notably in Québec. Yet the key question remains: did central Canada obtain and keep industrial mastery because of protection, at the expense of hinterland incomes? Not even economists with computers can really settle the point, or prove what might have been if the tariff had not been established. But an Albertan economist, Kenneth Norrie, has recently argued (to small applause in Alberta) that differences in regional income levels across the country are essentially due not to the tariff but to the inevitable workings of the capitalist market system, under which some get more and others less. Perhaps it might be different under socialism, but that is hardly the demand of the angriest westerners today in Alberta, who inveigh against the "socialist" policies of Ottawa. Besides, there is ample evidence of disadvantaged regions under all sorts of socialist or Communist régimes.

Still, the western assessment goes as follows: in the late nineteenth century, Canada was largely stagnant and depressed, until massive occupation of the West began around the century's end. Then, borne along by the rapid growth of the prairie wheat economy and the big new captive market it offered, the centre and its protected industries at last began to boom, aided as well by mining and logging developments in the Pacific West. In this version, the West saved and strengthened eastern power at its own cost of continued subservience.

But industrialization was advancing strongly in the East long before a significant western market existed. The late nineteenth century, in fact, far from being a time of stagnation, produced industrial expansion in central Canada, remarkably so in Ontario during the early 1880s. No doubt the 1879 tariff encouraged that growth, but considerable industrial progress had been made well before the tariff was even introduced; it was a result as well as a cause of the rise of manufacturing interests. There was an already sizable central Canadian population, providing an accessible market and work force, along with a well-developed regional transport system by both rail and water, and close links with the prosperous American heartland. Surely those factors had more to do with advancing central Canadian industrialism than did the tariff.

In the twentieth century the great western wheat boom undoubtedly created a valuable market for central industrialism, but eastern industry was already established. And it was sharing as well in the growing activities of much nearer pulpwood and mining frontiers, and benefitting from its own enlarging supply of cheap hydro.

It is short-sighted, in other words, to view the industrial rise of central Canada from a western perspective alone. The wider record indicates that central economic ascendancy was based on far more than any tariff grip on the West. And later years confirmed as much when the centre continued to expand despite western slowdowns — though in some degree, admittedly, because of north-south trade in the primary products of its resource-rich northern hinterlands.

There remains the claim that the tariff impaired manufacturing in the West. No doubt the record shows the struggles and failures of smaller western enterprises in the face of bigger, richer eastern rivals. But under free trade they would have faced the same competition, or worse, from even bigger American firms. Moreover, under the National Policy, Manitoba still built up decidedly valuable industries: effective units for the regional market, somewhat protected by distance from the East and by the tariff from the Americans. In fact, Manitoba, no less part of the West than its neighbours, has been predominantly favoured by protective rates; above all, in the Winnipeg area.

Western cities in general did well on the east-west flow of trade that was channelled behind the tariff barrier and along the Canadian transcontinental rail lines. Vancouver, as terminus of the CPR, was not only a direct creation of the national rail system, but was assured of regional dominance over the Pacific West by the tariff shield. Without it, markets on the coast and in the interior could have been tapped quite as well by American cities to the south. The Alaska boundary question of the early 1900s, for example, really involved whether Seattle or Vancouver would command trade access by water to the gold-rich Yukon, depending on where the Canada-U.S. border was drawn and which country's tariff wall would thus stand or be breached.

Western centres and their rising industries have gained a lot from a protective tariff, no less than in the East. A more diversified West might want a tariff even more. In that respect, the very push of Alberta to use its new wealth to build a broader-based economy and fatter home markets can only inspire mounting protectionist demands — most likely, in a separate Alberta state itself.

It follows that there is no inherent crime in pursuing a protectionist policy. For all its failings, protectionism historically has been a measure of political exigency, not of social injustice or regional oppression. Everyone looks for protection of his special interests — industrialists and farmers, easterners and westerners. One's own needs, of course, are essential and righteous, those of others self-seeking and immoral. But that too is in the historical record. And we are stuck with it.

Because of the West's dependence on long-distance land routes to markets or supplies, and its lack of water routes (like the Great Lakes-St. Lawrence system), westerners have always been crucially concerned with the cost of rail transport and the power of the great eastern-based railways. Even the recent rise of truck and air traffic has changed this in only a limited

67

way, because the bulk and low unit-value of the West's primary products make rail transport still most economic. Nor have pipelines essentially altered the historic pattern. Accordingly, the railway rate structure and the near-monopolies of the big rail corporations behind it have figured large in western complaints.

Rates and railway power were targets of attack from the early years of settlement, through the western farmers' movement of Progressivism in the 1920s, the bleak era of Depression, and down to the present. The eastern-centred traffic octopus, strangling the free peoples of the West, supplied a potent theme of protest. Lower or more preferably arranged freight rates, of course, were sometimes realized through political pressure, but this seemed only to demonstrate the need to fight the central power complex of politicians and business. Yet campaigns for adjustment were more often concerned with advantages for particular western interests or places than with equal justice for all. Certainly the main centres, such as Winnipeg and Vancouver, have enjoyed favourable rates in their time. In any case, westerners again have acted like other Canadians in trying to improve their own special positions in the national traffic system. The system may be focused historically in the more densely occupied centre, but it depends on serving all the country.

The West made one striking gain with the Crow's Nest Pass rates of 1897, an agreement by which the federal government secured low rates for western grain traffic by rail to the Lakehead, in return for subsidizing a costly extension of the CPR through southern British Columbia mountains. This agreement, ended by 1922, was revived largely due to the western Progressives' pressure — and thereby grew the "statutory grain rates" which still today, despite the enormous increase in all kinds of costs, move western wheat at antique price levels. Effectively, the Canadian government (and taxpayers) have provided a western subsidy, huge over the years, which has compensated for many of the higher charges the West has claimed to suffer from tariff and rail subservience. But to draw a balance sheet that covers every factor in the accounting is impossible. No one can deny the worth of the grain-rates arrangement in the national as well as the regional context, but the issue nevertheless demonstrates once more that the record has more than one side.

The same economist mentioned earlier, Kenneth Norrie (a maverick in an Alberta famed for its mavericks), has argued that the West would not have done better if it had not been forced by tariff and railway policy to use the Canadian routes. American rail rates, in fact, were higher. This fact upsets the long-held idea of the West's exploitation by the national transport system. Norrie also points out that in recent years some seventy per cent of western shipments from the region moved in the cheapest rate categories, scarcely overburdening producers' incomes; that the prairies receive rates no different from those of the rest of the country for mineral products and manufactures they send out; that the higher charges on their inbound processed goods afford a degree of protection for western industries; and that there is no basis for the view that discriminatory rates are impairing the development of those industries.

All this may not cover every aspect of the cost-of-transport case; notably, differences between the water-accessible Pacific West and the great land-locked interior. In general, however, one still is led to this conclusion: the rail and rate problems of the West owe far more to physical environment than historical mistreatment. The relative remoteness of the whole territory; the costs levied by distance, mountain barriers, and the vast Precambrian shield along its eastern margins; the lack of alternative water routes across its inland sweep — these were far greater hindrances than any human arrangements could be. Without doubting the facts of corporate self-interest, the devious effects of political deals, and the creaky clumsiness of rate regulation and adjustment, we can still conclude that geography is the main factor behind the historic freight-rates issue in the West.

The old but newly heated question of control of natural resources goes back to the very entry of the West into Confederation. At that time, the existing eastern provinces held title over their own unsettled lands and whatever natural wealth those lands might contain. So did British Columbia, since it joined Canada as a province already in being. But the prairies came in as territory transferred from the imperial British government and the Hudson's Bay Company. And while a small Manitoba was immediately erected — the so-called "postage stamp" province — it did not receive control over its own landed resources. Nor did Saskatchewan or Alberta when, thanks to the spread of settlement, they too were set up by federal law as provinces in 1905. The great plains country was treated as a national estate, to be opened, developed, and exploited under central, federal direction.

Almost certainly, there was no other way at the beginning. Quite certainly there was no thought of another way, given the nearly empty West of the day; the new-made Manitoba had only about 12 000 settled inhabitants. Western lands would be laid out, policed, and granted under federal authority. Some land would be used to support schools, some allocated to the Hudson's Bay Company as part of the transfer bargain. And more would go to help fund the railway lines so crucially required to open the West. Thus the CPR was initially granted 25-million acres, along with $25-million, to support the task of construction. The subsequent wealth that company gained by selling off this great land tract might later seem to the West extravagant overpayment out of its own birthright. This was easy enough to feel after the railway was built, and westerners began fuming about its privileged power; but not so easy to feel when a shaky young company was pushing forward in the 1880s in constant danger of financial collapse, its rewards far in the future. Memory is indeed selective.

Under federal management the lands of the West were successfully taken up, in a process greatly stimulated in the early twentieth century by

69

flourishing world demands for resource supplies, including food. Federal resource controls were not seriously challenged in the region until its post-war slowdown in the 1920s, when the Progressives attributed so many western troubles to outside power. Prairie dwellers came to see themselves as downgraded, kept in colonial status by the federal sway over their resources, unequal to the citizens of other provinces. British Columbians could share that sentiment also, since they had transferred large amounts of provincial railway lands to federal jurisdiction back in the 1880s.

At last, in 1929-30, the natural resources of all the western provinces were handed over to them. But the years of controversy, at times agitated and embittered, left sharp memories. And now, these memories have been revived as the question of resource control reemerges over federal policies affecting the revenues from oil- and gas-producing western lands — a new invasion, westerners feel, of their hard-won birthright. Without examining the present issue, one can see how deep its roots reach into the past.

70 The question is whether the historic record justifies the "victim" attitude of the West. Not, I think, for most of the early years of growth. Given the scope of the task of western settlement and the weakness of actual prairie jurisdictions, central resource control was both justifiable and effective; and federal authority had an aura of successful national leadership right up to the First World War.

Afterwards, it was different. The resources questions emerged amid the involved political manoeuvres of a far less dynamic federal régime. The final settlement looked more like a tardy concession wrung from central expediency than a positive recognition of regional equality. The West had overcome resource control by its own determined stand. Today Ottawa faces such a view once more.

There remains the long-perceived sway of eastern banks and investment houses over western financial life; the roles of eastern-centred media and cultural organizations, held to have neglected or inhibited western cultural developments. Far more critical is the West's sense of its own lack of political power in a federal system that has largely rested on central Canada votes — and never more obviously than today. On this, one still might say that representation based on population has been a powerful historical principle in this country, and it is hard to run democracy except by rule of the majority. Yet, apart from aligning with a political majority, a region with a minority population in a federal system can look to the provincial sphere of powers — and can hope for its own population to increase. For the West, this last looks promising, as economic forces continue to shift Canadian population westward.

Whatever the history behind the West's current alienation, history itself is at work to settle the matter. The West that has grown so far has not escaped geography; but the impact of geography is changing over time, as the whole demographic and economic orientation of North America moves westward. This shift may not make grass grow on Yonge Street — a cheerful western fantasy — but it will change the whole Canadian balance.

The centre's dominance, not a sinister plot but a joint product of history and geography, will be modified and offset. The current metropolitan rise of Vancouver, Calgary, and Edmonton, and the new wealth, diversity, and energy of their own western hinterlands, proclaims as much.

What we need, really, is more time to defuse angry issues. We could also use a shrewdly adaptable John A. Macdonald to wangle new political combinations, even a skilfully delaying Mackenzie King, rather than urgent confrontationists in power. If the Canadian genius (of seeming anything but genius) does come through, western alienation could subside without explosions. And history may then confirm that western discontents, while deep in memory, should be seen as no true basis for a belief in steady victimization.

Louis Riel: Patriot or Rebel?*

GEORGE STANLEY

The Essence of the Riel Question

Few characters in Canadian history have aroused such depth and bitterness of feeling as that of the métis chieftain, Louis "David" Riel. The mere mention of his name bares those latent religious and racial animosities which seem to lie so close to the surface of Canadian politics. Despite the fact that he identified himself, not with the French Canadians of Quebec, but with the mixed-blood population of the western plains, Louis Riel became, for a few years, the symbol of the national aspirations of French Canada and the storm-centre of political Orangeism. French-speaking Canadians elevated him to the pedestal of martyrdom; English-speaking Canadians damned him as a rebel. In Riel the people of Quebec professed to see another Papineau, a heroic patriot defending on the far away prairies the cause of Canadians living in the valley of the St. Lawrence; the people of Ontario saw in him only the dastard murderer of an Ontario Protestant. Even today the racial controversies which emerged from Riel's actions in Manitoba in 1869–70, and the political turmoils stirred up by his trial and execution in Saskatchewan fifteen years later, make it difficult to assess fairly the contribution of this strange and rather pathetic creature, whose remains now lie but a few steps from those of his grandparents, in the peaceful cathedral yard of St. Boniface.

In essence the troubles associated with the name of Louis Riel were the manifestation, not of the traditional rivalries of French Catholic Quebec and English Protestant Ontario, but of the traditional problems of cultural conflict, of the clash between primitive and civilized peoples. In all parts of the world, in South Africa, New Zealand and North America, the penetration of white settlement into territories inhabited by native peoples has led to friction and war; Canadian expansion into the North-West led to a similar result. Both in Manitoba and in Saskatchewan the métis had their own primitive society and their own primitive economy. They hunted the buffalo, they trafficked in furs, they freighted goods for the Hudson's Bay Company, and they indifferently cultivated their long narrow farms along the banks of the rivers. Few of them were equipped by education or experience to compete with the whites, or to share with them the political responsibilities of citizenship. When faced with the invasion of civilization they drew together; they did not want to be civilized; they wanted only to survive. Their fears and bewilderment drove them into resistance which, when reduced to armed conflict, held small chance of success.

Fundamentally there was little difference between the métis and the Indian problems. Even less than the mixed-bloods were the native Indians prepared to take a place in the highly competitive civilization of the white men. To the Indian and métis alike, civilization meant the destruction of their culture, with assimilation or extinction as their ultimate fate. The Riel risings were not, as the politicians said and believed, a war between French and English, but between plough and prairie. But these facts were hidden from the Canadian public by the timidity and prejudices of politicians; and the visionary defender of an obsolete cultural epoch in Western Canadian history became the martyr of a race.

The dates of the two risings associated with the name of Louis Riel are not without significance. The first, 1869–70, coincided with the passing of the Hudson's Bay Company as the governing power of the North-West. The second, 1885, coincided with the completion of the Canadian Pacific Railway, an event which definitely marked the end of the old order in the North-West. With the suppression of the last effort on the part of Canada's primitive peoples to withstand the inexorable march of civilization, and the execution of Riel, the domination of the white man was forever assured. Henceforth the history of Western Canada was to be that of the white man, not that of the red man or of the half-breed.

Simple as are the conflicts of 1869 and 1885 when viewed as episodes in the history of the cultural frontier, they have always been complicated by the enigmatic personality of their leader. A man with a real popular appeal and considerable organizing ability, Riel was able to give unity and corporate courage to his followers. In him the self-assertive tendencies of the métis were liberated; to him they owed that self-confidence which they had never previously possessed and were never to possess again. Whether Riel was mad will ever remain a matter of debate. Medical opinion inclines to the view that his grandiose visions, his obsessional neurosis, his intense egotism, his intolerance of opposition, were all symptoms of a paranoid condition. It must be remembered that primitive aggressiveness and hostility lurk deep in the minds of all of us. Unless these tendencies can get adequate sublimation they reveal themselves in strong self-assertion, ruthless desire for power, delusions of persecution, irrational fixations and megalomania. That Louis Riel fits into this pattern there seems little real doubt. Perhaps the psychologist has the final answer to the problem of Riel's personality when he suggests that a repressed primitive aggressiveness explains, in part at least, Riel's behaviour in 1869 and in 1885.

The Basic Cause of the Red River Rising

The half-breeds of the Hudson's Bay Company Territories were a remarkable people. Children of the fur traders and the Indian women of the plains, they combined many of the best qualities of both races. Physically they excited the admiration of visitors. They were as much at home on the prairie as any Indian tribesmen and in their elaborate organization for the buffalo hunt they had a self-made military organization as efficient for its own purpose as the Boer Commando. Despite their semi-nomadic life and their mixed blood they were not savages. They were religious and reasonably honest; and in the golden days of the Red River Settlement serious crime was unknown. The authority of the Hudson's Bay Company was almost entirely moral; and when left to themselves the métis got on well with the Indians, with each other and with their rulers.

The serpent in this Eden was progress. For a long time the menace came from the south. American settlement proceeded faster than Canadian, and while there was still an empty wilderness between Fort Garry and Western Ontario there were fast growing settlements in the United States. Developments south of the frontier made it difficult if not impossible to enforce the fur monopoly; and developments south of the frontier meant the end of the buffalo and the demoralization of the Indians.

The newly created federation of Canada, fearful — and with ample justification — of American expansion northwards and of the intrigues of Senator Alexander Ramsey and the Minnesota party, finally concluded an agreement with the Hudson's Bay Company for the transfer of the Company's territories to Canada. To Canada and to the Canadians the acquisition of the North-West was a logical and necessary corollary to confederation; but to the people of Red River it meant their transfer to a "foreign" government whose interests were very different from their own. Evidence of these differences was soon afforded by the arrival in Red River of a party of Canadian surveyors who proceeded to lay out the land in a symmetrical pattern, taking little or no heed of the irregularities of the métis holdings, and precursing, in any event, close settlement, the destruction of the buffalo and the end of the wandering life of the prairie. The sons of Isaac were advancing on the lands of the sons of Ishmael. A clash was inevitable.

Louis Riel Organizes the Métis

Louis Riel, the man who organized the resistance of the Red River métis, was born in St. Boniface, October 22nd, 1844. His mother, Julie Lagimodière, was the daughter of the first white woman in the North-West, and his father, a métis, had been the leader of the "free trade in furs" movement in the forties. A serious, somewhat introspective boy, Louis Riel was selected by Bishop Taché of St. Boniface with several other métis boys, to be educated in Eastern Canada. As a scholar at the Collège de Montréal his studies were satisfactory, particularly in rhetoric, although his lack of humility in the eyes of his ecclesiastical tutors unfitted him for a religious vocation. He remained, as he always was, aloof, egotistical, without real friends among his comrades. These were years of intense political activity in the Canadas, years of constitutional deadlock, of "Rep by Pop", "No Popery", "Double Majority", and "Confederation". Riel's patrons, the Masson family, were well known in Canadian political circles and it is not surprising that young Louis Riel should have shown a greater interest in politics than in religion. He worked for a brief time as a student-at-law; then in 1867 he went back to the west, to St. Paul, where he remained until his return to Red River a year later.

Riel did not stir up the métis to the insurrection that occurred in 1869. He only assumed the leadership of an already existing discontent, moulded it, and gave it form according to his judgment or his impulse. His education, his eloquence, his knowledge both of the English and French languages, and his genuine belief in the justice of the métis cause marked him out at once as the obvious leader of his people, and to him the frightened, confused métis turned. Their obvious need for leadership gave young Louis confidence, and he was able, in turn, to inspire them with a sense of national destiny. Small secret meetings developed into large political gatherings, and when news reached the Settlement that a Canadian Lieutenant-Governor, William McDougall, with a ready-made government and several cases of rifles, was approaching Red River by way of Pembina, the aroused métis met at the house of the abbé Ritchot in St. Norbert determined to organize their resistance. John Bruce, a man of little consequence, was elected president of the métis "National Committee"; Louis Riel, the real leader, was named secretary. A barricade was then erected across the road and on October 21st a warning was sent to McDougall not to attempt to enter the country without the express permission of the "National Committee". Having taken the first step towards armed resistance, the second came easily enough. The Hudson's Bay Governor, William McTavish, mortally ill, had virtually abdicated all authority and Riel's organization was able not only to cut McDougall off from the small but noisy group in Winnipeg favouring annexation to Canada, but to intercept all mails and parties entering the Settlement.

The day of decision for Riel was November 2nd. On that day he and a band of armed métis occupied Fort Garry without opposition. It was a daring and decisive act. Situated at the junction of the Red and Assiniboine rivers, with ample stores of food and munitions, and defended by stone walls, Fort Garry was both the geographical and strategic centre of the Red River Settlement. Whoever controlled the fort controlled the colony.

Meanwhile McDougall, much to the delight of the Americans who continually poked unkind fun at him in their newspapers, fretted and fumed at Pembina. He had been told to proceed with all convenient speed to Fort Garry and there to make arrangements for the completion of the transfer which had been fixed for December 1st, 1869. His line of duty to him was clear. Unaware of the fact that the Canadian government had at the last moment postponed the date of transfer, McDougall issued, on December 1st, in the name of Queen Victoria, a proclamation announcing the transfer of the North-West to Canada with his own appointment as Lieutenant-Governor, and he commissioned Colonel J. S. Dennis to raise a force to deal with the insurgents.

To proclaim a transfer which had not been effected was meaningless; but to propose to overcome by armed force the people whom he expected to govern, was dangerous both for McDougall and for the country he represented. It was fortunate that the response to McDougall's appeal fell far short of what he had hoped for. Henry Prince and a few Saulteaux Indians turned out, ready to fight the métis or anyone else, and the Canadians who had settled in the vicinity of Winnipeg displayed a genuine eagerness to enlist; but the great body of settlers, both mixed-blood and white, held back. Dennis soon realized the folly of any attempt to overthrow the Riel movement by force of arms and told McDougall so. But the enlisted Canadians, forty-five of them, led by Dr. John Schultz, believed themselves stronger than they were, and ignoring Dennis's advice they occupied a fortified house in Winnipeg. When, however, they found themselves faced with the muskets of six hundred métis even Schultz could see the force of the argument; they therefore emerged from "Fort Schultz" and dragged themselves between the files of Riel's ragged soldiery towards the cells of Fort Garry.

75

The First Convention, November 1869

Meanwhile Louis Riel had been seeking to broaden the basis of his support. Hitherto his movement had been limited to the French-speaking métis. Almost equal in number to the métis were the English-speaking half-breeds, whose interests, while differing in detail, were ultimately the same as those of their French-speaking kindred. It was thus Riel's aim, not to fight Canada, but to unite the whole body of mixed-blood settlers who formed over eighty per cent of the population of Red River, in a demand that Canada negotiate with them the terms of their entry into the Canadian federation. It was with this end in view that he invited the several parishes of the colony to send representatives to meet in convention at Fort Garry on November 16th.

From Riel's standpoint the convention was only a partial success. He had prepared no agenda; his supporters, most of them unschooled buffalo hunters, lacked any real knowledge of parliamentary procedure, and the English-speaking half-breeds to whom he was appealing, had no clear cut ideas as to what their role should be. Much time was wasted in fruitless disagreement over the question of forming a "Provisional Government" to take over the authority previously exercised by the Hudson's Bay Company. The English half-breeds were inclined to suspect the nature of Riel's motives although the continued presence of the Union Jack above the walls of Fort Garry and the moderation which characterized the "List of Rights" which Riel submitted for discussion, did much to minimize the disagreements between the two half-breed groups. However, McDougall's proclamation renewed the doubts of the English-speaking members of the convention, and, intolerant of any further delay, Riel, on December 8th, issued a "Declaration of the People of Rupert's Land and the North West" to the effect that, since the Hudson's Bay Company had, without the consent of the settlers, sold the country to a "foreign power", the people of Red River were, in the absence of any legal authority, free to establish their own government "and hold it to be the only and lawful authority now in existence in Rupert's Land and the North-West, which claims the obedience and respect of the people". In other words, the métis National Committee was the only "lawful" as well as the only "effective" government in Red River. The Declaration continued, however, by expressing the willingness of the people to "enter into such negotiations with the Canadian government as may be favourable for the good government and prosperity of this people". On December 23rd, John Bruce resigned and Louis Riel became the titular president of the National Committee. He was now complete master of the Red River Settlement.

76

The Canadian Government Attempts to Placate the Métis

Five days previously McDougall had quitted the inhospitable village of Pembina. In Ottawa the Prime Minister, Sir John A. Macdonald, wrote to one of his colleagues, "McDougall is now at St. Paul's and leaves this morning for Ottawa. He has the redoubtable Stoughton Dennis with him. The two together have done their utmost to destroy our chance of an amicable settlement with these wild people." Sir John A. Macdonald and the others completely misunderstood the real nature of the métis grievances. They viewed the troubles in Red River primarily as an expression of French-Canadian particularism, and so they sent as peace messengers to Red River a French-Canadian priest and a French-Canadian soldier from Eastern Canada. Neither Grand Vicar Thibault nor Colonel de Salaberry accomplished anything. Riel quickly found that the Canadian emissaries possessed no real authority to treat with the National Committee, and he would not, therefore, permit them to carry out their intended role of spreading propaganda on behalf of Canada.

Of far greater significance was the appearance in the Settlement towards the end of December 1869 of Donald A. Smith, the chief representative of the Hudson's Bay Company in Canada. Smith had offered his services to the Canadian Government in November, and his offer had been accepted.

Smith was a man of drive, ambition and resource, a cold and unemotional master of business. He had distinguished himself as administrator of the Company's Labrador District and was, at this time, manager of the Montreal District. Although fifty years of age, he was just crossing the threshold of that remarkable career which saw him enter parliament, make possible the building of the Canadian Pacific Railway, receive a peerage, and become High Commissioner for Canada in London. He had never before visited the North-West, but he had married a Red River girl and his name was well known to Company servants and métis alike.

As representative of the Company, Smith found little difficulty in entering the Settlement. Although his freedom of movement was circumscribed by a suspicious Riel, he had frequent visits from "some of the most influential and most reliable men in the Settlement", who not only made known to the people generally "the liberal intentions of the Canadian Government", but who helped Smith distribute no less than £500 among the French métis in those quarters where it would be most to the advantage of Canada. He had taken care to leave his official papers at Pembina in order to prevent their seizure, and by spreading word of their existence and implying that he possessed the power to negotiate, Smith finally compelled Riel to call a general meeting of the inhabitants of Red River to hear a public statement of Canada's position.

77

The Second Convention and the Establishment of the Provisional Government, January-February 1870

Despite the cold — the temperature was near to twenty degrees below zero [−29°C] — upwards of a thousand men, French métis, English half-breeds and Scotch settlers, assembled in the snow-packed square of Fort Garry on January 19th and 20th. The chairman of the meetings was Thomas Bunn, an English half-breed who was nominated for the position by Louis Riel. Riel himself acted as interpreter. At first it seemed as though the mature, experienced Scot had gained the upper hand, but by the second day it became clear that the young and inexperienced métis still retained his ascendancy over the people of Red River. His proposal that another convention should meet at Fort Garry to consider "the subject of Mr. Smith's commission and to decide what would be best for the welfare of the country" was seconded by A. G. B. Bannatyne, a white settler, and carried unanimously. The unity which Riel had sought before Christmas without achieving it now appeared to be on the point of realization; and the métis leader's suggestion that the proposed convention should include both French and English in equal numbers was a popular one. The fact is that on fundamental problems the mixed-blood population thought alike. Despite the failure of the first convention there had been no real difference of opinion over the proposed "List of Rights". The only real division was between the half-breeds and the "Canadians", who were cordially disliked by the old settlers of Red River, both French and English-speaking.

The convention met on January 25th. For seventeen days the representatives discussed the "rights" which they should claim from Canada. On several occasions Riel's proposals were rejected, much to his indignation and annoyance. In the end a new "List of Rights" was drawn up, delegates were appointed to carry it to Ottawa, and a Provisional Government was established under the presidency of Louis Riel. Towards midnight on February 9th the cannon of Fort Garry belched forth a salute and fireworks, which the Canadians had purchased to celebrate the arrival of McDougall, were exploded in honour of Riel and his associates. The métis leader's star was at its zenith.

The Execution of Thomas Scott, March 1870

There was, however, a cloud upon the horizon. Even while the members of the convention were still sitting at Fort Garry, the Canadians at Portage la Prairie had started a second counter-Riel movement. It was largely the work of one Thomas Scott, a Canadian who had been taken prisoner in December and who had succeeded in escaping from Fort Garry. A small band of these Canadians marched towards Kildonan where Dr. Schultz, who had likewise escaped from Riel's hands, was doing his best to enlist the sympathies and persons of the Scottish settlers; but they decided against armed resistance. Unfortunately the métis, believing an attack to be imminent, began to round up the Canadians as they were marching back to Portage la Prairie. The latter quietly submitted to being taken to the Fort and thrust into the prison rooms from which the first group of prisoners had only recently been freed.

The outcome of the Canadian action — which Macdonald called both "foolish" and "criminal" — was the trial and execution of Thomas Scott. The métis court martial which condemned him was no judicial tribunal; and the execution was both senseless and cruel. "Consider the circumstances. Let the motives be weighed," pleaded Riel at a later date. The métis leader justified the execution of Scott by declaring that he had been guilty of disorderly conduct the previous autumn, that he had twice been involved in offensive actions against the Provisional Government, and that he had been abusive to his guards and incited the other prisoners to insubordination; but these were hardly offences calling for the death penalty. A more honest explanation may be found in Riel's words to Donald A. Smith: "We must make Canada respect us." Both Riel and the métis, despite their swagger and apparent self-assurance, felt inadequate to the situation in which they found themselves. Fundamentally they were suffering from an inferiority complex and from it they sought to escape by a deliberate act of self-assertion.

The Despatch of Delegates to Ottawa, March 1870

Five days after the death of Scott, on March 9th, Bishop Taché, who had been absent during this critical period in the history of the North-West while attending the Oecumenical Council at Rome, arrived back in the Settlement. He had answered the urgent appeal of the Canadian government to lend his influence towards restoring peace and order to the country. There was little, however, at this point, that Taché could do. The death of Scott had occasioned but small excitement in the colony, and both English-speaking half-breeds and French-speaking métis continued to work together in the Convention and in the Provisional Government. Final discussions on the demands to be sent to Ottawa and preparations for the despatch of the delegates to Canada occupied the energies of the Convention. The last-minute addition of a demand for separate schools to the already familiar requests for provincial status, a general amnesty, the protection of local customs, the equality of French and English languages, treaties with the native Indian tribes and federal financial concessions, was, however, doubtless the Bishop's work.

The Manitoba Act, May 1870   79

On March 23rd, the delegates set out. On May 2nd, 1870, a bill called the Manitoba Bill, incorporating most of the features of the métis "List of Rights", was introduced into the Canadian House of Commons by Sir John A. Macdonald. Ten days later, it received the royal assent. When the news reached Fort Garry, a twenty-one gun salute was fired, and a special session of the Provincial Legislature, upon the motion of the métis Louis Schmidt, unanimously agreed to accept the terms of entry of Red River into the Dominion of Canada. With the troubles now virtually at an end the completion of the transfer could be effected, and on July 15th, 1870, the North-West territories formally became part of Canada, with that small portion of which Red River was the centre being admitted as the fifth province of the Canadian federation.

Were this the whole story, the question whether Riel may be looked upon as a patriot or a rebel would be a simple one. Unfortunately, however, as the excitement in Red River waned, that in Canada waxed increasing great. The execution of Thomas Scott had ramifications beyond anything anticipated by Louis Riel and his colleagues. Admittedly Scott was not a popular figure, even among the Canadians in Red River. He was hot-headed and aggressive. Donald A. Smith called him a "rash, thoughtless young man whom none cared to have anything to do with." But he was from Ontario; and he was an Orangeman. As the news of his death became known in Ontario, the latent hatreds of race and religion burst forth. A storm of indignation swept over the province. Schultz and other "refugees" from Red River, screamed for "justice" for Scott; the Orange lodges loudly demanded that no truck be had with the "rebels", no treaty with the "traitors", and no negotiations with the "murderers". Riel's delegates had no sooner arrived in Ontario than they were arrested for complicity in the "murder" of Scott on a warrant sworn out by Scott's brother, but lacking evidence to support the charge they had been discharged.

The negotiations had gone ahead to a successful conclusion, but the rancour remained.

Wolseley's Red River Expedition, May-August 1870

Partly to assist public opinion in Ontario and partly to provide armed support for the new Canadian administration, which was to be set up under the new Lieutenant-Governor, A. G. Archibald, the Canadian government decided to send a military force to Red River. Early in May this force, under the command of Sir Garnet Wolseley, and comprising two battalions of Canadian militia in addition to a force of British regulars, set out over the rocky waterways which led from Lake Superior to Fort Garry. On August 24th, Wolseley and the troops entered the Fort. Despite the assurances of pacific intent upon the part of the federal authorities, Louis Riel had been warned that the troops, particularly the militia, were hostile, and together with several companions he fled across the river. Thus, when Wolseley's soldiers, who had spent ninety-six gruelling days forcing their way through a wilderness of forests, rivers, lakes and portages, entered the stone gate of Fort Garry, they were greeted, not by armed métis but only by "a half-naked Indian, very drunk" who stood by to watch the rain-drenched British regulars form up on the empty square. Not far away Riel muttered bitterly, "he who ruled in Fort Garry only yesterday is now a homeless wanderer with nothing to eat but two dried fishes."

Louis Riel's Achievement in Red River

But for the execution of Scott, Louis Riel today would probably be looked upon by English and French, white and métis, as the father of the province of Manitoba. The "rebellion" would have passed for a patriotic demonstration in arms of the unwillingness of the people of Red River to be sold like a piece of landed property.

Wherever our sympathies lie, we cannot with justice deny the achievement of the métis leader. That Manitoba should have achieved provincial status and responsible government in 1870 — for good or for ill — was the work of Louis Riel. A glance over the subsequent history of the North-West Territories is enough to set aside any fond belief that the federal government would willingly have conceded provincial status to the infant half-breed colony at the time of the transfer of the territories to Canada, had it not been for Riel's protest.

Even more important was the part played by Louis Riel in preserving the western plains for Canada. The northern states were keenly interested in the acquisition of that area, and in 1868 the Minnesota legislature protested formally against the proposed transfer of the Hudson's Bay Company territories to the new Dominion. In 1869, J. W. Taylor, who had inspired this protest, was appointed by the State Department as United States Secret Agent in the Red River Settlement. From the outset the small but aggressive American party within the colony did everything it could to direct the Riel movement towards annexation. H. N. Robinson, in the pro-Riel newspaper, the *New Nation*, at Fort Garry, wrote vigorously in favour of "independence" and full union with the United States; Oscar Malmros, the American consul at Winnipeg, asked the State Department to give financial support to the métis resistance to Canada — a demand which was backed up by Senator Ramsey's appeal to President Grant. The Fenian, W. B. O'Donoghue, who was one of Riel's councillors, consistently intrigued for annexation. At first Riel was disposed to welcome American support. Encouragement from every source was grist to the métis mill: but with the strengthening of the métis position and the appointment of delegates to Ottawa, Riel's attitude towards the United States underwent a change. The *New Nation* dropped its pro-American tone, and under the editorship of a Canadian, became very British. On April 23rd the Union *81* Jack was raised over Fort Garry on Riel's orders. When O'Donoghue endeavoured to tear it down, a métis guard was stationed beneath the flag with strict orders to shoot anyone who should endeavour to remove it. There is little doubt that, for several months, the fate of Red River hung precariously in the balance. Weaker men than Riel would, under the circumstances, the provocations and irritations, have yielded to the blandishments and intrigues of the Americans and become the tool rather than the master of the Yankee wirepullers at Fort Garry, Pembina and St. Paul.

The Political Aftermath, 1870–1875

One of the terms of the métis "List of Rights" had been a general amnesty to all who had participated in the troublous events of 1869–70. No statement with regard to an amnesty had been inserted in the Manitoba Act, but verbal assurances of an amnesty had been given both to Bishop Taché, while in Ottawa on his way back to Red River, and to the métis delegates who had been sent to negotiate the terms of federation in 1870. That undertakings committing the government to secure an amnesty were actually given there seems little doubt, after a review of the evidence which was subsequently made public in 1874 by the Select Committee appointed to inquire into the causes of the Riel insurrection: that the Canadian government could not, in view of the intensity of public opinion in Ontario, give immediate effect to these undertakings is equally clear. Therein is to be found the dilemma of the next five years.

As the rumours of an amnesty began to circulate through the country, the anti-Riel agitation grew more and more violent. Ontario was ablaze with fury and Liberal party politicians welcomed what to them was a heaven-sent opportunity to turn the popular indignation to political account and capture the normally Conservative Orange vote. As the anti-

French, anti-Catholic, agitation developed in Ontario, so too did an anti-English, anti-Orange agitation develop in Quebec. The attacks upon the métis "rebels" were interpreted as an attack upon French Canada and Roman Catholicism. What Ontario regarded as a criminal act, Quebec began to look upon as a patriotic deed. The virulence of the Ontario press was matched by that of the Quebec press, and Sir John found himself between the upper and nether millstone of racial and religious conflict. For promising an amnesty he was denounced in Ontario; for neglecting to proclaim it he was denounced in Quebec.

But Macdonald had ridden out political storms before and reasoned that no action at all was often better than one which might permanently impair the future of the new political union which he had done so much to bring about. Yet Riel seemed to be an ever-present nemesis for past sins of omission and commission in the North-West. In the autumn of 1871 he opened old wounds by returning to Red River and offering the services of himself and several companies of métis horsemen to defend the province against a filibustering raid inspired by the ex-Fenian, ex-Provisional Government treasurer, ex-American agent, O'Donoghue. It was embarrassing to Macdonald that the Lieutenant-Governor of Manitoba should publicly have thanked Riel for this offer. It was even more embarrassing when the Liberal government in Ontario proceeded to offer $5000 reward for the apprehension of the métis leader. To avoid the crisis which an arrest would bring, Macdonald forwarded secret service funds to Bishop Taché to induce Riel to go to the United States; and then, to appease a wrathful Ontario, he righteously said, "Where is Riel? God knows: I wish I could lay my hands on him!"

Had Riel been content to remain quietly in the United States, at least until the political storm had blown itself out, it is possible that the problem might have yielded to Macdonald's solution. He had, however, developed within himself a strong sense of grievance at the continued postponement of the promised amnesty. He returned to Manitoba to stand for the constituency of Provencher, but on receiving assurances regarding the promulgation of his amnesty he temporarily withdrew in favour of Sir George Cartier. Following the latter's sudden death he came forward again and was elected both in the by-election of 1873 and in the general election of 1874. Then, once more, he was forced to flee across the border when an ambitious lawyer, Henry J. Clarke, anxious to cultivate the growing Orange vote in the province, obtained a warrant for his arrest.

In March 1874 Riel went to Ottawa, where he succeeded in signing the members' register, thus qualifying to take his seat. After a heated debate in the House of Commons, however, a motion for his expulsion was carried by a majority of 56 votes on a division along racial and not party lines.

Twelve months later, in 1875, five years after the Red River troubles, a general amnesty was proclaimed by the Governor-General entirely upon his own authority. It was a qualified amnesty, one hedged in with the condition that Riel remain in exile for five years.

82

Riel's Period of Exile, 1875–1884

Always introspective by nature, Louis Riel brooded over the events of 1869–70 and the years of persecution, as he viewed them, which followed. It was a period of strong religious feeling, this period of the struggle between Catholic liberalism and resurgent Ultramontanism, and Riel in his moments of heightened religious experience began to dream of a vast new Catholic state on the prairies with Bishop Ignace Bourget of Montreal as the Pope of the New World. The idea of a religious mission, casually mentioned by Mgr. Bourget in a letter, became an obsession or mental fixation with Riel. He adopted the name of "David", and, in the eyes of his French-speaking friends in the United States, he became more and more irrational both in his actions and in his views. As a result, he was committed, early in 1876, to the St. Jean de Dieu asylum at Longue Pointe, and several months later to the asylum at Beauport near Quebec under fictitious names.

83

In January 1878 Riel was discharged from Beauport and certified as cured, but he was warned to avoid excitement. For several months he followed this advice. He lived quietly at Keeseville, N.Y., where he became engaged to marry one Evelina Barnabé; but there was nothing there for him to do. Thus it was that he turned his eyes once more towards the west, where alone he was at home.

From St. Paul he went to St. Joseph near Pembina and then to the métis country in the upper Missouri. He tried his hand at trading, at interpreting for Indians and whites, and, according to the North-West Mounted Police, at selling liquor to the Indians. He lived with and like the métis. Within a few years his name became well-known in the territory of Montana. He threw in his lot with the Republicans and sought to deliver the métis vote for that party. He forgot his British allegiance — after all what had it done for him? — and became a United States citizen. He even forgot Evelina and married a métisse. One thing he could not forget; it was always somewhere in the background of his mind, the idea of his "mission".

In 1883 Riel paid a brief visit to Manitoba. Here he learned from the disconsolate and distressed métis the full story of their failure to adapt themselves to the new civilization which had descended upon Red River in the wake of the Manitoba Act. Then came appeals to the old days of the Provisional Government, to his patriotism, and to his egotism. He returned to Montana and met the old Fenian leader, J. J. Donnelly. There was talk of freeing the métis from the baneful yoke of Ottawa, of petitions, and of arms. Then on June 4th, 1884, four men rode into the little settlement in Sun River County where Riel was teaching at the Jesuit mission school. They were Gabriel Dumont, Michel Dumas, Moïse Ouellette and James Isbister. They had ridden over 600 miles and with them they carried an urgent invitation to the former president of the Provisional Government to return to the North-West to lead another protest movement against the government of Canada.

Discontent in Saskatchewan, 1870–1884

Although Riel had achieved many of his objectives during the Manitoba rising, the sad fact was that no legislative safeguards or grants of scrip for lands could really enable the métis to compete with the new settlers who poured into Manitoba after the formation of the province. Within a few years the métis were outnumbered and their homeland remade into something alien to their culture and to their inclination. Sullen, suspicious, embittered over the failure to adapt themselves and estranged from the civilization of the new settlers, many métis sold their scrip for a small portion of its value and sought new homes. Westward they moved, like the buffalo; and in the valley of the Saskatchewan they founded new settlements: St. Laurent, St. Louis and St. Antoine (Batoche). Here, once more, they were able to live for a few short years the old life of the plains, the semi-primitive existence which they had enjoyed before the arrival of the Canadians in Red River.

But the civilization they feared was close upon their heels. As early as 1873, only three years after the transfer of the North-West to Canada, a bill was introduced into the Canadian House of Commons to found a semi-military police force called the North-West Mounted Police. In 1874 three hundred policemen in scarlet tunics and pill box caps set out across the plains towards the hilly country of what was to become southern Alberta. They were the forerunners of civilization, with its surveyors, its colonization companies and its railway. Civilization meant the end, both for the Indians and the métis, of the old way of life in the North-West: it meant the end of the hunt and the chase, and the end of the buffalo; it meant the establishment of Indian reserves; it meant the filling up of the country with immigrants.

There may have been excuses for Sir John A. Macdonald in 1869; there could be none in 1885. For the problem which faced the Prime Minister was the same one which had faced him earlier; the problem of conflicting cultures, of reconciling a small primitive population with a new complex civilization. But Sir John had other things upon his mind — he was building the Canadian Pacific Railway — and the Ministry of the Interior, Sir John's own ministry, starved the Indian services and failed to allay the fears and suspicions of the métis that they would lose their rights as the original holders of the soil. And to add to the bewilderment of the native peoples came the subtle suggestions of those white settlers, who, beggared by early frosts, poor crops and low prices for grain, were prepared to use the métis grievances as a means of belabouring an apparently indifferent government. Thus it was that the settlers of the North Saskatchewan, mixed-blood and white, English and French-speaking, joined together to invite Louis Riel to take charge of their campaign for the redress of western grievances.

Riel's Agitation in Saskatchewan, 1884–5

Riel was nervous when he began his agitation in the North Saskatchewan valley in the summer of 1884. He felt unsure of himself when addressing white settlers and the recollections of his past relations with Canadians were not very happy. But as the weeks passed he acquired more confidence. His programme was a moderate one. It was directed towards the white settlers as well as to the half-breeds, and his secretary, Henry Jackson, was Ontario-born. Under Riel's direction a petition was drafted; on December 16th it was sent to Ottawa. This petition embodied the grievances of all the elements then supporting Riel. It demanded more liberal treatment for the Indians, scrip and land patents for the half-breeds; responsible government, representation at Ottawa, reduction in the tariff, modification of the homestead laws and construction of a railway to Hudson's Bay for the white settlers. It also contained a lengthy statement of Riel's personal grievances against Ottawa. Receipt of the petition was acknowledged and in January it was announced that a commission would be appointed to investigate and report upon western problems.

It would be an error to suppose that Riel's agitation was carried on with the whole-hearted support of all western people. The Riel movement began to acquire a definite party colour with the support of such well-known Liberals, as the Jacksons; and the adherents of Macdonald, even those, who, like the editor of the Prince Albert *Times*, had formerly expressed their sympathies with the métis, condemned Riel's leadership in no uncertain terms. The old feelings engendered by the execution of Scott in 1870 had never subsided and there were many who disliked and distrusted Riel for no other reason. From the clergy, however, came the greatest opposition. They were suspicious of the métis leader and feared that the North-West reform movement, under his leadership, might well get out of control. Riel's eccentricities troubled them and they doubted whether on matters of faith and politics he was really quite sane.

That a serious situation was developing in the North-West was by no means unknown to the Canadian government. Police, government officials and private individuals appealed unceasingly to Ottawa. Admittedly the appointment of a commission to look into the complaints from the North-West had been promised, but Macdonald's delays were notorious and the mere promise of a commission of inquiry seemed to hold out but small hope of early redress. In any event it was not until March 30th that the government finally decided to name the members. By that time it was too late.

Originally Riel had not intended to stay long in Canada, but as his enthusiasm for the political agitation waxed, his desire to return to Montana waned. Late in February 1885 he went as far as to propose that, should his supporters desire it, he should turn the leadership over to someone else; but it is doubtful whether he really expected or desired that his offer of resignation should be accepted. He turned towards a more active and more dangerous course of action. Ordinary constitutional methods

85

were too slow, too ineffective. Bold action, the policy of 1869–70 would arouse the government out of its lethargy. Riel therefore decided to follow the same formula which had been successful on the previous occasion. He would form a Provisional Government, put his supporters under arms, and compel the federal authorities to negotiate a revision of the terms which had brought the North-West into Confederation. It was the scheme of a mad man. The methods which had succeeded, in part at least, in Manitoba could never succeed again. There was now a military force in the country to support the government where formerly there had been none in 1869 to assist the Hudson's Bay Company; there was now a railway to bring men and arms from Eastern Canada. Riel ignored the changed conditions and embarked upon the desperate gamble which was to take him to the scaffold.

From Agitation to Rebellion, March 1885

The decisive day was March 19th, the feast of St. Joseph, the patron saint of the métis, and it was to be celebrated by the baptism of Henry Jackson. Métis from nearby settlements flocked into Batoche, carrying their rifles with them. The moment was opportune and Riel took advantage of it. With all the fire and spirit which he could command in his speech, he told the assembled gathering that the Mounted Police were preparing to attack them and suppress their movement. Alarm spread like panic and preparations were made for defence. A Provisional Government was immediately proclaimed, Riel nominating the members and the métis signifying their approval. Pierre Parenteau was elected president; but the real leaders were Gabriel Dumont, who was appointed "adjutant-general", and Louis Riel himself. With a group of excited followers Riel rushed towards the church, thrust aside the protesting priest and took possession of the building as his headquarters. "Rome has fallen" cried Riel. The rebellion had begun.

Riel was in no way disturbed by the alienation of the clergy — he had, after all, his own ideas of a religious organization for the métis — but he was disturbed by his failure to retain the support of the English half-breeds. The whites may have been willing to use him for their own purposes, and the English half-breeds to support him in a constitutional agitation, but they would not follow him as far as taking up arms or forming a Provisional Government. Several times he appealed to their old loyalties. "Gentlemen, please do not remain neutral. For the love of God help us to save the Saskatchewan," he wrote. "A strong union between the French and English half-breeds is the only guarantee that there will be no bloodshed." His appeals met with no response. Riel would have to go on alone — except perhaps for the Indians.

The Indians had found themselves in an even more desperate condition than the métis as a result of the white immigration, and many of them were in an ugly mood owing to the indifference displayed by the government towards their appeals for help. The summer of 1884 had almost seen an Indian outbreak, and during the autumn of that year a number of Indians turned to Louis Riel for advice and leadership. At first he restrained them but as his temper changed so too did theirs. From them at least he might hope for support in arms.

The Military Events, March-June 1885

The fighting began on March 26th at Duck Lake. Here Gabriel Dumont and the métis ambushed a force of Mounted Police, compelling them to abandon Fort Carlton and to retire to the principal settlement of Prince Albert. Further west Cree Indians from the Poundmaker and Little Pine Reserves broke into and pillaged the Hudson's Bay Company store and other buildings in the town of Battleford. They do not appear to have had in mind an attack upon the town, probably nothing more than a demonstration in force to obtain concessions and supplies; but the Stonies from the Eagle Hills, who joined them, murdered their Farm Instructor and a white settler and set up a "soldiers' lodge". Even the Stonies, however, did not propose to attack a fortified position and the Indians contented themselves, during the next few weeks, with prowling around the neighbourhood while the police and settlers watched with anxious eyes from the barricaded Mounted Police barracks. Further up the Saskatchewan the Crees of Big Bear murdered several men at Frog Lake, including the Indian agent and two missionaries, then descending the Saskatchewan river they terrified the inhabitants of Fort Pitt into surrender.

Thus the situation stood at the end of April. Everywhere the métis and Indians had met with surprising success. They had defeated the white men in pitched battle. Fort Carlton and Fort Pitt had fallen without even a fight. The white men had been driven into the narrow confines of Prince Albert and Battleford. These successes had not been the result of any concerted plan; they were entirely spontaneous and fortuitous. The métis were in no position to carry on a long war. They lacked numbers, supplies and wholehearted support. The Indians, held together by no strong principle of cooperation and with no central authority to combine their strength, were likewise incapable of sustained effort. Moreover, by far the greater number of Indian nations were prepared to wait and watch, while accepting and enjoying the gifts so freely handed out by the Indian Department to ensure their neutrality.

Meanwhile the Canadian government had taken prompt action. A military force numbering nearly 8000 men was mobilized and despatched to the North-West under the command of General Frederick Middleton. Three columns of troops were sent against the three principal centres of disaffection. The first, under the command of Middleton himself, was directed against Riel's capital at Batoche. It fought an indecisive action with the métis at Fish Creek on April 24th and was held up there for two weeks. The second, under the impetuous Colonel Otter, speedily relieved Battleford. The third, under Major-General Strange, moved against Big

87

Bear marching from Calgary by way of Edmonton and the North Saskatchewan river. In none of these operations did the commanding officers distinguish themselves. Middleton's movements in particular were
slow and his dispositions questionable. Little use was made of cavalry in a
country made to order for mounted warfare. Much of the responsibility
for the ponderous conduct of the campaign must rest upon the shoulders
of an uninspired commander-in-chief; but part, too, must be attributed to
the lack of training on the part of the troops and their inexperience in
warfare.

In the face of these developments Riel made desperate efforts to concentrate all his forces. He had been disappointed that the Indians of Alberta,
in particular the associated Blackfoot tribes, had yielded to the persuasions of Father Lacombe, and sought anxiously to persuade Big Bear and
Poundmaker to join the métis at Batoche without delay. But the Indians
could not arrive at a rapid decision, and before any concentration was
achieved both Poundmaker and Big Bear were attacked separately by
Otter and by Strange. Marching at night from Battleford Otter almost
caught the Indians unawares. As the troops rushed to seize the high
ground known as Cut Knife Hill the Indians spread out through the
coulées surrounding it, taking full advantage of the only cover available.
All day militia and Indians fought at full rifle range, until Otter, realizing that his unprotected situation would be particularly precarious when
night should fall, cleared his line of retreat with a charge and made his
way back to Battleford. His retirement might have become a rout had not
Poundmaker held back his warriors and prevented them from cutting the
retreating column to pieces.

Meanwhile, on May 7th, Middleton began to move from Fish Creek
towards Riel's capital. He had with him about 850 men; his opponents
could probably muster at the most about 350. On May 9th the attack
began. An attempt to use the steamer *Northcote* as an armed vessel to
attack simultaneously with the land troops proved to be a fiasco, and the
land attack was halted by the métis riflemen in trenches which Dumont
had constructed in the reverse slope leading down to Batoche. Middleton
himself declared, on inspecting the field after the action was over, "I was
astonished at the strength of the position and at the ingenuity and care
displayed in the construction of the rifle pits". These pits or trenches were
Dumont's work; for Riel was no military leader. He had not been present
at Fish Creek, and at Duck Lake he had watched the fighting armed only
with a crucifix.

For three days the fighting at Batoche continued. By May 12 the métis'
supplies of ammunition were almost exhausted; so too was the patience of
Middleton's troops who, exasperated at the general's cautious tactics, took
matters into their own hands and charged the enemy. With gathering
momentum the Canadian militia dashed through the métis lines and down
the hill towards Batoche. The métis fled to the woods. On May 15th Riel
gave himself up. Dumont and several others fled on horseback towards the
United States.

88

There still remained the Indians. Poundmaker surrendered to Middleton on May 23rd, after learning of Riel's defeat; but Big Bear was at large up the North Saskatchewan with his mixed force of Plains and Wood Crees. His band was split on the issue of continued resistance, and it was while the chiefs were endeavouring to heal the rupture that they were attacked by General Strange at Frenchman's Butte, on May 28th. After offering stout opposition the Indians finally fled from the field, just as Strange called off the attack. The heavy guns had taken the edge off their fighting enthusiasm. With their prisoners and their loot they began a disorderly retirement northwards through the woods.

Strange made no real effort to follow his retreating foe. He had no intention, as he often said, of "committing Custer", and it was not until the arrival of Middleton that the troops were once more sent into action. Steele's mounted scouts had proved their worth in keeping in touch with the Indians, but Middleton continued to rely upon his infantry. He ignored offers of assistance from the Mounted Police and set out with his wagons and his soldiers through a country which even light-burdened Indians found difficult to traverse. On June 9th the commander abandoned the pursuit. The Indians, however, did not continue together as a fighting force. They released their prisoners and broke up into small bands. On July 2nd Big Bear himself surrendered to a surprised police sergeant at Fort Carlton. The rebellion was at an end.

89

The sequel was a bitter one. The métis were not only defeated, as a politically cohesive group they were practically destroyed. Their homes were burned and their property looted or destroyed. Those who had taken part in the Provisional Government were sentenced to terms of imprisonment. A number of métis were compelled to seek entrance to the Indian treaties by virtue of their Indian blood; others moved westwards, towards Northern Alberta, to escape the merciless pressure of civilization. Those who did not join the rebellion received the scrip and patents which Louis Riel had demanded — tacit admission of the justice of the métis grievances. But just as the Manitoba half-breeds had done so too the Saskatchewan métis disposed of their scrip to eager and unscrupulous buyers. They lived only for the present and forgot about the future. What did it hold for them? Destitute and disillusioned, unable to compete with the white men either as traders or farmers, they gradually sank further and further in the social scale, their life, society and spirit crushed and destroyed.

The Indians suffered less from the rebellion than did the métis. Of the leaders some went to the gallows, others, including Big Bear and Poundmaker, went to prison. The rebels were deprived of their annuities until the destruction wrought by the rising had been made good and their horses and rifles were taken from them. However, in 1886 a general amnesty was declared for all who were not actually under sentence, and in the following year Big Bear and Poundmaker were released from prison. Several years later negotiations were undertaken with the United States for the return to Canada of those Indians who had sought refuge in Montana after the collapse of the rebellion.

The Trial and Execution of Louis Riel

On July 6th, 1885, a formal charge of treason was laid against Louis Riel, then in gaol at Regina. This was the beginning of that trial which was to have such drastic consequences, not only for Riel himself, but for the whole of Canada. The jury was entirely Anglo-Saxon and Protestant, the defendant French and, by training at least, Catholic. Here were the old familiar elements of discord. And into the little courtroom stalked the ghost of Tom Scott, whose memory his Orange brethren had never permitted to rest. As the howl for vengeance grew louder in Orange Ontario so too did the cry for clemency in Catholic Quebec. A madman, a heretic, a métis he might be, to the people of Quebec Louis Riel was nevertheless a French Canadian, a victim of Anglo-Saxon persecution. Even while shots were still being fired at Canadian soldiers on the plains, Quebeckers had expressed admiration for Riel's heroic battle for the rights of his people, and when he surrendered they sprang to his defence and provided him with eminent counsel.

The argument adopted by the defence lawyers was that Riel was insane. It was pointed out that he had twice been in asylums, that he had committed the folly of attacking the church, that he had planned the establishment of a Canadian Pope and spent valuable time during the actual rising changing the names of the days of the week. But Riel would not accept this defence. He repudiated the plea of insanity. "I cannot abandon my dignity!" he cried. "Here I have to defend myself against the accusation of high treason, or I have to consent to the animal life of an asylum. I don't care much about animal life if I am not allowed to carry with it the moral existence of an intellectual being . . . " Twice he addressed the court in long rambling speeches; but the jury was only bored, and after one hour and twenty minutes deliberation they declared him guilty. Henry Jackson, despite similar denials of insanity and an expressed desire to share the fate of his leader, was acquitted within a few minutes. To an English-speaking jury the English-speaking Jackson must obviously have been insane to have taken part in the rebellion. There was much truth in the statement made by one of the jurors fifty years later: "We tried Riel for treason, and he was hanged for the murder of Scott."

As the date set for Riel's execution approached feelings throughout Canada became more and more intense. Efforts to save the métis leader were redoubled in Quebec; efforts to ensure his death never slackened in Ontario. The Prime Minister temporized. He was uncertain what course to follow. The execution was postponed, and then put off again while a medical commission examined the question of Riel's sanity. But the terms of reference of the commission limited it to a determination of Riel's capacity to distinguish right from wrong and did not allow an investigation of his delusions; and when the report of the commission was published it was published in a truncated form. Throughout the autumn months petitions and letters from all parts of the world poured into Ottawa. Sir

John had not a jot of sympathy for Riel, but he had to balance the political consequences of death or reprieve. There was danger of political disaster if Riel were hanged, but perhaps Sir John could trust to the loyalty of his French Canadian colleagues, Hector Langevin, Adolphe Caron and Adolphe Chapleau, and to the support of a Catholic hierarchy offended at Riel's apostasy. There might be still greater danger of political disaster if Riel were not hanged with every Orangeman in Ontario baying for his death. So Riel was hanged. On November 16th, once more a son of the church, the métis, Louis Riel, mounted the gibbet of Regina. The madman became a martyr.

The Political Consequences of Riel's Death

It is hard to escape the conclusion that Riel's execution, to some extent at least, was determined by political expediency, that, in the final analysis, it represented the careful assessment by the Canadian government of the *91* relative voting strengths and political loyalties of the two racial groups in Canada. If this were so then, for the moment, Macdonald's choice was not unsound. Admittedly the "nationalists" in Quebec, led by Honoré Mercier, succeeded in 1886 in overthrowing the provincial Conservative govern- ment in an election fought largely on the Riel issue; but in the federal election of 1887 Macdonald, with the support of his French Canadian ministers, still retained a sufficient number of Quebec seats to keep in power.

Yet he had lost ground. And even if he did not recognize it, the election results were an ominous warning of the fate which awaited the Conserva- tive party in Quebec. In the long run the trial and execution of Louis Riel and the racial bitterness which it engendered led to a profound revolution in Canadian politics. As a result of the crisis of 1885 the most conservative province in Canada swung over to the Liberal party, a change in political allegiance which was cemented by the selection of a French Canadian, Wilfrid Laurier, as leader of that party. This shift in the political weight in Quebec, not as the result of any fundamental change in political outlook, but under the stress of a racial emotion, brought about a new orientation in Liberal policy. The old radical tradition of Clear Grittism and Rougeism was swamped by a basic rural conservatism; and for over seventy years the paradox endured of the backbone of the Liberal party being provided by rural Quebec.

Conclusion

Louis Riel was not a great man; he was not even what Carlyle would call a near great. Nevertheless he became, in death, one of the decisive figures of our history. By historical accident rather than by design he became the symbol of divisions as old as the Franco-British struggle for the control of northern North America. It is this historical accident which has obscured the fundamental character of the two risings which bear Riel's name; for the Riel "rebellions" were not what the politicians argued and what the people believed, a continuation on the banks of the Red and the Saskatchewan of the traditional hostilities of old Canada. They were, instead, the typical, even inevitable results of the advance of the frontier, the last organized attempts on the part of Canada's primitive peoples to withstand what, for want of a better word, may be termed progress, and to preserve their culture and their identity against the encroachments of civilization. To present-day Canadians Riel appears, no longer as the wilful "rebel" or "murderer" of Thomas Scott, but as a sad, pathetic, unstable man, who led his followers in a suicidal crusade and whose brief glory rests upon a distortion of history. To the métis, the people whom he loved, he will always be, mad or sane, the voice of an inarticulate race and the prophet of a doomed cause.

Topic Four

Continentalism, Imperialism, and Nationalism

In the late nineteenth century Canada faced great difficulties. Tensions between French and English Canadians were high as a result of the execution of Louis Riel, the implementation of the Jesuit Estates Act and the disagreement over the Manitoba Schools question. The National Policy had failed to generate prosperity or to integrate the nation, and the country continued in its economic depression. Politicians seemed unable to find solutions to these problems. To many Canadians, particularly Canadian intellectuals, Canada appeared a failure as a nation.

Three major alternatives were put forward by Canadian political commentators at the time: union with the United States, imperial federation, or independence. Carl Berger's introduction to *Imperialism and Nationalism, 1884–1914: A Conflict in Canadian Thought* (Toronto: Copp Clark, 1969) sets the context in which to understand these opposing views of Canada's destiny.

The strongest proponent of union with the United States, or continentalism, was Goldwin Smith, formerly Regius Professor of History at Oxford University, who resided in Canada from 1871 until his death in 1910. He put forward his ideas most forcefully in *Canada and the Canadian Question* (1891), considered by one historian to be the most pessimistic book written about Canada. The following excerpts, taken from his book and from an article, "The Political History of Canada," that he wrote for *The Nineteenth Century* in July 1886, present the essence of Smith's views on the question of continental union.

An alternative to continentalism was imperial federation, an idea popularized by a group of Canadian imperialists who were founding members of the Imperial Federation League in Canada in 1887. Encouraged by the growing desire in Britain to consolidate the Empire, and aroused by patriotic fervour to defend the Empire from external threats as witnessed in the Boer War of 1899, these imperialists advocated closer union of Canada with Britain. Stephen Leacock, better known for his career as a humourist than as a political scientist, presents a serious but emotionally charged argument for imperial union. In his article in the *Canadian Magazine* in 1907 he advises Canadian politicians, about to embark for England to attend the fourth Colonial Conference, on the imperialist stance they should take.

A French-Canadian view is presented from the writings of Henri Bourassa, the influential Quebec politician who was the grandson of Louis-Joseph Papineau. Beginning as a Liberal, he broke party ranks over the sending of Canadian troops to the Boer War and the establishment of a Canadian navy to be used in imperial wars. In an article written for *The Monthly Review* in 1902, Bourassa reveals his views of British imperialism and his opinions of the Boer War.

94   To appreciate fully the depth and magnitude of Goldwin Smith's argument, students are encouraged to read his book, *Canada and the Canadian Question,* first published in 1891 but still relevant today. The ideas of Canadian imperialists are examined in Carl Berger's *The Sense of Power: Studies in the Ideas of Canadian Imperialism, 1867–1914* (Toronto: University of Toronto Press, 1970). Henri Bourassa's nationalist views can be found in *Henri Bourassa on Imperialism and Bi-culturalism: 1900–1918,* edited by Joseph Levitt (Toronto: Copp Clark, 1970) and in M. P. O'Connell's "The Ideas of Henri Bourassa," *Canadian Journal of Economics and Political Science* 19 (1953):361–376. André Laurendeau provides an excellent portrait of Bourassa in *Our Living Tradition,* Fourth Series, edited by R. L. McDougall (Toronto: University of Toronto Press, 1962):135–158.

Imperialism and Nationalism: 1884–1914*
CARL BERGER

Introduction

Imperialism in Canada presented many faces and its story has been told from various perspectives. Its aim was to consolidate the British Empire through military, economic and constitutional devices. Those Canadians who supported imperial unity, or imperial federation, believed that Canada could attain national status only by maintaining the connection with the Empire and by acquiring an influence within its councils. Their opponents were convinced that imperialism was incompatible with Canada's national interests, internal unity, and self-government. The conflict between these two forces was a major theme in Canadian life in the thirty years before the First World War, and the struggle was bitter and divisive. It was fought out in many arenas, in Parliament, at Colonial and Imperial Conferences and in polemical literature, and it centered upon several issues — commercial

*Introduction to *Imperialism and Nationalism, 1884–1914*, edited by C. Berger. Copyright 1969 by Copp Clark Publishing Co. Reprinted by permission.

policy, participation in the Boer War, and military and naval preparedness. But it was above all fought out in the minds of Canadians, and it is from this point of view, as a problem in Canadian intellectual history, that it is presented in this book. The questions raised here do not concern, at least not primarily, elections, the formulation of tariff policy or the problems of military co-operation. These readings are intended rather to bring into sharper focus the guiding ideas and divergent conceptions of the Canadian future that underlay the clash between imperialism and nationalism.

Imperialism and nationalism are vague words which must be defined in terms of their historical context. The organized movement for imperial unity originated in the later 1880's. The cumulative impact of the long depression, the failure of Macdonald's National Policy to generate prosperity and economic integration, and the cultural crisis that followed the execution of Louis Riel, produced a widespread feeling of pessimism about Canada's future. The commitment of the Liberal party to unrestricted reciprocity, or free trade with the United States, climaxed the fears of those who, rightly or wrongly, identified such a policy with continentalism. It was at this point — in 1887 and 1888 — that branches of the Imperial Federation League, an organization founded in England in 1884, were set up in Canada, and they quickly became the centres of a perfervid British Canadian patriotism. As a countermeasure to reciprocity, the supporters of imperial unity advocated the idea of an economic union of the Empire to be secured through preferential tariffs. Imperial preference remained the central plank in the agenda of Canadian imperialism long after unrestricted reciprocity was defeated in the election of 1891, and long after the Liberal party rejected it in 1893. Canadian imperialists were far more emphatic on the commercial aspects of imperial unity than were their counterparts in England. In fact the difference of opinion between those who stressed imperial preference and those who placed their faith in military and naval co-operation was one of the chief reasons why the Imperial Federation League disintegrated in 1893. Its branches in Canada, however, were simply reconstituted as organs of the British Empire League. When in 1897 the new Liberal government of Wilfrid Laurier extended a preference on British manufactured commodities entering Canada, the action was widely hailed as a practical implementation of the imperial ideal.

Imperial unity was as much a state of mind as a political platform, and the appeals of those who underlined the necessity for Canada to maintain and strengthen the British connection customarily transcended commercial and economic arguments. The leading spokesmen of imperial unity — Colonel George T. Denison of Toronto, a police magistrate and military thinker, George R. Parkin, a New Brunswick born teacher and writer, and Rev. George M. Grant, Principal of Queen's University — all believed that Canada could only grow and survive if it held fast to the imperial connection. They were convinced, or they convinced themselves, partly through their reading of Goldwin Smith's plea for continental union, *Canada and the Canadian Question* (1891), that though unrestricted reciprocity might bring prosperity it would also ultimately end in political extinction. As a consequence, their arguments against a particular trade policy moved away from a discussion of the comparative prices of eggs in Toronto and Pittsburg to an attempt to awaken an appeciation for, and an attachment to, those traditions and institutions which in their minds made the Canadian nationality worthy of preservation. In this sense imperial unity began as a defence of Canada.

In the later eighties and early nineties imperial unity found its main support in the older section of English Canada and particularly among the descendants of the United Empire Loyalists. Both Denison and Parkin traced their roots back to the Loyalists who were described, in the mythology of the day, as 'Canada's Pilgrim Fathers.' Though the Imperial Federation League in 1889 counted one quarter of the members of the Dominion Parliament in its ranks, its most vocal and devoted supporters were drawn from a narrow group of politicians, lawyers, teachers, and Protestant ministers. It received no support from labour or the farming population, and in French Canada its progress was viewed firstly with indifference, then alarm, and finally with massive hostility. This is hardly surprising. Members of the Orange Order, who interpreted imperial federation to mean Protestant supremacy, were often members of the League, and D'Alton McCarthy, the leader of the Equal Rights Movement which endeavoured to limit French language rights and separate schools to Quebec alone, was prominent among the adherents of imperialism. Not all imperialists, of course, were supporters of Orangeism and Equal Rights. One of the most sympathetic defences of the state-supported separate schools of Manitoba was penned by G. M. Grant, who had been instrumental in deposing McCarthy from his position in the League because he had jeopardized the cause of imperial unity. Yet in general, the obvious racial overtones of the imperial sentiment, and the strange allies with whom the imperialist consorted, were enough to alienate French Canada.

Born in a period of doubt and despair, imperialism by the late 1890's had become more impatient, assertive and bellicose. The appointment of Joseph Chamberlain to the Colonial Office in 1895 signalized the increasing seriousness of purpose of British imperialism. In 1899, in spite of his own personal predisposition to remain uninvolved, Laurier was forced by public pressure in English Canada to dispatch Canadian soldiers to fight in the Boer War. This action was in itself a testimony to the growing strength of the imperial cause. Fourteen years before, Macdonald had shrugged off similar suggestions that Canada aid Britain in the Soudan and his reaction was endorsed by Denison, one of the most militant of Canadian imperialists who was never one to miss a war if he could help it. The Boer War was the decisive event in the history of Canadian imperialism. To many English Canadians it was not a matter of aiding England. For them that experience was invested with all the enthusiasm of nationalism. Canada's participation, niggardly though some thought it was, marked the entry of the Dominion into world politics. She had become a force within the Empire and her path forward was straight and clear. Now that Canadians had demonstrated their willingness to support the Empire with more than emotional speeches, was it not only fair that they be accorded some influence over the direction of imperial foreign policy? French Canadians saw the matter very differently. The spectacle of Canadians fighting in so remote a war, one waged against a non-British minority with which they so easily identified themselves, generated an imperialist reaction which grew and gained momentum. Some time before, the nationalist Premier of Quebec, Honoré Mercier, had warned that the imperial federationists wanted "us to assume, in spite of ourselves, the responsibilities and dangers of a sovereign state which will not be ours. They seek to expose us to vicissitudes of peace and war . . . ; to wrest from our arms our sons, . . . and send them off to bloody and distant wars, which we shall not be able to stop or prevent."[1] And the prophecy had come true. In 1899 Henri Bourassa left the Liberal Party charging that Laurier had capitulated to pressure from the Colonial Office and had thereby established a precedent, fatal to Canadian self-government, that Canada must fight in all imperial wars. In 1903, in conjunction with a group of young French Canadian nationalists, Bourassa founded the *Ligue Nationaliste* to combat the imperial menace. The zest with which imperialists had supported the South African war was proof to them of the essentially colonial-minded character of English Canada.

97

These two extremes, the one demanding that Canada take up imperial obligations and be accorded a voice in Empire affairs, the other insisting on Canadian neutrality and freedom from such burdens, were not easily reconciled, and for some time Laurier did not try to reconcile them. He turned aside Chamberlain's suggestions at the Colonial Conference of 1902 that co-operation be institutionalized. Though he declared in the same year that Canada must take some steps to ensure her security, and though in 1903, after the unpopular Alaska Boundary decision, he also urged that the Dominion make her own foreign policy, Laurier made no fundamental decisions in either direction, except for taking over the management of the naval bases at Halifax and Esquimalt. The imperial question lay quiescent until the "naval scare" of 1909 made postponement impossible. The threat that the German ship-building programme would undermine the supremacy of British seapower set off a wide-ranging and acrimonious debate over what stand Canada should take. The imperialists contended that Canada, now strong and prosperous, should help sustain the force upon which her own security depended; to the anti-imperialists this appeared as the payment of tribute to the motherland whose interests were very different from Canada's. In reality the debate was more complex than this, for even imperialists were in disagreement about the exact extent and nature of Canada's contribution to imperial defence. But Laurier's proposal for the creation of a Canadian navy which in times of crisis would become part of the British fleet angered both extremes and in part accounted for his defeat in 1911. Long before this time Bourassa had come to think of Laurier as the main instrument of the imperialist conspiracy. On July 13,

1911 he wrote in *Le Devoir*: "English and African soldiers fell on the veldt for the glory of Chamberlain; women and children died of shame and misery for the grandeur of Laurier; children's entrails were cut out in the Concentration camps for the honour of the Empire." From the imperialist Stephen Leacock, on the other hand, came this greeting at the news of Laurier's defeat:

Sir Wilfrid, it may be said, with all the gentleness of speech which is becoming in speaking of such a man on such an occasion, touched in this election upon the one point on which he never fully enjoyed the confidence of the Canadian people — our relations to the British Empire. It has been his fortunate lot to represent us on great occasions. He has ridden for us in coaches of State, to the plaudits of a London multitude. He has coined phrases for us, of summoning us to Imperial councils and the like, grandiloquent in the utterance, but meaning less and less as they recede into retrospect. That he never really understood the feelings of his English-speaking fellow citizens of Canada towards their Mother Country, that he never really designed to advance the cause of permanent Imperial unity — these things may well be doubted . . . We are . . . groping for something which we desire but still seek in vain. The great problem of our common future is to find an organic basis of lasting union.[2]

Such was the burden of the two extremes which tore apart the man who searched for the fragile consensus.

In the thirty years before 1914, the difference between nationalism and imperialism was much more complicated than the desire for Canadian autonomy on the one hand and a willingness to live under Downing Street rule on the other. Not even the anti-imperialists thought it was that simple. John Ewart, for example who defined nationalism as the end of subordination of one state to another, remarked that those Canadian imperialists with whom he was acquainted were really Canadian nationalists. And within the terms of his own definition he was right. What divided those who called themselves nationalists from those who preferred to be known as imperialists was not the question of whether Canada should manage her own affairs and have the power to formulate a foreign policy expressive of her interests; what divided them was disagreement over how these powers were to be acquired and for what purposes they were to be employed. The imperialists saw the British Empire as the vehicle in which Canada would attain national status; the anti-imperialists were so convinced of the incompatability of imperial and Canadian interests that they saw all schemes for co-operation as reactionary and anti-national. In a fundamental sense, therefore, the differences between, say, Stephen Leacock and Henri Bourassa stemmed from their very different ideas about Canada, her history, and place in the world. The only way to understand the conflict between the positions these two men embodied is to understand the divergent conceptions which underlay them.

There are some limitations to the purpose of these articles as well as some particular problems that are raised by such an approach. They are not intended as self-contained presentations of every facet and ramification of the nationalist-imperialist conflict. Such a project would require several volumes. Nor does the approach suggest that intellectual history offers some magical key that will unlock all the puzzles and problems raised by the theme. And certainly it is not intended to supersede all other approaches. Someone has said that the practice of intellectual history is like trying to nail jelly to the wall, and indeed the entities that are subject to examination are nebulous and intangible. Any exact and scientific way of measuring the force and impact of ideas, furthermore, has yet to be devised, and the question must always arise as to the connection between ideas and the motives of those active men of power who made the crucial decisions. Yet when all this is said our understanding of Canadian history would be narrow indeed if we left out of account the climate of opinion in which the battle between imperialism and anti-imperialism took place. In the accounts, of the Boer War crisis or the naval debate, for example, one invariably encounters allusions to the "imperialist pressure from English Canada" for this or that policy; yet one often comes away with the impression that we are told a good deal more about how extreme positions were accommodated or compromised at the centre than we learn about the extremes themselves. If we want to understand what imperialism and nationalism meant we must look to those who were the exponents and interpreters of these beliefs and try to grasp what these convictions meant to them. Only by doing so can we appreciate why their opposition was so fundamental and why Canadian historians are still divided as to the meaning of imperialism as a factor in Canadian history.

99

Notes

1. Quoted in George R. Parkin, *Imperial Federation - The Problem of National Unity* (London, 1892), pp. 85–6.
2. Stephen Leacock, *The Great Victory in Canada*, (reprint from *The National Review*, London, 1911), p. 12.

Canada and the Canadian Question*
GOLDWIN SMITH

Whoever wishes to know what Canada is, and to understand the Canadian question, should begin by turning from the political to the natural map. The political map displays a vast and unbroken area of territory, extending from the boundary of the United States up to the North Pole, and equalling or surpassing the United States in magnitude. The physical map displays four separate projections of the cultivable and habitable part of the Continent into arctic waste. The four vary greatly in size, and one of them is very large. They are, beginning from the east, the Maritime Provinces — Nova Scotia, New Brunswick, and Prince Edward Island; Old Canada, comprising the present Provinces of Quebec and Ontario; the

*From "The Political History of Canada," *The Nineteenth Century*, XX (May 1886), and *Canada and the Canadian Question* (Toronto: Hunter Rose, 1891), by Goldwin Smith. Adapted by C. Berger for *Imperialism and Nationalism, 1884–1914*. Copyright 1969 by Copp Clark Publishing Co. Reprinted by permission. Selections from "The Political History of Canada" have been placed within brackets.

newly-opened region of the North-West, comprising the Province of Manitoba and the districts of Alberta, Athabasca, Assiniboia, and Saskatchewan; and British Columbia. The habitable and cultivable parts of these blocks of territory are not contiguous, but are divided from each other by great barriers of nature, wide and irreclaimable wildernesses or manifold chains of mountains. The Maritime Provinces are divided from Old Canada by the wilderness of many hundred miles through which the Intercolonial Railway runs, hardly taking up a passenger or a bale of freight by the way. Old Canada is divided from Manitoba and the North-West by the great freshwater sea of Lake Superior, and a wide wilderness on either side of it. Manitoba and the North-West again are divided from British Columbia by a triple range of mountains, the Rockies, the Selkirks, and the Golden or Coast range. Each of the blocks, on the other hand, is closely connected by nature, physically and economically, with that portion of the habitable and cultivable continent to the south of it which it immediately adjoins, and in which are its natural markets — the Maritime Provinces, with Maine and the New England States; Old Canada, with New York and with Pennsylvania, from which she draws her coal; Manitoba and the North-West, with Minnesota and Dakota, which share with her the Great Prairie; British Columbia, with the States of the Union on the Pacific. Between the divisions of the Dominion there is hardly any natural trade, and but little even of forced trade has been called into existence under a stringent system of protection. . . . Between the two provinces of Old Canada, though there is no physical barrier, there is an ethnological barrier of the strongest kind, one being British, the other thoroughly French, while the antagonism of race is intensified by that of religion. Such is the real Canada. Whether the four blocks of territory constituting the Dominion can for ever be kept by political agencies united among themselves and separate from their Continent, of which geographically, economically, and with the exception of Quebec ethnologically, they are parts, is the Canadian question. . . .

[Canada is called a British colony, and over all her provinces waves the British flag. But as soon as you approach her for the purpose of Imperial Federation you will be reminded that a large part of her is French. Not only is it French, but it is becoming more French daily, and at the same time increasing in magnitude. . . . The French are shouldering the British out of the city of Quebec, where not more than six thousand British inhabitants are now left, and out of the Eastern Townships, which have hitherto been a British district; they are encroaching on the British province of Ontario, as well as overflowing into the adjoining states of the Union. The population multiplies apace. There, as in Ireland, the Church encourages early marriage, and does not teach thrift; and were it not for the ready egress into the States, we might have Irish congestion and misery in French Canada. Had French Canada been annexed to the United States, it would no doubt have been absorbed and assimilated, like other alien nationalities, by that vast mass of English-speaking population.

As it is, instead of being absorbed or assimilated, the French element rather absorbs and assimilates. Highland regiments disbanded in French Canada have become French. In time, apparently, there will hardly be anything British left in the province of Quebec, except the commercial quarter of Montreal, where the more energetic and mercantile race holds its ground. Had the conqueror freely used his power at first, when the French numbered only about sixty thousand, New France might have been made English; but its nationality has been fostered under the British flag, and in that respect the work of conquest has been undone. It is difficult indeed, if Canada remains separate from the United States, to see what the limits of French extension will be.

French Canada (now the province of Quebec) is a curious remnant of the France before the Revolution. The peasantry retain with their *patois* the pre-revolutionary character, though, of the allegiance once shared between the king, the seigneur, and the priest, almost the whole is now paid to the priest. There were seigneuries with vexatious feudal incidents; but these have been abolished, not by legislative robbery, in which the rude Canadian is inexpert, but by honest commutation. The people are a simple, kindly, and courteous race, happy on little, clad in homespun, illiterate, unprogressive, pious, priest-ridden, and, whether from fatalism or from superstition, averse to vaccination, whereby they brought upon themselves and their neighbours the other day a fearful visitation of small-pox. They are all small, very small farmers; and, looking down from the citadel of Quebec upon the narrow slips of land with their river fronts on the St. Lawrence, you see that here, as in old France, subdivision has been carried to an extreme.

It has been said that the Spaniards colonised for gold, the English for freedom, the French for religion. New France, at all events, was religious, and it has kept the character which the Jesuit missionary impressed on it. The Church is very strong and very rich. Virtually it is established, since to escape tithe you must avow yourself a Protestant. Clerical influence is tremendously powerful. . . . It is due to the clergy to say that they seem to make the people moral, though in ecclesiastical fashion. What they deem immorality they put down with a high hand; they restrain dancing and thunder against opéra bouffe. The Church has a strong hold on the peasant's heart through its ceremonial, which is the only pageantry or poetry of peasant life. Till lately the Church of French Canada was Gallican, and lived, like the old national Church of France, on perfectly good terms with the State. But now comes the Jesuit, with the Encyclical and the declaration of Papal Infallibility in his hand. There is a struggle between Jesuitism and Gallicanism under the walls of the citadel of Gallicanism, the great Sulpician Seminary at Montreal. The Jesuit, having all the influences of the day upon his side, prevails. A new chapter of history is opened and troubles begin between Church and State. . . .

The conqueror might have suppressed French nationality. Instead of this, he preserved and protected it. He gave the conquered a measure of his own liberty, and perhaps as large a measure as at that time they who had known nothing but absolute government could bear. He gave them a representative assembly, trial by jury, Habeas Corpus, an administration generally pure in place of one which was scandously corrupt, deliverance from oppressive imposts, and an appeal in case of misgovernment to Parliament instead of Pompadour. He gave them liberty of opinion and introduced among them the printing press. The one successful colony of France owes its success to British tutelage. French writers are fain to acknowledge this, and if some of them complain because the half-measure of liberty was not a whole measure, and the conquering race kept power in its own hands, the answer is that conquest is conquest, and that the monarchy of Louis the Fourteenth was neither unaggressive nor invariably liberal to the vanquished. . . . The Englishman in Canada has in the main got on perfectly well with the conquered Frenchman; even if there has been sometimes political antagonism between them, their social relations have been good. The French fought for England in the revolutionary war, and again in the war of 1812. If the hostile attitude of the Puritans of New England towards their religion decided them in the first case, it can hardly have decided them in the second; at least, the rule under which they had lived in the interim can hardly have been oppressive. It was one of their leaders, Etienne Taché, who said that the last gun fired in favour of British dominion on the continent would be fired by a French Canadian. The late Sir George Cartier, the political chief of French Canada in his day, was proud to call himself a British subject speaking French. . . .

There is, I believe, no feeling whatever among the French Canadians against England. But French nationality grows daily more intense and daily finds more political as well as literary expression. We had trouble with it the other day, when Quebec sympathised on national grounds with the rising of the French half-breeds under Riel in the North-West, as she had with previous attempts to secure that vast realm for the French race and religion. Regiments from Quebec were sent to the theatre of war, but they were not sent to the front. . . .]

. . . Not only has New France shown no increase of tendency to merge her nationality in that of the Dominion; her tendency has been directly the other way. She has recently . . . unfurled her national flag, and at the same time placed herself as the French Canadian nation, under the special protection of the Pope, who accepts the position of her ecclesiastical lord. At her head, and to all appearances firmly seated in power, is the chief of the Nationalist and Papal party, who bids Blue and Red blend themselves in the tricolor and restores to the Jesuits their estates. The old Bleu or Conservative party, associated with the clergy of the Gallican school, which by its union with the Tories in the British provinces linked Quebec politically to the Dominion, has fallen, as it seems, to rise no more. What life is left in it is sustained largely by Dominion subsidies of which the Ottawa Government makes it the accredited channel. "The complete autonomy of the French Canadian nationality and the foundation of a French

102

Canadian and Catholic state, having for its mission to continue in America the glorious work of our ancestors," are the avowed aims of the Nationalist and Ultramontane press. Greybeards of the old Conservative school protest that all this means nothing, that no design of autonomy has been formed, and that it is unjust to speak of French nationality and theocracy as dangers to Confederation. Whether the design has been distinctly formed or not matters little if the tendency is manifestly there and is gaining strength every day. Let those who prophesy to us smooth things take stock of the facts. When one community differs from another in race, language, religion, character, spirit, social structure, aspirations, occupying also a territory apart, it is a separate nation, and is morally certain to pursue a different course, let it designate itself as it can. French Canada may be ultimately absorbed in the English-speaking population of a vast Continent; amalgamate with British Canada so as to form a united nation it apparently never can. . . .

From British as well as from French Canada there is a constant flow of emigration to the richer country, and the great centres of employment. Dakota and the other new States of the American West are full of Canadian farmers; the great American cities are full of Canadian clerks and men of business, who usually make for themselves a good name. It is said that in Chicago there are 25 000. Hundreds of thousands of Canadians have relatives in the United States. Canadians in great numbers — it is believed as many as 40 000 — enlisted in the American army during the civil war. There is a Lodge of the Grand Army at Ottawa. A young Canadian thinks no more of going to push his fortune in New York or Chicago than a young Scotchman thinks of going to Manchester or London. The same is the case in the higher callings as in the lower: clergymen, those of the Church of England as well as those of other churches, freely accept calls to the other side of the Line. So do professors, teachers, and journalists. The Canadian churches are in full communion with their American sisters, and send delegates to each other's Assemblies. Cadets educated at a Military College to command the Canadian army against the Americans, have gone to practise as Civil Engineers in the United States. The Benevolent and National Societies have branches on both sides of the Line, and hold conventions in common. Even the Orange Order has now its lodges in the United States, where the name of President is substituted in the oath for that of the Queen. American labour organizations . . . extend to Canada. The American Science Association met the other day at Toronto. All the reforming and philanthropic movements, such as the Temperance movement, the Women's Rights' movement, and the Labour movements, with their conventions, are continental. Intermarriages between Canadians and Americans are numerous, so numerous as scarcely to be remarked. Americans are the chief owners of Canadian mines, and large owners of Canadian timber limits. The railway system of the continent is one. The winter ports of Canada are those of the United States. Canadian banks trade largely in the American market, and some have branches there. There is almost a

103

currency union, American bank-bills commonly passing at par in Ontario, while those of remote Canadian Provinces pass at par only by special arrangement. American gold passes at par, while silver coin is taken at a small discount: in Winnipeg even the American nickel is part of the common currency. The Dominion bank-bills, though payable in gold, are but half convertible, because what the Canadian banks want is not British but American gold. Canadians go to the American watering-places, while Americans pass the summer on Canadian lakes. Canadians take American periodicals, to which Canadian writers often contribute. They resort for special purchases to New York stores, or even those of the Border cities. Sports are international; so are the Base Ball organisations; and the Toronto "Nine" is recruited in the States. All the New-World phrases and habits are the same on both sides of the Line. The two sections of the English-speaking race on the American continent, in short, are in a state of economic, intellectual, and social fusion, daily becoming more complete. Saving the special connection of a limited circle with the Old Country, Ontario is an American State of the Northern type, cut off from its sisters by a customs line, under a separate government and flag. . . .

104

To force trade into activity between the Provinces and turn it away from the United States, giving the Canadian farmer a home market, and consolidating Canadian nationality at the same time, were the ostensible objects of the adoption in 1879 of a Protective tariff. The real object perhaps was at least as much to capture the manufacturer's vote and his contributions to the election fund of the party in power. . . .

The isolation of the different Canadian markets from each other, and the incompatibility of their interests, add in their case to the evils and absurdities of the protective system. What is meat to one Province is, even on the protectionist hypothesis, poison to another. Ontario was to be forced to manufacture; she has no coal; yet to reconcile Nova Scotia to the tariff a coal duty was imposed; in vain, for Ontario after all continued to import her coal from Pennsylvania. Manitoba and the North-West produced no fruit; yet they were compelled to pay a duty in order to protect the fruit-grower of Ontario 1500 miles away. Hardest of all was the lot of the North-West farmer. His natural market, wherein to buy farm implements, was in the neighbouring cities of the United States, where, moreover, implements were made most suitable to the prairie. But to force him to buy in Eastern Canada 25 per cent was laid on farm implements. As he still bought in the States, the 25 per cent was made 35 per cent. . . .

Without commercial intercourse or fusion of population, the unity produced by a mere political arrangement can hardly be strong or deep. It will, for the most part, be confined to the politicians, or to those directly interested in the work of Dominion parties. . . .

In the want of a real bond among the members of Confederation, the antinational attitude of Quebec, the absence of real Dominion parties, and the consequent difficulty of holding the Dominion together and finding a basis for the administration must be found the excuse, if any excuse can be found, for the system of political corruption which during the last twenty years has prevailed. "Better Terms," that is, increased subsidies to Provinces from the Dominion treasury, Dominion grants for local railways and other local works and concessions to contractors, together with the patronage including . . . appointments to the Senate, have been familiar engines of government. . . .

. . . The Government, which, it is justly said, ought in the matter of public works to act as trustee for the whole people, in effect proclaims that public works will be regulated by the interest of constituencies whose support it receives. That "the whole North-West of Canada has been used as one vast bribery fund" is a statement just made by a leading member of the Opposition, who can point to at least one recent and most flagrant instance in proof of his sweeping accusation. But what corruption can be more pestilential or more dangerous to the commonwealth than the surrender of the commercial policy of the country to private interests, in return for their votes and the support of their money in elections? . . .

105

[The thread of political connection is wearing thin. This England sees, and the consequence is a recoil which has produced a movement in favour of Imperial Federation. It is proposed not only to arrest the process of gradual emancipation, but to reverse it and to reabsorb the colonies into the unity of the Empire. No definite plan has been propounded, indeed, any demand for a plan is deprecated, and we are adjured to embrace the principle of the scheme and leave the details for future revelation — to which we must answer that the principle of a scheme is its object, and that it is impossible to determine whether the object is practically attainable without a working plan. There is no one in whose eyes the bond between the colonies and the mother country is more precious than it is in mine. Yet I do not hesitate to say that, so far as Canada is concerned, Imperial Federation is a dream. The Canadian people will never part with their self-government. Their tendency is entirely the other way. They have recently . . . asserted their fiscal independence, and by instituting a Supreme Court of their own, they have evinced a disposition to withdraw as much as they can of their affairs from the jurisdiction of the Privy Council. Every association, to make it reasonable and lasting, must have some practical object. The practical objects of Imperial Federation would be the maintenance of common armaments and the establishment of a common tariff. But to neither of these, I am persuaded, would Canada ever consent; she would neither contribute to Imperial armaments nor conform to an Imperial tariff. Though her people are brave and hardy, they are not, any more than the people of the United States, military, nor could they be brought to spend their earnings in Asiatic or African wars. . . . Remember that Canada is only in part British. The commercial and fiscal circumstances of the colony again are as different as possible from those of the mother country. . . .

Why not leave the connection as it is? Because, reply the advocates of Imperial Federation, the connection will not remain as it is; the process of separation will go on and the attenuated tie will snap. Apart from this not unreasonable apprehension, there are, so far as I know, only two reasons against acquiescence in the present system. One of these may be thought rather vague and intangible. It is that the spirit of a dependency, even of a dependency enjoying the largest measure of self-government, is never that of a nation, and that we can make Englands only in the way in which England herself was made. The other is more tangible, and is brought home to us at this moment by the dispute with the Americans about the Fisheries. The responsibility of Great Britain for the protection of her distant colony is not easily discharged to the distant colony's satisfaction. To Canadians, as to other people, their own concerns seem most important; they forget what the Imperial country has upon her hands in all parts of the globe; they have an unlimited idea of her power; and they expect her to put forth the whole force of the Empire in defence of Canadian fishing rights, while perhaps at the same moment Australians are calling upon her

to put forth the whole force of the Empire in defence of their claims upon New Guinea. Confiding in Imperial support, they perhaps take stronger ground and use more bellicose language than they otherwise would. But the more democratic England becomes, the more impossible will it be to get her people to go to war for any interests but their own. The climax of practical absurdity would be reached if England were involved in war by some quarrel arising out of the Canadian customs duties, imposed partly to protect Canadian manufacturers against British goods. . . .]

Annexation is an ugly word; it seems to convey the idea of force or pressure applied to the smaller State, not of free, equal, and honourable union, like that between England and Scotland. Yet there is no reason why the union of the two sections of the English-speaking people on this Continent should not be as free, as equal, and as honourable as the union of England and Scotland. We should rather say their reunion than their union, for before their unhappy schism they were one people. Nothing but the historical accident of a civil war ending in secession, instead of amnesty, has made them two. . . .

That a union of Canada with the American Commonwealth, like that into which Scotland entered with England, would in itself be attended with great advantages cannot be questioned, whatever may be the considerations of the other side or the reasons for delay. It would give to the inhabitants of the whole Continent as complete a security for peace and immunity from war taxation as is likely to be attained by any community or group of communities on this side of the Millenium. Canadians almost with one voice say that it would greatly raise the value of property in Canada; in other words, that it would bring with it great increase of prosperity. . . .

On the other hand, there is the affection of the Colonists for the mother country, which has always been kind to them in intention, even if she has not had the power to defend their rights and her interference has ceased to be useful. This might prevail if union with the rest of the race on this

Continent, under the sanction of the mother country, would really be a breach of affection for her. But it would be none. It would be no more a breach of affection than the naturalisation, now fully recognised by British law, of multitudes both of Englishmen and of Canadians in the United States. Let us suppose that the calamitous rupture of the last century had never taken place, that the whole race on this Continent had remained united, and had parted, when the time came, from the mother country in peace; where would the outrage on love or loyalty have been? Admitted into the councils of their own Continent, and exercising their fair share of influence there, Canadians would render the mother country the best of all services, and the only service in their power, by neutralising the votes of her enemies. Unprovoked hostility on the part of the American Republic to Great Britain would then become impossible. . . .

Nor need Canada give up any of the distinctive character or historical associations which she has preserved through the continuance of her connection with the mother country. . . . The Federal system admits wide *107* local diversities, and if Ontario or Nova Scotia clings to the British statute-book, to the British statute-book it may cling. There is no reason even why Canadians, who like to show their spirit by military celebrations, should not celebrate Canadian victories as the Scotch celebrate Bannockburn. Americans would smile. Of the antipathy to Americans sedulously kept up within select circles and in certain interests, there is absolutely none among the Canadian people at large. It would be strange if there were any, considering that half of them have brothers, sons, or cousins on the American side of the Line. . . .

Again, Canadians who heartily accept democracy wish that there should be two experiments in it on this Continent rather than one, and the wish is shared by thoughtful Americans not a few. But we have seen that in reality the two experiments are not being made. Universal suffrage and party government are the same, and their effects are the same in both Republics. Differences there are, such as that between the Presidential and the Cabinet system, of a subordinate kind, yet not unimportant, and such as might make it worthwhile to forgo for a time at least the advantages of union, supposing that the dangers and economical evils of separation were not too great, and if the territorial division were not extravagantly at variance with the fiat of Nature. The experiments of politicial science must be tried with some reference to terrestrial convenience. Besides, those who scan the future without prejudice must see that the political fortunes of the Continent are embarked in the great Republic, and that Canada will best promote her own ultimate interests by contributing without unnecessary delay all that she has in the way of political character and force towards the saving of the main chance and the fulfilment of the common hope. The native American element in which the tradition of self-government resides is hard pressed by the foreign element untrained to self-government, and stands in need of the reinforcement which the entrance of Canada into the Union would bring it. . . .

There is a conflict of forces, and we must judge each for himself which are the primary forces and likely to prevail. Prevail the primary forces will in the end, however long their action may be suspended by a number of secondary forces arrayed against them. In the case of German and in that of Italian unity the number and strength of the secondary forces arrayed against the event were such, and the action of the great forces was so long suspended by them, that it seemed even to sagacious observers as if the event would never come. It came, irresistible and irreversible, and we see now that Bismarck and Cavour were the ministers of destiny.

In the present case there are, on one side, geography, commerce, identity of race, language, and institutions, which with the mingling of population and constant intercourse of every kind, acting in ever-increasing intensity, have brought about a general fusion, leaving no barriers standing but the political and fiscal lines. On the other side, there is British and Imperial sentiment, which, however, is confined to the British, excluding the French and Irish and other nationalities, and even among the British is livelier as a rule among the cultivated and those whose minds are steeped in history than among those who are working for their bread; while to set against it there is the idea, which can hardly fail to make way, of a great continent with an almost unlimited range of production forming the home of a united people, shutting out war and presenting the field as it would seem for a new and happier development of humanity. Again, there are bodies of men, official, political, and commercial, whose interests are bound up with the present state of things, whose feelings naturally go with those interests, who in many cases suffer little from the economical consequences of isolation, and who, gathered in the capital or in the great cities exercise an influence out of proportion to their numbers on public opinion and its organs. . . .

. . . However, if the primary forces are working towards an event, sooner or later the crisis arrives; the man appears, and the bidding of Destiny is done.

108

Greater Canada: An Appeal
Let Us No Longer Be A Colony*
STEPHEN LEACOCK

Now, in this month of April [1907], when the ice is leaving our rivers, the ministers of Canada take ship for this the fourth Colonial Conference at London. What do they go to do? Nay, rather what shall we bid them do? We — the six million people of Canada, unvoiced, untaxed, in the Empire, unheeded in the councils of the world, — we, the six million

*First published in 1907 by the Montreal News Company. Abridged by C. Berger for *Imperialism and Nationalism, 1884–1914*. Copyright 1969 by Copp Clark Publishing Co. Reprinted by permission.

colonials sprawling our over-suckled infancy across a continent, — what shall be our message to the motherland? Shall we still whine of our poverty, still draw imaginary pictures of our thin herds shivering in the cold blasts of the North, their shepherds huddled for shelter in the log cabins of Montreal and Toronto? Shall we still beg the good people of England to bear yet a little longer, for the poor peasants of their colony, the burden and heat of the day? Shall our ministers rehearse this worn-out fiction of our 'acres of snow,' and so sail home again, still untaxed, to the smug approval of the oblique politicians of Ottawa? Or, shall we say to the people of England, "The time has come; we know and realize our country. We will be your colony no longer. Make us one with you in an Empire, Permanent and Indivisible."

This last alternative means what is commonly called Imperialism. It means a united system of defence, an imperial navy for whose support somehow or other the whole Empire shall properly contribute, and with it an imperial authority in whose power we all may share. To many people in Canada this imperialism is a tainted word. It is too much associated with a truckling subservience to English people and English ideas and the silly swagger of the hop-o'-my-thumb junior officer. But there is and must be for the true future of our country, a higher and more real imperialism than this — the imperialism of the plain man at the plough and the clerk in the counting house, the imperialism of any decent citizen that demands for this country its proper place in the councils of the Empire and in the destiny of the world. In this sense, imperialism means but the realization of a Greater Canada, the recognition of a wider citizenship.

109

I, that write these lines, am an Imperialist because I will not be a Colonial. This Colonial status is a worn-out, by-gone thing. The sense and feeling of it has become harmful to us. It limits the ideas, and circum-scribes the patriotism of our people. It impairs the mental vigor and narrows the outlook of those that are reared and educated in our midst. The English boy reads of England's history and its glories as his own; it is *his* navy that fought at Camperdown and Trafalgar, *his* people that have held fast their twenty miles of sea eight hundred years against a continent. He learns at his fireside and at his school, among his elders and his contemporaries, to regard all this as part of himself; something that he, as a fighting man, may one day uphold, something for which as a plain citizen he shall every day gladly pay, something for which in any capacity it may one day be his high privilege to die. How little of this in Canada! Our paltry policy teaches the Canadian boy to detach himself from the England of the past, to forget that Camperdown and Copenhagen and the Nile are ours as much as theirs, that this navy of the Empire is ours too, ours in its history of the past, ours in its safe-guard of the present.

If this be our policy and plan, let us complete our teaching to our children. Let us inscribe it upon the walls of our schools, let us write it in brass upon our temples that for the Navy which made us and which defends us, we pay not a single penny, we spare not a solitary man. Let us add to it, also, that the lesson may bear fruit, this "shelter theory" of Canada, now rampant in our day; that Canada, by some reason of its remoteness from European sin and its proximity to American republicanism, is sheltered from that flail of war with which God tribulates the other peoples of the world, sheltered by the Munroe Doctrine, by President Roosevelt and his battleships, sheltered, I know not how, but sheltered somehow so that we may forget the lean, eager patriotism and sacrifice of a people bred for war, and ply in peace the little craft of gain and greed. So grows and has grown the Canadian boy in his colonial status, dissociated from the history of the world, cut off from the larger patriotism, colourless in his ideas. So grows he till in some sly way his mind opens to the fence-rail politics of his country side, with its bribed elections and its crooked votes — not patriotism this, but 'politics,' maple-leaf politics, by which money may be made and places and profit fall in a golden shower. . . .

110   . . . The time has come to be done with this *colonial* business, done with it once and forever. We cannot in Canada continue as we are. We must become something greater or something infinitely less. We can no longer be an appendage and outlying portion of something else. Canada, as a *colony,* was right enough in the days of good old Governor Simcoe, when your emigrant officer sat among the pine stumps of his Canadian clearing and reared his children in the fear of God and in the love of England — right enough then, wrong enough and destructive enough now. We cannot continue as we are. In the history of every nation, as of every man, there is no such thing as standing still. There is no pause upon the path of progress. There is no stagnation but the hush of death.

And for this progress, this forward movement, what is there first to do? How first unravel this vexed skein of our colonial and imperial relations? This, first of all. We must realize, and the people of England must realize, the inevitable greatness of Canada. This is not a vainglorious boast. This is no rhodomontade. It is simple fact. Here stand we, six million people, heirs to the greatest legacy in the history of mankind, owners of half a continent, trustees, under God Almighty for the fertile solitudes of the west. A little people, few in numbers, say you? Ah, truly such a little people! Few as the people of the Greeks that blocked the mountain gates of Europe to the march of Asia, few as the men of Rome that built a power to dominate the world, nay, scarce more numerous than they in England whose beacons flamed along the cliffs a warning to the heavy galleons of Spain. Aye, such a little people, but growing, growing, growing, with a march that shall make us ten millions tomorrow, twenty millions in our children's time and a hundred millions ere yet the century runs out. What say you to Fort Garry, a stockaded fort in your father's day, with its hundred thousand of today and its half a million souls of the tomorrow? What think you, little river Thames, of our great Ottawa that flings its foam eight hundred miles? What does it mean when science has moved us a little further yet, and the wheels of the world's work turn with electric force? What sort of asset do you think then our melting snow and the roaring river-flood of our Canadian spring shall be to us? What say you, little puffing steam-fed industry of England, to the industry of Coming Canada. Think you, you can heave your coal hard enough, sweating and grunting with your shovel to keep pace with the snow-fed cataracts of the north? Or look, were it but for double conviction, at the sheer extent and size of us. Throw aside, if you will, the vast districts of the frozen north, confiscate, if you like, Ungava still snow-covered and unknown, and let us talk of the Canada we know, south of the sixtieth parallel, south of your Shetland Islands, south of the Russian Petersburg and reaching southward thence to where the peach groves of Niagara bloom in the latitude of Northern Spain. And of all this take only our two new provinces, twin giants of the future, Alberta and Saskatchewan. Three decades ago this was the 'great lone land,' the frozen west, with its herds of bison and its Indian tepees, known to you only in the pictured desolation of its unending snow; now crossed and inter-crossed with railways, settled 400 miles from the American frontier, and sending north and south the packets of its daily papers from its two provincial capitals. And of this country, fertile as the corn plains of Hungary, and the crowded flats of Belgium, do you know the size? It is this. Put together the whole German Empire, the republic of France and your England and Scotland, and you shall find place for them in our two new provinces. Or take together across the boundary from us, the States of Maine, New Hampshire, Vermont, Massachusetts, Rhode Island and Connecticut, — all the New England States — and with them all the Middle States of the North — New York, New Jersey, Pennsylvania, Delaware, Ohio, Indiana, Michigan, Illinois and Wisconsin, — till you have marked a space upon the map from the Atlantic to the Mississippi and from the Ohio to the lakes — all these you shall put into our two new provinces and still find place for England and for Scotland in their boundaries.

111

This then for the size and richness of our country. Would that the soul and spirit of its people were commensurate with its greatness. For here as yet we fail. Our politics, our public life and thought, rise not to the level of our opportunity. The mud-bespattered politicians of the trade, the party men and party managers, give us in place of patriotic statecraft the sordid traffic of a tolerated jobbery. For bread, a stone. Harsh is the cackle of the little turkey-cocks of Ottawa, fighting the while as they feather their mean nest of sticks and mud, high on their river bluff. Loud sings the little Man of the Province, crying his petty Gospel of Provincial Rights, grudging the gift of power, till the cry spreads and town hates town and every hamlet of the country-side shouts for its share of plunder and of pelf. This is the tenor of our politics, carrying as its undertone the voice of the black-robed sectary, with narrow face and shifting eyes, snarling still with the bigotry of a bygone day. This is the spirit that we must purge. This is the demon we must exorcise; this the disease, the canker-worm of corruption, bred in the indolent security of peace, that must be burned from us in the pure fire of an Imperial patriotism that is no theory but a passion. This is our need, our supreme need of the Empire — not for its ships and guns, but for the greatness of it, the soul of it, aye for the very danger of it.

Of our spirit, then, it is not well. Nor is it well with the spirit of those in England in their thoughts of us. . . . Can they not see, these people of England, that the supreme English Question now is the question of Canada? that this Conference of the year of grace 1907 might, if it would, make for us the future of the Empire? Or will they still regard us, poor outlying sheltered people of Canada, as something alien and apart, sending us ever of their youngest and silliest to prate in easy arrogance of 'home,' earning the livelihood their island cannot give, still snapping at the hand that feeds them?

And what then can this Colonial Conference effect, after all, it is asked? . . . if we pay for this our Navy that even now defends us, and yet speak not in the councils at Westminster, then is that Taxation without Representation . . .[?]

So there we stand, we and you, pitched fast upon the horns of a dilemma. You cannot tax us, since you will not represent us. We cannot be represented because we will not be taxed. . . .

Yet is the difficulty perhaps not impossible of solution. The thing to be achieved is there. The task is yours to solve, men of the council table. . . .

Nor is guidance altogether lacking in the task. For at least the signs of the times are written large as to what the destiny of Canada shall *not* be. Not as it is, — not on this *colonial* footing, — can it indefinitely last. There are those who tell us that it is best to leave well alone, to wait for the slow growth, the evolution of things. For herein lies the darling thought of the wisdom of the nineteenth century, in this same Evolution, this ready-made explanation of all things; hauled over from the researches of the botanist to meet the lack of thought of the philosopher. Whatever is, is: whatever will be, will be, — so runs its silly creed. Therefore let everything be, that is: and all that shall be, shall be! This is but the wisdom of the fool, wise after the fact. For the solution of our vexed colonial problem this profits nothing. We cannot sit passive to watch our growth. Good or bad, straight or crooked, we must make our fate.

Nor is it ever possible or desirable that we in Canada can form an independent country. The little cry that here and there goes up among us is but the symptom of an aspiring discontent, that will not let our people longer be colonials. 'Tis but a cry forced out by what a wise man has called the growing pains of a nation's progress. Independent, we could not survive a decade. Those of us who know our country realize that beneath its surface smoulder still the embers of racial feud and of religious bitterness. Twice in our generation has the sudden alarm of conflict broken upon the quiet of our prosperity with the sound of a fire-bell in the night. Not thus our path. Let us compose the feud and still the strife of races, not in the artificial partnership of an Independent Canada, but in the joint greatness of a common destiny.

Nor does our future lie in Union with those that dwell to the Southward. The day of annexation to the United States is passed. . . .

Not Independence then, not annexation, not stagnation: nor yet that doctrine of a little Canada that some conceive, — half in, half out of the Empire, with a mimic navy of its own; a pretty navy this, — poor two-penny collection, frollicking on its little way strictly within the Gulf of St. Lawrence, a sort of silly adjunct to the navy of the Empire, semi-detached, the better to be smashed at will. As well a Navy of the Province, or the Parish, home-made for use at home, docked every Saturday in Lake Nipigon!

Yet this you say, you of the Provincial Rights, you Little Canada Man, is all we can afford! — we that have raised our public charge from forty up to eighty millions odd, within the ten years past, and scarce have felt the added strain of it. Nay, on the question of the cost, good gentlemen of the council, spare it not. Measure not the price. It is not a commercial benefit we buy. We are buying back our honour as Imperial Citizens. For, look you, this protection of our lives and coast, this safe-guard from the scourge of war, we have it now as much as you of England: you from the hard-earned money that you pay, we as the peasant pensioners of your Imperial Bounty.

Thus stands the case. Thus stands the question of the future of Canada. Find for us something other than mere colonial stagnation, something sounder than independence nobler than annexation, greater in purpose than a Little Canada. Find us a way. Build us a plan, that shall make us in hope at least, an Empire Permanent and Indivisible.

113

The French-Canadian in the British Empire
HENRI BOURASSA

The present feeling of the French-Canadian is one of contentment. He is satisfied with his lot. He is anxious to preserve his liberty and his peace. . . . . Upon any proposed modification of the constitutional system of Canada he is disposed to look with distrust, or at least with anxiety. He cannot forget that all changes in the past were directed against him, except those that were enacted under such peculiar circumstances as made it imperative for the British Government to conciliate him. He asks for no change — for a long time to come, at least. And should any change be contemplated, he is prepared to view it, to appreciate its prospective advantages and inconveniences, neither from a British point of view nor from his own racial standpoint, but to approach the problem as it may affect the exclusive interests of Canada. He has loyally accepted the

* First published in *The Monthly Review*, IX (October 1902). Abridged by C. Berger for *Imperialism and Nationalism, 1884–1914*. Copyright 1969 by Copp Clark Publishing Co. Reprinted by permission.

present constitution; he has done his ample share of duty by the country; and he feels that he is entitled to be consulted before any change is effected.

How thoroughly and exclusively Canadian the French-Canadian is should never be forgotten by those who contemplate any change in the constitutional or national status of Canada. This is so patent a fact, so logical a consequence of historical developments, that nothing short of absolute ignorance or wilful blindness can justify the language of those who talk of drawing him either by persuasion or by force to a closer allegiance to the Empire. As a matter of fact, he constitutes the only exclusively Canadian racial group in the Dominion. A constant immigration from the British Isles has kept the English-speaking Canadians in close contact with their motherland; so that even now they still speak of the "Old Country" as their "home," thus keeping in their hearts a double allegiance. On the soil of Canada, his only home and country, all the national aspirations of the French-Canadian are concentrated. "Canadian" is the only national designation he ever claims; and when he calls himself "French-Canadian," he simply wants to differentiate his racial origin from that of his English, Scotch, or Irish fellow citizen, who, in his mind, are but partially *Canadianised*.

When he is told that Canada is a British country, and that he must abide by the will of the British majority, he replies that Canada has remained British through his own loyalty; that when his race constituted the overwhelming majority of the Canadian people, Canada was twice saved to the British Crown, thanks to him and to him only; that he has remained faithful to Great Britain because he was assured of certain rights and privileges; that his English-speaking fellow citizens have accepted the compact and should not now take advantage of their greater numerical strength to break the agreement; that when settling in Canada, newcomers from the British kingdom should understand that they become citizens of Canada, of a Confederacy where he has vested rights, and should not undertake to make the country and its people more British than Canadian. . . .

Independence is to his mind the most natural outcome of the ultimate destinies of Canada. But so long as the present ties are not strengthened he is in no hurry to sever British connection. He realises that time cannot but work in favour of Canada by bringing to her population and wealth, and that the later she starts on her own course the safer the journey. . . . .

Now, apart from his instinctive reluctance to contemplate any political evolution, what are the feelings of the French-Canadian with regard to Imperial Federation or any form of British Imperialism?

First, as may be naturally expected, sentimental arguments in favour of British Imperialism cannot have any hold upon him. To his reason only must appeals on this ground be made. That the new Imperial policy will bring him, and Canada at large, advantages that will not be paid by any infringement on his long-struggled-for liberty, he must be clearly shown.

Towards Great Britain he knows that he has a duty of allegiance to perform. But he understands that duty to be what it has been so far, and nothing more. He has easily and generously forgotten the persecutions of the earlier and larger part of his national life under the British Crown. He is willing to acknowledge the good treatment which he has received later on, though he cannot forget that his own tenacity and the neighbourhood of the United States have had much to do with the improvement of his situation.

In short, his affection for Great Britain is one of reason, mixed with a certain amount of esteem and suspicion, the proportions of which vary according to time and circumstances, and also with his education, his temperament, and his social surroundings.

Towards the Empire he has no feelings whatever; and naturally so. The blood connection and the pride in Imperial power and glory having no claims upon him, what sentiment can he be expected to entertain for New Zealand or Australia, South Africa or India, for countries and populations entirely foreign to him, with which he has no relations, intellectual or political, and much less commercial intercourse than he has with the United States, France, Germany, or Belgium?

By the motherland he feels that he has done his full duty; by the Empire he does not feel that he has any duty to perform. He makes full allowance for the blood feelings of his English-speaking partner; but having himself, in the past, sacrificed much of his racial tendencies for the sake of Canadian unity, he thinks that the Anglo-Canadian should be prepared to study the problems of Imperialism from a purely Canadian standpoint. Moreover, this absence of racial feelings from his heart allows him to judge more impartially the question of the relations between Canada and the Empire.

He fully realises the benefits that Canada derives from her connection with a wealthy and mighty nation. He is satisfied with having the use of the British market. But this advantage he knows that Canada enjoys on the very same terms as any other country in the world, even the most inimical to Britain. From a mixed sense of justice and egotism he is less clamorous than the British Canadian in demanding any favour, commercial or other, from the motherland, because he has a notion that any favour received would have to be compensated by at least an equal favour given.

His ambition does not sway him to huge financial operations. Rather given to liberal professions, to agricultural life, or to local mercantile and industrial pursuits, he is more easily satisfied than the English-speaking Canadian with a moderate return for his work and efforts. He has been kept out of the frantic display of financial energy, of the feverish concentration of capital, of the international competition of industry, which have drawn his English-speaking fellow citizen to huge combinations of wealth or trade; and therefore, he is not anxious to participate in the organisation of the Empire on the basis of a gigantic co-operative association for trade. He would rather see Canada keep the full control of her commercial policy and enter into the best possible trade arrangements with any nation, British or foreign.

He is told that Canada has the free use of British diplomacy, and that such an advantage calls for sacrifices on her part when Britain is in distress. But considered in the light of past events, British diplomacy has, on the contrary, cost a good deal to Canada. So far the foreign relations of Canada, through British mediation, have been almost exclusively confined to America. That the influence and prestige of Great Britain were of great benefit to Canada in her relations with the United States is hardly conspicuous in the various Anglo-American treaties and conventions in which Canadian interests are concerned.

Not only did the American Republic secure the settlement of nearly all her claims according to her pretentions, but Canadian rights have been sacrificed by British plenipotentiaries in compensation for misdeeds or blunders of the British Government.

In fact, the Reciprocity Treaty of 1854 stands as the only convention entered into by Great Britain and the United States in which Canada stood at an advantage. But when the Secession War came, Great Britain gave to the slave-owning States a half-hearted moral support, too weak to turn the tide of fortune on their side, but strong enough to raise the ire of the victorious Government. Canada paid the price of revenge. Not only was the treaty of 1854 denounced, never to be renewed, but in the Washington Treaty of 1871 Canadian fisheries were made accessible to the Americans at a time when they were most profitable, in order to reconcile the United States and pay for the protection offered by Great Britain to privateers of the Southern States. True, Canada was awarded a money compensation; but the United States was none the less given a valuable privilege within the limits of Canadian territory, and one upon which the Canadian Government had always relied to procure trade reciprocity with the Americans. This unfair transaction was strenuously opposed by Sir John A. Macdonald, Prime Minister of Canada, who acted on that occasion as one of the British plenipotentiaries. He went to the length of threatening either to resign or to withold the sanction of the Canadian Parliament from the treaty. At last he gave way under the pressure of his colleagues, Lord de Grey, Sir Stafford Northcote, and Sir Edward Thornton who convinced him that Canadian rights had to be sacrificed for the sake of Imperial interests.

Now with regard to disputes over boundaries. In the Treaty of 1842, whereby the northern frontiers of the State of Maine were delimitated, a large portion of Canadian territory was abandoned to the Americans by Lord Ashburton, who jocosely observed that he did not care for a few degrees of latitude more or less. Later on, the Oregon boundaries were also fixed in a way which Canada claimed was unjust to her; although it must be admitted that this time the Americans endeavoured to get more territory than they actually secured. Not later than last year the Clayton-Bulwer convention was denounced without any settlement of the Alaskan boundary being reached. Canada had no right under that treaty; but she always claimed that the anxiety of the United States for its removal offered a most propitious occasion for a fair application in her favour of the famous Monroe doctrine, so dear to the heart of the Americans. Great Britain waiving her rights in a treaty dealing with questions of a purely American nature — in the geographical sense — Canada rightly expected that this abandonment should be compensated by the settlement of another exclusively American problem. This view was strongly urged by the Canadian authorities upon the Home Government; it has even been stated that this was one of the primary conditions of the unfruitful negotiations carried on at Quebec and Washington in 1898–1899, under the presidency of Lord Herschel, but evidently all in vain.

It may be argued that all those concessions, made by Great Britain at the expense of Canada, were imposed by circumstances. It may be said also that by those same concessions Canada at large was affected, and that the French-Canadians had no greater cause of complaint than their English-speaking fellow citizens. But that exclusive Canadian sentiment which I have described makes the French-Canadian feel more deeply any encroachment upon the integrity of Canada. Unlike the Anglo-Canadian, he does *117* not find in the glory of Empire a compensation and a solace for the losses suffered by Canada. That he entertains any rancour against Britain on that account would, however, be a false conclusion. For the international intricacies in which Great Britain has been and is still entangled he makes full allowance. With his strong sense of self-government, he does not expect the motherland to endanger her own position on behalf of Canada. But if Great Britain is either unable or unwilling to take risks for the sake of Canadian interests, he does not see why Canada should assume new obligations towards Great Britain and run risks on her behalf.

As far as war and defence are concerned, he is still less disposed to consent to any Imperial combination. First there is that aversion to militarism that I have mentioned. Then he has a notion that all the sacrifices he may make on this ground will be so much that Canada will give without any probable return.

When he turns towards the past, what does he find? He finds that for the hundred and forty years that he has been a British subject, no more than his English-speaking fellow citizen has he ever been the cause, near or distant, of any trouble to Great Britain. Never did Canada involve the Empire in any war or threat of war. But the policy, right or wrong, of the British Government did cause his country to be the battlefield of two Anglo-American struggles. Upon those two occasions Canada was saved to the British Crown, thanks to the loyalty of his own race. During the Secession war, the peace of Canada came very near being disturbed once more, and her territory was threatened with invasion because of the attitude of Great Britain. And if he has been spared this and other bloody contests, it was only by the granting to the United States of such concessions as are referred to above.

So much for the past. When he considers the present and the future, the French-Canadian does not see any reason why he should enter into a scheme of Imperial defence.

The argument that if Canada stands by the Empire, the Empire will stand by Canada, cannot have much weight with him; and his objections on that ground are founded both on past events and on prospective developments. In the South African War he has witnessed an application of the new doctrine. Of the expenditure of that war he has been called upon to pay his share — a small one if compared with that of the British Kingdom, but a large one when it is remembered that he had no interest whatever in the contest, and no control over the policy which preceded the conflict, or over its settlement. Should the principle of military Imperialism predominate, he foresees that he may find himself involved in wars occasioned by friction between Australia and Japan, between New Zealand and Germany, between Great Britain and France in Europe, or between Great Britain and Russia in Asia. He does not see any eventuality in which the Empire may be called upon to help Canada.

118

He is ready now, as he was in the past, to support a sufficient military force to maintain internal peace and to resist aggression on the territory of Canada. But these eventualities are most unlikely to occur in the near future. The enormous area as well as the vast resources of the country offer such opportunities to the care and activity of its population, that social struggles are almost impossible in Canada for many years to come. Foreign invasion, from the United States excepted, is most improbable. The Canadian territory is easy to defend against attacks on her sea borders, which would offer great difficulties and little benefit to any enemy of the Empire. Moreover, from a purely Canadian standpoint such occurrences are most unlikely to happen. Left to herself Canada has no possible cause of conflict with any other nation but the United States. On the other hand, by entering into a compact for Imperial defence, she may be involved in war with several of the strongest Powers. Therefore, as far as concerns any country outside America, the French-Canadian feels that the scheme of Imperial defence brings upon him new causes of conflict not to be compensated by any probable defensive requirement.

It is worthwhile mentioning here one possible conflict in which, if Imperialism carries the day, the racial problem of Canada might cause serious trouble. Although happily checked by a large interchange of material interests, the possibility of a war between France and Great Britain is not altogether removed. Were such a conflict confined to these two Powers, the French-Canadian could be counted upon to stand loyally neutral. Should even the French navy, by the most improbable of war fortunes, attack the coast of Canada, the French-Canadian could be relied upon for the defence of his country. But should the principle of Imperial solidarity obtain, were Canada called upon to contribute to an Anglo-French war in which she had no direct interest, the French-Canadian would no doubt resent most bitterly any such contribution in men or money as could be voted by the Federal Parliament. This would no longer be the defence of his home — which he is prepared to undertake even against France — it would mean his contributing to the slaughter of his own kith and kin in a quarrel which was foreign to him. It would hurt the

French-Canadian in that most peculiar and sentimental love for the French national soul which I have already mentioned.

There remains to be dealt with the eventuality of a war with the United States. Rightly or wrongly, the French-Canadian is inclined to think that, in order to avert such a calamity, Great Britain would even go to the length of abandoning all British rights in America. And should British sentiment and British policy undergo such a change as would warrant Canada in counting upon the armed help of the Empire against the United States, the French-Canadian entertains some doubt as to the possibility of keeping up the struggle and carrying it to a successful issue.

Should the most sanguine expectations be realised; should the American Navy be annihilated even as a defence force; and were the British Navy to succeed in blockading and bombarding the American ports — the only effective blow which might be struck at the enemy — nothing could prevent the American army from occupying the central portion of Canada, and probably invading most of her territory. Canada would therefore, at all events be the sufferer in the fight. Moreover, her ways of transportation from the Western graingrowing country would be interrupted; and whilst the Americans would get from their untouched territory unbounded resources of food supply, the British people would be at once deprived of American and Canadian breadstuffs. This alone, in spite of any military success in other ways, would force Great Britain to accept the terms of the American Republic.

119

Another point to be considered with reference to an Anglo-American War is the fact that there are now as many French-Canadians living under the star-spangled banner as under the Union Jack. Many of those migrated Canadians have become as loyal and devoted citizens of the American Republic as their brothers have remained loyal and devoted citizens of Canada. Although prepared to do his full duty in the defence of his land, the prospect of his becoming the murderer of his own brother is sufficient to prevent the French-Canadian from exposing Canada and the Empire to any war with the United States.

From all those considerations the French-Canadian concludes that Canada has never been, and never will be, the cause of any display of Imperial strength, with the single exception of a possible encounter with a nation that he is not desirous of attacking, and against which, in his mind, the Empire would be either unwilling or incapable of defending him. He does not therefore feel bound to assume military obligations towards any other part of the Empire.

The stronger Canada grows in population and wealth, the slighter will be the dangers that may threaten her security, and the greater her contribution to the welfare and glory of the Empire. The French-Canadian thinks therefore that the best way in which he can play his part in the building up of the Empire is not by diverting the healthiest and strongest portion of its population from the pursuits of a peaceful and industrious life and sending them to fight in all parts of the world. He does not believe in fostering in

Canada the spirit of militarism. He is only anxious to make his country attractive and prosperous by keeping aloof from all military adventures.

Indifferent as he is to commercial Imperialism, hostile as he is to military Imperialism, the French-Canadian cannot be expected to wish for any organic change in the constitution of Canada and to look favourably upon any scheme of Imperial Federation.

For years he fought to obtain full control of his laws, of his social system, of his public exchequer. With the principles of self-government, of self-taxation, of direct control over the legislative body, no other citizen of the British Empire is more thoroughly imbued than he is. His local organisation, in Church, educational or municipal matters, is still more decentralised and democratic than that of the English provinces of Canada. He likes to exercise his elective franchise and to keep as close as possible to the man, the law and the regulation that he votes for. He cannot view with favour a scheme by which any power that has heretofore been exercised by his own representative bodies may pass under the control of some Council sitting in London.

120

There remains to be considered the question of annexation to the United States.

As I have stated, left to himself, the French-Canadian is not eager for a change. He requires nothing but quietness and stability in order to grow and develop. He is satisfied with and proud of his Canadian citizenship. But should a change be forced upon him by those who aspire to a greater nationality, he would rather incline towards Pan-Americanism.

For a long time annexation to the United States was most abhorrent to the French-Canadian. In fact, when an agitation in that direction was started by several leading English-speaking Canadians, his resistance proved to be the best safeguard of the British connection. But should his past fidelity be now disregarded, and Canadian autonomy encroached upon in any way, should he be hurried into any Imperial scheme and forced to assume fresh obligations, he would prefer throwing in his lot with his powerful neighbour to the South. His present constitution he prizes far above the American system of Government; but if called upon to sacrifice anything of his Federal autonomy for the working of the Imperial machinery, he would rather do it in favour of the United States system, under which, at all events, he would preserve the self-government of his province. Should Imperial re-organisation be based on trade and financial grounds, he would see a greater future in joining the most powerful industrial nation of the world than in going into partnership with the British communities; and this sentiment is gaining greater force from the present influx of American capital into Canada. The fact that the union of Canada and the United States would bring again under the same flag the two groups, now separated, of his nationality has no doubt greatly contributed towards smoothing his aversion to annexation.

I have so far analysed the sentiments of the higher classes among the French-Canadian people, of those who control their feelings by historical knowledge or by a study of outside circumstances, political, military or financial. If I refer to the masses, mostly composed of farmers, I may say that they entertain similar feelings, but instinctively rather than from reflection. The French-Canadians of the popular class look upon Canada as their own country. They are ready to do their duty by Canada; but considering they owe nothing to Great Britain or any other country, they ask nothing from them. Imbued with a strong sense of liberty, they have no objection to their English-speaking fellow countrymen going to war anywhere they please; but they cannot conceive that Canada as a whole may be forced out of its present situation. They let people talk of any wise and wild proposal of Imperialism; but if any change were attempted to be imposed on them, they would resist the pressure, quietly but constantly.

To sum up, the French-Canadian is decidedly and exclusively Canadian by nationality and American by his ethnical temperament. People with world-wide aspirations may charge him with provincialism. But after all, this sentiment of exclusive attachment to one's land and one's nationality is to be found as one of the essential characteristics of all strong and growing peoples. On the other hand, the lust of abnormal expansion and Imperial pride have ever been the marked features of all nations on the verge of decadence.

121

Topic Five

Immigration and Western Settlement

Between 1896 and 1914 over two million immigrants arrived in Canada, the majority of them settling in the West. A large proportion of these were from Britain and the United States and assimilated relatively easily into Canadian society. A significant number, however, came from continental Europe and found it more difficult to adjust because of cultural and linguistic differences.

The expansion of immigration to Canada in this period was partially the result of changed world conditions. The American frontier of settlement had closed by the 1890s when the best homestead land had been settled, forcing immigrants to consider the Canadian prairies — "the last best West" — as a viable alternative. This was also a period of world-wide prosperity that enabled more immigrants to come to Canada.

Equally influential were the efforts of the Liberal government of Wilfrid Laurier, elected in 1896, to settle the West. Under the leadership of Clifford Sifton, the minister of the interior, the Liberals launched a vigorous campaign to recruit immigrants. Sifton doubled and redoubled the expenditures of the Immigration Branch, sent government agents to Britain, the United States, and various European countries armed with propagandist literature that extolled the virtues of Western Canada, offered special bonuses to steamship agents willing to book immigrants to take passage to Canada, and encouraged various ethnic and sectarian groups to believe that they would be able to establish block settlements and continue their customs in the new world.

Many Anglo-Canadians saw "foreign" immigrants as posing a serious threat to their culture. Howard Palmer analyses the various attitudes and assumptions that underlay anglo-conformist views and indicates the varied reaction to the different ethnic groups who arrived. The chapter from John Marlyn's novel, *Under the Ribs of Death*, tells the immigrant's side of the story — the difficulties of, yet desire for, acceptance in Canada.

For a good overview of immigration to Western Canada, see the chapter

"Opening Up the Land of Opportunity" in R. C. Brown and R. Cook's *Canada: 1896–1921: A Nation Transformed* (Toronto: McClelland and Stewart, 1974), pp. 49–82. *Immigration and the Rise of Multiculturalism*, edited by H. Palmer (Toronto: Copp Clark, 1975), contains a good selection of primary readings on the subject of immigration. The immigrant's view can be further examined in R. F. Harney and H. Troper's *Immigrants: A Portrait of the Urban Experience: 1890–1930* (Toronto: Van Nostrand Reinhold, 1975). The Department of the Secretary of State is currently publishing individual histories of some thirty ethnic groups in Canada.

Reluctant Hosts:
Anglo-Canadian Views of Multiculturalism
in the Twentieth Century*

123

HOWARD PALMER

Introduction

The way in which Anglo-Canadians have reacted to immigration during the twentieth century has not simply been a function of the numbers of immigrants or the state of the nation's economy. The immigration of significant numbers of non-British and non-French people raised fundamental questions about the type of society which would emerge in English-speaking Canada; hence, considerable public debate has always surrounded the issue of immigration in Canada. The questions which have repeatedly been raised include the following: Were the values and institutions of Anglo-Canadian society modelled exclusively on a British mold and should immigrants be compelled to conform to that mold? Or, would a distinctive identity emerge from the biological and cultural mingling of Anglo-Canadians with new immigrant groups? Would cultural pluralism itself give English-speaking Canada a distinctive identity? These three questions reflect the three theories of assimilation which have dominated the twentieth century debate over immigrant adjustment.

The assimilation theory which achieved early public acceptance was Anglo-conformity. This view demanded that immigrants renounce their ancestral culture and traditions in favour of the behaviour and values of Anglo-Canadians. Although predominant prior to World War II, Anglo-conformity fell into disrepute and was replaced in the popular mind by the "melting pot" theory of assimilation. This view envisaged a biological merging of settled communities with new immigrant groups and a blending of their cultures into a new Canadian type. Currently, a third theory of

*Revised by the author from an address to the Second Canadian Conference on Multiculturalism. First published in the conference report, *Multiculturalism as State Policy*, by the Canadian Consultative Council on Multiculturalism. Reprinted by permission of the Minister of Supply and Services Canada.

assimilation — "cultural pluralism" or "multiculturalism" — is vying for public acceptance. This view postulates the preservation of some aspects of immigrant culture and communal life within the context of Canadian citizenship and political and economic integration into Canadian society.[1]

There has been a recent burgeoning of historical and sociological research on Anglo-Canadian attitudes toward ethnic minorities. Much of this research contradicts the view which has been advanced by some Anglo-Canadian historians[2] and politicians that Anglo-Canadians have always adopted the "mosaic" as opposed to the American "melting pot" approach. Much of this rhetoric has simply been wishful thinking. Perhaps immigrant groups did not "melt" as much in Canada as in the United States, but this is not because Anglo-Canadians were more anxious to encourage the cultural survival of ethnic minorities. There has been a long history of racism and discrimination against ethnic minorities in English-speaking Canada, along with strong pressures for conformity to Anglo-Canadian ways.

124

The "Settlement" Period and the Predominance of Anglo-conformity: 1867-1920

Among the several objectives of the architects of the Canadian confederation in 1867, none was more important than the effort to accommodate the needs of the two main cultural communities. There was virtually no recognition of ethnic diversity aside from the British-French duality. This is, of course, somewhat understandable since at the time of confederation, only eight percent of the population of three and one half million were of non-British[3] or Non-French ethnic origin. There were, however, significant numbers of people of German and Dutch origin, well-established black and Jewish communities as well as a few adventurers and entrepreneurs from most European ethnic groups now in Canada.

The proportion of people of other than British, French, or native origin in Canada remained small until nearly the turn of the century; the United States proved more attractive for most European emigrants. In fact it was attractive for many Canadians as well, and the Dominion barely maintained its population. But with the closing of the American frontier which coincided with improving economic conditions in Canada and an active immigration promotion campaign by Wilfrid Laurier's Liberal government, many immigrants began to come to the newly opened land of western Canada in the late 1890's.[4] Immigration policy gave preference to farmers, and most non-British immigrants came to farm in western Canada. However, some immigrants ended up working in mines, laying railway track, or drifting into the urban working class.[5] During this first main wave of immigration between 1896 and 1914, three million immigrants, including large numbers of British laborers, American farmers, and eastern European peasants, came to Canada. Within the period of 1901 to 1911, Canada's population rocketed by 43 percent and the percentage of immigrants in the country as a whole topped 22 percent. In 1911, people of non-British and non-French origin formed 34 percent of the population of Manitoba, 40 percent of the population of Saskatchewan, and 33 percent of the population of Alberta.

Throughout the period of this first large influx of non-British, non-French immigrants, (indeed up until World War II), anglo-conformity was the predominant ideology of assimilation in English-speaking Canada.[6] For better or for worse, there were few proponents of either the melting pot or of cultural pluralism. Proponents of anglo-conformity argued that it was the obligation of new arrivals to conform to the values and institutions of Canadian society — which were already fixed. During this period when scarcely anyone questioned the verities of God, King, and country, there was virtually no thought given to the possibility that "WASP" values might not be the apex of civilization which all men should strive for.

Since at this time the British Empire was at its height, and the belief in "progress" and Anglo-Saxon and white superiority was taken for granted throughout the English-speaking world, a group's desirability as potential immigrants varied almost directly with its members physical and cultural distance from London, (England) and the degree to which their skin pigmentation conformed to Anglo-Saxon white. Anglo-Canadians regarded British and American immigrants as the most desirable.[7] Next came northern and western Europeans who were regarded as culturally similar and hence assimilable. They were followed by central and eastern Europeans, who in the eyes of Clifford Sifton and immigration agents, had a slight edge on Jews and southern Europeans, because they were more inclined to go to and remain on the land. These groups were followed in the ethnic pecking order by the "strange" religious sects, the Hutterites, Mennonites, and Doukhobors, who were invariably lumped together by public officials and the general public despite significant religious and cultural differences between them. Last, but not least (certainly not least in the eyes of those British Columbians and their sympathizers elsewhere in the country who worried about the "Asiatic" hordes) were the Asian immigrants — the Chinese, Japanese, and East Indians (the latter of whom were dubbed "Hindoos," despite the fact that most were Sikhs). Running somewhere close to last were black immigrants, who did not really arise as an issue because of the lack of aspiring candidates, except in 1911, when American blacks were turned back at the border by immigration officials because they allegedly could not adapt to the cold winters in Canada; a curious about-face for a department which was reassuring other American immigrants that Canadian winters were relatively mild.[8]

As might be expected, prevailing assumptions about the relative assimilability of these different groups were quickly transformed into public debate over whether immigrants whose assimilability was problematic should be allowed into the country. During this first wave of immigration, considerable opposition developed to the entry of central, southern and eastern European immigrants, Orientals, and to the three pacifist

125

sects. Opposition to these groups came from a variety of sources, for a variety of reasons. But one of the most pervasive fears of opinion leaders was that central, southern and eastern Europeans, and Orientals would wash away Anglo-Saxon traditions of self-government in a sea of illiteracy and inexperience with "free institutions."[9] Many English-Canadian intellectuals, like many American writers at the time, thought that North America's greatness was ensured so long as its Anglo-Saxon character was preserved. Writers emphasized an Anglo-Saxon tradition of political freedom and self-government and the "white man's" mission to spread Anglo-Saxon blessings.[10] Many intellectuals and some politicians viewed Orientals and central southern and eastern European immigrants as a threat to this tradition and concluded that since they could not be assimilated they would have to be excluded. The introduction in Canada of a head tax on Chinese immigrants, a "gentlemen's agreement" with Japan which restricted the number of Japanese immigrants, the passing of orders-in-council which restricted immigration from India, the gradual introduction of restrictive immigration laws in 1906, 1910, and 1919 relative to European immigration and the tightening of naturalization laws was based in considerable part on the assumptions of anglo-conformity — immigrants who were culturally or racially inferior and incapable of being assimilated either culturally or biologically, would have to be excluded.[11] Those who rose to the immigrants' defence argued almost entirely from economic grounds: immigration from non-British sources was needed to aid in economic development, not because it might add anything to Canada's social or cultural life.

Although the trend toward restrictionism during the early 1900s seemed to indicate a government trend toward anglo-conformity in response to public pressure, for the most part between 1867 and 1945, there was no explicit federal government policy with regard to the role of non-British and non-French ethnic groups in Canadian society. It was generally assumed, however, that immigrants would eventually be assimilated into either English-Canadian or French-Canadian society. A recent careful study of Clifford Sifton's attitudes toward immigrant groups in Canadian society concludes Sifton assumed that central and eastern Europeans ". . . would be 'nationalized' in the long run through their experience on the land . . .".[12] The federal government's concern was tied to the economic consequences of immigration, while schools, the primary agents of assimilation, were under provincial jurisdiction. The federal government had encouraged Mennonites and Icelanders to settle in blocks in Manitoba during the 1870's and had given them special concessions (including local autonomy for both and military exemptions for the Mennonites) to entice them to stay in Canada rather than move to the United States.[13] But this was not because of any conscious desire to make Canada a cultural mosaic, nor was it out of any belief in the value of cultural diversity. Block settlements, by providing social and economic stability, were simply a way of getting immigrants to settle in the west and remain there.[14] The govern-

126

ment policy was pragmatic and concerned primarily with economic growth and "nation building;" there was little rhetoric in immigration propaganda picturing Canada as a home for oppressed minorities who would be able to pursue their identities in Canada.

Provincial governments were faced with the problems of assimilation more directly than the federal government since the provinces maintained jurisdiction over the educational systems. The whole question of the varying attitudes of provincial authorities toward assimilation is much too complex to outline in this article; suffice it to say that with some notable exceptions (like the bilingual school system in Manitoba between 1896 and 1916, and the school system which was established for Hutterites in Alberta), anglo-conformity was the predominant aim of the public school system and was an underlying theme in the textbooks.

Anglo-conformity was most pronounced during World War I as nationalism precipitated insistent hostility to "hyphenated Canadianism" and demanded an unswerving loyalty. For many Anglo-Canadians during the war, loyalty and cultural and linguistic uniformity were synonymous. During the war, western provincial governments acted to abolish the bilingual schools which had previously been allowed.[15] The formation of the Union government of Conservatives and Liberals during the first World War was an attempt to create an Anglo-Saxon party, dedicated to "unhyphenated Canadianism" and the winning of the war; even if this meant trampling on the rights of immigrants through press censorship and the imposition of the War Time Elections Act which disfranchised "enemy aliens" who had become Canadian citizens after March 21, 1902.[16] Various voluntary associations like the YMCA, IODE, National Council of Women, Canadian Girls in Training, Girl Guides, Big Brothers and Big Sisters Organizations and Frontier College, as well as the major Protestant denominations also intensified their efforts to "Canadianize" the immigrants, particularly at the close of the war when immigrant support for radical organizations brought on anti-radical nativist fears of the "menace of the alien."[17] The pressures for conformity were certainly real, even if English-Canadians could not always agree completely on the exact nature of the norm to which immigrants were to be assimilated.

All the major books on immigration prior to 1920, including J. S. Woodsworth's *Strangers Within Our Gates*, J. T. M. Anderson's *The Education of the new Canadian*, Ralph Connor's *The Foreigner*, Alfred Fitzpatrick's *Handbook for New Canadians*, C. A. Magrath's *Canada's Growth and Some Problems Affecting It*, C. B. Sissons, *Bilingual Schools in Canada*, and W. G. Smith, *A Study in Canadian Immigration*, were based on the assumptions of anglo-conformity. To lump all these books together is of course to oversimplify since they approached the question of immigration with varying degrees of nativism (or anti-foreign sentiment), and humanitarianism. Nor were all of the voluntary organizations' attempted "Canadianization" work among immigrants motivated solely by the fear that immigrants would undermine the cultural homogeneity of English-speaking Canada.

127

Many of these writers and organizations saw their work with the immigrants as a means of fighting social problems and helping immigrants achieve a basic level of political, social, and economic integration into Canadian society. But it cannot be denied that their basic assumption was that of anglo-conformity. Cultural diversity was either positively dangerous, or was something that would and should disappear with time, and with the help of Anglo-Canadians.

Perhaps it should be emphasized that the individuals advocating anglo-conformity were not just the reactionaries of their day. Protestant Social Gospellers (including J. S. Woodsworth, later one of the founders of the CCF) who played such a prominent role in virtually all the reform movements of the pre-World War I period (including women's rights, temperance, and labor, farm, and penal reform) believed that immigrants needed to be assimilated to Anglo-Canadian Protestant values as part of the effort to establish a truly Christian society in English-speaking Canada.[18] Women's groups pushing for the franchise argued that certainly they deserved the vote if "ignorant foreigners" had it, and joined in the campaign to Canadianize the immigrants who "must be educated to high standards or our whole national life will be lowered by their presence among us."[19]

But there was a central contradiction in Anglo-Canadian attitudes toward ethnic minorities. Non-Anglo-Saxon immigrants were needed to open the west and to do the heavy jobs of industry. This meant not only the introduction of culturally distinctive groups, but groups which would occupy the lower rungs of the socio-economic system. The pre-1920 period was the period of the formation of, and the most acute expression of what was later called the "vertical mosaic." Anglo-Canadians were not used to the idea of cultural diversity, nor the degree of class stratification which developed during this period of rapid settlement and industrialization. The answer to all the problems of social diversity which the immigrants posed was assimilation. The difficulty however with achieving this goal of assimilation was not only the large numbers of immigrants, or the fact that not all (or even a majority) of them wanted to be assimilated. One of the major factors preventing assimilation was discrimination by the Anglo-Canadian majority.

The basic contradiction, then, of Anglo-Canadian attitudes as expressed through the "Canadianization" drives was the tension between the twin motives of humanitarianism and nativism — between the desire to include non-British immigrants within a community and eliminate cultural differences and the desire to stay as far away from them as possible because of their presumed "undesirability." This contradiction was graphically revealed at the national conference of the IODE in 1919. The women passed one resolution advocating a "Canadianization campaign" to "propagate British ideals and institutions", to "banish old world points of view, old world prejudices, old world rivalries and suspicion" and to make new Canadians 100 percent British in language, thought, feeling and impulse." Yet they also passed another resolution protesting "foreigners" taking British names.[20]

It does not appear that this was simply a case of the Anglo-Canadian majority being divided between those who wanted to pursue a strategy of assimilation, and those who wanted to pursue a strategy of subordination and segregation. Certainly there was some division along these lines, but as suggested by the IODE resolutions, discrimination and anglo-conformity were often simply two different sides of the same coin — the coin being the assumption of the inferiority of non-Anglo-Saxons.

What developed throughout English-speaking Canada during this period was a vicious circle of discrimination. Non-Anglo-Saxons were discriminated against because they were not assimilated, either culturally or socially, but one of the reasons they were not assimilated was because of discrimination against them. As one researcher noted in a 1917 report on "Social Conditions in Rural Communities in the Prairie Provinces," the group "clannishness" of immigrants which was so widely deplored by the public was caused as much by the prejudice of the "English" as it was by the groups' desire to remain different.[21]

There is no need to catalogue here the extensive patterns of social, economic and political discrimination which developed against non-Anglo-Saxons.[22] Patterns of discrimination parallelled preferences of immigrant sources with northern and western Europeans encountering relatively little discrimination, central and southern Europeans and Jews encountering more discrimination and non-whites encountering an all pervasive pattern of discrimination which extended to almost all aspects of their lives. Discrimination was one of the main factors which led to the transference (with only a few exceptions) of the same ethnic "pecking order" which existed in immigration policy to the place each group occupied in the "vertical mosaic," with the British (especially the Scots) on top, and so on down to the Chinese and blacks who occupied the most menial jobs.[23] Non-British and non-French groups not only had very little economic power; they also would not even significantly occupy the middle echelons of politics, education or the civil service until after World War II.

The ethnic stereotypes which developed for eastern European and Oriental groups emphasized their peasant origins. These stereotypes played a role in determining the job opportunities for new immigrants and functioned to disparage those who would climb out of their place. Opprobrious names such as "Wops," "Bohunks" and especially "foreigner" indicated class as well as ethnic origin and these terms were used as weapons in the struggle for status. The very word "ethnic" carried, for many people, such an aura of opprobrium that even recently there have been attempts to expurgate the use of the word. Ethnic food and folklore were regarded by most Anglo-Canadians as not only "foreign," but "backward" and lower class. Folklorist Carole Henderson has aptly described the views of Anglo-Canadians toward folklore, (views which continue to the present day): "Except for members of some delimited regional and usually ethnic, subcultures such as Newfoundlanders or Nova Scotian Scots, most Anglo-Canadians simply fail to identify folklore with them-

129

selves, and tend to consider such materials to be the . . . unimportant possessions of the strange, foreign or 'backward people in their midst'."[24]

The 1920s and the Emergence of "Melting Pot" Ideas

The 1920s brought the second main wave of non-British and non-French immigrants to Canada and saw the emergence of the second ideology of assimilation, the "melting pot." During the early 1920s both Canada and the United States had acted to further restrict immigration from southern, central and eastern Europe and from the Orient. Chinese were virtually excluded from Canada, and central, southern and eastern Europeans were classified among the "non-preferred" and restricted category of immigrants. But by the mid-1920s several powerful sectors of Canadian society, including transportation companies, boards of trade, newspapers and politicians of various political persuasions, as well as ethnic groups, applied pressure on the King government to open the immigration doors.[25] These groups believed that only a limited immigration could be expected from the "preferred" countries and that probably only central and eastern Europeans would do the rugged work of clearing marginal land. The railways continued to seek immigrants to guarantee revenue for their steamship lines, traffic for their railways and settlers for their land. With improving economic conditions in the mid-twenties, the Federal government responded to this pressure and changed its policy with respect to immigrants from central and eastern Europe.

While continuing to emphasize its efforts to secure British immigrants, in September 1925, the Liberal government of Mackenzie King entered into the "Railways Agreement" with the CPR and CNR which brought an increased number of central and eastern Europeans. The Government authorized the railways to encourage potential immigrants of the "non-preferred" countries to emigrate to Canada and to settle as "agriculturalists, agricultural workers and domestic servants."[26]

Through this agreement, the railways brought to Canada 165 000 central and eastern Europeans and 20 000 Mennonites. They represented a variety of ethnic groups and a diversity of reasons for emigrating. Most of the Ukrainian immigrants were political refugees. Poles, Slovaks, and Hungarians were escaping poor economic conditions. German-Russians and Mennonites were fleeing civil war, economic disaster, and the spectre of cultural annihilation in Russia.[27] Often they chose Canada since they could no longer get into the United States because of its quota system and the Canadian route was the only way they could get to North America. With this new wave of immigration, the proportion of the Canadian population that was not of British, French, or native origin, rose to more than 18 percent by 1931.

In responding to this new wave of immigration, many opinion leaders held to an earlier belief that Canada should be patterned exclusively on the British model, and continued to advocate anglo-conformity. In national periodicals and newspapers during the 1920s, the emphasis which was placed on the need to attract British immigrants was related to this assumption that anglo-conformity was essential to the successful development of Canadian society. "Foreign" immigrants had to be assimilated and there needed to be enough Britishers to maintain "Anglo-Saxon" traditions.[28] R. B. Bennett, later to become the Conservative prime minister during the early 1930s, attacked melting pot ideas in the House of Commons and argued "These people [continental Europeans] have made excellent settlers: . . . but it cannot be that we must draw upon them to shape our civilization. We must still maintain that measure of British civilization which will enable us to assimilate these people to British institutions, rather than assimilate our civilization to theirs . . ."[29]

The influx of new immigrants from central and eastern Europe during the mid and late twenties also aroused protests from a number of nativist organizations such as the Ku Klux Klan, The Native Sons of Canada, and The Orange Order who were convinced that Canada should "remain Anglo-Saxon."[30] Nativist sentiment in western Canada was most pronounced in Saskatchewan where one of its leading spokesmen was George Exton Lloyd, an Anglican bishop and one of the founders of the Barr colony at Lloydminster.

In a torrent of newspaper articles and speeches, Lloyd repeated the warning that Canada was in danger of becoming a "mongrel" nation: "The essential question before Canadians today is this: Shall Canada develop as a British nation within the empire, or will she drift apart by the introduction of so much alien blood that her British instincts will be paralyzed?"[31] According to Lloyd, Canada had but two alternatives: it could either be a homogeneous nation or a heterogeneous one. The heterogeneous or "melting pot" idea had not worked in the United States (as evidenced by large numbers of unassimilated immigrants at the outbreak of World War I), and could not, he argued, work in Canada. With Lloyd, as with other individuals and organizations promoting anglo-conformity at this time, one gets the distinctive feeling that they were on the defensive. Like other English-speaking Canadians who had a strong attachment to Britain and the Empire, Lloyd saw a threat to Canada's "British" identity, not only in the increasing numbers of "continental" immigrants, but also in the declining status of things British as Canadians moved towards a North American based nationalism which did not include loyalty to the British Empire as its primary article of faith.[32]

During the late 1920s, a new view of assimilation, the melting pot, developed greater prominence. This view of assimilation, which arose partly as a means of defending immigrants against nativist attacks from people like Lloyd, envisioned a biological merging of Anglo-Canadians with immigrants and a blending of their cultures into a new Canadian type. Whereas Lloyd and other nativists argued that since immigrants could not conform to Anglo-Canadian ideals they should be excluded, a new generation of writers argued that assimilation was indeed occurring,

131

Barr Colony

but to a new Canadian type.[33] Since assimilation was occurring, nativist fears were unwarranted. Indeed, immigrants would make some valuable cultural contributions to Canada during the process of assimilation. Although these writers did not all use the "melting pot" symbol when discussing their view of assimilation, one can lump their ideas together under the rubric of the "melting pot" because they did envisage the emergence of a new society which would contain "contributions" from the various immigrant groups.

Most of these writers who defended "continental" European immigration did not seriously question the desirability of assimilation. Robert England, a writer and educator who worked for the CNR had read widely enough in anthropological sources to be influenced by the cultural relativism of Franz Boas and other anthropologists and did in his writing question the desirability of assimilation.[34] But most of these writers were concerned primarily with attempting to promote tolerance toward ethnic minorities by encouraging their assimilation, and many became involved in programs to facilitate this assimilation.

Advocates of anglo-conformity and the melting pot both believed that uniformity was ultimately necessary for unity, but they differed on what should provide the basis of that uniformity. Advocates of the melting pot, unlike the promoters of anglo-conformity, saw assimilation as a relatively slow process, and saw some cultural advantages in the mixing that would occur.

There was not, however, always a clear distinction between anglo-conformity and the melting pot. Rhetoric indicating that immigrants might have something more to offer Canada than their physical labor was sometimes only a thinly veiled version of anglo-conformity; the melting pot often turned out to be an Anglo-Saxon melting pot. For example John Blue, a prominent Edmonton promoter and historian, wrote in his history of Alberta in 1924 that the fears about foreign immigration destroying Canadian laws and institutions had proved groundless. "There is enough Anglo-Saxon blood in Alberta to dilute the foreign blood and complete the process of assimilation to the mutual advantage of both elements."[35]

There were a variety of reasons for the development of melting pot ideas during the 1920s.[36] The growth during the 1920s of an autonomous Canadian nationalism helped the spread of melting pot ideas. Some English-Canadian opinion leaders began to discuss the need for conformity to an exclusively Canadian norm rather than a "British" norm. One of the arguments that John W. Dafoe, the influential editor of the *Winnipeg Free Press* and J. S. Ewart, a constitutional lawyer, used in support of their view of Canadian nationalism was that non-British immigrants could not be expected to feel loyalty to the British Empire.[37]

Melting pot advocates tended to be people who had some personal experience with immigrants, and recognized both the intense pride that immigrants had in their cultural backgrounds as well as the rich cultural sources of those traditions. But they also lived in a time when recognition

132

of ethnicity meant mostly Anglo-Canadian use of ethnicity as a basis of discrimination or exploitation. It was also a time when some ethnic groups were still close enough to their rural peasant roots that ethnic solidarity was often not conducive to upward mobility. The view of most melting pot advocates that the disappearance of ethnicity as a basis of social organization would increase the mobility opportunities of the second generation was based on a sound grasp of the realities of the day. The life-long campaign of John Diefenbaker for "unhyphenated Canadianism" and "one Canada" grew out of this experience with ethnicity as something that could be used to hinder opportunities, and was consistent with his emphasis on human rights, rather than group rights.[38]

The 1930s

Although immigration was severely cut back during the depression of the 1930s, the role of ethnic minorities in English-speaking Canada continued to be a major public concern. Paradoxically, although the depression witnessed the high point of discrimination against non-Anglo-Saxons, it was also during the 1930s that the first major advocates of cultural pluralism in English-speaking Canada began to be heard.

The depression affected non-Anglo-Saxon immigrants more than most other groups in the society. These immigrants because of their language problems and lack of specialized skills, were concentrated in the most insecure and therefore most vulnerable segments of the economy. Since immigrants were the last hired and the first fired, a large proportion were forced onto relief. Government officials were gravely concerned about the way immigrants seemed to complicate the relief problem. Calls by some officials for deportation as the solution to the relief problem were heeded by the federal government; sections 40 and 41 of the Immigration Act (still essentially the same act as the one which existed in 1919) provided for deportation of non-Canadian citizens on relief and government officials took advantage of the law to reduce their relief rolls.

While there was some continuing concern over the assimilation of non-British and non-French immigrants during the 1930s, most Anglo-Canadians were more concerned about protecting their jobs.[39]

Prior to the depression, most Anglo-Saxons were content to have the "foreigners" do all the heavy work of construction, and the dirty work of the janitors and street sweepers. But as the economy slowed down, these jobs became attractive. Whereas the pre-depression attitude was "let the foreigners do the dirty work," the depression attitude became "how come these foreigners have all of our jobs?" The 1930s also saw the high point of anti-semitism in English-speaking Canada as the patterns of discrimination which had hindered the desires of second generation Jews for entry into the professions, were extended into a vicious and virulent anti-semitism by fascist groups.[40]

Barry Broadfoot's book *Ten Lost Years* also makes it very clear that

133

discrimination and prejudice flourished during the depression. In the transcripts of his interviews with the "survivors" of the depression, one is struck by the all-pervasiveness of derogatory ethnic epithets in interviewees' recollections of their contact with immigrants. One does not read of Italians, Chinese or Poles. One reads of "Dagos," "Wops," "Chinks," "Polacks," "Hunyaks."[41] One "survivor" of the depression, waxing philosophical, gives explicit expression to the prevailing attitudes of the time. He compares how the depression affected people from R. B. Bennett down to "the lowest of the low," "some bohunk smelling of garlic and not knowing a word of English. . . ."[42] Another "survivor" recalls that her boy had great difficulty finding work during the depression, and went berserk because of the blow to his self-esteem when the only job he could find was "working with a bunch of Chinks . . ."[43]

134

The vicious circle of discrimination became perhaps even more vicious during the 1930s as non-Anglo-Saxons' political response to the depression further poisoned attitudes toward them. The discrimination and unemployment which non-Anglo-Saxons faced was an important factor in promoting the support of many for radical political solutions to the depression, in either communist or fascist movements. Indeed the vast majority of the support for the communists throughout Canada, and for the fascists in western Canada came from non-Anglo-Saxons.[44] Ethnic support for these two movements, and the conflict between left and right within most central and eastern European groups and the Finns was seen as further evidence of the undesirability of non-Anglo-Saxons. The existence of fascist and communist movements in Canada was not of course due simply to the presence of immigrants bringing "old world" ideas. The leaders in both movements were predominantly of British origin,[45] and their "ethnic" support came more from immigrants reacting to depression conditions than from immigrants bringing to Canada "old world" ideas. But the depression gave further support to the notion of non-Anglo-Saxons being unstable politically; one more proof along with immigrant drinking, garlic eating and the legendary violence at Slavic weddings, that non-Anglo-Saxons were in dire need of baptism by assimilation. Deporting immigrant radicals was seen as one alternative to assimilation and the federal government did not hesitate to use this weapon.[46]

The relationship in the public mind between ethnicity, lower social class origins, and political "unsoundness" explains why during the late 1920s so many second generation non-Anglo-Saxons who were anxious to improve their lot economically made deliberate attempts to hide their ethnic background, such as changing their names. Ethnic ties were clearly disadvantageous for those non-Anglo-Saxons seeking economic security or social acceptance. The experience of the second generation in English-speaking Canada was similar to the second generation experience as described by a historian writing about ethnic groups in the United States. "Culturally estranged from their parents by their American education, and wanting nothing so much as to become and to be accepted as Americans, many second generation immigrants made deliberate efforts to rid themselves of their heritage. The adoption of American clothes, speech, and interests, often accompanied by the shedding of an exotic surname, were all part of a process whereby antecedents were repudiated as a means of improving status."[47]

Despite the continuing dominance of the old stereotypes concerning non-Anglo-Saxons and the continuing dominance of assimilationist assumptions, the 1930s also saw the emergence of the first full blown pluralist ideas in somewhat ambiguous form in John Murray Gibbon's book, *The Canadian Mosaic* and in the writings of Watson Kirkconnell, then an English professor at the University of Manitoba. These writers were much more familiar than earlier writers with the historical backgrounds of the ethnic groups coming to Canada, and they were influenced by a liberalism which rejected the assumptions of Anglo-Saxon superiority. Gibbon, a publicity agent for the Canadian Pacific Railway, wrote his book as an expansion of a series of CBC radio talks on the different ethnic groups of Canada. He traced the history of each group and related their "contributions" to Canadian society. Although he was concerned with the preservation of folk arts and music, he also went out of his way to alleviate fears of unassimilability by discussing individuals' assimilation as well as the "cement" of common institutions which bound the Canadian mosaic together. Although Gibbon was not the first writer to use the mosaic symbol, he was the first to attempt to explore its meaning in any significant way.

Kirkconnell was an essayist, poet, and prolific translator of European verse from a number of European languages. His writing on ethnic groups was based on a different approach than Gibbon's. He tried to promote tolerance toward "European Canadians" by sympathetically portraying the cultural background of the countries where the immigrants originated and by demonstrating the cultural creativity of European immigrants in Canada through translating and publishing their creative writing.[48] In his writing he attacked the assumptions of anglo-conformity, and advocated a multicultural society which would allow immigrants to maintain pride in their past.

". . . it would be tragic if there should be a clumsy stripping-away of all those spiritual associations with the past that help to give depth and beauty to life . . . If . . . we accept with Wilhelm von Humboldt 'the absolute and essential importance of human development in its richest diversity,' then we shall welcome every opportunity to save for our country every previous element of individuality that is available."[49]

Kirkconnell was not advocating complete separation of ethnic groups so that they might be preserved. He believed that assimilation needed to occur in the realm of political and economic values and institutions but he hoped that some of the conservative values and folk-culture of immigrants could be preserved.

Kirkconnell did not ignore the political differences within ethnic groups. Indeed, with the outbreak of World War II he wrote a book in which he attempted to expose and combat both fascist and communist elements in different ethnic groups.[50] But he was also active in attempts to bring various other factions of eastern European groups together in order to alleviate public criticism of divisions within ethnic groups.[51]

These advocates of pluralism believed that ethnic diversity was not incompatible with national unity. Unity need not mean uniformity. They believed that recognition of the cultural contributions of non-Anglo-Saxon groups would heighten the groups' feeling that they belonged to Canada and thus strengthen Canadian unity. But Gibbon and Kirkconnell were voices crying in the wilderness — a wilderness of discrimination and racism.

After World War II: The Emergence of Multiculturalism

136   The war period and early post-war period was a transitional time with respect to attitudes toward immigration and ethnicity. Although the war brought renewed hostility toward enemy aliens, a number of developments during the war eventually worked to undermine ethnic prejudice. During the arrival of the third wave of immigration in the late 1940s and 1950s, many pre-war prejudices lingered, and ethnic minorities encountered considerable pressures for conformity. But for a variety of intellectual, social, and demographic reasons, the ideology of cultural pluralism has been increasingly accepted in the post-World War II period. The post-war decline of racism and the growing influence of theories about cultural relativism opened the way for the emergence of pluralist ideas. The arrival of many intellectuals among the post-war political refugees from eastern Europe and the growth in the number of upwardly mobile second- and third-generation non-Anglo-Canadians, some of whom felt that they were not being fully accepted into Canadian society, increased the political pressures at both federal and provincial levels for greater recognition of Canada's ethnic diversity. Some suggested that this could be achieved through the appointment of senators of a particular ethnic origin, or through the introduction into the school curriculum of ethnic content and of ethnic languages as courses (and sometimes as languages of instruction).[52]

These demands for greater government recognition of "other ethnic groups" increased during the 1960s in response to the French-Canadian assertion of equal rights and the Pearson government's measures to assess and ensure the status of the French language and culture. In 1963 the Royal Commission on Bilingualism and Biculturalism was appointed to "inquire into and report upon the existing state of bilingualism and biculturalism in Canada and to recommend what steps should be taken to develop the Canadian Confederation on the basis of an equal partnership between the two founding races, taking into account the contribution made by the other ethnic groups to the cultural enrichment of Canada." Many non-British, non-French groups, but particularly Ukrainians, opposed the view that Canada was bicultural. By 1961, 26 percent of the Canadian population was of other than British or French ethnic origin; over two hundred newspapers were being published in languages other than French and English; there were fairly well-defined Italian, Jewish, Slavic and Chinese neighbourhoods in large Canadian cities, and there were visible rural concentrations of Ukrainians, Doukhobors, Hutterites and Mennonites scattered across the western provinces: thus, how was it possible for a royal commission to speak of Canada as a *bi*cultural country?

This feeling that biculturalism relegated all ethnic groups who were other than British or French to the status of second-class citizens helps explain the resistance some of these groups expressed to the policies and programs that were introduced to secure the status of the French language in Canada. The place of the so-called "other" ethnic groups in a bicultural society became a vexing question for federal politicians, who had originally hoped that steps to ensure French-Canadian rights would go a long way towards improving inter-ethnic relations in Canada. The partial resolution of this dilemma was the assertion in October 1971 by Prime Minister Trudeau that, in fact, Canada is a *multi*cultural country and that steps would be taken by the federal government to give public recognition to ethnic diversity through the introduction of a policy of multiculturalism. Several provinces with large numbers of non-Anglo Canadians have also initiated their own policies of multiculturalism.

137

Although most political leaders in English-speaking Canada have accepted and proclaimed the desirability of Canada's ethnic diversity, the Canadian public has not given unanimous support to pluralism. The debate over the place of ethnic groups in Canadian life continues, focusing on such questions as: Does the encouragement of pluralism only serve to perpetuate the vertical mosaic, in which class lines coincide with ethnic lines, or does it help break down class barriers by promoting acceptance of the legitimacy of cultural differences? Are the goals of current government policy — cultural pluralism and equality of opportunity — mutually compatible? Does the encouragement of ethnic group solidarity threaten the freedom of individuals in these groups, or can ethnic groups provide a liberating, rather than a restricting, context for identity? Does the encouragement of cultural diversity serve to perpetuate old-world rivalries, or will the recognition of the contributions of Canada's ethnic groups heighten their feeling that they belong in Canada and thus strengthen Canadian unity? Is government talk of multiculturalism just a way to attract the "ethnic vote," or is positive action necessary to preserve cultural pluralism when cultural diversity throughout the world is being eroded by the impact of industrial technology, mass communication and urbanization? Does the encouragement of multiculturalism simply heighten the visibility of the growing numbers of non-whites in the country and hinder their chances of full acceptance as individuals into Canadian life, or is a public policy of multiculturalism essential to an effective campaign against racism? The nature of these arguments suggest that the prevailing assumptions about immigration and ethnicity have changed over time in English-speaking Canada. They also suggest that the discussion about the role of immigration and ethnic groups in Canadian life is still an important, and unfinished, debate.

Notes

1. For a discussion of these three ideologies of assimilation in the United States, see Milton Gordon. *Assimilation in American Life* (New York, 1964).
2. L. G. Thomas, "The Umbrella and the Mosaic: The French-English Presence and the Settlement of the Canadian Prairie West," in J. A. Carroll ed., *Reflections of Western Historians*, (Tucson, Arizona, 1969) pp. 135–52; Allan Smith, "Metaphor and Nationality in North America," *Canadian Historical Review*, Vol. 51 #3, September, 1970.
3. The Canadian census has consistently classed the Irish as part of the "British" group.
4. Howard Palmer, *Land of the Second Chance: A History of Ethnic Groups in Southern Alberta*, Lethbridge, 1972; Norman Macdonald, *Canada Immigration and Colonization, 1841–1903*, Toronto, 1967; Harold Troper *Only Farmers Need Apply*, Toronto, 1972.
5. Donald, Avery, "Canadian Immigration Policy and the Foreign Navvy", *Canadian Historical Association Reports*, 1972; Edmund Bradwin, *Bunkhouse Man*, New York, 1928, H. Troper and R. Harney, *Immigrants*, Toronto, 1975.
6. Donald Avery, "Canadian Immigration Policy, 1896–1919: The Anglo-Canadian Perspective," Unpublished Ph.D., University of Western Ontario, 1973. Cornelius Jaenan, "Federal Policy Vis-à-Vis Ethnic Groups", unpublished paper, Ottawa, 1971; Howard Palmer, "Nativism and Ethnic Tolerance in Alberta, 1880–1920", unpublished M.A., University of Alberta, 1971; "Nativism and Ethnic Tolerance in Alberta, 1920–1972, unpublished Ph.D., York University, 1973.
7. H. Palmer, "Nativism and Ethnic Tolerance in Alberta, 1880–1920", unpublished M.A. University of Alberta, 1971, Chapters 1 and 2; H. Troper *Only Farmers Need Apply* (Toronto, 1972); D. J. Hall, "Clifford Sifton: Immigration and Settlement Policy, 1896–1905" in H. Palmer, ed., *The Settlement of the West* (Calgary, 1977), pp. 60-85.
8. H. Troper, "The Creek Negroes of Oklahoma and Canadian Immigration, 1909–11". *Canadian Historical Review*, September, 1972, p. 272–288.
9. Rev. George Bryce, "Past and Future of Our Race", *Proceedings*, Canadian Club of Toronto, 1911, p. 6–7; C. A. Magrath, *Canada's Growth and Problems Affecting It*, (Ottawa, 1910); Goldwin Smith in *Weekly Sun*, Feb. 1, 1899, Sept. 17, 1902, Sept. 23, 1903, May 18, 1904, Aug. 16, 1905; W. A. Griesbach, *I Remember*, Toronto, 1946, pp. 214–217, 220–221.
10. Carl Berger, *Sense of Power*, Toronto, 1970, p. 117–188.
11. Morton, *In A Sea of Sterile Mountains*, Vancouver, 1974; W. P. Ward, "The Oriental Immigrant and Canada's Protestant Clergy, 1858–1925", *B.C. Studies*, Summer, 1974 p. 40–55; Ted Ferguson, *A White Man's Country*, Toronto, 1975.
12. D. J. Hall, "Clifford Sifton: Immigration and Settlement Policy: 1896–1905", in H. Palmer, ed., *The Settlement of the West* (Calgary, 1977), pp. 79–80.
13. W. L. Morton, *Manitoba*, A History, Toronto, 1957, p. 161, 162.
14. J. B. Hedges. *Building the Canadian West*, New York, 1939; Frank Epp, *Mennonites in Canada*, 1786–1920, Toronto, 1974.
15. Cornelius J. Jaenen, "Ruthenian Schools in Western Canada 1897–1919" *Paedagogica Historica*, International Journal of the History of Education, X.3; 1970, pp. 517–541. Donald Avery, "Canadian Immigration Policy", pp. 374–420.
16. Avery, Ibid. p. 408.
17. Kate Foster, *Our Canadian Mosaic*, Toronto, 1926; J. T. M. Anderson, *The Education of the New Canadian*, Toronto, 1918; C. B. Sissons, *Bi-Lingual Schools in Canada*, Toronto, 1917; W. G. Smith, *Building the Nation*, Toronto, 1922. For a discussion of some of the concrete activities involved in these "Canadianization" programs, see R. Harney and H. Troper, *Immigrants* Chapter 4.
18. J. S. Woodsworth, *Strangers Within our Gates*, Winnipeg, 1909; Marilyn Barber, "Nationalism, Nativism and the Social Gospel: The Protestant Church Response to Foreign Immigrants in Western Canada, 1897–1914" in Richard Allen ed. *The Social Gospel in Canada*, Ottawa, 1975, pp. 186–226.
19. Quoted in Barbara Nicholson, "Feminism in the Prairie Provinces to 1916", unpublished M.A. University of Calgary, 1974, p. 71. For the views of womens' groups on immigration and the role of immigrants in Canada society, see Ibid. pp. 83–85, 86, 114, 121, 133, 165–169, 186–187.
20. Reported in *Lethbridge Herald* May 29, 1919.

21. J. S. Woodsworth, "Social Conditions in Rural Communities in the Prairie Provinces", Winnipeg, 1917, p. 38.
22. For a fairly extensive chronicling of patterns of discrimination against a number of minority groups see Morris Davis and J. F. Krauter, *The Other Canadians*, Toronto, 1971.
23. For an analysis of the various causes of ethnic stratification (settlement patterns, time of arrival, immigrant and ethnic occupations, ethnic values, language barriers and discrimination and exploitation) see Book IV, *Report of the Royal Commission on Bilingualism and Biculturalism*, Ottawa, 1969, Chapter 2.
24. Carole Henderson, "The Ethnicity Factor in Anglo-Canadian Folkloristics", *Canadian Ethnic Studies*, Vol. VII No. 2, forthcoming.
25. *Canadian Annual Review*, 1923, p. 264–265; 1924–25, p. 190–192.
26. *Canada Year Book*, 1941, p. 733.
27. Olha Woycenko, *The Ukrainians in Canada* (Winnipeg, 1967); Victor Turek, *Poles in Manitoba* (Toronto, 1967), p. 43; J. M. Kirschbaum, *Slovaks in Canada* (Toronto, 1967), p. 101; Edmund Heier, "A Study of German Lutheran and Catholic Immigrants in Canada formerly residing in Czarist and Soviet Russia", unpublished M.A. (University of British Columbia, 1955) Chapter 3.
28. R. B. Bennett, House of Commons *Debates*, June 7, 1929, p. 3925–7.
29. Ibid.
30. H. Palmer, "Nativism in Alberta," 1925–1930, *Canadian Historical Association Reports*, 1974, pp. 191–199.
31. G. E. Lloyd, "National Building", *Banff Crag and Canyon*, Aug. 17, 1928.
32. A. R. M. Lower, *Canadians in the Making*, Don Mills Ontario, 1958. Chapter 22, 27.
33. J. S. Woodsworth, "Nation Building," *University Magazine*, 1917 pp. 85–99. F. W. Baumgartner, "Central European Immigration", *Queen's Quarterly* (Winter, 1930), p. 183–192; Walter Murray, "Continental Europeans in Western Canada", *Queen's Quarterly*, 1931; P. M. Bryce, *The Value of the Continental Immigrant to Canada* (Ottawa, 1928), E. L. Chicanot, "Homesteading the Citizen: Canadian Festivals Promote Cultural Exchange", *Commonwealth*, May, 1929, pp. 94–95; E. K. Chicanot, "Moulding a Nation", *Dalhousie Review*, July, 1929, pp. 232–237. J. H. Haslam, "Canadianization of the Immigrant Settler", *Annals*, May, 1923, pp. 45–49; E. H. Oliver, "The Settlement of Saskatchewan to 1914" *Transactions of the Royal Society*, 1926, pp. 63–87; Agnes Laut, "Comparing the Canadian and American Melting Pots", *Current Opinion*, Vol. 70, April, 1921, pp. 458–462; Kate Foster *Our Canadian Mosaic* (Toronto, 1926). Robert England, "Continental Europeans in Western Canada", *Queen's Quarterly*, 1931.
34. Robert England, *The Central European Immigrant in Canada* (Toronto, 1929).
35. John Blue, *Alberta Past and Present* (Chicago, 1924), p. 210.
36. There were some advocates of the melting pot prior to 1920, but it did not gain widespread acceptance until the 1920's. See H. Palmer, "Nativism in Alberta, 1880–1920" Chapter 1. Marilyn Barber, "Nationalism, Nativism, and the Social Gospel".
37. Douglas Cole, "John S. Ewart and Canadian Nationalism", *Canadian Historical Association Report*, 1969, p. 66.
38. John Diefenbaker, *One Canada*, Toronto, 1975, p. 140, 141, 218–19, 274.
39. H. Palmer, "Nativism in Alberta, 1920–1972" Chapter 3.
40. James Gray, *The Roar of the Twenties*, (Toronto, 1975) Chapter 11; Lita-Rose Betcherman, *The Swastika and the Maple Leaf*. (Don Mills, Ontario) 1975.
41. Barry Broadfoot, *Ten Lost Years*, p. 25, 70, 76, 132, 156–164, 186, 279.
42. Ibid p. 132.
43. Ibid p. 186.
44. Ivan Avakumovic, *The Communist Party in Canada: A History*, (Toronto, 1975) p. 66–67; Lita-Rose Betcherman, *The Swastika and the Maple Leaf*, Chapter 5.
45. Ibid.
46. H. Palmer, "Nativism in Alberta, 1920–1972" Chapter 3.
47. M. A. Jones, *American Immigration*, (Chicago, 1960) p. 298. For fictional treatments of the second generation's repudiation of the ethnic past in an attempt to become accepted see John Marlyn, *Under the Ribs of Death*, (Toronto, 1951) and Magdalena Eggleston: *Mountain Shadows*, (New York, 1955) p. 122. See also *Change of Name*, Toronto: Canadian Institute of Cultural Research, 1965.
48. Watson Kirkconnell, *The European Heritage, A Synopsis of European Cultural Achievement*, London, 1930; *Canadian Overtones*, Winnipeg, 1935. For a complete listing of Kirkconnell's work, see the list in his memoirs, *A Slice of Canada* (Toronto, 1967) p. 374–375. For an assessment of his work see J. R. C. Perkin ed. *The Undoing of Babel*. (Toronto, 1975).
49. W. Kirkconnell, Trans., *Canadian Overtones*, preface.
50. Watson Kirkconnell, *Canada Europe and Hitler*, (Toronto, 1939).
51. W. Kirkconnell, *A Slice of Canada*.
52. For documentary evidence of changing ethnic attitudes in the post-war era and the emergence of multiculturalism as an idea and as a governmental policy, see H. Palmer, *Immigration and the Rise of Multiculturalism* (Toronto, 1975), chapter 3.

139

Under the Ribs of Death*

JOHN MARLYN

For hours on end he sat on the roof of the woodshed silently contained within himself, re-living Saturdays that had come and gone, lost in unfolding fantasies that formed themselves sometimes about Eric, sometimes about his mother. He moved from the far circumference of her life to its centre. He related himself to her, subjected her to a thousand perils and saved her from them all — and sighed at their unlikelihood. Her presence hovered about him. Enough that she liked cleanliness; he washed himself half a dozen times a day: that she had once frowned at his manner of speech, and she accomplished by the mere lowering of a brow what school teachers and his father and Mr Crawford had tried in vain to do.

140

The outer aspects of his life receded. He held himself proudly aloof from the affairs of his family. He moved through his neighbourhood with unseeing eyes.

The summer holidays arrived. He remained alone, snug and secure in the cocoon he had woven about himself.

One night, sitting in his accustomed place, he overheard his parents talking in the yard below. With an air of supreme condescension he raised his head and listened. It appeared that his father had made the last payment on Onkel Janos' ticket. Sandor curbed his excitement. It was undignified and out of keeping with his highborn rôle.

But a week or so later he became aware that his mother was planning a party, and from the evidence that had begun to accumulate, a party such as Henry Avenue had never known.

The attitude he had imposed upon himself began to show signs of strain. A telegram from his uncle shattered it.

Early that Sunday morning on which his uncle was to arrive, the kitchen began to fill with women — friends and acquaintances who had been invited to the party and had come to help. It was sweltering outside; in the kitchen the heat was almost unbearable. The women moved around in their petticoats, long shapeless affairs with flounces and lace, black and purple and yellow — an amusing sight to Sandor who stood in a corner laughing until his mother sent him upstairs to make sure that his uncle's room was in order. Mr Schwalbe had consented to sleep in the outer attic so that Frau Hunyadi's brother would have a room to himself, for the first few days at least.

In the doorway of the attic, Sandor paused. All the beds had been covered with thick flannel sheets and on them, sucking their thumbs in sleep, squalling, pink and gurgling or blue with moist anger, lay the babies. Watching over them were the grown-up daughters of the women downstairs.

Once he might have stopped to listen to them. Now he simply looked into Mr Schwalbe's cubicle and passed them by. They reminded him too much of the maids he had seen in Eric's neighbourhood. They laughed too loud and too long. Their clothes were too bright and too fancy.

He went into the toilet, took a small fragment of mirror out of his hiding-place under the floorboards and, holding it at arm's length, examined his new blue serge sailor-suit which his mother had bought — by instalments — with the money he had earned. He straightened the collar and continued to look at himself until he heard his mother calling to him from the foot of the stairs. It was time to go. He was to meet his father at the station.

A few minutes later he was on his way. He came to the hotel and reverting to his former rôle, passed proudly and sedately below the windows of the lobby.

141

Then he saw the crowd moving toward the station and became Sandor Hunyadi again, pressing excitedly and eagerly to the great doors. He saw his father standing there in his best black suit which he wore at Christmas and New Year. It was like new. Whenever he removed it from the closet, he smiled and stroked it and clicked his tongue at Old-Country craftsmanship.

Sandor waved to him. His father waved back. They had been on good terms ever since the summer holidays had started. His father took him by the hand.

They followed the crowd into the vast echoing cavern to a rope barrier. Sandor had been here before and it had always been crowded, but now for the first time he sensed the expectancy of the people around him. Now and then the station reverberated to the jargon of the train-caller. On the platform above, he heard the familiar, ponderous clatter of the engines. The suppressed excitement of the crowds began to affect him. He heard his father call out a greeting to a friend and realized that his father was as excited as he was. His father did not quite approve of Onkel Janos. Was it only because he was an adventurer, or were there other hidden reasons?

From the upper level came the interminable slow creak and groan of a train coming to a stop. Behind him the crowd strained forward, pressing him against the rope barrier. All was still. There reached them the shrill cry of a child; a voice in English giving directions. Then the long-awaited tramp of feet, growing louder and louder, reaching the head of the stairs, and finally the first of the new arrivals emerged from the gates and looked about them timidly and fearfully, bent under the weight of their belongings. Reluctantly they moved forward, pushed ahead by those who came behind.

Sandor turned pale at the sight of them. They stood there, awkward and begrimed, the men in tight-fitting wrinkled clothes, with their wrists and ankles sticking out, unshaven and foreign-looking, the women in kerchiefs and voluminous skirts and men's shoes . . . exactly the way his grandmother looked in that picture in the front room. And it was this that was frightening. They were so close to him. Only a few months or years — a few words and recently acquired habits — separated his parents from them. The kinship was odious. He knew how hard it was for his parents to change their ways. But they were changing. They used tinned goods sometimes at home now, and store-bought bread when they had enough money. English food was appearing on their table, the English language in their home. Slowly, very slowly, they were changing. They were becoming Canadians. And now here it stood. Here was the nightmare survival of themselves, mocking and dragging them back to their shameful past.

Sandor looked up at his father. His lips trembled at the expression on his father's face. It was as though the embers of something long forgotten had been stirred into flame by the sight of these people and now cast an ardent glow upon his features. His eyes half-closed, he murmured something to himself in his native tongue. Sandor tugged at his arm. His father never noticed. Sandor turned back and glanced at the newcomers. The foremost among them had faltered and finally come to a stop at the sight of the crowd in front of them.

The two groups stared at one another. Then a man's voice cried "Ilonka!" The new arrivals wavered. A woman shifted the child in her arms and waved. The man called to her again, and before they were in each other's arms the barrier was down and the two groups were one. The station echoed their gladness in many tongues. They touched one another and cried. They embraced and smiled and stood apart and stared into eyes familiar and yet grown strange.

Sandor scowled. There were probably dozens of people here who could call his father "landsmann." As he followed his father with reluctant steps to the foot of the stairs, he wondered with a sudden shudder of disgust whether his uncle was as foreign-looking and as dirty as these others. Off to one side of him, he heard someone calling his father by his first name. He caught sight of a tall, dark man moving towards them, with an enormous wickerwork trunk on his shoulders and a miscellaneous array of packages and boxes in his hand. His teeth against dark lips and a swarthy complexion flashed in a dazzling smile. Onkel Janos, Sandor thought with a sinking heart. He was unshaven; he wore a collarless shirt, and a faded green jacket that looked as though it had once been part of a uniform. Ten feet away he shouted a greeting at them, dropped his belongings, and sprang forward to meet them with outstretched hands.

"By gollies, hullo," he shouted, and laughed uproariously. The two men began shaking hands and talking excitedly in Hungarian. Sandor caught the sound of his mother's name, and once, while his uncle's glance swept appraisingly over him, his own. He stood still while his uncle patted him on the head and shouted "Kolossal." For his uncle everything was evidently "kolossal." Sandor crept around behind his father and waited. The only thing to look forward to now was the food and possibly, though not very probably, his uncle's present.

The two men began collecting the parcels and boxes. On the street, Sandor dropped a few paces behind them. Gollies hullo, he moaned. So this was the Pirate Uncle. This was how an adventurer looked and smelled. This was the man who had fought the Turks — who had been captured by the Arabs and who had been a millionaire several times over.

He had arrived just in time. With his ticket paid for they were just beginning to lay aside a little money every week. Now they would probably have to buy him clothes and feed him until he found a job.

Half a dozen steps or so behind them, Sandor stood still while his uncle looked about him. He drew a little nearer when he discovered that they were speaking German. His uncle wanted to know if there was a place where he could wash and shave before going on. Joseph Hunyadi explained that he had already thought of that. He hoped Janos wouldn't mind; he had taken the liberty of buying him a few things: underwear, a shirt, a pair of socks.

Yeah. That's how it was with his father, Sandor thought. He could make a gesture worthy of a millionaire and borrow the money to do it.

143

There was a place only a few blocks away, his father continued, where Janos could have a bath and a shave.

Sandor walked on behind until they reached the barber shop. His father and his uncle went downstairs. He sat down despondently in the empty pool room until a barber who had once lived with them as a non-paying boarder called to him and asked him if he wanted a haircut. The boss was out, he explained. Sandor nodded, and thanked him as he walked back into the barber shop. He sat down and closed his eyes. It was warm and quiet here, the air filled with the odours of the lotions and the soap. A fly droned on the ceiling. From the basement came the faint hiss of escaping steam; above him, the rhythmic snick of the scissors.

He had been up since early morning. He nodded and fell into a light slumber, from which he was awakened by the sound of laughter. He opened his eyes to discover his father, two barbers, and a stranger, all smiling at him. Sandor blinked, smiled back weakly, and felt his hair. It was cool and moist. He blinked again, and then turned back to the stranger, who was still laughing. He was tall and elegantly dressed. There was an air of distinction about him.

Sandor rubbed his eyes. The stranger laughed uproariously and cried, "Kolossal!" It was a complete transformation. His uncle was a foreigner no longer. He reminded Sandor strongly of the men in the hotel lobby.

He jumped to his feet. "Onkel Janos!" he cried.

His uncle bent down and with a swoop raised him aloft. "Hullo," he roared.

"Hullo," Sandor cried joyfully.

"By gollies, hullo hullo, hullo," his uncle echoed. "I spik English? You will learn me, ya?"

Sandor nodded, too happy to speak.

He felt as though he were walking on air as they left the barber shop.

The wickerwork trunk had been left behind to be picked up later. But the shoe-box, Onkel Janos said as he thrust it into Sandor's hands with a promising wink, this box was to be handled carefully. Sandor winked back and tucked it under his arm; it felt reassuringly heavy and solidly packed. He took his uncle's hand as they turned down Logan Avenue.

He snorted impatiently as his father and uncle began talking Hungarian again. Finally, he caught his uncle's eye. "Onkel Janos," he said, "please talk German. I can't understand."

"You don't speak Hungarian?"

Sandor shook his head. "I've forgotten."

"I've tried to teach him Hungarian," Joseph Hunyadi said. "Maybe when he's a little older . . . "

"But you speak English?" Onkel Janos asked, turning to Sandor.

"I talk English very well," Sandor said, and repeated it in German.

"Of course, you speak English. And why not? This is an English-speaking country isn't it? You want to get on. I can see just by looking at you that you're the kind of boy who's going to get ahead."

He turned away from Sandor and looked across at Joseph Hunyadi. "What does the boy want with Hungarian?" he asked. "Take my advice, Joseph, don't addle his brains."

Sandor tightened his grip on his uncle's hand. They turned down Henry Avenue, and walked on. A few hundred feet from the house, Onkel Janos suddenly raised his head. "I smell goulash," he roared, and lengthened his stride.

"The back way," Sandor cried, tugging at his hand. "Ma said to use the back door."

The back yard was full of children. On the roof of the woodshed sat the sons of the invited guests, taunting those who now gathered below, having nosed their way to the origin of the odours that had been drifting through the neighbourhood all morning. In their midst stood Frau Hunyadi handing out cookies. The invited urchins screamed. They were not being given any on the fantastic ground that it would spoil their appetites. From their perch on the roof they yelled down their defiance and threats.

As Frau Hunyadi turned back to the screen door, she caught sight of her brother. In an instant she was in his arms. "Ach, Janos, Janos." She held him close to her. They embraced and beheld each other at arm's length as well as their tears would allow. The children grew silent. Sandor shifted uncomfortably. His mother and Onkel Janos began to talk to one another in Hungarian.

Now a woman's face appeared at the window, and then another. Frau Hunyadi, catching sight of them, whispered something to her brother. To Sandor's relief they spoke German. It was very hot in the kitchen, his mother explained. And the front room was filled with tables and chairs. They had arranged a little party. Would Janos mind . . .

Onkel Janos kissed her. The women streamed into the back yard from the kitchen, red and smiling. And behind them came their husbands, their hands and faces burned dark with the sun, painters and carpenters and sewer-diggers; and a pale shoe-maker, a Hegelian philosopher and close friend of Joseph Hunyadi.

The women began gathering around Onkel Janos, to be introduced. Sandor grinned from ear to ear at his uncle's performance. He had drawn himself erect. Now he twirled the ends of his moustache, and with a faint click of his heels and a slight bow, bent over and kissed Frau Szabo's hand. Frau Szabo flushed and giggled. Then Frau Gombos.

Their husbands smiled indulgently. The kids on the roof looked on in silent delight. Sandor laughed to himself. He felt he was beginning to understand. His uncle had a way with him that made people smile.

When the introductions were over, the women returned to the house; there were still a few things to be done in the kitchen. The men had been told to stay where they were. They pulled some logs off the woodpile and settled down to a comfortable smoke.

Sandor followed his mother and uncle upstairs into Mr Schwalbe's *145* cubicle. He remained in the doorway while they seated themselves on the cot. To his annoyance they began to talk in Hungarian again, and they talked for a long time. He caught the names of other uncles and distant relations. His mother began to cry. Sandor shifted impatiently. Finally his uncle noticed him, reached out, and took the shoe-box from him.

"Guess what?" he asked as he broke the string.

Sandor smiled and shook his head. This was going to be something, a real present. He knew it. Everything his uncle did exceeded one's expectations.

Onkel Janos opened the box and handed him a long shining cardboard tube, gaily decorated with laughing fishes and mermaids, with sailing ships and benign, droll monsters cavorting in a sky-blue sea.

Sandor eyed it with dismay. It looked like a kid's toy. From the expression on his uncle's face, he suspected that a joke was being played on him. "What it it?" he asked.

"Kolossal!" his uncle shouted, and burst into laughter.

"It's a joke," Sandor cried. "It's not my present at all."

Onkel Janos slapped his knees and roared with laughter. "Here, I'll show you," he said at last. "It's called a kaleidoscope. Look." He took the tube, held it up to the light, and peered through it. "So," he said, and handed it back.

Sandor placed his eye to the peep-hole and gasped.

"Turn it," his uncle said.

He turned it. There was a click, and behold, a new world. Another turn and another in a riot of colour, like a splintered rainbow; cool, deep-green gems, and frivolous pink ones, water-blue and orange jewels in triangles and squares and crescents glittering and flashing before his eye, ever changing, ever new.

He set it aside, finally, and gazed across at his uncle with a look of deep affection.

"Thank your uncle, Sandor," his mother said.

"Ho, something for you too," Onkel Janos cried, handing her a small leather case.

She opened it. A slow flush came over her cheeks. Sandor craned his neck and saw a pair of gold ear-rings with small red stones, and a brooch. She kissed her brother tenderly. "You shouldn't have done this, Janos," she said. "You know you shouldn't. But they are beautiful."

Onkel Janos was already engrossed in pulling out more shredded paper from his shoe-box. "For Joseph," he said, extracting an amber-stemmed pipe. "I'll give it to him later."

"You really shouldn't have done this, Janos. You've spent all your money, haven't you? . . . And a new suit," she exclaimed. "I never even noticed. It's very becoming."

Onkel Janos grasped her hand. "Here. Feel," he said. "English tweed."

"It reminds me of so many things to see you sitting here like this," she said quietly. "You haven't changed a bit."

"And neither have you. You're as beautiful as ever, Helena."

Sandor's eyebrows rose. He watched the colour ebb and flow on his mother's cheeks.

She laughed softly and shook her head. Her laughter had a girlish trill. Sandor's incredulity grew. He had never heard his mother laugh like this.

"The whole village went into mourning the day Joseph took you away," Onkel Janos continued. "At least, the young men did . . . The girls? Hmm!" He rolled his eyes, raised his right hand, and gave his moustache a twirl.

Frau Hunyadi laughed.

Sandor looked on in astonishment. His mother's lips, always so tightly pressed together, were now parted softly in a smile. He scarcely knew her. She looked strange and beautiful. He shifted uneasily.

As she raised her arm to fit her ear-rings in place, he bent over impulsively, threw his arms about her, and kissed her.

"Why, Sandor!" she said in surprise. He drew away, embarassed, and looked at his uncle, who merely laughed and caught him between his knees and rumpled his hair some more.

His mother rose to her feet. "There's so much to talk about, I don't know where to start," she said. "But I'll have to go downstairs now . . . Come, Sandor. Onkel Janos is going to have a little nap."

Sandor wandered about the kitchen until his mother asked him to leave. The men in the yard were talking about the Old Country. With the exception of Willi Schumacher, the kids on the roof were all too young to play with. He went into the lane and looked into his kaleidoscope until his arm grew numb holding it to his eye. He smiled to himself as he lowered it. Next Saturday he would take it along and show it to Eric, and maybe even lend it to him for a week.

As he walked back into the yard, Willi Schumacher called down to him, asking him what he was carrying. Sandor paused. The thought that flashed across his mind was fully developed by the time he was up on the roof.

Five minutes later he was doing a roaring business. None of his customers had any ready money, but their fathers were down there in the yard below and feeling in an expansive mood. A few of the boys came back with nickels. These were permitted to hold the tube in their own hands. Some, who had been able to raise only a few coppers, found their exclamations dying in their throats, the tube was snatched away so fast.

When it was over, Sandor thrust his hand into his pocket and let the coins trickle through his fingers. In fifteen minutes, he had made forty-three cents — almost as much as he earned for a morning's work. As he climbed down, he caught sight of his father and Onkel Janos looking down at him from the attic window. Onkel Janos was smiling. But in that brief glance at his father, he knew that there was going to be trouble. His father motioned to him to come upstairs.

Sandor walked slowly through the yard, wondering what was wrong. He shrugged his shoulders and went upstairs. They were waiting for him behind Mr Schwalbe's cubicle. If he was going to be shamed, he thought, at least it was not going to be in the presence of all those girls . . . .

147

His father turned on him the moment he appeared. His face was livid. He raised his hand, dropped it — and Sandor, looking straight ahead, saw the clenched fingers in a convulsive fist, darkly veined, opening and closing and opening again.

"You demand money of your friends before you would let them see your gift?" his father asked in German.

Sandor looked up at him in astonishment.

"Sure," he said. "Why not?"

"You're not ashamed," his father asked, "to make your friends pay?"

"They're not my friends," Sandor replied. "And anyway, what did I do that's wrong? They'da done the same to me if they were in my place . . . ."

"They are our guests," his father shouted. "You sent them down to their parents for money to pay you. Have you no shame at all? Your gift has not been an hour in your possession and already you have turned it into something dirty by contaminating it with money."

Sandor lowered his head. To be humiliated like this in front of his uncle, on the day or his arrival, and for no reason that he could understand!

"I didn't do anything wrong," he cried tearfully. "Anybody woulda done the same as I did." He saw his uncle shaking his head at him, but with a faint sympathetic smile on his lips. "It's my present, isn't it?" he shouted. "I can do what I like with it."

He fled into Mr Schwalbe's cubicle. At the door, he saw Onkel Janos remonstrating with his father, and as he closed it, caught a glimpse of his brother on one of the beds outside, lying peacefully there on his back, playing with his toes.

Poor little punk, he thought. He doesn't know yet what kind of a family he's in . . .

He lay down on the cot, his eyes tight against the threatening tears, his mind filled with the familiar pain and pleasure of crushing his father and humiliating him as he himself had been humiliated. Then he thought of how things might have been if he had been older. And he remembered that Eric too had trouble with his father. It was something you had to bear until you were grown up. He thought of how his uncle had taken his part. He wiped his eyes.

The door opened suddenly and his uncle entered the room. He sat down, sighed, and removed his shoes. Then he yawned, flinging out his arms as far as they would go, which was not very far, for the cubicle was only five feet wide and as a result the knuckles of his left hand struck the beaverboard partition a blow that seemed to Sandor to rock the entire attic. The plaster between the sheets of beaverboard shot out against the far wall. Sandor began to smile. His uncle merely raised his eyebrows and asked Sandor to move over. The springs groaned under his weight.

"Your father has great plans for you," he began. "A fine life is in store for you. A good education, an established position. Some day people will call you Herr Doktor. You will be a wealthy man. Does this please you?"

148   Sandor shook his head. "Pa doesn't want me to be rich," he cried. "He wants me to be like him, instead of like other people. He thinks everything that's got anything to do with money is wrong. Honest-to-God, Onkel Janos," he continued passionately, "Pa won't ever make enough money for me to go to University. He just talks like that . . . . And even if I could go, I wouldn't. You don't have to go to University to get rich."

His uncle stared up at the ceiling for a long time. "But your father works very hard," he said at last.

Sandor raised himself on one elbow. "Pa works hard," he admitted. His voice broke. "But he doesn't make enough," he continued. "And what makes Ma so mad is that he takes in boarders even when they don't pay."

His uncle turned and looked at him in silence. "I see," he said.

"Some day, I'm going to make a lot of money," Sandor said. "And Ma won't have to worry any more. I won't let her take in any boarders, and Pa won't have to work. I'll look after the whole family."

His uncle smiled and nodded. "So? That's fine," he said "It's good to hear such things. But how will you earn this money?"

Sandor flushed. "I'm going to quit school as soon as I can, and get a job. In an office. That's how people get rich in this country. Working in offices. And I'm already earning money," he added. "A dollar every week, cutting grass for rich people. Next week maybe I'll be making a dollar and a half when I get another customer."

"But that's a great deal of money," his uncle said.

"That's how things are in this country," Sandor explained.

Onkel Janos sighed and pulled a package of cigarettes and a box of matches from his pocket. He flicked the package open and popped a cigarette into his mouth, then lit it and letting the cigarette dangle from his lower lip, he gave a snort and blew at the flame of the match in a great sweeping gust that quite extinguished it and sent a shower of sparks and ashes into the air intermingled with the smoke from the bright-glowing end of the cigarette.

Sandor looked at him, hungrily intent upon the mighty inhalation which caused the cigarette so visibly to shorten, almost tasting the long-drawn, thin blue smoke streaming slowly and deliciously out of his uncle's hairy nostrils. His uncle had a way about him, a special way. Everything he did was just right. You felt that the way he did a thing was the only way it could ever be done.

He lay on his back watching the smoke trickle out of his uncle's nostrils. He watched until he could stand it no longer. "Onkel Janos," he pleaded, "give me a puff, will you?"

His uncle raised his eyebrows. "You smoke already?"

"I've been smoking for years."

His uncle looked at him thoughtfully as he handed him a cigarette. "And girls, too," he said "I suppose you know all about girls."

"What is there to know?" Sandor asked. "They're all the same, aren't they?"

"You think so?" his uncle inquired, and nodded. "Maybe you're right." he said.

149

Sandor felt himself flushing. Out of the corner of his eyes he glanced at his uncle to see if he was laughing at him. But Onkel Janos was very soberly crushing the remains of his cigarette in the lid of a jam tin.

"So you're already earning a dollar and a half a week," he said. "You've been smoking for years and you know all about girls. It is as I said to your father. He doesn't have to worry about you. You're the kind of boy who's going to get along in this country."

"And so will you," Sandor cried. "You look like an English millionaire in your new suit. Nobody could tell you just came to Canada a few hours ago."

Onkel Janos laughed. Grabbing him by the middle he lifted him in the air for a moment, then dropped him on the cot and pretended to wrestle with him. Sandor screamed with pleasure.

He was weak with laughter when his uncle finally let him go. He was about to retrieve his cigarette which had fallen to the floor when he heard the sound of footsteps on the lower front stairs. He listened intently and crushed his cigarette in the jam-tin lid. "It's Ma," he said.

His uncle grinned. "Go and tell her you'll wake me," he whispered, and winked. Sandor winked back. He opened the door and ran down the steps to the first landing. His mother stopped and looked up at him.

"You want me to call Onkel Janos, Ma?"

"Yes, call him Sandor. Everything's ready now."

Sandor ran back upstairs. Onkel Janos was lying on his side, breathing heavily. Sandor smiled softly.

"Onkel Janos. It's all right now," he said.

His uncle rose, combed his hair, and put on his shoes. They went downstairs.

Sandor's mouth fell open as he entered the living-room. All the tables they had borrowed from their neighbours that morning had been placed end to end. With wedges under their legs they were now all the same height, and since they were covered with several white tablecloths whose edges overlapped, the whole thing looked like one table, long and immense in the little room. The linen gleamed, the dishes sparkled. But Sandor's attention was fastened upon the head of the table where, in all its splendour, stood the Hunyadi geranium. For the occasion, the jam tin in which it stood was covered with a piece of green crepe.

Sandor looked at it in astonishment. Against the cool crisp background, where everything glistened so invitingly, it seemed to have taken on fresh colour and life. Its blood-red blossoms gave an air of festivity to the room. How it had ever managed to survive at all was a mystery. Year in and year out, it stood on the front-room window-ledge. In winter, the panes froze over; in summer they were black with rain-smeared grime. The Hunyadis had not only to water the plant, but also, since the window faced the freight-yards, to dust its thick limp leaves and blow away the specks of soot that lay like so many black sins upon its petals. Sometimes, they forgot to water it; sometimes in the winter when they were short of coal for the frontroom stove it was kept above the kitchen range. His mother had tried to grow other things, delicate fragile things with subtle odours and gracious forms, but one season on Henry Avenue and they were dead. Only the geraniums survived. And in window after window on Henry Avenue they stood, earthy and sturdy, throwing up leaves so that they might blossom and give their colour in lonely splendour to a neighbourhood whose only workaday tone was an abiding grey.

Now it stood at the head of the table to welcome Onkel Janos who, as he passed by, plucked a blossom and stuck it in his lapel.

Sandor followed suit and trotted after his uncle into the kitchen.

A moment later he heard the strains of an accordion in the back yard. The screen door banged as Long Thomas, a neighbour, entered with his accordion, flanked on either side by one of the Nemeth twins. Long Thomas was well over six feet tall, sad and gaunt. The great bald nodding heads of the twins came scarcely to his elbows. With their fiddles under their arms, they walked sedately beside him, their dark eyes infinitely guileless. Upon a few rare occasions Sandor had visited them in their shack by the river. In the winter they made raffia baskets; in the summer, willow flower-stands. But no matter what the season, there was always time for music. No party was complete without them. By long-established custom their fee had come to consist of all the beer they could drink and as much food as they could eat.

Behind them swarmed the children, screaming with laughter. Long Thomas stopped, flung an incredibly long leg into the air, did a short little jig, and walked into the front room.

As though guided by some infallible sense, the twins made straight for the corner where the beer barrel stood. They drank in a way that made Sandor's mouth water even though he hated the smell of beer.

When they had finished, they sat down with their mugs of beer beside them, adjusted their instruments, and began to play. They played with verve, gusto, sweat, and love. Their eyes closed, their bodies swayed, their pink domes nodded, their fingers flew. Long Thomas finished his beer and joined them.

But now without warning the song changed to a Hungarian dance. Played by the Nemeth twins to a houseful of Hungarians, it was irresistible. From the kitchen came the sound of shouting and laughing and the impatient clacking of heels. Then to the loud delight of Sandor and the children, who had gathered around the musicians, Onkel Janos came waltzing into the front room with Frau Szabo in his arms. Sandor could not make up his mind whether to look at his uncle or receive the admiring glances of those around him for possessing such a relative. For Onkel Janos did not merely dance. There were times when Sandor could have sworn that neither Onkel Janos nor his partner had their feet on the ground. He spun her around, did a series of weird little sidesteps and then, while she whirled alone, leaped up, snapped his fingers, clicked his heels in mid-air, and shouted incomprehensible rhymes in Hungarian. Frau Szabo's face grew flushed. She smiled happily. Her bosom strained alarmingly against the fabric of her bodice.

151

The twins, watching them, nodded and grinned. Then their eyes and their mouths closed simultaneously and sublime smiles settled on their faces. The tempo of their playing became frenzied. More and more of the guests came from the kitchen and back-yard; a man would laugh, look shyly at his wife, and step out. The room grew so crowded one could scarcely move. The narrow aisle between the wall of children and the row of tables was filled with people dancing.

But no one danced as his uncle did, Sandor thought. Everything he did became appropriate, but only because he himself had done it.

When the music stopped, Sandor followed him to the corner where the twins were. With a few words, he had them laughing uproariously. They looked droll with their pink tongues flickering in the dark caverns of their mouths.

But now the guests were beginning to respond to Frau Hunyadi's pleas. They were gradually seating themselves at the table. Frau Hunyadi's friends helped her to serve.

Sandor pushed his way forward to the table set up for the older children. He sat down where he could watch his uncle.

The food arrived, the hot steaming fragrance of it filling the room, savoury and varied and as spicy as an adventure, rich with the treasured cooking-lore of the whole of Europe. Crumb by crumb the women had garnered the skills and details, the piquant flavours and the subtle aromas from a thousand sources — small ingenuities that came from poverty, recipes taken from the vanquished and imposed by conquerors, graciously given by neighbours or stolen from friends, handed down from mother to daughter so that at last in Frau Hunyadi's kitchen there came to fruition an age-long process, proudly, lovingly, and painstakingly fulfilled.

Soup came first. But this was merely to prepare the guests for the more serious business of eating. Immediately after, there appeared an enormous bowl of chicken goulash, steaming hot in its red sauce of paprika, with great fat globules floating on the surface. As a side dish for soaking up the gravy there was a mound of home-made noodles, accompanied by small green gherkins with flesh clear as glass from their long immersion in brine, with the pungent aroma of dill and garlic and the young tender leaves of horse-radish. And there were pickled red peppers — for the adults who knew how to get them into their mouths without touching their lips — and horse-radish grated into crushed beetroot that went with the sausages, which were made by a landsmann who had been a butcher in the Old Country and who could be depended upon to season them liberally with paprika and garlic among other things.

152

Sandor rose after every course, with twitching nostrils breathing in the food that was carried past him, following it with his eyes to the adults' table, listening to his uncle's exclamations and the remarks of guests with a deep feeling of pride. This was a party. Not one — not one guest — had been asked to bring anything. The pickles and preserves and things were offered out of friendship. Their equivalent would some day be returned. A fleeting image of the Kostanuiks, Mary and her mother and father, came to him. He saw them, their long-drawn hungry faces pressed to the front room window, their eyes imploring him for food. "Yaah," he muttered, "that would be good for them."

He sat down, satisfied, only to spring up again as the aroma of another dish came to him. Sarma, it was called, made of ground meat and rice flavoured with paprika and chopped onions, wrapped in sauerkraut leaves. The thought of the paprika seeping through the finely shredded kraut almost made him swoon. He sat down. When he had finished the last course, he closed his eyes.

The clatter around him slowly diminished. Above the murmuring voices he heard his uncle's laughter. The twins began once more to play. He smelled coffee — real coffee with no chicory in it. His eyes opened.

The dishes had been cleared away; the cakes and pastry were brought in, heaping platters of kupfel, the bright outer pastry caressingly flaked around apricot, cherry, or plum centres. Mohn strudel — ground poppy seeds with sugar and raisins, enfolded in a pastry like a jelly-roll. Then apfel strudel and other tidbits, crisp bubbles of fruit-sugar and egg-white beaten to a froth and browned, with a walnut or an almond in the centre.

And last of all, the crowning achievement, the Torte, made of ground hazelnuts and a few spoonfuls of flour with five whipped-cream layers and a glazed dark chocolate covering. Sandor bit into it ecstatically. He felt as though he were eating his way into heaven. A few gulps later it was gone. He sipped his coffee and discovered that there was real cream in it.

At the adults' table, the men were getting up and beginning to smoke. Sandor got to his feet, just as the change of shift occurred at his table. The children were told to go outside and play. The girls who had been watching the babies upstairs, and the women who had helped to serve, seated themselves while the neighbours waited on them. Sandor sauntered slowly to the corner where the men were talking.

He sat down on the floor beside his uncle and listened, and watched the coming and going of people, and leaned back against his uncle's chair, contented.

Unfortunately, his uncle was speaking Hungarian. He got up after a time, passed a woman, a neighbour from across the way, who alone among the guests did not appear to be enjoying herself, and glared at her ferociously as he passed by.

The kitchen was full of women washing dishes and cleaning up. He helped himself to a handful of assorted pastries. Beside the dish stood a decanter and a brandy bottle with a few thimblefuls left at the bottom. He uncorked it and a sweet pungent odour reached his nostrils. He had never tasted brandy. His mouth began to water. He unbuttoned his blouse, thrust the bottle into it, and ran happily upstairs into his uncle's cubicle. He sat down, smoked the remainder of his cigarette, and then, raising the bottle to his lips, swallowed its contents in a gulp that suddenly sent him leaping to his feet to go reeling and gasping around the cubicle, clutching his throat. In trying to get cold air into his lungs, he tore open the door and staggered across the attic and down the stairs.

At the bottom, just as suddenly, he stopped. From the pit of his stomach there began to spread the most agreeable feeling he had ever known, a warm, satisfying glow that rose languidly to his head and darted like little tongues of flame in his veins, slowly to his loins. He sat down and grinned vacantly. A great peace came over him. Above he heard the sound of footsteps. He turned and saw two girls come mincing down the stairs, one of them Emma Schumacher. Emma's name had been a byword in the gang. Fragments of sex lore flashed through his mind, but most of them had become established as neighbourhood fact only so that they might fit into the sorry scheme of some dirty joke or other, and they only made things more confusing. He looked up. He caught a glimpse of the margin of Emma's black cotton stockings and above them the pink flesh of her thighs. Emma was small and slender, but the size of her thighs was appalling. He grew frightened lest in some future time he should prove unequal to what would be demanded of him. But then he remembered. The last time he had gone swimming with the gang, it had not escaped his notice that he was almost as big as Hank and certainly as big as Louis.

Emma's skirt swished past his ears and for the first time in his life he felt an unmistakable tremor in his loins, as though of a power long dormant now stirring at last to brief wakefulness, to fill him with a delight that was indescribable, that seemed to transport him to a region deep within him, where his passionate affection for himself, far from laughter and derision, could unfold and flower.

As though entranced he returned to the front room to his place beside his uncle's chair. Distantly he heard the party coming to life. He felt his uncle's hand on his head and fell asleep.

When he awoke, it was to the sound of his uncle's voice singing a

153

Hungarian song. Onkel Janos stood in the centre of the room, keeping time with a glass of beer to the music. The refrain consisted of a few bars of laughter. His uncle's voice, Sandor thought, no less than his laughter, was deep and rich and splendid. It was fine to see him standing there.

The assembled guests clapped loudly when he had finished. He lowered his glass and in bowing caught sight of Sandor who had risen to his feet to applaud. With a shout Onkel Janos swooped down on him, caught him under the armpits, and raised him to his shoulders.

"A toast," he cried; the rest was a Hungarian rhyme.

And Sandor looked down at the smiling, friendly faces upturned to him, all happy, all willing to raise their glasses to him, and thought that it was only fitting that they should do so, that they should look up at him. Somehow he felt he had deserved it. He saw his parents smiling up at him and in that moment he forgave them everything.

154

Topic Six:

The Impact of Industrial Growth

Between 1890 and 1920 Canada underwent its industrial revolution. It was the result of a unique combination of circumstances. At last there was an upswing in the economy, an expanding agricultural sector, and a growing population creating a much larger domestic market. In addition, millions of dollars of investment money was available for new transportation and service facilities and for the development of the extensive mineral resources in the Canadian Shield. Factories were established across the country and particularly in the urban centres of Central Canada. Benefiting from the larger Canadian market for their products and the government's tariff protection, many businesses made fortunes. Wealthy new suburbs developed in the large cities as a direct result of the increased prosperity. However, not all shared in the new opportunities.

There emerged from this industrial growth a new class of Canadian citizens, the "urban poor." Living in congested and filthy slum areas, they were exposed to disease and impure water. They worked long hours at monotonous jobs in cramped and poorly ventilated factories. Unlike the "rural poor," many became wholly dependent on others for the basic necessities of food, shelter, and work. A large number were recent immigrants who lacked skills and were not unionized. They were at the mercy of their employers, who could pay the lowest of wages and lay them off at any time. To stay above the poverty line, women and even children joined the labour force.

The following readings look at the negative side of industrial growth. David Bercuson, in "Labour Radicalism and the Western Industrial Frontier: 1897–1919" examines conditions in the mining industries in the West. In *Hogtown*, Greg Kealey describes working-class conditions in Toronto at the turn of the century. Fernand Harvey discusses the same time period in "Children of the Industrial Revolution in Quebec."

There are three excellent primary sources for a study of the impact of industrial growth in Canada at the turn of the century. The first is *The*

Royal Commission on the Relations of Labour and Capital, 1889. An abridged version has been published, *Canada Investigates Industrialism*, edited and with an introduction by Greg Kealey (Toronto: University of Toronto Press, 1973). The other two sources are collections of documents: *The Workingman in the Nineteenth Century*, edited by M. S. Cross (Toronto: Oxford University Press, 1974), *The Canadian Worker in the Twentieth Century*, edited by I. Abella and D. Millar (Toronto: Oxford University Press, 1978). A worthwhile collection is *Essays in Canadian Working Class History*, edited by G. Kealey and P. Warrian (Toronto: McClelland and Stewart, 1976). A counterpart to Kealey's essay on Toronto is Terry Copp's "The Conditions of the Working Class in Montreal: 1897-1920," Canadian Historical Association *Historical Papers* (1972): 157–180. On labour radicalism in the West, see D. J. Bercuson's *Fools and Wise Men: The Rise and Fall of the One Big Union* (Toronto: McGraw-Hill Ryerson, 1978) and *Confrontation at Winnipeg* (Montreal: McGill-Queen's, 1974) as

156   well as A. R. McCormack's *Reformers, Rebels, and Revolutionaries: The Western Canadian Radical Movement: 1899–1919* (Toronto: University of Toronto Press, 1977).

Labour Radicalism and the Western Industrial Frontier: 1897–1919 *

DAVID JAY BERCUSON

The rapid growth of the Canadian west from the mid-1890s to the start of World War I was based upon the arrival and settlement of millions of immigrants. [Throughout this essay the term is applied generally to all those who migrated to the frontier including central and eastern Canadians.] The agricultural frontier attracted prospective farmers from every corner of the globe and their settlement saga has held the attention of a generation of Canadians. The frontier has been called a great leveller which broke down class distinctions because men were equal, free and far from the traditional bonds and constraints of civilization.[1] On the frontier every 'Jack' was as good as his master. But the settlement of the agricultural frontier was only part of the total picture of western development. An urban-industrial and a hinterland-extractive frontier was being opened at the same time which underwent spectacular productive expansion and attracted many thousands of pioneer workers. Most of these men had gone to the frontier pushed by the same ambitions and seeking the same opportunities as other immigrants. But once in western Canada most entered into closed and polarized communities and were forced to work in dangerous or unrewarding occupations. For these men there was little

* From *Canadian Historical Review*, LVIII (1977): 154–175. Reprinted by permission of University of Toronto Press.

upward mobility, little opportunity for improvement. They were not free and were not as good as their masters.

The pioneer workers had come a long way to improve themselves. Most lost the inhibitions and inertia which usually characterized those who stayed behind. They were ready to work hard and live frugally, to sacrifice, to do what was necessary to win the rewards they had come to seek.[2] But their way was usually blocked, their efforts thwarted not because of their failures but by a system. They usually faced a big difference between what they had sought and what could be achieved. Some immigrants came from such poverty and desperation that anything was an improvement and they were satisfied. But most eventually decided to break out of the closed systems which bound them or, if they could not break out, to smash them. The system thus lost its claim to their hearts and minds and labour radicalism emerged.

Were western workers really more radical than those in central Canada and the maritime provinces? The answer depends upon the definition of radicalism because major, prolonged, and violent strikes, as well as political insurgency, can be found in all regions of Canada during this period.[3] The dictionary is precise: Radicalism is 'the quality or state of being radical' while radical is 'favoring fundamental or extreme change; specifically, favoring such change of the social structure; very leftist.' Militancy is 'the state or quality of being militant' while militant is 'ready and willing to fight; warlike; combative.'[4] These definitions allow the conclusion that up to 1919 western workers were more radical than those of other regions though they were, perhaps, no more militant. Their radicalism emerged in several ways, which involved efforts to effect radical change. For example, the Socialist Party of Canada, which called for the elimination of capitalism and its replacement by the dictatorship of the proletariat, had its headquarters in Vancouver, the bulk of its membership in the west, and, after 1914, the official endorsation of District 18 of the United Mine Workers of America. Major Socialist party supporters could be found in the leading ranks of western unions — George Armstrong, Robert B. Russell, Richard Johns in Winnipeg, Joseph Sanbrooke in Regina, Joseph Knight and Carl Berg in Edmonton, William Pritchard, Jack Kavanagh, Victor Midgley, A. S. Wells in Vancouver. Support for other left-wing socialist parties, such as the Social Democratic party, was also centred primarily in western Canada. Though union members in other parts of the country engaged in independent political action, only in the west was their politics so definitely and unmistakable Marxian. Radical industrial unionism and syndicalism also flourished in the west. The Industrial Workers of the World [IWW], the United Brotherhood of Railway Employees, the American Labour Union, and the One Big Union all attained varying degrees of success in western Canada but almost none in Ontario, Quebec, or the maritimes. The west's attraction to these forms of unionism was also reflected in its experiments with general strikes.[5]

Western radicalism reached the peak of its influence in 1919. Conventions of the British Columbia Federation of Labor, the Alberta Federation of Labor, and District 18 of the United Mine Workers passed resolutions advocating worker control of industry, the formation of syndicalist-oriented unions, and general strikes to achieve political change. The workers pointedly expressed sympathy and support for Russian and German revolutionaries.[6] These three gatherings were prelude to the now famous Western Labor Conference held in March 1919 at Calgary and to the emergence of the One Big Union.[7] In each case large and representative bodies of western workers declared that their unions must be instruments for social change. This was the essense of western labour radicalism.

There were, to be sure, radicals in central Canada and the maritimes. The coal miners of Cape Breton were susceptible to radical ideas, particularly after 1917 when the Provincial Workmen's Association [PWA] was disbanded. In 1919 there was some experimentation with general strikes on a limited scale and some scattered sympathy for the One Big Union idea.[8] But, for the most part, Nova Scotia miners responded to the exigencies of militancy, not political radicalism. Syndicalism, with its rejection of electoral politics, went against the grain of a group of workers 'content to remain within the rules.'[9] When the Nova Scotia Independent Labour party was formed in 1919, it advocated traditional progressive reform such as the initiative, referendum, recall, and proportional representation.[10] J. B. McLachlan, a radical Scottish miner who led the drive to destroy the PWA in the coal fields, tried to lead District 26 of the United Mine Workers into the Red International of Labor Unions in the early twenties.[11] He was personally popular but stood outside the mainstream and his views alienated others and eventually undermined his own support.[12] There was a tradition of independent political activism amongst island miners but it tended towards labour-oriented reform, not socialist or marxist radicalism. Outside the coal fields even this tradition was almost non-existent.

In a 1966 article, and later in his history of the IWW, Melvyn Dubofsky sought to explain labour radicalism in the American west particularly amongst miners. He asserted that rapid industrialization, the introduction of technological innovations, ethnic homogeneity of the workforce, and other factors created class polarization in the mining industry. Polarization led to class war which, in turn, led to the development of class ideology. Dubofsky did not agree with the idea that western American radicalism was 'the response of pioneer individualists to frontier conditions.'[13]

The validity of this argument is something which American labour historians are more competent to judge but its applicability to Canada should be seriously questioned. There was certainly rapid industrialization in the Canadian west but there was no technological revolution in mining because most coal and hardrock mining began *after* the major technological changes in the western United States had occurred. Americans were mining for metals on a large scale in the 1870s and when Canadian hardrock mining did begin in the 1890s it was initially financed and directed largely by Americans who generally applied what they had already learned.[14] Most western Canadian coal mines were too small to benefit from the major advances of the day and mechanization was not widespread prior to 1919. The ethnic homogeneity pointed to by Dubofsky did not exist in western Canada. In the Kootenay region, for example, 34 per cent of the male population in 1911 were Canadian, 24 per cent British, 25 per cent European, 10 per cent American, and 4 per cent Asian.[15] In Vancouver 28 per cent were Canadian, 33 per cent British, 9 per cent European, 7 per cent Asian, and 9 per cent American. If Dubofsky's ideas are to be applied to the Canadian west, they will have to be significantly altered because the opening of the western Canadian mining frontier and the settlement, growth, and industrialization of western Canadian cities occurred at least two decades later than in the United States.

Paul Phillips has put forward arguments rooted in Canadian experience. He asserted that the character of western labour developed in response to the nature of the resource-based economy.[16] The National Policy of tariff protection to manufacturers raised the costs of primary production, encouraged investment in commerce and transportation but provided 'little or no scope for industrial expansion in the west . . .' Employers developed 'a short-term rather than a long-term view toward labour issues' and were not greatly interested in 'developing a permanent and peaceful relation with the labour force.' Phillips believed these factors, combined with regional isolation, created 'greater insecurity of employment and wages . . .' primarily because 'frontier employers . . . wanted to shift as much of the entrepreneurial risk onto the employees as possible.' In this way the resource-based economic structure of the region created 'a very much more militant and class-conscious type of union.'

If Phillips' thesis is to hold it must apply to the miners because they were clearly the vanguard of radicalism. The National Policy may have forced an inordinate concentration on resource extraction in the west and pressured employers into 'short-term' attitudes but resource extraction was also significant in Nova Scotia which, in this period, produced more coal than Alberta and British Columbia combined.[17] The mine workforce in Nova Scotia in 1910 was slightly more than 17 000 out of a total labour force of just over 173 000. This was a far larger proportion of the workforce than in either Alberta or British Columbia or even the two together.[18] The miners of Nova Scotia should have been under the same constraints and difficulties as those of the west because if the National Policy put difficulties in the path of western resource extraction industries, it also created problems for maritime resource extraction industries. Indeed, Nova Scotia coal operators, even the giant Dominion Coal (and British Empire Steel and Coal which succeeded it), could not compete in the lucrative markets of Ontario against Pennsylvania and West Virginia coal because of insufficient tariff protection.[19] If the National Policy was responsible for labour radicalism in western Canada,

159

why not Nova Scotia? Nova Scotia miners were often very militant but prior to 1919 showed little radicalism.

The capital structure of mining in western Canada was actually far from being unsophisticated or 'frontier-like.' Andy den Otter observed that 'although Alberta's coal deposits were vast, mining ventures did not realize quick, high returns but required very careful planning and large scale, long-term financing.' Thus the federal government granted Sir Alexander Tilloch Galt large tracts of land to subsidize his combined railway and coal mining operations in the Coal Banks (Lethbridge) area and enabled him to attract the British investment capital needed for expansion in the 1890s.[20] Investors such as Barings and Glyn and Company, the Grand Trunk Railroad, the Industrial and General Trust, and other like concerns could hardly have held short-term, quick return, expectations. Similarly, railway companies such as the CPR could not have acted the role of 'frontier employers' in their ownership of, or investment in, large mining properties. Canadian Pacific took over F. Augustus Heinze's smelter at Trail (and the railways and land grants that went with them) in 1897.[21] This was the beginning of Consolidated Mining and Smelting (Cominco), which combined Heinze's operation with large Canadian Pacific investments and acquired valuable properties such as the Sullivan mine at Kimberly, British Columbia.[22] Cominco soon became the largest employer of miners and smeltermen in the region and was clearly intended to be a long-term capital venture. The Crows Nest Pass Coal Company, with a capitalization in 1911 of $3.5 million, had an agreement with Canadian Pacific, concluded in 1897, to provide coal for smelting and other purposes.[23] This mining concern earned large profits[24] selling coal and coke to smelters in the west Kootenay and Boundary regions and was typical of many mines in the area.

The mineral economy of the British Columbia interior quickly developed a complex inter-related structure. Coal mines supplied coal and coke to the smelters while hardrock mines supplied ores.[25] As long as the smelters operated profits were made. The smelter concerns may have had to sell their products in an unprotected world market but there were few uncertainties associated with this phenomenon in the period under examination. The mines in the region were prosperous and went through phenomenal growth up to the end of World War I. New smelters were opened, rail lines laid, mines dug, and camps, towns, and cities expanded.[26] The key to the region's success was the low cost of extraction and the high grades of ore. Even world depressions had little impact in the region's hot house economic atmosphere. One observer commented: 'During the past summer [1897] the rapid decline in the value of silver, that proved so disastrous to other silver countries, had little effect on our silver mines, other than to check investment, as the ores were usually of such high grade, as to leave, even at the lowest price, a good margin of profit.'[27] What was true of silver was also true of copper. The size of the deposits and the heavily mechanized nature of the industry, combined with cheap railway charges, kept

160

profits high. Another observer claimed that 'nowhere on the continent can smelting be carried on more cheaply given fair railroad rates and fuel at a reasonable cost.'[28] Both conditions existed and business boomed except for a brief period just after the turn of the century. Some of the mine owners blamed the downturn on restrictive mining legislation and labour agitators (there was a major strike at Rossland that year) but the *British Columbia Mining Record*, leading journal of the industry, attributed the condition to swindling, mismanagement, and over-taxation.[29] Stagnation there was — for a few years — but the factor which most often closed down the smelters and caused a back-up of ore and production cuts in the hardrock mines was strikes in the coal fields supplying fuel to the area.[30]

The collieries of Vancouver Island do not easily fit a general picture of struggling and uncertain resource extractors. The largest operator was the Dunsmuir family who sold out to Canadian Collieries in 1911. The Dunsmuirs enjoyed steady markets in the United States at the turn of the century and were able to sell as much as 75 per cent of their production in San Francisco. This was true for all the collieries on the island.[31] During these years 30 to 40 per cent of the coal consumed in California was mined in British Columbia — the largest amount from any one source.[32] Profits to the Dunsmuirs from coal were enhanced by land grants and subsidies acquired from the British Columbia government to build the Esquimalt and Nanaimo Railway.[33] When the Dunsmuirs sold out to a syndicate headed by Sir William Mackenzie, co-owner of the Canadian Northern Railway, the new company, Canadian Collieries (Dunsmuir) Limited, was capitalized at $15 million.[34] Mackenzie's interest in coal was not confined to Canadian Collieries. He and Sir Donald Mann, his partner in the Canadian Northern, provided half the capital to develop the Nordegg Field in Alberta through Mackenzie, Mann and Company Limited. The other half of the money came from the German Development Company, which was sole owner of the Brazeau Collieries in the same area.[35] These mines, like many that were opened in western Canada, were 'steam' coal operations which sold everything they could produce to the railways. The greatest market problem facing most of these mines prior to World War I was the increased use, particularly in California but also in Canadian coastal areas, of California fuel oil to replace coal.[36] This problem was, however, seriously aggravated by the serious production cuts in the island collieries resulting from the 1913 coal strike.[37] Up to this point island coal production showed a slow but steady increase.[38]

The mining industry may not have been protected by National Policy tariffs but it was frequently given generous subsidies by provincial and federal governments. It also had little trouble attracting capital from Britain and the United States as well as major Canadian companies such as Canadian Pacific. Some of the region's most intransigent employers were the largest. Canadian Collieries and Granby Consolidated Mining and Smelting were probably the most 'hard nosed' operators in western Canada and yet were large, heavily capitalized, and secure. Their attitude

161

to industrial relations may have been short-sighted but could hardly have been prompted by insecurity. They shifted risks to their workers because they, like most employers, wanted to and, unlike some employers, were able to. The National Policy had little to do with it.

The argument could be made that the National Policy was the culprit behind most labour problems in the area because it had produced a resource-based economy in the west and such economies are riddled with labour problems. This is clearly so simplified that it explains nothing. Industry in the west was primarily resource-based because that was where the resources were (and still are). In this period there had been no appreciable industry established in urban areas but the west was still very young and industrial output was expanding at tremendous rates.[39] It is an interesting but fruitless exercise to speculate if, in this period, the economy would have been resource-based anyway or whether the National Policy was already suppressing the growth of secondary industry. The key problem here is whether western manufacturing had yet reached the point where it was large enough to be restricted by the National Policy. So far, there is no answer to the question.

What about the 'domestic' coal operators — those smaller mines producing coal for heating purposes? These mines in the east Kootenays and Alberta had more limited markets.[40] They could not compete with Pennsylvania anthracite in Winnipeg or points east because American coal, though usually slightly higher in price, was better quality.[41] They were also unable to compete in the coastal trade, in Canada or the United States, and had no entry to the northern California market. The prairies, northern Idaho, and eastern Washington were their domain. These operators sold in a less certain market than the steam coal producers or the Vancouver Island collieries and their uncertainty *was* at least partly due to the absence of sufficient tariff protection. However, they were the most reasonable for their employees to deal with and were less reluctant to sign agreements recognizing unions.[42] Perhaps the very uncertainty of their markets prompted them to avoid serious labour troubles, unlike a powerful giant such as Canadian Collieries.

Phillips asserts that western employers tended to take short-run, commercial views of their relations with their workers primarily because they purchased capital goods in a high-priced, protected market and sold their raw materials in unprotected world markets,[43] like the prairie grain farmers. But the parallel was superficial in reality whatever it may be in theory. Perhaps Phillips has explained why there were some uncertainties amongst western resource extraction employers at certain times, but even this tells little. There was no necessary connection between these uncertainties (when they did occur) and the rise of labour radicalism. There is, in fact, no real evidence that mine owners or smelter operators, with large capital investments in their enterprises, acted any differently from industrial capitalists anywhere. Conversely, there is no evidence that manufacturers in central Canada, when faced with the inevitable uncertainties of busi-

162

ness, acted any differently from the resource extractors. Unions were fought and demands resisted by most businessmen when the cost of the struggle fell within economically acceptable limits. Unions were tolerated and their demands considered when the cost of resisting was greater than the price of capitulation. When mine owners in the Crowsnest Pass area faced a strong union (organized before the scattered operators had a chance to unite against it) in the reality of a limited labour supply and uncertain markets, they chose to deal with their workers. But the large operators at Vancouver Island, with a ready surplus of Chinese labour, assured markets, and facing a struggling union, dug in their heels.

The men who worked the mines of western Canada were mostly immigrants. This is in sharp contrast to the mine workforce in Canada's other major mining area — Nova Scotia. The 1911 federal census revealed that almost three-quarters of the mine employees in Nova Scotia were Canadian born compared to 12 per cent in Alberta and 16 per cent in British Columbia mine workers.[44] This picture is reflected in the male population of two Nova Scotia coal counties, Cumberland and Inverness. Eighty-one per cent of Cumberland men and 92 per cent of Inverness men were Nova Scotia born. In British Columbia 22 per cent of the men in Nanaimo District and 11 per cent in Kootenay District were native to the province. Conversely, only 19 per cent of Cumberland and 8 per cent of Inverness men were immigrants, while immigrants accounted for 78 per cent of the males of Nanaimo District and 89 per cent in Kootenay District. The western mines and mining communities were almost exactly opposite in composition to the mines and mining communities of the east. In addition, as Donald MacGillivray has pointed out, the strong presence of the Roman Catholic church in Cape Breton, with its belief in an organic, structured society, was important. Conservative religious traditions added to the influence of conservative metropolitan centres such as Halifax and Antigonish. His picture is one of an 'essentially conservative community' with a 'thread of radicalism.'[45]

The pioneer immigrant nature of western mining society is reflected in other statistics. In the two Nova Scotia counties the ratio of men to women was 1.04:1. In Nanaimo District the ratio was 1.7:1 and in Kootenay District 1.9:1. The average age of mine employees in the west was higher than in Nova Scotia. Eighty per cent of British Columbia mine employees were between twenty-five and sixty-four years of age, while 70 per cent of Alberta and 65 per cent of Nova Scotia mine employees were in the same range. Literacy rates were also higher in the western mining regions for Canadian- and British-born miners. A composite emerges: in Nova Scotia young men born in the mining communities, or living in towns or on farms close by, went into the collieries at the earliest opportunity. They had travelled little, were younger, and less educated than western miners. They probably worked for the company their fathers had served before them and had few expectations about improving their immediate environment. In western Canada the miners had come from Ontario or Idaho or Wales or Italy or Austria to make their fortune. Perhaps they simply sought more cash to send back to the village. Troper and Harney have pointed to a crisis in rural village life in late nineteenth-century Europe as a factor causing young men to seek opportunities elsewhere[46] and many were clearly refugees from economic hardship.[47]

The British and Americans who came to the mining communities were usually skilled miners as were some Canadians from Nova Scotia.[48] The vast majority of European miners had been peasants and had no experience in mining. One result was that better paying jobs — miners in the hardrock mining industry, contract miners in the coal fields — usually went to Anglo-Saxons while the lower paying positions — muckers (ore loaders) in hardrock mining and 'day men' in the collieries — were taken up by the Europeans.[49] Contract mining was an especially skilled occupation in the coal fields since a miner had to know the best way to work a seam, shoring and bucking, safety techniques, coal quality, and other factors in order to earn an above standard wage. In hardrock mining the use of machinery such as air drills rendered many old skills unnecessary but certain semi-skilled procedures and techniques were still required for the use of air drills, blasting, and other jobs.

The urban workforce was also mostly immigrant during this period. The composition of western cities contrasted sharply with those of the east and more closely reflected the ethnic and demographic profile of the western mining regions. The 1911 census showed that only slightly more than 12 per cent of Vancouver men and 18 per cent of the women were British Columbians.[50] In Halifax about 88 per cent of the men and 89 per cent of the women were born in Nova Scotia. Hamilton, one of the county's most heavily industrialized cities, contained a larger proportion of immigrants than Halifax — about 41 per cent of the men and 33 per cent of the women (primarily from the British Isles), but most of the population was born in Ontario. Calgary closely matched Vancouver in that 90 per cent of the men and 84 per cent of the women were immigrants, most from Great Britain but with a very large number of Canadians. Here, about 12 per cent of the men and 14 per cent of the women were from the United States and approximately 12 per cent of the men and 8 per cent of the women were from Europe. Though Winnipeg was the oldest, largest, and most industrialized western city its profile closely followed the other western urban areas. Seventy-nine per cent of the men and 73 per cent of the women were immigrants. The British were the largest group — 32 per cent of the men, 26 per cent of the women — followed by Canadians and Europeans. The ratio of men to women was also disproportionately high in the two most western cities, reflecting their frontier character: 1.5:1 in Vancouver, 1.6:1 in Calgary. In Winnipeg the ratio was 1.2:1. The ratios were more normal in the east: 1.1:1 in Hamilton, 1:1 in Halifax.

Immigrants responded differently to the industrial frontier. Those who came from deplorable conditions of poverty, powerlessness, and oppression sometimes found the new cities and mining communities of the west considerably better than whatever they had left behind. Most of the Italians in British Columbia were from southern Italy, an area of grinding rural poverty.[51] They probably felt a distinct improvement in their situation simply because of the steady wages. Many never intended to remain in Canada and only stayed as long as necessary to earn cash to bring home. Donald Avery has called them sojourners.[52] They constituted a conservative element: in the radical and tumultuous environment of the Kootenay country, Trail, with a heavy Italian immigrant population, was an island of labour tranquillity.[53] Managers welcomed Italians to the mining communities because of their excellent (or infamous?) reputation as strikebreakers.[54] The Chinese were in much the same position. They too found Canada to be a heaven compared to what they had left. It is impossible to tell whether their strikebreaking activities resulted from exclusion from unions by white workers or vice versa but their conservative temper and exclusiveness mirrored the attitudes of many Italians.

At the other end of the scale were the British, Canadians, and Americans who had been reared in liberal democratic societies, were used to a democratic franchise, and might well have been involved in trade union or radical activities. These workers enjoyed an additional advantage over Europeans since they knew English and were familiar with the methods and mores of the political system. They were usually the most radical in their response to hardships and inequities and always provided the leadership for the socialist and syndicalist movements that vied for the allegiance of western workers. When the Social Democratic party was formed in 1911 a large majority of its membership was European but every one of its public leaders was Anglo-Saxon.[55]

British and American workers brought well-developed traditions of trade unionism and radicalism to western Canada. The British labour movement had been undergoing continuous change, growth, and increased militancy and radicalism since the London dock strike of 1889. Amalgamation and industrial unionism vied with socialism, syndicalism, and anarchism as theories and ideas were adopted, discarded, re-examined and adopted again. Leaders such as Keir Hardie, Tom Mann, James Connolly, and other worker-philosophers kept British labour in ideological turmoil.[56] The British labour movement, from which thousands of western workers had graduated, was in constant search for new directions and more effective means of bringing the organized power of the workers to bear.

Much the same sort of thing was happening in the United States, particularly the western mining states which sent the bulk of the American hardrock miners to the British Columbia interior. These men had no use for the business unionism and conservative moderation of Samuel Gompers and formed radical industrial unions such as the Western Federation of Miners and the United Brotherhood of Railway Employees. They founded the American Labor Union to challenge the AFL and supported socialist and syndicalist causes.[57]

These British and American workers drew on a rich heritage of trade unionism and radicalism developed in industrial and/or urban contexts. When they found themselves closed in by their adopted society, their unions beset upon by courts and governments, their employers using police, spies, dismissals, evictions from company towns, and alliances with governments against most efforts to organize, they responded with all the fury of the militancy and the radicalism they brought with them.

The new societies of the western mining camps were totally polarized as were the economic regions in which mining was carried out. Company towns were a feature of the region because most of the coal and ore deposits were far from normal settlement areas. It was not possible for miners to live in Lethbridge or Victoria and work in the collieries nearby, even when they were close. The company camps grew immediately adjacent to the collieries and the miners were forced to spend most of their lives in these controlled towns. The company town could be a wretched place, with stinking outhouses, no fresh water supply, dilapidated shacks, and cold, damp bunkhouses. There may have been no medical facilities, no schools, bad food, lice-ridden blankets, and frequent attacks of typhoid.[58] Or a company town could have been the epitome of paternalism. Nordegg, in the Coal Branch area of Alberta, was planned as 'a modern and pretty town' with the best equipped hospital west of Edmonton, bathrooms in the larger cottages, a poolroom, a miners club, and several company stores.[59] Martin Nordegg, who laid out the town, decided to paint the miners' cottages in different pastel shades.[60] In the British Columbia interior the Granby Consolidated Mining and Smelting Company offered cottages with electric lights, running water, and sanitary facilities. Their town had a recreation hall, meeting hall, tennis court, reading room, baseball diamond, and moving pictures.[61] All the towns and camps scattered throughout Alberta and British Columbia had one thing in common — they were closed societies, highly polarized, which isolated the workers and made them as dependent on each other above the ground as they were below. In Nordegg, for example, it was not long before company officials and their families occupied the cottages on the heights and refused to mix with the miners.[62] In the Granby camp the velvet glove concealed a company policy of ejecting 'agitators.'[63] On Vancouver Island the Dunsmuirs' favourite tactic for dealing with labour unrest was to eject miners from the company towns.[64] There was never any question about who owned and controlled. The miners faced this reality every time they went to the company store, used company scrip (which was still circulating in Nordegg as late as 1915), or availed themselves of any company facility.

The polarization of the camps was enhanced by the newness of society on the mining frontiers. The only important social institutions were the companies and the unions. That which the company did not provide the union did. The unions built their own halls, which served as the major recreation area for the men — a place where they could bitch and drink away from company ears. The union provided compensation, helped with legal fees in suits brought by accident victims, or provided burial funds.

166

In the BC interior the only hospital for miles was apt to be owned and financed by the union as was the case in Sandon.[65] The unions, whether the Western Federation of Miners or the United Mine Workers, were organized on the basis of a lodge for each colliery, mine, or smelter. The lodge was, therefore, locally organized and supported. The men were the local and the local was the men — identification was complete. When the United Mine Workers fought wage reductions in Alberta and the Crowsnest Pass in the years 1924–5, the miners who disagreed with this policy did not leave their unions, they withdrew their locals and established 'home locals'[66] which survived to be reunited in a rejuvenated District 18 in the early 1930s.

Mining society was raw. There was no established tradition of servitude or corporate paternalism handed from generation to generation such as existed in many Nova Scotia coal communities. In most company-owned towns and camps the presence of church and other moderating social institutions was weak while the class structure of the community reflected its totally mine-oriented existence. There were miners and their families and the managers. There were no teachers, clerks, merchants, priests, salesmen, artisans, doctors, or other professionals. And if there were they too were company employees. Mining was the only industry and the entire social and economic structure of the region depended upon the labour of the miners or the smeltermen. In southern Alberta mining communities were often located near agricultural districts but this did not lessen the polarity of the camps because the professional miners resented the farmers who came looking for work after the harvest, found employment in the mine, and undercut the earnings of the permanent miners.[67] Some mining towns — Rossland and Sandon in the British Columbia interior, Drumheller in south central Alberta — were open communities not under direct company control. A handful of tailors, drygoods merchants, tobacconists, hoteliers, barmen, and preachers set up shop to service the miners' needs. Well-stocked bars in small frame hotels and enterprising prostitutes provided 'recreation'[68] as did miners' day parades and, in the hardrock country, July Fourth celebrations. Relay races, rock drilling contests, and union band concerts drew large crowds and eager participants. These towns offered more individual freedom — the men could come and go if they were single and debt-free — and more class diversity than closed company camps. But they were always isolated, by miles of open prairie or by the high mountains and thick forests of the rainy Kootenays. And though not owned, they were dominated by the mining companies whose managers formed a close bond with the handful of local independent businessmen. Costs to the miners in these towns were high — for room, board, or recreation[69] — and the everpresent closeness and isolation helped make them pressure-cookers of discontent.

The polarization of these communities was also reflected in the limited opportunities for improvement available to the workers. Day men (paid a flat daily wage) might become contract miners (paid by the amount of coal

TABLE I — **Fatalities per million tons of coal mined over one decade**

	1907	1908	1909	1910	1911	1912	1913	1914	1915	1916	Avg
BC	13.96	8.53	23.75	8.92	7.30	9.25	10.5	9.39	26.36	11.26	12.92
ALTA	10.35	5.96	4.14	20.08	4.13	6.09	6.50	54.68	5.24	4.30	12.15
NS	5.61	6.09	5.82	5.05	5.18	4.46	5.95	4.72	5.74	3.99	5.26
US	na	5.97	5.73	5.62	5.35	4.53	4.89	4.78	4.27	3.77	4.99

Sources: Nova Scotia, *Annual Report on Mines 1940* (Halifax 1941), 114; ibid. (1944), 186; Alberta, *Annual Report of the Department of Public Works of Alberta 1916* (Edmonton 1917), 110; British Columbia, *Annual Report of the Bureau of Mines 1910* (Victoria 1911), 230; ibid. (1920), 358.

dug, graded as suitable and weighed at the pit head) but this was as far as they could go. In the hardrock mines a mucker might become a miner, an even less important promotion than that from day man to contract miner in the coal fields.

Working conditions were uniformly poor. Death rates in western coal mines were more than twice those of Nova Scotia (see Table 1). The miners were newer than those in Nova Scotia and the men and their managers had less expertise in how to extract the mineral.[70] It was not discovered until after several major disasters, in which hundreds of miners were killed, that the coal of the east Kootenay region was fifteen times more gaseous and therefore much more likely to cause explosions than comparably-graded bituminous in Pennsylvania.[71] In the hardrock mines heat, unstable explosives, faulty machinery, unguarded shafts, flooded sumps, cave-ins, and mining related diseases took a constant toll of lives.[72] Here conditions were about the same as those of the American hardrock mines.

When conditions in mining camps and in the mines themselves were intolerable, there were few places to escape. The skilled miners were tied to their occupations (if not to the company store) and faced lower wages as unskilled workers in cities or as agricultural labour. American hardrock miners could always migrate back across the border, and many appear to have done so, but mines there were just as dangerous and the communities just as polarized as in Canada. Those miners with families had little mobility to begin with. The unskilled single miners did have options, but very restricted ones.

Southern Alberta coal mines were located near agricultural areas and even those not so near were a short train ride away. But agricultural labour, when available, was twenty-four hour a day work at low wages. Farmers gained unsavoury reputations amongst migratory agricultural workers from both sides of the border because of the treatment meted out to their employees. Added to this was competition from small farmers needing additional cash[73] and immigrants who wanted to learn homesteading before filing on a piece of their own land.[74] Every fall thousands of men were brought west by the railways to help bring in the harvest.

168

Even if work was available under decent circumstances it would rarely be steady since farms were still small and extra labour requirements were seasonal. For the single miners of the BC interior or Vancouver Island, however, even this was not an option.

The other escapes were railway construction work and migration to the cities. Railway construction workers — navvies or 'bunkhousemen' — were just above slaves in the general scheme of things. Under the direction of brutish foremen, navvies worked from dawn past dusk clearing rights of way, laying track, hauling rock and gravel. The work was gruelling and the pay negligible. The food was usually bad — though a charge was always deducted for it, the sleeping conditions fit for animals: bunks rigged up in old box cars with almost no heat, proper ventilation, or space to move. Sanitary facilities were nonexistent. The workers on these construction jobs were closely watched to assure that 'agitators' would not get close to them.[75] It was a wise policy. When the IWW managed to get a foothold in the construction camps in the Fraser River canyon in 1912 two long strikes of navvies, one on the Grand Trunk Pacific, the other on the Canadian Northern, gave these wretched men an opportunity to protest their deplorably bad working and living conditions.[76]

The cities offered the greatest chance to escape. Here, at least, there was recreation, companionship, freedom to roam about, and, during this period, usually plentiful work. But if the city offered good opportunities for advancement and the chance to forge a decent life for the skilled worker, it offered barely enough to get by for the unskilled. Urban slums blighted the new cities of the west and in times of depression, when there was no work to be had, primitive and patchwork welfare schemes offered little hope.[77] In truth, western cities were also closed and polarized societies for many thousands of industrial workers.

Every western city had an 'across the tracks.' In Calgary there were tent towns in Hillhurst or near the Centre Street Bridge. In Edmonton frame shacks were thrown up along the Grand Trunk Pacific main line, near the Calder Yards, or east of Mill Creek. In Vancouver tenements scarred the urban landscape along the waterfront to the southeast of Stanley Park. In Winnipeg there were the tenements and broken down hovels of the 'North End' where overcrowding, lack of sanitary facilities, and a near absence of fresh water created one of the highest infant mortality and death rates per thousand persons on the continent.[78] For the unskilled these slums were a dead end.

The skilled fared better. They built modest homes in Calgary's Mount Pleasant or Winnipeg's Ward 4 near the Point Douglas Yards. Many eventually went into business on their own and started printing shops, contracting firms, and other small enterprises. A few became successful in politics. The skilled workers quickly formed themselves into an aristocracy of labour, their exclusive and conservative craft unions presiding over respectable Trades and Labor Councils.

For the unskilled there were no unions since the crafts would not stoop

169

to attempting mass organization. They had no political voice because of restrictive franchises. Many of the Europeans sought out ethnic-based socialist clubs and in Winnipeg Jews and Ukrainians organized vigorous and active left-wing parties[79] but they had no real power. This was a common frustration which affected both the skilled and the unskilled: the cities of western Canada were tightly controlled by commercial élites who ran them like closed corporations.[80] Winnipeg offers the best though certainly not the only example and this was reflected in the restricted franchise, based upon property qualification. In 1906, when Winnipeg contained over 100 000 persons, only 7784 were listed as municipal voters.[81]

This situation was particularly hard for workers. The city government was reluctant to spend money to improve facilities in the North End. It provided little impetus for the privately owned but municipally chartered street railway system to operate adequate services in working-class areas. It was not receptive to requests for improved health and building bylaws or minimum wage schedules from the local labour movement. The imbalance of electoral power also assured the election to office of men such as Thomas Russell Deacon who, in the midst of the depression of 1913–15, opposed giving his policemen a day's rest in seven and told his city's unemployed to 'hit the trail' but struggled hard to obtain a municipal vote for property-owning corporations.[82] Men like Deacon were representative of and supported by a commercial élite which constantly stymied and frustrated the working people's attempts to make their jobs safer, their homes more secure, their lives better.

Nevertheless, the cities were clearly the best places to be on the industrial frontier, especially for skilled workers. They could find the jobs and build the homes and families they had come to the west for. Unless and until they were thwarted in their own drives for improvement they remained moderate, though reform minded. The unskilled were better off in the cities but just barely. They were still powerless, living in bad conditions, earning low wages, and living in fear of unemployment. The cities were significantly different from the mining communities in that they offered some middle ground between polarized extremes. Here there were churches, religious and social clubs, city missions, ethnic self help societies, socialist and free thought clubs, and libraries.[83] Here, also, there appeared to be a middle class — clerks, salesmen, priests, professionals — lacking in the mining communities. The mix was not as volatile, the chances for improvement better, the edges not so rough. Perhaps this is why radicalism took longer to dominate the cities.

All western workers were not radicals. Those who were did not become radical at once. The coal miners of Vancouver Island, the Crowsnest Pass, and Alberta and the hardrock miners of the British Columbia interior were the vanguard of radicalism in the west, founding it, nurturing it, and lending its spirit of revolt to other western workers. These miners early rejected reformism and swung behind marxist political organizations, particularly the Socialist Party of Canada. They also provided the most

170

fertile ground in the west for doctrines of radical industrial unionism and syndicalism and were amongst the strongest supporters of the Industrial Workers of the World. The miners formed a large and cohesive group in British Columbia and they quickly overwhelmed, dominated, and greatly influenced the urban crafts and railroad lodges. Radicals were more influential in Vancouver prior to 1914 than other western urban centres. In Alberta the urban crafts formed the Alberta Federation of Labor partly to offset the radical influence of the coal miners who dominated the labour movement in the south,[84] but by 1918 the miners had become undisputed masters of the provincial labour movement. Radicalism, therefore, emerged first and was strongest in the highly polarized and closed mining communities. In these camps workers with a common employer and common interests were grouped into a single community. Their struggle with their bosses did not begin with the morning whistle and end when the shift was over because the entire area was controlled by their employer and they were forced to cope with the company on a twenty-four hour basis. Since they were grouped into one place a little radical propaganda went a long way.

171

The situation in the cities was, as we have seen, different and radicalism took much longer to dominate, even though it was always present. Prior to the war urban workers were ready to defend the rights of groups such as the IWW but, for the most part, refused to endorse their aims. Urban workers even elected radicals to important positions, particularly in Vancouver, but would not support radical objectives. Though a socialist such as R.P. Pettipiece was editor of the *B.C. Federationist*, a moderate such as W.R. Trotter (a trades congress organizer), was a regular contributor. In part this was the result of indecisiveness and ideological uncertainty. Christian Sivertz, socialist and a leader of the British Columbia Federation of Labor, demonstrated this lack of clarity when he wrote that a general strike (contemplated to support the Vancouver Island coal miners in 1913) would make employers aware that such a weapon existed and they would then be 'more amenable to reasonable consideration of the demands of organized labor.'[85] This one radical leader only supported a general strike to force the bosses to be more reasonable. Clearly the pressures of polarization and limited opportunities were not yet great enough or had not yet been perceived by enough workers to have thoroughly radicalized the Vancouver labour movement. Radical strength existed in that radicals had achieved important positions, but there was no concerted radical purpose. In the other major urban centres — Calgary, Edmonton, and Winnipeg — radicals played second fiddle to men such as Alex Ross, Alfred Farmilo, and Arthur W. Puttee. All this changed after 1914.

The emergence of radicalism as the dominant factor in the urban labour movement was primarily due to the war. The domestic industrial and political situation convinced many urban workers that opportunity and mobility were illusions. Inflation and manpower shortages prompted moves to increased organization, union recognition, and higher wages but these drives were usually stymied by court injunctions, federal orders in council, and the indifference or hostility of the Imperial Munitions Board. Many otherwise economic and industrial issues, such as higher wages for railway shopcraft workers, became politicized as worker hostility towards the war itself became the major issue. Western urban labour turned increasingly against the war and, conversely, more supportive of radical alternatives.[86] Urban labour leaders were also immigrants and now reacted in a fashion similar to their brothers in the mines. By September 1918 the urban-industrial and the extractive-hinterland labour movement was united behind radical leadership.

Western labour radicalism was born when immigrant industrial pioneers entered into the closed, polarized societies of the mining communities and the western cities. Once settled there was little chance for improvement. Many of these individuals could not accept their change in status from free immigrants, some of them from a rural background, to regulated and enclosed industrial workers.[87] In Nova Scotia and in central Canada, by contrast, radicalism was slow to develop. Its signs were not apparent in Nova Scotia until sixty years after mining began in earnest and at least two generations had worked in the mines. Young men growing up in the closed communities of the Nova Scotia coal towns knew little else and expected little better. They too would go down in the mines and would live in the company towns as did their fathers before them. If not, they would themselves emigrate. In central Canadian cities radicalism was never a dominant factor though it was always present. But in the west most workers did expect better. Those who had worked the land in Europe, who had survived the mining wars of the American frontier, who escaped the turbulence, insecurity, restrictiveness, and polarization of British society, or the falling wages and lower productivity of the Welsh coal fields, had come to the Canadian frontier for a new start and better opportunities. But they soon found themselves victims of a new oppression. This was the frontier; but the mining communities were pockets of industrial feudalism denying the opportunity of the frontier to those who sought it while the cities were only slightly better. This deep frustration provided fertile soil for the socialists and syndicalists who offered radical change and abolition of 'wage slavery.' The freedom which was sought, but not found, could be found yet in the commonwealth of toil. It became apparent to those with little patience that the traditional methods of business unionism — organization, negotiation, strike, arbitration, and so on — won no battles. Even the few victories that were achieved changed little; perhaps a slightly higher wage or shorter hours, but the company town, the slum, the whole polarized and closed environment continued to exist. In one sense the entire labour system in the west was a closed environment. Thus the one apparent hope — the unions — offered little real hope.

For many who sought improvement the only answer lay with those who attacked the basic structure of the system that held immigrant workers in thrall: the political socialists who preached the dictatorship of the proletar-

172

iat and scorned reformism; the syndicalists who advocated use of the trade unions as instruments for radical change; the radical industrial unionists who advocated general strikes to overcome the combined power of employers and state. These solutions offered hope to men who refused to wait for gradual, evolutionary improvement. Far from becoming a leveler, the Canadian industrial frontier was the chief stimulus to the development of class consciousness and radical working-class attitudes in the Canadian west.

Notes

I am grateful to Ramsay Cook, David McGinnis, and Ian Fuge for their helpful comments and suggestions.

1. The classic statement is 'The Significance of the Frontier in American History' in Frederick Jackson Turner, *The Frontier in American History* (New York 1920). A Canadian discussion is included in M. S. Cross, ed., *The Frontier Thesis in the Canadas: The Debate on the Impact of the Canadian Environment* (Toronto 1970), 104–25.
2. Some immigrant attitudes can be found in H. Palmer, ed., *Immigration and the Rise of Multiculturalism* (Toronto 1975), 82–111. A good account of a Ukrainian pioneer worker is A. B. Woywitka, 'Recollections of a Union Man,' *Alberta History*, autumn 1975, 6–20.
3. See S. M. Jamieson, *Times of Trouble: Labour Unrest and Industrial Conflict, 1900–1966* (Ottawa 1968), 62–151.
4. Taken from *Webster's New World Dictionary of the American Language, College Edition* (Cleveland and New York 1968).
5. For examples see P. Phillips, *No Power Greater* (Vancouver 1967), 60, 72–3; M. Robin, *Radical Politics and Canadian Labour* (Kingston 1968), 127–32; E. Taraska, 'The Calgary Craft Union Movement, 1900–1920' (unpublished MA thesis, University of Calgary, 1975), 69–70; D. J. Bercuson, *Confrontation at Winnipeg* (Montreal 1974), 58–65, 83.
6. See British Columbia Federation of Labour, *Proceedings of the Ninth Annual Convention* (Calgary, 1919), 2, 4, 5, 7; Alberta Federation of Labor, *Proceedings of the Sixth Annual Convention* (Medicine Hat 1919), 41; 'Sixteenth Annual Convention District 18 United Mine Workers of America' (typewritten), 133.
7. One Big Union, *The Origin of the One Big Union: A Verbatim Report of the Calgary Conference, 1919* (Winnipeg nd), 10–12.
8. I am grateful to E. R. Forbes for bringing these events to my attention. See his 'The Maritime Rights Movement, 1919–1927: A Study in Canadian Regionalism' (unpublished Ph D thesis, Queen's University, 1975, 88–9.
9. D. MacGillivray, 'Industrial Unrest in Cape Breton 1919–1925' (unpublished MA thesis, University of New Brunswick, 1971), 35, 44.
10. Ibid., 33
11. H. A. Logan, *Trade Unions in Canada* (Toronto 1948), 334–5
12. MacGillivray, 'Industrial Unrest,' 226
13. M. Dubofsky, 'The Origins of Western Working Class Radicalism, 1890–1905,' *Labor History*, spring 1966, 131–54.
14. R. M. Longo, ed., *Historical Highlights of Canadian Mining* (Toronto 1973), 21–3; M. Robin, *The Rush for Spoils* (Toronto 1972), 25–6.
15. Canada, *Census of Canada*, 1911, II, 377–8 [hereafter *Census*]
16. P. Phillips, 'The National Policy and the Development of the Western Canadian Labour Movement,' in A. W. Rasporich and H. C. Klassen, eds., *Prairie Perspectives 2* (Toronto 1973), 41–61
17. *Census*, V, 106–9, 118–19
18. Ibid., 10–11
19. E. S. Moore, *The Mineral Resources of Canada* (Toronto 1933), 188–92
20. A. A. den Otter, 'Sir Alexander Tilloch Galt, the Canadian Government and Alberta's Goal,' *Historical Papers* 1973, 38
21. R. Chodos, *The CPR: A Century of Corporate Welfare* (Toronto 1973), 63–5
22. J. L. McDougall, *Canadian Pacific* (Montreal 1968), 143–8
23. Chodos, *The CPR*, 63–4
24. Public Archives of Canada, Sir Thomas Shaughnessy Papers, Canadian Pacific Railway Letterbooks, Shaughnessy to Elias Rogers, 4 March 1903. I am grateful to Donald Avery for bringing this source to my attention.

25. Ibid., Shaughnessy to W. Whyte, 27 March 1907
26. H. A. Innis, *Settlement and the Mining Frontier* (Toronto 1936), 282–320, contains the best description of the region's growth.
27. Ibid., 280
28. Ibid., 284
29. Robin, *Spoils,* 76
30. This emerges constantly in Innis. See, for example, pages 284, 285, 288, 289. He notes that the 1911 Crowsnest Pass coal strike necessitated the importation of 41 000 tons of coke from Pennsylvania (285).
31. British Columbia, *Annual Report of the Minister of Mines* (for the year ending 31 December 1914) (Victoria 1915), 333 [hereafter *Mines Reports*]
32. *Mines Reports,* 1902, 1202
33. Robin, *Spoils,* 79–80
34. *Mines Reports* 1915, 348
35. A. A. Den Otter, 'Railways and Alberta's Coal Problem, 1880–1960,' in A. W. Rasporich, ed., *Western Canada Past and Present* (Calgary 1975), 89–90
36. C. J. McMillan, 'Trade Unionism in District 18, 1900–1925: A Case Study' (unpublished MA thesis, University of Alberta, 1968), 23
37. *Mines Report* 1914, 329
38. Ibid., 1915, 426
39. *Census,* III, XI-XIII
40. den Otter, 'Railways,' 84
41. Canada, 'Evidence Presented to the Royal Commission on Industrial Relations, 1919' (typewritten). Testimony of Jesse Gough, 690–2, and C. G. Sheldon, 1003–6 [hereafter 'Royal Commission Evidence']
42. Jamieson, *Times of Trouble,* 99, 126–32
43. Phillips, 'National Policy,' especially 41–3
44. *Census,* II. All these statistics were compiled from Table XV. Literacy rates were obtained from Table XXXV.
45. MacGillivray, 'Industrial Unrest,' 23–4
46. H. Troper and R. Harney, *Immigrants* (Toronto 1975), 8
47. See, for example, H. Palmer, *Land of the Second Chance* (Lethbridge 1972), 29–30, 71–2, 194; Woywitka, 'Recollections,' 6
48. For American examples see A. R. McCormack, 'The Emergence of the Socialist Movement in British Columbia,' *B.C. Studies,* spring 1974, 6; A. R. McCormack, 'The Origins and Extent of Western Labour Radicalism: 1896–1919' (unpublished Ph D thesis, University of Western Ontario, 1973), 24, 104.
49. D. Avery, 'Foreign Workers and Labour Radicalism in the Western Canadian Mining Industry, 1900–1919' (paper presented to the Western Canadian Urban History Conference, Winnipeg, October 1974), 4–5, 8–9
50. *Census,* II, Table XV
51. Palmer, *Chance,* 174; J. S. Woodsworth, *Strangers within our Gates* (Rep. ed., Toronto 1972), 133
52. Avery, 'Foreign Workers,' 7, discusses this and the 'padrone' system.
53. I am grateful to Professor S. H. Scott for his impressions of the role of the immigrants in the Trail labour movement.
54. Avery, 'Foreign Workers,' 8
55. Robin, *Radical Politics,* 104–15, tells of the birth of the SDP.
56. H. Pelling, *A History of British Trade Unionism* (London 1963), 94–100; McCormack, 'Emergence,' 6
57. V. H. Jensen, *Heritage of Conflict: Labor Relations in the Non Ferrous Metals Industry up to 1930* (New York 1950), 61–2, 64–70
58. Glenbow Alberta Institute [GAI], United Mine Workers of America, District 18 Papers. 'Report of Alberta Coal Mining Industry Commission, Dec. 23, 1919' contains valuable information concerning the state of Alberta coal towns.
59. M. Nordegg, *The Possibilities of Canada are Truly Great* (Rep. ed., Toronto 1971), 176–7
60. Ibid., 184
61. 'Royal Commission Evidence,' 393–5, 405–7
62. Nordegg, *Possibilities,* 196–8
63. 'Royal Commission Evidence,' 396–7
64. Phillips, *No Power,* 5–9
65. University of British Columbia Special Collections [UBC], *By Laws and Sketch of Sandon Miners' Union Hospital* (Sandon, nd)
66. F. P. Karas, 'Labour and Coal in the Crowsnest Pass' (unpublished MA thesis, University of Calgary, 1972), 36–51, 129–33
67. GAI, United Mine Workers of America, District 18 Papers, 'Special Convention held at Calgary, June 14–16, 1921' 101–5, 108
68. James Gray discusses prostitution in Drumheller in *Red Lights on the Prairies* (Toronto 1971). See also Provincial Archives of British Columbia, Cominco Papers, Add. MS 15/8/3, 'St. Eugene Arbitration.'

69. For Kootenay town living costs see 'St. Eugene Arbitration,' and Cominco Papers, Add. MS 15/9/2.
70. McMillan, 78–82, summarizes some of the dangers and the evolution of safety legislation.
71. British Columbia, *Special Report on Coal Mine Explosions, 1918* (Victoria 1918), 529–30
72. R. E. Lingenfelter, *The Hardrock Miners* (Los Angeles 1974), 12–26, tells of conditions in American hardrock mines in the period prior to 1896. For evidence that many of these conditions existed in British Columbia mines see UBC, Orchard Interviews. Interview of William Byers, 7–10. Byers worked in the Phoenix and Rossland area. See also *By Laws and Sketch of Sandon Miners' Union Hospital*.
73. D. P. McGinnis, 'Labour in Transition: Occupational Structure and Economic Dependency in Alberta, 1921–1951' (paper read to the Western Canadian Studies Conference, Calgary, Alberta, March 1975), 4–6.
74. This was a close to universal experience. See G. Shepherd, *West of Yesterday* (Toronto 1965), 17–18, for one example.
75. E. Bradwin, *The Bunkhouse Man* (Rep. ed., Toronto 1972), 63–90
76. Jamieson, *Times of Trouble*, 143–6
77. J. Taylor, 'The Urban West: Public Welfare and a Theory of Urban Development,' in A. R. McCormack and I. Macpherson, eds., *Cities in the West* (Ottawa 1975), 298–301
78. A. F. J. Arbitise, *Winnipeg: A Social History of Urban Growth, 1874–1914* (Montreal 1975), 223-45.
79. Ibid., 163–5
80. J. M. S. Careless, 'Aspects of Urban Life in the West, 1870–1914,' in A. W. Rasporich and H. C. Klassen, eds., *Prairie Perspectives*, 2, 32–5
81. Artibise, *Winnipeg*, 38
82. *The Voice* (Winnipeg), 9 and 16 Jan. and 9 Oct. 1914
83. Artibise, *Winnipeg*, 113–65
84. Taraska, 'Calgary Craft Union Movement,' 38–40
85. *B.C. Federationist*, 'Wage Workers' Forum,' 12 Sept. 1913
86. See Phillips, *No Power*, 61–77; Bercuson, *Confrontation*, 32–77.
87. This phenomenon has been explored in Herbert G. Gutman, 'Work, Culture, and Society in Industrializing America, 1815–1919,' *American Historical Review*, June 1973, 531–87.

Hogtown: Working Class Toronto at the Turn of the Century*

GREGORY S. KEALEY

The history of the Canadian working class remains largely unwritten. In the United States and Great Britain the broad contours of industrialization have been carefully studied and in the past two decades the active role of the working class in this process has been realized.[1] Canadian historians, however, must return directly to the sources even to begin discussing the history of the working class. This paper is a distillation of an earlier essay on the creation of an industrial working class in late Victorian Toronto. Its focus will be on working and living conditions during the transition to industrial capitalism, a necessary prelude to any discussion of working class consciousness.

Toronto's population grew from 30 775 in 1851 to 144 023 in 1891.[2] Accompanying this rapid urbanization was the transition from artisanal production for a local market to industrial production for a hinterland.[3] The lives of workers and their families were affected both by the change in the system of production and by the rapid growth of the city.

Canada prides herself on the ease of her industrial transition. We applaud our humanity and point to the horrors of British and American industrialization. Canadian historians have refused to analyze and deal with the destructiveness of the Canadian process. As Barrington Moore points out in his discussion of British industrialization:

> That the violence and coercion took place over a space of time, that it took place mainly within a framework of law and order, and helped ultimately to establish democracy on a firm footing must not blind us to the fact that it was a massive violence exercised by the upper classes against the lower.[4]

Working Conditions

Skilled Labour

176

New industries grew up around trades with long independent histories. The industrial transformation destroyed the integrity of the old craftsmanship. These trades had possessed the earliest union organizations. Artisans adapted these older organizations and used them to fight industrialization. The resistance to the transition to industrial production in Toronto can be seen in the tailors' strike against Singer Sewing Machines in 1852 and in the strength of the Knights of St. Crispin among shoemakers in the late 1860's and early 1870's.[5] Although initially successful in fighting the incursions of mechanization, both the tailors and the shoemakers eventually lost. By the 1880's, shoemaking, once a trade in which an individual artisan performed the entire operation, had been transformed into an assembly-line process in which each article passed through fifty hands.[6] The Knights of St. Crispin and other similar organizations are often viewed as hopelessly reactionary in their resistance to mechanization. Many of the Knights' demands, however, demonstrate that their real concern was not the advent of the machine, but rather the loss of individual power. They demanded that the workers "should exercise the right to control [their] labour and be consulted in determining the price paid for it".[7] Their constitution emphasized the antagonisms of capital and labour and asserted "that labour is capital, and the only capital that possesses the power to reproduce itself".[8] Their solution was to propound co-operation as "a proper and efficient remedy for many of the evils of the present iniquitous system".[9]

The militancy of the skilled artisans can be seen in an analysis of Toronto strikes. In the years between 1867 and 1892 Toronto workers fought 141 strikes. Artisans struck most often: shoemakers nine times; moulders eight times; carpenters seven times; plasterers seven times; tailors and cigarmakers six times each.[10] The testimony of skilled workers before the Royal Commission of 1889 suggests the leading issues in these strikes: the cost of housing, sanitation, industrial accidents, seasonal unemployment and wages. Even for skilled workers the price of housing in Toronto was prohibitive; "respectable areas", "close to work" were not available to them. Bad sanitation and dangerous machinery both threatened

the worker's life. Above all the uncertainty of continuous employment —
the frequent shutdowns for repairs or over-production, the short season in
the outdoor trades, the ever-threatening presence of the unemployed —
was the major source of insecurity for the skilled worker.

The early organizational efforts of skilled artisans in response to these
problems yielded mixed results for the Toronto working class as a whole.
It afforded the skilled certain kinds of limited protection but simultaneously bred the labour aristocracy and labour elitism. Consequently
much early organization did not touch the industries where exploitation
was most rampant.

Child and Female Labour

In turning to the unskilled workers we are immediately confronted with
the pervasiveness of female and child labour. Table I outlines the child-
and female-intensive industries. It is clear from this data that child and
female labour was not only used extensively in marginal operations and
declining trades (tobacco, straw), but was also important in major areas
of Toronto's industrial growth especially in the various segments of the
clothing industry. Child labour was the harshest product of industrialism
and aroused considerable indignation. Nevertheless this cheap pool of
labour provided approximately 11% of the work force in 1871 and 1881
and still provided 5% ten years later despite the passage of the 1886
Factory Act.[11] The Act forbade the employment of males under twelve
and females under fourteen in Ontario. Outlawing child labour however,
greatly increased the number of women workers, as Table I shows. Table

177

TABLE I – Some Child and Female Intensive Toronto Industries

Industry	1871 No. of Factories	No. of Employees 16 and over M	F	under 16 M	F
Bakeries	33	132	19	36	
Book Binding	5	80	140	5	25
Boot and Shoe	47	1032	361	87	84
Corsets					
Dressmaking	25		164	3	26
Furriers	10	42	114	9	7
Hosiery	1	11	60	3	3
Printing	11	331	100	72	
Paper Bag					
Shirts					
Straw	2	27	255	19	30
Tailors	51	466	764	22	47
Tobacco	9	180	60	84	40

Industry	1881 No. of Factories	No. of Employees 16 and over		under 16	
		M	F	M	F
Bakeries	45	263	61	27	27
Book Binding	6	135	190	16	22
Boot and Shoe	76	838	269	91	34
Corsets	2	19	232	4	8
Dressmaking	72	7	393	7	76
Furriers	15	85	197	5	3
Hosiery	2	26	49	9	3
Printing	32	862	116	223	24
Paper Bag	8	40	82	14	28
Shirts					
Straw	2	19	29	3	2
Tailors	61	537	927	16	23
Tobacco	13	237	80	63	9

Industry	1891 No. of Factories	No. of Employees 16 and over		under 16	
		M	F	M	F
Bakeries	98	500	208	35	7
Book Binding	9	225	254	8	1
Boot and Shoe	149	576	152	13	1
Corsets	6	40	372	2	11
Dressmaking	402	30	1547	15	85
Furriers	30	340	412	4	1
Hosiery	4	21	64	13	29
Printing	74	1790	441	147	6
Paper Bag	6	94	163	1	7
Shirts	19	53	535	2	
Straw					
Tailors	216	1034	1575	28	17
Tobacco	4	107	22		

Source: Canada, *Census*, 1871, 1881, 1891.

II shows that employers turned to women as an alternative source of cheap labour when forced to cease employing children. Wage data drawn from Ontario Bureau of Industry Reports and from the Royal Commission of 1889 show that children received one-quarter to one-third the pay of adult males in the same trades and that women drew from one-third to one-half.

Formal government responses suggest the growing public distaste for such conditions and provide important statistical information. In 1882 a commission was appointed by the federal government to investigate "the

TABLE II – **Composition of Labour Force in Toronto**

Year	Child Labour		Female Labour		Children & Women as % of Total Work Force
	Total No. of Children Employed	Total % of Work Force	Total No. of Women Employed	Total % of Work Force	
1871	917	11%	2164	22%	33%
1881	1385	11%	3048	24%	35%
1891	1070	5%	7117	29%	34%

Source: Canada, *Census*, 1871, 1881, 1891.

working of mills and factories in the Dominion and the labour employed therein".[12] The commissioners, William Lukes and Alf Blackeby, were horrified by the conditions they found. The tone of their report suggests a mixture of indignation and incredulity. Could these things happen in "this fair Dominion"? Their account of children working in factories at eight and nine — unaware of their ages, completely illiterate — is filled with pathos. Lukes and Blackeby pointed out that "the employment of young persons in mills and factories is extensive and largely on the increase, the supply being unequal to the demand". They found, in addition, that "the children invariably work as many hours as the adults" and that "the appearance and condition of the children in the after part of the day . . . was anything but inviting or desirable". As for the Ontario Compulsory School Act, "we were unable to find any place in which this act is enforced". Child labour also disgusted the Royal Commission of 1889. Its discoveries of horrible conditions in the Montreal tobacco industry lent its recommendations a biting edge.[13] Ontario Bureau of Industry Reports provide earlier evidence. The 1884 report described children who received two to four dollars for a sixty hour week. In 1886 the Toronto Bureau statistician noted:

179

One matter of special import to the working people is the continuous employment of minors of both sexes in large numbers by employers of cheap labour in defiance of the Factory Act and the Public School Act. This should be remedied by the active enforcement of such laws.[14]

James R. Brown, an Ontario factory inspector, reported to the 1889 Royal Commission that he had found forty girls under fourteen, six boys of nine, and many of ten and eleven working in the factories in his district in 1887. Twenty years later, an Ontario legislative committee concluded that "certain abuses exist and that they have arisen, first, because our compulsory education law has lacked adequate enforcement".[15] The inadequacies of the early factory acts were: the age limits were still too low — twelve for males, fourteen for females — and the laws only applied to factories with more than twenty employees (1886). This meant that children of all ages were allowed to work in offices or retail shops. W. H. Pearson, a child clerk, recalled his experiences:

I was only fifteen years of age when I went into the post office and as considerably over one-half of my time during five years service was spent in this wretched dumpy hole with its foul atmosphere, together with the close confinement, Sunday work, no holidays, and irregular meal hours, the effect it had upon my health can be readily understood and after a few years I became a confirmed dyspeptic and almost a nervous wreck and I sometimes wonder that I lived through it all.[16]

The labour of women also began to draw attention in this period. As early as 1867 the Toronto *Globe* discussed female labour and differentiated between work done at home with the aid of children, and that done in factories. The *Globe* expressed compassion:

There is another class of female labour whose earthly prospects . . . are not so bright, these are the widows and orphans . . . at the will of employers who even here, with presumable plenty to do for all, do not scruple to extract the last farthings worth of bodily energy from the dependents of their will.[17]

180

The article also described vividly the problem of the off-season: "in the dead of winter when the trade in the retail is slack . . . the prospect for those who are left suddenly to their own resources is, for the time, miserable indeed . . . even then the many expedients to economize are not sufficient to ward off the same experiences in succeeding winters".[18]

The parliamentary commission of 1882 reported that "female labour is very extensively employed not only in mills and factories but also in private houses and what may be described as workshops, which are very difficult to find, sometimes being in the attic of a four-story building, at others in a low damp basement where artificial light has to be used the entire day".[19] The Royal Commission of 1889 noted that:

To arrive at the greatest profit for the smallest expenditure the mills and factories are filled with women and children to the practical exclusion of adult males. The reason for this is obvious. Women and children may be counted on to work for small wages, to submit to petty and exasperating exactions and to work uncomplainingly for long hours.[20]

The Bureau of Industry Reports vividly portrayed some of the conditions under which women worked. In 1885 the Toronto correspondent noted that "female employees are subject to fainting and spasms apparently through being obliged to work in standing position". He also wrote that in the dress-making trade, "there is no proper ventilation and twelve girls are stuck in a room 12' x 14' with no washrooms or closets attached".[21] In 1886 he described the same problem:

The greatest sufferers from poor ventilation appear to be women and girls employed in the cities in shirt factories, tailorshops, and such places. They are often crowded into small rooms which receive the suggestive appellation "sweat shops".[22]

In a later passage we find that "any man who has been in charge of a large number of girls could portray suffering . . . all who have had experience will admit that a large number of girls have contracted disease of some kind in their working experience".

Similarly in 1887 the report noted that "young women and girls who work in factories (especially in paper box and envelope making) suffer through failing health". This concern led him to consider why they worked:

Many work through necessity that they may live, others that they may help their parents, while no inconsiderable number are daughters of country farmers who prefer city life and fixed hours of work, even at low wages, rather than remain at home, on the farm.

He saw a simple reason for employing women: "they can be had for much less wages than men can be hired for";[23] and, as a cigar manufacturer from London pointed out in 1889, "they do not cause trouble".

Women workers also suffered from long hours on their feet. Shop girls often worked from 8:00 a.m. until 9:00 or 10:00 at night.[24] Dr. William Oldright of the Toronto Board of Health and the University of Toronto School of Hygiene, in testimony before the Royal Commission of 1889 indicated that this was a health hazard that led to illnesses he had often dealt with in his medical practice.

A report in 1892 by Joan T. Scott on female labour in Toronto provides both an interesting policy study of the Factory Laws and an equally interesting amount of descriptive material. In her examination of factories employing women in Toronto, she found that the range of hours varied greatly, as Table III shows.[25]

One can clearly see that the nine-hour movement of 1872 and all the labour agitation which followed had been far from successful, especially in the industries employing women. Scott's description of extended female labour in retail outlets was also notable. The predominant attitude that women workers have been unable to organize was challenged by Scott's description of two local assemblies of the Knights of Labour organized by and made up solely of women — the Hope Assembly and the Silver Fleece Assembly. Here again we find the claim that oppression was worst at the margins of industrial capitalism: "both men and women in stores and small work shops suffer more . . . than the workers in larger accommodations". However, her own description of Bell Telephone where "the hours are extremely complicated and arduous", and where "there can be little doubt that they are capable of simplification and reduction" implicitly undercuts her position.[26] The position is further damaged when one realizes that much of this so-called marginal sweat-shop trade was actually being produced on order by such "honest" men as Timothy Eaton.[27]

181

TABLE III – **Female Labour Hours**

Number of Hours	Number of Factories
60 and over	10
55–59	14
50–54	30
44–49	6

Source: Joan T. Scott, "The Conditions of Female Labour in Ontario"

Government reports on the Bell Telephone and the "Sweating System" clarify the issue of whether conditions were bad solely in "marginal segments". Obviously telephones were not marginal and equally obviously sweat shops are only marginal by a definition that ignores their direct relation to places like "the house that Timothy built".[28]

The Bell Telephone Commission of 1907 is beyond the period that we are directly concerned with, but the allusions to Bell in Scott's article suggest that, if anything, the conditions at Bell revealed in 1907 were improvements over conditions in the late eighties and early nineties. In 1907 the company attempted to lower the wages of its employees in a disguised way by changing the hours of work. Unimpressed, the women walked out. W.L. MacKenzie King's new Department of Labour investigated and documented a devastating case against Bell. The evidence the bosses supplied was startling:

Q. . . . during the past three years Bell Telephone Company has not been paying wages sufficiently [sic] to enable these operators to pay the cost of their living?
A. . . . I think you are right, with this qualification, I'm not sure that it goes back three years or later.
Q. . . . a woman could not make a sufficient amount to really properly pay her living expenses?
A. . . . Not of the class we wanted.
Q. . . . 30–40% were not receiving a sufficient amount?
A. . . . Yes.
Q. . . . Any self respecting woman wanting employment would naturally turn away?
A. . . . Most decidedly.[29]

These answers were supplied by the manager of the Toronto branch of the Bell Telephone Company. Later the key question was addressed to both the Montreal and the Toronto managers.

Q. . . . Do you think they [wages and profits] should be associated?
They answered that they should not be.[30]

Workers described the hazardous physical design of the switchboards and conditions which led to nervous breakdowns from overwork. A supervisor of operators, Maude Orton, testified.

Q. . . . Were [the operators] worked within their capacity?
A. . . . They were worked to their extreme limit and more than that in some cases.

Even more damaging was evidence of hospitalization, heart failure, and deafness caused by frequent shocks received from the boards, especially by long-distance operators. The testimony of various medical experts appended to the report confirmed the evidence given by the workers.

The Commission report's conclusion was uncompromising:

One looks in vain for any reference which would indicate that the health or well-being of the operators was a matter of any consideration . . .

To the extent to which the Bell Telephone Company has profited by the necessities of its operators . . . to this extent the profits of the Company have been derived from a species of sweating. That the company has profited in this manner is sufficiently proved by the admission of its own managers that the wages paid were not sufficient . . . and that the operators had been obliged to work at a pace which was absolutely detrimental to their health.

At least 32 operators each day were expected to work, not five hours only but six or nine hours and and this for the rate of remuneration fixed for the five hour period.[31]

"We believe," added the commissioners "that where it's a question between the money making devices of a large corporation and *the health of young girls and women* business cupidity should be compelled to make way".[32]

The Sweating System

Equally revealing was the *Report Upon the Sweating System in Canada*.[33] The sweating system worked this way: retailers such as Eaton's had three alternative sources of clothing — they could buy direct from a manufacturer; they could set up their own factories; or they could contract out their work to contractors, who had small shops and who in turn let the work to men and women to do at home. As the Commission report pointed out, "in Toronto . . . the proportion of work done in private homes is greater" than that done by contractors' shops and far surpassed that done by factories.[34] The report goes on to suggest that "it seems inevitable that such a system must result in bringing the wages down to the lowest point at which the employee can afford to work". This effect is "rendered the more certain by the fact that the separation of the workers where they work in their own homes" prevents not only union organizing but even wage comparison.[35] The workers understood and "almost invariably prefer [ed] the factory system" since they realized a contractor was "less likely to be deterred from cutting wages", "less likely to have regard for the health and comfort of his employees" and because they held that "all the profit the contractor makes must come out of the sum which would go to the workers as wages did they work directly for the manufacturer".[36]

The sweating system resulted in several advantages for retailers like Eaton's: it avoided the embarrassment of directly hiring and supervising cheap labour and diminished the potential for organized strikes and other methods of collective resistance. It allowed such firms, when challenged, to deny any knowledge of conditions in the shops they bought their work from. "In no case", said the Report, "did . . . the manufacturers take any measures to keep themselves informed as to conditions of the shops or houses in which the goods were made".[37] Thus Eaton was not incriminated, even though shops doing his business "were far from being cleanly", had ventilation that "was often bad", and "rooms [that] were too small for the number of people employed".[38] Even conditions in factories were far from ideal. One report cited

A factory where nearly 200 females were operating sewing machines driven by power, seated on each side of long tables so closely together that it was impossible for air to circulate and the foul air would accumulate . . .[39]

183

But smaller shops were even worse:

> I will tell you of a place, over the Army and Navy Store on King Street. I went into the shop and could hardly breathe for steam, heat and the smell from the gas irons; I could not even see the girls . . . There is a place on Elizabeth Street where you can go at 11 or 12 at night and 5 a.m. in the morning and still find them working.[40]

Not covered by the terms of the Factory Act, these places remained invisible to the public. Even the manufacturers seldom bothered "inquiring as to the workshops where their work was done . . . People work for them for years and bosses and foremen know nothing of them beyond the street and the number of the house in which they reside."[41] All of this ensured the high profits which were all that counted. The commissioner found that "the tendency is towards lower wages", "that 60 hours a week is the usual time worked in factories but in private homes the time is irregular and the number of hours of work usually more". He recommended extension of the Factory Acts and "the substitution of factory work for the contract system", but that if this was impossible, then the latter was far better than the home system practiced so widely in Toronto.[42]

184

The success of the Factory Acts was called into question by the Royal Commission of 1889 which reported that "laws regulating the employment of children and women in Ontario and Quebec . . . as far as could be learned . . . are largely inoperative".[43] Ineffective regulation intensified the brutality of early Canadian capitalism. Exploitation of children and women as sources of cheap labour then, was not restricted to the marginal sectors of the economy. Indeed, it was an integral part of the whole process of early industrialization.

We have discussed in detail child and female labour in Toronto in the eighties and nineties, but what of the other 65% of the work force? What kind of working conditions did they enjoy?

Male Labour

Industrial work presented an extreme physical hazard to the life of male workers throughout the period. Not until the Ontario Factory Act of 1886 was there legislation prohibiting the cleaning of machinery while it was in motion, and forcing owners to cover machines, to protect elevator shafts, and to introduce some semblance of sanitation and ventilation inside the factories. Each deserves separate discussion in turn: machinery, general safety, ventilation, and finally, sanitation.

The 1882 parliamentary committee found "dangerous machinery" to be "quite common"; "Gearing, fly wheels, pulleys, belts and steam engines, are in many cases entirely unprotected and many accidents have resulted".[44] An instance was cited where "in one factory two men fell through the opening of a hoist within two years and the proprietor had taken no precaution against further accidents from the same cause".[45] They recommended fire escapes, unlocked factory doors, and inspection of boilers.[46]

The Ontario Factory Inspectors found similar hazards. In 1885 one inspector noticed "much unsafe machinery".[47] The next year a different inspector observed that "some firms are in the habit of putting green hands from the country on machines they know nothing about".[48] The statistics on industrial accidents in their annual reports between 1888 and 1893 revealed the personal irresponsibility of many employers. Most accidents occurred in two types of industries: those employing power presses, such as in the manufacturing of tin and iron, and those employing circular saws, such as used in carpentry and box making. In 1889 these industries accounted for one third of the accidents in one inspector's territory and 60 of 85 in another's in 1890, despite the fact that safety equipment for both power presses and circular saws was discussed in voluminous detail in these reports.

Testimony before the Royal Commission of 1889 highlights many of these same features. John Callow, a carpenter, testified that he had "worked in factories where machinery wasn't guarded . . . and I say that machinery ought to be guarded and it is not guarded".[49] Dr. William Oldright pointed out in his testimony that "machinery is not properly guarded" and that many boys were injured because of it "in machine shops, box factories, carpenter shops and planing mills".[50] One of the workers in a box factory, Hugh Burke, described this process:

185

In Toronto, the general system is to take a foreigner, for an employer gets him cheaper than the usual run of city hands. If he can get him to run a planing machine for a couple of weeks he'll do it . . .

Isn't this dangerous, asked a commissioner?

Yes, but it is very seldom taken into account. If one man is injured they can get another for the same wages as the first and they don't have to pay anything for getting him run through.[51]

When a box manufacturer, Joseph Firstbrook, testified, he admitted that boys worked on the machines and that he also sometimes put new men from the country on them. Yet he blamed the two fatalities at his plant on the carelessness of the men. He also testified that the Factory Inspector had forced changes in his operations in the interest of safety. Perhaps it is not surprising then, that Firstbrook was one of the most hostile capitalists and claimed that "organized labour was organized tyranny".[52]

The minutes of the Toronto and District Labour Council record a similar case of using untrained boys on machines:

She [his mother] had arranged for him to learn the cabinet business and the first morning he started the Boss placed him to work a shaper machine, the boy not having worked, or had anything to do with the machine before. Such machines being dangerous to an experienced hand and more especially to a boy of no experience, within two hours of his starting work, he was under chloroform having all the fingers of his left hand amputated. The Boss, Mr. McGuire, refused to compensate or do anything to assist the boy.[53]

It is not surprising that the Royal Commission of 1889 recommended that "compensation should be recoverable even in cases where negligence on the part of the employer or his agents, or defects in the machinery have not caused the accident. The owners of machinery benefit from its use and should be primarily responsible for accidents caused by it".[54]

We have already discussed ventilation in connection with the sweat shops, but the problem was not limited to them. The 1886 Bureau of Industry complained that "it seems to be the special object of the manufacturer to adopt methods in their factories and workshops to shorten life by having unhealthy workshops, no regard for ventilation, cleanliness or fire escapes and above all long hours" and as an example it cited the bookbinding trade, "where 9/10 of the men die of consumption caused by long hours and unhealthy workshops, where the constant inhalation of glue does little for their lungs".[55] Dr. Oldright, in his testimony before the Royal Commission of 1889, singled out print shops with night work as especially bad because of the gas lighting and insufficient ventilation.[56] The testimony of two iron moulders, Joseph Hunt and David Black, revealed similar problems in their trade where cold, wet and draughty plants resulted in the deaths of two apprentices and one man.[57] Black described "the condition of other shops" as being "not all that can be desired" and pointed out that "in casting at night, gas and smoke come off which are very injurious and have a very irritating effect on the lungs" because the shops are "poorly ventilated".[58]

Sanitation was another subject that angered and depressed the investigators. The 1882 Commission found "inadequate and unsatisfactory provisions", "insufficient closet accommodation", and even "two or three cases where women were employed and no provision whatever" was made. They commented that "very often on entering a mill or factory our senses have been convincingly informed of imperfect ventilation and drainage of closets".[59] Bureau of Industry Reports complained each year that "the number of washrooms in workshops and factories is not as large as circumstances call for" and that often those that existed were unsanitary. These kinds of problems may seem petty, but as the Factory Inspector's Report in 1888 noted, closet accommodation "has nevertheless been the cause of much suffering and serious injury to the health". Stewart J. Dunlop, a printer, testified before the Royal Commission that some printing shops "are wretchedly bad" in sanitary matters and that "in particular I was in a shop today in which I held my nose till I got out".[60]

Moulding shops were just as bad according to the testimony of Joseph Hunt who said that "some of the shops [he had] been working in [were] not fit for a horse to stop in".[61] Factory Inspector Brown mentioned in his testimony: "with reference to closets, in some cases we found them very filthy, especially those which were outside in pits".[62] The Toronto Board of Health inspectors also found conditions abhorrent. In 1887 they found that about 25% (68 of 278) were unsatisfactory. Again in 1891 the report angrily attacked "large factories where many men are employed", with nothing but "an immense pit in use".[63]

Slaughter houses also came under attack throughout the period, but the most vivid description is in the 1884 report:

186

There is slaughtered here from 30 to 35 cattle each week, besides some sheep; the blood and water arising therefrom is all poured into the Don. The construction for holding the offal, which is taken away every night, the box drains for carrying the blood (and frequently pieces of offal) to the Don, and the ground around, are all in a very foul state and a fruitful source of danger to the public health. The space between the buildings and the stream is considerable and is all saturated with organic filth.[64]

Living Conditions

Having looked briefly at certain aspects of working conditions in Toronto, let us now look at the living conditions of the workers. There are several built-in difficulties in this pursuit. Describing a life style which can be said to be "typical" is attended by certain problems because, as noted before in distinguishing the skilled from the unskilled worker, there were significant income variations within the working class. Moreover, attempts to relate income to standard of living are hazardous in any case, because so little is known of the day to day details of life in this period. Far more work must be done toward understanding the proletarian lifestyle before we can utilize the copious material on prices and wages with any degree of accuracy. (There is a certain comfort in finding, in the testimony before the Royal Commission, that there was much contemporary confusion on these issues. Some of the workers questioned felt that life became significantly better through the period of industrialization; others felt things became decidedly worse.) With these caveats in mind let us proceed to a discussion of such concrete matters as housing (and the related questions of job security and family size), home sanitation and diet.

187

Housing

Two things are very clear for Toronto in this period: rents and housing costs had skyrocketed and the two key variables in economic security were family size and continuity of employment. There was much evidence given before the Royal Commission in 1889 and nearly universal agreement that rents had nearly doubled in ten years in Toronto, and that it was increasingly difficult for workers to purchase homes. The Bureau of Industry statistical data on income versus costs (Table IV) is convincing when it correlates failure to save with family size and with number of days employed.

TABLE IV–Economic position related to family size and work time

Economic Position	Average No. of Dependents	Days Employed
Surplus	3.34	277.89
Even	3.70	263.40
Deficit	4.01	233.29

Source: Ontario, Bureau of Industry, *Annual Report*, 1888

TABLE V–**Workers' savings after essential expenses**

Year	Savings or Deficit After Expenses		No. of Workers
1887	surplus over	$20	261
	surplus under	$20	109
	even		79
	deficit under	$20	87
	deficit over	$20	118
			654
1888	surplus over	$20	132
	surplus under	$20	50
	even		76
	deficit		43
			301

Source: Ontario, Bureau of Industry, *Annual Reports*, 1887, 1888

188

Table V shows how marginal the existence of many Toronto workers was in 1887 and 1888. The data demonstrate quite clearly that many lived in poverty, many more were faced with it as a continual menace, and a very few were getting rich. The upswing in the 1888 data is probably accounted for by a break in the depression.

The problem of finding continual employment loomed large in this period as one of the key factors in family life. As the 1887 Bureau of Industry Report stated: "each year almost every factory or shop of any considerable productive capacity closes for repairs, cleaning up, etc. The time thus occupied usually runs from three to six weeks."[65] Owing to depression in trade, in several cases the time referred to was extended by several weeks in Toronto. As always, the winter was extremely difficult for the outdoor trades. John Callow, a carpenter, noted: "in the eight years I've been in Toronto, I've never had the privilege of working through a winter. I'm off now [November]. I never start to do much until April". He went on to say he averaged six to eight months of work a year.[66] Edward Gurney, a Toronto foundry owner, told the commissioners in his testimony that his plant was shut down for about two months a year and that there was absolutely no way to avoid this. Employment was quite uncertain at all times.

It is little wonder then, that housing presented large problems for Toronto workers. The most often mentioned complaints in the hearings in 1887 concerned excessive rents and impossibly high-priced houses. The commissioners reported in 1889:

The question of rent, the increase of which has been almost continual during the last years, and has exceeded what labouring men have gained in increase of wages, will be settled only when workers become owners. It is undeniable that workers are badly lodged in houses badly built, unhealthy, and rented at exorbitant prices.[67]

Earlier they noted that advancing rents were adding a serious burden "to those borne by people struggling for a living".[68] As John Callow testified: "rents . . . have gone up like a balloon".[69]

Home ownership seems to have been rare among the working class as can be seen in Table VI:

TABLE VI–**Workers' housing patterns in Toronto**

Year	Owners	Tenants	Tenants & Boarders	Boarders
1886	22	167		166
1887	35	278		341
1888	21		280	
1889	44	223		210

Source: Ontario, Bureau of Industry, *Annual Reports*

189

A printer testified in 1887 that "with very strict economy [he] might purchase a home . . . in the course of a few years . . . with constant employment".[70] The catch, of course, was "constant employment". Expert testimony by Charles Pearson, a real estate agent, corroborated the testimony given by many workers. Rents, he said, had doubled in the previous ten years and workers were forced to put up "with poorer houses". They also frequently lived in over-crowded situations:

I know of some four or five room houses with more than one family. I know some houses where the basement has one family and another lives above. There is a row where there are two families in every house.

He concluded that very poor housing such as in St. John's Ward, the centre of working class housing in Toronto, was "a source of great profit for the landlord".[71]

W. H. Howland, the Toronto reform Mayor of 1886–1887, also mentioned housing in St. John's Ward in his testimony. There "you will find houses built in front and then others built in at the back end, the result being that there's no space or air room and that they are very unwholesome". He also commented on their extreme profitability and noted that "they are now largely falling into the hands of people who own a number of houses and the system is wrong in every way". He recommended government inspection to the committee.[72]

Housing and land values were uppermost in many people's minds and much of the testimony of radicals focussed on this issue. Thus the spokesmen from the Anti-Poverty League of Toronto, W. A. Douglas and Richard T. Lancefield, recommended the appropriation "of ground rentals for public purposes" and "a simple land-tax and the abolition of all others". They noted that the "part of society which produces the most must be contented with the smallest share"; that the "landowner becomes rich because of the impoverishment of the rest of the community" and that increase in land values was derived from "other people's toil".[73]

Phillips Thompson, a Toronto labour reformer, focused on this question in his testimony and while noting that "I don't exactly put my faith in all that Henry George says", he still made heavily George-like recommendations: "There should be an appropriation of the land value or a considerable proportion of the land value by the government or the state".[74] David Black, a moulder, noted movingly the plight of a worker with a large family who "can't bring up a family respectably and live in a respectable way and make both ends meet at the wages paid". Connecting the housing problem with land speculation which caused high land prices and forced contractors to build housing "not suitable for working men", he recommended that land speculation be stopped.[75] An analysis of the housing problem was not lacking; it just seemed insoluble given the assumptions of the system.[76]

Frank Beer's writing of 1914 isolated the same problems and suggested similar solutions to those noted in 1887, all under an illusion of new discovery and fresh insight. "The intensive use of land" said the Toronto urban reformer,

> has leant itself to the creation of slums and the scarcity of small houses has resulted in a doubling up of families in houses, so that two, three, and in some cases even five families are housed in a building constructed for one family only and with but one set of sanitary conveniences.

The state must act, said Beer, for "we have lost all faith in the so-called law of supply and demand as an automatic remedy for conditions arising from human need on one side and an imperfect social organization and money greed upon the other".[77] An interesting progression from 1887 — 27 years later the problem is discovered by middle-class reformers.

Even the tax structure was biased against the working class as the Royal Commission of 1889 reported: "In some cities, if not all, the houses of the comparatively poor are in proportion to their value more highly taxed than those of wealthy people. This is unjust".[78] Later it noted that "Toronto and many other cities have lent and given money to railroads . . . and protect and aid capital. Why should they not protect and aid labour?" It added that "municipalities instead of protecting their workers seem to have established their taxes in such a fashion as to strike, in preference, the contributors least wealthy."[79]

Sanitation

Sanitation was another serious problem connected with working class housing. The Royal Commission of 1889 noted:

> In many places no effectual means are taken to secure proper sanitary conditions in workingmen's dwellings . . . These homes yield to their owners a much larger revenue than houses of a better class, and certainly landlords can afford to make them safely habitable . . . The letting of a house in bad sanitary condition should be forbidden by law.[80]

Later passages were even more critical:

In the large cities very exhaustive evidence was taken showing that the poorer classes are labouring under a serious disadvantage in regard to sanitary inspection of their homes . . . In most of the large cities and towns there are municipal laws having reference to sanitary matters but these laws are to a great measure inoperative.[81]

Dr. William Oldright of the Board of Health emphasized these problems in his testimony when he noted that many landlords refused to make sanitation adjustments in their property and on receipt of a complaint would change tenants instead. In his testimony on the links between disease and sanitation he noted: "I could point out dozens of cases in this city where I know of diptheria having been caused by a direct communication from the drain to the interior of the house and also there being no trap to intercept the sewer gas."[82] The technical literature on waste-removal often included assertions such as this: "The ordinary privy-vault is an abomination. It has caused more deaths in this country than war or famine."[83]

191

An 1884 survey conducted by the Toronto Board of Health found the following conditions. Of 5181 Toronto houses inspected there were 201 foul wells, 278 foul cisterns, 814 full privies, 570 foul privies, 739 cases of slops being thrown into privies, 668 cases of slops in the streets, 1207 cases of no drainage whatsoever and 503 cases of bad drainage. Only 873 of the 5181 houses had water closets. The report recommended that privies be abolished and suggested earth closets as opposed to water because of the horrible sewer system. The report noted that "Toronto Bay is a disgrace to the city" and that "the limpid bay of half a century ago has been converted into what is little better than a cesspool".[84]

In 1886 the report recommended draining all lots, closing all wells and cisterns, abolishing all privy pits, and sanitary inspection for all buildings. None of these recommendations were implemented. Each year the reports complained especially about privies. In 1891, with the outbreak of a severe diphtheria and typhoid epidemic traceable to specific unsanitary conditions, the Board made a new concerted effort. It noted that "the presence of foul privy pits has been the most prolific source of these diseases and promises to be the most permanent evil the Department will be called upon to deal with". Its authors understood the source of the difficulties: "Here", they said, "we meet the opposition of a formidable array of landed interest."[85] They noted the horror of privies where "the fluids soak through into the earth, saturating it with filth and remaining there after the privy is emptied".

The report also pointed out that "in certain sections privies are so numerous and so close to houses as to be a menace". The inspectors noted that "the denser the population, the fewer the water closets, the most closely built sections having nearly all the pits"; "in many cases there are houses built in the rear" and "the privy is placed just where the kitchen door is located". Later they were specific: "In one block in St. John's Ward of

67×200 yards, a physiological calculation shows that there are deposited annually 14 to 18 tons of solid excreta. What must be the condition of the soil?"[86] The working class, then, not only faced sanitation and health problems where they worked but also where they lived. The hardships of Nineteenth Century proletarian life did not begin or end at the door of the factory.

Diet

Another aspect of working class life which we can only hint at is diet, although middle class eating patterns can be roughly established from the numerous contemporary cook books. Let us cite just one week of what is referred to as an economic diet:

Sunday	roast beef, potatoes, greens, pudding
Monday	hashed beef, potatoes, pudding
Tuesday	broiled beef, vegetable, apple pudding
Wednesday	broiled pork, beans, potatoes, rice pudding
Thursday	fowl, cabbage, potatoes, pie
Friday	fish, tomatoes, potatoes, pudding
Saturday	beef, potatoes, vegetable, pudding[87]

This can be contrasted with the food bought for one week by a working class girl for her mother, herself and two sisters:[88]

```
bread at 14¢ a loaf . . . . . . . . . . . . . . .85
oatmeal . . . . . . . . . . . . . . . . . . . . . . .25
milk at 6¢ a quart  . . . . . . . . . . . . . . .42
sugar . . . . . . . . . . . . . . . . . . . . . . . .10
butter  . . . . . . . . . . . . . . . . . . . . . . . .20
lard  . . . . . . . . . . . . . . . . . . . . . . . . .12
meat . . . . . . . . . . . . . . . . . . . . . . . . .25
potatoes . . . . . . . . . . . . . . . . . . . . . .15
currants . . . . . . . . . . . . . . . . . . . . . .06
coal oil . . . . . . . . . . . . . . . . . . . . . . .10
soap and salt . . . . . . . . . . . . . . . . . .10
                              $2.60
```

An American recommended the following cheap but healthy diet for workers at 79¢ per capita for a week:

1. 26 oz. bread, 2 oz. oatmeal, 1pt. milk, 1 oz. sugar, 24 oz. potatoes, 4 oz. beans, 2 oz. lard

2. 26 oz. bread, 2 oz. cheese, 1 pt. milk, 16 oz. potatoes, 4 oz. beans, 1 oz. lard, 3×5 oz. cups tea

3. 16 oz. bread, 4 oz. oatmeal, 1 pt. milk, 1 oz. sugar, 32 oz. potatoes, 1 oz. lard, 5 oz. cheese

4. 16 oz. bread, 6 oz. oatmeal, 1 pt. milk, 1 oz. sugar, 4 oz. beans, 32 oz. potatoes, 1 oz. lard, 3×5 oz. cups tea

5. 25 oz. bread, 2 oz. rice, 1 egg, 1 oz. lard, 4 oz. beans, 4 oz. cheese

6. 26 oz. bread, 10 oz. macaroni, 4 oz. beans, 32 oz. potatoes, 1 oz. lard, 4 oz. cheese, 1 oz. sugar, 3×5 oz. cups tea

The same source offers a second diet for 81¢ a head per week which adds cod, bacon and coffee to the above. Also there are two more expensive diets at $1.10 and $1.90. The former includes beef, mutton, butter, pork and sausage; the latter, fruit, salmon, mackerel and chicken.[89]

The first two diets with the heavy starch content probably approach most closely the dietary style of the Toronto working classes, for they are very similar to English and Irish working class diets of the period.[90]

Conclusion

How does one sum up this type of description of working class conditions? One could be moralistic and inveigh against the evils of capitalism, but that is only naive. Any claims that industrialism came easily — that the worst evils were avoided — can exist only as an ideological rationalization for horrors that can be documented with relative ease. The Royal Commission of 1889 summed up its report in a way that is highly instructive:

193

In acquiring the industry at one bound we have become possessed just as quickly of the evils which accompany the factory town and which in other lands were the creatures of gradual growth . . . They spring from the desire to acquire vast fortunes in the shortest possible interval of time, regardless of the suffering which might be caused . . . [91]

The task which remains is to correct our vision of the working class as objects and to restore to them their active, subjective role in history. Historians should be interested in understanding how men responded to their situations and how they worked out the possibilities of their lives. Much work lies ahead of us before the lived experience of the Canadian working class is really known.

Notes

1. For a synthetic look at United States working class history see Herbert Gutman, "Work, Culture and Society in Industrializing America, 1815–1919", *American Historical Review*, 78 (June 1973), p. 531–588. See also Herbert Gutman and Greg Kealey, *Many Pasts: Essays in United States Social History* (2 vols), Englewood Cliffs, N.J., 1973. The Gutman essay discusses in passing the stimulating work of Edward Thompson and Eric Hobsbawm that has inspired so much of the new social history in America. For a discussion of the historiography of the Canadian working class see the Introduction to Russell Hann *et al*, *Primary Sources in Canadian Working Class History*, Kitchener, 1973.
2. Canada, *Census*, 1851; 1891.
3. See D. C. Masters, *The Rise of Toronto, 1850–1890*, Toronto, 1947 and Stanley Ryerson, *Unequal Union*, Toronto, 1968.
4. Barrington Moore, *The Social Origins of Dictatorship and Democracy*, Boston, 1966, p. 29.
5. For the tailors' strikes see Connor, "Trade Unions in Toronto", in J. E. Middleton, ed., *The Municipality of Toronto*, Toronto, 1923; Douglas Kennedy, *The Knights of Labour in Canada*, London, 1956; and H. A. Logan, *History of Trade Union Organization in Canada*, Chicago, 1928. For the shoemakers see D. D. Lescohier, *The Knights of St. Crispin*, Madison, 1910. See also Greg Kealey, "Artisans Respond to Industrialism: Shoemakers, Shoe Factories and the Knights of St. Crispin in Toronto", Canadian Historical Association, *Historical Papers*, 1973.
6. Canada, *Royal Commission on the Relations of Labour and Capital*, Report and Evidence, Ottawa, 1889. Hereafter cited as *Labour and Capital*. For an edited version of this commission see Greg Kealey, *Canada Investigates Industrialism*, Toronto, 1973.
7. Lescohier, *op. cit*.
8. *Ibid*.
9. *Ibid*.

10. For lists of strike activity see Connor and Kennedy, *op. cit.* and Charles Lipton, *The Trade Union Movement in Canada*, Montreal, 1968. Additional data compiled from survey of Toronto press 1867–1892.
11. *Census*, 1871, 1881, 1891.
12. Canada, *Sessional Papers*, 1882, IX, No. 42.
13. *Labour and Capital*, Quebec evidence, pp. 20–80, gives a description of child beating and imprisonment in dark cellars. The commissioners referred to this as "the darkest pages in the testimony" and noted that the "lash and the dungeon are accompaniments of manufacturing in Ontario".
14. Ontario, Bureau of Industry, *Annual Report*, 1886, p. 40.
15. Ontario, Legislative Assembly, *Report of the Committee on Child Labour*, Toronto, 1907.
16. W. H. Pearson, *Recollections and Records of Toronto of Old*, Toronto, 1914, p. 181.
17. *Globe*, March 27, 1867.
18. *Ibid.*
19. Canada, *Sessional Papers*, 1882, *op. cit.*
20. *Labour and Capital*, Report, p. 87.
21. Ontario, Bureau of Industry, *Annual Report*, 1885.
22. *Ibid.*, 1886, p. 34.
23. *Ibid.*, 1887, p. 28ff.
24. These hours were true only of the small stores by the 1880's and 1890's. Large stores were generally open from 8:00 to 6:00 and later on Saturdays.
25. Joan T. Scott, "The Conditions of Female Labour in Ontario", *Toronto University Studies in Political Science*, No. 3, 1892.
26. *Ibid.*, pp. 16–18.
27. George Nasmith, *Timothy Eaton*, Toronto, 1923. A eulogistic biography which does not do justice to this Canadian financial wizard who fined his employees regularly for tardiness and who farmed out much of his textiles and clothing to sweat shops.
28. *Report of the Royal Commission on a Dispute Regarding House of Employment Between the Bell Telephone Co. and U.S. Operators at Toronto*, Ottawa, 1907.
29. *Ibid.*, pp. 29–30.
30. *Ibid.*, p. 35.
31. *Ibid.*, pp. 29, 37, 39.
32. *Ibid.*, p. 97, emphasis mine. One wonders if men are excluded from this conclusion.
33. Canada, *Sessional Papers*, 1896, XXIX, No. 61.
34. *Ibid.*, p. 6.
35. *Ibid.*, p. 7.
36. *Ibid.*, p. 6.
37. *Ibid.*, p. 7.
38. *Ibid.*, p. 9.
39. Ontario, *Report of the Factory Inspectors*, 1888, p. 7.
40. Testimony of L. Gurofsky before the Commission on Sweating, *op. cit.*, pp. 24, 30.
41. *Ibid.*, p. 22.
42. *Ibid.*, p. 9–11.
43. *Labour and Capital*, Report p. 79.
44. Canada, *Sessional Papers*, 1882, *op. cit.*
45. *Ibid.*
46. Locking the doors to the factory seems to have been one rather primitive method of ensuring your employees maintained discipline and didn't wander. Not terribly good if there was a fire of course, but c'est la vie.
47. Ontario, Bureau of Industry, *Annual Report*, 1885.
48. *Ibid.*, 1886, p. 53.
49. *Labour and Capital*, Ontario evidence, p. 57.
50. *Ibid.*, p. 93.
51. *Ibid.*, p. 262.
52. *Ibid.*, pp. 311–315 and 326.
53. As quoted in Doris French, *Faith, Sweat and Politics*, Toronto, 1962, p. 84.
54. *Labour and Capital*, Report, p. 12.
55. Ontario, Bureau of Industry, *Annual Report*, 1886, p. 40.
56. *Labour and Capital*, Ontario evidence, pp. 91–98.
57. *Ibid.*, p. 148.
58. *Ibid.*, p. 151.
59. Canada, *Sessional Papers*, 1882, *op. cit.*
60. *Labour and Capital*, Ontario evidence, p. 45.

61. *Ibid.*, p. 148.
62. *Ibid.*, p. 317.
63. Ontario Board of Health, *Annual Reports*, 1887, 1891, p. 101.
64. *Ibid.*, 1884, p. 99.
65. Ontario, Bureau of Industry, *Annual Report*, 1887.
66. *Labour and Capital*, Ontario evidence, p. 53.
67. *Labour and Capital*, Report p. 29.
68. *Ibid.*, p. 8.
69. *Ibid.*, Ontario evidence, p. 57.
70. *Ibid.*, p. 44.
71. *Ibid.*, pp. 254–257.
72. *Ibid.*, pp. 159–169.
73. *Ibid.*, pp. 13–28. This single tax group was heavily influenced by Henry George and part of a continent-wide network of Anti-Poverty Leagues.
74. *Ibid.*, pp. 98–103.
75. *Ibid.*, pp. 151–156.
76. One might add that seemingly not much has changed in Toronto in the last 80 years.
77. G. Frank Beer, "Working Men's Houses and Model Dwellings in Canada", *Garden Cities and Town Planning*, IV (May, 1914), pp. 104–109, (November, 1914) pp. 261–262.
78. *Labour and Capital*, Report, p. 8.
79. *Ibid.*, p. 30.
80. *Ibid.*, p. 8.
81. *Ibid.*, p. 84.
82. *Labour and Capital*, Ontario evidence, p. 95.
83. Victor Vaughan, *Healthy Homes and Foods for the Working Classes*, Concord, N.Y., 1886.
84. Ontario Board of Health, *Annual Report*, p. 98.
85. *Ibid.*, 1891, p. 103.
86. *Ibid.*, 1891, p. 103.
87. *Toronto Home Cook Book*, Toronto, 1877, p. 384.
88. Scott, "Conditions of Female Labour", *op. cit.*
89. Victor Vaughan, *Healthy Homes, op. cit.*
90. For Edwardian working class diets see Margharita Laski, "Domestic Life" in *Edwardian England*, London, 1964.
91. *Labour and Capital*, Report, p. 112.

Children of the Industrial Revolution in Quebec*

FERNAND HARVEY

Translated by Robert Russell

Much has been written about the family in Quebec from both the ideological and scientific points of view. That is easily understood if it is realized that the family has always been considered, until the mid 1960's, as the basic unit of Quebec society. It is rather unusual therefore that the child itself has not been the subject of study. It all seems as though the child could not be considered independently of the family.

To undertake a history of the child in Quebec is thus to break new ground. It seems that no historian or sociologist has yet shown systematic interest in the field. I will thus outline the topic by specifically limiting my subject to the role and function of children in the process of industrialization in Quebec.

* From *The Professions: Their Growth or Decline?* edited by J. Drufresne et al. Copyright 1979 by Société de publication Critère. Reprinted by permission.

Recent studies on the history of workers, as well as former research on traditional societies, suggested a hypothesis to me: children of the industrial revolution in Quebec as victims were doubly constrained: by a traditional society based on family solidarity, and by a capitalist society based on the technical division of labour and the exploitation of cheap manpower.

At the end of the 19th century, minds opened to social concerns, especially among philanthropists and some journalists, denounced the shameless exploitation of child labour in factories, but a silent majority seemed resigned to its fate and accepted the situation as an established fact. We will see that child labour was indeed not a new reality in Quebec society.

Quebec's Industrial Revolution at the End of the 19th Century

To best understand the condition of a child at work during the last century, several steps in the economic evolution of Quebec should be recalled.

Under the French Regime and the beginnings of English rule, Quebec's economy comprised three main activities: agriculture, fishing and the fur trade. Of those three sectors, the fur trade provided a generative product and consituted the bulk of the colony's exports to the home country. Artisanry was little developed and limited to a domestic market. However, from the beginnings of New France an apprentice system was created and developed that had been inspired by a French model but adapted to a Canadian context, as has been shown in a recent study by Hardy and Ruddel.[1]

From the beginning of the 19th century, the economic structure of Lower Canada underwent profound changes as the forestry industry developed. Without going into details, the period from 1800 to 1880 may be characterized as the period during which commercial capitalism in British North American colonies grew and peaked.

In Quebec the true origin of the timber industry goes back to 1803 when Britain, fighting the Napoleonic Wars, set a special tariff on Canadian rough-hewn timber. For over thirty years lumbering was the mainstay of the Quebec economy. Then, especially after 1850, Canada's timber industry redirected its output to profit from the rapid development of the American mid-West and captured new markets.[2]

Here it should be emphasized that the timber industry provided the momentum for other production sectors such as iron tooling, shoes and clothing.

The period from 1800 to 1880 also saw creation of important transportation facilities. A series of canals constructed between 1825 and 1840 made the St. Lawrence navigable from Montreal to the Great Lakes. After 1850, railways were built linking the various colonies of British North America.

In 1876 the Intercolonial Railway joining Sarnia (Ontario) and Halifax (Nova Scotia) by way of Rimouski was completed.

Two comments should be made regarding the development of commercial capitalism, of which I have only sketched the important aspects, that were related to this article. First, it should be noted that construction of the transportation facilities required cheap, abundant, unskilled labour. Quebec's first proletariat composed mainly of Irish, English and Scottish immigrants was created in this fashion. French Canadians were said to show little interest in wage employment, preferring farming. They would later emigrate to New England, never entering the urban proletariat in masses until the first significant wave of industrialization in Quebec in the 1880's.[3]

Almost nothing is known about the children of those first proletarians. Did they work alongside their parents building canals and railways or did they remain at home? More research is required to deal with such questions.

A second comment, however, must be made regarding the evolution of Canadian commercial capitalism: its expansion allowed development of artisanry and a modest beginning of manufacturing industries. Child labour, especially apprenticeships, was affected by the situation.

From the end of the 19th century, Quebec and Ontario began significant industrialization. The first signs of that industrialization were already appearing from 1850 onwards in milling, ironwork and timber with their related industries, and shoes; its actual beginning occurred in the 1880's with the tariff policy of Federal Prime Minister John A. Macdonald known as the "National Policy".

After that period which coincided with what several authors term the Second Industrial Revolution, the industrial profile of modern Quebec may be discerned. The availability of cheap, willing labour encouraged capitalist entrepreneurs in the Province to develop sectors such as textiles, clothing, tanning, shoes and tobacco or in current political economic terminology, the soft sectors. Other industrial sectors were also developed: food products, iron and steel products especially rolling stock for railroads etc.

On a parallel with industrialization went rapid urbanization in Quebec. In 1851 the rate of urbanization was 15%, in 1891, 29% and after 1921 over 50%. Thus, in 70 years Quebec's population that had been massively rural, became mainly urban.

Child Labour before Industrialization

The elements of economic history already presented enable us to better situate the evolution of child labour in Quebec during the 19th century. The condition of the working child before industrialization should be examined first.

The historian Claude Folhen properly notes that child labour is "far

197

from being an invention of the industrial revolution, for in all economic systems, children always assisted their parents in family occupations."[4] The same comment applies to rural Quebec. From the early beginnings of the colony, children contributed to maintaining the family farm since many family heads were unable to resist the attractions of the fur trade, leaving the home for months at a time while the wife remained in charge of the family.

As agricultural activity was consolidated in the 18th and 19th centuries, child labour on the farm was a necessity inasmuch as the hiring of farm labourers remained a rare and marginal occurrence. The evolution of child labour is best seen in the artisanry sector for that type of work was linked to an apprenticeship system found in all traditional societies and which in Quebec was recognized by notarized contract.

Of what exactly did apprenticeships comprise? In an era in which there were no technical institutes, the only way to pass on a trade was through on-the-job training in an artisan's shop. In their study of the evolution of apprenticeships in Quebec, Hardy and Ruddel[5] note that the age apprentices were accepted varied with the trades but rarely dipped below 12. A child was placed by his parents with a master who undertook the child's training in the different branches of the trade. In addition, the master agreed to provide bed and board and at times, clothing and linen. The apprentice agreed to obey his master and not to leave without permission.

Before expansion of commercial capitalism in Canada, artisans' shops were of limited size comprising the master, his family, one or two apprentices and perhaps a labourer. At that time artisan production was directly linked to local and individual demand in response to the request by a client for a pair of shoes or for construction of a house. Stock was not accumulated by the artisan system due to the limited size of its market.

After 1800, development of commercial capitalism that was linked to the timber industry and later to the construction of canals and railroads increased demand for manufactured goods. Already by 1840 artisan enterprises were rapidly expanding and the first manufactured goods appeared, although admittedly of modest quantity. Following that development, the number of apprentices in some trades such as shipbuilding, bakeries, blacksmiths, shoemaking, pilots and milling increased.

The work conditions imposed on the apprentices were relatively difficult if compared with contemporary standards but the amount of work required was certainly comparable to that demanded of children on farms. An apprentice in the previously-mentioned trades signed on for three years and worked 11 hours a day in winter and 12 hours a day in summer. Some contracts specified that the child was to perform certain household chores requested by the master.

Two consequences of the expansion of the commercial economy concerning children deserve mention. First, young wage earners appeared. In fact, little by little, the master was transformed into a small capitalist entrepreneur, tending to drift from the model of paternalistic apprentice-

198

ship. He thus willingly released himself from the obligation to feed, clothe and lodge his apprentice by paying a small compensating salary. This tendency became the rule with the creation of workshops and mechanized production after the 1880's.

In addition, the development of business and increase in the number of apprentices created a problem of discipline at work even before the mechanization of factories. Wishing to best profit from child labour, masters and entrepreneurs adopted a very strict attitude regarding time lost by apprentices. For example, in some trades, every day of lost work, whether justified or not, was to be compensated by two days of additional work.

The social control of apprentices was partly assumed by the State. The law was used to punish apprentices absent from work. In 1802 the Assembly of Lower Canada first adopted a bill respecting trades and apprentices. The intent of the law was to control apprentices, domestics, servants and journeymen and to govern and direct them. The government intended at the same time to establish laws and regulations fixing the conduct of masters towards their apprentices.[6] The law underwent few amendments and remained in effect throughout the 19th century. After 1865, in Montreal, the law, entitled the Act respecting Masters and Servants, was enforced through Recorders Court. In this instance the terminology used reveals the inertia of the legal apparatus when faced with the realities of industrial life, since apprentices and even workers continued to be designated as servants until the end of the 19th century. It is hardly necessary to stress that this first industrial relations law was conceived and interpreted in favour of the employer. Apprenticeship as it evolved in the first half of the 19th century already exhibited some characteristics of child labour found in the early part of Quebec's period of industrialization.

Children and Work at the Beginning of Industrialization

The actual beginning of industrialization in Canada and Quebec as stated earlier was in the early 1880's. Quebec's entry into industrialization coincided with the Second Industrial Revolution in the world.

The first industrial revolution occurred in England after 1760 and spread to the rest of Europe at the beginning of the 19th century. It remained linked to the manufacturing phase of industrialization. Marx aptly described the twofold origin of manufacture as either the assemblage in one workshop under the control of a single capitalist of labourers belonging to various independent artisans to produce, as for example, in the manufacture of carriages; or in the assemblage in one workshop of a large number of artificers who all fabricate the same object, such as the making of type.[7]

The second Industrial Revolution was the result of accelerating technological developments and diversifying production methods. During the second phase of industrialization corresponding in general to the change from manufacturing to mechanized factories, two technical elements play a determining role: development of the steam engine and that of machine tools.[8]

The evolution in technology caused by development of capitalist means of production created in consequence a constantly increasing technical division of labour. Thus, for reasons at one and the same time technical and economic, child labour became a generalized phenomena in Quebec factories at the end of the 19th century. The use of machine tools in certain sectors of industry in effect enabled employing women and children in places where qualified skilled workers were previously required. The skills and physical effort formerly required were replaced by rapidity and a simple initiation into the operation.

Testifying before the Royal Commission on the Relations of Capital and Labour, instituted by the Federal Government between 1886 and 1889, a skilled worker expressed his fears of the invasion of the cigar industry by children in these terms:

200

> Manufacturers found they could get cigars made more cheaply by children, and that is how so many children are employed in the trade. Before that time there were only a certain number of apprentices employed according to the number of men in the shop, as is the case in Upper Canada at present. (. . .)
> If shops are allowed to continue under their present system, with this machinery that makes 5500 bunches in one day, with a little girl working at it, I ask what will become of cigar-makers?[9]

The evidence is significant in several respects. Technological advancement of course is mentioned. Also demonstrated is the interest employers have in hiring children: manpower that could be paid less than skilled workers, thus increasing profits. For skilled workers, however, the invasion of certain trades by children and labourers constituted a real tragedy. Powerless, they witnessed the disappearance of their trade. The situation was even more tragic in that trade unionism proved powerless to protect their interests. How could it react in mechanized sectors in which the new organization of the factory made all work positions interchangeable?

That leads us to deal with the evolution of apprenticeship in Quebec at the end of the 19th century. In the trades most affected by technical change, the apprenticeship system as it existed in traditional society was only a memory. Legal constraints imposed on both the employer and the apprentice became too rigid during the rapid evolution of the economy and society. For all practical purposes, the child working in a large factory became a skilled worker at the same level as a labourer except that the child was paid less and worked at repetitive or control tasks that did not require appreciable physical effort.

The notorious exceptions to that general tendency were the Montreal cigar factories. In that industrial sector, the formal apprenticeship system continued but in a legal form devoid of content. The apprentice cigar maker was placed by his parents with the owner of a factory after a contract for a period of three years was notarized. The salary was $1.00 a week for the first year and $3.00 a week by the third year compared to the average adult salary of $7.00 a week. The interest of employers in child labour is understandable.

In general there was an emptiness in apprenticeship training in Quebec at the end of the 19th century. The former apprentice system had practically disappeared in the most industrialized sectors but no solution for their replacement yet existed, such as a network of technical schools. It would not be until the beginning of the 20th century that the situation would evolve in that direction. In addition, it is quite conceivable that the former artisan system continued into the 20th century in trades little affected by technical change or in regions in Quebec that were not immediately industrialized.

It is difficult at this stage in our research to quantify the evolution of child labour in Quebec during the 19th century. The federal census of 1891 indicates that in Quebec there were 9500 children under 16 employed in industrial establishments or 8% of the local manpower in the sector.[10] Child labour was most used in the textile and tobacco industries. The conditions of work for children in the factories were arduous. Witnesses before the Royal Commission on the Relations of Capital and Labour in 1888 provoked a veritable scandal at that time in the national press. The apprentice cigar makers of the Montreal Fortier factory constituted in that respect one of the summits of the investigation.[11] The meagre salaries, long work hours, brutality of the foremen, numerous fines and occasional imprisonment were the lot of the children employed in that factory and many others.

201

Work conditions of that sort, to which must also be added the problem of poor health conditions posed the problem of work discipline. Industrialization in Quebec, as elsewhere, entailed putting a proletarian army, still undisciplined, to work. At that time, theories of management did not hinder anyone; for management theory did not develop in an operational manner until the creation of Taylorism at the beginning of the 20th century. The factory at the end of the 19th century had the traits of a totalitarian institution: all was subject to the iron rule of maximum production. In that context, the foremen were free to use any methods deemed necessary to maintain discipline within the organization. The children then became the private targets of foremen and owners inasmuch as their power to fight back was practically non-existent.

With those facts established, it is possible to conclude that child labour was not a new phenomenon linked to the industrialization of Quebec. Its origins go back to the beginnings of the colony and are linked to the organization of work in traditional society. However, the development of commercial capitalism at the beginning of the 19th centuy and especially industrial capitalism in the 1880's changed the nature and function of child labour in the working classes. Children became, with their parents, wage earners serving the accumulation of capital. As their parents, they were subjected by mechanization to an *objective organization of work* in contrast to the former system of work.

The Child and Society in General

It is difficult in the current state of research to evaluate the status of the child within the Quebec family at the end of the 19th century. Without a doubt the level of valorization of the child must be distinguished by social class, type of milieu and ethnic group. A child was undoubtedly valued more in the middle classes than in the working class or on the farm. It may also be supposed that the child was more valued in the Anglo-Protestant than in the French Catholic milieu especially with respect to education.

To better evaluate the condition of the child in Quebec's working class at the end of the 19th century, it should be situated with respect to the family.

It seems evident that in Quebec proletarianization did not break family unity. Indeed entire families of French Canadians left the country for the city: first for cities in New England and later in Montreal and Quebec. For example, witnesses before the Commission on Labour stated that an agent of the Hochelaga Cotton Company was to recruit whole families of workers in the Saguenay drawing them to the factory with false promises of the salary to be earned. The first generation proletarians called the "Saguenay" were, it seems, favoured by employers because of their greater obedience at work to the detriment of urban workers.[12]

Taking into account the late industrialization of Canada in respect to other countries, it seems that Quebec society avoided the preliminary stages of industrialization regarding child labour. It is known that in England, at the end of the 18th century, orphans and abandoned children from parishes were recruited by the hundreds and crowded into workhouses in the service of manufacturers.[13] Nothing similar occurred in Quebec, at least with respect to French Canadians.

Moreover, even in England, the situation had evolved by the second half of the 19th century. That is the opinion of historian Peter Laslett who affirms that during that period of family solidarity: "children stayed at home and joined their income to that of their parents."[14]

In Quebec, a child of the working class also profited from family solidarity, a heritage undoubtedly of rural life. But he was also a victim of the solidarity to the extent that he had to work by the age of ten or even earlier in a factory with his father, mother, brothers and sisters in order to meet the family budget.

In fact the father's meagre salary did not suffice for the essentials of food, clothing and shelter. The family was always at the mercy of the unforeseen: a work accident, unemployment, death of the father could plunge the family into misery in an era during which insurance and social security were non-existent for the working class.

It may be assumed in that context that education, even at primary level, was a luxury not allowed working families. The factory was the only

202

opening for children of the proletariat — the only cultural gathering place in effect. In that respect pressure by parents was great on the employer, as witnessed by a foreman of a cotton factory drawn from the minutes of the Royal Commission on the Relations of Capital and Labour.

You can understand, in regard to small help, that it is as one of the overseers said to me: "I have more trouble to keep the small help out of my room, than I have to keep them in it". A man will be working at the mill, and his daughter working there also, and he may have a small child, whom he desires to have there, for instance, in the spooling room. Often you don't want to take the child, but if you do not, he and his daughter will go out, and they will go to some mill where the whole three will be employed.

The same witness added later:

When young girls come to the mill their mothers often come with them, and beg the chance of getting them on to work. For instance, there was a mother brought a girl the other day. I said she was small. The mother replied: "I went into the mill at about that age."[16]

203

Should the parents be accused of being greedy? Although some parents may have abused their children by making them work, such a moralizing accusation risks taking the cause for the effect. It is the economic system instead that is the primary cause of the miserable conditions for working class children in the 19th century.

What did the State do in such circumstances? Very little in fact. All during the 19th century, labour relations in Quebec were governed by the out-moded Act respecting Servants and Masters. The law permitted an employer or his foreman to take to Recorder's Court any apprentice accused of misbehaviour, breaking property or absence from work. The law provided a fine and imprisonment for the apprentice found guilty. An apprentice could also bring his employer before the Court for reason of brutality. In that case, the employer found guilty was fined or condemned to prison. The complacency of judges however renders problematical the condemnation of an employer.

More striking than the injustice of the law is its anachronistic and paternalistic character. As the good father of a family that he considered himself, the Montreal City Recorder, Judge B.A.T. de Montigny, established the principle that the "master" had a right to correct his "apprentice" or "servant" provided it was a "reasonable correction".[17] This occurred in 1888, less than a century ago.

As for industrial and social legislation, it was almost non-existent in the 19th century. Quebec passed its first law requiring inspection of factories in 1885 but the law remained ineffective for many years because of the limited number of inspectors and the weak penalties provided for employers. It was not until the 20th century that Quebec set 14 as the minimum age for children in factories. That "victory" was not followed up until the law compelling educational instruction was adopted in 1940. Thus, little by little, the development of industrialization permitted the transfer from the factory to the school of the methods of acculturation and social control of children.

Notes

1. Jean-Pierre Hardy and David-Thiery Ruddel, *Les apprentis artisans à Québec, 1660–1815*. Montréal, Presses de l'Université du Québec, 1977, pp. 9–84.

2. Noël Vallerand, "Histoire des faits économiques de la Vallée du St-Laurent 1760–1866", in *Economie québécoise*, Montréal, Presses de l'U.Q., 1969, pp. 71–72.

3. See H. C. Pentland, "The development of a Capitalistic Labour Market in Canada", *Canadian Journal of Economic and Political Sciences*, 25 (1959):459–60.

4. Claude Folhen, "Révolution industrielle et travail des enfants", *Annales de Démographie historique*, (1973):320.

5. *Op. cit.*

6. J. P. Hardy and D. T. Ruddel, *op. cit.*, p. 89; 170–171.

7. Karl Marx, *Le Capital*, Livre premier, T. II, Paris, Editions Sociales, 1967, p. 30.

8. H. Pasdermadjian, *La deuxième révolution industrielle*. Paris, P.U.F., 1959, p. 152.

9. Canada, *Royal Commission on the Relations of Capital and Labour*, Quebec, Ottawa, Queen's Printer, 1888, pp. 59 and 65.

10. *Recensement du Canada*, 1891, pp. 383–387.

11. For further details on that Commission, see: Fernand Harvey, *Révolution industrielle et travailleurs. Une enquête sur les relations entre le capital et le travail au Québec à la fin du 19e siècle*. Montréal, Boréal Express, 1978, 350 p.

12. Fernand Harvey, *op. cit.*, p. 113.

13. Claude Folhen, *op. cit.*, p. 321.

14. Peter Laslett, "L'attitude à l'égard de l'enfant dans l'Angleterre du XIXe siècle", *Annales de Démographie historique*, (1973): 317.

15. See: Terry Copp, *Classe ouvrière et pauvreté. Les conditions de vie des travailleurs montréalais, 1897–1929*. Montréal, Boréal Express, 1978.

16. Quoted in: Fernand Harvey, *op. cit.*, p. 186.

17. F. Harvey, *op. cit.*, pp. 162–163.

Topic Seven:
The Rise of Cities

Cities have had a profound influence on Canada's development. They have served as focal points of identity in the various regions and as centres of growth in a sparsely populated nation. The most recent approach to the interpretation of Canadian history is metropolitanism—the study of the impact of cities on their respective hinterlands.

Urban communities have existed in Canada since the beginning of European settlement, but the rate of their growth has varied from region to region and from one period to another. Urban historians generally agree that the "take off" period for the emergence of the modern city was from 1850 to 1914, from the end of the mercantile system of trade up to and including the rise of the industrial city. For the Maritimes the growth tended to be more pronounced in the earlier decades of this period, while for Central Canada and the West it was in the later decades.

By 1921, the census showed more Canadians living in urban centres than in rural areas. There existed in all regions the same essential features: commercial buildings and industrial factories in the city centre; slums; growing suburban areas; and the network of streets, inner-city transportation, and railways.

The following three readings discuss the evolution of cities in three different regions during this period. In "Aspects of Metropolitanism in Atlantic Canada", J. M. S. Careless analyses the metropolitan roles of the three principal Atlantic cities, Saint John, Halifax, and St. John's from the mid-nineteenth to the early twentieth century. Peter Goheen's "Currents of Change in Toronto" outlines the growth of Toronto from a colonial to a commercial and industrial city from 1850 to 1900. Alan Artibise discusses the kaleidoscopic history of prairie towns and cities from before 1850 to 1930, in "The Urban West: The Evolution of Prairie Towns and Cities to 1930."

A brief but informative overview of the history of cities in Canada can be found in J. M. S. Careless's *The Rise of Cities in Canada before 1914*,

Canadian Historical Association Booklet No. 32 (Ottawa, 1978). *The Canadian City: Essays in Urban History,* edited by G. A. Stelter and A. F. J. Artibise (Toronto: McClelland and Stewart, 1977), is an excellent anthology of articles in Canadian urban history and contains a good bibliography of recent publications organized according to regions. Students should also consult the journal *The Urban History Review/Revue d'histoire urbane (UHR/RHU)* (Ottawa: National Museum of Man, 1972–   ). On the methodology of urban history, see G. Stelter's, "Current Research in Canadian Urban History," *UHR/RHU* 13 (1976):27–36.

Aspects of Metropolitanism in Atlantic Canada*

J. M. S. CARELESS

206

I

Metropolitanism, the pattern of reciprocal relations whereby large urban communities focus broad areas on themselves, is intimately associated with regionalism. For regions usually centre on metropolitan communities, which largely organize them, focus their views, and deal with outside metropolitan forces on their behalf. Indeed, much of what is often called regionalism may be better expressed in terms of metropolitan relations and activities. In that belief, this discussion of metropolitanism in Atlantic Canada is offered. Because the subject is so large, it has been limited to the period from the mid-nineteenth to the early twentieth centuries, and to a selective consideration of the metropolitan roles of the three principal Atlantic cities, Saint John, Halifax, and St. John's during that period.

This time span is long enough to allow a considerable process of change to be examined, still highly significant today. Although its limits are inevitably imprecise, there is some validity in starting with the 1850's, after the end of the Navigation Acts and the old imperial system, and closing before the First World War brought striking new developments to the Maritimes and Newfoundland. As for the subject-matter, there seems no less validity in studying the three largest communities of the Atlantic region in themselves: both as regional leaders, and because we might well pay more regard to urban history in Canada.

The fact is that, land of vast frontiers and wilderness or not, urban communities long played a large part in Canadian development and this is no less true for the Atlantic region. Nor need the cities in question be huge and teeming by modern standards. It is far more the proportion of their population to the total in their regional community that has meaning. In 1861, for instance, Saint John had a population of 27 315 to 252 045 for all

*From *Regionalism in the Canadian Community, 1867–1967*, Canadian Historical Association Centennial Seminars, edited by M. Wade. Copyright 1969 by University of Toronto Press. Reprinted by permission.

New Brunswick, or a proportion of close to 1 in 9; Halifax had 25 025 to 330 885 in Nova Scotia, or roughly 1 in 13; St. John's 30 475 to 122 635 in Newfoundland, or a remarkable proportion of almost 1 in 4. A century later, by the Canadian census of 1961, Saint John stood at something over 1 in 8, Halifax at about 1 in 8, St. John's around 1 in 9. Plainly then, even by present standards, each city has represented a decided concentration of population in its provincial community; not to mention a concentration of capital and labour that would enable it to fulfil metropolitan functions.

These functions or attributes of metropolitan stature have broadly been held to comprise, first, the provision of commercial facilities for the import and export trade of the city's dependent region or hinterland (on which, of course, it in turn depends); second, the establishment of industries to process products of, or imports for, the hinterland; third, the development of transport services to channel traffic to and from the urban centre; and fourth, the creation of financial facilities for investment and development in the region. All these attributes can be seen in greater or less degree within the three cities under inquiry. But to these economic characteristics might also be added those of political power or military authority often centred in the metropolis; and, quite as frequently, the exercise of religious, educational, and intellectual leadership for the regional community, along with press influence over its opinion.

207

Indeed, to a great extent a metropolitan system is inherently a system of communications, whether this carries goods, people or money, orders or ideas. As a result, it may be deeply affected by changes in technology; a point as true for the age that experienced the introduction of the steamship, railway, and telegraph as for that of automobility, jet transport, and television.

The effect of technological change on communications is notably clear in the case of Atlantic Canada. Although in assessing it, this general survey must to some extent put together material that is far from new, yet it is hoped that a restructuring in terms of metropolitan patterns and pulls will make the data more meaningful. And it is thought that a comparative analysis of the development of the three major Atlantic centres can promote new queries concerning their regional functions. The procedure will be to start with Saint John, then move out to sea, so to speak, in a properly Toronto-centred view of the globe.

II

In the mid-nineteenth century, Saint John held a prominent role in an Atlantic communications system extending to Liverpool and London in one direction, Boston and New York in another. It was the commercial metropolis for much of New Brunswick, exporting the timber wealth of the Saint John River from its position at the entrance to that long waterway, importing the British manufacturers or American provisions needed for a hinterland heavily based on forest production. It was a focus of industry also, that utilized the chief product of its hinterland region in large-scale wooden shipbuilding. And through wealth acquired from the timber trade or the sale of Saint John ships in England, the city's business community was able to provide significant financial services, including by the later fifties three locally owned banks and four local marine, fire, or general insurance companies.

Yet Saint John's metropolitan stature had clear limits. First, although New Brunswick was past the frontier expansionist stage, the province was relatively poor and undiversified in depending on its forest staple. Second, since the whole region was largely composed of a series of separated river valleys, Saint John's sway over its own river and Bay of Fundy area by no means extended to the province's north shore. And third, since the city was not the seat of government, it could not enjoy the pervasive influence of a centre of political authority. Nor did it really exercise social or cultural headship, which remained with the genteel society of little Fredericton up-river.

Saint John's own leading elements composed a substantial, overlapping business élite of import merchants, timber traders, shipbuilders, and shipowners. The same individuals reoccurred in lists of the directors of banks, insurance firms, and other joint stock enterprises such as the Saint John Gas, Light, Electric, Telegraph or South Bay Boom Companies: men such as William Parks, President of the Commercial Bank, or shipbuilders and shipowners such as Wright, DeVeber, and Zebedee Ring.[1] Nor did this Saint John business community lack strong political ties. Out of its background came such major political figures as R. L. Hazen and R. D. Wilmot, W. H. Steeves, a father of Confederation, G. E. King, provincial premier of the seventies — or Samuel Leonard Tilley himself, partner in the prominent firm of Peters and Tilley, merchants.

The business élite of Saint John was perhaps more limited in its outlook than its counterparts in either Halifax or St. John's. The New Brunswick port's outside connections largely ran to Portland as an intermediary for Boston, or else focussed on Liverpool; hardly a city of light. A scion of the mid-century élite (son of the president of the Bank of New Brunswick) recalled that Saint John businessmen would cross to Liverpool and Manchester twenty times "without ever going on to London."[2] Yet the sober, workaday masters of Saint John were lively and enterprising enough when it came to the city's main industrial activity, shipbuilding.

In the prosperous fifties, stimulated by the gold rush to Australia, Saint John yards turned out a splendid succession of large sailing vessels for Liverpool owners. There was James Smith's famed *Marco Polo,* hailed as the fastest ship in the world, after her 68-day voyage from Liverpool to Melbourne in 1852; or the *Morning Light,* of over 2 300 tons, launched by William and Richard Wright in 1855, which remained for twenty years the largest ship constructed in British North America. By 1858, of 100 major vessels over 1 200 tons sailing out of Liverpool, 32 had been built in Saint John and the pace continued through the sixties.

Successful as it was in ocean transport, the city entered a whole new phase of problems when it looked to railways to improve its land communications in the prosperous mid-century years. Saint John interests were deeply involved in the scheme to build the European and North American Railway, which would link the Bay of Fundy port overland with the Atlantic shore at Shediac, and in the other direction with Portland, Maine, there connecting with the rails to Boston and with the Atlantic and St. Lawrence to Montreal, open since 1852. Saint John was thus to become the focus of a great international overland route between coasts close to Europe, New England, and Canada. It was a bright vision, often more appealing than the alternative Intercolonial Railway project from Nova Scotia through New Brunswick to Quebec — though, conceivably (in the brightest moments of vision) both lines might be built, and tied together at Saint John. Of course, John A. Poor, the Portland capitalist who expressed his own city's metropolitan ambitions, had other hopes as to the final focal point of the railway scheme he was promoting. But in any case it did not succeed.

209

Neither Portland nor Saint John could organize the capital for so large a design, and construction problems had been underestimated. The European and North American was completed only between Saint John and Shediac by 1860, and then as a publicly owned road. Moreover, Saint John was not really well placed to dominate overland routes to the interior of the continent, a fact of growing ominous significance in the spreading railway age. When again in 1865, an attempt by a new company under William Parks shortly failed to build the "Western Extension" from the city to Maine, it was no wonder that many in Saint John viewed with disdain the coming of Confederation, and its concomitant bargain to build the Intercolonial, but via New Brunswick's distant north shore. Indeed, they might sense that an oceanic metropolitan system in which their city had flourished was passing away, to be replaced by new continental patterns with which they were less equipped to deal.

Yet Confederation was more coincident than causal in regard to changes that affected the whole functioning of Saint John as a metropolis. In fact, the changes did not plainly reveal themselves until after the depression of 1873 began. Most vital was the shift from wood to iron technology in transport. It was not the steamship that drastically affected Saint John's shipping industry, but the iron-built vessel. British yards had begun turning out cheap, capacious iron and steel steamships in quantities. They doomed Saint John's Liverpool sales and attacked the lucrative charter business of wooden sailing craft, secure while the steamship itself had been limited to fairly small wooden hulls, carrying fuel as well as cargo on a relatively few high-cost ocean runs. And while it had once been economic to build wooden ships in New Brunswick instead of England, now the great British iron and steel capacity made it increasingly uneconomic to do so. The effects came gradually. A peak year for Saint John yards was 1873, and as late as 1888, 2 000 men were still employed there.[3] But through the seventies and eighties, the city's major industry inexorably declined.

One should recall, of course, that the sweep of technological change also affected wealthier adjacent American centres. Thus New England's magnificent but costly clippers could not compete, and the region failed to build an iron ship industry. This in part was because Boston capital had turned from marine to railway investment, in efforts to organize and dominate continental routes west that proved only somewhat less abortive than Saint John's hopes of the European and North American. Portland declined. Boston itself was not so well placed to collect the traffic from the ever growing continental hinterland. It could be the chief regional metropolis of New England, but not a great deal beyond.[4] Railways, which had made inland western development so much more feasible and valuable, had shifted the emphasis from ports chiefly well located for the exchange of water-borne coastal and ocean traffic to those which also offered the most effective land access to broad continental territories

210

All this was true for Saint John in the advancing railway age — itself another aspect of triumphant steel technology. Again the city was not in a position to benefit. Its own hinterland did not provide fuel or raw material for new heavy industry. And along with the relative down-grading of its timber resources went a decline in their quality, as the best pineries were cut over. Even in the 1860's it was becoming difficult to get good timber for large ships at Saint John yards.[5] Hence these underlying changes, affecting the commercial position, industrial enterprise, and even hinterland supply of the New Brunswick metropolis, were much more basic than any effects of Confederation, the National Policy of 1879, or the long depression of the later nineteenth century.

No doubt the lean depression years made the impact of change harder, especially for a city swept by the disastrous fire of 1877 that destroyed two-fifths of Saint John and $27 000 000 in property.[6] No doubt the protective tariff offered little to the business enterprises of a community largely geared to primary production, except for a declining industry tariffs could not protect. But world depression created none of Saint John's essential problems. And National Policy or not, the smaller business units of the Maritime centres would surely have faced powerful competition from much larger aggregations of capital and labour, once the age of overland communication by rail had tied them into major continental traffic systems. Here indeed lay the essential significance of the later nineteenth-century years for Saint John and its region; it was the difficult era when the old Atlantic system was failing and the New Brunswick metropolis had not yet adjusted to the new forces of continental dominance.

That adjustment came in the early twentieth century. It was, perhaps, only relatively successful, in that it could not restore all Saint John's vanished eminence, but it has largely endured to the present. Its effect was economic, yet it was achieved largely by political means for political reasons: not in spite of, but because of, the Atlantic region's membership in Canada. And it was built on the advantage the Atlantic region had to offer within that membership, year-round access to the ocean.

The Canadian federation had a political, national, need for winter ports of its own. In a sense, the process of developing them was a valid complement to the National Policy. For that programme, as Professor R. C. Brown has emphasized, must truly be seen as an expression of national aspirations, however much it might also enhance central Canadian metropolitan power.[7] If the federal state could pursue nation-building by tariffs, it could equally do so by railway and port development, by subsidies and preferential rail rates, to aid enterprises and areas disadvantaged by distance or tariffs. It was all a natural response to the problem of integrating regions within a Canadian continental entity.

The process of adjustment for Saint John really began when in 1887 business leaders in its Board of Trade opened a campaign to shift the winter terminus of the Dominion-subsidized mail steamers from Portland to the New Brunswick city. Then in 1890 the completion of the Canadian Pacific's Short Line from Montreal across Maine to Saint John meant that the Fundy port now had fairly direct access to central Canada, as well as by the more circuitous Intercolonial, intersected by the Saint John–Shediac line at Moncton. Now there indeed was hope that Canadian winter traffic still moving via Portland could be diverted to Saint John. Hence that city invested in building large ocean docks, to the extent of $1 000 000 by 1895.[8]

Late that year came the key political step. When city delegations repeatedly had failed to bring the federal government to grant a mail subsidy to a Saint John-based steamship line, the city's two MPS, J. D. Hazen and J. A. Cheslay, bluntly indicated they would resign their seats if nothing were done.[9] The Conservative cabinet, already in turmoil, and nearing highly doubtful elections, forthwith provided an annual subsidy of $25 000 to the Beaver Line for fortnightly service between Saint John and Liverpool. The Donaldson Line quickly followed in shifting its terminus from Portland; others soon did the same. Almost in months in 1896 Saint John emerged as a major winter port.

Thereafter, as the western Canadian boom developed, prairie grain flowed out of the port and imports for central Canada came in. Both the city and the CPR repeatedly enlarged the harbour facilities in a veritable race to keep up with cargoes. In 1910, the federal government entered directly into building ocean berths itself.[10] And though Saint John's old shipbuilding industry did not re-emerge, it gathered repair yards, railway shops, sugar refineries and lumber mills. Finally, another technological change benefited it and its provincial hinterland. The development of wood-pulp mills gave a new significance to forest resources, especially those that had been inferior, such as spruce.

By 1914, accordingly, the New Brunswick city had moved far in adjusting to continental pulls, and had succeeded in making connections inward to share in western and central Canadian hinterlands. Its commercial future as a Canadian outlet and gateway would still largely depend on deliberate political policy, as in the provision of preferential railway rates. Industrial — and financial — pre-eminence had decisively moved to central Canadian metropolitan centres. Yet in the national continental system that had replaced the colonial and Atlantic one, Saint John clearly continued to play a metropolitan role within its own region.

III

Halifax and St. John's can be dealt with more briefly — not in any way as less significant, but as variations on a theme that has been established. The theme, of course, is the role of these communities in an Atlantic metropolitan system, and the effects technological change and continental pulls had upon them. However, there is more to say of Halifax during the period to be covered, since the changes in question affected St. John's later and more slowly.

212

The Nova Scotian city of the mid-nineteenth century did not have as full commercial control of an immediate hinterland area as did its New Brunswick neighbour. There was no long Saint John Valley to dominate; the open Atlantic coasts of the Nova Scotian peninsula enabled many lesser places to share in Halifax's importing or exporting functions, although at the same time no part of the province was wholly remote from its influence. Moreover, Halifax did not develop industry on the scale of Saint John; either wooden shipbuilding, or later enterprises. On the other hand, it was a notably larger focus of shipping interests and financial power. It was also political capital, intellectual centre — and perhaps social arbiter — as Saint John was not. Finally, Halifax, of course, was an imperial citadel and naval base: a transatlantic bastion of British metropolitan power that had strong ties to sustain and pounds sterling to spend. Still closely akin to Boston, despite the breach of the Revolution, the Haligonian descendants of Loyalist and pre-Loyalist New Englanders were happy to view London in their midst, in the fashionable society of the garrison.

As Saint John had grown with timber and the large shipbuilding it fostered, so Halifax had grown with the fishing staple and the schooners it required. The location of Halifax's superb harbour, at the corner of the continent adjacent to the main northwest Atlantic fishing grounds made it an excellent base for a fishing fleet. It was also well placed as a first mainland port of call for ships bringing imports on the great circle route from Europe to America; and for trading fish to the West Indies, in return for tropical products to be re-exported by coastal or transatlantic shipping. This extensive trading pattern, well settled by the mid-century, had made Halifax a major centre of shipping rather than shipbuilding, a commercial and financial emporium, and the wealthiest, most advanced metropolitan city in the British Atlantic provinces — focus of a fairly diversified regional society matured beyond the frontier phase.

The metropolitan stature of Halifax was evinced in the wealth and power of its merchants, notably its West Indies merchants, and in its banking institutions. In the 1850's and 1860's these included the long-established Halifax Banking Company, the Bank of Nova Scotia, the Union Bank, and the Merchants Bank, begun in 1864, which would become the Royal Bank of Canada. Again their directors and those of Halifax insurance, gas, and water companies formed a business élite interwoven with wholesale merchants, shipping magnates, and steamship operators.[11] Men such as Enos Collins, Samuel Cunard, W. A. Black, and M. B. Almon were prominent. Their political pedigree was evident also. Although the old days of the Halifax oligarchy and the Council of Twelve had vanished, other potent names like Uniacke, Fairbanks, Kenny and Tobin also revealed the strong connections of the Halifax business world with Nova Scotian politics. As for wealth, Collins died in 1871 worth $6 500 000; Cunard in 1865 worth $5 000 000; and many others amassed sizeable fortunes.[12]

213

Cunard might have moved to England to direct his burgeoning steam-ship line, but the foundations of his fortune had been laid in Halifax. He had no less benefited his native city by establishing his "ocean ferry" (steamships running to schedule as sailing ships could not), and making it the first port of call in the regular steam service from Liverpool to Boston, begun in 1840. Boston was thoroughly grateful for the Cunard Line, with good reason; Halifax had reason also.[13] At the same time Halifax and Cunard could thank the British metropolitan concern for improved Atlantic communications that produced the vitally needed imperial mail contract and subsidy. Still further, Cunard might thank the imperial dockyard at Halifax for a lucrative coal contract to supply steam warships.[14] And all the Halifax merchants could appreciate the dockyard contracts for provisions, or the imperial expenditures on Halifax defences which exceeded £170 000 in the later sixties.[15] These investments in steam communications or improved facilities at Halifax were aspects of British metropolitan influence wholly beneficial to the Nova Scotian centre.

Yet the wooden paddlewheeler was the forerunner of the iron screwsteamer, which in the seventies began to exert its effects on Halifax. No longer need the larger iron vessels call at the port for fuel after crossing the ocean; the tendency was to concentrate through runs at larger ports. Thus even in 1867 the main Cunard route ceased its stop at Halifax: an unfortunate coincidence with the inception of Confederation. And although Halifax had no major wooden ship industry to suffer, its functions as a wholesale centre did. For the ubiquitous iron tramp steamer could readily take cargoes direct to hinterland ports, instead of via Halifax warehouses. In fact, by the 1880's the ease of ordering goods direct by telegraph and the speed of steamship delivery was seriously affecting Halifax as an *entrepôt*.[16] Moreover, the decline in the West Indies sugar economy increasingly harmed Halifax shipping and fishing interests.

Again, the old oceanic trading pattern was failing, while the Nova

Scotian capital was being opened to rising continental influences. The Intercolonial was completed through to Halifax in 1876; the National Policy came three years after. Far from gaining the flow of western trade that had been hoped for, Halifax firms seemed chiefly to have acquired increasing competition from larger central Canadian firms — all this, and world depression, and the British government reducing expenditures on the Halifax base.

Nevertheless, the wealth and power of Halifax business were such that it was a case of slowed growth rather than absolute decline. New industries were started, some aided by tariff protection: cotton mills, shoe factories, sugar refineries.[17] But the important response was as that of Saint John: to make the city an effective part of the Canadian continental system as a winter port. The work began as early as 1882, when indeed the dominion government built a grain elevator at Halifax. But more important were the building of the big Halifax drydock in 1887–89, and the steady development of the Intercolonial's deep water terminus, which by 1899 could handle twelve large ocean steamers at once.[18]

With first-class port facilities and improving rail connections, Halifax was now equipped to take its own considerable share of the Canadian boom of the early twentieth century. It prospered vigorously, able to hold its own with Saint John — and hold as well the Atlantic margins of New Brunswick, more susceptible to its own rail connections. In fact, it made little difference when in 1905 a long era ended for Halifax, and Britain, concentrating her naval forces, gave up the Halifax naval base. Formal transfer of the naval dockyard to a largely store-keeping Canadian regime came in 1910, to mark another aspect of advancing continental dominance. Still another sign of that advance came in the financial field. In 1900 the general manager's office of the Bank of Nova Scotia was transferred to Toronto, in 1907 that of the Royal Bank to Montreal, and in 1903 the august Halifax Banking Company became part of Toronto's Bank of Commerce as it invaded the Maritimes.[19]

Still, if Halifax was thus being incorporated in the continent, it retained its essential strategic importance as a focal point for transatlantic communication. That was made abundantly plain only a few years thereafter, when the port was again called upon to prove its significance in naval war, as it had not been required to do since 1814. But that is another story.

IV

To conclude with St. John's: its metropolitan role might seem the least significant of the three Atlantic cities. Certainly its own hinterland was thinly populated and scarcely developed but for the fringe of fishing outports; it had virtually no industrial base apart from the cod and seal fisheries; and its financial services were limited by the backward state of the Newfoundland region in general. And yet, in other respects, St. John's had a decidedly powerful metropolitan role, as the great commercial and shipping *entrepôt* of the island. Its merchants and shipowners financed the fishing staple, marketed dried cod from the West Indies to the Mediterranean, imported and distributed foodstuffs and manufactures for the outports and through the use and abuse of the credit system tied the fishing population closely to the business houses of Water Street. Here was a compact urban élite, notably internationally minded, whose social predominance was unrivalled. One cannot doubt the enduring influence of the great dynasties of the St. John's business world, the Bowrings, Job Brothers, the Ayres, Newman and Company.[20] And one need scarcely assert the political ascendancy of St. John's figures like Charles Fox Bennett and Amrose Shea, Robert Thorburn and Robert Bond, when all the class and religious friction of the province found its focus in politics at the capital.

The city, moreover, was well integrated in the old Atlantic nineteenth-century system, traditionally linked with Liverpool, London, and Bristol, increasingly with the Maritimes and Boston. Yet it was still remote from the continent, buying supplies rather than selling there, and little affected by continental forces — as the flat rejection of Confederation with Canada might show. The state of the fishing and sealing catches also affected it far more immediately than the world process of technological change. Indeed, for much of the later nineteenth century St. John's was generally flourishing. It had four banks by the mid-seventies, direct steam service with England from 1869, the Atlantic cable since 1866, and regular steamship sailings to Halifax.[21] The eighties brought the beginning of railway building with the line to Harbor Grace and stimulated many small-scale industrial enterprises, of which Colonial Cordage survived.

But the well-being of St. John's continued to rest ultimately on the uncertain fortunes of the fisheries; its metropolitan ventures into industrial and transport development proved shaky and premature. After the Great Fire of 1892, that burned out most of the city's commercial firms and left 11 000 homeless, the whole strained overextended financial system was in deep trouble.[22] The bank crash of 1894 that followed, the failure of renewed Confederation negotiations with Canada the next year, left the city in financial chaos and considerable bitterness over apparent Canadian indifference to the gravity of the problem. When recovery came, with prosperous world trade in the new century, and a Newfoundland boom based on railway building and the development of pulpwood and mineral resources, it seemed that St. John's had again decisively turned its back on Canadian continental connections.

But had it? With hindsight, one could say that the connections had only been delayed; or rather, that they were so far premature for an island community which, in remoteness, had not yet felt the full impact of technological change in its communications system. The decline of the old-style Newfoundland fishery in face of modern big-ship operations would not become fully apparent until the bad years between the two world wars. Commission government might then be regarded as a final, reluctant exercise of British metropolitanism; the establishment of American and Canadian bases on the island in the Second World War as a function of extending continental metropolitan dominance — to be consolidated politically in the Confederation settlement of 1949.

Furthermore, again with hindsight, one may note the growth of continental pulls upon St. John's even from the 1890's; above all, the fact that Canadian banks took over in the city after the collapse of its own financial institutions.[23] Also, the very Newfoundland railway boom was shaped, if not captured, by R. A. Reid, fresh from his building for the CPR. And the pulpwood and iron-mining developments that began at last to diversify the Newfoundland region were largely in accord with Canadian continental interests. The real point is that St. John's, like its sister cities of the Atlantic region, was going to join the continent; each in varying ways, perhaps, but decisively — with changes in metropolitan patterns of communications which involved them all. What remain are questions. There is no intention here to put forward technological change as a kind of simplified economic determinism — but how far did it relate to the decision-making processes both of business and of government? How far was it the factor that made urban business élite in the Atlantic metropolitan centres aware of their own need to respond to change and make adjustments? How far did they utilize political influence to do so, and what were the reactions in their own regional communities? We need a great deal more study of the role of these urban élites, in the Atlantic region as elsewhere in Canada: more urban history, more business history, more study of the political and social interweavings of these entrepreneurial elements — which will inevitably carry us further into regional socio-cultural history as well. In sum, the restructuring in this inevitably sketchy paper (that still leaves so much out) of things we already know, should only make us aware of how much we do not know, when we look at regionalism in terms of metropolitanism.

Notes

1. See *Saint John Business Directory and Almanac for 1857, et seq.* (Saint John 1857).
2. J. W. Millidge, "Reminiscences of Saint John from 1849 to 1860," *New Brunswick Historical Collections*, no. 10 (Saint John 1919), 135.
3. F. W. Wallace, *Wooden Ships and Iron Men* (London n.d.), 309.
4. A. P. Langtry, ed., *Metropolitan Boston* (New York 1929), 1067.
5. Millidge, *loc. cit.*, 131.
6. D. R. Jack, *Centennial Prize Essay on Saint John* (Saint John 1883), 151.
7. See R. C. Brown, "The Nationalism of the National Policy," in P. Russell, ed., *Nationalism in Canada* (Toronto 1966), 155–63.
8. F. W. Wallace and I. Sclanders, *The Romance of a Great Port* (Saint John 1935), 37.
9. *Ibid.*, 44.
10. *Ibid.*, 46.
11. See *Beecher's Farmers Almanack for 1850, et seq.* (Halifax 1850).
12. A. W. H. Eaton, *Chapters in the History of Halifax* (New York 1915), 839.
13. F. L. Babcock, *Spanning the Atlantic* (New York 1931), 48.
14. P. H. Watson, "The Two Hundredth Anniversary of the Halifax Dockyard," *Occasional Papers of the Maritime Museum* (Halifax 1959), 21.
15. *Ibid.*, 32.
16. P. R. Blakeley, *Glimpses of Halifax, 1867–1900* (Halifax 1949), 24.

17. *Ibid.*, 38–45.
18. *Ibid.*, 28.
19. See *McAlpine's Halifax City Directory for 1907–08* (Halifax 1907).
20. See *Year Book and Almanack of Newfoundland, 1913* (St. John's 1913); also C. R. Fay, *Life and Labour in Newfoundland* (Toronto 1956), 13–37.
21. P. Toque, *Newfoundland as it was and is* (London 1878), 76–87.
22. A. B. Perlin, "St. John's," *Atlantic Advocate* (June 1960), 47.
23. R. A. MacKay, ed., *Newfoundland* (Toronto 1946), 459.

Currents of Change in Toronto, 1850–1900
PETER G. GOHEEN

During the half century following 1850 Toronto welcomed the age of iron and steam, experienced the revolution of industrialization, and outgrew both its old shell and perhaps its old ways. The colonial city which had been isolated by dint of geography and politics from the mainstreams of economic life on the continent became a commercial and industrial capital of first rank. The new city was distinguished from the old by its size, by its communications, and by its social and economic organization. Toronto in 1851 housed 30 775 persons; in 1901 the figure was 208 040,[1] a population increase of almost 700 percent within fifty years.

217

Among the most important innovations which appeared in the urban landscape during these fifty years were those features around which the economic system of production reorganized itself. Additionally, a few remarks indicating what can be gleaned from already available information about the social landscapes of the city throughout the period. Scadding anticipated the social importance of change in defining the character of the city after mid century when, in 1873, he perceptively titled his book *Toronto of Old*.[2] The new Toronto was only beginning its history of transition in the 1870's; the process would continue for the remainder of the century.

The Economic Dimensions of Change

By mid-century, certain old and respected realities of Canada's commercial life had been fundamentally altered. The system of trade and the organization of the commerce of Britain's northern American colonies had been shattered. The commercial aggressiveness of the colonies' southern neighbour, in concert with the revocation by the British of the concept of commercial protection for colonial goods, as witnessed in the repeal of the Corn Laws and the subsequent abrogation of the Navigation Acts, served to kill the old arrangements of trade and commerce by which the Canadian commercial system had so long survived. In particular, the system of commerce by which Montreal had been granted privileges amounting to a monopoly on the export trade of Canada was ended. Of this ending, Creighton has written:

> With the repudiation of its past and this denial of its ancient principles, the history of the Canadian commercial state comes to a close. . . . 1849 meant the conclusion of an entire drama. . . . The commercial empire of the St. Lawrence was bankrupt. . . . The failure to win the international commercial empire of the west and the forfeiture of part of the trading monopoly of western Canada had come home to a commercial generation whose historic weapons were broken in their hands and whose traditional support had vanished. . . . The design of the St. Lawrence, as the Canadian merchants had always conceived it in the past, had been shattered beyond redemption. . . . Canada had ceased to be an imperial trade route which sought its source of supply in the international American west, which built its political structure in the interests of commerce and which found its markets and its final court of appeal in the ample resources of the British Empire.[3]

218

In this collapse of an old Imperial design lay the possibilities for Toronto's rise: Toronto was provided with an opportunity to challenge the Montreal merchants for control of their old Empire up and down the St. Lawrence valley. To meet this challenge meant that new communications would be required and this, in the middle years of the nineteenth century, meant railways.

The promise of the rails

Railroad iron is a magician's rod in its power to evoke the sleeping energies of land and water.[4]

The story of the railroads introduces Toronto at the point when its first energies were about to be directed toward creating those conditions that would make possible its eventual and successful rise to the status of a great city. The transformation of the city from a quiet commercial centre into a metropolis in which the commerce of the province would concentrate and the industry of a great city would prosper may date from the collapse of the old strategy of trade which had worked so well against the interests of Toronto and so fitfully for the commercial growth of Montreal. The destruction of the old commercial system of the "Empire of the St. Lawrence" presented Toronto with new opportunities to exploit its long appreciated geographical position and its newly developed relationships with the Canadian West, with New York, and with Ontario.

Most importantly, an opportunity now arose for alternate systems of transportation to contest the monopoly previously enjoyed by Montreal as a port for shipping the staples of the interior to the market of Britain. Now there were no laws insisting that exports destined to Britain cross the Atlantic in British bottoms, now the possibilities of using the Erie Canal and New York as a route to European markets were available. This alternative was attractive because the costs of shipping from New York to Europe were considerably less than the costs from Montreal to the same markets. Without the protection of the old British mercantile system, Montreal was subject to direct competition for the exports of the West. Further, although shipping costs from the West to Montreal were less than those from the West to New York, New York enjoyed a great advantage in overseas shipping rates.[5] New York's competitive position for the trade from the Canadian and United States agricultural interiors was greatly enhanced when British ports were opened to commodities shipped from American ports and in American ships as well as goods arriving from Canadian ports in British ships. Toronto was in an ideal position to take advantage of these new opportunities. For some time, Toronto had been able to import directly from New York, but now she was able to explore the possibilities of exporting via that port as well.

Toronto's competitive position as the Canadian terminal for trade from the West and from Ontario was now greatly enhanced. She could herself compete for some benefits from the carrying trade. As one author put it, the "Toronto Carrying Place" was now becoming, once again as in the days of the French traders, a route of trade. Exports from Toronto increased greatly, and the exportation was predominantly through the United States. In 1859, only two percent of the shipments of wheat and flour from Toronto went to Montreal and Quebec, the rest went out by Oswego and the American ports.[6] A sign of the increasing importance of this trade to Toronto is the increasing number of merchants engaged in the import and export of various items, including lumber, grain, livestock, hardware and consumer goods.[7] This trade was possible in good measure because of the railroads which were being built to Toronto.

219

Building the railways

Toronto's desire for trade made it necessary to build railroads. Toronto's campaign for trade from the St. Lawrence basin and from the opening West was pursued by the construction of railway lines which were built first into peninsular Ontario in an attempt to capture the trade of this growing area, then to Ontario ports in an effort to funnel the Western trade via the upper Great Lakes into the city, and finally to a few United States ports in an effort to create cheap routes along which to channel the exports of the great Western hinterland destined eventually for overseas markets. Toronto's greatest enthusiasm in the optimistic days of the early and mid 1850's was reserved for those lines which would extend the city's influence into the hinterland of Ontario and the West. George Brown, editor of *The Globe*, perhaps Toronto's leading newspaper, was convinced that the city's commercial influence would spread along the rail lines.[8]

The city's first railway was incorporated in August of 1849 under the name of the Toronto, Simcoe, and Huron Railway Company. The first sod was turned on October 15, 1851 and on 15 May, 1853, the road was first opened to the public. The Northern Railroad, as it became known, opened the 53 miles from Toronto to Barrie in 1853, and on June 2, 1855, the route was complete to Collingwood, a port on Georgian Bay some 95 miles distant from Toronto.[9] Toronto's first railway sought to exploit those particular advantages of the city's situation which had been appreciated from the earliest days of European settlement along the shores of Lake Ontario.[10] An old understanding was being realized, belatedly, under the impulses of a new policy.

The railway was built by city businessmen in an effort to secure the trade of Ontario and more especially of the West, thereby gaining an advantage in the competition for this trade over Buffalo and New York.[11] Brown saw in this the splendid realization of the strategy of Simcoe: that the Toronto Passage would be an important overland route for trade. The wealth of the western continent would "come pouring down its rails to a mighty Toronto entrepôt."[12] The dreams were realized, though not immediately. Collingwood was a terminus for trade gathered from the Upper Great Lakes on both sides of the international border. By 1861, Collingwood maintained a tri-weekly steamer service to Lake Michigan ports. So successful was this port in siphoning the trade of the lakes and funnelling it on to Toronto that the town was moved to protest its status as a mere outport of the larger city. Grain now moved from Chicago to Toronto with great efficiency, untouched by human hands.[13] For the first time since the French regime, the Toronto Passage was a significant route and Toronto was beginning to realize advantages others had long seen in its situation.

220

The second railway to enter the city provided it with links to the American ports. In early December of 1855 Toronto was connected with the Great Western Railway system. Now the city had direct rail connections with Buffalo and Windsor. The Great Western was designed to be part of a system which would carry traffic from Michigan to New York state, passing on the shortest route between these points. That route, it happened, lay through Ontario along the north shore of Lake Erie. Toronto interests had not sponsored this line nor had they supported it financially to the degree that they had invested in the Northern Railway. This was not Toronto's businessmen's brainchild, but nevertheless the city's connection with the trunk line proved to be very important from a variety of perspectives. This railway was particularly important for Toronto, not only for its long distance connections, but because it linked the city with the major competitor for trade in South Central Ontario. This was the city at the head of the lake, Hamilton. Toronto was now able directly to challenge the commercial position of Hamilton in peninsular Ontario. Although Hamilton had enjoyed rail connections with the Great Western before Toronto had, the stronger commercial interests in the larger city asserted their position with the consequence that Hamilton suffered from the competition. The Great Western was the principal instrument for the early extension of Toronto's commercial hinterland into rapidly growing Southern Ontario.[14] It is significant in this context that Toronto was connected with New York state by rail before it had similar ties with Montreal. In part, this advantage over its Canadian sister city helped Toronto preserve its trading area against the competitive powers of the largest city of Canada. This was particularly true for the development of a substantial wholesaling business in Toronto, for the city aggressively sought the job of supplying the merchants of Ontario. Further, Toronto continued to import through New York, avoiding dependence upon Montreal and the expenses of transport on the St. Lawrence River.

The third railway to enter Toronto arrived in the autumn of 1856. At last Toronto was connected by rail with Montreal. The railway had been largely designed as a substitute for the inconvenience and inefficiencies caused by the canal system of the St. Lawrence River, which was icebound several months of every year. The railway would, it was hoped, overcome the need to transship cargo *en route* to Montreal. The line was extended to Sarnia from Toronto in late 1859, further aiding the Ontario city in its efforts to establish itself as the undisputed commercial centre of agricultural Ontario. The Grand Trunk Railway was predominantly a Montreal venture and was an important expression of that city's effort to extend its commercial hinterland to the limits of the old commercial empire of the Saint Lawrence. The railway was not an immediate success. Progress toward creating an effective system by which to capture the trade of the new West was extremely slow. It was not until early in 1880 that the Grand Trunk developed direct connections with Chicago, for example. In 1882 the Grand Trunk and the Great Western systems merged in a belated effort to improve their financial positions.[15] By this time the prospects of the trunk railways had been reappraised and were found not to be so promising. One reason why the trunk lines failed to meet the expectations of their success was that they never succeeded in attracting the inbound trade which continued to reach most of Canada via New York. Furthermore, as was soon realized, the railways of Ontario were not so much complementary to the canal system of the St. Lawrence as they were competitive with it.[16]

221

The attention of Toronto's businessmen continued to focus on the opportunity to capture the trade of the growing hinterland of Southern Ontario. The Great Western had revealed the possibilities afforded by direct rail connections with a growing hinterland and had further revealed the ability of Ontario's first city to compete with any other provincial towns for commercial dominance. The building of local lines was, therefore, indulged in at great expense and with even greater hopes. It was thought that a well developed system of feeder rail lines focusing on Toronto would offset the weaknesses of the canal and railway system which had largely failed to secure for the city a major role in the handling of through traffic. In 1868 the Toronto and Nipissing was chartered under the guiding influence of George Laidlaw, a prominent Toronto investor. The railroad was designed to tap the timber stands, which would bring trade to Toronto from east of Lake Simcoe and Georgian Bay. In 1872 it had reached as far as Coboconk, east of Lake Simcoe. At about this time the railway promoters were busy with schemes designed to tap the Lake Huron trade as well. Among others, the Grey and Bruce was undertaken reaching from Toronto to Owen Sound. Likewise, the Wellington, Grey, and Bruce Railway was built to tap the Ontario hinterland. Meanwhile, the Northern was being extended along Georgian Bay from Collingwood to Meaford, another small port.

Within twenty years of the first line into Ontario the province was crisscrossed by railroads; some were trunk lines designed to carry through traffic and sprout towns along the way, others were designed to trap the local trade of their regions and funnel this into the metropolis. By 1880 the enthusiasm for new lines was dying.[17] Toronto was not the only city to have been active in spawning rail lines, and eventually the network was overextended. Numerous lines were later to be consolidated in the effort to reduce losses, but in the meantime, there had sprung into existence a well articulated system of transport which could be used to collect the produce of the land and to distribute in return the commerce and, later, the manufacturers, of the city. In 1860 the united provinces of Canada were traversed by 1880 miles of track. In 1875–76, the figure was 5157 miles, under the control of no less than 37 companies.[18] The system was substantially complete. Its importance was not unappreciated, for as one Toronto writer put it: "no other one thing has contributed so materially in building up the city. It has made it really the metropolis . . . the mart of Ontario."[19]

222 **The growth of industries**

The growth of industries in Toronto in the last decades of the nineteenth century provided further evidence of a new era in the life of the town. The industrial establishments which intruded into the old urban landscape were but the bulkiest symbols of the process by which the life of the city was being reorganized.

Two sets of statistics document the changing economic complexion of the city: in 1870, 9400 industrial employees produced articles valued at $13 093; in 1901, 42 515 industrial employees produced goods valued at $58 415 498.[20] Industrial growth during these thirty years was not steady and there remains some mystery as to how the industrialization of the city proceeded so rapidly during a period of general economic depression.[21] Nonetheless, the achievement of an industrialized economy by 1900 cannot seriously be questioned. Industry was by 1900, perhaps, the single most important source of employment and of income in the city.

The growth of employment in industry and the development of the factory system were the fruits of patient labouring. The momentum of change built up slowly. The first industrial production-lines in the city date from no later than 1850 and perhaps much earlier. By 1856, however, factory operatives were beginning to be conspicuous among the artisans and craftsmen who formerly had monopolized industrial employment within the city.[22] The factory system was first adopted in the manufacture of materials and products the demand for which was created by the newly developed nineteenth-century technology. Steam and iron were responsible for creating the first factory-industry in the city. The Toronto Locomotive Works, established in 1852, was among the first major industrial establishments to be organized as a large scale factory.[23] In 1860 the city was still properly characterized as a place of craftsmen and artisans. These skilled workers were the last to abandon their well established system of production in favour of the regimentation and scale economies achieved by the

TABLE I – **Population and industrial growth of Toronto, 1860 to 1901**

Year	Population	Industrial Statistics		
		Number of Establishments	Employees	Value of Articles Produced (in dollars)
1860	44,821[a]			
1870	56,092[b]	497[f]	9 400	13 686 093
1880	86,415[c]	932[g]	12 708	19 100 116
1890	144,023[d]	2,109[h]	24 480	42 489 352
1901	208,040[e]	847[i]	42 515	58 415 498

[a]Canada, Board of Registration and Statistics, *Census of the Canadas, 1860–61*, I, 48.
[b]Canada, Department of Agriculture, *Census of Canada, 1870–71*, I, 16–17.
[c]Canada, Department of Agriculture, *Census of Canada, 1880–81*, I, 73.
[d]Canada, Department of Agriculture, *Census of Canada, 1890–91*, I, 66.
[e]Canada, Census and Statistics Office, *Fourth Census of Canada, 1901*, I, 22.
[f]The industrial statistics for 1870 are derived from the *Census of Canada, 1870–71*, III, 290–445.
[g]The industrial statistics for 1880 are given in the *Census of Canada, 1880–81*, III, 503.
[h]The industrial statistics for 1890 are given in the *Census of Canada, 1890–91*, III 385.
[i]The industrial statistics for 1901 are given in the *Fourth Census of Canada, 1901*, III, 329. These statistics refer only to establishments employing five or more persons.

223

factory. Gradually, however, the jobs of the skilled were reorganized.

As the population of the city grew, so also did the number of industries. In 1871, a city of just over 56 000 people was the home of 497 industries. By 1881, 932 manufacturing establishments were located in a city of over 86 000 population (Table 4). Despite the numerical increase of establishments, evidence suggests that no fundamental change in the scale of manufacturing operations had taken place in the decade prior to 1880. In 1871, there were, on the average, 19 employees per establishment; in 1881 the number remained about the same, declining to roughly 13 per establishment. The large-scale factory continued to be a somewhat exotic feature in the economic landscape, although the number and size of these establishments continued to increase. In its annual review of commerce in Toronto, *The Globe*, in February of 1886 noted the existence of a number of large factories in the city.[24] This review identified several firms employing over one hundred persons. Among these were the Toronto Rolling Mills, manufacturing nails and employing, according to *The Globe*, some 300 men; for another, a boiler and still factory employed 120 men. By this time, several factories not engaged in metal fabricating were large as well. The Gooderham and Worts Distillery employed 160 hands, Jacques and Hay cabinet factory had 400 men working, and a meat packing plant was said to have 300 workers.

The first signs of rapid industrial growth in the city were noted during the succeeding decade, from 1880 to 1890, when the real turn in the fortunes of the city occurred. The population of the city almost doubled in the decade and the value of articles produced more than doubled. By 1890, over forty million dollars value came from the factories and shops of the city (Table 1). The number of employees per factory, averaged over the entire range of industry, remained small, but important new large-scale industrial establishments were now in operation. Of these, one of the most noteworthy was the Massey Manufacturing Company. Daniel Massey had established an agricultural implement business in nearby Newcastle in 1847. In 1879, the entire business was moved to Toronto.[25] By 1890, the census taker recorded that at the one firm in the city manufacturing agricultural implements there were 575 persons employed.[26]

By 1900, the factory system had been introduced to Toronto not only as a means of organizing the production of those materials the demand for which was created by new uses of iron and steam but also as the system for manufacturing those goods which had for many years constituted the industrial product of the city but which had until now been manufactured in small workshops by craftsmen and artisans. A whole new scale of production was now becoming evident through a process by which the factory replaced the small scale shop. The scale shifts in manufacturing are revealed in the statistics for 1890, 1901, and 1905. In 1901, an average of 50 men laboured in each city factory, defined for census purposes as a manufacturing establishment employing five or more persons (Table 1). A special 1905 census of manufacturing confirms the trend to large-scale factory production. In that year, when all establishments of every size were enumerated, 38 persons on the average were employed per work place.[27] When compared with the 11 or 12 workers per plant averaged in 1890, the dimensions of the change begin to be clear. This represented a second stage in the industrialization process. In the first, the value of products manufactured had increased greatly, along with a rise in the number of establishments in the city, but without a change in the overall scale of the unit of production. The second stage, the period in which the number of employees per establishment increased dramatically, corresponded with the adoption by many kinds of manufacturing enterprises of the factory system of production. This process involved not only enlarging the scale of production but also the consolidation of many small workshops into larger factories.

Toronto's industrial growth began slowly and had a late start. Among the possible explanations for this, two of the most important relate to her difficulties in securing economical ties with the West and the correlation between her own prosperity and that of the Ontario hinterland. Toronto's efforts to secure for herself a portion of the trade of the West were marked by much frustration following the initial success at appropriating a share of the grain trade of the Lakes via Collingwood and the Northern Railway. Subsequent to this, attempts to gain access by rail to Chicago were delayed until 1880 and the completion of Grand Trunk, by which time the cost advantage formerly enjoyed by the Toronto-Montreal route over New York for grain shipment from Chicago had been reversed.[28] To a consider-

224

able degree, the inefficiencies of the St. Lawrence canal system contributed to the uncompetitive character of the Canadian route. Furthermore, Toronto was deprived of her important Georgian Bay timber hinterland after 1883 when the tolls on the Erie Canal were removed without similar steps being taken to end Welland Canal charges.[29] Ontario timber then took the American route to Europe. No precise analysis has been made of Toronto's reliance upon her own immediate hinterland as a source of trade and as a market, but there have been suggestions that the city's commercial and industrial prosperity was linked to the growth of Southern Ontario which, by the 1880's boasted a dense network of small rail lines many of which radiated out from Toronto.[30]

In her struggle to win a share of the Canadian West's trade Toronto experienced considerable difficulty. Initially, Toronto interests were unsuccessful in securing the charter for the Canadian Pacific Railway which was to connect British Columbia with central Canada. After the original charter for the railway was cancelled and a new company organized for the same purpose in 1880, Toronto business interests again failed to win the contract. Montreal became, in fact, the eastern terminus for the Canadian Pacific Railway, although a feeder line was built northward from Toronto to connect the city with the transcontinental line. Having experienced difficulty securing good overland connections with the West, Toronto's business community displayed interest in the Great Lakes. In 1886 when grain elevators were built at Port Arthur on Lake Superior, Owen Sound became a grain port providing Toronto with the shortest possible route between the Great Lakes and the St. Lawrence River outlet.[31] Symptomatic of Toronto's improving competitive position by the end of the decade, foreign imports to the city rose substantially between 1884 and 1889.[32]

Toronto's industrial prosperity would have been impossible without the system of transportation which made it possible for the city's industries to serve efficiently and compete for a sizeable trading hinterland. The success of the city in the competition for markets is revealed in statistics showing localization of manufacturing in the city. Even before 1880 the advantages offered by Toronto as a convenient and cheap transportation hub were appreciated by at least a few industrialists. The availability of low cost transportation and its attendant advantages in the search for markets have been cited as inducements attracting the Massey Company to Toronto in 1879.[33] As other factories found Toronto convenient and attractive because of access to the Ontario markets, both urban and rural, numerous types of industry began to localize within the city. In particular, the manufacture of consumer goods became localized in the city. Clothing, secondary wood products, and non-ferrous metal products became increasingly localized in the city as did such services as printing and publishing. By contrast, in such resource processing activities as primary food and beverage production and the handling of primary wood products, Toronto was of declining importance.[34] When evaluated in the context of the

225

TABLE II – **Value added in manufacturing, by industry, for York County, in 1870, 1880 and in 1890**[a]

Industry	Value Added, in Thousands of Dollars, by Year		
	1870	1880	1890
Clothing (textiles and furs)	844 (11.0)[b]	1 362 (11.6)	4 037 (17.7)
Iron and steel production	1 313 (17.0)	2 791 (23.7)	3 481 (15.2)
Food and beverages (secondary)	1 526 (19.8)	1 282 (10.9)	2 593 (11.4)
Printing and publishing	653 (8.5)	1 158 (9.9)	2 332 (10.2)
Wood products (secondary)	364 (4.7)	500 (4.2)	1 282 (5.6)
Non-metallic mineral products	178 (2.3)	362 (3.1)	1 161 (5.1)
Leather products	822 (10.6)	851 (7.2)	996 (4.4)
Textile products	86 (1.1)	273 (2.3)	928 (4.1)
Wood products (primary)	390 (5.0)	641 (5.5)	922 (4.0)
Chemical and allied products	85 (1.1)	336 (2.9)	919 (4.0)

[a]Data are given in Edward J. Chambers and Gordon W. Bertram, "Urbanization and Manufacturing in Central Canada, 1870–1890," in *Papers on Regional Statistical Studies*, ed. Sylvia Ostry and T. K. Rymes, Canadian Political Science Association: Conference on Statistics, 1964 (Toronto: University of Toronto Press, 1966), pp. 242–53.
[b]Statistics in parentheses indicate the value added as a percentage of the total value added for York county.

226

industrialization of Central Canada, Toronto's growth is impressive. For York County, in which Toronto was situated, the ratio of value added in all manufacturing over value added in all manufacturing in Central Canada was 9.72, 11.09 and 13.45 in 1870, 1880 and 1890.[35]

If we look at the relative importance of the various manufacturing sectors to the county itself it can be seen that the same generalizations apply (Table II). Clothing ranks first in 1890 while other consumer and service sectors contribute heavily to the total of value added. The Table reveals the declining significance for Toronto of such industry groups as primary wood products, leather products and iron and steel production. Primary food and beverages, not shown on the table, also declined in their importance to the creation of value added in manufacture in Toronto.

What these statistics index is the growing importance of Toronto as an industrial centre of Canada and the growing significance for the city itself of manufacturing industry by the end of the century.[36] Whereas Toronto in 1850 was a small trading center, by 1900 she had achieved the rank of a great manufacturing and industrial centre.

Elements of the Social Landscapes

Street railways

The symbol of progress and pride perhaps most widely adopted by cities and towns in the latter half of the nineteenth century was the street railway. This visible and dramatic innovation in mass transit had appeared on the streets of several American cities by the early 1850's and was to be seen in Toronto after 1861. Toronto was among the first cities on the continent to grant a charter for construction of a street railway and to witness its building.[37]

When the rails were laid on the streets of Toronto in the early 1860's they did not initiate public transportation in the city. In 1850 there already were several omnibus lines radiating out from the centre of the city in various directions. The omnibuses had been in operation in the city since at least the early 1840's, but soon ceased operation after the introduction into the city of the first street car.[38]

In October of 1860, Alexander Easton, an Englishman resident of the suburb of Yorkville applied to the Toronto city council for a license granting him exclusive rights to build and operate a street railway in the city. In March of 1861 the council was pleased to grant the license and a thirty-year franchise for the operation of a street railway under certain conditions stipulating the frequency of service and routing of the lines. Three lines were to be built: along Yonge Street, from King to Bloor (the northern boundary of the city), along Queen Street from Yonge to the Asylum in the western part of the city, and along King Street from the Don River in the east to Bathurst Street in the west. The company was duly incorporated in May of 1860 and began operations in September of the same year. The first company report, dated December 31, 1861, indicated that six miles of track had been laid. On Yonge Street, tracks stretched from King Street to the suburban Yorkville Town Hall, on Queen from Yonge to Dundas Street (Ossington Street today), and on King Street the few blocks from the St. Lawrence Market to Yonge Street. The same report indicated that the average daily passenger load numbered 2000 persons.[39]

Despite this early activity and construction, the railway soon proved to be unremunerative and the company asked for financial relief. In 1869 an act for the relief of the Toronto Street Railway Company was passed and the property sold to new owners. The transfer of ownership brought no rapid expansion of the system which was not yet operating all of the lines called for in the initial contract of 1861. It was not until 1874 that any more building of lines was undertaken.[40] In that year a cautious expansion was undertaken in order to improve service to the more prosperous northern suburbs of the city. By 1880, nineteen miles of track had been laid in Toronto. The railway still was far from serving the whole city. The stimulus for rapid expansion of the network was still largely absent, but expansion of the system had begun.

The decade of 1880–1890 saw a remarkable growth in the population of the city and it was during this ten years that the street railway system first realized expansion on a large scale. Despite the difficulties occasioned at the end of the decade, owing to the expiration of the franchise and the reluctance of the company prior to the termination of their charter in 1891 to extend the company lines, the decade witnessed a rapid growth in service. By 1891 there was a total of 68 1/2 miles of track traversing the city. Every part of the city was now within reasonably easy access of the railway. The system carried over 16 million revenue passengers in 1890, or an average of between 50 000 and 60 000 every working day of the week.[41] At least by 1890, there was no question that the street railway was a vital part of the transportation system of the city, without which its economic life could hardly have been carried on.

Exercising its rights of purchase, the city bought the street railway company at the expiry of the thirty-year franchise in 1891. Late the same year the company was sold to a group of private interests who were granted another 30 year franchise. From 1891 to 1894, in accord with the terms of the franchise agreement, the entire system was electrified.[42] From 1891 to 1897 new additions were made to the system, but disagreements arose as to the legal responsibilities of the company to extend lines to areas of the city incorporated after the date of franchising of the company. The company was upheld by the Privy Council in its interpretation that it had no legal obligation to extend its lines beyond the boundaries of the city as they were defined in 1891. As a result, the expensive job of laying new lines into the newer suburbs of the city was left to subsidiary companies which, subsequently, were purchased and operated by the city.[43] By 1900, numerous companies were operating lines to all areas of the city. The requirements of a growing population were being met by a series of companies; no longer could the indifference of a single traction company deny the city the service it demanded.

The story of street railways in large cities has been told as a serial success story. The rails created the divided city, they exercised a "moral influence"[44] over the townspeople. Such were the accomplishments of the suburbanization made possible by the streetcar ride into the country. In contrast, the story of the building of the street railway in Toronto is told as a series of legal battles and bankruptcies and interruptions to service. The eventual destruction of most of the records of the main traction company leaves many details of the history unavailable for all time. Despite an unquestionably unhealthy climate of operation which was created in part by the thirty-year franchises which were in the habit of expiring at just those times when major investments were called for, and despite the late beginning of rapid population growth which resulted in the early unprofitability of the lines, there is reason to believe that the street car lines were of great importance to Toronto. A few threads of evidence on the passenger use of the facilities suggest this. Other evidence points to the early service afforded the better suburban districts of the city. It is of more than passing interest that the first franchise holder was a resident of Yorkville, Toronto's first high class suburb, an area of some settlement already in 1860. The first impulses came more from a desire for service in the suburbs than from a realization of the potential impact of the lines on the mobility habits of the central city population. Thus, Toronto is thoroughly typical in that the desire to gain access to the centre of the city on the part of a few well-to-do suburbanites preceded the desire to escape the city by its residents.

A substantial expression of enthusiasm for suburban living was only to materialize when the city spawned a growing middle class which could afford the luxury in cost and time of reaching the outer limits of the city. But it was this ground swell of enthusiasm, created many years after the initial laying of the rails, which was to turn the crude system into a modern, efficient, and profitable one. In the years following the middle class use of the rails, the working people of the city gained the habit as well. The first evidence which is available for Toronto to suggest that the streetcar had become a route of access for laboring people comes in 1891 at the time when the city had exercised its right to purchase the expired franchise of the railroad. As a condition of contract, the city instructed the corporation to whom it leased the lines for operation that working-class reduced fares were to be instituted in the early morning and early evening hours.[45] This thread of evidence is virtually all that remains to indicate that before the end of the century Toronto's street railways were used by all classes as an economic necessity. Clarification of the role of the railways and of their impact will be obtained from an evaluation of the evidence provided in the course of examining the growth of Toronto in detail. It is impossible to "test" a hypothesis of railway determinism in any precise way, for the railway was only one of the significant innovations altering the way people lived in the city in the late nineteenth century. It is possible, however, to evaluate in some statistically less precise manner the patterns of development and the availability of the city's first rapid and mass transportation system. It is reasonable to expect that this was, indeed, as important an innovation as many authors have claimed it to be.[46]

229

The population: its changing composition and enduring mood

The social map of Toronto during the last half of the nineteenth century remains almost completely unencumbered with meaning. The grosser features of the changing landscape have been recognized and the institutions which created them have been briefly investigated. There is no correspondingly simple procedure, however, by which to assess the changing ways in which people lived in the city, and no evidence now survives which would permit a simple evaluation of the impact of each of these developments upon the changing modes of city life.

Toronto was, in 1860, and, at the turn of the century, continued to be a British city. This fact provides perhaps the most important clue to the social character of the place. Indeed, Toronto might be thought to have

TABLE III – **Population of Toronto, 1860 to 1901, by Origin and Religion**[a]

	1860	1870	1880	1890	1901
Total population	44 821	56 092	86 415	144 023	208 040
By religion:					
Anglican	14 125	20 668	30 913	46 084	62 406
Baptist	1 288	1 953	3 667	8 223	11 898
Congregational	826	1 186	2 018	3 102	3 658
Jews*	153	157	534	1 425	3 083
Lutheran	167	343	494	738	972
Methodist	6 976	9 606	16 357	32 505	48 278
Presbyterian	6 604	8 982	14 612	27 449	41 659
Roman Catholic	12 135	11 881	15 716	21 830	28 994
Other and unspecified	2 547	1 316	2 104	2 677	7 092
By origin:					
English			34 608		94 021
Irish			32 177		61 527
Scotch			13 754		34 543
Other British					785
French			1 230		3 015
German			2 049		6 028
Other			2 597		8 121
By Nativity:					
English	7 112	11 089		22 801	
Irish	12 441	10 366		13 347	
Scotch	2 961	3 263		6 347	
French	66	61		114	
German	336	336		799	
Native to Canada	19 202	28 424		93 162	
Other	2 703	2 553		7 435	

[a]Sources for this table are the following: Canada, Board of Registration and Statistics, *Census of the Canadas, 1860–61*, I, 48–49, 128–129; Canada, Department of Agriculture, *Census of Canada, 1870–71*, I, 114–17, 266–67; Canada, Department of Agriculture, *Census of Canada, 1880–81*, I, 276–77, 174–75; Canada, Department of Agriculture, *Census of Canada, 1890–91*, I, 282–83, 345; Canada, Census and Statistics Office, *Fourth Census of Canada, 1901*, I, 218–19, 222–23, 344–45, 348–51.

*The term used in the Censuses.

been exclusively British, so great was the proportion of the total population that was of British stock. In 1860, out of a population that was of roughly forty thousand, less than five thousand of the city's inhabitants traced their origins outside of Britain (Table 3). There were less than one hundred persons resident in Toronto in 1860 who were born in France. Roughly half of the city's population of that year was native to Canada, but of this number a mere four hundred were of French extraction. What was true of

Toronto in 1860 remained true for the rest of the century. In 1870, of a total population of roughly fifty-six thousand, some twenty-eight thousand were native to Canada. Of these, only a thousand were from the province of Quebec, while but a few hundred had immigrated to Toronto from France. By 1901, out of a total of 208 040 people in the city, some 94 021 were of English origin and a further 96 070 were of Scottish or Irish descent. A mere three thousand and fifteen traced their roots to France. Germans comprised the only other numerically significant minority group in the city in 1900.

The immigration to the city which occurred toward the end of the century failed to upset the British quality of Toronto even though the migrants came from many countries of Europe. The migration late in the century created subtle and important changes, however. The first massive migration to the city had been a result of the Irish famines of the late 1840s. This mass movement had profound effects on the city. A revealing statistic for Toronto in 1860 shows that, in that year, the city contained more persons who were by birth Irish than who were born English. At that time the city housed few persons of Scottish ancestry. The immigration of the 1860s and later years changed this balance and by 1870 the Irish no longer outnumbered the English in the city. The Census of Origins in 1880 reveals that at that date there were still almost as many Irish as English, however. By 1890 the immigrant population was distinctly more English than Irish. Thus, following the initial flood of immigrants out of Ireland, the city was a destination for persons from all parts of the British Isles. Nevertheless, the early characterization of the town as an Irish city was to have lasting consequences in attitudes developed and long maintained during subsequent years when conditions were much changed.

231

As an immigrant city, Toronto was unique within Canada. Immigration contributed a much larger proportion of people to total population of the city than was the case for any other major urban place in the country. Whereas in 1890 there were 50 861 foreign born in Toronto out of a total population of 144 023, in Montreal the foreign born numbered only 31 843 of a total city population of 182 695.[47] Thus, to be correct, Toronto must be characterized both as a peculiarly British city and also as a city of newcomers. None of the cities of Ontario or Quebec rivalled it as a destination for immigrants.[28] In large part, its attractiveness to migrants may be considered to be owing to the rapid growth of industry and a strong demand for labour in the city. At a time when the interior of the provinces was still absorbing new immigrants it is probable that there was no surplus of farm sons to fill city jobs, whereas labour was obtainable from the ships as they landed.[29] The continuing immigrant character of Toronto is of great importance if one is to understand the development in the city of a set of attitudes which explain the persistence of some of the important institutions of the time. Whereas the citizens of the city shared British backgrounds and constituted a homogeneous group by most standards, they did not share a history of common experience in this city. There was no very substantial tradition of Canadian life for many, indeed, for the majority, of those living in the city. The divisions were transferred from Europe along with its population.[50]

The religious composition of the city shows a weave of finer strands. The Church of England and the Roman Catholic Church were, in 1860, the two large religious groups in the city (Table 3). The Roman Catholic population had only very recently arrived. In 1850 there had been but 7940 Catholics in Toronto and by 1860 that number had increased to 12 135.[51] This rate of growth in the decade 1850 to 1860 was by far the highest in the city. Presbyterians and Methodists were present in substantial numbers as well, but at this time were small confessional groups in comparison with the two leading denominations. As immigration from Ireland to Toronto slackened and a greater proportion of the immigrants came from the other parts of Britain, the proportion of the total population which was Catholic shrank correspondingly. In 1870 there were over 20 000 Anglicans in the city and only 11 881 Catholics, an actual drop in their numbers during the decade. By this time, Methodist and Presbyterian numbers had swelled so that they were each about as large as the Catholic group. This trend continued for the rest of the century. By 1880 there were more Methodists than Catholics in the city and by 1890 both the Methodist and Presbyterian churches claimed more adherents than did the Roman Catholic Church. By this time, then, the Protestant and English Church groups dominated the religious scene. Among these, the Anglicans were by far the largest group, constituting over a quarter of the total population.

232

Given the increasingly Protestant character of the city one might expect that a measure of religious toleration would be achieved in the city. Evidence suggests that, with respect to the Catholics of Toronto, this was not the case. The first signs of the Orange Order in the city had already been noted. This organization, embodying as it did religious zeal and bigotry, played an important and conspicuous role in the life of the city in the late decades of the century. There is no evidence that the Order lost vigor as the Catholic population of the city declined in proportion to the total. The answer to the continuing vitality of the Orangemen can perhaps be found in the immigrant spirit of the city in the late nineteenth century. The early support for the Order derived from the antipathy felt by the Protestant Irish toward the Irish Catholics, and most of the Catholics in Toronto at that time were Irish.[52] The verve of this organization was to manifest itself in rather spectacular ways at various moments from 1860 to 1900. In 1860, the visit to Toronto of the Prince of Wales, a figure well revered by all the city's British population, was interrupted by crowds of Orangemen jeering the Catholics of his entourage. The Duke of Newcastle, in charge of the Prince's itinerary, was Catholic.[53]

The Orange Order responded to external stimuli as well as to local opportunities. The Red River Insurrection was a case in point. A most uneasy relationship existed in the Red River settlements between the

Canadians from Upper Canada, who were, in the 1860s, beginning to populate the region, and the Métis who comprised most of the population. The surveying of the area by parties sent out by the Canadian government led to much friction because the surveyors abused the local settlers. Amid the tensions of the time, an "Ontario Orangeman, Thomas Scott,"[54] was murdered. This event, in distant Manitoba, inspired the protests of Toronto Orangemen who demanded that the murder of a Protestant Orangeman by the forces of Catholicism must quickly be repaid with "justice." The slow speed at which the Dominion government acted prompted a Toronto Orange Lodge to insist that "the blood of Scott should not pass unavenged."[55] In this murder a singularly noted Canadian Catholic, Louis Riel, was implicated. The case of Riel made the event "the most determinative specific political incident between Confederation and the Great War."[56] It also preluded the most notable outburst of anti-French and anti-Catholic feeling in Toronto in the late nineteenth century. The same raw edges of Western expansionism which touched off the Red River troubles in 1870 recurred in the West on the Prairies in the 1880s. The same man, Riel, returned to lead a new group of local Prairie dissidents in 1885. The eventual result of the encounter between the federally sponsored troop and the protesting Saskatchewan Métis was that the militia, "after losing nearly all the skirmishes to the rebels, crushed them by sheer weight."[57] Riel surrendered. Here was fresh kindling for the highland Ontario temperament, as the Orangemen of Toronto once again revealed their stripes. To be a supporter of Riel meant, in their interpretation, that one was "bent upon precipitating a war of the races."[58] It is probable that most of Toronto shared in the sentiment that Riel had to be found guilty.

233

In contrast with the anti-Catholic sentiment which lasted throughout the nineteenth century, Toronto showed little hostility toward its miniscule but growing Jewish community. The Jewish population of the city remained small throughout the century, increasing from 153 persons in 1860 to 3083 in 1901 (Table 3). This small group represented one of the important clusters of Jewry in Canada in the nineteenth century, comprising roughly 20 percent of the Canadian total by 1901.[59] In 1860, the Jewish population of Toronto was composed of immigrants from Britain, the German states, and the United States predominantly. The community spoke English and adopted pro-English, or pro-British, attitudes. Relations were developed with London and not with New York or Cincinnati. Many members of the Jewish community in the city were British educated; British rabbis were appointed to the synagogue and, in numerous ways, Anglophile attitudes were encouraged.[60]

Migration in the 1880s brought to the city the first Jewish people from Eastern Europe and Russia. These immigrants were not Anglicized and came from a culture which was altogether unlike that of Toronto. Despite this introduction into Toronto of a most foreign cultural group, the overt hostility which characterized the Protestant attitude toward Catholics was not directed toward them. The reason for this may perhaps be found in the steps taken within the Jewish community itself to assure the harmonious integration into the life of the city of the Russian Jews. In the beginning, as one author has pointed out, Toronto's Jews were "Jews by religion and not by culture."[61] When, soon after the arrival in the city of large numbers of Russian Jews, a new and orthodox synagogue was formed, its membership included, in addition to most of the recent immigrants to the city, some of the established families of the city. These members withdrew from the original synagogue after reforms had been instituted there. This small group of English-speaking Jews played a very important role in the new congregation. They "gave to an immigrant congregation that stemmed from the Russian political and cultural sphere a handy core-group already trained in British parliamentary procedure and possessing a recognized status, assets that were to become of much value in the development of Toronto's other great congregation."[62] This "stroke of fortune" may have had much to do with the maintenance within the Toronto Jewish community of a common effort toward social and economic betterment and of a common identity. As it was perceived by the city, the community maintained its old identity and there were no serious problems of assimilation. The middle class, Anglophile tag had been firmly affixed to the group and apparently remained as the characterization, in the eyes of the city, of Jewish Toronto up until 1900.

234

Evidence of the social prestige of the various religious groups within the city is scant, but it is true to say that the importance socially of some religious groups was notably above that of others. The Anglican Church included in its confession the families of old Toronto, the early leaders in the city. Many of the first families of the city continued to belong to this group. The immigration, late in the century, of many English people, added a working-class element to it, however. Presbyterianism was directly associated with the Scottish population of the city, and counted among its members some of the prominent socially. By contrast, Methodism was more identified with the working class population of Toronto. "To become a member of that Church was to some extent to lose caste . . . . There were very few professional men connected with the body, and none who were wealthy."[63] Methodism claimed only the Masseys. The Baptists and Congregationalists also apparently failed to share with the Church of England the connotation of prestige. The hostility toward Catholics manifested in the Orange Order was most probably an amalgam of religious prejudice and feelings of social superiority on the part of the Protestants. In the absence of concrete evidence, however, no conclusions can be drawn from these snips of information. Instead, these scanty data concerning hostilities and bias provide some hints which suggest that religious denominationalism warrants serious consideration as a probable means of identification of various groups in the latter part of the nineteenth century. Religion was important in the era, investment in real estate and buildings alone would convince any observer of that fact, but the task remains to find out in what ways religion influenced and was correlated with the broader social and economic issues of the time.

The social imprint on the map

The maps of Toronto in the years from 1860 to 1900 suggest three important attributes of the changing landscapes of these years. These features are the changing scale of the city, and a changing heterogeneity of small areas within the city, and a changing orientation of the physical landscape.

The city in 1860 was small in area, comprising a patchwork of old patterns and new developments (Figure 1). The city was still seen at its best when reached from the lake which remained, as in the earliest of days, the principal avenue of approach and the main entrance route for new arrivals to the city. By 1860 the first railway tracks had been laid on the Esplanade, but the consequences of this action for the amenities of the waterfront were not yet fully realized. Toronto in 1860 extended along the north shore of the lake for a distance of about three miles, reaching westward from the mouth of the Don River toward Bathurst Street, a concession line surveyed through the former Garrison Reserve. The encroachment on the former Reserve lands continued, some fields still awaiting their absorption into the land-consuming process of city-building. To the north, the city had struggled almost to the bottom of the line of bluffs, the most distinct break in the generally flat plain on which the city was being built. The bluff, marking the eroded shorelines of the enlarged lake which in glacial times overspilled the limits of Lake Ontario, long proved to be a difficult obstacle in the northward expansion of the city. The town boundaries had been extended as far north as Bloor Street, one and a quarter miles north of Queen Street and about a mile and a half from the shoreline in 1860. To the north of this line small suburbs had risen, spreading along the main streets and struggling over the brow of the bluffs whence the finest prospects of the city were to be seen once the amenities of the waterfront had been despoiled by the greatest of the mid-century's symbols of progress. Yonge Street had been surveyed in Simcoe's time but remained a slow axis of expansion; the city preferred to sprawl along the lakeshore flats, tending only to avoid the minor streams which provided the only major barriers to construction along the shoreline.[64]

Within the roughly four square miles which comprised the built-up city in 1860, about fifty thousand people lived, worked, maintained their warehouses and constructed the institutions around which they organized their society. What is most notable about this compact city is not the density of the settlement, for this was not particularly high, but rather the heterodox quality of the map. By comparison with the end of the century, the city was a jumble of confusion in 1860. Commerce, industry and high class residential properties were tightly intermixed. The central commercial district was also the locus for the larger industrial plants of the city, and many of the estates of the wealthiest and most prominent citizens. The map of Toronto in 1860 reveals clearly this mix of land uses. The Anglican Cathedral was constructed on some of the city's most valuable real estate in the centre of the most prosperous commercial development, along King

236

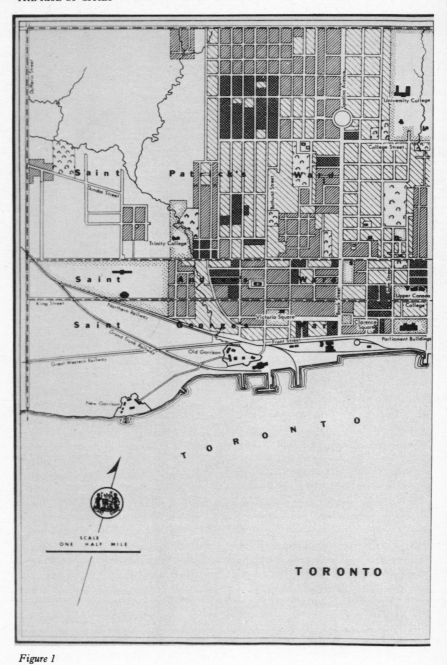

Figure 1

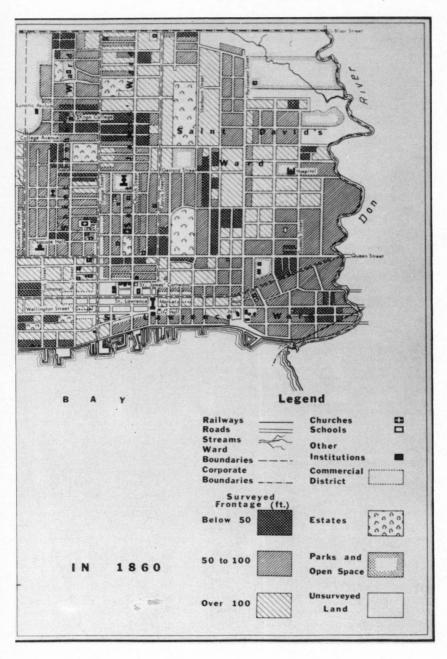

Street.[65] Factories along the quays were immediately adjacent to the commercial district and workshops occupied many commercial lofts.

Immediately adjacent to the commercial and institutional core of the city and to the west was located one of the high prestige residential areas of the city, localized around some of the most important of the urban institutions, the Parliament Building and the private preparatory school, Upper Canada College. Here the Bishop's Palace was located along with some large estates, shown on Figure 1. This district was the first of many tracts laid out as the town expanded, and the generous lot sizes combined with the amenities provided by the lake created a high social valuation in the district. In 1860 some of this prestige remained despite the incursions of commerce, waterfront industry and railways. To illustrate this, the occupations of persons living on several blocks of Wellington Street are listed below. Wellington Street, on the north side from Clarence to John Streets contained the homes of the following: a barrister, a professor, a

238   surgeon, a merchant, a widow, a boarding housekeeper and an accountant. On the south side of the street between Peter and Bay Streets there lived 3 gentlemen, 3 merchants, a professor, a broker, a registrar, a civil engineer, an auctioneer and a widow. In addition, at the corner of Bay and Wellington Street, in the heart of this district, there were already several prestigious commercial developments, notably barristers' offices and a bank. This range of occupations typified the high class district's main streets. By contrast, and to emphasize the characteristic diversity to be found even in the districts of wealth in the city, the occupations of persons living on a small side street just one block away from the previous example are listed: 6 labourers, 2 widows and a tailor, a shoemaker, a cooper, a moulder, an innkeeper, a clerk and a carver.[66] This social and economic diversity within a small area was characteristic of the waterfront area, but less forceful examples could be drawn from other parts of the city as well. The pattern of segregation appears to have been finely detailed and to have been responsive to the variations in prestige attached to very precisely defined sites.

Another highly visible aspect of the large-scale complexities of the urban map of 1860 is the multitude of unco-ordinated surveys, each of which was characterized by an individual and frequently deranged street plan plus accompanying lot surveys. The map north of Queen Street is covered with evidence of these speculative surveys undertaken at different times and various scales for numerous entrepreneurs. Adding to this collage of surveys and plans were the efforts at overbuilding the old surveys by subdividing properties to ensure the maximum use of land. South of Queen Street and east of Yonge ample evidence of this process was to be found in the development of tiny streets lined by tinier lots. North of Queen Street there remained, in 1860, a random scattering of undivided land and of remnant estates. In contrast to the general confusion of development was the property owned by the Allan family, originally a park lot. By 1860 only this one property, located just west of

Sherbourne Street, extending from Queen to Bloor Streets, reveals the dimensions of the original park lots, most of the one hundred acres of the original grant still being unsubdivided. The old park lots were consumed not only by housing but also by the institutional acreages of a growing city. The landscape is speckled with church sites, many donated for particular purposes and needs. Educational institutions occupied the largest fragments of several old estates, however. By 1860, University College had been built in the northwestern quarter of the city adjacent to the old King's College which after 1856 saw service as a Lunatic asylum. The University of Trinity College was established on the southern portion of another park lot after 1851. Most of the nineteenth-century institutions established in Toronto after the first years of settlement eventually came to occupy property in this area north of Queen Street, and the pattern of institutional land use in this part of the city remained in 1960 about as it was in 1860.

Whereas the development north of Queen Street of educational complexes served to localize institutions of higher learning in the city for over a century, the intrusion of other activities onto Toronto's waterfront destroyed old patterns and altered dramatically the social valuation of this part of the city. The residual prestige still attached to this district in 1860 was to be short lived. The death of the waterfront as an amenity was part of the gradual reorientation of the city away from the lake. The new high status districts were located in the northern suburbs. The waterfront was destroyed by the railways and their attendant industry as well as by the expanding commercial activity of this entrepot town. By 1870 the small estates had disappeared from the lakeshore and only the old Parliament Buildings, the Bishop's Palace and Upper Canada College survived as ossified remainders of a vanished district (Figure 2).

Other subtle indications of the changing orientation of the city can be gleaned from the maps. For some time the new religious establishment had been avoiding the lake front. St. Basil's and St. Michael's Colleges were begun in 1856 at the northern edge of the city. Knox College moved from Front Street to quarters in the northern fringes after 1856 as well. These only add to the examples already mentioned. St. Michael's Cathedral, begun in 1848, was north and east of the old waterfront district on part of the same park lot on which the Metropolitan (Methodist) Church was built in 1872. Investment in amenities unconnected with religion also reflected the changing direction of growth and prestige. The first street railway in the city was constructed, not along the broad east-west waterfront axis of the city, but along the shorter north-south spine to the fashionable northern periphery. In all, these trends probably contributed significantly to the abandonment by the citizens of the old districts and to the new orientation of the city. The town no longer focused on the waterfront. Here the commerce and industry of the city remained and expanded, but by 1870 residential growth had taken a different direction.

The map of 1880 reveals, in a general manner, the continuation of the

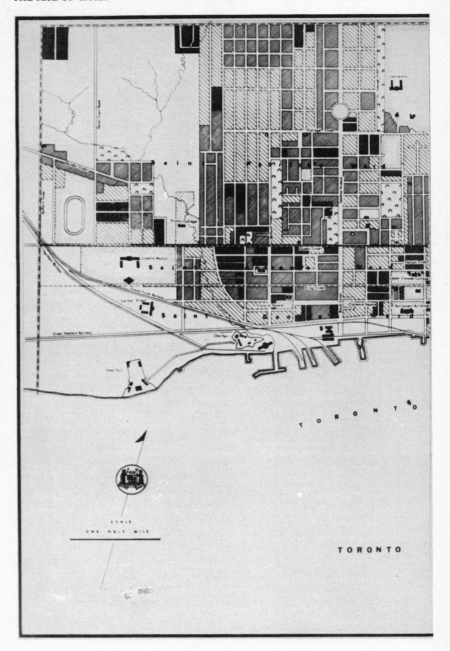

Figure 2

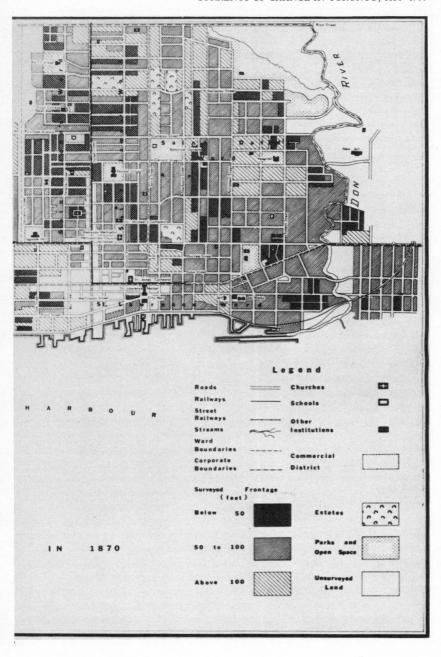

Legend

Roads		Churches	
Railways		Schools	
Street Railways		Other Institutions	
Streams			
Ward Boundaries		Commercial District	
Corporate Boundaries			

Surveyed Frontage (feet)

Below 50		Estates	
50 to 100		Parks and Open Space	
Above 100		Unsurveyed Land	

H A R B O U R

I N   1 8 7 0

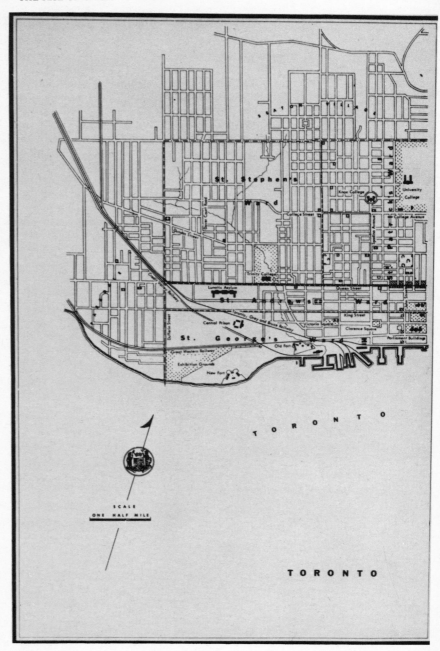

Figure 3

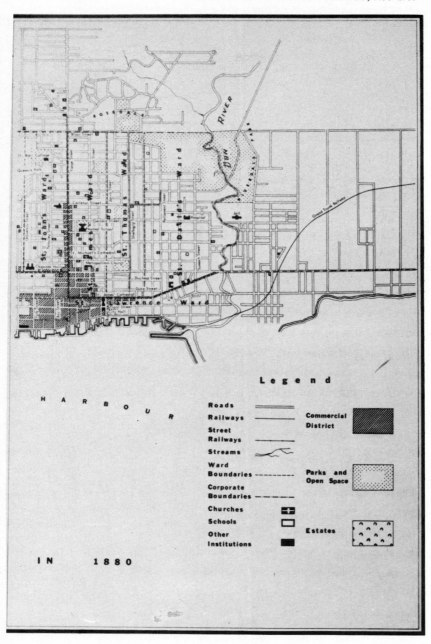

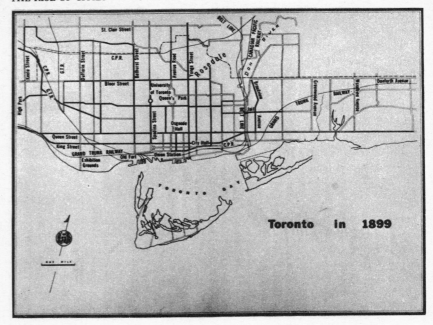

Figure 4

244

trends, discerned already (Figure 3). The waterfront was becoming more industrialized and the commercial core was continuing to expand yet further into the old western suburb. The institutions previously planted in the northern part of the city were flourishing and expanding while the remnant estates in the old city continued to shrink. Land south of Bloor Street continued to be parceled out under the influence of the speculative subdividers so that by 1900 the process was virtually complete. The same procedures were then reiterated in all the newer and more distant suburbs. The city continued to grow by the piecemeal plans of speculative realtors.

The changing scale of the city becomes quite apparent when the map of 1899 is compared with that of 1860 (Figures 4 and 1). In 1899 the new and expanded plan was being held together by the growing mileage of streetcar lines. Following the old design, the lines first reached into the northern suburbs and only later were they built to the more distant but less fashionable areas of the city. In 1880 the best served district in Toronto was the newly fashionable northern area just south of Rosedale. By 1899, however, the major achievement of the transport system was that it had effectively reached to the limits of the populated areas of the city, tying the sprawling new metropolis together.

Industrial development, population growth, and the changing system of internal transportation were three of the most conspicuous agents of change in the late nineteenth-century urban landscape of Toronto. Each created opportunities, influenced the character of the new city, and provided the broad context within which the city grew. The social characteristics of different parts of the city developed not only within these broad constraints but also under the more intimate influences of social taste and the prevailing definition of prestige. The attributes of these social worlds were a product of the interplay of the general economic context of life in the city and of the more particularistic conceptions which were derived from the immediate urban environment.

Notes

1. Canada Board of Registration and Statistics, *Census of the Canadas, 1851–52*, I, p. 30; Canada, Census and Statistics Office, *Fourth Census of Canada*, 1901, I, pp. 218–19.
2. Henry Scadding, *Toronto of Old* (Toronto: Oxford University Press, 1966).
3. D. G. Creighton, *The Commercial Empire of the St. Lawrence* (Toronto: Ryerson Press, 1937), pp. 382–84.
4. Ralph Waldo Emerson, quoted in Asa Briggs, *Victorian Cities* (Harmondsworth, England: Penguin Books Ltd., Pelican Books, 1968). p. 13.
5. The costs of shipping from Montreal to Europe as against the costs from New York to Europe were the subject of investigation in Canada. New York already controlled the bulk of the import trade into Canada, and had for some time been able to do this because of relaxation of the Navigation Laws as they applied to shipping on the Great Lakes. Thus, there was special urgency in the investigation. The findings and later reports are discussed by Innis in H. A. Innis and A. R. M. Lower, eds., *Select Documents in Canadian Economic History* (Toronto: University of Toronto Press, 1933), p. 473.
6. Innis and Lower, *op. cit.*, p. 492.
7. A discussion of the various merchants engaged in the trade is found in D. C. Masters, *The Rise of Toronto, 1850–1890* (Toronto: University of Toronto Press, 1947), p. 60.
8. The attitudes of Toronto's leading editor, who was also an avid railway supporter, toward the railways are discussed in J. M. S. Careless, *Brown of the Globe*, Vol. I: *The Voice of Upper Canada 1818–1859* (Toronto: Macmillan Co. of Canada, 1959), pp. 211–12.
9. These details are according to *The Handbook of Toronto* (Toronto: Lovell and Gibson, 1859), pp. 201, 221.
10. Details of the gateway functions of early settlements near Toronto are given in Percy J. Robinson, *Toronto During the French Regime 1615–1793* (Toronto: Ryerson Press, 1933).
11. Careless, *op. cit.*, p. 229; Innis and Lower, *op. cit.*, p. 489.
12. The words are those of Careless describing Brown's idea. Careless, *op. cit.*, p. 212.
13. Details of this trade may be found in Innis and Lower, *op. cit.*, p. 494.
14. *Ibid.*, p. 664.
15. *Ibid.*, p. 490
16. *Ibid.*, p. 493
17. Masters, *op. cit.*, pp. 178–80.
18. Of this total trackage, 228 miles were operated in the United States. Innis and Lower, *op. cit.*, p. 497.
19. C. Pelham Mulvany, *Toronto: Past and Present* (Toronto: W. E. Caiger, 1884), p. 59.
20. Figures given are in the *Census of Canada, 1870–71*, and the *Fourth Census of Canada, 1901*. For the complete statistics for the thirty years, see Table 1.
21. D. C. Masters discusses the general depression that hung in the rooms of the business community. See Masters, *op. cit.*, pp. 142–72. The general argument of a depression is countered by Chambers and Bertram who dispute the evidence offered concerning a prolonged business malaise. See Edward J. Chambers and Gordon W. Bertram, "Urbanization and Manufacturing in Central Canada, 1870–1890," in *Papers on Regional Statistical Studies*, ed. Sylvia Ostry and T. K. Rymes, Canadian Political Science Association: Conference on Statistics, 1964 (Toronto: University of Toronto Press, 1966), pp. 225–58.
22. An inspection of the city directory published by William Brown for 1856–57 led Guillet to the conclusion that factories had begun to "supplant" the city's small tradesmen. See Edwin C. Guillet, *Toronto — From Trading Post to Great City* (Toronto: Ontario Publishing Co., 1934), p. 273.
23. *Ibid.*, p. 268.
24. Quoted in D. C. Masters, *op. cit.*, pp. 61–62.
25. John E. McNab, "Toronto's Industrial Growth to 1891," *Ontario History*, XLVII (1955), p. 73.
26. Canada, Department of Agriculture, *Census of Canada 1890–91*, III, p. 385.
27. Canada, Census and Statistics Office, Bulletin 2: *Manufactures of Canada*, 1907.
28. Innis and Lower, *op. cit.*, p. 477.
29. Masters, *op. cit.*, p. 173.

THE RISE OF CITIES

30. *Ibid.*, p. 147. Masters suggests that the growth of Toronto's hinterland may have played an important role in the timing of its late prosperity.
31. *Ibid.*, p. 172. In efforts to control the trade of Georgian Bay, Toronto interests had built a railway connecting Owen Sound with the larger city. The significance of this line was enhanced once the C.P.R. had finished its line to Fort William-Port Arthur. Innis and Lower, *op. cit.*, p. 490.
32. Masters, *op. cit.*, p. 172.
33. Innis and Lower, *op. cit.*, pp. 596–97.
34. For a fuller discussion of industrial localization and specialization in Toronto and in Central Canada from 1870 to 1890, see Edward J. Chambers and Gordon W. Bertram, "Urbanization and Manufacturing in Central Canada, 1870–1890," in Ostry and Rymes, *op. cit.*, pp. 225–58.
35. *Ibid.*, p. 258.
36. Chambers and Bertram cite statistics for the percent of value added in manufacturing within Ontario and Quebec accounted for by York county. These data are as follows: 1870 — 9.72 percent; 1880 — 11.09 percent; 1890 — 13.45 percent. See Chambers and Bertram *op. cit.*, pp. 244, 248, 252.
37. Street railway lines had been installed in only seventeen cities in America prior to the construction of Toronto's first line. Dates of construction of street railways in the cities of the United States and Canada are given in Arthur J. Krim, "The Innovation and Diffusion of the Street Railway in North America" (unpublished Master's dissertation, Department of Geography, University of Chicago, 1967), p. 63.
38. Guillet, *op. cit.*, p. 121.
39. *Ibid.*, pp. 121–31.
40. Louis H. Pursley, *Street Railways of Toronto, 1861–1921*, Interurbans Special: Interurbans, Vol. XVI, No. 2 (Los Angeles: Electric Railway Publications, 1958), p. 7.
41. *Ibid.*, p. 9.
42. According to Pursley, the agreement had called for the electrification of the system within one year of franchising. The first electric line was installed in the city in August of 1892, on Church Street leading to a fashionable northern suburb, *Ibid.*, p. 16.
43. *Ibid.*, p. 22.
44. The words are those of Henry M. Whitney of Boston, quoted in Sam B. Warner, *Streetcar Suburbs* (Cambridge Mass.: Harvard University Press, 1962), p. 26. A moderate interpretation of the impact of local railways is found in D. A. Reeder, "A Theatre of Suburbs: Some Patterns of Development in West London, 1801–1911," in *The Study of Urban History*, ed. H. J. Dyos (London: Edward Arnold, 1968), pp. 253–71.
45. This fact is mentioned in Frederic W. Speirs, *The Street Railway System of Philadelphia: Its History and Present Condition*, Johns Hopkins University Studies in Historical and Political Science. Vol. XV (Baltimore: John Hopkins Press, 1897), pp. 70–71.
46. Some of the more important works discussing the role of street railways in reforming the morphology of cities are listed in Goheen, *Victorian Toronto*, p. 74, footnote 2.
47. Canada, Department of Agriculture, *Census of Canada, 1890–91*, I, pp. 349, 357.
48. Since Toronto was the second city of the country, it is not surprising that there should be more migrants there than in smaller places. By comparison, in 1890, Hamilton contained 15 596 foreign-born as against 31 649 Canadian-born residents, a proportion close to Toronto's ratio. Ottawa numbered 6431 foreign-born and 30 838 Canadian-born residents in the same year. *Ibid.*, pp. 343, 347.
49. There is at present no information on this procedure relating to Toronto in the nineteenth century. The process was not, however, unusual. Details of its application in Boston are given in Oscar Handlin, *Boston's Immigrants* (New York: Atheneum, 1968).
50. The recency of the arrival in Canada of Toronto's population is given added support by numbering children of foreign-born fathers as well as the foreign-born population itself. In 1890, there were 111 489 in these categories, only 32 534 being born in Canada of native fathers. Canada, Department of Agriculture, *Census of Canada 1890–91*, II, p. 230.
51. Figures quoted in Masters, *op. cit.*, p. 33.
52. *Ibid.*, p. 37.
53. *Ibid.*, p. 85.
54. Arthur R. M. Lower, *Colony to Nation, a History of Canada* (Toronto: Longmans Canada, 1946), p. 352.
55. Quoted from the *Globe*, Feb. 18, 1871, in Masters, *op. cit.*, p. 128.
56. Lower, *op. cit.*, p. 352.
57. *Ibid.*, p. 382.
58. Remarks of the *Orange Sentinel* were reprinted in the paper *Week*, Oct. 1, 1885 and are quoted from Masters, *op. cit.*, p. 192.
59. In 1901, 18.9 percent of the Jewish population of Canada lived in Toronto. Louis Rosenberg, "A Study of the Changes in the Geographic Distribution of the Jewish Population in the Metropolitan Area of Toronto, 1851–1951," *Canadian Jewish Population Studies, Jewish Community Series*, II (1954), p. 1.
60. Ben Kayfetz, "The Jewish Community in Toronto," in *A People and Its Faith*, ed. by Albert Rose (Toronto: University of Toronto Press, 1959), pp. 14–29.

246

61. Sidney S. Schipper, "Holy Blossom and Its Community," *Ibid.*, p. 31.
62. *Ibid.*, p. 34.
63. Quoted in Guillet, *op. cit.*, p. 376. Remark made in 1914.
64. For several decades scholars have followed Griffith Taylor in his assertions that these tiny streams have controlled the early development in Toronto. Taylor asserts that, "the evolution of the city of Toronto . . . [is] determined by the minor topographic features" of the plain. Griffith Taylor, "Topographic Control in the Toronto Region," *Canadian Journal of Political Science*, II (1936), p. 493.
65. St. James Cathedral was actually constructed on land set aside for the purpose in the plans for the enlargement of the city plot drawn up by The Honorable Peter Russell soon after the founding of the town. Not all of the land so designated, however, was preserved by the Church for its own use.
66. This street is Melinda Street, one block long and extending west of Yonge Street south of King. The description of the occupations are taken from the "Asssessment Roll for the Ward of St. George, City of Toronto, 1860," pp. 14–18, p. 22.

Sources of the Figures

Figure 1 is drawn from the "Plan of the City of Toronto Showing the Government Survey and the Registered Subdivision into Lots According to Plans Filed in the Office of the City Registrar," made by H. J. Browne under the direction of J. O. Browne, Civil Engineer and P. L. Surveyor in 1862. Details have been corrected for 1860 from the Assessment Rolls of that year.

Figure 2 is drawn from "Wadsworth and Unwin's Map of the City of Toronto," compiled by Maurice Gaviller, C.E. and P.L.S. from plans filed in the Registry Office and the most recent surveys in 1872, and corrected for 1870 from the Assessment Rolls of 1870.

Figure 3 is drawn from a map titled "City of Toronto," published in Toronto by R. L. Polk and Co., 1887, and corrected for 1880 from the Assessment Rolls, City of Toronto, 1880.

Figure 4 is derived from an untitled map in the collection of the Baldwin Room, Toronto Public Library, drawn in 1899 by J. G. Foster and Co.

247

The Urban West: The Evolution of Prairie Towns and Cities to 1930*

ALAN F. J. ARTIBISE

The urban frontier was one of the vital elements in Canada's western expansion. Towns and cities introduced a dynamic and aggressive element into the prairie West and played a key role in transforming a sparsely settled fur-trading expanse into a settled and well-integrated region. In this process, the interdependent relationship of city and countryside was clearly evident. But the urban centres were the driving force in the massive changes that occurred in the six decades following Confederation.

I

The process of prairie urban development in the years before 1930 can best be outlined by examining it in four distinguishable phases. The first was a pre-urban stage that lasted for almost two centuries, ending only in the early 1870s when a series of political decisions — Confederation, the sale of Rupert's Land by the Hudson's Bay Company to the Canadian government, and the creation of the Province of Manitoba — opened a new era in western Canadian history. Prior to these dramatic events, the prairie

* From *Prairie Forum*, 4 (1979): 237–262. Reprinted by permission.

West had no urban centres.[1] The economic base of the region was the H.B.C. fur trade and any agriculture that was practised was at the subsistence level. The only commercial centres were scattered H.B.C. posts managed by a few traders, and these could scarcely claim urban stature. In this pre-railway age, settlement was associated with rivers and the various population concentrations were linked only by boat or by the Red River carts which plied the Carleton Trail.

Five settlements dating from this pre-urban age, however, were destined to become towns and cities in the post-1870 period. At the eastern terminus of the Carleton Trail were located the Red River Colony and Fort Garry. The former had been begun by Lord Selkirk in 1811–1812; the latter was established by the H.B.C. in 1835. Neither of these settlements can be regarded as the basis for urban growth, however, for the lack of immigration and efficient linkages with the outside world resulted in very slow development. It was not until the 1860s that developments occurred which soon led to the establishment of a distinct urban centre. During this decade a small commercial centre named Winnipeg emerged near Fort Garry to compete with the Company in servicing incoming plains traders and supplying the needs of the Red River Colony. By 1870, Winnipeg consisted of a few frame structures and some 100 inhabitants, and offered a number of services, several hotels and specialized retail outlets.[2]

Across the Red River from Winnipeg was the St. Boniface mission. It had been established in 1818 by two Quebec priests, and it soon became one of the most urban communities on the prairies. Catholic missionaries from central Canada erected a chapel and a school in 1818, and by 1827 the latter was well established and on its way to becoming the College of St. Boniface. By 1870, the population of this settlement was approaching 800, far exceeding that of Winnipeg.[3]

To the west, along the banks of the Assiniboine River, was Portage la Prairie, established as a mission in 1853. A H.B.C. trading post was erected at the site in 1856 but neither mission nor fort attracted a concentration of settlement. Although all trade for the western area passed through Portage, the settlement was in most respects an offshoot of the settlement at Fort Garry.[4]

To the west and north of Portage, another mission and H.B.C. post were located in close proximity; both Prince Albert Mission and Fort Albert were established in 1866. By 1870, there were approximately 100 inhabitants dispersed along the banks of the North Saskatchewan River but no service centre nucleus had yet developed.[5]

At the western terminus of the Carleton Trail and also on the banks of the North Saskatchewan River was Edmonton House, one of the H.B.C.'s most important entrepôts. This fort acted as a collection centre for furs for the Saskatchewan District and as the distribution centre for goods from Winnipeg. The population of Edmonton House was approximately 150 by Confederation, although this small size belied its administrative and distributive importance.[6]

248

TABLE I – Rural and Urban[a] Population Growth in the Northwest Territories and Prairie Provinces, 1871–1931 (in thousands)

			Northwest Territories		Manitoba		Total Prairies		
			Rural	Urban	Rural	Urban	Rural	Urban	% Urban
1871			48	—	25	—	73	—	0
1881			56	—	52	10	108	10	8
1891			95	4	111	41	206	45	18

	Alberta		Saskatchewan						
	Rural	Urban	Rural	Urban	Rural	Urban	Rural	Urban	% Urban
1901	61	12	86	6	192	64	339	81	19.3
1911	264	110	413	80	269	193	946	383	28.8
1921	411	177	630	128	341	269	1,382	574	29.3
1931	504	228	735	187	357	343	1,596	758	32.2

Notes: (a) In 1871, 1881, and 1891, the urban category includes all incorporated villages, towns, and cities, regardless of size. From 1901–1931, urban population includes incorporated cities, towns, and villages of 1000 and over and incorporated municipalities of this size range surrounding the larger cities which were later defined as parts of the census metropolitan areas.
Sources: *Census of Canada, 1931*; and *Census of Canada, 1956* — "Analytical Report: Rural and Urban Population," p. 26.

By 1870, then, the prairie West contained only a few settlement nodes. The entire population of the region was about seventy thousand persons, virtually none of whom could be counted as urban dwellers. Change was in the air, however, and during the next three decades the fur trading economy with its few small posts was replaced by a commercial agricultural economy organized by and around numerous villages, towns, and cities.

249

II

Between 1871 and 1901, the population of the prairies jumped from 70 000 to more than 400 000, and almost 20 per cent lived in urban centres with populations exceeding 1000 (Table I). By this date the region also had three incorporated cities, twenty-five towns, and fifty-seven villages.[7] More than eighteen of these centres had populations exceeding 1000, six had populations exceeding 5000, and one had a population in excess of 40 000 (Tables II, III, IV).

TABLE II – Population Growth in Incorporated Villages, Towns, and Cities in Manitoba, 1871–1931[a]

Urban Centre	Date of Incorporation			Population										
	Village	Town	City	1871	1881	1886	1891	1901	1906	1911	1916	1921	1926	1931
Beauséjour	1908	1912	—	—	—	—	—	—	—	847	879	994	996	1 139
Brandon	—	—	1882	—	—	2 348	3 778	5 620	10 408	13 839	15 215	15 397	16 443	17 082
Brooklands	1921	—	—	—	—	—	—	—	—	—	—	—	—	2 462
Carman	1899	1905	—	—	—	—	—	1 439	1 530	1 271	1 426	1 591	1 385	1 418
Dauphin	1898	1901	—	—	—	—	—	1 135	1 670	2 815	3 200	3 885	3 580	3 971
Killarney	1903	—	—	—	—	—	—	585	1 117	1 010	989	871	901	1 003
Minnedosa	—	1883	—	—	—	549	614	1 052	1 299	1 483	1 833	1 505	1 681	1 680
Morden	—	1903	—	—	—	—	1 176	1 522	1 437	1 130	1 261	1 268	1 354	1 416
Neepawa	—	1883	—	—	—	255	774	1 418	1 895	1 864	1 854	1 887	1 833	1 910
Portage la Prairie	—	1880	1907	—	—	2 028	3 363	3 901	5 106	5 892	6 766	6 513	6 597	
St. Boniface	—	1883	1908	817	1 283	1 449	1 553	2 019	5 119	7 483	11 021	12 821	14 187	16 305
Selkirk	—	1882	—	—	—	—	705	950	2 188	2 701	2 977	3 399	3 726	4 201	4 486
Souris	—	1903	—	—	—	—	—	839	1 413	1 854	1 845	1 710	1 612	1 661
Stonewall	1906	1908	—	—	—	—	—	589	1 074	1 005	1 152	1 112	1 043	1 031
Le Pas	—	1912	—	—	—	—	—	—	—	—	1 270	1 858	1 925	4 030
Transcona	—	1912	—	—	—	—	—	—	—	—	3 356	4 185	5 218	5 747
Tuxedo	—	1913	—	—	—	—	—	—	—	—	192	1 062	717	1 173
Virden	1890	1904	—	—	—	—	606	901	1 471	1 550	1 618	1 361	1 380	1 590
Winkler	1906	—	—	—	—	—	—	391	530	458	547	812	971	1 005
Winnipeg	—	—	1873	241	7 985	20 238	25 639	42 340	90 153	136 035	163 000	179 087	191 998	218 785

Notes: (a) Includes only those centres with a population exceeding 1000 in 1931.
Sources: *Censuses of Canada, 1871–1931*; and *Censuses of the Prairie Provinces, 1906–1926*. Also, various other sources have been used to provide data for the period of 1871–1891. Unfortunately, I have been unable to locate data on all the communities in existence during these years.

TABLE III – Population Growth in Incorporated Villages, Towns, and Cities in Saskatchewan, 1881–1931[a]

Urban Centre	Date of Incorporation			Population								
	Village	Town	City	1881–1882	1891	1901	1906	1911	1916	1921	1926	1931
Assiniboia	1912	1913	—	—	—	—	—	—	719	1 006	1 245	1 454
Battleford	1899	1904	—	—	—	609	933	1 335	1 436	1 229	1 018	1 096
Biggar	1909	1911	—	—	—	—	—	315	830	1 535	2 034	2 369
Canora	1905	1910	—	—	—	—	169	435	835	1 230	1 121	1 179
Estevan	1899	1906	—	—	—	141	877	981	2 140	2 290	2 336	2 936
Gravelbourg	1912	1916	—	—	—	—	—	—	463	1 106	1 201	1 137
Herbert	1907	1912	—	—	—	—	—	559	950	827	997	1 009
Humboldt	1905	1907	—	—	—	—	279	859	1 435	1 822	1 751	1 899
Indian Head	—	1902	—	—	—	768	1 545	1 285	1 334	1 439	1 313	1 438
Kamsack	1905	1911	—	—	—	—	204	473	1 202	2 002	1 948	2 087
Kindersley	1910	1910	—	—	—	—	—	456	770	1 003	987	1 037
Lloydminster[b]	1903	1907	—	—	—	—	389	441	494	469	847	1 516
Maple Creek	1896	1903	—	—	—	382	687	936	1 140	1 002	930	1 154
Melfort	1903	1907	—	—	—	—	351	599	971	1 746	1 605	1 809
Melville	1908	1909	—	—	—	—	—	1 816	2 100	2 808	3 352	3 891
Moose Jaw	—	1884	1903	c.100	1 200	1 558	6 249	13 823	16 934	19 285	19 039	21 299
Moosomin	—	1887	—	—	—	868	1 152	1 143	1 329	1 099	1 121	1 119
North Battleford	1906	1906	1913	—	—	—	824	2 105	3 154	4 108	4 787	5 986
Prince Albert	—	1885	1904	c.500	1 009	1 785	3 005	6 254	6 436	7 558	7 873	9 905
Radville	1911	1913	—	—	—	—	—	233	621	883	1 082	1 005
Regina	—	1883	1903	c.800	1 681	2 249	6 169	30 213	26 167	34 432	37 329	53 209
Rosetown	1909	1911	—	—	—	—	—	317	731	865	1 142	1 553
Rosthern	1898	1903	—	—	—	413	918	1 172	1 200	1 074	1 273	1 412
Saskatoon	1901	1903	1906	—	—	113	3 001	12 004	21 048	25 739	31 234	43 291
Shaunavon	1913	1914	—	—	—	—	—	—	897	1 146	1 459	1 716
Sutherland	1909	1912	—	—	—	—	—	421	940	961	1 010	1 148
Swift Current	1904	1907	1913	—	—	121	554	1 852	3 181	3 518	4 175	5 296
Tisdale	1905	1920	—	—	—	—	61	250	458	783	846	1 069
Watrous	1908	1909	—	—	—	—	—	781	843	1 101	1 172	1 303
Weyburn	1900	1903	1913	—	—	113	966	2 210	3 050	3 193	4 119	5 002
Wilkie	1908	1910	—	—	—	—	—	537	815	778	1 041	1 222
Wynyard	1908	1911	—	—	—	—	—	515	682	849	833	1 042
Yorkton	1894	1900	1928	—	—	700	1 363	2 309	3 144	5 151	4 458	5 027

Notes: (a) Includes only those centres with a population exceeding 1000 in 1931.
(b) Until 1930, population is split between Alberta and Saskatchewan. Amalgamated with Alberta in 1930.
Sources: See Table II.

TABLE IV – **Population Growth in Incorporated Villages, Towns, and Cities in Alberta, 1881–1931**[a]

Urban Centre	Date of Incorporation			Population								
	Village	Town	City	1881	1891	1901	1906	1911	1916	1921	1926	1931
Beverley	–	1914	–	–	–	–	–	–	813	1 039	931	1 111
Blairmore	1901	1911	–	–	–	231	449	1 137	1 219	1 552	1 609	1 629
Calgary	–	1884	1893	100	3 867	4 398	11 967	43 704	56 514	63 305	65 291	83 761
Camrose	1905	1906	–	–	–	–	412	1 586	1 692	1 892	2 002	2 258
Cardston	1898	1901	–	–	–	639	1 001	1 207	1 370	1 612	2 034	1 672
Claresholm	1903	1905	–	–	–	–	680	809	687	963	956	1 156
Coleman	1904	1910	–	–	–	–	915	1 557	1 559	1 590	2 044	1 704
Drumheller	1913	1916	1930	–	–	–	–	–	312	2 499	2 578	2 987
Edmonton	–	1892	1904	263	700	2 626	11 167	31 064	53 846	58 821	65 163	79 187
Edson	1911	1911	–	–	–	–	–	497	500	1 138	1 493	1 547
Fort Saskatchewan	1899	1904	–	–	–	306	585	782	993	982	943	1 001
Grand Prairie	1914	1919	–	–	–	–	–	–	337	1 061	917	1 464
Hanna	1912	1914	–	–	–	–	–	–	711	1 364	1 400	1 490
High River	1901	1910	–	–	–	153	1 018	1 182	1 182	1 198	1 377	1 459
Innisfail	1899	1903	–	–	–	317	643	602	838	941	944	1 024
Lacombe	1896	1902	–	–	–	499	1 015	1 029	1 047	1 133	1 151	1 259
Lethbridge	–	1890	1906	–	–	2 072	2 936	9 035	9 436	11 097	10 735	13 489
Macleod	–	1892	–	–	–	796	1 144	1 844	1 811	1 723	1 715	1 447
Magrath	1901	1907	–	–	–	424	884	995	938	1 069	1 202	1 224
Medicine Hat	1894	1898	1906	–	–	1 570	3 020	5 608	9 272	9 634	9 536	10 300
Olds	1896	1905	–	–	–	218	554	917	730	764	1 003	1 056
Pincher Creek	1898	1906	–	–	–	335	589	1 027	1 026	888	1 003	1 024
Raymond	1902	1903	–	–	–	–	1 568	1 465	1 205	1 394	1 799	1 849
Redcliff	1910	1912	–	–	–	–	–	220	1 294	1 137	916	1 192
Red Deer	1894	1901	1913	–	–	323	1 418	2 118	2 203	2 328	2 021	2 344
Stettler	–	1906	–	–	–	–	570	1 444	1 168	1 416	1 127	1 219
Strathcona[b]	–	1899	1907	–	–	1 550	2 921	5 579	–	–	–	–
Taber	1905	1907	–	–	–	–	578	1 400	1 412	1 705	1 342	1 279
Vegreville	1906	1906	–	–	–	–	344	1 029	1 156	1 479	1 721	1 659
Vermilion	1906	1906	–	–	–	–	623	625	929	1 272	1 203	1 270
Wainwright	–	1910	–	–	–	–	–	788	818	975	1 028	1 147
Wetaskiwin	1899	1902	1906	–	–	550	1 652	2 411	2 048	2 061	1 884	2 125

Notes: (a) Includes only those centres with a population exceeding 1000 in 1931.
(b) Annexed to Edmonton in 1911. The Edmonton total in 1911 includes Strathcona.

Sources: See Table II.

The reasons for this substantial growth in the number of urban centres are complex and cannot be adequately analyzed here.[8] What is readily apparent, however, is that virtually all the centres which sprang up or grew significantly in this second era of development were located on railway lines or along the paths of projected lines (see Map 1). The fact was that the 1870s were the beginning of a new era for the prairies in which subsistence agriculture was replaced by the production of agricultural surplus for export. The development of commercial agriculture — indeed, the mere anticipation of it — brought about the rise of centres of distribution. The reciprocal relationship between town and country was clear.

The prairie pioneer was no self-sufficient farmer but an agricultural industrialist engaged in commercial trading. He produced a large surplus of grain and was a heavy consumer of manufactured goods. He needed grain shipping depots, farm implements, hardware goods, wagons, harnesses, lumber and other supplies. He needed banking services to finance these investments. He needed consumer goods that he could not produce himself: clothing and staple foodstuffs. As a result, every rural community needed a town, both as a shipping point that gathered surplus grain, and as a distribution point that fanned manufactured goods back into the countryside.[9]

To survive and to grow, incipient service centres needed capital, agricultural hinterlands, and transportation connections. The most important of these essentials for every aspiring metropolis was the railway. "Railways and continually improving transportation were as essential as rain and sun to progressive settlement on the Canadian prairie. Nearness to railways and projected railways was of first importance to the settler."[10]

In the three decades following 1870, approximately 3600 miles of rail were laid in the prairie West.[11] The most dramatic growth of settlement occurred along the main line and branch lines of the Canadian Pacific Railway, and among these settlements none grew as rapidly as Winnipeg. The first railway reached Winnipeg in 1878, connecting the community with St. Paul and Chicago. By 1883, the C.P.R. stretched north of the Great Lakes to link Winnipeg with eastern Canada, and two years later the first transcontinental line was complete. Winnipeg was also a nodal point for several branch lines in Manitoba, and together these external and internal linkages contributed to its growth and dominance. By 1881, Winnipeg's population was 8000; during the next decade it more than tripled. Wholesaling was organized during these years, and with the growing number of towns and service centres in the prairie West Winnipeg merchants were soon establishing branch offices. Financial, retail and merchandising operations also increased in number. In 1881–1882, Winnipeg experienced a tremendous real estate boom; although the boom soon collapsed, real growth did take place, and the initial physical infrastructure of an urban centre — railways, hotels, warehouses, offices, stores — had been acquired. By the early 1880s, Winnipeg was firmly established as the dominant western urban centre.

Elsewhere in Manitoba, new centres appeared and older centres grew, although nowhere was change as substantial as in Winnipeg. St. Boniface was incorporated as a town in 1883 but, given its proximity to Winnipeg, was to remain in that city's shadow in subsequent years. Portage la Prairie grew more rapidly and established itself as a second-order centre. Incorporated as a town in 1880 and situated on the main line of the C.P.R., Portage grew steadily in the early part of that decade and by 1901 was the third largest settlement in Manitoba. The second largest town was Brandon. Established by the C.P.R. in 1881 and incorporated as a city in 1882 (with a population of 3000), this centre was evidence of the magic of railways.[12] It was known to most westerners that the C.P.R. would establish a divisonal point some 100 miles west of Winnipeg. But when speculators attempted to sell a proposed townsite to the C.P.R. for what the company felt was an unreasonable sum, the company simply moved two miles west and created the instant town of Brandon. When other incipient centres tried to compete with the new boom town they were destined to fail, since no-one was going to buy lots in a town where the train did not stop. The C.P.R. thus became a significant builder of prairie towns, and the Brandon story was repeated many times.[13]

253

Two other Manitoba centres also learned of the power of the railway during these years, but with less pleasant results than Brandon. Emerson (the former site of Pembina) was surveyed in 1874 when it was believed that its intervening location between Winnipeg and out-of-province centres would guarantee its future. Its rail connection with Winnipeg and the anticipation of further branch-line connections led to the incorporation of Emerson as a town in 1880, and by the spring of 1882 it had a population of 2500 and was thriving as the supply base of southwestern Manitoba. But when a railway was constructed to Morris and Morden, bypassing Emerson, the town's growth halted and a long period of population decline set in. By 1886 Emerson was a dull place with empty warehouses and stores, and vacant homes. People had simply left to establish businesses in the new towns along the C.P.R.'s Pembina Branch.[14]

Selkirk's early history was similar, although its story is more dramatic since it had hoped to become the hub of railway operations in the West. Until 1880 it was the plan of the C.P.R. to cross the Red River at Selkirk, not at Winnipeg, placing the former community on the main line and excluding the latter. This anticipation caused a surge of growth in Selkirk until the Winnipeg business community marshalled their forces and succeeded in having the decision changed.[15] Thus, when the C.P.R. crossed the Red River at Winnipeg, Selkirk had to be content with remaining the centre of steamboat, lumbering and fishing operations on Lake Winnipeg. It was, at best, a poor second prize. By 1901 Selkirk's population was barely 2000.

The rise and growth of towns and cities in the remainder of the prairie West in this era were also closely related to railways. The most dramatic growth occurred along the C.P.R. main line where the towns of Regina, Moose Jaw, Swift Current, Medicine Hat, and Calgary suddenly came to life. All except Calgary were creations of the C.P.R.

Few other western urban centres illustrated the power of the C.P.R. so well as Regina. It possessed no natural advantages as a townsite since it was situated on a treeless plain with only the meandering Pile of Bones (Wascana) Creek as a nearby source of water. Furthermore, the site had not previously possessed any commercial importance; until 1882 the nearest settlement was the H.B.C. post on the Qu'Appelle Lakes, thirty-five miles to the northeast. Yet by 1883 Regina was incorporated as a town and by 1888 it claimed a population of 1400.[16]

The C.P.R.'s ability to control townsite selection and land sales on the prairies was well known. The choice of Regina, however, was not unchallenged. In 1882, Edgar Dewdney, federally appointed Lieutenant-Governor of the North West Territories, was authorized to select a site for a new capital to replace Battleford, the choice for capital in 1876 when the C.P.R. had been projected to follow a northern route along the North Saskatchewan River. Dewdney and several colleagues had earlier purchased several sections of the H.B.C. land adjacent to the route of the C.P.R. Not surprisingly, it was alleged that in selecting the site of the capital he had been influenced by his investments rather than by the merits of the site. The C.P.R., rarely outmanoeuvred in such matters, located its station two miles from the Dewdney property and, since the railway station was always a focal point in a new settlement, its land sales soon outstripped those of its rivals. The Lieutenant-Governor retaliated by pressuring Ottawa to establish all public buildings on his land, but without much success. At the urging of the C.P.R., the customs office, post office, and dominion land office were all located near the station and it was here that the centre of the new city remained. The C.P.R. also struck back at Dewdney by situating its divisional point forty miles to the west at Moose Jaw. This move ended hopes for early branch line construction out of Regina and dampened its chances for future growth.[17] Some growth did take place, however, since by the end of 1882 Regina had a population of "around 800 or 900." There was little settlement in the vicinity of Regina, though, and the town functioned mostly as an administrative centre and shipping point rather than as a service centre with a local hinterland. By 1901 it was still only a small town with a population of 2249.[18]

The complicated manoeuvres of Dewdney and the C.P.R. spurred the rise of Moose Jaw which, unlike Regina, also possessed some natural advantages. The site on the Moose Jaw Creek had long been used as an Indian camp and it was situated on several well-used trails. Thus, in anticipation of the railway passing through the Moose Jaw region, prospective settlers and speculators located in the area in July, 1881. But it was the actual arrival of the C.P.R. the next year that "changed Moose Jaw within a matter of months from an outpost on a lonely trail to a bustling prairie boom town of tents, shacks, and small stores."[19] By 1884 Moose Jaw was incorporated as a town with a population of about 700. In the next fifteen years, however, the town grew slowly; by 1901 it had a population of but 1557. Like most other prairie communities, Moose Jaw suffered from the slowness of settlement in the region in these early years, but

254

evidence exists to suggest that the town's citizens themselves did not always do all that they could to promote and develop their own community.[20]

Swift Current and Medicine Hat were also in large part products of the C.P.R.; both were chosen as divisional points by the company, and during the 1880s and 1890s the C.P.R. payroll sustained both hamlets. Swift Current's growth was painfully slow. By 1901, it had a population — according to the federal census — of a mere 121, and it did not obtain village status until 1904.[21] Medicine Hat developed slightly more rapidly; it became a village in 1894 and a town in 1898, and by 1901 had a population of 1570.[22] At the turn of the century, however, both communities were still waiting for substantial development to take place.

In contrast, the growth of Calgary was remarkable. The site of Fort Calgary, at the junction of the Bow and Elbow Rivers, was chosen by the North West Mounted Police in 1875, and soon H.B.C. and other traders "clustered under the protective wing of the law to form the settlement first known as the Elbow." In the next seven years, the community acted as a focal point linking the fur trade of the North with American distributing centres, and by 1881 it had a population of about 100. In the next two years, however, dramatic growth occurred with the approach and, in August 1883, the arrival of the C.P.R. line. The railroad changed Calgary from a police post to an urban centre, as the power of the C.P.R. was again demonstrated. The company, rather than locating its station on or near the site of the fort, where a nucleus of permanently settled residents existed, chose a spot three quarters of a mile west of the fort. Despite objections, Calgary businessmen soon followed and many even moved their buildings nearer the station. By 1884, incorporation as a town was secured and Calgary's continued survival and growth seemed assured. In the next few years it quickly grew to become the dominant urban centre on the western plains.[23]

The construction of the main line of the C.P.R. also spawned a number of other, smaller communities during these crucial years. But for most settlements off the main line the period was one of stagnation or decline. Only those which received branch lines, or had other sources of growth, experienced progress. South of Calgary, Lethbridge experienced slow but steady growth. Between 1882 and 1890 the various enterprises incorporated by Sir Alexander Galt established several collieries near Lethbridge and constructed two railways, one to the C.P.R. main line near Medicine Hat, the other to the Great Northern railway at Great Falls, Montana. During peak periods the Galt companies employed as many as a thousand workers, creating a transient male-dominant population and a local economy entirely dependent upon the companies. The railways, however, were subsidized by the federal government, with nearly a million acres of land located south of Lethbridge; when this acreage proved too dry for agricultural settlement, elaborate irrigation works were constructed, a project completed by 1900. Once irrigated, the lands attracted a large number of settlers and thereby transformed Lethbridge from a mere dormitory for

255

the mines to a service centre for its agricultural hinterland. By 1901, shortly after the Crowsnest Pass Railway was built, the incorporated town of Lethbridge had a population of 2072 — the third largest centre in what was soon to become the province of Alberta.[24]

To the north, Edmonton experienced virtually no growth in the 1880s. With the completion of the main line to Calgary, Edmonton lost much of its function as the depot for the northern fur trading posts. Future prospects brightened considerably in July, 1891, however, when the Calgary and Edmonton Railway reached a point across the river from Edmonton.[25] But the C. & E.R. then announced that its northern terminus would remain across the river from Edmonton, a decision which would give rise to the rival community of Strathcona. During the next decade the rivalry between the two incipient urban centres was constant. Although Edmonton's growth continued to surpass that of Strathcona, the prize of northern metropolitan status was still in some doubt by 1901.[26]

256

Like Edmonton, other pre-railway settlements experienced difficult times in the 1880s and 1890s. In anticipation of being on or close to the main route of the C.P.R., immigrants moved into the northern prairies in considerable numbers until 1881. The re-routing of the line slowed northern growth considerably. Although a townsite was laid out around the Prince Albert Mission in 1882, incorporation as a town did not come until 1885. At the end of that year, with the Riel Rebellion over, Prince Albert settled into a dull existence as a frontier town 200 miles from the nearest railway. There were few signs of progress in the late 1880s although a Board of Trade was established in 1887; more numerous and conspicuous were the signs of decline, including a drop in population. Despair among the citizens of Prince Albert yielded to confidence only in 1885 when the first sod was turned on the Qu'Appelle, Long Lake and Saskatchewan Railroad. The colonization railway, incorporated in 1883, finally reached Prince Albert in September, 1890. In large part as a result of this linkage, Prince Albert was able to experience modest progress during the 1890s.[27]

The construction of the Qu'Appelle, Long Lake and Saskatchewan Railway also had a significant impact on another prairie community. The site of Saskatoon was chosen in 1882 by the Temperance Colonization Society, which acquired a grant of some 500 000 acres in a block traversed by the South Saskatchewan River. By August, 1883, a townsite had been laid out and settlers began to arrive. The provisioning of the settlers was at first carried out from Medicine Hat, via the South Saskatchewan River, but the hopes of the Society to develop a strong and rapidly growing community did not materialize. There were several reasons. Transportation problems existed from the outset; the South Saskatchewan River was difficult to navigate because of its shallow water and numerous shoals and, although railways got closer to the colony, they passed to the south and channeled prospective settlers away from Saskatoon. The colony was saved from probable extinction when the Qu'Appelle, Long Lake and Saskatchewan Railway, building its line from Regina to Prince Albert,

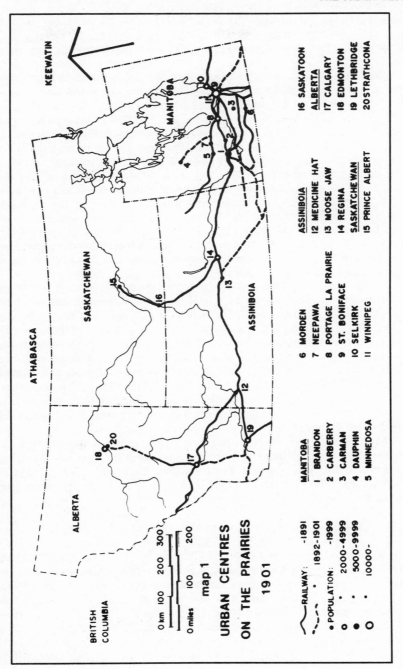

KEEWATIN

BRITISH
COLUMBIA

ALBERTA

ATHABASCA

SASKATCHEWAN

MANITOBA

ASSINIBOIA

0 km 100   200   200   300
0 miles   100   200

map 1

URBAN CENTRES
ON THE PRAIRIES
1901

RAILWAY: -1891
           1892-1901
POPULATION: -1999
           2000-4999
           5000-9999
           10000-

MANITOBA
1 BRANDON
2 CARBERRY
3 CARMAN
4 DAUPHIN
5 MINNEDOSA

6 MORDEN
7 NEEPAWA
8 PORTAGE LA PRAIRIE
9 ST. BONIFACE
10 SELKIRK
11 WINNIPEG

ASSINIBOIA
12 MEDICINE HAT
13 MOOSE JAW
14 REGINA
SASKATCHEWAN
15 PRINCE ALBERT

16 SASKATOON
ALBERTA
17 CALGARY
18 EDMONTON
19 LETHBRIDGE
20 STRATHCONA

257

passed through Saskatoon. But, though the railway was fundamental to Saskatoon's continued existence, it did not bring about rapid development in the 1890s. By 1901, the settlement still had a population of only about 100.[28]

While Prince Albert and Saskatoon received second prize in the railway stakes of this era — branch lines rather than location on the main line — another community not only received no rail connection, it lost another prize as well. Battleford was established in 1874 as a camp for the survey parties working on the line of the proposed transcontinental railway. In 1875, surveyors and contractors located their permanent headquarters and supply depot near the mouth of the Battle River and threw up "a collection of roughly constructed log huts with mudded walls and thatched roofs."[29] This primitive work camp on the flats acquired status only in October, 1876, when the Canadian government chose it as the capital of the North West Territories.[30] Within a year the lieutenant-governor's mansion, residences for the judiciary and court officials, and barracks for the N.W.M.P. were under construction. Battleford's future seemed assured and land values and construction boomed. The fertile countryside around attracted numerous settlers in the 1870s and 1880s.

Two decisions soon changed this bright future to a bleak one. There was great disappointment when the C.P.R. was built through the southern prairies instead of along the North Saskatchewan River. It was a long cart haul to Battleford from the nearest point on the railway. Further, in order to facilitate governmental administration the capital of the territories was moved to a site on the railway. Although the selection of Regina was not confirmed until March 1883, instructions to ship government house furniture were received by local civil servants in October 1882. Together, these two decisions drastically changed Battleford's immediate future, and for two decades the town merely survived; it did not prosper. Population grew slowly, and village status was not secured until 1899.[31]

By the end of the nineteenth century, the railways had opened the prairie West to settlement and the basic outline of the region's urban pattern had emerged (see Map I). It was an outline that still needed to be filled in; but that process occurred with great rapidity in the years after the turn of the century.

III

The period between 1900 and 1914 stands in sharp contrast with the previous era. The pre-1900 era was, at best, a period of slow progress. The subsequent era was one of dramatic growth and prosperity. After decades of hesitation, the prairie West suddenly began to realize the potential that so many Canadians had long believed it possessed. A number of important events in widely disparate areas occurred which, when taken together, propelled the region forward. The problems of farming in a semi-arid region were, by 1900, largely solved and the future of prairie agriculture

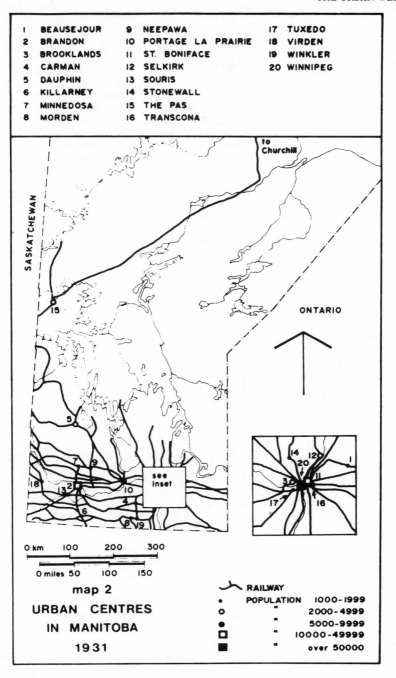

1	BEAUSEJOUR	9	NEEPAWA	17	TUXEDO
2	BRANDON	10	PORTAGE LA PRAIRIE	18	VIRDEN
3	BROOKLANDS	11	ST. BONIFACE	19	WINKLER
4	CARMAN	12	SELKIRK	20	WINNIPEG
5	DAUPHIN	13	SOURIS		
6	KILLARNEY	14	STONEWALL		
7	MINNEDOSA	15	THE PAS		
8	MORDEN	16	TRANSCONA		

map 2

URBAN CENTRES

IN MANITOBA

1931

0 km   100   200   300

0 miles 50   100   150

RAILWAY

POPULATION   1000-1999
                      2000-4999
                      5000-9999
                      10000-49999
                      over 50000

1 ASSINIBOIA	12 LLOYDMINSTER	23 ROSTHERN
2 BATTLEFORD	13 MAPLE CREEK	24 SASKATOON
3 BIGGAR	14 MELFORT	25 SHAUNAVON
4 CANORA	15 MELVILLE	26 SUTHERLAND
5 ESTEVAN	16 MOOSE JAW	27 SWIFT CURRENT
6 GRAVELBOURG	17 MOOSOMIN	28 TISDALE
7 HERBERT	18 NORTH BATTLEFORD	29 WATROUS
8 HUMBOLDT	19 PRINCE ALBERT	30 WEYBURN
9 INDIAN HEAD	20 RADVILLE	31 WILKIE
10 KAMSACK	21 REGINA	32 WYNYARD
11 KINDERSLEY	22 ROSETOWN	33 YORKTON

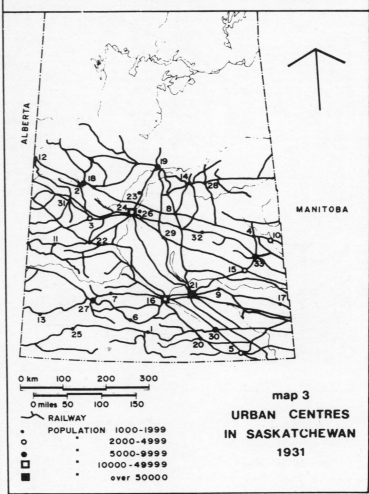

0 km   100   200   300

0 miles 50   100   150

⌇ RAILWAY

. POPULATION 1000-1999
o   "   2000-4999
●   "   5000-9999
□   "   10000-49999
■   "   over 50000

map 3
URBAN CENTRES
IN SASKATCHEWAN
1931

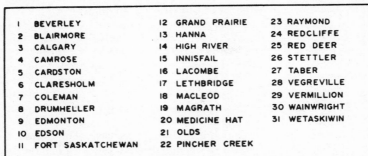

1	BEVERLEY	12	GRAND PRAIRIE	23	RAYMOND
2	BLAIRMORE	13	HANNA	24	REDCLIFFE
3	CALGARY	14	HIGH RIVER	25	RED DEER
4	CAMROSE	15	INNISFAIL	26	STETTLER
5	CARDSTON	16	LACOMBE	27	TABER
6	CLARESHOLM	17	LETHBRIDGE	28	VEGREVILLE
7	COLEMAN	18	MACLEOD	29	VERMILLION
8	DRUMHELLER	19	MAGRATH	30	WAINWRIGHT
9	EDMONTON	20	MEDICINE HAT	31	WETASKIWIN
10	EDSON	21	OLDS		
11	FORT SASKATCHEWAN	22	PINCHER CREEK		

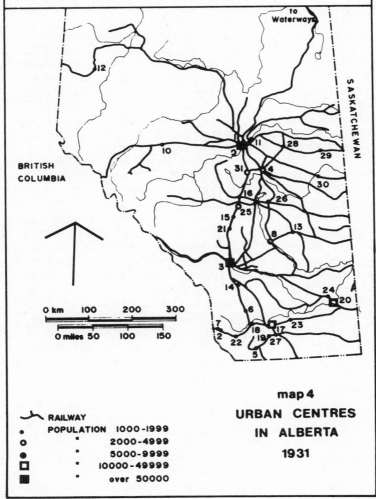

261

map 4

URBAN CENTRES
IN ALBERTA
1931

RAILWAY
POPULATION 1000-1999
" 2000-4999
" 5000-9999
" 10000-49999
" over 50000

at last seemed assured. Under the direction of an expansive new federal government, immigrants poured into the area in record numbers. Railways were built on an extensive scale; almost 7000 miles of track were laid in the prairie West between 1901 and 1913, increasing the mileage in the region to well over 10 000.[32] In addition to the building of numerous locally and provincially sponsored lines, the C.P.R. constructed branch lines, and two new transcontinental railways — the Canadian Northern and the Grand Trunk Pacific — rapidly found their way across the prairies. Capital for these and other projects was readily available at low interest rates. There were important political changes as well. The North West Territories received responsible government in 1897; in 1905 the provinces of Alberta and Saskatchewan were created; and in 1912 Manitoba's boundaries were extended to 60°N and to Hudson Bay.

The expansion and consolidation of prairie settlement were both aided by and reflected in the growth of villages, towns, and cities. The rapid urban growth of the period was apparent in four significant trends. First, a filling-in process occurred as the prairie region quickly became dotted with hundreds of new urban centres. Most were fairly small service centres, often founded before farmers arrived in the area, or else developing simultaneously with the influx of rural pioneers. These communities usually began with a train station, a grain elevator, and a general store. As soon as settlers moved on to nearby homesteads, attracted both by available land and by the urban centre itself, the general store was duplicated and then supplemented by more specialized businesses such as a lumber yard, hardware store, blacksmith shop, harness and wagon business, an implement dealer, and a bank. Rapid population growth soon led to the construction of a post office, schools and churches; the establishment of a newspaper and a Board of Trade; and, sooner or later, to incorporation as a village, town, or city. Finally, other less essential services appeared: barber shops, hotels and beer parlours, cafés, pool halls, and real estate offices. This pattern of development was repeated over and over. Between the censuses of 1901 and 1916, the number of incorporated cities increased from three to seventeen; incorporated towns from twenty-five to 150; and incorporated villages from fifty-seven to 423.[33]

In addition to the rise of new centres, communities already in existence by 1901 experienced substantial growth in the next decade. Winnipeg strengthened its hold as the chief metropolis of both Manitoba and the prairie region. A medium-sized centre in 1901, it had become the country's third largest city by 1913, with a population of about 150 000 (Table V). Brandon and St. Boniface also more than doubled their population in these years while other Manitoba towns and cities experienced rapid but less spectacular growth (Map 2 and Table II). In Saskatchewan (Map 3), Saskatoon emerged after 1901 to become a focal point for growth in the rich agricultural belt of central Saskatchewan. In rapid succession it was incorporated as a village, town, and city, and by 1911 it was the third largest centre in the province. Regina, as provincial capital, retained its dominant position as the chief city of the province while Moose Jaw,

Table V-**Rank of Selected Canadian Cities by size, 1901–1931**

Rank	1901	1911	1921	1931
1	Montreal	Montreal	Montreal	Montreal
2	Toronto	Toronto	Toronto	Toronto
3	Québec	WINNIPEG	WINNIPEG	Vancouver
4	Ottawa	Vancouver	Vancouver	WINNIPEG
5	Hamilton	Ottawa	Hamilton	Hamilton
6	WINNIPEG	Hamilton	Ottawa	Québec
7	Halifax	Québec	Québec	Ottawa
8	Saint John	Halifax	CALGARY	CALGARY
9	London	London	London	EDMONTON
10	Vancouver	CALGARY	EDMONTON	London
11	Victoria	Saint John	Halifax	Windsor
12	Kingston	Victoria	Saint John	Verdun
13	Brantford	REGINA	Victoria	Halifax
14	Hull	EDMONTON	Windsor	REGINA
15	Windsor	Brantford	REGINA	Saint John
16	Sherbrooke	Kingston	Brantford	SASKATOON
17	Guelph	Peterborough	SASKATOON	Victoria
	—	—	—	—
36	—	SASKATOON	—	—
	—	—	—	—
73	CALGARY	—	—	—
	—	—	—	—
77	EDMONTON	—	—	—
	—	—	—	—
97	REGINA	—	—	—
	—	—	—	—
110	SASKATOON	—	—	—

263

Prince Albert, and Yorkton expanded as regional supply centres (Table
III).[34] The changes in Alberta, however, were the most dramatic (Map 4).
In 1901, Calgary and Edmonton were the most populous places in what
was soon to become the province of Alberta, but they were still small
service centres, not much different from many others in the western
interior. By 1913, however, it was clear that they were to have no competition as the dominant centres of economic activity in the newly formed
province.[35] Calgary continued to have an edge over Edmonton, but the
latter city's amalgamation of rival Strathcona in 1911 brought the northern
metropolis added prominence in the years immediately before the Great
War.[36] Between Edmonton and Calgary, only Wetaskiwin and Red Deer
attained city status during these years, but their growth paled in comparison to that of the two major centres.[37] South of Calgary, however,
Lethbridge and Medicine Hat expanded their roles as regional service
centres (Table IV).

Table VI–Population Growth in Selected[a] Prairie Cities, 1871–1931

City	1871	1881	1891	1901	1906	1911	1916	1921	1926	1931
Winnipeg	241	7 985	25 639	42 340	90 153	136 035	163 000	179 087	198 998	218 785
Calgary	—	100	3 867	4 398	11 967	43 704	56 514	63 305	65 291	83 761
Edmonton[b]	—	263	700	4 176	14 088	31 064	53 846	58 821	65 163	79 187
Regina	—	c.800	1 681	2 249	6 169	30 213	26 167	34 432	37 329	53 209
Saskatoon	—	—	—	113	3 001	12 004	21 048	25 739	31 234	43 291
Moose Jaw	—	c.100	1 200	1 558	6 249	13 823	16 934	19 285	19 039	21 299
Brandon	—	—	3 778	5 620	10 408	13 839	15 215	15 397	16 443	17 082
St. Boniface	817	1 283	1 553	2 019	5 119	7 483	11 021	12 821	14 187	16 305
Lethbridge	—	—	—	2 072	2 936	9 035	9 436	11 097	10 735	13 489
Medicine Hat	—	—	—	1 570	3 020	5 608	9 272	9 634	9 536	10 300
Prince Albert	—	c.500	1 009	1 785	3 005	6 254	6 436	7 558	7 873	9 905
Portage la Prairie	—	—	3 363	3 901	5 106	5 892	5 879	6 766	6 513	6 597
North Battleford	—	—	—	—	824	2 105	3 154	4 108	4 787	5 986
Swift Current	—	—	—	121	554	1 852	3 181	3 518	4 175	5 296
Yorkton	—	—	—	700	1 363	2 309	3 144	5 151	4 458	5 027
Weyburn	—	—	—	113	966	2 210	3 050	3 193	4 119	5 002

Notes: (a) Table includes only those centres which were incorporated as cities by 1931 and had a population in excess of 5000.
(b) Beginning in 1901, figures for Edmonton include Strathcona. See Table IV.
Sources: See Table II.

264   While substantial growth occurred in virtually all prairie centres between 1900 and the Great War, one of the most spectacular developments was the rise of the large prairie city. In 1900, with the exception of Winnipeg, it was not altogether clear which prairie towns would expand to become booming cities. By 1914, Regina, Calgary, Edmonton, and Saskatoon had joined Winnipeg as the region's dominant cities (Table VI). The growth of these metropolitan centres was a response both to massive rural settlement and to the rise of villages and towns, for just as farmers needed service centres, so in turn towns needed cities. Large cities performed a variety of specialized services. They acted as central shipping and distribution points and were the location of such key facilities as railway marshalling yards, roundhouses, locomotive shops, grain terminals, stockyards, warehouses, and wholesale businesses. Cities also provided a complex set of professional and commercial services in the offices of engineers, architects, bankers, insurance and real estate agents, doctors, lawyers, and accountants. The cities were the main repositories of skilled and unskilled labourers, meeting the demands of farmers, railway contractors, bush camp operators, building contractors, and even village and town councils. Manufacturing was also included in the range of city functions. By 1911, Winnipeg was a major centre of manufacturing, and the other large cities were increasing their production of commodities manufactured for the prairie market. Finally, it was in the cities that the region's political and legal institutions (legislatures, court houses, government offices) and educational institutions (universities, trade schools, teacher's colleges) were located. In short, by 1914 the prairies had five fairly large and sophisticated cities. These communities had compressed a century or more of eastern urban growth into a few short years and, together with demographic dominance, displayed considerable power over trade patterns, communications, and development processes in the region, and exercised growing political, social and cultural influence.

The fourth notable trend in this era was the rapid degree of urbaniza-

Table VII–**Per Cent of Population Urban**[(a)] **in Canada's Regions, 1901–1931**

Region	1901	1911		1921		1931	
British Columbia	46.4	50.9	(4.5)[(b)]	56.1	(5.2)	67.3	(11.2)
Prairies	19.3	28.8	(9.5)	29.3	(0.5)	32.2	(2.9)
Ontario	43.6	52.8	(9.2)	60.7	(7.9)	65.3	(4.6)
Quebec	38.2	45.9	(7.7)	52.0	(6.1)	59.7	(7.7)
Maritimes	26.2	32.7	(6.5)	37.9	(5.2)	38.9	(1.0)

Notes: (a) See definition in Table IV, note (a).
　　　 (b) Bracketed figures represent increase in percentage points for decade.
Source: *Census of Canada, 1956* — "Analytical Report: Rural and Urban Population,"
p. 26.

tion. No other region of Canada experienced such vigorous urban growth   *265*
during any one decade as did the prairie provinces between 1901 and 1911
(Table VII). In gross terms, urban residents in the prairie region increased
from 19.3 per cent of the total population in 1901 to 28.8 per cent in 1911.
While less than 100 000 persons lived in urban centres in 1901, almost
400 000 could be so classified by 1911, a reflection of the facts that the
prairie provinces were undergoing a period of massive change and that the
area's urban centres were playing an integral part in the development of
the region.

IV

1913 was a pivotal year in the history of prairie urban development.
Before, there had been prosperity and rapid growth; after, there came
several decades of relative stagnation and almost continual crisis. Although
there were a few short years of prosperity in the 1920s, the period from
1913 to 1930 can be characterized as one of either uncertainty or modest
growth for the region's urban centres. This trend was apparent in a number of ways. The prairies switched from being the fastest to the slowest-
growing region in the country in terms of urban concentration (Table
VII). Between 1911 and 1931, the urban percentage of the prairie population increased by only 3.4 percentage points — far behind the other regions.

　　This sharp relative decline took place within the context of general
economic difficulties. A severe recession in 1913 was followed by the
dislocation of war and a slow recovery, all events which adversely affected
the villages, towns, and cities of the prairie region, which were far from
booming between 1913 and 1930. The recession immediately preceding
the Great War coincided with the slowing down of the great agricultural
expansion of the West. The wheat economy — with its commercial and
transportation infrastructure and its main institutions — was established
and in place. Filling-in and investment in powered farm machinery was

carried on in the 1920s, but the scale and rate of expansion was at a much reduced level. As V. C. Fowke notes: "The investment boom which had characterized the early years of the twentieth century had exhausted itself by 1913, and serious economic difficulties faced Canada and the prairie provinces as a result."[38] While the war created an artificial stimulus that temporarily averted the effects of contraction in the growth rate,[39] these effects were felt soon enough. Economic distress characterized the early 1920s, distress caused by inflation, a sharp recession, and a prolonged drought.

In contrast to the early years of the decade, the later 1920s was a period of relative prosperity and expansion. Contemporary observers regarded the developments of these years as a continuation of the conditions that had been interrupted by the recession of 1913 and the war. In terms of urban centres, there were several important developments that received impetus from the comparative prosperity of the period after 1924. The major mechanical revolution that took place on prairie farms, with horse-driven machinery giving way to trucks, tractors, and combine harvesters, increased the dependence of farmers on urban services and skills. It was in these years as well that the road system of the prairies was taking shape, changing dramatically the relation of city and country. Similarly, the aeroplane was beginning to give larger cities additional transportation links. The prairies, it seemed, were apparently again on the road to rapid expansion.

266

The similarities between the late 1920s and the pre-war boom, however, were more apparent than real. Although many individual activities were much the same as they had been before 1914, their collective significance was vastly different.

Collectively the economic processes associated with the wheat frontier had been of a magnitude before 1914 sufficient to vitalize and integrate the entire Canadian economy and to diffuse this economic vitality throughout the North Atlantic trading area. In absolute quantities the immigration, occupation and improvement of land, and capital formation which were associated with the wheat economy in the latter half of the 1920s were smaller than before the war. In relative terms, however, the diminution was greater still, for other frontiers [in northern Quebec and Ontario and in British Columbia] had meanwhile risen to prominence within the Dominion and the wheat frontier was no longer of unique importance. Possibilities for agricultural settlement in western Canada were no longer adequate to focus attention throughout the Dominion or to serve as the integrating force within the Canadian economy.[40]

The impact of these trends on prairie urban centres was substantial. In general terms, the population of the region's cities grew by only 47.5 per cent between 1916 and 1931 (408 000 to 602 000), compared to an increase of nearly 700 per cent between 1901 and 1916 (52 000 to 408 000). Towns grew by 30.5 per cent (121 000 to 158 000), compared to 278.0 per cent (32 000 to 121 000) in the earlier period. Villages increased by only 64.5 per cent (76 000 to 125 000), compared to an increase of 300 per cent (19 000 to 76 000) between 1901 and 1916.[41] The number of new cities (2), towns (14), and villages (121) incorporated since 1916 was in sharp contrast to the rapid increase in numbers in the earlier era. In terms of the ranking of Canadian cities by size, several larger prairie cities dropped to lower positions, including Winnipeg, Brandon, Portage la Prairie, Regina, Moose Jaw and Yorkton;[42] however, none of the region's cities suffered an absolute loss in population between 1911 and 1931.[43] It was a period in which the larger centres gained population, but only gradually. Some towns and villages, however, actually lost citizens (Tables II, III, IV). Such communities, and others which experienced very slow rates of growth, were those whose prosperity largely depended upon supplying a restricted agricultural hinterland that was floundering. In contrast, the larger prairie cities, and especially Winnipeg, Regina, Calgary, Edmonton, and Saskatoon, had reached the point where their extra-provincial relations coupled with their intra-provincial services ensured slow but steady growth.

The growth of the cities between the end of rapid expansion in 1913 and the major economic crisis of the Depression was thus unremarkable. But there were several important changes in the prairie urban system which deserve notice, even if they were changes of "degree" rather than of "kind." Most important was the decline in Winnipeg's metropolitan position as a result of several events, including the opening of the Panama Canal in 1914 (which allowed Vancouver to penetrate the western prairies); the diffusion of Winnipeg's commercial functions in the wheat economy with the formation of provincial wheat pools in the 1920s (dispersing control and income from Winnipeg head offices of the private grain trade); the erosion of the city's preferential freight-rate structures (resulting in the gradual takeover by other prairie cities of some of the commercial and supply functions formerly centred on the city); and a decline in the importance of grain and an increase in such non-grain products as meat, butter and cheese (areas where Winnipeg's metropolitan position was challenged by other prairie cities).[44] All these changes diminished Winnipeg's financial and commercial hinterland but they did not presage any major alterations in the basic urban system of the prairies. While there was a gradual westward shift in urban population,[45] and while the role of other prairie cities in the region grew considerably, the urban structure in place by 1913 — with Winnipeg at its apex — maintained a high degree of stability through to and beyond 1930.

In spite of this stability, the onset of drought and the Depression in 1929–1930 marked the end of an era for prairie urban development. Although dramatic urban growth in the region had ended as early as 1913, contemporaries had continued to hope — indeed to believe — throughout the 1910s and 1920s that prosperity would soon return. In particular, the short periods of prosperity in the 1920s were seen as the beginning of a new surge of growth. The Depression, however, soon dimmed the hopes of even the most optimistic. By the mid-1930s, prairie urban centres were concentrating, for the first time in their history, not on growth, but on survival.

Notes

1. Defining what is meant by "urban" is a complex issue. In this article, I shall use two basic characteristics. First, an urban community consists of a concentration of people organized at a specific site who carry on various functions or services differentiated from the surrounding countryside, functions which may be economic, political, social or cultural in nature and which usually involve some combination of these factors. Second, while it is an arbitrary figure, this article concentrates on those communities which had a population of 1000 or more. For a succinct discussion of the definition problem see James and Robert Simmons, *Urban Canada*, 2nd ed. rev. (Toronto: Copp Clark, 1974), pp. 8–11.
2. Alan F. J. Artibise, *Winnipeg: A Social History of Urban Growth, 1874–1914* (Montreal: McGill-Queen's University Press, 1975), Chapter 1, "The Origins and Incorporation of Winnipeg."
3. There is no comprehensive history of St. Boniface available. See, however, W. L. Morton, *Manitoba: A History* (Toronto: University of Toronto Press, 1957), *passim*.
4. Margaret J. Bell, "Portage la Prairie to 1907," M. A. Thesis (University of Manitoba, 1926). See also Evelyn Baril, "The Hudson's Bay Company and the Urbanization of the Prairies, 1870–1888," B. A. Thesis (University of Winnipeg, 1978). This excellent thesis contains much detail on prairie urban centres in these early years.
5. Gary Abrams, *Prince Albert: The First Century, 1866–1966* (Saskatoon: Modern Press, 1966), Chapter 1, "A Mission in the Wilderness."
6. B. A. Ockley, "A History of Early Edmonton," M. A. Thesis (University of Alberta, 1932). See also J. G. MacGregor, *Edmonton: A History* (Edmonton: Hurtig, 1967); and Baril, "H.B.C. and the Urbanization of the Prairies."
7. *Census of Population and Agriculture of the Northwest Provinces, 1906*, p. xx.
8. There are a number of good accounts available. See, for example, Paul Voisey, "The Urbanization of the Canadian Prairies, 1871–1916." *Histoire sociale/Social History*, Vol. VIII, No. 15 (May 1975), pp. 77–101; J. M. S. Careless, "Aspects of Urban Life in the West, 1870–1914," in Gilbert A. Stelter and Alan F. J. Artibise, eds., *The Canadian City: Essays in Urban History* (Toronto: McClelland and Stewart, 1977), pp. 125–141; K. Lenz, "Large Urban Places in the Prairie Provinces — Their Development and Location," in R. L. Gentilcore, ed., *Canada's Changing Geography* (Toronto, 1967), pp. 199–211; L. D. McCann, "Urban Growth in Western Canada, 1881–1961," *The Albertan Geographer*, No. 5 (1969), pp. 65–74; and K. H. Norrie, "The Rate of Settlement of the Canadian Prairies, 1870–1911," *Journal of Economic History*, Vol. XXXV (June, 1975), pp. 410–427.
9. Voisey, "Urbanization of the Canadian Prairies," p. 78.
10. W. A. Mackintosh, *Prairie Settlement: The Geographical Setting* (Toronto: Macmillan, 1934), p. 46.
11. This figure is an estimation taken from tables in M. L. Bladen, "Construction of Railways in Canada to the Year 1885," *Contributions to Canadian Economics*, Vol. V (1932), pp. 43–60; and Bladen, "Construction of Railways in Canada from 1885 to 1931," *ibid.*, Vol. VII (1934), pp. 82–107.
12. See G. F. Baker, *Brandon: A City, 1881–1961* (Altona: Friesen, 1977).
13. Voisey, "Urbanization of the Canadian Prairies"; Baril, "H.B.C. and the Urbanization of the Prairies."
14. *Ibid.*; J. M. Richtik, "Manitoba Service Centers in the Early Settlement Period," *Journal of the Minnesota Academy of Science*, Vol. 34, No. 1 (1967), pp. 17–21; and John H. Warkentin, "Western Canada in 1886," *Transactions of the Historical and Scientific Society of Manitoba*, Series III, No. 20 (1963–1964), p. 91.
15. Artibise, *Winnipeg: A Social History*, Chapter 4. See also R. C. Bellan, "Rails Across the Red: Winnipeg or Selkirk," *Transactions of the Historical and Scientific Society of Manitoba*," Series III, No. 18 (1961–1962), pp. 69–77.
16. Two general accounts of Regina's history are available: E. G. Drake, *Regina: A History* (Toronto: McClelland and Stewart, 1955); and J. W. Brennan, ed., *Regina Before Yesterday: A Visual History, 1882–1945* (Regina: City of Regina, 1978).
17. Some branch lines were built out of Regina in later years, but they were local lines rather than C.P.R. branch lines. See Chester Martin, *"Dominion Lands" Policy* (Toronto: Macmillan, 1938), Chapter V.
18. Brennan, *Regina Before Yesterday*, pp. 3–4. The capital question is discussed in L. H. Thomas, *The Struggle for Responsible Government in the North-West Territories, 1870–97* (Toronto: University of Toronto Press, 1956), p. 107.
19. K. A. Foster, "Moose Jaw: The First Decade, 1882–1892," M. A. Thesis (University of Regina, 1978), p. 22.
20. *Ibid.* See also G. R. Andrews, "The National Policy and the Settlement of Moose Jaw, Saskatchewan 1882–1914," M. A. Thesis (Bemidji State University, 1977).
21. Don C. McGowan, *Grassland Settlers: The Swift Current Region During the Era of the Ranching Frontier* (Regina: Canadian Plains Research Center, 1975), *passim*.

22. J. G. MacGregor, *Alberta: A History* (Edmonton: Hurtig, 1972), pp. 157–158.

23. The best account of Calgary's development is M. Foran, *Calgary: An Illustrated History* (Toronto: Lorimer, 1978). It contains an excellent bibliography.

24. A. A. den Otter, "Lethbridge: Outpost of a Commercial Empire," in Alan F. J. Artibise, ed., *Town and City: Aspects of Western Canadian Urban Development* (Regina: Canadian Plains Research Center, 1981).

25. The Calgary and Edmonton Railway also led to the rise of Red Deer. See Wellington Dawe, *History of Red Deer* (Red Deer, 1953). The Calgary and Edmonton Railway is discussed in Martin, *"Dominion Lands" Policy*, p. 323 and *passim*.

26. John F. Gilpin, "The city of Strathcona, 1891–1912," M. A. Thesis (University of Alberta, 1978).

27. Abrams, *Prince Albert*. On the railway, see Martin, *"Dominion Lands" Policy*, p. 296 and *passim*.

28. John H. Archer, "The History of Saskatoon," M. A. Thesis (University of Saskatchewan, 1948); W. P. Delainey and W. A. S. Sarjeant, *Saskatoon: The Growth of a City* (Saskatoon: Saskatoon Environmental Society, 1974).

29. Arlean McPherson, *The Battlefords: A History* (Saskatoon: Modern Press, 1967), p. 35.

30. Thomas, *Struggle for Responsible Government*, p. 80.

31. McPherson, *The Battlefords*.

32. Bladen, "Construction of Railways in Canada from 1885 to 1931."

33. *Census of Prairie Provinces, 1916*, p. xix.

34. Yorkton's early history is discussed in J. W. McCracken, "Yorkton During the Territorial Period, 1882–1905," M. A. Thesis (University of Saskatchewan, Regina, 1972).

35. P. J. Smith and D. B. Johnson, *The Edmonton-Calgary Corridor* (Edmonton: Department of Geography, University of Alberta, 1978), p. 26 and *passim*.

36. John F. Gilpin, "Failed Metropolis: The City of Strathcona, 1891–1911," in Artibise, *Town and City*.

37. The origins and development of these two centres are discussed in Smith and Johnson, *Edmonton-Calgary Corridor*; A. Reynolds, *"Siding 16": An Early History of Wetaskiwin to 1930* (Wetaskiwin: Wetaskiwin Alberta — R.C.M.P. Centennial Committee, 1975); and Dawe, *Red Deer*.

38. V. C. Fowke, *The National Policy and the Wheat Economy* (Toronto: University of Toronto Press, 1957), p. 77 and *passim*.

39. Even the temporary prosperity of the war did not benefit the prairies as it did Canada's other regions. See John Herd Thompson, *The Harvests of War: The Prairie West, 1914–1918* (Toronto: McClelland and Stewart, 1978), Chapter Three.

40. Fowke, *The National Policy and the Wheat Economy*, p. 82.

41. *Census of Prairie Provinces, 1916*; and *Census of Canada, 1931*.

42. *Ibid.* Those included are cities with population in excess of 5000.

43. There were however, short-term losses in population. See Table VI.

44. Paul Phillips, "The Prairie Urban System, 1911–1961: Specialization and Change," in Artibise, *Town and City*.

45. In 1911, Manitoba had 42.7 per cent of the region's urban population. This declined to 35.7 per cent by 1931. Saskatchewan's urban population increased from 28.0 per cent to 32.9 per cent of the regional total, while Alberta's increased from 29.3 per cent to 31.4 per cent. *Census of Canada, 1931*.

269

Topic Eight

Social Reform Movements

270   The first two decades of the twentieth century witnessed the rise of a
number of significant social reform movements in Canada: social gospel,
women's suffrage, prohibition, and urban reform. All were closely related
and rested upon similar assumptions about the ideal Canadian society.

Attempts at social reform were a logical by-product of the growth of
urban-industrial Canada. As immigrants settled in the cities more rapidly
than they could be adequately accommodated, as industrial waste blighted
the urban environment, as women and children were compelled to enter
the work force, there arose groups of socially conscious individuals who
were concerned about the negative effects of industrialization and urbanization on the quality of Canadian life. Fundamentally optimistic that the
new society held great possibilities if properly directed, they were prepared
to lead it toward the desired social goals.

These reform movements were well established in the first decade of the
twentieth century. Supporters of the social gospel, a socially oriented
approach to Christianity that developed among the Protestant denominations, were having some success in arousing a concern about social problems. Urban reformers were equally active in making citizens aware of
the problems of urban growth and the possible solutions to them. The
campaigns for women's suffrage and prohibition were less successful at
this time but would witness significant achievements during the popular
movement for moral regeneration in the Great War — a war to end all wars
and the evils of society that lead to wars. These reform movements would
die out by the mid-1920s.

In "The Social Gospel and the Reform Tradition in Canada," Richard
Allen explains the historical context for the rise of the social gospel
movement, analyses its major assumptions, reveals its impact, and accounts for its decline. In "'The Beginning of our Regeneration': The
Great War and Western Canadian Reform Movements," John Thompson
describes the link between the success of the women's suffrage and prohibition movements and the Great War, and Paul Rutherford examines the

ideas of diverse groups of urban reformers active at the turn of the century in "Tomorrow's Metropolis."

The social gospel is discussed in greater depth in Richard Allen's *The Social Passion: Religion and Social Reform in Canada, 1914–28* (Toronto: University of Toronto Press, 1971). John Thompson further examines the social-reform movements of the war years in *The Harvests of War: The Prairie West, 1914–1918* (Toronto: McClelland and Stewart, 1978). Paul Rutherford has edited and written an introduction to a valuable collection of primary sources on urban reform, *Saving the Canadian City: The First Phase, 1880–1920* (Toronto: University of Toronto Press, 1974). Two articles give a different perspective and wider dimension to the urban-reform movement: John C. Weaver's " 'Tomorrow's Metropolis' Revisited: A Critical Assessment of Urban Reform in Canada, 1890–1920," in *The Canadian City: Essays in Urban History,* edited by G. A. Stelter and A. F. J. Artibise (Toronto: McClelland and Stewart, 1977), pp. 393–418; and Walter Van Nus's "The Fate of City Beautiful Thought in Canada, 1893–1930," Canadian Historical Association *Historical Papers* (1975): 191–210. R. C. Brown and R. Cook's *Canada: 1896–1921: A Nation Transformed* (Toronto: McClelland and Stewart, 1974) contains two chapters that give an excellent overview of social reform: "O Brave New World . . ." (Ch. 15) and ". . . That Has Such People In't" (Ch. 16).

271

The Social Gospel and the Reform Tradition in Canada, 1890–1928*

RICHARD ALLEN

The literature of social reform has not been extensive in Canada even though a sizable movement of reform was abroad in the land from the 1890s through the 1930s, a movement that was found in church and in secular society, and at municipal, provincial, and, progressively, federal levels. In the last chapter of his *Progressive Party in Canada,* Morton sees the decline of that party as a result in part of the waning of the impulse towards reform in society as a whole. Underlying and accompanying the movement towards reform through the political system had been the social gospel, a movement of which the most important function was to forge links between proposed reforms and the religious heritage of the nation, thus endowing reform with an authority it could not otherwise command. At the same time it attempted to create the religious and social attitudes thought necessary for life in a world reformed. But the world proved too intractable for the realization of the movement's high socio-religious hopes, and in the wake of the frustrating experiences of the early 1920s, supporters

*From *Canadian Historical Review*, XLIX (1968): 381–399. Reprinted by permission of University of Toronto Press.

of the social gospel, and other reform movements, took different paths; some withdrew from politics, some retreated to pragmatic politics, some transferred their enthusiasm to other causes (notably peace movements and personal religion), and others moved towards a new radicalism. The reform movement may be viewed from many standpoints, but only when it is looked at as a religious manifestation, a striving to embed ultimate human goals in the social, economic and political order, is its success and failure fully appreciated. The history of the social gospel in Canada is an account of that process.

The social gospel rested on the premise that Christianity was a social religion, concerned, when the misunderstanding of the ages was stripped away, with the quality of human relations on this earth. More dramatically, it was a call for men to find the meaning of their lives in seeking to realize the kingdom of God in the very fabric of society. It was a measure of the radicalism implicit in the Social Gospel that the Methodist church in 1918 called for complete social reconstruction by a transfer of the basis of society from competition to co-operation. It was a measure of the conservatism inevitably associated with such a call that even some of the most radical supporters of the social gospel believed that in the family as they knew it, and in the political democracy of their time, two essential elements of the society toward which Jesus pointed men were already in existence, or virtually so. Such a reduction was necessary to apply a pan-historical and transcendent concept to immediate needs. And without such reduction the reform movement would have enjoyed considerably less power.

272

The Protestant background out of which the Canadian social gospel had to emerge was one dominated overwhelmingly by the Anglican, Methodist, and Presbyterian churches. The similarities and disparities in the social outlook of these churches prior to the onset of depression in the late nineteenth century may be suggested by their reactions to a strike of the Toronto Printers' Union in 1872. The Anglican *Church Herald* condemned the labourers for usurping the role of the employer and blamed the strike upon "the insidious whimperings of a foreign-born league." The *Presbyterian Witness* argued that labour's campaign "strikes at the very root of . . . personal independence and perpetuates their social demoralisation. . . . No man ever rose above a lowly condition who thought more of his class than of his individuality." The Methodist *Christian Guardian* declared a profound sympathy with all honest workingmen and a sincere desire for their betterment, but went on to say: "we seriously question the wisdom and advantage of this movement — especially the strikes to which it is likely to lead."[1] When news of Henry George's Anti-Poverty Society reached Toronto in 1887, the other two churches would probably have echoed the response of the *Christian Guardian* on 29 June: "We have no faith in the abolition of poverty by any laws that can be made in legislatures. . . . The best anti-poverty society is an association of men who would adopt as their governing principles in life, industry, sobriety, economy and intelligence." Such an individualistic ethic was unable, however, to withstand the combined onslaught of extended depression, the rapid growth of industrial urban centres, and the spread of new social conceptions.

It has been argued that the social gospel in Canada was an indigenous development.[2] Although it is possible that a Canadian social gospel might have developed simply in response to domestic urban and industrial problems, it did not in fact happen that way. To be sure, the earliest expressions of the social gospel in Canada may still lie in sources untouched by historians' hands. And in those sources, the rise of the social gospel may be obscured by the gradual nature of its separation from older forms of Christian social expression characterized by a concern for church-state relations, education, political corruption, and personal and social vice. But almost all evidence regarding the emergence of the social gospel from this tradition points to currents of thought and action which were sweeping the western world, none of which originated in Canada. To trace this "North Atlantic triangle" of culture and religion underlying the social gospel at large and its transmission to and development within Canada is a worthy but massive project. In this paper, only a description of some of its salient features can be attempted.

273

The inspiration of the pioneers of the social gospel in Canada and the origin of some of its prominent institutions reveal the extent of its indebtedness. W. A. Douglass in the 1880s expressed his disagreement with individualistic methods of social regeneration by tirelessly campaigning for Henry George's panacea of the single tax.[3] Salem Bland, later to become the philosopher and mentor of the movement, was an omnivorous reader, and in the decade of the 1890s when he seems to have first formulated a social gospel outlook, was especially influenced by Carlyle, Tennyson, Emerson, Channing and Thoreau, by the historical critics of scripture, and by Albert Ritschl, the great German theologian whose optimistic theology played a great role in the emergence of a social gospel theology. At least as significant for Bland was the literature of evolution.[4] The notes for his first socialist lecture, "Four Steps and a Vision," acknowledge various works of Darwin, Drummond's *Ascent of Man,* and Kidd's *Social Evolution,* as well as *Fabian Essays,* Arnold Toynbee, Edward Bellamy, and Henry George.[5] Canadians had attended the three great interdenominational conferences in the United States on social problems in 1887, 1889, and 1893, and one follow-up conference had been held in Montreal in the latter year.[6] Institutional vehicles and expressions of the social gospel such as the Brotherhoods, institutional churches, settlements and labour churches derived ultimately from British models, although American mediation and modification took place in some instances. This pattern of influence continued throughout the life of the social gospel in Canada.

The optimism of the social gospel drew on more than a generalized sense of progress, and even on more than the influence of evolutionary concepts. One of the more significant religious developments of the nineteenth century was the expansion of evangelicalism — expressed variously in German pietism, the Methodism of the English-speaking world, the missionary movement, and American revivalism. As against the reformed tradition of Calvinism, evangelicalism stressed free will, an immanent God, religious emotion, and a restrictive personal and social morality which made its followers formidably austere. Among its doctrines was a belief in the possibility of personal perfection beyond the temptation of sin. In the course of the nineteenth century it made an immense impact on all Christian traditions, especially in North America. As evangelicalism became more diffused in the latter half of the century and awareness of the social problem arose, the individualism of the evangelical way seemed to many to be less and less appropriate.[7] The demand "save this man, now" became "save this society, now," and the slogan "the evangelization of the world in our generation" became "the Christianization of the world in our generation."[8] The sense of an immanent God working in the movement of revival and awakening was easily transferred to social movements, and hence to the whole evolution of society. Thus Josiah Strong in the United States could speak of the "great social awakening," and many could come to view secular social action as a religious rite.

Such combinations of ideas and impulses were apparent in a sermon given to the first Brotherhood group in Canada on 14 April 1895. Speaking on "Social Resurrection," J. B. Silcox argued that Jesus' "resurrection means that humanity shall rise . . . into higher, nobler, diviner conditions of life." He joined several British thinkers, preachers, and writers, he said, in predicting a worldwide revolution for the people in the twentieth century. "This uprising of the people is divine in its source. . . . God is in the midst of it. . . . To the ecclesiastical and industrial Pharaohs of today, God is saying, 'Let my people go.'" He concluded by calling for "a political faith in Jesus" based on the charter of the Sermon on the Mount.[9] C. S. Eby in *The World Problem and the Divine Solution* (1914) was somewhat more philosophical in expression. Jesus Christ was the "type of coming man on this planet." The ultimate reality of which Christ was the revelation was in and through all things: "the universal spirit of Christ would reconstruct man and mankind." Trade unionism, socialism, and business organization were a work of this spirit developing a new social order.[10] On this basis Eby built his Socialist church in Toronto in 1909.[11] Many influences from the world of letters, science, religion, and reform were held in solution in the social gospel in various proportions. Few distilled the solution as did Douglass, Bland, Silcox, and Eby, and while they might be more radical than most, their thought represented the tendency of the movement as a whole.

The pressures of the last years of depression in the early 1890s precipitated a quickening interest in new forms of social thought and action among a growing group of Christian ministers and laymen. One of the most important centres of this interest was the Queen's Theological Alumni

274

Conference, instituted by Principal G. M. Grant in 1893. At its annual meetings, the conference discussed papers on such topics as biblical criticism, economic development, the problems of poverty, socialistic schemes, the single tax, social evolution, interpretations of modern life by modern poets, studies of the prophets, Tolstoi, the relation of legislation and morality, and Christianity in its relation to human progress. As a Methodist minority among Presbyterians, Salem Bland was probably the most radical of the regular members.[12] At the beginning of the decade a pirated edition of General William Booth's *In Darkest England and the Way Out* was selling vigorously.[13] Booth's scheme, involving the establishment of labour exchanges, farm colonies and industrial towns, model suburban villages, paid holidays, and an intelligence service for processing useful social data, was branded by some as socialistic, but encouraged others to view social action as an essential part of true religion.[14] Two Canadian ministers, S. S. Craig and Herbert Casson, taking their cue from John Trevor in Manchester, attempted to found labour churches. Nothing more is known of Craig's venture in Toronto,[15] but Casson's attempt at Lynn, Massachusetts, lasted from 1893 to 1898, after which he became a well-known socialist lecturer in Canada as well as the United States.[16] The Congregationalist layman, T. B. Macaulay, in 1894 brought the Brotherhood movement from England to Montreal, whence its "brief, bright and brotherly" meetings, which mixed gospel songs with social reform, spread across the nation.[17]

275

Among social problems, those of slums and immigration prompted the larger part of the institutional response of the social gospel within the churches. Again, it was in the last decade of nineteenth century that the more ambitious innovations were undertaken with the establishment of St. Andrew's Institute in 1890 by the Presbyterian, D. J. Macdonnell, and the Fred Victor Mission in 1894 by a Methodist group under the impetus of the Massey family. Together providing facilities for night school, library, savings bank, nursery, clubrooms, gymnasium, medical centre, and restaurant, they reflected ventures pioneered in England, Scotland, and the United States in the previous decade.[18] Further institutional response to urban problems came after 1902 with the development of settlement houses by Miss Sara Libby Carson, working under the Presbyterian church. By 1920 there were at least thirteen settlements, in Canada, probably all of them formed under the impulse of the social gospel.[19] Where Miss Carson was not involved directly as organizer, she was often associated as consultant, as in the cases of the Toronto and McGill University settlements (1907 and 1909 respectively), which grew out of social concern in the student YMCAs. When the University of Toronto opened its Department of Social Service in 1914, the University Settlement provided the framework for practical work, and Miss Carson and the Rev. F. N. Stapleford of the Neighbourhood Workers' Association, among others, were recruited as lecturers.[20] Under J. S. Woodsworth, the settlement approach to the problems of north Winnipeg became a more potent spearhead of social reform, and the beginning, for Woodsworth, of an ever more radical formulation of the social gospel.[21]

In the 1890s, the churches were deeply involved in a mounting campaign against "drink." This was rationalized by leading figures such as F. S. Spence as part of the great gospel of liberty.[22] Significantly, however, a rude sort of environmentalism was creeping into the "ideology" of prohibition, placing it in the context of a reform programme based on the strategy of reform Darwinism: that the way to reform the individual was through alterations in his environment. As a wider array of social problems began to engage the minds of clergy and laymen alike, new committees and church structures were required. The Methodist Committee on Sociological Questions from 1894 to 1918 presented to general conference ever more progressive and comprehensive reports for church guidance. By 1914 committees or departments of temperance and moral reform had become full boards of social service and evangelism. The social task had been placed alongside that of evangelism in the official hierarchy of concerns of the Methodist and Presbyterian churches, and committees of social service were common in the other denominations. In 1913, when Methodists and Presbyterians combined in a programme of social surveys of major Canadian cities (and some rural areas), a systematic attack, chiefly upon the complex environment of the cities, was in the making.[23]

In the background of this escalation of social gospel enterprise was an ambitious effort at institutional consolidation. The Church Union movement, initiated in 1902, was making headway, and in 1907, an alliance of church and labour groups, having won the Lord's Day Act, blossomed into the Moral and Social Reform Council of Canada, jointly headed by J. G. Shearer and T. A. Moore, social service secretaries of the Presbyterian and Methodist churches respectively. Although until the middle of the second decade the provincial units of the council were largely engrossed in temperance campaigns, for several years thereafter they promoted a broad programme of social reform and community action that won the praise of young radicals like William Ivens and William Irvine.[24] In 1913 the national organization changed its name to the Social Service Council of Canada and further broadened its perspectives.[25]

These years were exciting ones for progressive churchmen. Not only were they advancing their campaign to win the churches to what they called sociological concepts, but they were also making significant progress in liberalizing the restrictive personal disciplines of their denominations and gaining ground for historical criticism and a reformation of theological curricula.[26] During and after 1908 a lively discussion on the relation of Christianity to socialism developed. The subject had been kept alive by a small group among whom were Bland, the Rev. Ben Spence, the socialist-prohibitionist who in 1904 managed A. W. Puttee's campaign to win a second term as a labour MP,[27] A. E. Smith, who endorsed labour candidates in successive pastorates at Nelson, B. C., and Winnipeg and Brandon, Manitoba,[28] and the Rev. W. E. S. James, who was general secretary from about 1905 of the Christian Socialist Fellowship in Ontario and organizer in 1914 of the Church of the Social Revolution in Toronto.[29] A wave of millennial socialism in Britain after the election of 1906, the controversy surrounding R. J. Campbell's *New Theology,*[30] and touring lecturers such as Keir Hardie (1908 and 1912) and the Rev. J. Stitt Wilson (1909 and 1910), who preached the message of socialism as applied to Christianity, undoubtedly spurred discussion in Canada.[31]

Both socialists and clerics picked up the theme. In 1909 W. A. Cotton, editor of the Canadian socialist journal, *Cotton's Weekly,* developed the notion that Jesus had been the original labour leader.[32] In 1910 a large meeting in Montreal heard an exposition of socialism based on the Bible, and the prominent socialist from British Columbia, E. T. Kingsley of the Socialist Party of Canada, declared Christianity and socialism to be identical. The current did not run all one way, of course. A group of Toronto socialists in November 1910 devoted at least one evening to the subject, "Why a Socialist Can Not Be a Christian."[33]

After 1908 professed socialists in the churches seem not to have been so isolated or so peripheral. In that year the Rev. Dr. D. M. Ramsey in Ottawa described socialism as "carrying into economic regions the Christian doctrine of human brotherhood."[34] The Rev. Elliott S. Rowe organized socialist leagues in Sandon and Victoria, B. C.[35] Bryce M. Stewart in his survey of Fort William in 1913 found a considerable number of Christians sympathetic to socialism, and observed: "It is beyond question that in purity of purpose, ethics, and scientific reasoning the socialist position is far beyond any other political organization, and should appeal especially to the Christian."[36] In the same year, the Rev. Thomas Voaden of Hamilton, in a series of lectures later published, presented the thesis that socialism was the effect of Christianity forced outside the churches.[37] But that socialism not entirely outside the churches was becoming more and more apparent. In a survey of London, Ontario, in 1913 by the Brotherhoods of that city, it was found to be common opinion in the churches that neither unions nor socialist groups threatened or interfered with the church's work, and further, men of both organizations were found among the church's workers.[38]

Given the groundswell that seemed to be building up for the social gospel as the twentieth century entered its second decade, it was not surprising that when the Social Service Council called a national congress on social problems for March 1914, the response was overwhelming. For three days over two hundred regular delegates from across the nation, representing welfare organizations, churches, farm and labour groups, municipalities, provinces, and the federal government, were subjected to a barrage of social statistics, social conditions, social challenges, and social exhortations.[39] Most of the forty Canadian speakers were from central Canada, and although the rural problem was considered, speakers overwhelmingly represented urban areas: social workers, city judges and politicians, city doctors, labour leaders, college professors, city clergy. Although city oriented, the world of business management and ownership was conspicuous by its absence.

This was primarily a professional man's conference. Its social sources lay outside and below the centres of power which were forging the new Canada. The lines of sympathy were clear in the enthusiastic response to the claim of a visiting speaker that "there is so much religion in the labor movement and so much social spirit in the Church, that someday it will become a question whether the Church will capture the labor movement or the labor movement will capture the Church."[40] Not all the speakers gave evidence of the social gospel, but when their concerns were related to other information about them, the inferences seemed clear: Dr. Charles Hastings, Toronto's medical health officer, was a Presbyterian elder, a past chairman of the Progressive Club, and a member of the Public Ownership League;[41] J. O. McCarthy, Toronto city controller, was a leading figure in the Canadian Brotherhood Federation and a member of the Methodist Board of Social Service and Evangelism;[42] James Simpson, vice-president of the Trades and Labor Congress, was a Methodist local preacher, a lecturer for the Dominion Prohibition Alliance, a vice-president of the Toronto branch of the Lord's Day Alliance, and a perennially successful socialist candidate for offices of city government in Toronto who was consistently supported in his campaigns by the Epworth League, the Methodist young people's organization.[43] In short, it seemed that to scratch a reformer at the congress was to find a social gospeller.

So popular were the evening open meetings that the *Ottawa Citizen* could not recall any recent visiting theatrical production to rival them and, when the tumult had subsided, concluded on 6 March that the congress had been "one of the greatest assemblages ever held in Canada to grapple with . . . social and economical problems." The congress represented the social gospel entering a crest of influence. C. W. Gordon (Ralph Connor), writing the introduction to the report, was excited by the challenge thrown down to the "economic and social conditions on which the fabric of our state is erected." He may not have been aware of the hint of incongruity in his conclusion that "there is in our nation so deep a sense of righteousness and brotherhood that it needs only that the light fall clear and white on evil to have it finally removed."[44] Was reform to be won so cheaply? An unevangelicalized Calvinist might have been pardoned his doubts.

During the generation of its ascent, from 1890 to 1914, the social gospel front had remained remarkably united. One could now discern three emphases or wings beginning to crystallize, however. The conservatives were closest to traditional evangelicalism, emphasizing personal ethical issues, tending to identify sin with individual acts, and taking as their social strategy legislative reform of the environment. The radicals viewed society in more organic terms. Evil was so endemic and pervasive in the social order that they concluded there could be no personal salvation without social salvation — or at least without bearing the cross of social struggle. Without belief in an immanent God working in the social process to bring his kingdom to birth, the plight of the radicals would surely have been desperate. Between conservatives and radicals was a broad "centre party" of progressives holding the tension between the two extremes, endorsing in considerable measure programmes of the other two, but transmuting them somewhat into a broad ameliorative programme of reform. The harmony of these wings was not to last. Between 1914 and 1928 the social gospel enjoyed and endured at one and the same time a period of crest and of crisis. Its growing differentiation in church, interdenominational, and secular organizations multiplied its impact on Canadian society, and at the same time initiated interaction between the various modes of its expression. These were the conditions of its potency. They were also the conditions of its crisis, for the encounter with social reality was the true test of social gospel concepts, and the very complexity of that reality and the conflict inherent within it inevitably set one wing of the social gospel in conflict with another. This involved process culminated in the years 1926–8, and the movement generally entered a period of weariness, reaction, and reconsideration. 279

The war of 1914–18 was the occasion, and in considerable measure the cause, of a crisis in relations between the radicals and the church. In the course of the war four radicals, then or later of some prominence, lost their professional posts: William Irvine, J. S. Woodsworth, Salem Bland, and William Ivens. The situation of each man was complex, but while they all believed their fate to be the result of increasing commercialism in the church and growing reaction in the state, and while Professor McNaught adopts the radicals' arguments as to what happened to them, the thesis is hardly acceptable.[45] It can only be maintained by slighting a number of facts: the acceptance of their radicalism, either prior to their appointment or without protest during a considerable period before severance of employment; the obvious support all had in the courts of the church; the complicating factor of pacifism in two cases; a host of evidence that Bland was more likely a victim of retrenchment in Wesley Theological College; and most important, the growing progressivism of the churches throughout the war period.

The evidence of church progressivism, 1914 to 1918, is more than substantial. All churches were dismayed by the outbreak of war, and the Methodists and Presbyterians at least condemned the profiteering that accompanied it. The Methodist general conference in the fall adopted the strongest reform programme to date and promised a further instalment in four years.[46] The Presbyterian Department of Social Service in 1916 regarded with hope the increase of nationalization and social control of industry in allied countries, and took heart at new Canadian legislation on prohibition, female suffrage, workmen's compensation, and protective legislation, the beginnings of provincial departments of labour, government encouragement of fishermen's co-operative societies in Nova Scotia, and the establishment of a bureau of social research under Woodsworth by the prairie provinces.[47] The Social Service Council sponsored regional congresses carrying on the spirit of its Ottawa success, added several more secular affiliates to its roster, and just prior to the war's end established the first national social welfare publication.[48] The church declarations of social policy in 1918 were further left than the manifestos of any major Canadian party, and approximated the British Labour party's programme for national minimum standards.[49] The Methodist call for a complete social reconstruction received international circulation, and, stated the *New Republic,* placed that church in the vanguard of reform forces.[50]

Radical social gospellers like Ernest Thomas of Vancouver, Bland, and A. E. Smith,[51] had played an important role in the formation of these church resolutions, but for the radicals the most important consequence of their mid-war crisis with church and state was the impact of their association, and hence of the social gospel, on agrarian and labour movements. J. S. Woodsworth was to be found addressing meetings of the Federated Labour party in Vancouver, and writing in the *B. C. Federationist.* William Irvine had become a leading figure in the Non-Partisan League in Alberta, editor of its journal the *Alberta Non-Partisan,* and a key person in the Dominion Labour party in Calgary. William Ivens in 1918 undertook an organizing tour in the prairie region for the Dominion Labour party,[52] stepped into the high priesthood, as the *Voice* put it, of labour forces at Winnipeg by founding a thriving labour church, and became editor of the *Western Labor News.*[53] From 1917 to 1919, Salem Bland contributed a regular column to the *Grain Growers' Guide,* and during the summer of 1918 addressed tens of thousands of westerners (with Henry Wise Wood) from the Chautauqua platform. Adding their voices to the journalism of reform were two more radicals of the social gospel, A. E. Smith as editor of the *Confederate* in Brandon,[54] and James Simpson as editor of the *Industrial Banner* in Toronto.

Despite the wartime crisis, the progressive and radical social gospellers had by 1918–19 reached a position of considerable power and consequence in the Canadian reform movement. And in the conservative wing, the progress of prohibition was startling. The war economy aided the cause, and in 1918 a government order-in-council prohibited further manufacture and sale of liquor until a year after the war's end. But it must be admitted that the temperance forces had won a national consensus on the subject. By 1919 only Quebec held out as a province, and it was at least two-thirds dry by local option. The farm organizations for some time had officially endorsed the reform, and now labour was finding near prohibition a stimulus to union membership.[55] Anglican publications joined other church journals in declaring that if prohibition was good in wartime, it was good in peace as well.[56]

There can be no doubt that the unrest, and especially the great Winnipeg strike of 1919, dealt the social gospel a rude jolt — and yet the impact can be easily exaggerated. The radicals, of course, were in the midst of it, sometimes carried to enthusiastic excesses of rhetoric which could easily be misunderstood. Their social millenialism undoubtedly contributed to the élan and discipline of the strike, but also to an element of unreality in which it was shrouded.[57] The Labour church provided its focus and strove as eight continuing churches in Winnipeg to maintain the essential unity of the left and the religious sense of labour's purpose which had been generated.[58]

The critical question, however, was how the progressive social gospel at large reacted to the events of 1919. The problem was complicated not simply by the growth of conservative reaction inside and outside the churches, but by the complex of attitudes in progressive minds to employers, unions, and social conflict. Generally sympathetic to labour, and persuaded that the spirit of Jesus was in social unrest calling the church to her true function as a defender of the oppressed,[59] they nevertheless believed that the "day of club and bludgeon is gone by," as Creighton described it in the *Christian Guardian*.[60] Misreading the face of power in industry, they were often, as was H. Michel in the *Canadian Churchman*, as pleased with the ending of a strike with improved conditions and shop committees as with recognition of a union and bargaining rights.[61] Nevertheless, the social gospel position held remarkably firm. Of the church press inclined toward the social gospel only the *Presbyterian and Westminster* attacked the Winnipeg strike outright.[62] The *Western Methodist Recorder* sympathized with labour and strike action but attacked the most radical element of strike leadership.[63] The *Churchman* reluctantly conceded the case in the face of government charges of sedition.[64] But the *Christian Guardian* and *Social Welfare* supported the strike throughout.[65] Clergy in and out of Winnipeg frequently spoke out on behalf of the strikers and questioned the government's interpretation and intervention. While the strike was on, numerous church conferences were in progress across the land, and it is difficult to find a case where social policies were modified in the face of unrest — quite the reverse.[66] S. D. Chown, superintendent of the Methodist church, in many addresses urged members to continue to cry out against injustice and to consider the social gospel the voice of prophecy in their time.[67] He has been charged with pronouncing a "ban" on the strikers.[68] He did not, but he was concerned that there was an indiscriminate injustice in the general strike weapon which he could not sanction, and believed that if labour continued such tactics the church might have to be more reserved in its support.[69]

Three events taken together served to heighten that reservation, however, to stalemate the progressives' programme for industrial peace and to perplex the social gospel. Even radicals of the social gospel had long argued that the very collective organization of industry bore out their arguments about the nature of society and hence the nature of the ethic required of modern man.[70] The businessman and industrial owner would surely come to recognize this. However, when in September 1919 the government gathered a national industrial conference with representatives from management, labour and the public, it was almost a total failure.[71] But when the churches conducted an immense Inter-Church Forward

281

Campaign in the winter and spring to equip them for their enlarged social role in the new era, it was an immense success.[72] Some, like Chown, saw in the success a new alliance for progress — the socially minded clergyman and the "new businessman."[73] For some months, the Methodist social service officers had been aware of a small flood of enquiries from businessmen asking guidance as to how to apply the church's policies to their business operations.[74] J. G. Shearer in *Social Welfare* was astonished at the number of plants that had instituted joint industrial councils, although he was suspicious that some at least were intended to forestall unionization.[75]

The dilution of progressivism such developments entailed was completed for many by the printers' strike of 1921, in the course of which the church publishing houses, the Methodist in particular, experienced at first hand the hideous complexities of industrial conflict. The Methodist house encouraged union membership. Depressed business conditions of 1921 precluded meeting all union demands. Nevertheless, with most other printing establishments in Toronto, it was struck on 1 June. Its manager allowed himself to be drafted as chairman of the employers' anti-strike committee and soon found himself in the midst of an outright open shop campaign. The union on the other hand not only rejected reasonable offers, but turned on the Methodists with special fury because they seemed not to be living up to their progressive declarations of 1918. Despite an outcry from Methodist summer schools, and frantic negotiations by Ernest Thomas of the Social Service Department, there was little that could be done. Neither the church nor any other business could live now on the terms of the envisaged economic order of social gospel prophecy.[76] Creighton concluded that strikes were simply stupid, and had no constructive word for labour in the great British Empire Steel and Coal Company conflicts of the mid-decade.[77] The Social Service Council drifted from its celebration of the significance of labour in its Labour Day issues to its calm notices of the day at the decade's end.[78] The United Church's pronouncement on industry in 1926 simply launched the new church on a sea of ambiguities, which many recognized, but which none could chart more accurately.[79] The bright vision of the social gospel seemed to be going into eclipse.[80]

For a time the upward course of the agrarian revolt and the Progressive party offered new opportunities. From the earlier days of E. A. Partridge, the social gospel had had an intimate role in the theory and practice of the agrarian movements.[81] The churches had attempted to foster social life and community ideals through institutes, conferences, and summer schools.[82] The *Guide* promoted the notion of the church as a community centre.[83] Farm leaders like Drury, Good, Moyle, and Henders were prominent members of social service councils.[84] Bland and the Congregationalist, D. S. Hamilton, worked closely with S. J. Farmer and Fred Dixon in Winnipeg on behalf of the single tax and direct legislation.[85] Henry Wise Wood counselled his farmers to look to the church for a social saviour, for it was just now beginning to recognize Jesus as a social leader as well as a personal saviour.[86] Wood's whole programme of civilizational reform was built on the theological assumptions of the social gospel.[87] Since 1903, from Wesley College, Winnipeg, Salem Bland had been sending out young ministers of the social gospel who frequently became members of local units of the Grain Growers' Associations.[88] By 1919 the social gospel had become, in effect, the religion of the agrarian revolt,[89] and its continued involvement in the process of party and policy formation was such that Norman Lambert, secretary of the Canadian Council of Agriculture, observed that religion and social work were inextricably linked with the farmers.[90]

The victories of the Progressive party can, then, be viewed in part as victories of the social gospel. But equally, the failure of the Progressives in 1926 must be weighed on the social gospel scales. In brief, it must be conceded that the social gospel belief that in the rise of such movements true religion and genuine democracy were triumphing together in the modern world contributed to the Progressive party's sense of being something other than a traditional party, and of fulfilling something more than a political role. This non-politics of hope inevitably was ground to pieces in a parliamentary world where alliances were necessary, but compromising, where decisions were mandatory, but the better alternative seldom clear.

283

At mid-decade, although the great accomplishment of Church Union brightened the horizon, that victory had been won at some cost. The drive to consolidate social service in the new church had worked to the disadvantage of other expressions of the social gospel. Support was withdrawn from the Brotherhood Federation, and the Social Service Council ran afoul of church financing and personal animosities. The former collapsed completely, and the latter, also hit by depression conditions, the counter-attacks against prohibition, and the death of its secretary, G. J. Shearer, lived on in a maimed condition.[91] The campaign for a national church made church social service leaders more hostile than they would otherwise have been to the labour churches which had spread to at least ten other cities before collapsing in 1924–5.[92] T. A. Moore of the Methodist Social Service Department had for three critical years of their life played a dubious role with the RCMP in its investigation of the churches.[93] The labour churches, however, died chiefly of their own inadequacy as a religious institution. After 1924 they followed their logical course, with a transfer of religious commitment and zeal to the creation of a more radical reform party via Woodsworth's Ginger Group, and in A. E. Smith's case, one might observe, to the Communist party.[94] Not only did Church Union further drain progressive social gospel energies in the task of institutional reconstruction, but on the morrow of Union, the critical battle in defence of prohibition had to be fought. One by one after 1920 the provincial temperance acts had gone down to defeat. In 1926 the last main stronghold, Ontario, was under attack. The church which was to rally the forces of social righteousness was already fighting a rearguard battle.

At stake was the survival of the conservative social gospel. In the aftermath of defeat the temperance forces were shattered beyond repair.[95] "Old Ontario" has died, declared Ernest Thomas as he launched a careful critique of temperance strategy.[96] The consensus, carefully built up over the years, had disappeared, just as the association of social work and religion so long nurtured under the social service formula was now giving way to secular organizations quite outside, and often severely critical of, the churches.[97]

It was no coincidence that the crisis in the social gospel coincided so nearly with the crisis in Progressive politics and in the reform movement at large. The categories in which they all worked, and the divinities which moved them all, lay shattered. Nevertheless, the lessons of the encounter with reality were not easily absorbed, in part owing to the ease with which the social gospel could transfer its passion from one cause to another. Partly as a positive expression of the social gospel, but also, one suspects, as a sublimation of frustration, much progressive zeal in 1923 transferred itself to a resurgence of pacifism, and after 1926 to a more broadly conceived peace movement.[98] Only among a few individuals like Ernest Thomas and leaders in the Student Christian Movement were penetrating questions being asked about the adequacy of social gospel concepts.[99] Prosperous church expansion in the later 1920s was accompanied by an introversion religiously and by small fellowship groups.[100] But out of the latter, the reconsiderations of the more critically minded, the struggles of the survivors of the political wreck of Progressivism, and a growing dialectic with more radical forms of socialist thought, was to come a new thrust of a reconstructed social gospel in the 1930s.

284

Notes

1. These reactions of the church press are cited in Stewart Crysdale, *The Industrial Struggle and Protestant Ethics in Canada* (Toronto, 1961), pp. 18–19. It is not unlikely that among the strikers and those who rallied to their support were some who were not prepared to accept the editors' opinions as to their Christian duty (See Doris French, *Faith, Sweat and Politics,* Toronto, 1962). For a fuller account of the social stance of Methodism and Presbyterianism in these years, see Marion Royce, "The Contribution of the Methodist Church to Social Welfare in Canada" (unpublished M.A. thesis, University of Toronto, 1940), and E. A. Christie, "The Presbyterian Church in Canada and Its Official Attitude Towards Public Affairs and Social Problems, 1875–1925" (unpublished M.A. thesis, University of Toronto, 1955).
2. Crysdale, *The Industrial Struggle and Protestant Ethics in Canada,* p. 22.
3. C. D. W. Goodwin, *Canadian Economic Thought* (Durham, N.C., 1961), pp. 32–8; *Toronto World,* 7 Feb. 1898; *Grain Growers' Guide,* 21 Nov. 1917, pp. 32–3.
4. United Church Archives, Toronto (UCA), reading lists in the Bland Papers.
5. Bland Papers.
6. C. H. Hopkins, *The Rise of the Social Gospel in American Protestantism, 1865–1915* (New Haven, 1940), pp. 110–15.
7. For an expression of this transition, see the introduction to General William Booth, *In Darkest England and the Way Out* (London: International Headquarters of the Salvation Army, 1890).
8. The distinction was between bringing the message and creating the social reality. For an illuminating discussion of this process, see Donald B. Meyer, *The Protestant Search for Political Realism, 1919–1941* (Los Angeles and Berkeley, 1960), chap. I.
9. UCA, J. B. Silcox, *Social Resurrection.*
10. C. S. Eby, *The World Problem and the Divine Solution* (Toronto: William Briggs, 1914).
11. W. S. Ryder, in a paper presented to the Pacific Coast Theology Conference, 1920; *Western Methodist*

Recorder, Sept. 1920, pp. 4–5. See also David Summers, "The Labour Church" (unpublished Ph.D. thesis, University of Edinburgh, 1958).

12. Kingston *Daily News,* 14 Feb. 1894; 13 Feb. 1896; 20 Feb. 1896; 11 Feb. 1897; *Queen's Quarterly,* V (April 1898), 316–18; VI (April 1899), 314–16; VII (April 1900), 332; VIII (April 1901), 388.

13. Robert Sandall, *The History of the Salvation Army* (3 vols; London, 1955), III, *Social Reform and Welfare Work,* 80.

14. Alexander Sutherland, *The Kingdom of God and Problems of Today* (Toronto: William Briggs, 1898), p. xiii.

15. Bland Papers. Salem Bland, Sermon at St. James Bond United Church, 31 Oct. 1937.

16. Summers, "The Labour Church," pp. 427ff; Hopkins, *The Rise of the Social Gospel in American Protestantism, 1865–1915,* pp. 85–7; French, *Faith, Sweat and Politics,* pp. 129–30.

17. *Social Welfare,* Oct. 1923, pp. 14–15; W. Ward, *The Brotherhood in Canada* (London: The Brotherhood Publishing House, [1912]). See also F. D. Leete, *Christian Brotherhoods* (Cincinnati: Jennings and Graham, 1912).

18. J. F. McCurdy, *The Life and Work of D. J. Macdonnell* (Toronto: William Briggs, 1897), pp. 23–4, 289–309; Minutes of the Toronto City Missionary Society of the Methodist Church, 29 Dec. 1894. 10 Dec. 1895. For the less well-known Scottish side of the story, see Stewart Mechie, *The Church and Scottish Social Developments, 1780–1870* (London, 1960).

19. *Social Welfare,* Feb. 1929, p. 113. *The Social Service Congress of Canada, 1914* (Toronto: Social Service Council of Canada, 1914), pp. 134–6.

20. *Canadian Student,* Oct. 1919, pp. 16–20; *Social Welfare,* Feb. 1929, p. 113; Murray G. Ross, *The YMCA in Canada* (Toronto, 1951), pp. 215–32.

21. Kenneth McNaught, *A Prophet in Politics* (Toronto, 1959), chap. IV.

22. *Social Service Congress of Canada,* p. 307.

23. UCA, Methodist Church of Canada and Presbyterian Church in Canada, *Reports of Investigations of Social Conditions and Social Surveys,* 1913–14: Vancouver, Regina, Fort William, Port Arthur, London, Hamilton, Sydney.

24. *Voice,* 8 Dec. 1916, p. 8; *The Nutcracker,* 17 Nov. 1916, p. 8.

25. UCA, Moral and Social Reform Council, *Minutes of the Annual Meeting.* 5 Sept. 1913.

26. See H. H. Walsh, *The Christian Church in Canada* (Toronto, 1956).

27. A. E. Smith, *All My Life* (Toronto: Progress Publishing Co. 1949), p. 33.

28. *Ibid.*

29. W. E. S. James, "Notes on a Socialist Church," in Summers, "The Labour Church," pp. 690–6.

30. For an able discussion of these factors in their British context, see Stanley Pierson, "Socialism and Religion: A Study of their Interaction in Great Britain, 1889–1911" (unpublished Ph.D. thesis, Harvard University, 1957).

31. *Canadian Annual Review (CAR),* 1908, p. 101; 1909, p. 307; 1910, p. 315; 1912, p. 277.

32. *Ibid.,* 1909, p. 306.

33. *Ibid.,* 1910, pp. 315–16.

34. *Ibid.,* 1908, p. 99.

35. Paul Fox, "Early Socialism in Canada," in J. H. Aitcheson, *The Political Process in Canada* (Toronto, 1963), p. 89.

36. Methodist and Presbyterian Churches, *Report of a Social Survey of Port Arthur* (n.p., 1913), p. 10.

37. Thomas Voaden, *Christianity and Socialism* (Toronto: Methodist Book Room, 1913).

38. Methodist and Presbyterian Churches, *Report of a Limited Survey of Educational, Social and Industrial Life in London, Ontario* n.p., 1913), p. 43.

39. *Ottawa Free Press,* 2 Mar. 1914; *Ottawa Evening Journal,* 3 Mar. 1914; and the record of the conference proceedings cited above, *Social Service Congress of Canada, 1914.*

40. Charles Stelzle, "Capturing the Labour Movement," *Social Service Congress of Canada,* pp. 35–8.

41. *Canadian Men and Women of the Time,* 1912.

42. UCA, Canadian Brotherhood Federation, *Constitution* [and list of officers and General Council], c. 1916.

43. *Canadian Men and Women of the Time,* 1912; *Canadian Forum,* Nov. 1938, p. 229; Summers, "The Labour Church," pp. 690–6.

44. *Social Service Congress of Canada, 1914.*

45. McNaught, *A Prophet in Politics,* pp. 79–85. For a detailed discussion from another point of view, see A. R. Allen, "The Crest and Crisis of the Social Gospel in Canada, 1916–1927" (unpublished Ph.D. thesis, Duke University, 1967), chap. II.

46. See for instance the early reactions of the Methodist Church, *Journal of Proceedings of the General Conference,* 1914, pp. 404–6; 1918, pp. 290–3.

47. Presbyterian Church in Canada, *Acts and Proceedings of the General Assembly,* 1916, Appendix, pp. 13–14.

48. *CAR,* 1918, p. 598. Social Service Council of Canada, *Minutes,* Annual Meeting. January 1918.

49. See the first issues of *Social Welfare*, beginning Oct., 1918; Methodist *Journal of Proceedings*, 1918, pp. 290–3; Statement of the Presbyterian Board of Home Missions and Social Service, *Presbyterian and Westminster*, 10 April 1919, p. 351.
50. *New Republic*, 8 Feb. 1919.
51. *Hamilton Spectator*, 12 Oct. 1918; *Western Methodist Recorder*, March 1919, pp. 5–6.
52. *Voice* (Winnipeg), 19 Apr. 1918.
53. *Ibid.*, 21 June 1918: 5 and 12 July 1918.
54. Summers, "The Labour Church," pp. 379–80.
55. *Edmonton Free Press*, 10 May 1919; *Industrial Banner*, 10 Oct. 1919; *Youth and Service*, Aug., 1919, pp. 114–15; *Western Methodist Recorder*, Oct., 1920, p. 3; *Alberta Labor News*, 25 Sept. 1920; *Christian Guardian*, 30 July 1919, p. 2, quoting John Queen of the Winnipeg strike committee.
56. *Canadian Churchman*, 28 Nov. 1918, p. 763.
57. See William Ivens' euphoric mixture of prophecy, platform rhetoric, and industrial tactics in *Western Labor News*, Special Strike Editions, e.g., No. 3, 19 May 1919.
58. For more extensive discussion of the Labour Churches in Canada, see McNaught, A *Prophet in Politics*, Allen, "The Crest and Crisis of the Social Gospel," Summers, "The Labour Church," and D. F. Pratt, "William Ivens and the Winnipeg Labor Church" (unpublished B.D. thesis, St. Andrew's College, Saskatoon, 1962).
59. Editorial, "I Was Hungry," *Christian Guardian*, 27 Nov. 1918, p. 6.
60. *Ibid.*, 5 Mar. 1919, p. 5.
61. *Canadian Churchman*, 27 Feb. 1919, p. 133; 10 Apr. 1919, pp. 234–5.
62. *Ibid.*, 29 May 1919, p. 344; 10 July 1919, p. 441.
63. *Western Methodist Recorder*, June 1919, p. 8.
64. *Presbyterian and Westminster*, 22 May 1919, p. 497; 29 May 1919, pp. 518–19; 5 June 1919, pp. 549–50.
65. *Social Welfare*, 1 Aug. 1919, pp. 266–70; *Christian Guardian*, 28 May 1919, p. 5; 4 June 1919, pp. 4–5; 11 June 1919, p. 3; 18 June 1919, p. 4; 25 June 1919, p. 4.
66. For a detailed discussion of the more general church reaction, see Allen, "The Crest and Crisis of the Social Gospel," chap. VI, VII.
67. *Western Methodist Recorder*, June 1919.
68. McNaught, *A Prophet in Politics*, p. 118.
69. *Christian Guardian*, 25 June 1919, p. 2; *Toronto Daily Star*, 12 June 1919, pp. 1, 8.
70. See for instance UCA, Bland Papers, Salem Bland, "Four Steps and a Vision."
71. *Social Welfare*, 1 Nov. 1919, p. 39; 1 Dec. 1919, p. 75; *Christian Guardian*, 1 Oct. 1919, p. 6.
72. *Canadian Baptist*, 1 May 1919, p. 4; 31 July 1919, p. 3; *Presbyterian and Westminster*, 19 June 1919, p. 603; 25 Dec. 1919, p. 594; *Christian Guardian*, 15 Oct. 1919, p. 22.
73. *Christian Guardian*, 30 June 1920, pp. 18–19.
74. *Western Methodist Recorder*, Oct. 1921, p. 4.
75. *Social Welfare*, 1 Sept. 1919, p. 287; 1 Aug. 1920, pp. 316–17; 1 Aug. 1922, p. 235.
76. See A. R. Allen, "The Crest and Crisis of the Social Gospel," chapter XI.
77. *Christian Guardian*, 25 Mar. 1925.
78. *Social Welfare*, Aug. 1927, p. 483; Aug. 1929, p. 242.
79. "The Christianization of Industry," *Social Welfare*, 1 Aug. 1927, pp. 488–9; see also, United Church, Department of Evangelism and Social Service, *Annual Report*, 1924–5, p. 10.
80. See Creighton's reflections on this possibility, *New Outlook*, 12 Jan. 1927, p. 19.
81. *Grain Growers' Guide*, 14 and 28 Aug. 1909; 30 Sept., 6 Oct. 1919.
82. McNaught, *A Prophet in Politics*, pp. 74, 74n.
83. *Grain Growers' Guide*, 7 June 1916; 20 Dec. 1916.
84. Moral and Social Reform Council, *Minutes*, 10 Sept. 1909; Social Service Council of Canada, *Minutes*, 5 Sept. 1913; Manitoba Conference of the United Church, *Minutes*, 1932, p. 42.
85. *CAR*, 1913, p. 578; Manitoba Conference, *Minutes*, 1929, p. 60; *The Single Taxer and Direct Legislation Bulletin* (Winnipeg), III, 8 (1916).
86. See his Circulars Nos. 9 and 10 for United Farmers of Alberta Sunday, 27 May 1917, Bland Papers, UCA.
87. *Grain Growers' Guide*, 29 Jan. 1917; 4 Dec. 1918.
88. *Christian Guardian*, 17 Mar. 1920, p. 25; 15 Dec. 1920, p. 14.
89. For further elaboration of this suggestion, see A. R. Allen, "Salem Bland and the Social Gospel in Canada" (unpublished M.A. thesis, University of Saskatchewan, 1961), chaps. V and VI.
90. *Presbyterian Witness*, 23 June 1921, pp. 10–11.
91. The documentation for this is too diffuse to be suggested through a few citations, but may be found in A. R. Allen, "The Crest and Crisis of the Social Gospel," chaps. XIV, XV, XVI.
92. *Ibid.*, chap. X.
93. See correspondence between Moore and Hamilton from 25 May 1920, to 25 April 1922, Papers on Methodist Industrial Relations, 1920–2, UCA.

94. A. E. Smith, *All My Life*, pp. 76–7.

95. United Church, Department of Evangelism and Social Service, *Annual Report*, 1927, pp. 24–5, 27–9; *New Outlook*, 21 Mar. 1928, p. 2; 8 Jan. 1930, p. 46; Dobson Papers, Union College Library, B.C., Hugh Dobson to L. C. McKinney, 30 April 1929.

96. *New Outlook*, 22 Dec. 1926, p. 5; 8 Jan. 1930, pp. 31, 44.

97. In 1926 the Canadian Association of Social Workers was formed, and in 1928 the Canadian Conference of Social Work held its first national meeting. The immediate shrinkage in size of the Social Service Council's annual meetings indicated the impact of these developments on the stature of the council. For an expression of the rationale upon which the council was founded, see *New Outlook*, 10 June 1925, p. 23. For expressions of the new social worker's outlook see J. D. Ketchum, "Judge and be Judged," *Canadian Student*, Nov. 1925; *Social Welfare*, June–July 1926, pp. 189–90; and for a warning about the dangers of a social work that had lost its sense of God, see United Church, Department of Evangelism and Social Service, *Annual Report*, 1927, p. 25. The social gospel stress upon the immanence of God of course abetted the very secularism about which some of them were now concerned.

98. See for instance, *Canadian Student*, Jan. 1924, p. 99; *Christian Guardian*, 20 Feb. 1924, and issues of subsequent months for discussion of the subject; *Social Welfare*, April 1923, pp. 137–9; *New Outlook*, issues of July through December 1925; *Canadian Churchman*, 21 Jan. 1926, p. 36.

99. *New Outlook*, 12 Aug. 1925, pp. 5–6; 12 Feb. 1930, p. 153; *Canadian Student*, March 1925, p. 163; March 1926; pp. 165–6. Student Christian Movement Archives, Minutes of the General Committee, 24–26 Sept. 1926.

100. [Ernest Thomas] *Fellowship Studies* (Toronto: United Church Department of Evangelism and Social Service [1927 or 1928]; *Canadian Student*, March 1926, p. 168; Dobson Papers, Dobson to Armstrong, 14 May 1928.

"The Beginning of Our Regeneration": The Great War and Western Canadian Reform Movements*

JOHN H. THOMPSON

I know nothing about Germany. But I do know something about our own people. I know how selfish and individualistic and sordid and money-grabbing we have been; how slothful and incompetent and self-satisfied we have been, and I fear it will take a long war and sacrifices and tragedies altogether beyond our present imagination to make us unselfish and public-spirited and clean and generous; it will take the strain and emergency of war to make us vigorous and efficient; it will take the sting of many defeats to impose that humility which will be the *beginning of our regeneration*.

Edith Duncan to Dave Elden in R. J. C. Stead, The Cow Puncher, *1918*.

The Western Canadian reform movement was not created by the enthusiasm released by the Great War. Associations advocating prohibition, woman's suffrage, and economic reform had existed in Manitoba and the North West Territories before the turn of the century. After 1900, the problems of immigration, rapid urban growth, and an expanding wheat economy gave the political, social, and economic dimensions of reformism increasing relevance. In the decade before the war, reform causes won new supporters, and became an important theme in Western Canadian life. The "reform movement" which espoused this theme was not a monolith. It was composed of a variety of pressure groups, dedicated to such diverse objectives as tariff reform, the single tax, direct legislation, prohibition,

* From *Canadian Historical Association Historical Papers*, 1972, 227–245. Copyright by Canadian Historical Association. Reprinted by permission.

and woman's suffrage. The movement's members belonged to no particular political party, and only in Manitoba did they find it necessary to capture a party to gain their ends. The movement's common philosophical denominator was the social gospel, which swept North American protestantism at the close of the nineteenth century.[1]

By 1914, Western reformers felt that they had made considerable progress toward their goals. Each Prairie Province had an active Social Service Council, committed to the eradication of the liquor traffic and prostitution, and to the amelioration of social conditions in Western cities. The Woman's Christian Temperance Union also spoke for prohibition, and was the leading force in demands for woman's suffrage. Direct Legislation Leagues promised to purify political life by using the initiative, referendum, and recall to make governments more responsive to their electorates. Grain Growers' Associations used their voice, *The Grain Growers' Guide*, to support these reforms and to promote tariff and tax reform as well.

288

But as of August, 1914, none of these causes had enjoyed significant success. No Western province had enfranchised its women or introduced prohibition.[2] Direct legislation had been partially implemented in Saskatchewan in 1912 and Alberta in 1913, but Saskatchewan's electorate had failed to endorse the Direct Legislation Act in a referendum.[3] In January, 1914, the *bête noire* of Western reformers, Premier R. P. Roblin of Manitoba, observed sanctimoniously to his Attorney General that "seemingly crime does not decrease, seemingly the world is getting no better, seemingly the efforts of social and moral reformers is [*sic*] not as effective as we would like."[4]

It was on Premier Roblin that reform eyes were fixed in July 1914. The Manitoba Liberal Party, in the grip of the provincial reform movement, was challenging Roblin's fifteen year old Conservative government. The Liberal Platform was a reformer's banquet, with direct legislation as an appetizer, woman's suffrage as the entrée, and a promised referendum on prohibition to conclude the meal. Roblin opposed each of these items, and, for the first time, reform and the status quo were presented to a Western electorate as clear-cut alternatives. C. W. Gordon of the Social Service Council described the significance of the confrontation for Western reformers:

On the one side are the Christian Churches, various [reform] organizations, social workers, and all the decent citizens, on the other the Roblin Government, the Liquor traffic, and every form of organized vice and crime.[5]

But "decent citizens" were apparently not a majority in Manitoba, for the Roblin Government was returned for a fifth consecutive term.

The defeat in Manitoba did not mean that reformers throughout the West faced a hopeless situation. The Liberals made significant gains in terms of seats and in their percentage of the popular vote. But the defeat did suggest that in a head to head confrontation with "the forces of reaction" (as Nellie McClung described those who opposed reform), reform ideas did not enjoy the support of a clear majority of the electorate. Although the reform movement had increased both in size and vigour, it had not succeeded in winning the enthusiastic endorsement of the general public. This endorsement was necessary if such reform objectives as prohibition and woman's suffrage were to be effectively implemented. It was in their quest for this broad public support that reformers were aided by the Great War.

A modern democracy with a literate population cannot engage in a major war without soliciting an enthusiastic mandate from its citizens. For this reason, the Great War was interpreted and described in terms very different from those applied to wars of the past. The Canadian Expeditionary Force was not fighting for territorial gain, but "in maintenance of those ideals of Liberty and Justice which are the common and sacred cause of the Allies" and for "the freedom of the world"[6]. Although "there may have been wars in the history of the British Empire that have not been justifiable", "there never was a juster cause" than the war against German autocracy.[7]

289

But if Canadian soldiers were giving their lives for "Liberty and Justice" in Flanders, was it not the duty of those who remained behind to see to it that these same things existed in Canada? Reformers argued that the Great War was an opportunity to accomplish this very thing, a sign given to Canada in order that "the national sins which are responsible for this awful carnage may be eradicated so righteousness and peace may be established."[8] As Mrs. Nellie McClung told her many readers, the war was necessary for national regeneration, for "without the shedding of blood, there is no remission of sin."[9] If the sacrifice was not to be wasted, the reform programme had to be implemented. Even Clifford Sifton, hardly an ardent reformer, recognized that the Great War made it necessary for both Eastern and Western Canada to "cast out everything that threatens its moral health." The war produced a transformation in public attitudes to reformism, changing them to the point that "men who scoffed a few years ago are the foremost now to demand reform."[10] The transformation was particularly pronounced in Western Canada. As Mrs. Irene Parlby told the Saskatchewan Grain Growers, "before the war the real spirit of the West had been smothered in materialism," and public action had been difficult. Because of the common goal of victory, "the big broad free spirit is beginning to emerge again."[11]

In addition to changing public attitudes to the idea of reform, the wartime experience changed attitudes to the role of the state as the enforcer of reform measures. Many reform objectives, most notably prohibition and changes in the system of taxation, called for a previously unacceptable degree of state intervention into the lives of its citizens. The expansion of governmental power necessary to meet the wartime emergency gave government intervention a sanction which it had not had before 1914. The state became "more than a mere tax-collector or polling clerk," it became an organization capable of vigorous, positive activities.[12]

An Alberta prohibitionist noted that "the European War has taught us that the State has a right to take such action as will best conserve its forces for the national good."[13] Because of the demands of war, no truly patriotic citizen could react to such action with "resentment or resistance"; the correct course was "a new and affectionate loyalty."[14] This new willingness to grant a more active role to government combined with the wartime ideal of redeeming Canadian society to produce a climate of opinion favourable to reform. It was this climate that the reform movement exploited to gain its ends, in some facets of the movement more successfully than in others.

The reform objective which received the greatest impetus from the wartime atmosphere was the prohibition of alcoholic liquors. Despite the social problems which liquor created in the rapidly expanding West, prohibitionists had been unable to convince the Western public or their provincial governments that prohibition was the necessary cure. The events of August, 1914, introduced a new factor into the equation. The Great War provided the necessary catalyst in the public reaction which brought about prohibitory liquor legislation, not only in Western Canada, but throughout North America. More than any other reform group, prohibitionists were able to use the exigencies of the wartime situation to lend new credence to their arguments and to exploit the desire to purify society which emerged as part of the domestic side of the war effort.

Prohibitionists had long been fond of military metaphors to describe their struggle. The cause itself was "*warfare* waged against ignorance, selfishness, darkness, prejudice and cruelty", while a successful referendum campaign might be compared to Wellington's victory at Waterloo.[15] Sara Rowell Wright of the W.C.T.U. liked to speak of her years as "a private in the rear ranks of the movement," and a book of temperance poems and songs was called *The Gatling*, in reference to the way its contents were to be deployed against the liquor traffic.[16] The war made these rhetorical flourishes a mainstay of temperance propaganda. The liquor traffic was clearly identified with the Kaiser and his brutal hordes as a force blocking the way to a more perfect society. Since a Westerner would "despise the Kaiser for dropping bombs on defenseless people, and shooting down innocent people", he should also despise the liquor traffic, since it had "waged war on women and children all down the centuries."[17] The techniques to be employed in the eradication of both the Kaiser and the liquor traffic were made to seem exactly the same. Rev. J. E. Hughson of Winnipeg urged Westerners to "use ballots for bullets and shoot straight and strong in order that the demon of drink might be driven from the haunts of men."[18] A cartoon in the *Grain Growers' Guide* carried on the analogy pictorially, depicting a 'war' on the entrenched liquor interests, with 'votes' being loaded into a field piece by the forces under the banner of "Temperance and Righteousness."[19]

It was not only the tone of prohibitionist rhetoric that was adapted to suit the Great War, its content was modified as well. The war provided the temperance movement with two important new arguments, with which to influence public opinion. The first concerned the moral and physical health of the thousands of young Westerners who had entered the army, many of whom were leaving home for the first time. What would happen to the decent boys from prairie farms when, befuddled by unfamiliar liquor, they fell victim to the prostitutes who haunted military camps in Canada and overseas? Blighted by horrible unnamed diseases, "thousands of clean-minded innocent young boys who would otherwise have been decent upright citizens will now be nothing but a scourge to their country when they return."[20]

One way to avoid such a result was to keep liquor out of the hands of soldiers. As the Medical Officer of Ralph Connor's *Sky Pilot* in *No Man's Land* pointed out, "Cut out the damned beer. Cut out the beer and ninety *per cent* of the venereal disease goes . . . [Soldier's] mothers have given them up, to death, if need be, but not to this rotten damnable disease."[21] To "cut out the beer", women's groups and W.C.T. Unions bombarded legislators and commanding officers with resolutions demanding that bars and 'wet' canteens be closed "for the sake of our soldiers."[22] It was not enough to restrict such protection to the period when they were in uniform, only to allow them to become victims of the liquor traffic once they were civilians again. It was the responsibility of every Westerner to see that the veterans found "a clean pure Province for them when they return to us, in which they may rest their shattered nerves and poor wounded bodies."[23] This could only be guaranteed if prohibition became a reality.

No one thought to ask the "clean minded innocent young boys" if they wanted to be rescued from the clutches of temptation. Evidence about the soldiers' opinion on the prohibition question is contradictory. During referenda on prohibition in Manitoba, Saskatchewan, and Alberta polls in military camps returned 'dry' majorities, and one Saskatchewan officer wrote Premier Scott to raise the provincial government's decision to make the liquor trade a public monopoly.[24] After prohibition was in force, however, a Calgary private wrote A. E. Cross of the Calgary Brewing and Malting Company that his comrades "would be solid for to have it back to the good old days again" on their return.[25] Soldier poets poked rude fun at both 'dry' canteens and prohibitionists. One particularly piquant rhyme entitled "From the Trenches", derided

Preachers over in Canada
Who rave about Kingdom Come
Ain't pleased with our ability
And wanted to stop our rum.
Water they say would be better
Water! Great Scott! Out here
We're up to our knees in water
Do they think we're standing in beer?[26]

Thus it would seem that soldiers were as divided in their opinions of prohibition as most Westerners had been before 1914. But among the public as a whole, the prohibitionist movement was rapidly making converts, and producing a consensus in favour of prohibition.

An important factor in producing this consensus was a second new temperance argument, again one peculiar to the Wartime situation. Canadians were told constantly by their governments that efficiency was a prerequisite for victory over Germany. Prohibitionists quickly capitalized on this theme, pointing to the production and consumption of liquor as a drain on Canada's ability to wage war. Not only did drunkenness squander the nation's human resources, it wasted its physical resources as well. A drunken soldier was unfit to fight, an alcoholic worker was unable to produce, and grain distilled into whiskey could not be used to feed starving Allies. Newspapers sympathetic to the war effort put this argument forcefully before the public, demanding that

the bar must be closed [because] the national existence is at stake. The ship must be stripped for action. All dead weight must go by the boards if we are to win.[27]

292

As well as providing prohibitionists with two new important arguments, the situation created by the Great War gave them new answers to two of the most effective defences of the liquor traffic. With thousands of Westerners dying in France to serve their country, criticism of prohibition as a violation of individual liberty lost most of its impact. *Manitoba Free Press* editor John W. Dafoe reflected the popular mood when he pointed out that "the propriety of subordinating individual desires to the general good need not be elaborated at this moment, when millions of men, representing the cream of British citizenship have put aside all their individual inclinations and ambitions."[28] Nellie McClung was even more blunt. "We have before us," she wrote, "a perfect example of a man who is exercising personal liberty to the full. . . . a man by the name of William Hohenzollern."[29] The second anti-prohibitionist argument routed by the Great War was the claim that prohibition would produce widespread unemployment by wiping out the liquor industry and its associated outlets. The wartime demand for manpower created a labour shortage that made this contention ridiculous.

With their own rhetoric refurbished to suit the wartime situation, and with their opponents' most effective weapons temporarily silent, prohibitionist organizations intensified their efforts to put their case to the public and to the provincial governments. The traditional mainstays of the movement, the W.C.T.U. and the Social Service Councils, were joined in their campaign by groups which had not formerly been associated with prohibition. The Orange Lodge, the I.O.D.E., the Anglican Church, the Winnipeg Canadian Club; all came to the conclusion that prohibition was "the best way of dealing with the liquor traffic *at the present time*", and became war converts to the cause.[30] These new allies meant that prohibitionists could apply increased pressure on Western governments, and the movement began to gain concessions rapidly.

In Manitoba, for example, the antiprohibitionist Roblin government raised the legal drinking age from sixteen to eighteen and suspended the licenses of seventy-two establishments found to be flouting the liquor laws.[31] The Liberal government of Saskatchewan engaged in the same sort of short term measures, but Premier Scott and his colleagues began to realize that the public was demanding more and that "the time [was] high ripe for action." The step on which they decided fell short of prohibition. In March, 1915, the government announced that the liquor trade in Saskatchewan was to become a state monopoly. Liquor was to be available only in provincially operated dispensaries, and all bars, saloons, and stores were to be closed. Scott viewed the decision as a frank concession to wartime public opinion, and confided to Senator James H. Ross that this opinion was so strong that "to stand still any longer meant suicide for this government."[32] Scott and his cabinet regarded their dispensary system as a radical step in the direction of prohibition. J. A. Calder considered introducing the dispensaries as "having decided to go the limit", and expressed "very grave doubts" as to whether a referendum on prohibition could ever be successful in Saskatchewan.[33] The events of the next two years were to show how rapidly the war could change public attitudes to prohibition, and make a mockery of the prediction of as astute a politician as Calder.

In July 1915, with the Saskatchewan dispensary system scarcely in operation, the voters of Alberta gave a solid endorsement to a prohibition referendum. All but sixteen of the fifty-eight provincial constituencies returned prohibitionist majorities, with 'wet' victories coming only in "primarily mining or remote northern areas", beyond reach of prohibitionist propaganda.[34] Manitobans followed suit seven months later, with an even larger majority. Only three constituencies remained 'wet' in a prohibitionist landslide.

Saskatchewan, which had been so proud of its system of government control, suddenly found itself to the rear of temperance sentiment on the Prairies. One prohibitionist warned W. R. Motherwell that the situation had changed, and that the public was

not satisfied with the working out of the Liquor Dispencery [sic] System. It is true that we are tremendously better off . . . this however does not alter the fact that more is needed. This is a matter which is receiving a good deal of unfavourable comment at this time. The people are ready for a total prohibition measure at this very time, let us have it.[35]

The Saskatchewan Liberal government responded once again to public demands, and Saskatchewan became the third Western Province to endorse prohibition by referendum, in December, 1916. The Saskatchewan majority was the largest of the three, demonstrating again that as the war against Germany became longer and more bitter, the war against booze enlisted more and more recruits.

There are several revealing similarities among the three referenda, in addition to the fact that all were resounding prohibitionist victories. In each campaign the Great War played an important rhetorical role, and temperance workers succeeded completely in convincing the Western public that prohibition and patriotism were synonymous. The referenda themselves were treated as an opportunity for those truly behind the war effort to stand up and be counted. As the Cypress River *Western Prairie* warned on the eve of the Manitoba balloting, "anyone who will vote in favour of liquor might as well enlist under the Kaiser as far as patriotism goes."[36]

This identification helped prohibitionists overcome opposition among a traditionally hostile group, the Catholic immigrants from Central and Eastern Europe. It had been "this very heavy foreign population" which J. A. Calder had thought would prevent a 'dry' Saskatchewan, and much of the opposition faced by prohibitionists during the war did come from this quarter.[37] But many of these people saw the prohibition referendum as a kind of loyalty test, through which they could prove that they were good Canadian citizens, even during this time of crisis. Prohibitionists encouraged this belief, and actively sought non Anglo-Saxon votes. For the first time, their efforts were rewarded. In Manitoba, the Ruthenian Catholic Political Club and the Slavonic Independent Society "spoke fervently in favour of temperance," while *The Canadian Farmer,* a Western Ukrainian weekly, urged its Saskatchewan readers to "get organized and vote against the [Liquor] stores!"[38] Not all non Anglo-Saxons were converted, but enough voted for prohibition in each of the three provinces to largely neutralize the ballots of their wet countrymen. After the Alberta referendum, the W.C.T.U.'s Superintendent of Work Among Foreigners "knelt in thanksgiving to our Heavenly Father that not all foreign-speaking people voted wet, but that right prevailed and carried the day, even in several of their own district communities."[39] North Winnipeg, perhaps the most aggressively 'foreign' community in the West, rejected prohibition by only sixty-five votes. The *Manitoba Free Press* made an observation which applied throughout the West when it noted with satisfaction that "the greatest disappointment of all to the wets was the foreign vote."[40]

The only group completely untouched by wartime arguments on behalf of prohibition was Western Canada's French Canadians. French Canadians and prohibitionists had never enjoyed cordial relations, partly because of its wholehearted support for unilingual education. Since most French Canadians had centuries of North American ancestry, the idea that they needed to prove their loyalty by accepting prohibition did not occur to them. As the French language *Le Manitoba* was careful to point out, this did not mean that French Canadians were "plus intemperant que les autres", simply that they resented the totalitarian techniques of prohibition and prohibitionists. In each Western Province, Francophones rejected prohibition in the referenda of 1915–16.[41]

The second important similarity between the referenda campaigns in Manitoba, Saskatchewan, and Alberta was the demoralization of the traditional opponents of prohibition. The Great War not only defused the arguments used by the defenders of liquor, it sapped the strength of the defenders themselves. In Alberta, liquor dealers had "very little success" in raising funds to oppose prohibition during wartime.[42] In both Manitoba and Alberta, the Licensed Victuallers' Association had to turn to the

United States for antiprohibitionist speakers. The Manitoba Association co-operated with the Bartenders Union to obtain Clarence Darrow, who received an enthusiastic reception from 'wet' faithful, but an icy one from the general public. The Alberta Victuallers did no better with A.C. Windle, an anti-war editor from Chicago. Windle's outspoken opposition to the Great War allowed prohibitionists to reemphasize their argument that 'wet' sympathy meant a lack of patriotism, and that booze and Kaiserism were inextricably intertwined.[43] In Saskatchewan's referendum campaign of 1916, there simply was no opposition to the prohibitionists. The Government Dispensary system, in effect for more than a year, had decimated the ranks of hotel keepers, who generally provided the 'anti' leadership.

Because of a combination of new factors, all of them attributable to the Great War, the Prairie Provinces adopted prohibitory liquor legislation during the first two full years of the war. Provincial prohibition was not total prohibition, however. The right to restrict interprovincial trade belonged to the Dominion Government, and for this reason provincial Temperance Acts could not prevent individuals from importing liquor from another province for home consumption. A thriving interprovincial export business rapidly developed. Liquor dealers like William Ferguson of Brandon informed customers in the neighbouring province that "having decided to remain in business, and having still a large stock of draught Brandies, Scotch and Irish Whiskies, Rum, Holland Gin, Port and Sherries, [I] will continue to fill orders for *Saskatchewan*."[44] So much liquor came into Alberta across the British Columbia border that Bob Edwards' *Calgary Eye Opener* included the satirical "Society Note" that

Percy M. Winslow, one of our most popular and dissipated young men, left Monday morning for Field, B.C., where he has accepted a lucrative position as shipping clerk in one of the wholesale liquor houses. We predict a bright future for Percy.[45]

Western prohibitionists were determined not to stop short of the ultimate goal. To plug the loopholes in provincial legislation, they turned to Ottawa. Petitions, letters, and resolutions reminded Members of Parliament of the gravity of the situation, and urged them to introduce measures to "abolish the sale and manufacture of alcoholic liquors during wartime."[46] Prohibitionists gave enthusiastic support to Unionist candidates throughout the West during the election of 1917. Dominion prohibition was one of the many reforms which they expected to emanate from Unionism, and the Union Government's bipartisan character and crusading style appealed to the prohibitionist mind. Many influential prohibitionists campaigned on behalf of Union Government, among them Dr. Salem Bland, Rev. C. W. Gordon, and Mrs. Nellie McClung. Their work was rewarded, for shortly after they took office the Unionists introduced federal prohibition as an Order in Council under the War Measures Act, to come into effect April 1, 1918.

This made the prohibitionist victory in theory complete. All that remained was the task of making certain that the hard-won legislation was enforced. The war aided prohibitionists in this respect as well, and 1917–18 became the most effective years of the prohibition experiment. Even before the Dominion Government put an end to importation, Manitoba could report that "drunkenness had been reduced 87% for the first seven months of the operation of the (Prohibition) Act . . . all other crime has been reduced by 32%" and that "the support accorded the Act has surpassed the most sanguine expectations of its friends."[47] A jubilant Saskatchewan farm wife wrote to Premier Martin that "our little town, which was formerly a drunkard's paradise, since the banishment of the bars and dispensaries has assumed an air of thrift and sobriety."[48] Alberta's Chief Inspector under the Temperance Act claimed that under prohibition arrests of drunks were reduced by ninety *per cent*, and drinking, crime, and drunkenness decreased in each Prairie Province during the last two years of the war.[49] Once the war ended, however, the prohibitionist solution to society's problems became increasingly less effective.[50] The assault on prohibition began almost as soon as the war ended, and prohibitionists no longer had the wartime situation to interest the public in their programme. By 1924 all three Western Provinces had replaced prohibition with government operated liquor stores.

How much of the prohibitionists' fleeting success can be attributed to the Great War? To describe the imposition of prohibition as a purely wartime phenomenon would do an injustice to the work done before 1914 to convince Westerners of the need for liquor restriction. The foundations laid before the war began were a vital factor in the eventual success. But it was the emotional atmosphere of wartime which completed the prohibitionists' work, and which allowed prohibition to operate reasonably effectively for two short years. It was the Great War's accompanying national reappraisal which made once indifferent citizens listen to temperance arguments for the first time. Once this was accomplished, the majoritarian zeal which marked the domestic war effort ensured the right "psychological moment to strike the blow."[51] The *Saskatoon Phoenix* understood this process completely. "The temperance party," said an editorial, "has the war to thank for bringing public opinion *to a focus* on the matter of temperance reform."[52]

The second reformist group aided significantly by the Great War was the movement for woman's suffrage. The prohibition and suffrage movements were so closely intertwined in both programme and personnel that what advanced one cause almost automatically had the same effect on the other. In the three Western Provinces, the W.C.T.U. played a leading role in both movements and an ardent prohibitionist was usually an ardent suffragette as well. In many parts of the Prairies, the pre-war suffrage movement was the Equal Franchise Department of the local W.C.T.U.[53]

The war's favourable effect on the achievement of woman's suffrage is paradoxical, for prior to 1914, the woman's movement had thought of itself as pacifistic, and regarded war as one of woman's greatest enemies. War was part of the scheme of masculine domination which denied women an effective voice in society. "History, romance, legend, and tradition," wrote Nellie McClung, "have shown the masculine aspect of war and have surrounded it with a false glory and have sought to throw the veil of glamour over its hideous face." It was for the "false glory" that men went to war, abandoning women to face the true responsibilities of life alone.[54]

The Great War challenged these pacifistic assumptions. The wars which women had so roundly condemned had been the wars with which they themselves were familiar; the South African War, the Spanish American War, and colonial wars in Africa or the Far East. This new war was something very different. Germany was not the tiny Transvaal Republic, but an aggressive modern industrial power. Canada was not fighting for colonial conquest, but for 'liberty', 'justice', her very survival. Had it not been "the Kaiser and his brutal warlords" who had decided to "plunge all Europe into bloodshed?" And what about Belgium, gallant little Belgium where "the German soldiers made a shield of Belgium women and children in front of their Army; no child was too young, no woman too old, to escape their cruelty; no mother's prayers no child's appeal could stay their fury!"[55] Surely such inhumanity had to be checked lest it dominate first Europe, then the world.

As with the prohibitionist movement, the Great War's first effect on the suffrage movement was on its rhetoric. As Aileen S. Kraditor has pointed out, pre-war suffrage arguments can be divided into two categories, those based on justice and those based on expediency. The older, justice-oriented theme contended that women had a natural right to vote, as did all citizens. Arguments which emphasized expediency stressed instead the good effects that women's vote could accomplish in society.[56] Both types of argument were suitable to adaptation to the wartime atmosphere.

The new significance which the Great War gave to arguments based on justice is obvious. If the war were really "the greatest fight for liberty since the Dutch and English broke the power of Spain in the 16th Century", why, women asked, could they not enjoy in Canada the same liberty for which their sons were fighting and dying? Since the war was to be the "vindication of democracy", should not the democratic rights of millions of Canadian women be vindicated at the same time? Men who indulged in such descriptions of the war found themselves caught on the hook of their own eloquence.[57] As W. L. Morton has succinctly pointed out, "those who would carry democracy abroad must see that it is without reproach at home."[58]

Arguments based on expediency gained more power in wartime as well. The public came to accept the idea that the war could be used to redeem Western Canada from her pre-war materialism. This might be accomplished without women's votes, but what would happen when the war ended, and reforming zeal dissipated? Women's votes were necessary to prevent backsliding, and a return to evil in the post-war era. If this should happen, all the sacrifice, all the bloodshed, would be in vain. As a "war widow" told R. J. G. Stead,

> We women, we women of the war — we have nothing left to be selfish for. But we have the whole world to be unselfish for. It's all different, and it can never go back. *We won't let it go back. We've paid too much not to let it go back.*[59]

To prevent this "going back", women demanded the vote.

Not only the rhetoric, but the organization of the woman's movement was profoundly changed by the war. Initially, suffragists thought that the war would postpone the achievement of their goal, since it would force them to devote less time to suffrage activities. In reality, however, women's war work proved to be the greatest organizational aid the movement had ever been blessed with. The motivation provided by patriotic work increased the membership of existing women's groups, such as the United Farm Women of Alberta and Manitoba, and the I.O.D.E. Groups not formerly concerned with suffrage were brought into contact with their more activistic sisters in associations like the W.C.T.U. As these women gathered to produce incredible quantities of towels and toques, socks and shirts, balaclavas and bandages, they did not sit mute. Quiet housewives conversed with ardent advocates of equal suffrage, and while

> the nimble fingers of the knitting women are transforming balls of wool into socks and comforters, even a greater change is being wrought in their own hearts. Into their gentle souls have come bitter thoughts of rebellion. . . . They realize now something of what is back of all the opposition to the woman's advancement into all lines of activity and a share in government.[60]

In their Annual Report of 1918, the United Farm Women at Manitoba credited "war relief and patriotic work" with the formative role in the development of "a spirit of national sisterhood".[61]

It was not knitting for the Red Cross alone which produced this new frame of mind. The Census of 1911 had already revealed a tendency for increasing numbers of women to seek employment outside their homes, a tendency accentuated by the wartime shortage of manpower. More important, Western women were entering fields which had formerly tended to employ men. The number of women engaged in professional occupations, mainly teaching, increased 130% between 1911 and 1921. Alberta employed 630 more female teachers in 1916 than in 1914. Wartime vacancies also gave women an opportunity in Government Service, and Western governments employed four times as many in 1921 as they had ten years earlier.[62] New opportunities for women did not stop with employment. Women began to infiltrate other areas regarded once as *de facto* male preserves. At the University of Manitoba, for example, the "two major honours", student presidency and newspaper editorship, went to women in 1917.[63]

In addition to this role as men's replacements, women pointed to the fact that they bore much of the war's real suffering. They were the ones who struggled to keep farms working and families together in their husbands' absence. They were also the ones who had to carry on after husbands and sons were killed or maimed in France. Wilson Macdonald caught this sense of sacrifice in verse:

Ah! the battlefield is wider than the cannon's sullen roar;
And the women weep o'er battles lost or won.
For the man a cross of honour; but the crepe upon the door
For the girl behind the man behind the gun.[64]

Suffragists enjoyed this image of the noble woman, quietly continuing with her duty and bearing her grief in silence. In reality, however, everything done for the war effort by woman was given the widest possible publicity and described in the most heroic terms possible. Women's pages of western dailies were filled with stories on patriotic service done by women. The caption accompanying a series of pictures featured in the *Winnipeg Tribune* provides an example:

It is the men'warriors who reap all the material rewards of war; it is the men who have medals pinned upon their breasts; it is the men whom the world lauds as heroes. What of the women who labor and suffer at home in the cause of justice and freedom? In Winnipeg there are thousands of women who are doing as much to win battles as their soldier fathers, brothers, husbands and sons. There are women who are devoting every waking hour to the provision of comforts for boys at the front, and to planning for their care when they return.[65]

Magazine articles publicized the female side of the war effort, making it clear that women "count it an honour to engage in an occupation that strengthens the hands of our Empire."[66] Politicians especially were not allowed to forget women's contributions to the struggle with Germany. Letters reminded them how "truly and nobly our women have shown themselves equal to any emergency", and urged that women be given still greater responsibilities.[67]

Because of this surge of publicity, and partly by direct contact with the new woman, the image men held of women began to change. Some resented the fact that the Red Cross and other activities fell largely into female hands. F. W. Rolt, secretary of the Edmonton Red Cross, found woman's new assertiveness so alarming that he resigned his position, claiming that although "I don't wish to control the ladies, still less do I wish to be controlled by them."[68] But most men, even if they shared Rolt's fears about female domination, were grudgingly forced to concede that women were proving that they deserved equal citizenship. When the Dominion Parliament debated the question in 1917, for example, R. B. Bennett reversed his former opposition to woman's suffrage. Since women during the war were "discharging their full duties with respect to service", he felt that they must be admitted, "side by side with the male population . . . to exercise the highest rights and the highest functions of citizenship." Two Western members from the other side of the House voiced enthusiasm for Bennett's conversion. W. A. Buchanan stated simply that he was "in favour of women [sic] suffrage . . . because I believe the women have earned the right to that franchise since the war commenced." Michael Clark added that Bennett's opinion would be well received in the West, since it was "in accordance with the opinions of the vast majority of the people of Western Canada."[69]

It was the provincial governments, however, which acted first on the suffrage question. During the opening months of 1916, each Western Province granted its women the provincial franchise. Manitoba came first in January, and in March Alberta and Saskatchewan followed suit. Only one vote was cast against woman's suffrage in all three provinces, that by a French Canadian member of the Alberta House. Albertans made up for this by returning Mrs. Louise McKinney to the Legislature in the provincial election of the following year, and by naming Mrs. Emily Murphy as the first woman magistrate in the British Empire.[70]

300

The federal franchise was not to come as suddenly or as completely. The Dominion Government's grant of woman's suffrage came in stages. It was established in principle by the Military Voters Act, which gave the vote to women serving in the Armed Forces, or as nurses. The controversial Wartime Elections Act, enfranchising close female relatives of men serving overseas, established it further, but still not completely. Those women who gained the ballot, especially those in Western Canada, used it to vote for the government which had given it to them. Complete woman's suffrage, like prohibition, was one of the many things reformers hoped for from the newly elected Unionists. Suffragists were not disappointed. Prime Minister Borden personally introduced a franchise bill in April, 1918, and parliamentary assent followed rapidly. On January 1, 1919, less than two months after the war ended, the crusade for woman's suffrage was over, as far as the Prairie Provinces were concerned.

Woman's suffrage would have come without the Great War. There can be little doubt that the women of the Western Provinces would have gained the provincial franchise before too many years had passed, and the federal franchise would have followed eventually, although probably after a much longer struggle. But the Great War, with its impact on the suffragists' rationale, organization and public image, speeded the victory at both levels. Perhaps, however, the war's real importance to the woman's movement extends beyond the primary question of the right to vote. The dislocations of war won for women a foothold in fields of endeavour formerly reserved for men, and the traditional pattern of domestic service as the working woman's principal occupation. With these new opportunities came a new self-respect. By changing the average woman's image of herself and her position in a world dominated by men, the war advanced the cause of women in ways not simply political.

No other reform group was able to exploit the wartime situation as successfully as were the advocates of woman's suffrage and prohibition. The direct legislation movement enjoyed a brief moment of elation in

1916, when Manitoba's Norris government introduced an Initiative and Referendum Act. The Act was not accompanied by any large-scale campaign based on the mid-war enthusiasm for democracy, but was the fulfilment of a commitment Norris had made while Leader of the Opposition. The Saskatchewan Conservative Party attempted to resurrect the direct democracy issue during the 1917 Provincial Election, but were unable to use it to gain any political advantage.[71] This was in part because of the fact that a substantial number of those who had originally supported the initiative and referendum had done so as a means to obtain prohibition, not because of a strong belief in direct legislation for its own sake. By 1917 these people were satisfied, and saw no need to campaign for a tool they no longer needed to use.

The economic reforms sought by Western reformers proved even more difficult to obtain. Unlike prohibition, woman's suffrage, and direct legislation, most of these had to come from the Dominion Parliament, a body not as easily influenced as a provincial government. The war did pave the way for some specific objectives. During 1917 the first Canadian tax on incomes was imposed, and the principle of railway nationalization as exemplified by the case of the Canadian Northern was also well received in the West. Western support for Union Government was based on the assumption that more such action would be forthcoming, most particularly a reduction in the tariff. In this respect, and on the question of economic reform in general, Westerners were to be sadly disillusioned during the final year of war.

301

Notes

1. A. Richard Allen, *The Social Passion* (Toronto, 1971) Chapter 1, *passim*.
2. In Saskatchewan, for example, only six of the twenty-six local option referenda conducted in December, 1913, resulted in prohibitionist victories. Erhard Pinno, "Temperance and Prohibition in Saskatchewan", (unpub. M.A. Thesis, University of Saskatchewan, 1971) p. 29.
3. E. J. Chambers, "The Plebiscite and Referendum in Saskatchewan", (unpub. M.A. Thesis, University of Saskatchewan, 1965) Chapter 1.
4. Provincial Archives of Manitoba (P.A.M.) Colin H. Campbell Papers, R. P. Roblin to Colin H. Campbell, 9.1.14.
5. *Canadian Annual Review* (*C.A.R.*), 1914, p. 598.
6. The first phrase is from a resolution passed by the Manitoba Legislature on the third anniversary of the War's declaration, while the second is included in a circular written by W. R. Motherwell on behalf of the 1918 Victory Loan. P.A.M. Norris Papers, Box 2, Archives of Saskatchewan (A.S.), Motherwell Papers, p. 26267.
7. Rev. Canon Murray, "Canada's Place in the War", in Canadian Club of Winnipeg, *Annual Report 1913–14*, p. 71.
8. Mrs. Louis McKinney, "President's Address", in Alberta W.C.T.U. *Report of the Annual Convention 1915*.
9. Nellie L. McClung, *In Times Like These* (New York, 1915), p. 161.
10. Clifford Sifton, "Foundations of the New Era", in J.O. Miller, *The New Era in Canada* (Toronto, 1918), pp. 37–38.
11. A. S., Saskatchewan Grain Growers Association, *Convention Report*, 12.2.17.
12. Mrs. H. V. Plumptre, "Some Thought on the Suffrage", in Miller, *New Era*, pp. 328–9.
13. Archives of the Glenbow Foundation (Glenbow) Alberta W.C.T.U. Collection no. 1, f.35, *Report of the Annual Convention, 1915*, p. 30.
14. Plumptre, *op. cit.*, p. 329.
15. McClung, *In Times Like These*, p. 5, R. E. Spence, *Prohibition in Canada* (Toronto, 1919), p. 71.

16. Sara Rowell Wright, "The W.C.T.U. Program" in *The Social Service Congress of Canada* (Ottawa, 1914), p. 322.
17. McClung, *In Times Like These*, p. 165.
18. *Manitoba Free Press*, 6.3.16.
19. *Grain Growers' Guide*, 16.6.15.
20. Frances M. Beynon in *Ibid.*, 30.5.17.
21. Ralph Connor, *The Sky Pilot* in *No Man's Land* (New York, 1917) pp. 149–50.
22. A.S., Martin Papers, Ladies of North Battleford Methodist Church to W. M. Martin, 7.11.16, p. 31654. See also Alberta W.C.T.U. Minute Book, 2.1.15; and P.A.M., Manitoba W.C.T.U. Collection, Winnipeg District Minute Book, 9.12.14.
23. Motherwell Papers, Mrs. W. R. Motherwell, Address at Lemberg, Sask. 5.12.16. p. 123.
24. A.S., Walter Scott Papers, Capt. J. L. R. Parsons to Scott, 25.3.15, p. 59695. See also Pinno, *op. cit.*, p. 121; John H. Thompson "The Prohibition Question in Manitoba, 1892–1928", (unpub. M.A. Thesis University of Manitoba, 1969), p. 2; and R.I. McLean, "Temperance and Prohibition in Alberta, 1875–1915", (unpub. M.A. Thesis, University of Calgary, 1970); p. 134.
25. Glenbow, Calgary Brewing and Malting Collection, W. Towers to A. E. Cross, 1.1.18, f.577.
26. *Manitoba Free Press*, 7.3.16.
27. *Edmonton Bulletin*, 20.7.15. See also *Regina Leader*, 24.2.15.
28. *Manitoba Free Press*, 7.3.16.
29. McClung, *In Times Like These*, p. 170.
30. This quotation is from a resolution of the Manitoba Rural Deanery of the Church of England, *Manitoba Free Press*, 1.3.16. The Anglican conversion to prohibition is discussed in McLean, *op. cit.*, pp. 111–112. For the Orange Order's opinion, see *C.A.R.*, 1915, p. 665 and P.A.M., R. P. Roblin Papers, J. J. Stitt to R. P. Roblin, 3.3.15. For an I.O.D.E. attitude see Provincial Archives of Alberta (P.A.A.). Beaverhouse I.O.D.E. Minute Book, 1.10.14. The Winnipeg Canadian Club's views are expressed in its *Annual Report*, 1913–14, pp. 6–7.
31. Lionel Orlikow, "A Survey of the Reform Movement in Manitoba, 1910–1920", (unpub. M.A. Thesis, U. of Manitoba, 1955), p. 150.
32. Scott Papers, Scott to Willoughby, 1.12.14, p. 48455; Levi Thomson to Scott, 8.4.15, p. 48503; Motherwell to Scott, 18.12.14, p. 12889; Scott to S. G. Hill, 1.7.15, p. 13300; Scott to J. H. Ross, 12.4.15, p. 13650.
33. A.S., J. A. Calder Papers, Calder to G. H. V. Bulyea, 23.3.15, G4, p. 11.
34. R. I. McLean, *op. cit.*, p. 135.
35. Motherwell Papers, T. A. Mitchell to Motherwell, 22.1.16, f. 71(2).
36. *The Western Prairie* (Cypress River, Manitoba), 2.3.16.
37. Calder to Bulyea, 23.3.15, Calder Papers, G. 4, p. 11. Opposition to prohibition during wartime was notable among those of German birth or descent. The German language *Der Courier, Der Nordwesten*, and *St. Peters Bote* all editorialized against prohibition, and the German Canadian Alliance of Saskatchewan publicly denounced the "aggressive and unscrupulous agitation" of the prohibitionists. See Erhard Pinno, *op. cit.*, pp. 121–3. Thompson, *op. cit.*, pp. 28–9, and *C.A.R.*, 1914, p. 630.
38. *Manitoba Free Press*, 6.3.16: *Canadian Farmer*, November, 1916, translation in Martin Papers, pp. 31616–8.
39. Alberta W.C.T.U. *Annual Report*, 1915, p. 60.
40. *Manitoba Free Press*, 14.3.16.
41. Pinno, *op. cit.*, p. 122; *Le Courrier de l'Ouest* (Edmonton), 1.7.16; *Le Manitoba*, 13.4.16. The comparative effectiveness of patriotic arguments for prohibition on French Canadians and non-Anglo Saxon immigrants can be demonstrated by an examination of referendum results in the Alberta Constituencies of Victoria, Whitford, St. Albert, and Beaver River. All four rejected prohibition, but Victoria and Whitford, with heavy Ukrainian populations, did so by the relatively narrow margin of 1392 to 1022. St. Albert and Beaver River, with largely French Canadian electorates, recorded a combined majority of 889 against prohibition, 1484 to 595.
42. Calgary Brewing and Malting Collection, A. E. Cross to D. R. Ker, 24.3.15, f.550.
43. *Edmonton Bulletin*, 6.7.15.
44. Advertisement in Motherwell Papers, f. 71(2).
45. *Calgary Eye Opener*, 8.7.16.
46. Manitoba W.C.T.U. Collection, Recording Secretary's Book, 15.2.16.
47. Province of Manitoba, *Annual Report on the Temperance Act*, Sessional Paper no. 13, 1917.
48. Martin Papers, Mrs. G. V. Jewett to Martin, 23.4.17, p. 31759.
49. R. E. Popham and W. Schmit, *Statistics of Alcohol Use and Alcoholism in Canada* (Toronto, 1958), pp. 48–53. See also James H. Gray, *The Boy from Winnipeg* (Toronto, 1970), p. 126 and *Red Lights on the Prairies* (Toronto, 1971), pp. 149–151.
50. Alberta W.C.T.U. Collection no. 1, Social Service Council Convention Minutes, 18.2.19 f. 7.
51. Scott Papers, Levi Thomson to Scott, 8.4.15, p. 48503.

52. *Saskatoon Phoenix*, 19.3.15. Richard Allen has suggested that prohibition was "almost predictable" in Manitoba and Saskatchewan before the war began in 1914, (*Social Passion*, p. 22). This judgment seems exaggerated, given the lack of success of local option ballots, the defeat of the Norris Liberals in Manitoba, and comments such as those of Calder and Scott cited above, p. 10.

53. See June Menzies, "Votes for Saskatchewan's Women", in N. Ward ed., *Politics in Saskatchewan* (Don Mills, 1968), p. 90, Thomson, *op. cit.*, pp. 59–60, and C. L. Cleverdon, *The Woman Suffrage Movement in Canada* (Toronto, 1950), pp. 49–64.

54. McClung, *In Times Like These*, p. 14. See also Carol Lee Bacchi Ferraro, "The Ideas of the Canadian Suffragists, 1890–1920", (unpub. M.A. Thesis, McGill University, 1970), pp. 109–111.

55. McClung, *op. cit.*, p. 27.

56. Aileen S. Kraditor, *The Ideas of the Woman Suffrage Movement* (New York, 1965), p. 38–63.

57. The first phrase is from P.A.C., Dafoe Papers, Clifford Sifton to J. W. Dafoe, 21.9.14. The second is from Stephen Leacock, "Democracy and Social Progress", in J. O. Miller, *New Era*, p. 13.

58. W. L. Morton, "The Extension of the Franchise in Canada; A Study in Democratic Nationalism", *Canadian Historical Association Report*, 1943, p. 79.

59. R. J. C. Stead, *The Cow Puncher* (Toronto, 1918), p. 342.

60. McClung, *In Times Like These*, pp. 28–29. For some examples of the effects of the war in increasing the membership of women's organizations, see Glenbow, United Farmers of Alberta Collection, f. 35; Scott Papers, Eva Sherrock to Scott, 14.2.16, p. 59505; *Manitoba Free Press*, 27.2.15. For a good example of the cooperation among organizations promoted by the war, see Alberta W.C.T.U. Collection no. 2, North West Calgary Union, Minutes, 4.11.15, f. 5.

61. P.A.M., United Farmers of Manitoba Collection, United Farm Women report, 1918.

62. The Census of 1921 revealed a sixty-three *percent* increase in the number of women in the western provinces employed outside their homes. For comparative figures see Canada. *Fifth Census*, 1911, vol. VI, p. 10, passim, and *Sixth Census*, 1921, vol. IV, p. 10 passim. The statistics on women teachers in Alberta are taken from Alberta Department of Education, *Annual Report*, 1916, pp. 16–17.

63. *Manitoba Free Press*, 4.10.17.

64. Wilson Macdonald, "The Girl Behind the Man Behind the Gun", in *Song of the Prairie Land* (Toronto, 1918), pp. 124–6.

65. *Winnipeg Tribune*, 9.10.15.

66. P.A.A., Miriam Elston Scrapbooks, "The Home Shall be an Honoured Place", *Everywoman's World*, November 1916.

67. Scott Papers, Ella B. Carroll to Scott, 1.2.16, p. 59492; Norris Papers, W. R. Wood to T. C. Norris, 26.1.18, Box 2. In his work on the domestic impact of the war on Great Britain, Arthur Marwick describes British women as "a gigantic mutual-admiration circle" during wartime. Marwick, *The Deluge* (London, 1965), p. 96. Marwick's comment can be applied to their Canadian counterparts as well.

68. University of Alberta Archives, Henry Marshall Tory Papers, F. W. Rolt to H. M. Tory, 15.15.15. f 14082A.

69. Canada, House of Commons, *Debates*, 1917, vol. II, pp. 1515–19.

70. L. G. Thomas, *The Liberal Party in Alberta* (Toronto, 1959), p. 165. For a detailed description of the passage of each suffrage act, see Cleverdon, *op. cit.*, pp. 46–83.

71. Chambers, "Plebiscite and Referendum", p. 63.

Tomorrow's Metropolis: The Urban Reform Movement in Canada, 1880–1920 *

PAUL RUTHERFORD

Between the census of 1881 and the census of 1921, the urban population of Canada increased in absolute terms from 1.1 million to 4.3 million, and in proportional terms from one-quarter to one-half the total population.[1] This demographic revolution was largely unexpected. True, the Canadians

* From *Canadian Historical Association Historical Papers*, 1971, 203–224. Copyright by Canadian Historical Association. Reprinted by permission.

of the 1860s had envisaged a great and populous future, but as an agricultural nation with a vast western frontier, not an urban frontier. As early as the 1870s, however, newspapers commented upon the steady drift of population towards the cities and by the turn of the century the theme of rural depopulation had become common throughout eastern Canada. Worse, urban growth led more to the expansion of cities than towns, which threatened to change the whole economic and social character of the Dominion. In a prophetic passage, J. S. Woodsworth warned that the railway, the telephone, and similar technological innovations were carrying the city into the countryside, a process which would ultimately give the whole nation a metropolitan image.[2]

The Canadian response to the urban fact, especially to the appearance of the "big city", was generally unfavorable. At one level, it it true, cities were regarded as the physical embodiment of progress, the home of literature and the arts. Yet many people, looking to the sad experience of Europe and America, feared the further spread of the city.[3] Rural apologists emphasized the debilitating influences of city life upon the individual.[4] Social conservatives inveighed against the rampant materialism of the new culture.[5] Even urban writers admitted that there was a dark side to the city where disease, crime, prostitution, and general misery flourished.[6] In the city all the ills of modern society were concentrated and highly visible. By the beginning of the twentieth century, it was widely accepted that urban growth posed a serious menace to the future of the nation.

It is only in retrospect that reform seems the logical solution to the urban crisis. Well into the twentieth century, there were public leaders who continued to hope that a new wave of agricultural development would direct the city dweller back to the farm.[7] It took four decades of agitation before the reform movement achieved a national prominence. During the 1880s, various daily newspapers, the exponents of what was called "people's journalism", turned to the idea of urban reform, then attracting considerable attention in the United States.[8] These papers appealed to the expanded reading public of their cities, which was as interested in urban affairs as in provincial and national problems. The Montreal *Star* launched a series of crusades against municipal corruption and incompetence and sponsored such welfare projects as the "Fresh Air Fund" to send poor women and children out of the city in the summer months. The Toronto *World* appeared as the champion of the interests of the people in the city's many battles with local monopolists and utility companies. The Vancouver *News-Advertiser* argued the case of labor and demanded the increased political involvement of all city dwellers (excepting, of course, the Chinese) in civic affairs. Though inspired as much by hopes of a higher circulation as civic spirit, these papers popularized the idea of reform long before intellectuals discovered urban problems.

By 1900, however, the journalist had been replaced by the expert. In 1897 Herbert Ames, a businessman, published *"The City Below the Hill,"* a statistical analysis of social conditions in Montreal. A decade later, another businessman, S. Morley Wickett of Toronto, edited an anthology

304

on municipal government with wide-ranging suggestions for reform. In 1910 in Quebec a somewhat different study of municipal government by a one-time *bleu* journalist and provincial minister, G.-A. Nantel, was published posthumously by friends. This book, *La Métropole de Demain*, proposed a scheme of metropolitan federation and civic beautification for the island of Montreal, based upon the experience of Paris. And in 1911 appeared J. S. Woodsworth's *My Neighbor*, an impassioned plea for the reform of living conditions in Canada's cities.

These works were only a portion of the material which reached the public. No annual session of the Canadian or Empire Clubs, those so eminent representatives of opinion in English Canada, seemed complete without one address on urban problems — and not only by Canadians, but by visitors from Britain and the United States.[9] These were supplemented by conferences sponsored by the churches, women's organizations, and eventually town planning and civic improvement associations. Specialized magazines, like the *Municipal World* and the *Western Municipal News*, appeared as house organs of municipal government and consistent advocates of reform. Even academics joined the movement: in 1913 the new Canadian Political Science Association held a special seminar on municipal government, involving American and Canadian municipal officials.[10]

Urban reform was less a single creed and more a common approach to a wide variety of urban problems. Early reformers concentrated upon the redemption of the urban environment, a theme which extended back to the mid-century. The old ideal of civic improvement had emphasized the construction of stately buildings, colleges and academies, eventually libraries and museums, to bolster the prestige of the city.[11] But as the cities became more and more congested, this concern was replaced by the attempt to make the city healthy, moral, and equitable.

Public health reform was founded upon the sanitary ideal, a British doctrine long popular in Canada. Originally the sanitarians concentrated upon the issues of pollution and pure water. Even before the acceptance of the germ theory, it was widely recognized that water pollution was a public hazard and waterworks were one of the first utilities subject to direct municipal improvement. In the 1870s Toronto invested some $2 000 000 in the construction of an effective waterworks system.[12] By this time, of course, the city was moving into the general field of health control, with an emphasis upon the prevention of disease. After 1880 reformers tackled the problems of vaccination, pure food, and living conditions, especially as these related to the health of the poor and the proletariat.[13] Such reform was not always welcomed — in 1885 during the short but severe Montreal smallpox epidemic, spokesmen for the francophone proletariat fiercely opposed the whole idea of vaccination.[14] Ideally, reformers hoped to impose a strict code of public health upon all city dwellers. Without pure environment, they warned, the city would soon die. Charles Hastings, the medical officer of Toronto during the war, pointed out that the contamination of any class would soon lead to the infection of the rest of the community. Disease did not respect social standing.[15]

During the 1880s clergymen, temperance societies, and women's organizations set out on a long crusade to purify city life. William Howland, elected in 1885 as Toronto's first reform mayor, was a stout advocate of moral reform — in fact, he founded that city's department of morality — and he left an influential party on city council which carried on his work for decades. These crusaders were most famous for their attacks upon organized sin — the saloon, the gambling den, the house of prostitution, even the theatre. They were convinced that vice was so much a fact of city life that it menaced the national destiny.[16] They managed to persuade provincial and municipal authorities to pass laws to stamp out immorality, to regulate the behaviour of the wealthy as well as the poor and the immigrants, and to protect the youth of Canada.[17] They sponsored a variety of moral clean-up campaigns in each city to enforce these laws, a task which was not always easy or successful. In Winnipeg, after an initial assault on prostitution, the chief of police contacted the leading madam of the day, Minnie Woods, and re-established a segregated red-light district, where the police could at least control the activities of prostitutes.[18] In Halifax war-time prohibition closed down legal bars but left the city to "blind pigs" (illegal saloons), generally in league with brothels, which expanded to meet the needs of thousands of soldiers and sailors.[19] Still it is little wonder that these reformers were despised by many — C. S. Clarke, an opinionated Torontonian, denounced them as a small group of pious fanatics who bothered the respectable and terrorized the weak.[20] Moral reform was an experiment in social engineering, an attempt to force the city dweller to conform to the mores of the church-going middle class.

In attitude and in personnel, moral reform was closely connected with social welfare. Howland, for example, throughout his civic career, was devoted to the cause of the underprivileged. Traditionally the care of the urban poor was the task of the churches and private charities with some relief services supplied by the municipalities and the provincial government.[21] As with so many other institutions, this welfare system collapsed under the impact of urban growth. In both his books, *My Neighbor* and *Strangers at Our Gates*, J. S. Woodsworth drew upon his own experiences and those of others to paint what to contemporaries must have been an incredible picture of spiritual and physical degradation in Canada's big cities. Some humanitarian reformers like J. J. Kelso of Toronto, who had been active since the 1880s, concentrated upon child welfare. They reasoned that by saving the young, they could ultimately save the future, an idea which particularly appealed to middle-class Canadians. These people saw the child as tomorrow's hope for a better society and invested heavily in education as an instrument of social and moral improvement. Thus the concern for a special children's charter, boys' camp, parks and recreational centres, and new schools, all to protect the innocence of the child and to mold his character according to the rational ethic.[22]

But other reformers, notably J. S. Woodsworth, refused to forget the adult generation of poor. Woodsworth rejected the notion that the majority of the poor were undeserving, that they had failed because of some weakness in their make-up. Rather, social and economic conditions, perhaps the very structure of society, had prevented the poor from achieving any kind of success. Surely the fruits of progress could be more evenly distributed? Woodsworth called upon the well-off to recognize their responsibility to the underprivileged — thus the title *My Neighbor*. In fact, civic authorities did respond to the misery of the poor. Speaking to an Ottawa audience in 1914, Mayor Hocken of Toronto claimed that his city had taken up a wide variety of "human services" — public recreation, the care of the feeble-minded, food inspection, unemployment relief, and the like.[23] This "new spirit", as Hocken called it, was laying the foundations of the welfare state.

In 1902, in his classic survey of city government, S. Morley Wickett concluded that the "corporation question" in all its manifold aspects was of overshadowing importance to urban reform. By the "corporation question" he meant utility regulation and ownership, issues which had became more and more pressing towards the end of the nineteenth century. Waterworks, street railways, electric power, and the telephone systems, all constituted the physical plant of the city and the basis for continued urban expansion. The "utility base" of the cities had been largely developed by the efforts of private capital, usually on extremely generous terms to the entrepreneurs. Even though most utility companies performed with reasonable efficiency, there seemed an inherent conflict between civic requirements and business profits.[24]

It was this assumption which gave rise to the long controversy over municipal ownership. Drawing upon American and British experience, reformers like Wickett concluded that civic authorities must take control of the utility base. They argued that utility development was very different from other kinds of business endeavor. The utilities were in fact natural monopolies since any competition was both wasteful and expensive. Companies were able to exploit this captive market with little regard for the interests of the city. Because of their wealth, they could thwart any efforts to regulate their activities. Municipal ownership would allow the city to extend utilities into suburban areas, reduce service rates, and increase civic revenues.[25] Of course, not all Canadians agreed with this appraisal. However argued, municipal ownership was an assault upon the national ethic of individual enterprise. Theoretical questions aside, one noted economist, James Mavor of the University of Toronto, warned that public ownership everywhere had failed. Because they were essentially political bodies, subject to the changing impulses of the public mind, governments simply could not manage a business enterprise. Efficient, cheap service was lost in a welter of bureaucratic red-tape and noisy rhetoric.[26]

Whatever the merit of his conclusions, Mavor had taken up a losing cause. True, the campaign for municipal ownership was not immediately victorious. In Montreal between 1904 and 1909, the utility companies easily overcame a threat of municipalization and remained largely untouched

307

for the next thirty years.[27] In 1910, after running its power and transport utilities for fifteen years, Moncton returned these facilities to a private company, apparently to save money.[28] But these were exceptions. As early as 1893 Guelph had purchased its gas works and electric light and power plants.[29] In 1901 delegates from Quebec and Ontario, led by O. A. Howland, mayor of Toronto, founded the Union of Canadian Municipalities specifically to combat the machinations of utility companies.[30] In 1905 the new Whitney Government in Ontario organized the Public Hydro Commission to provide cheap power for industries and cities.[31] In 1907 the Manitoba government purchased the young provincial telephone system and expanded it across the province.[32] By 1920 the idea of municipal control, if not always municipal ownership, had won numerous converts in cities and towns.

308   After 1900 urban reformers, inspired by the town planning craze, became aware of their ability to mold the physical character of Canadian cities. The concept of town planning originated in the so-called City Beautiful and Garden City movements common to Europe, Britain, and the United States and popular ever since the Chicago Exposition of 1893 and the Letchworth experiment in England in 1903.[33] The City Beautiful movement updated the old ideal of civic improvement — the elimination of unsightly civic architecture and its replacement by attractive buildings, widened streets, promenades, parks, and trees. G.-A. Nantel wished to turn Montreal into this kind of City Beautiful. The Garden City and Garden suburb ideas were more drastic attempts to create communities separate from existing urban centres and without their problems. These schemes were an extension and a rationalization of the movement to the suburbs and an attempt to revive the ideal of the village community.[34] In 1912 at the Canadian Club of Montreal, Adam Shortt unveiled a fantastic scheme of urban depopulation to redeem the life of the city dweller throughout Canada. Envisaging a network of rapid transit systems, he imagined the movement of city workers out to country homes where they could enjoy the benefits of rural life and perhaps indulge in a little farming to supplement their incomes.[35] In essence, he was proposing the ruralization of the city. Such nostalgia for country life was implicit in all these schemes.

Many town planning experts, like the influential Thomas Adams, a Scotchman attached to the Commission of Conservation, were very conscious of the need to disassociate their projects from this kind of nostalgia. Their sensibility was injured by the disjointed civic topography left in the wake of the early developers, who in their rush to accommodate new industry, the rural migrant, and the foreign immigrant cared little whether they created a livable environment.[36] These town planners emphasized that they were not merely concerned with the aesthetic but with pressing economic and health problems. Town planning, noted Clifford Sifton, was "a rational scheme of supervising the conditions in which the people of our great cities live."[37] It was practical and economical, involving the doctor, the engineer, and the businessman as well as the artist and the architect.

Just prior to World War I, more and more municipal and provincial authorities became converts of the movement and an incredible number of town plans were initiated throughout Canada — for example, the proliferation of special zoning by-laws to protect residential areas, the Halifax reconstruction scheme after the disastrous explosion of 1917, and the new steel town of Ojibway projected for Southwestern Ontario.[38]

Perhaps the most publicized scheme was that put forward by the Toronto Harbor Commission. At an estimated cost of twenty-five million dollars, using civic and federal capital, the Commission proposed to redevelop the Toronto waterfront as a multiple-use site with improved warehousing and commercial facilities, room for industrial growth, better housing for workers, and a recreational area, all tied to the rest of the city by means of an expanded rapid transit system. Although controlled by the Commission, the project was in fact an alliance of private and public interests — the all-important railway companies had early given their approval — so that all might profit. It was an expensive investment in the future, but the initial cost would soon be recouped by the attraction of new business to Toronto. Waste lands, then largely valueless, would become industrial areas. And Torontonians as a whole would benefit from the use of the waterfront as a public park.[39]

309

The Toronto harbor project, of course, stood in a long tradition of developmental schemes with which Canadians and businessmen were very familiar.[40] A more novel concern of town planners was urban congestion and the appearance of the slum and the immigrant ghetto. In the years after 1895 a series of studies by such people as Herbert Ames, J. J. Kelso, J. S. Woodsworth, and Bryce Stewart showed that all major cities, even small centres like Port Arthur and Fort William, housed an urban proletariat, in part foreign-born, generally poor and concentrated in crowded subdivisions, slums, or shanty-towns.[41] Like the United States, suggested Charles Hodgetts, we had "our Little Italys, our Little Londons, and our Chinatowns, devoid of the simplest of modern sanitary requirements."[42] These slums were "cancerous sores" on the body politic, "sources of bacteria" spreading disease, crime, and discontent throughout the city. They menaced the moral and physical character of Canadian manhood and thus the racial future of the whole nation. Some alarmists even feared a red revolution sparked by the disgruntled proletariat and the immigrants. But all reformers charged that slums were a reflection upon the nation; no civilized society could allow its citizens to suffer in this way.[43]

Yet, without tremendous expenditures, how could the nation end the slum problem? Clifford Sifton pointed out that the much-heralded suburban movement was no solution; it was actually a movement of the prosperous, not the poor, away from the urban core.[44] Some reformers tried to meet the problem with new housing laws to control tenements and to maintain minimum standards of hygiene and health — in effect to check the further spread of the slum and to ameliorate conditions within it.[45] Others attempted to get business interests involved in cheap housing, a primitive form of urban renewal. Herbert Ames advocated such a plan of privately financed workers' homes and this was apparently carried out on a limited scale by G. Frank Beer in Toronto. During the post-war reconstruction clamour, there was a demand for direct state involvement in the housing business. In fact Thomas Adams did head a commission which co-ordinated a joint federal-provincial loan scheme for cheap housing, essentially to meet the needs of returned soldiers.[46] All of these reformers, it should be emphasized, were convinced of the moral and physical virtues of the single-family dwelling — they wanted a nation of homes, not of apartment houses.

The steadily expanding services expected of city governments resulted in mounting costs and in increased tax burden, neither of which were popular. In 1907 Wickett pointed out that "the annual expenditure of Winnipeg clearly exceeds that of Manitoba; Montreal's that of the province of Quebec; and until the present year Toronto's that of the province of Ontario."[47] Reformers and municipal officials constantly searched for new methods of meeting tax requirements. Some of the impetus behind the campaign for municipal ownership was this desire for greater revenue. Most cities switched from the confused personal property tax system to a more specific and just business tax. Between 1890 and 1910, western cities experimented widely with variants of Henry George's single tax idea, exempting at least part of the value of improvements upon land.[48] Of course, all civic leaders paid at least lip-service to economy and retrenchment, but it was impossible to implement these axioms with any permanent success. Businessmen were particularly outraged by the casual attitude which civic authorities adopted towards new expenditures. Sir Frederick William-Taylor of the Bank of Montreal insisted that "the outstanding matter calling for municipal reform in this country is with regard to borrowing powers."[49] He believed that Canadian cities, especially in the west, had accumulated debts at a per capita rate out of all proportion to the rest of the world.

The success of the reform idea was heavily dependent upon the active support of municipal government. Only the state had sufficient authority to impose order on the chaos of city life. But even before 1880 it was clear that the existing councils of untrained aldermen were ill-equipped to deal with the multiplicity of new problems. Too often they were dominated by ward-heelers and partymen — individuals who were more concerned with private gain, local interests, and politics than with the city's welfare.[50] Worse, the expansion of civic responsibilities had vastly increased the opportunities for and the profits of municipal corruption. These evils seemed so pressing that for some time the urban reform movement was closely identified in the mind of public at large with the reform of municipal government.

In 1885 W. H. Howland, a business leader and child welfare advocate in Toronto, and H. Beaugrand, editor of Montreal's Liberal paper *La Patrie*, won the mayoralty of their respective cities as declared reform candidates.

310

But they and later reform mayors found it difficult to realize their promises. It was hard to overcome civic apathy, to maintain reform morale and cohesion, and to get rid of the "old guard" politicians. During the mid-1890s in Montreal, to meet these problems, Herbert Ames and like-minded English civic leaders constructed a political machine to combat the "old guard' at the ward level.[51] Thus began a battle which lasted two decades between, on the one hand, a reform coalition, supported by many English voters, certain businessmen, and French-Canadian progressives like Bourassa and Asselin, and, on the other hand, a mixed bag of opportunists who had the backing of most French Canadians, especially the clerical and artisan classes. In 1914 this classic battle ended with the victory of Médéric Martin, a colourful and unscrupulous cigar-maker, who during his long rule crushed the reform-progressive coalition.[52] Elsewhere in Canada, the conflict was rarely so fierce or reform so decisively beaten. In fact, municipal politicians generally paid lip-service to reform, though their active support for the idea was ofttimes sporadic and self-interested.[53] It was this hyprocrisy which Stephen Leacock brutally satirized in his account of "the great fight for clean government."

As the early reformers learned to their chagrin, the mere election of honest men did not ensure the ability of the council to handle the rapacious utility companies or to foster civic improvement. In the 1890s reformers began a search for new governmental structures. To ensure continuity, the ward system was rationalized and the length of term for aldermen increased. To enlarge the powers of the executive, the Board of Control was instituted first in Toronto (1897) and later in several cities as a kind of municipal cabinet.[54] Some enthusiasts, like the young Frank Underhill, supported the American idea of commission government, rule by a small body of elected or even appointed officials.[55] These measures were an attempt to divide legislative and executive functions and to fix responsibility, thereby reducing political influences. Of course, this emphasis upon structures produced its own reaction. Throughout, some reformers, especially those who were actually involved in municipal government, argued that "good men" were essential, no matter the structure. Ultimately, it was the quality of elected officials who would determine the character of municipal government.[56]

Whether concerned with structures or men, reformers agreed that city government must be more responsive to the interests of the whole community. They looked upon the city as a single entity. Urban society was founded upon interdependence: "City life," claimed J. S. Woodsworth, "is like a spider's web — pull one thread and you pull every thread."[57] Thus all urban problems, not merely those relating to utilities and town planning, had a general import. In the past, argued reformers, too much attention had been paid to particularist interests. Wealthy neighbourhoods had benefited from local improvement schemes at the expense of slums and suburbs. Entrenched neighbourhood politicians had hindered the implementation of general reform measures necessary to the city's welfare.[58] It was essential to subordinate the neighbourhood to the city. In future, the civic leadership must look to the whole electorate and not to its constituent elements.

Then as now, reformers were continually foiled by civic apathy. Even when they managed to win over municipal officials they found it difficult to mobilize public support, especially if their suggestions required increased expenditures. Not surprisingly, frustrated reformers were inclined to blame such defeats upon a conspiracy of the cruder elements in municipal politics. There was a significant though muted fear of the urban proletariat and the immigrant vote, both of which could lead to the dominance of American-style city bosses. Some reformers, like Wickett, seemed to favour the restricted franchise which would give the respectable property-holder decisive power in civic affairs.[59] One of the reasons for proposals to rationalize the ward system, particularly by creating enlarged wards, was in the hope of undermining the strength of the lower-class vote.[60] On the whole, though, reformers placed greater emphasis upon popular involvement in municipal politics through civic organizations, a lowered franchise, and the plebiscite — in Regina and Edmonton, civic leaders even experimented with "direct democracy" incorporating the referendum system in their respective city charters.[61] Time after time, reformers called upon municipal leaders to educate the public, to make the electors aware of civic problems. Reformers seemed convinced, at least at the level of rhetoric, that a vigorous "civic patriotism" would eventually overcome particularism and partisanship, freeing municipal government from the corrupting influence of special interests.[62] In reality "civic patriotism" meant a blanket commitment to the schemes of the reformers.

More and more, the reformers placed their final trust in the bureaucratic method, that essential handmaiden of modern collectivism. The bureaucratic method was a radically new approach to society and problem-solving. At the theoretical level, it was founded upon the burgeoning science of statistics. This science, in vogue since the last quarter of the nineteenth century, seemed able to rationalize the complex and mysterious world created by the new urban-industrial order. The statistician broke down situations into their constituent elements, transferred these results to paper, and thereby rendered understandable the "real world."[63] In his study of a particular area in Montreal, Herbert Ames analysed the inhabitants as an economic class of varying income units, as ethnic groups, and as home-owners, piling category on top of category, and eventually creating a composite picture of their physical needs. Although very ambitious, Ames' survey was only one of the innumerable municipal studies sponsored by reform organizations and individuals, dealing with relief cases, crime and disease, municipal finances, and so on. Such studies were essential as a means of educating the public and projecting sound reform programmes — without statistics, complete and standardized, there could be no effective planning, no slum clearance, no tax reform.[64]

At the institutional level, the bureaucratic method required the creation

312

of an autonomous and trained administration dedicated to the twin ideals of economy and efficiency. To the reformers expert knowledge was a near panacea. This was the beginning of the age of the specialist and the professional. The reformers hoped to minimize the influence of the amateur in all departments of civic government, to take administration out of politics.[65] Wickett pointed to Germany where leading civic adminstrators were trained before they took office.[66] There were suggestions that Canadian academics become involved in municipal research and the training of municipal experts. Reformers demanded the multiplication of bureaucratic structures, special and permanent commissions, advisory posts and the like, to deal in detail with the community.[67] Responding to reform pleas, especially after 1900, municipal governments did create formidable civic bureaucracies to control police, public health, utilities, parks and recreation, and social welfare.[68] To a degree, this appeared to be a devolution of authority; in fact, it was a centralization of authority in the hands of professionals, well-nigh independent of the electorate, with a vested interest in the success of the reform movements. This latent authoritarianism was tempered by the assumption that the bureaucrat would move in accordance with a right-thinking public.

313

The reform idea had an import far beyond the immediate urban setting. Some reformers and municipal officials, it is true, did seem to favour the separation of the city and the wider provincial community. These "home rulers" argued that provincial assemblies were dominated by rural members and therefore the provincial governments were largely indifferent to municipal problems. W. D. Lighthall, secretary of the Union of Canadian Municipalities, believed that the cities must have complete control over all their utilities.[69] W. F. Maclean, owner of the Toronto *World*, argued that Toronto should extend its control over the surrounding countryside and regulate its own affairs without outside interference.[70] Similarly, G.-A. Nantel wished to consolidate all major governmental functions on the island of Montreal under one general scheme of metropolitan federation. Such beliefs led to experimentation with existing incorporation and municipal acts — in Toronto a call for a special charter to meet the city's peculiar needs, in Edmonton a less specific grant of municipal powers to ensure flexibility and freedom.[71]

But "home rule" never secured as much support in Canada as in the United States. As most reformers recognized, it was hardly practicable to establish an inflexible division between civic and provincial affairs. Cities were legal creatures of the provinces and schemes for municipal reorganization, public health, or social welfare required provincial approval. Battles between the cities and utility companies, such as the public hydro controversy in Ontario, the campaign against corporate domination in Montreal, and the drive for provincialization of telephones in Manitoba and Alberta, all involved province-wide interests and consequently these battles were transferred to the legislative assemblies. Thus reformers pressured provincial governments to take an active hand in urban reform. In response, provinces passed special laws and gradually established a new bureaucracy to deal with municipal matters.[72]

Towards the end of the period, more and more reformers demanded a national response to urban problems. Most wanted a federal commission modelled on the British Local Government Board with extraordinary powers to co-ordinate schemes for civic improvement. To a degree, this desire was satisfied by that strange federal body, the Commission of Conservation, which existed between 1909 and 1921. Although in theory only advisory, under the energetic direction of Clifford Sifton the Commission delved into all kinds of issues, not the least being urban reform. It held a number of special hearings on housing and public health, sponsored conferences on town planning and civic improvement, and engineered the founding of the Civic Improvement League of Canada. Between 1914 and 1921, it published a quarterly magazine, *Conservation of Life*, to investigate town planning, housing and public health. It attempted to co-ordinate the plans of reformers and provincial and federal administrators and to establish national codes for housing and health. The range of activities included within the purview of the Commission was astonishing. It had tried to deal with all the problems of the new urban-industrial order. Unfortunately, it has also invaded the preserves of other government departments and even challengd the politicians — the result was its abolition in 1921.[73]

Urban reform should not be considered in isolation. It was part of a movement international in scope and general to Canadian society. Urban problems were common to all industrialized nations. The ties between Canadian reformers and American progressives are obvious. In a long discussion of American influences on Canadian government, delivered at the University of Toronto in 1929, the Harvard political scientist William Bennett Munro concluded that Canadian city government, if not the idea of municipal reform, was modelled upon the American system with its checks and balances, administrative profusion, and divided authority.[74] While there was some truth in this assertion, Canadian reformers had in fact imported ideas and techniques from everywhere. Much of the theory of town planning in Canada was inspired by the British experience, perhaps because of the influence of Thomas Adams. G.-A. Nantel praised Paris as the prototype for the City Beautiful in the Dominion. Morley Wickett looked upon German cities as a model of efficient government. The advocates of social purity looked to Britain and the United States for inspiration. The idea of reform in Canada, or for that matter anywhere, had only a limited nationalist content.

In his book *The Search for Order, 1877–1920*, Robert Weibe has argued that the challenge of social and economic change during the late nineteenth century led to the disruption of the loosely-knit American society based upon a network of "island communities". In the following decades, he maintains, it was reordered, more properly integrated, by the new urban middle class along collectivist lines. There is every reason to believe that

314

a similar process, perhaps not so drastic, occurred in Canada. To control a society both fluid and complex, Canadians searched for some new method of ensuring stability. The answer for many, whether radical or moderate, anglophone or francophone, business, labor, and farm, lay in collectivism. The rise of the professions, the proliferation of business combinations and associations, trade unionism and agrarian organization, all were aspects of the same collectivist urge.[75] Urban reform was only one of many phenomena like civil service reform, the social gospel, and conservation, which together constitute the progressive tradition in Canada.[76] By 1920 organization and bureaucracy flourished at all levels.

Although the idea of urban reform appealed to an ever-widening constituency, it drew its leadership from the spokesmen of the new middle class concentrated in Canada's, especially central Canada's big cities. Speaking very generally, this class was itself a collection of at least three elements: old and new professionals proud of their particular expertise; businessmen, committed to the efficient exploitation of the nation's resources; and women, in many cases the wives of professionals and businessmen, determined to carve out their own place in society. Each group saw the ideal city in a somewhat different light. Much of the early initiative came from journalists like Hugh Graham of the Montreal *Star,* John Ross Robertson of the Toronto *Telegram,* and W. F. Maclean of the Toronto *World.* These self-proclaimed tribunes of the people were most conscious of political corruption and vaguely distressed by the squalor of urban life. Businessmen, like Herbert Ames and S. Morley Wickett, and particularly their fellows in the Boards of Trade, desired an attractive community, run on principles of economy and efficiency. Women's organizations, clergymen, and humanitarians concentrated their efforts upon the moral and social uplift of the underprivileged. And the ultimate victors, the bureaucrats like Thomas Adams, Charles Hastings, and Charles Hodgetts pictured the city as a poorly-functioning mechanism which had to be streamlined and regulated.

Still these people held much in common. The distinction between, say, humanitarian and town planner or sanitary and municipal reformer was always blurred, especially in the heat of battle. They were all motivated by a generalized sense of crisis, founded on a variety of fears, such as the spread of moral decay, the threat of class hatreds, and the growth of vested interests. They were inspired by the possibilities of improvement, by a belief in their ability to mold the urban environment and to create a humane, rational society. Though this was an essentially secular goal, their values, moral, humanitarian, political, and economic — in a phrase, their cultural baggage — was defined within a Christian context and jumbled together in the drive for social reconstruction. They fostered a concept of the public interest based upon the primacy of the civic community, social justice and social order, and good government. They tried to impose this concept upon all city dwellers, rich and poor. Most significant, they institutionalized reform at the three levels of government, thereby creating

315

a bureaucracy which systematically carried forward their work.

The story of urban reform does not end here. It would be unwise to assume that reform doctrine was wholly accepted by the urban middle class, nevermind by other groups within Canadian society. The rural myth, more especially the image of the "evil city", retained a strong hold upon the Canadian mentality. Moreover, some critics feared that reform would subvert the individualistic ethos which underlay Victorian Canada, while others warned that it would solidify the class domination of city life. Such attitudes have not died. In fact, the very success of the urban reform movement has inspired new anxieties. For the price of order was a reduction in the freedom of the individual and the neighbourhood. Since 1960 centralization, bureaucracy, even expertise have become the targets of a new dissenting movement based upon radically different propositions. Ironically, we are now witnessing a general reaction against collectivism which threatens to undo the work of the urban reformers.

Notes

1. M. C. Urquhart, *Historical Statistics of Canada* (Toronto: 1965), pp. 14–15.
2. J. S. Woodsworth, *My Neighbor* (Toronto: 1911), p. 37.
3. A good example of this ambivalent approach to the city can be found in the speech of Martin Burrill, minister of agriculture, to the sixth national conference on town planning: "But we have all got to remember that the cities of the past and many of the cities of the present have been responsible for the building up of the greater forces of our modern and our past civilization, that the impact of mind on mind and the interplay of moral and intellectual forces which are associated closely together in our great centers are responsible for the advance that civilization has made in all ages. It is perfectly true that there is a darker side to our city life, and it is not without some poignancy of regret to every man who believes that from the great country homes of the land the streaming forces that uplift the whole of the national life must and do mainly come, [sic] it must be a matter of regret that in Canada, essentially an agricultural country today, there are 45 per cent of our people living in urban homes. In speaking of that, one cannot forget that the great cities of the world are characterized too often by squalor and by a dismal poverty that must rob man of his manhood and point to nothing but dismay." *Proceedings of the Sixth National Conference on City Planning* (Boston: 1914), pp. 315–316.
4. See Thomas Conant, *Life in Canada* (Toronto: 1903), pp. 227–243 and W. C. Good, "Canada's Rural Problem", *Empire Club Speeches*, Toronto, 1915–16/1916–17, pp. 299–302.
5. C. C. Berger, *The Sense of Power* (Toronto: 1970), p. 177–198.
6. C. S. Clarke's scurrilous account of Toronto in 1898 contains an excellent description of this "dark side". Clarke was particularly intrigued by the extent of the social evil, prostitution and the like in Toronto. C. S. Clarke, *Of Toronto the Good*, Toronto: Coles reprint, 1970.
7. For critical comments on this movement see "The Back-to-the-land Movement", *Conservation of Life*, Toronto, October, 1914, pp. 30–31 and John A. Cormis, "Back to the Land", *University Magazine*, April, 1918, pp. 197–203.
8. These papers were the Montreal *Star*, the Toronto *Telegram*, the Toronto *World*, the Toronto *News*, The Ottawa *Journal*, the Vancouver *News-Advertiser*, and to a lesser extent the Winnipeg *Sun*. They were less partisan, more sensationalist, more chauvinist, and much cruder than the regular party journals. These people's papers set a new tone in journalism which eventually affected the whole of the urban press. It should be added that regular journals did not neglect municipal affairs, but their concern was rarely so continuous.
9. For example, in 1910 the Canadian Club of Ottawa was addressed by Charles J. Bonaparte, ex-attorney general of the United States, on the purification of city politics and by Henry Vivian, a British m.p., on city planning.
10. Canadian Political Science Association, *Papers and Proceedings*, vol. 1, 1913.
11. This had first been championed by the civic booster, the spokesman for local business interests, who was committed to the material growth of his community. But by the late 1870s and early 1880s, when the public library issue arose in Montreal and Toronto, there was a much more obvious reform tone to civic improvement, a concern with popular culture as well as prestige.

12. J. E. Middleton, *The Municipality of Toronto: A History*, vol. 1 (Toronto and New York: 1923), pp. 301–302.
13. For a chronological account of the advance of public health in the city of Toronto, see *Events and Factors in the Advance of Public Health Measures in Toronto, 1866–*, a special report, Department of the City Clerk, September 18, 1968.
14. The English papers in Montreal were the most vociferous advocates of vaccination — the Montreal *Herald* was the target of a riot for its "advanced" views. But so-called respectable francophone opinion, represented by Mayor Beaugrand, was equally committed. Vaccination was as much a class issue as a race issue, involving the physical imposition of the wishes of the educated upon the lower orders.
15. Charles J. Hastings, "The Modern Conception of Public Health Administration", *Conservation of Life*, October, 1917, p. 88.
16. For an elaboration of the ideas of these moral reformers see G. A. Warburton, "The Moral Conditions of Toronto", Canadian Club. Toronto, *Proceedings*, 1915–16. pp. 17–25 and "Commercialized Vice and the White Slave Traffic" and "Temperance", Social Service Congress, *Report of Addresses and Proceedings*, (Toronto: 1914), pp. 199–237 and 303–326. Another valuable source are the yearbooks of the National Council of Women, especially with regard to the social purity movement. These yearbooks indicate the wide variety of interests involved in moral reform, especially its concern with the immigrants, the under-privileged, and social welfare.
17. These laws related to prostitution and seduction, liquor and prohibition, gambling, night curfew, pernicious literature, tobacco and narcotic sales, sabbatarianism, and the police. The morale reform movement had a national import: the anti-gambling legislation of Blake, Charlton's campaign against seduction, the Dominion Lord's Day Act, and of course prohibition. "Blue Laws" won considerable support in cities, towns, and farming districts — more often from English Canada than Quebec. The moral reform campaigns in the cities were only a part of a movement throughout English Canada.
18. James H. Gray, *The Boy from Winnipeg* (Toronto: 1970), pp. 5–8.
19. Thomas H. Raddall, *Halifax, Warden of the North* (Toronto: 1948), pp. 260–261.
20. C. Clarke, *Of Toronto the Good*, pp. 86–131.
21. Richard B. Splane, *Social Welfare in Ontario, 1791–1893*, (Toronto: University of Toronto Press, 1965).
22. See the comment of W. J. Hanna, an Ontario cabinet minister to the new Civic Improvement League of Canada: "The nation is the individual in the aggregate. Surround the individual with the proper conditions and most of the real problems, the social problems, will cease to exist. Before the individual is born, make such labour laws and establish such conditions as will ensure him a healthy mother . . . . Suitable town-planning and enforced housing laws will give him a home with sunshine and fresh air on all sides . . . . We must also give him supervised playgrounds. Failing playgrounds and open spaces, he should have a quiet street with now and then a hurdy-gurdy . . . . Where he goes to school he should be put in his proper class; he should not have to sit beside a consumptive or a defective. Manual training should be part of his school course. His sister should be taught mothercraft, cooking and sewing; at the same time she ought to be given some practical education that would enable her to become a skilled wage-earner. Give the boy a school bank if you can, that he may learn the first principle of thrift. Introduce him to the public library with its Saturday afternoon story talks and moving pictures and get his parents in to read the magazines. Censor his movies so that he will not choose the wrong hero. Give him compulsory military training. If you launch him with this equipment, he is not likely to prove a serious civic problem. Launch a generation of him and your civic problems are largely solved." Civic Improvement League of Canada, *Report of Conference*, 1916, pp. 31–32. See also J. J. Kelso, "Neglected and Friendless Children", *Canadian Magazine*, vol. 2, 1893–94, pp. 213–216; C. J. Atkinson, "The Boy Problem", Canadian Club, Toronto, *Addresses*, 1909–10, pp. 52–60: and "Child Welfare", Social Service Congress, *Report of Addresses and Proceedings*, (Toronto: 1914), pp. 89–115.
23. H. C. Hocken, "The New Spirit in Municipal Government", Canadian Club, Ottawa, *Addresses*, 1914–15, pp. 85–97.
24. S. Morley Wickett, "City Government in Canada", *Municipal Government in Canada*, ed. S. Morley Wickett (Toronto: 1907), p. 23. This article was first written in 1902. See also A. C. Thompson, "The Taxation of Franchises", *Canadian Magazine*, vol. 24, 1904–05, pp. 463–465.
25. S. Morley Wickett, "Present Conditions", *Municipal Government in Canada*, pp. 157–162; W. F. Maclean, "A Greater Toronto", *Empire Club Speeches*, Toronto, 1907–08, pp. 84–89; and F. S. Spence, "Some Suggestions as to Toronto Street Railway Problems", Canadian Club, Toronto, *Addresses*, 1908–09, pp. 37–40.
26. James Mavor, "Municipal Ownership of Public Utilities", reprint, a paper read at the joint meeting of the Michigan Political Science Association and the League of Michigan Municipalities (Ann Arbor: 1904); James Mavor, *Government Telephones: The Experience of Manitoba, Canada*, New York: Moffat, Yard and Company, 1916; and Edward Harris, "A Review of Civic Ownership", Toronto: William Briggs, 1908.
27. For a fuller description of the abortive campaign against corporate dominance in Montreal, see

317

J. I. Cooper, *Montreal: A Brief History* (Montreal and London: 1969), pp. 120–121 and Joseph Levitt, *Henri Bourassa and the Golden Calf* (Ottawa: 1969), pp. 47–56.

28. Lloyd A. Machum, *A History of Moncton, Town and City 1855–1965* (Moncton: 1965), p. 218 and 222.

29. W. J. Bell, a local civic booster, claimed that Guelph was "the first Canadian Municipality to own and successfully operate all of its public utilities." W. J. Bell, "Municipal Ownership and Civic Government" (Guelph: 1909), p. 3.

30. J. E. Middleton, *The Municipality of Toronto*, p. 364 and W. D. Lighthall, "Valedictory of W. D. Lighthall, K.C., On Retiring from the Honorary Secretaryship of the Union of Canadian Municipalities, August, 1919".

31. Even before this, Ontario towns had been purchasing their electric power utilities. Acording to R. N. Beattie, twenty towns and cities between 1899 and 1902 had commenced operation of their own facilities. R. N. Beattie, "The Impact of Hydro on Ontario", *Profiles of a Province* (Toronto: 1967), pp. 167–168.

32. The telephone question was a problem unto itself. Bell Telephone had a Dominion charter which could not be touched by the provinces. Furthermore, Bell controlled the trunk lines between cities, upon which an efficient and extensive telephone system depended. It seemed almost impossible for cities to handle Bell on their own, thus the interest in provincial and national control.

33. For a discussion of the significance of these movements see Charles N. Glaab and A. Theodore Brown, *A History of Urban America* (New York and London: 1967), pp. 260–263 and 289–291. Jane Jacobs, the noted urban philosopher, argues that the town planners, in fact urban reform generally, never overcame the myths created by the City Beautiful and Garden City ideas. Jane Jacobs, *The Death and Life of Great American Cities*, Random House, 1961, pp. 16–25.

34. Henry Vivian, "Garden Suburbs and Town Planning", Canadian Club, Toronto, *Addresses*, 1910–11, pp. 35–40 and G. Trafford Hewitt, "Canada and the United States as a Field for the Garden City Movement", *Proceedings of the Sixth National Conference on City Planning* (Boston: 1914), pp. 180–189. Hewitt was the president of the Province of Nova Scotia Land Corporation, Limited and he claimed that he planned to build a Garden City in Canada. Purportedly, Lindenlea, outside Ottawa, was a garden suburb. See B. Evan Parry, "Ottawa Garden Suburb", *Town Planning and Conservation of Life*, July-September, 1920, p. 68.

35. Adam Shortt, "The Social and Economic Significance of the Movement from the Country to the City", Canadian Club, Montreal, *Addresses*, 1912–13, pp. 70–71.

36. James Gray gives an amusing description of the chaos left by the developers in Winnipeg after the boom in the early twentieth century. James H. Gray, *The Boy from Winnipeg*, pp. 1–5.

37. Clifford Sifton, "Address of Welcome", *Proceedings of the Sixth National Conference on City Planning* (Boston: 1914), p. 12. One writer argued that Canadians were following the broader scheme of town planning along the British model rather than the American, which tended more towards the aesthetic. "The Meaning and Practical Application of Town Planning", *Conservation of Life*, July, 1915, pp. 74–76.

38. As an appendix, the magazine *Conservation of Life* carried a summary of town planning exploits throughout the nation.

39. R. S. Gourlay, "Some Aspects of Commercial Value to the City of Toronto of the Proposed Harbor Improvements", *Empire Club Speeches*, Toronto, 1912–13/1913–14, pp. 129–145; R. S. Gourlay, "Basic Principles of Water Front Development as Illustrated by the Plans of the Toronto Harbor Commission", *Proceedings of the Sixth National Conference on City Planning* (Boston: 1914), pp. 17–31; and L. H. Clarke, "Putting a New Front on Toronto", *Canadian Magazine*, vol. 42, 1913–14, pp. 205–215.

40. The CPR and the Grand Trunk had sponsored development schemes in Moncton, Toronto, Winnipeg and Vancouver, though these railway companies had not been especially concerned with the idea of town planning.

41. For a short but effective description of the problem of immigrant ghettoes see Bryce Stewart, "The Housing of Our Immigrant Workers", Canadian Political Science Association, *Proceedings and Papers*, vol. 1, 1913, pp. 98–111.

42. Charles Hodgetts, "Unsanitary Housing", Commission of Conservation, *Addresses, 1911*, p. 33. See also G. F. Chipman, "Winnipeg: The Melting Pot" and "The Refining Process", *Canadian Magazine*, vol. 33, 1909, pp. 409–416 and 548–554.

43. P. H. Bryce, "Civic Responsibility and the Increase of Immigration", *Empire Club Speeches*, Toronto, 1906–7, pp. 186–197; W. D. Lighthall, "Toronto and Town Planning", *Empire Club Speeches*, *1910–11*, pp. 233–234; and J. W. Macmillan, "Problems of Population", *Empire Club Speeches*, 1911–12, pp. 75–79. It seems that the prosperous urbanites who attended Empire Club proceedings were interested in the slum problem. Comment after Bryce's paper, however, revealed that at least three members were more concerned with keeping out undesirable immigration than with solving the existing problem.

44. Clifford Sifton, "Address of Welcome", *Proceedings of the Sixth National Conference on City Planning* (Boston: 1914), p. 8. The suburban movement had been a feature of Canadian life for some years by 1914. Developers had been quick to realize the possibilities of exploiting the dissatisfaction of

318

prosperous urbanites with their cities. But in terms of urban reform, the suburban movement further fragmented the city into poor and rich districts and did not solve the problem of congestion within the poor districts.

45. Charles Hodgetts discussed the character of housing laws in Canadian provinces. They usually established regulations with regard to space, ventilation, and sanitation and they made provision for some kind of permanent inspectorate. Hodgetts noted that where applied these acts had the desired effect, but unfortunately many boards of health had not exercised their powers to the fullest extent Charles Hodgetts, "Unsanitary Housing", *Addresses 1911*, Commission of Conservation, pp. 43–51. For a more general discussion of town planning and slum reform see G. Frank Beer, "A Plea for City Organization", *Addresses, 1914*. Commission of Conservation.

46. Thomas Adams, "The Housing Problem", Canadian Club, Montreal, *Addresses*, 1918–19, pp. 178–187 and C. B. Sissons, "A Housing Policy for Ontario", *Canadian Magazine*, vol. 53, 1919, pp. 241–248.

47. S. Morley Wickett, "Present Conditions", *Municipal Government in Canada*, p. 343.

48. For a long discussion of the conversion to business taxes and the single tax experiment, see J. H. Perry, *Taxes, Tariffs, and Subsidies; A History of Canadian Fiscal Development* (Toronto: 1955), pp. 124–136. The western variant of single tax was not in fact a true application of Henry George's principles and it was based upon an extravagant land boom which constantly raised the value of land. There were many absentee landowners and speculators in the west, not the least being the Canadian Pacific Railway. When the land boom ended after 1910, western towns soon turned to the business tax and other more regular taxation systems. There was some discussion of the western variant in Ontario, especially in Toronto where it received approval in principle in a plebiscite, but the provincial government refused to allow its adoption. Perry indicates, however, that in practice improvements were under-assessed in many municipalities.

49. Civic Improvement League of Canada, *Report of Preliminary Conference at Ottawa*, 1915, p. 8.

50. For example, municipal politics in Toronto in the 1880s seems to have been based upon a network of localist influences, religious and ethnic factions like the Orange Order, and sporadic business interest, all overlayed by the partisan loyalty of civic leaders and the press to the Conservatives or Liberals.

51. H. B. Ames, "The Machine in Honest Hands", *Canadian Magazine*, vol. 3, 1894, pp. 101–109.

52. See W. H. Atherton, *Montreal, 1535–1914* (Montreal: 1914), vol. 2, pp. 184–191; Leslie Roberts, *Montreal: From Mission Colony to World City* (Toronto: 1969), pp. 263–270 and 304–316; and J. I. Cooper, *Montreal*, pp. 96–103, 119–121, and 130–144.

53. E. A. Macdonald, mayor of Toronto in 1900, is an excellent example of this kind of "reform" politician. Throughout the 1880s he constantly sniffed out scandal among his opponents in a finally successful campaign to secure the mayoralty. An account of his chequered career, albeit inadequate, can be found in J. E. Middleton, *The Municipality of Toronto*, vol. 1, pp. 339–357.

54. This innovation was peculiar to Canadian cities. It spread from Toronto to Hamilton and Ottawa and was temporarily adopted by Montreal, Winnipeg, and London. S. Morley Wickett, "City Government in Canada", *Municipal Government in Canada*, pp. 12–13 and H. L. Brittain, *Local Government in Canada* (Toronto: 1951), pp. 52–53.

55. F. h. Underhill, "Commission Government in Cities", *The Arbor* (University of Toronto), vol. 1–2, 1910–11, pp. 284–294; W. J. Bell, "Municipal Ownership and Civic Government by Commission"; Oliver Asselin, "Le Problème Municipal" (Montreal: 1909); and Goldwin Smith "Municipal Government: A Letter to the World", reprint, 1905 (?).

56. During the 1880s, when certain reformers were trying to change the structure of city government, the Toronto *Telegram* constantly argued the case for "good men" over reformed institutions. Toronto *Telegram*, January 12, 1893, p. 4; February 27, 1896, p. 4; and March 28, 1896, p. 5. Mayor R. D. Waugh of Winnipeg told the Civic Improvement League of Canada in 1916 much the same thing: "The citizen does not, as a rule, take any of the blame or responsibility for mismanagement himself. It is almost invariably "the system" or "the Council" that is wrong. But you hear it in Ottawa, Toronto, Montreal, Winnipeg, everywhere, the old story, "The city government is no good." There is always a clamour more or less loud for a change. We all know that there is room for great improvement, but when we get down to the question of "How?" one says one thing, one another, but it is just threshing out the same old straw. We try new schemes, elect new men, but still the main result is the same.

No, the system is not altogether to blame for the result. It matters little about the system after all — the man is the main consideration. Poor men with a good system will not insure good government, but good man may, no matter what the system." Civic Improvement League of Canada, *Report of Conference*, 1916, p. 22.

57. Woodsworth, *My Neighbor*, p. 26.

58. Underhill, "Commission Government in Cities", pp. 286–287.

59. Wickett, "City Government in Canada", *Municipal Government in Canada*, pp. 9–11.

60. In Toronto, there was a proposal that all wards be drawn from the harbour to the northern city limits. Such would create "heterogeneous" wards and break down the influence of lower-class neighbourhoods.

61. Wickett, "Present Conditions", *Municipal Government in Canada*, p. 351.

62. This point was continually raised at the two conferences on civic improvement: Civic Improvement League of Canada, *Report of Preliminary Conference at Ottawa*, 1915, p. 12 (Thomas Adams) and pp. 35–36 (S. Morley Wickett); and Civic Improvement League of Canada, *Report of Conference*, 1916, pp. 24–25 (R. D. Waugh, mayor of Winnipeg) and pp. 35–36 (W. J. Hanna).

63. See "Community Engineering", The Citizen's Research Institute of Canada, Ottawa, 1920. This was a pamphlet put out by the Institute to attract interest in statistical research into municipal problems. For a price the Institute was willing to carry out studies of particular communities.

64. S. Morley Wickett, "Municipal Publicity Through Uniformity in Municipal Statistics", Eighth Annual Convention of the Union of Canadian Municipalities, Montreal, 1908 and J. A. Cooper, "The Municipal Survey", *Canadian Political Science Association*, vol. 1, 1913, pp. 124–131.

65. Mrs. Adam Shortt: "But I think none of us will disagree in this, that in almost all municipal councils, at least, so far as we have known, from Halifax to Vancouver, there is an element of politics which enters into municipal administration and sometimes ties up the machinery, which, at its best and without politics, might be more efficient. Moreover, this entrance of politics into the municipal situation frequently leads to the appointment of men for outstanding positions which affects our morality, our beauty and our efficiency — not because they are men fitted for the positions, but because they are men who, for some reason or other, it is thought must have a job. It is, in many cases, as has been said, not the man's fitness for the occupation, but there is an occupation to which they may fit the man who needs a job." Civic Improvment League of Canada, *Report of Preliminary Conference at Ottawa*, 1915, p. 2.

66. S. Morley Wickett, "The Problems of City Government", *Empire Club Speeches*, Toronto, 1907–08, p. 113.

67. Initially this demand was only for a special post like City Engineer and Medical Officer or a commission for police or waterworks. But after 1900 reformers were concerned with the development of a complete municipal civil service. See J. O. Miller, "The Better Government of Our Cities", in *The New Era in Canada*, ed. J. O. Miller (Toronto: 1917), pp. 368–370.

68. For example, in 1919 a handbook on Ottawa listed 10 permanent officials — city clerk, commissioner of works, city collector, city treasurer, city auditor, fire chief, assessment commissioner, city solicitor, charity officer, and market inspector. J. H. Putnam, "City Government Ottawa", Ottawa: James Hope & Sons, Limited, 1919.

69. W. D. Lighthall, "Valedictory . . . . ", 1919.

70. W. F. Maclean, "A Great Toronto", *Empire Club Speeches*, Toronto, 1907–08, pp. 81–90.

71. S. Morley Wickett, "Civic Charters: The Question of a Charter for Toronto and of Civic Charters in General", *The Municipal World*, January, 1905, pp. 8–10. Wickett claims that the act incorporating Edmonton was written by the editor of *The Municipal Manual*, a former city solicitor of Toronto — Wickett, "Present Conditions", *Municipal Government in Canada*, pp. 151–152.

72. These included liquor licensing and prohibition, public health, municipal financing, utilities and highways, town planning and housing.

73. J. W. Dafoe, *Clifford Sifton in Relation to His Times* (Toronto: 1971), pp. 444–445. Dafoe deals mainly with the involvement of the commission in resource development.

74. W. B. Munro, *American Influence on Canadian Government* (Toronto: 1929), pp. 99–142.

75. For a discussion of the collectivist urge and economic groups see J. M. Bliss, "The Protective Impulse: An Approach to the Social History of Mowat's Ontario", a paper delivered at the Mowat Seminar, Kingston, November, 1970.

76. Recently historians have begun to investigate this progressive tradition. R. Craig Brown has pointed out that Robert Borden expressed the ideals of bureaucratic reform in national politics. R. C. Brown, "The Political Ideas of Robert Borden", *The Political Ideas of the Prime Ministers of Canada*, ed. M. Hamelin (Ottawa: 1969), pp. 87–97. Joseph Levitt has argued that one can find a progressive response to social and economic problems in French Canada in the writings of Bourassa and the *nationalistes*. J. Levitt, *Henri Bourassa and the Golden Calf*, Ottawa: Les Editions de L'Université d'Ottawa, 1969. And of course, Richard Allen has discussed in some detail the rise and decline of the social gospel in Canada. R. Allen, "The Social Gospel and the Reform Tradition in Canada, 1890–1928", *Canadian Historical Review*, vol. 59, Dec., 1968, pp. 381–399.

320

Topic Nine

World War I and the Conscription Crisis

The First World War initially united and later divided Canadians. Canada's significant contribution to the war effort aroused a sense of nationalism, particularly among English-speaking Canadians. However, the controversial conscription issue intensified the age-old conflict of English and French Canadians.

Canada joined the war in August of 1914 as a colony of Britain. At the outset, Canadians were united behind the war effort. Even those who were anti-imperialistic, like Henri Bourassa, initially agreed to support Britain so long as men were not conscripted to serve. Canadians from every province volunteered. But as the fighting continued on from months to years, voluntary enlistment declined, and enthusiasm for Canadian involvement waned. In particular, French Canadians questioned the rationale for fighting in a European war under the direction of Britain. After living three hundred years in North America, French Canadians did not have the emotional links with Britain and Europe that English Canadians had.

There were internal problems as well that increased tensions between French and English Canadians. For one thing, recruiting was handled badly, and many French Canadians were obliged to serve under English-speaking officers in English-speaking regiments. For another, French Canadians were being pressured to fight for democracy in Europe at the very time that they were forced to defend their rights to French-language schools in Ontario and Manitoba. As a result, recruitment in Quebec declined drastically, much to the annoyance of English Canadians.

By 1917 the recruiting situation was critical. Because of heavy casualties at the front and declining voluntary enlistment, Canada was falling behind in her contribution of men. Britain was also pressuring the prime minister, Robert Borden, to step up the Canadian effort. With support from English-speaking conscriptionist Liberals, the Conservative government passed the Military Service Act in Parliament on 18 May 1917, allowing for the implementation of conscription. Anti-conscriptionists rioted in Montreal on 24 May.

In the article that follows, Matthew Bray outlines the evolving English-Canadian patriotic response to the war. Two different French-Canadian viewpoints are presented in "An Open Letter from Capt. Talbot Papineau to Mr. Henri Bourassa" and in "Mr. Bourassa's reply."

For an overview of the war years, see the relevant chapters in R. C. Brown and R. Cook's *Canada: 1896–1921: A Nation Transformed* (Toronto: McClelland and Stewart, 1974) and D. Morton's *Canada and War: A Military and Political History* (Toronto: Butterworth, 1981). A number of biographies of key politicians during the First World War touch on the war years. The most important are R. C. Brown's, *Robert Laird Borden: A Biography*, Vol. II, 1914–1937. (Toronto: Macmillan, 1980); J. Schull's *Laurier: The First Canadian* (Toronto: Macmillan, 1965); Robert Rumilly's *Henri Bourassa* (Toronto: Chantecler, 1953); and R. Graham's *Arthur Meighen*, Vol. I: *The Door of Opportunity* (Toronto: Clarke Irwin, 1960).

322   On the issue of conscription, see Elizabeth Armstrong's *The Crisis of Quebec, 1914–18* (New York: Columbia University Press, 1937) and J. L. Granatstein and J. M. Hitsman's *Broken Promises: A History of Conscription in Canada* (Toronto: Oxford University Press, 1977).

'Fighting as an Ally': The English-Canadian Patriotic Response to the Great War*

R. MATTHEW BRAY

Writing to Sir Wilfrid Laurier in mid-November 1916 John M. Godfrey, a Toronto lawyer and activist in a wide range of civilian recruiting organizations, observed that 'what a difference it would have made in this war if we [Canada] had fought as a nation and an ally. In the first place we should have been bound to put our whole strength into the war. Fighting as an ally there could be no such thing as a limited liability.'[1] Godfrey's lament made little impression on the veteran Liberal leader, but it did summarize succinctly the patriotic viewpoint of a growing number of urban, professional, middle-class English Canadians who were becoming increasingly dissatisfied with their country's contribution to the Great War.[2] Yet at the outbreak of the conflict in August 1914 most of those same Canadians had been perfectly content with the ancillary role assumed by Canada, just as they had enthusiastically endorsed the voluntary principle on which the war effort was organized. In the intervening two years, however, events had served to render in their eyes both that role and that type of war effort inadequate. To understand these radically altered perspectives it is neces-

*From *Canadian Historical Review*, LXI (1980): 141–168. Reprinted by permission of University of Toronto Press.

sary to trace the evolution of the English-Canadian patriotic response to the Great War by focussing on its various journalistic and organizational manifestations in the period from 1914 to 1917.

Like people the world over, most Canadians were taken very much by surprise by the events of July-August 1914, but though the country was neither psychologically nor materially well prepared for it, the decision of the federal government to commit Canada to war, symbolized in the mobilization of the Canadian Expeditionary Force, was welcomed with an unforeseeable degree of unanimity.[3] Even predictable sources of opposition such as Henri Bourassa, editor of the influential Montreal daily, *Le Devoir,* and chief antagonist over the previous decade to greater Canadian collaboration in imperial affairs, did not materialize immediately.[4] Yet though Canadians may have been relatively united about the necessity for their country's involvement in the conflict, they differed over the reasons for participation. Castell Hopkins suggested in the *Canadian Annual Review, 1914,*[5] that amongst the partisan press — and therefore possibly amongst its readers — there was a critical divergence of opinion, that Conservative newspapers interpreted Canada 'to be fighting for the Empire, and incidentally, for British ideals of peace and liberty,' while Liberal journals portrayed her as 'fighting for the liberties and peace of the world, and incidentally, for the British Empire of which the Dominion was a part.' A careful survey of the Canadian daily press indicates that Hopkins made the mistake of assuming that Toronto was representative of the rest of Canada, for while that city's six major newspapers did divide roughly along the lines he drew, this was not the case elsewhere in the country.[6] Outside the Ontario capital, in fact, only the *Grain Growers' Guide* and the *Manitoba Free Press,* both published in Winnipeg, expressed the nationalistic viewpoint he found principally in the *Globe* of Toronto.[7] Otherwise the Canadian press took the more colonially-minded position that Canada was both legally and morally at war because of her place in the British empire; on this issue there was little difference between Liberal and Conservative newspapers, between French and English journals, or between the press in western, central, and eastern Canada.[8] And if a lack of evidence to the contrary may be used as a measure, what was true of the press was equally true of English Canadians generally. Few and far between were those individuals who argued that it was Canada's obligation as a nation in her own right to share in the defence of the principles and liberties for which the allies were fighting.[9]

An accurate assessment of what motivated English Canadians to endorse their country's war effort is vital, because more than anything else, perhaps, that factor shaped their expectations about the nature and extent of the Canadian contribution. So long as it was believed that the rationale for Canada's participation was the colonial tie to Great Britain, it was also assumed that her role in the conflict would be a subordinate, subsidiary one. The Canadian government, for example, was not expected to play any significant part in the organization and direction of the Allied war effort, not even with respect to the mobilization of the Canadian Expeditionary Force; that was left entirely in British hands. As the *Toronto Mail and Empire* explained in mid-October 1914 vis-à-vis the recruitment of the second Canadian contingent: 'For all practical purposes the wishes of the British War Office govern the raising of Canadian contingents. The Dominion Department of Militia is the executive which carries into effect the design of organization that the British authorities suggest. Until the War Office indicates the composition of the desired contingent the Canadian authorities are held back in their call for recruits.'[10] In voicing this point of view the *Mail and Empire* was very much representative of other Canadian newspapers during the first months of the war; with but a few exceptions, Canada was not perceived to be an 'ally' in the sense that Great Britain, France, and Russia were allies, but rather was looked upon as an adjunct to Great Britain whose place in the war, as in the empire, would be secondary to that of the mother country.[11] While Canada would do her 'duty' to the utmost of her ability, that duty was clearly thought to be circumscribed by the constraints of her colonial status. Herein lay the basis of later complaints about the 'limited liability' mentality that prevailed at the outset of the war.

324

Expectations about the auxiliary nature of the Canadian war effort were reinforced by the popular belief that the conflict would be of extremely short duration. As the minister of finance, Thomas White, later recalled, at the outbreak of war few people in Ottawa thought that it would last longer than a year.[12] Newspaper articles like that in the *Saint John Telegraph* headlined 'Shortest War on Record Says U.S. Military Expert' tended to confirm the widely-held conviction that the armies of the Triple Entente would easily rout their Austro-German foe.[13] Such optimistic though myopic predictions buttressed the view that Canada's role would indeed be a minor one; given the country's lack of military preparedness, the mobilization of an effective overseas force would take several months, by which time, presumably, the end would be in sight.

If one of the chief assumptions about the Canadian war effort was that it would be ancillary to that of Great Britain, another was that it would be totally voluntary in nature. On the military side no one seriously suggested during the first months of hostilities that a selective draft might be the most equitable means of enrolling the Canadian Expeditionary Force; as the *Globe* of Toronto so self-righteously declared: 'Canada wants no unwilling defenders. Coercion is wrong — in Toronto as in Berlin.'[14] Of course, there were also practical reasons for dismissing out of hand the conscription option, the most obvious of which was that Canadians, or at least residents of Canada, had responded in huge numbers to the call for volunteers issued by the minister of militia, Sam Hughes, in the second week of August 1914.[15] Then, too, it was not clear that compulsory military service could be legally implemented. As Sir Robert Borden himself informed the Halifax Canadian Club on 18 December 1914: 'under the laws of Canada, our citizens may be called out to defend our own territory, but cannot be required to go beyond the seas except for the defence of Canada itself. There has not been, there will not be compulsion or conscription.'[16] So long as Canada was assisting in the defence of the empire and not fighting primarily on her own behalf, the prime minister was saying, conscription would not — indeed, could not — be introduced by his Conservative government.

Other aspects of the Canadian war effort were also expected to be carried out voluntarily by the Canadian people. It was predictable, perhaps, that the making of field comforts — scarves, socks, handkerchiefs, and the like — would become a national pastime among the women of Canada.[17] It was even predictable that a great deal of public energy would go into collecting monies for organizations such as the Canadian Red Cross, the Young Men's Christian Association, and the Belgian and Serbian Relief funds, all of which sought to relieve the suffering of both combattants and civilians discomfitted by the war.[18] More surprising was the extent to which private groups also undertook responsibilities that might properly have been left to governmental authorities. A prime example was the Canadian Patriotic Fund. Designed, according to its Act of Incorporation, 'to provide a fund for the assistance, in the case of need, of the wives, children and dependent relatives of officers and men, residents of Canada, who, during the present war, may be on active service with the naval and military forces of the British Empire and Great Britain's allies,' the fund offered the first opportunity for Canadians, and particularly middle-class English Canadians, to demonstrate the strength of their patriotic fervor.[19] And demonstrate it they did; the national executive of the fund read like a *Who's Who* of Canadian society, headed as it was by the governor general, HRH the Duke of Connaught, and the nine lieutenant-governors of the provinces, while in cities and towns all across Canada affiliated branches were established by the local business and professional élites.[20]

325

Interestingly, there was very little popular discussion of the idea that the support of the soldiers' dependents, like that of the men themselves, ought to be borne by the federal government so as to ensure that the financial burden would be shared equally by all Canadians. In the press only the *Calgary Herald* and the *Edmonton Bulletin,* the one Conservative and the other Liberal, put forward this argument, and even they were less concerned about the matter of principle than desirous that the aid not have the appearance of charity.[21] Otherwise, the voluntary approach was accepted without question. Evidently, the same amalgam of sentiments that necessitated Canada's military commitment be met without resorting to conscription also required the financing of the Patriotic Fund by means of voluntary subscriptions. Genuine patriotism, it was thought, must spring spontaneously from the hearts of individual Canadians.

Over the course of the next two years all of the major premises underlying the English-Canadian patriotic outlook — the brevity of the war, the ancillary nature of the Canadian role, the efficacy of the voluntary system — were to be challenged. The first to be tested was the belief that the conflict would be concluded successfully within a few months. Indeed, even in the autumn of 1914 it became apparent that this hope was not soundly based, and consequently the adequacy of the Canadian contribution also came to be questioned. The 25 000-man Canadian Expeditionary Force, for example, which had seemed in early August to be such a generous expression of Canadian solidarity with the empire, had come by October to be the subject of a good deal of complaint, both in representations to the office of the prime minister and in the press, Liberal and Conservative.[22] Borden himself admitted privately to the acting Canadian high commissioner in London, Sir George Perley, that his government's decision to enrol a second contingent had been made 'urgently necessary' by the weight of public opinion.[23] Even this failed to silence those who, like the *Montreal Star,* believed that 'it ought not, in reality, to be a question of a first and a second contingent at all — it ought to be a question of an unending chain of contingents, drawn steadily from the bosom of our loyal and patriotic people . . .'[24] Though such critics were partially appeased by the announcement in mid-October of a new policy whereby a minimum of 30 000 (raised in November to 50 000) men would be kept in continuous training within Canada, newspapers like the *Financial Post,* the *Toronto Star,* the *Halifax Chronicle,* the *Manitoba Free Press,* and the *Victoria Times* continued to express the fear that the Canadian war effort was not being pressed with sufficient foresight or vigour.[25]

326

Throughout the winter of 1914–15 the English-Canadian press also turned its attention to the quality of the Canadian Expeditionary Force, two aspects of which were found to be disturbing. One was the fact that most volunteers resided in cities and towns, meaning that the rural areas of Canada were under-represented in the overseas contingents. Though this did not worry everyone — *Saturday Night* took the position that the urban unemployed should be enlisted before the working farm population — it did raise objections from those like the *Globe* of Toronto who maintained that the military burden should fall equally on all parts of the country.[26] A much more serious problem with the composition of the CEF was the relatively small percentage of recruits who were actually native-born Canadians. Public awareness of this anomaly in the so-called 'Canadian' war effort was particularly heightened in February 1915 when the *Montreal Star* began to publish a daily Roll of Honor listing the names, places of residence, and places of birth of volunteers in the Montreal area, which illustrated quite graphically the extent to which the men in the force had been born in the United Kingdom and then emigrated to Canada in later life.[27]

Concern about these faults in the make-up of the Canadian Expeditionary Force was especially great in southern Ontario, or more specifically in Toronto, and led to the establishment of the first formal civilian association designed to provide an organizational framework for all facets of the Canadian patriotic response to the war, including the systematic recruitment of volunteers for overseas service. Founded in March 1915 under the patronage of Lt-Gov. John S. Hendrie of Ontario, the Central Ontario branch of the Speakers' Patriotic League was the joint brainchild of N. F. Davidson, a lawyer and Conservative party organizer from Toronto, and H. B. Ames, the Conservative MP for St Antoine in Quebec and honorary secretary of the Canadian Patriotic Fund.[28] Davidson originally proposed the formation of a centralized speakers' bureau in early February because, in his words, 'it is absolutely true that in many parts of the country districts [of Ontario] they have not yet come to realize that we are at War.'[29] Ames welcomed the idea because it had been his experience too that 'those counties which have given fewest men were also weak so far as contributions to the Patriotic Fund were concerned.'[30] Together the two men persuaded Hendrie to convene on 2 March a meeting of Toronto professional and business men, at which time the decision was made to create a civilian league, under the chairmanship of Judge C. A. Masten of the Supreme Court of Ontario, with the objectives: 'To educate public opinion throughout the country as to the pressing needs of the Empire for men and money; to co-ordinate and stimulate all the various activities working to this end, and to augment the various patriotic funds without however establishing any fund of its own.'[31] Ames hoped that eventually there would be seven such branches of a semi-national Speakers' Patriotic League, one for each of the military divisions in eastern Canada, but this plan never fully materialized.[32] Only in Kingston and Montreal, head-quarters for Military Divisions #3 and #4, were other affiliates set up, and that in Montreal did not survive beyond the fall of 1915.[33] Those in Toronto and Kingston, in contrast, served as central clearing-houses for all patriotic and civilian recruiting activities in their respective areas for the duration of the war.[34]

327

Paradoxically, the attempt to bring some order to the voluntary Canadian war effort by establishing the Speakers' Patriotic League came at a time when the material and military demands being made of Canada were relatively light. During the first quarter of 1915 the Canadian Expeditionary Force was deployed, when at all, in a secondary sector of the war theatre, so that losses were few and replacement figures low.[35] The British War Office had still not requested further military assistance from Canada, and regular enlistment was going ahead at a rate which the federal authorities claimed was beyond their capacities of supply.[36] Even the Canadian Patriotic Fund was prospering; according to its executive secretary, Phillip Morris, 'during the first five months of 1915 . . . each monthly period showed an excess of income over expenditure.'[37] Late in April, however, all that was changed by the full-scale engagement of the Canadian Expeditionary Force in the costly and tragic defence of the Ypres salient.

For Canada one of the most important consequences of the German spring offensive was the mid-May decision of the British War Office that 'no numbers which the Dominion Government are willing and able to provide with arms and ammunition would be too great for His Majesty's Government to accept with deep gratitude.'[38] No longer could Prime

Minister Borden respond to those calling for a more aggressive Canadian war effort with the declaration that his administration's actions were strictly controlled by the British. In effect, for the first time since the outbreak of war ten months earlier, the Canadian contribution — military and otherwise — became a function not of a need abstractly perceived by the imperial authorities, but of the country's own resources and of its willingness to commit them to the cause.

Equally as significant, the sense of direct, personal loss engendered by the horrendous Canadian casualties at St Julien and Langemarck, Festubert and Givenchy during the spring and summer of 1915 altered the focus of the English-Canadian patriotic perspective. As Castell Hopkins noted, up to that time 'it was difficult [for Canadians] . . . to understand that the War was what the speakers called 'our war' . . . to realize that Canada was no longer an insignificant, dependent, unknown colony, but a British nation with a nation's responsibilities and wealth . . .'[39] The new immediacy of the war had the effect of diminishing that difficulty. With regard to the press, for example, in contrast to 1914 when only a few journals like the *Globe* of Toronto and the *Manitoba Free Press* had treated the conflict as a genuinely Canadian one, in the course of 1915 a number of other Liberal papers such as the *Saint John Telegraph*, the *Hamilton Times*, the *Edmonton Bulletin*, the *Montreal Herald*, and the *London Advertiser*, as well as several Conservative organs including the *Montreal Star*, the *Ottawa Journal*, the *Winnipeg Telegram*, and *Saturday Night* adopted that nationalistic stance.[40]

Other indices of the English-Canadian patriotic viewpoint also suggested that during the summer of 1915 a Canadianization process was beginning to take place with respect to the war. That this must happen, certainly, was the implication of the national survey commissioned by Sir George Foster, the acting prime minister during Borden's visit to Great Britain. Foster, who was personally convinced that 'Canada is slowly recruiting — but unaroused to the necessities and something unusual must be done,' arranged via the Canadian Press Association to have three Toronto advertising agencies canvass the country to find out what was wrong with recruiting and then to suggest remedies.[41] The conclusions of the three firms, McConnell and Ferguson Ltd, J. J. Gibbons Ltd, and A. McKim Ltd were enlightening, because all were agreed that the major factors discouraging enlistment were a 'lack of a sufficiently deep realization of Canada's interest and stake in the war,' and a 'disbelief in an unfavourable outcome of the war.'[42] Foster's determination to resolve this difficulty and to bring home the reality of the war to Canadians by means of a nation-wide newspaper recruiting campaign was, however, thwarted by none other than the minister of militia himself who refused to admit that such propaganda was either necessary or effective; as Hughes awkwardly but expressively explained to Borden in mid-September, 'recruits must come from inspiration from within.'[43]

A popular manifestation of English-Canadian patriotic fervor also occasioned by the dramatically heightened import of the Great War was the machine-gun campaign initiated in July 1915. Begun in response to rumours that the Canadian Expeditionary Force lagged far behind the enemy in terms of automatic weaponry, this campaign caught the public imagination particularly after the acting minister of militia, Senator J. A. Lougheed, assured a *Toronto Mail and Empire* interviewer on 19 July that the federal government welcomed all voluntary donations of money to be used for the acquisition of additional machine-guns.[44] From one end of Canada to the other, individuals, private groups, and even lower levels of government took up the cause, so that within a few weeks over a million dollars had been voluntarily subscribed for that purpose.[45] Though upon his return to Canada in September Sir Robert Borden moved quickly to put a halt to this campaign on the grounds that, as a matter of principle, 'the Treasury ought properly to bear all the cost of equipping and maintaining our forces in the field,' the whole episode did provide a valuable measure of the ever-growing concern of English Canadians from all regions of the country about Canada's place in the war.[46]

329

Illustrative of the intensified English-Canadian patriotic spirit, too, was the proliferation of civilian recruiting associations modelled on the Speakers' Patriotic League but more narrowly confined to a specific geographical area — city, town, county — throughout Canada in the last half of 1915 and the first quarter of 1916. The rationale for this development was later explained by S. F. Washington, a Hamilton lawyer, who argued that: 'The Recruiting Leagues of this Province and throughout the Dominion were formed because the men required to furnish Overseas Battalions were not coming, as we thought, fast enough. The first call was promptly responded to by the best and the bravest, the men who saw their duty without Recruiting Leagues or recruiting speeches. The first 100 000 came easily. We found other men were not coming.'[47] What had happened was that the federal government had responded to Great Britain's request for further military assistance by augmenting the total complement of the Canadian Expeditionary Force to 150 000 in June 1915; but that decision had come at the very time of year when, because of expanded seasonal employment opportunities, the task of recruiting had become more difficult.[48] The resulting — and entirely unforeseen — convergence of increased demands and diminishing returns raised the prospect that Canada was in danger of reneging on its manpower commitment to the war effort. The civilian recruiting organizations were designed to ensure that this did not occur.

Fear that the Canadian patriotic zeal was beginning to falter was most prevalent among the local military authorities, and it was they who took the initiative and appealed for the collective assistance of prominent civilians in their areas. Typical was the case of Hamilton which prided itself on having established the first civic recruiting league in all of Canada at the beginning of July. According to a pamphlet published by that Recruiting League, 'in the summer of 1915 . . . the flow of recruits began to show signs of sluggishness, and the Militia authorities became concerned.

The idea of civilian cooperation, with a view to rousing public interest in the state of the war and Canada's obligations, originated in the fertile brain of Col. S. C. Mewburn.'[49] The Department of National Defence records indicate that Mewburn's example was followed by local military officials — usually divisional GOCs — in other parts of Canada as well.[50] But while these recruiting associations were organized at the behest of the military establishment, once in existence they drew their strength, both in terms of personnel and enthusiasm, from the business and professional middle class of English Canada.

Certainly there was no doubt that the civilian recruiting movement was essentially an English-speaking one. Theoretically, for example, there were both English- and French-speaking branches of the Citizens' Recruiting Association of Montreal established in September 1915, but in fact the latter was ineffectual.[51] Only in Quebec City, where in January 1916 l'Association Civile de Recrutement was set up, was there anything comparable to the elaborate organizational structures created in places like Halifax, Saint John, Fredericton, Ottawa, Toronto, Hamilton, London, Winnipeg, Regina, Vancouver, and Victoria; and nowhere in the province of Quebec were there the many town and municipal leagues that came into being in the other provinces.[52] Just as assuredly, the civilian recruiting organizations were dominated by middle-class Canadians. Very much representative in this respect was the Winnipeg Citizens' Recruiting League, founded in February 1916, which grew out of a preliminary committee of one hundred drawn from the local Board of Trade, the University of Manitoba, the credit associations, the manufacturers, doctors, lawyers, judges, the Grain Exchange, the Canadian Club, and the military authorities.[53] The same class of citizens, and in many cases the same individuals, who had filled the ranks of the Canadian Patriotic Fund Association at the outset of the war manned the civilian recruiting leagues when, by the summer of 1915, their patriotic necessity had become evident.[54]

The spread of the civilian recruiting movement across Canada during the last half of 1915 marked a new stage in the English-Canadian patriotic response to the Great War. Long gone were the confident expectations of a quick and easy allied victory; receding into the past, too, was the belief that Canada need play only a subordinate, ancillary role in the conflict. Perhaps the most articulate spokesman for the new patriotic viewpoint that was beginning to emerge was the *Edmonton Bulletin* which, on 14 October 1915, called upon the Borden administration to be absolutely clear as to whether Canada was merely assisting Great Britain or was fighting on her own behalf; the difference, it maintained, was crucial because 'Whichever of these two views prevails at Ottawa determines which amount of energy it is proper for us to exert. If we are merely lending a hand in order to save our kinsmen and friends in Great Britain from the unpleasantness of what has happened to Belgium, our contribution has undoubtedly been a striking testimonial to our neighborliness and our loyalty to kith and kin. But if we are fighting, as the people of Great

330

Britain are fighting, to preserve our national liberties and our individual lives and rights, the case is somewhat different. On that understanding we are required to put ourselves into the conflict as though we were fighting to protect our homes and country and all that we have to lose.'[55] If the conflict were really a Canadian one, the *Bulletin* was arguing, nothing less than a total war effort should be expected of the country.

As events of the next year and a half would demonstrate, the concept of a total Canadian war effort would severely challenge and ultimately triumph over another of the basic tenets of the original English Canadian patriotic outlook — the inviolability of the voluntary system. In some respects, in fact, the inadequacies of that approach were becoming apparent as early as the winter of 1915–16, though to be sure at that time there was still no real concern that it could not be relied upon to furnish a sufficient number of recruits, not even when, on 1 January 1916, Prime Minister Borden suddenly raised the total Canadian military commitment to the war to half a million men.[56] In the opinion of a growing number of English-Canadian businessmen, rather, the problem was that the voluntary system was not selective, and that consequently the military and industrial manpower needs of the country were beginning to conflict.[57] In Parliament, in the press, and in representations to Borden the most frequently advanced solution was for the federal government to take a survey of all adult, male Canadians in order to determine who were employed in industries essential to a healthy war economy, and who could be spared for military service.[58] The assumption of many of those pressing for such a national registration was that the voluntary system would only have to be temporarily set aside, that once the census had been completed it would simply be a matter of appealing directly to the patriotic consciences of those who had been declared eligible for overseas duty, and thereby the ranks of the CEF would be filled without serious disruption to the domestic scene.

For activists in the civilian recruiting movement, the situation was not nearly so straight-forward. Starting in December 1915 citizens' recruiting associations in many English-Canadian cities such as Hamilton, Toronto, London, Saint John, Berlin, and Winnipeg had taken surveys of the manpower resources in their own communities, but their efforts had not yielded much in the way of results.[59] In large measure this was because the returns of their censuses were fragmentary, a fact that most certainly underlined the necessity for a compulsory, nationwide registration. Yet at the same time, their experiences also suggested that by itself such a national inventory of manpower would not be of much value. Even on the basis of the incomplete information their enquiries elicited they were able to discover, at least to their own satisfaction, the names of some individuals who could readily be freed for military service, and had made direct, personal appeals to them. Too often, those appeals had been ignored.[60] For those frustrated in this manner the only logical answer was to couple national registration with the application of compulsory military service.

Taking the lead in the demand for the twin policies of registration and

331

conscription was the Hamilton Recruiting League which, on 7 March 1916, adopted the following resolution:

To the Right Hon. Sir Robert Laird Borden, P.C., G.C.M.G., K.C., L.D., Premier of the Dominion of Canada. The Memorial of the Hamilton Recruiting League Respectfully Sheweth:
That the Dominion of Canada is engaged in a war involving the very existence of British institutions — a war that calls for the most rigid economy of men and means — a war that can be successfully concluded by the fullest utilization of our resources.
That under the present voluntary system there is great waste of the Nation's resources. Therefore your Memorialists pray that a Commission be appointed for the purpose of:
Taking a census of all men in the Dominion from eighteen years of age and upward, specifying those married and unmarried.
Classifying the men according to their occupations or their fitness or preference for certain kinds of work.
Classifying the industries with a view to the restriction or the ultimate elimination of such as are non-essential to the welfare of the country or are not economic factors.
It being understood that the foregoing is urged with a view to the immediate application of some just and comprehensive system of draft, whereby the men necessary to complete the Canadian Expeditionary Forces may be readily secured.[61]

332

That this memorial was not simply the whim of a single, isolated group of Hamiltonians was shown in the fact that by the time of its presentation to Prime Minister Borden on 14 April 1916 it had been formally endorsed by nearly sixty other recruiting associations including both the Eastern and Central Ontario branches of the Speakers' Patriotic League, as well as by a number of civic Boards of Trade, municipal councils, and mass meetings.[62] Though most of that support came from Ontario, the presence of delegates from Winnipeg, Halifax, and Saint John in Ottawa on that second Friday in April demonstrated there was some enthusiasm for registration and conscription in the other provinces as well.

By his own admission, Borden's response to the various arguments put forward on behalf of the memorial — the voluntary system was scored for being wasteful, inefficient, indiscriminate, expensive, unbusinesslike, un-British, and inadequate — was cautious and diplomatic.[63] He began and ended his brief remarks by praising the work of the civilian recruiting leagues, but devoted most of his time to arguing that because, in his view, the pace of recruiting was already more than satisfactory, it would be inadvisable to introduce controversial and bureaucratically difficult measures such as those being proposed.[64] For some of the delegates like John Godfrey, however, the government's position was more candidly explained by Sir George Foster with whom they later met privately on Friday afternoon. 'Sir George,' Godfrey recalled, 'laid particular emphasis on the fact that the government could do nothing on account of the attitude of Quebec. He led us to believe that from their information serious trouble would result if drastic measures were taken.'[65]

In view of Prime Minister Borden's reluctance to accept the merits of the case pressed upon him by the Hamilton memorialists it was decided to create an association whose purpose would be to mobilize Canadian public opinion behind the policies of registration and conscription. Accordingly, the representatives of the various recruiting leagues met at the Chateau

Laurier on the evening of 14 April and established the Canadian National Service League, with Chief Justice T. G. Mathers of the Manitoba Court of King's Bench as honorary president, John Godfrey as president, and A. H. Abbott of the University of Toronto as secretary.[66] This executive moved quickly to fulfil its mandate, publishing in early May a pamphlet entitled *Canada and National Service* which outlined the details of the Hamilton memorial and its presentation to Borden, and then calling a public meeting at the National Club in Toronto to consider other means of popularizing the goals of the CNSL.[67] The decision then made to hold a series of mass public rallies, beginning with one in Massey Hall later in May, was invalidated by a directive from the federal Department of the Interior urging the Canadian press not to report popular agitation for conscription because such stories were adversely affecting the flow of immigrants from the United States.[68] Justifiably alarmed by this challenge to the *raison d'etre* of the National Service League, Godfrey and several of his associates journeyed to Ottawa on 10 May to discuss the matter with Borden once again. To their dismay, they learned that the prime minister was generally sympathetic to the controversial directive, although he claimed not be have been consulted about its release; furthermore, he remained adamantly opposed to conscription on the grounds that it was unnecessary, that it would be unenforceable so long as the United States remained neutral, and that it would cause serious difficulties in Quebec.[69] As Godfrey later commented, 'these reasons were so cogent that the delegation had to accept Sir Robert's view, with the result that the National Service League launched with such enthusiasm a few weeks before was left stranded with nothing to do.'[70]

333

Undoubtedly contrary to what Borden had hoped, the decision of the Canadian National Service League to cancel, at least for the time being, its campaign in support of registration and conscription did not remove those topics from the realm of public discussion, because the factor chiefly responsible for giving rise to their demand — the clash between the domestic and military manpower needs of the country — increasingly occupied English-Canadian attention during the summer of 1916. Individual civilian recruiting bodies like the Central Ontario branch of the Speakers' Patriotic League simply ignored the official forbearance of the CNSL and worked to keep those issues before the public eye.[71] Similarly, in the English-Canadian press, many of the same newspapers that had extolled the virtues of a national registration scheme at the beginning of the year continued to pressure the Borden government to take action.[72] Most importantly, a multiplicity of groups and associations that had previously remained silent on these matters began to make themselves heard. At the annual summer conferences of the Anglican, Presbyterian, Methodist, and Congregational Union churches, resolutions calling for registration and/or conscription were passed with barely a murmur of opposition.[73] Organizations such as local branches of the National Council of Women and affiliates of the Women's Emergency Corps — an association established earlier in the year to facilitate the substitution of women for men in the workplace and thereby free the latter for military service — sponsored mass meetings in Toronto, Hamilton, Calgary, Edmonton, London, and Montreal, all of which endorsed the taking of a national manpower census.[74] So too did a number of business and governmental organizations, the most notable of which were the Canadian Manufacturers' Association, the Union of Saskatchewan Municipalities, and the Ontario legislature's Organization of Resources Committee.[75] Throughout June, July, and August 1916, finally, public meetings of the local military authorities in Toronto, Edmonton, London, and Montreal all came to the conclusion that the half million men promised by Sir Robert Borden could only be efficiently recruited by means of a national registration.[76]

The growing crescendo of support in English Canada for some sort of legislative action by the federal authorities to rationalize the allocation of Canada's limited manpower resources was reinforced by the private appeals made to Prime Minister Borden and his colleagues. The minister of finance, Sir Thomas White, was most impressed by the argument of Ontario businessmen that they were suffering by comparison to their Quebec competitors because the former province was being denuded of skilled labour while the latter was not, a situation that could only be rectified by registration and/or conscription.[77] Although Sir Sam Hughes continued to dismiss such fears as groundless, and although Borden himself was convinced that 'reg[istratio]n means in end conscription and that might mean civil war in Quebec,' by the middle of June the prime minister had finally decided that something would have to be done.[78] The eventual outcome of that decision was the establishment of what came to be known as the National Service Board in mid-August 1916, although it was not until the second week of October that the board actually got down to work.[79]

The public reception accorded to the National Service Board was mixed. In the English-Canadian press even newspapers of the Conservative persuasion were not overly enthusiastic, although most did breathe a grateful sigh of relief that action of some sort was being taken, while those with Liberal leanings either reserved judgment or were highly critical of the fact that the national census to be taken under the board's auspices was to be voluntary rather than compulsory.[80] For activists in the Canadian National Service League such as John Godfrey and Lt-Col. Lorne W. Mulloy, the blinded veteran of the Boer war and lecturer in military history at Royal Military College, the decision not to make the registration compulsory for all Canadians was totally incomprehensible and condemned the whole scheme to inevitable failure.[81]

Part of the explanation for the uneasiness about the National Service Board was that by the autumn of 1916 the voluntary system of recruitment was coming under attack for a new and much more urgent reason. By that time the Canadian Expeditionary Force had been expanded to four complete divisions, with a fifth in the planning stages.[82] Yet the first two years of the war had demonstrated that wastage on the line was extremely high — perhaps as high as 25 per cent — which meant that a Canadian Corps consisting of five divisions would require about 25 000 men per month as reinforcements alone.[83] Such a rate of replacement may have seemed feasible at the beginning of 1916 when, as in March, a record 35 000 volunteers came forward, but by October when the corresponding figure was 6000, expectations of this kind could no longer be realistically maintained.[84] If this progression were to continue, the voluntary system would be hard pressed even to supply reinforcements for the four divisions already in the field. In light of these circumstances it was not surprising that when, during the winter of 1916–17, the monthly gap between military losses and enlistment figures continued to widen at an alarming rate — the difference in February 1917 was over 15 000 although it averaged around the 5000 mark — a very intense and widespread movement developed throughout English Canada for the adoption of some form of compulsory military service.[85]

As had often been the case throughout the previous two years, in the forefront of this new (or for the civilian recruiters, renewed) expression of the English-Canadian patriotic outlook was the press. Generally there were two options proposed by those newspapers which had become convinced that the voluntary system had run its course, both of which were spawned by the continued uncertainty as to whether the existing Militia Act permitted the conscription of Canadians for overseas military service. The one, supported by the *Toronto World* and at least a dozen other English-Canadian daily papers, was for the Militia Act to be applied for home defence only.[86] This more limited form of compulsion was thought to have several advantages; not only would it facilitate in an authoritative manner the rational allocation of manpower, but it would also immediately release for overseas duty the 50 000 volunteers who were being retained in Canada as a home defence force; and, in addition, there was the hope that the conscripted troops, once they had experienced military life, could be persuaded to join the Canadian Expeditionary Force.[87]

The other alternative counselled by the English-Canadian press was for the Borden administration to enact new legislation providing for conscription for overseas service. Chronologically, this proposal had first been put forward by both Liberal newspapers like the *Regina Leader* and the *London Advertiser* and Conservative journals like the *Toronto Telegram* and the *Ottawa Journal,* but during the first quarter of 1917 it had taken second place to the idea of applying the Militia Act for home defence.[88] By mid-April 1917, however, several new factors had arisen to bring it into favour once again. Chief among these were the dismal failure of the government's plan to recruit voluntarily a special Canadian Defence Force, the national pride in the Canadian Expeditionary Force engendered by the widely reported battle honours won at Vimy Ridge on 9 April, and the adoption of conscription by the latest entrant into the Great War, the United States.[89] Well before Prime Minister Borden's 18 May announce-

335

ment of his government's decision to introduce compulsory military service, these developments had prompted at least thirty English-Canadian papers to conclude that such a course of action was unavoidable.[90] Considering that another dozen newspapers were also demanding the application of the Militia Act, it is clear that by the beginning of May 1917 the English-Canadian press had finally been forced to disavow the voluntary system of recruitment.

Disillusionment with the system in English Canada was by no means restricted to the press. During the winter of 1916–17 a plethora of organizations and clubs also speaking for the English-Canadian patriotic mentality began to espouse conscription. Most of the civilian recruiting leagues had already publicly declared themselves on the issue, so there was little more they could do, although at least one, the Greater Vancouver Recruiting League, chose in January 1917 to reconstitute itself into the 'War and National Service League,' with the objective to 'advocate and do all in its power to secure the immediate introduction of compulsory military service ...'[91] But while the recruiting associations played a relatively minor role in the growing popular demand for compulsion, either for home defence or for overseas military service, other groups — Boards of Trade, municipal councils, church organizations, women's clubs, fraternal orders, veterans' associations, local military establishments — were correspondingly much more vocal in pressing those options on the federal government.[92]

The outcry for compulsory military service that overtook English Canada during the winter of 1916–17 was only one measure of public dissatisfaction with the voluntary war effort to which the Borden administration was so resolutely adhering. Another, equally important, was the emergence of a popular movement to replace that administration by a 'national,' 'win the war' government. Though there were both partisan and political considerations that gave rise to this proposal — for example, the determination of some English-Canadian Liberals to get rid of what they thought to be a highly incompetent Conservative administration without handing the reins of power over to their own party, whose leadership they no longer trusted, and the desire of some politicians, Liberal and Conservative, to avoid what they deemed a needless and potentially divisive wartime election — a factor of some significance as well was the patriotic belief that partisanship itself was responsible for the flagging Canadian war effort.[93] Essentially it was feared that party rather than national concerns were determining the actions, and inactions, of Borden and his colleagues, and that this situation would not be greatly altered by putting Laurier and the Liberal party in their stead. As the *Toronto Star* explained, what the country desperately needed was 'a patriotic War Ministry, non-partisan and efficient, prepared to unite the whole people and centre all the nation's energies on the winning of the war and the handling with courage of those problems which a party Government to-day trembles and fears to touch.'[94] That this demand should have been articulated precisely at the time when public support for conscription was growing throughout

336

English Canada was not merely coincidental. So long as the recruitment of the Canadian Expeditionary Force had remained voluntary and therefore in a sense extra-governmental in nature, the fact that there was a party government in Ottawa was not of much concern; but when the voluntary approach began to fail and it was realized that only the federal administration possessed the moral and legal authority to enforce compulsory military service, then a debate about the suitability of a partisan government became inevitable.

Behind the national government idea, too, was the belief that the war was a truly Canadian one that could only be won by the resolute marshalling of the country's entire resources. In the words of John W. Dafoe, editor of the *Manitoba Free Press*:

The view, amply justified by events, that disaster would be escaped by a narrow margin through unlimited sacrifice by the nations, was widely and passionately held in Canada; and to those who held it, it seemed in 1917 that the time was near at hand when the brave talk about the last man and the last dollar would have to be made good. It was from them that the demand for a national government and for measures that would put the last reserves of the country into the furnace came. These were the people who believed that Canada was in the war as a principal; that we had not gone into the war to oblige or to assist any other nation; and that the country could not set any limits to its exertions that fell short of the totality of its powers.[95]

337

In addition to the *Free Press*, support for the national government plan was forthcoming from a number of other Liberal newspapers, including the *Toronto Star*, from several independent journals like the *Grain Growers' Guide*, and from a few Conservative papers like the *Toronto World*, the *Hamilton Herald*, and the *Vancouver News-Advertiser*.[96] From an organizational perspective, only in Winnipeg was there an outburst of enthusiasm for the proposal, which was likely attributable to the fact that two of the city's three daily newspapers were boosting it.[97] Yet the absence of petitions and resolutions approving the scheme elsewhere in English Canada did not necessarily mean that it was unpopular, because during the same period that it was being discussed by the press, Ontario activists in the civilian recruiting movement were able to stir up a good deal of public support for yet another patriotic campaign that was designed to lead to the same end.

The suggestion that a national 'Win the War' convention might serve as 'the best means of unifying, organizing and expressing the intense patriotism which undoubtedly exists all over Canada' was first seriously discussed at a meeting of about forty professional and business men at the National Club in Toronto on 9 February 1917, but the genesis of the idea was to be found in Prime Minister Borden's scuttling of the Canadian National Service League in May 1916.[98] Though Borden had cited a variety of reasons why the CNSL should drop its plan to popularize registration and conscription, the one that had seemed to league president, John Godfrey, to be uppermost in the prime minister's mind was fear of the French-Canadian reaction to those policies. Accordingly, in mid-June, Godfrey had undertaken to channel the unused patriotic resources of the CNSL into a project to send a delegation of Ontario businessmen on a good will tour of Quebec. Privately his hope was that 'as a result of this visit we [will] . . . be able to form in Quebec branches of the National Service League. It is then proposed that from these branch organizations a large and representative deputation of French Canadians go to Ottawa and ask the government for national registration and compulsory selection which will include Quebec.'[99] In fact, nothing of the sort eventuated from what came to be known as the 'Bonne Entente' exchanges of October 1916 and January 1917 between the Ontario and Quebec business communities, and consequently Godfrey and his associates turned to the Win the War proposal.[100]

Though it was to suffer from many of the same misunderstandings that plagued the Bonne Entente exchanges, from the viewpoint of its English-Canadian organizers the Win the War movement embodied all of the measures necessary to remedy the ills of the Canadian war effort.[101] Godfrey himself, for example, was convinced that the conference would call for the formation of a national government, but he recognized that this could not be publicized beforehand because, for political reasons, 'it would handicap such a convention to have a National Government programme outlined in advance.'[102] John W. Dafoe, who threw the editorial support of the *Manitoba Free Press* behind both, also associated the two campaigns when he wrote privately that the proposed congress 'was really a part of the National Government movement and it is expected to bring it to a head.'[103] Similarly, although here again there was a reluctance on the part of its English-speaking proponents to say so publicly, the Win the War idea was closely tied to the demand for compulsory military service that was spreading throughout English Canada. While Godfrey claimed to have devised a compulsory national registration scheme that would obviate the need for outright conscription, most of his fellow Win the Warriors remained firmly on the compulsion bandwagon, though few were as forthright as Frank Fetherstonhaugh, a Conservative lawyer from Toronto, who declared that the whole objective was to 'make our French Canadian fellow Citizens appreciate the necessity of Conscription.'[104]

By the time that the approximately 300 English-Canadian Win the War delegates had joined an equal number of their French-speaking confrères in Montreal on 23 May, the whole exercise had been rendered redundant by other, more momentous developments. The need to proclaim the virtues of conscription, for example, had been considerably lessened by Prime Minister Borden's announcement of that policy a few days before. Shortly, too, the Win the Warriors' other chief objective — the formation of a national government — seemed about to come to fruition when rumours began to circulate publicly of Borden's coalition offer to the leader of the official opposition, Sir Wilfrid Laurier.[105]

Yet as a measure of the matured English-Canadian patriotic response to the Great War, the Win the War idea was without parallel. For as *La Presse* of Montreal correctly perceived, the English-Canadian Win the Warriors were 'animés seulement par la pensée . . . que cette guerre est notre guerre et que le travail de la victoire est notre tâche'; and because they believed it was Canada's war, they refused to accept anything less than a total war effort which, they had concluded, could only be provided by a national government fearlessly implementing a fair and equitable system of compulsory military service.[106] Consequently, when Laurier rejected Borden's coalition overtures early in June and announced his opposition to the proposed Military Service Act, Win the War associations such as those in Ontario and the four western provinces were galvanized into action once again, reaffirming their faith in a 'non-party Government' and resolving 'to oppose the election of any candidate who does not publicly agree to support every measure calculated to bring the full strength of the country in men, money and resources into effective use for winning the war . . .'[107] That determination interacted with, and was reinforced by, a similar resolution on the part of the English-Canadian press, and together these two depositories of the English-Canadian patriotic perspective worked throughout the summer of 1917 to assist Prime Minister Borden in his quest for a 'Union' administration.[108] And so it was that in the general election of December 1917 English-Canadian patriots helped to return to power a government which they believed was created in their own image and dedicated, like themselves, to ensuring that Canada would fight 'as a nation and an ally.'

339

Notes

The preparation of this paper has been assisted by Canada Council research funds administered by Laurentian University. Special thanks must also be given to Professor Craig Brown and Mr. Henry Borden for their permission to consult the Borden Diaries.

1. Godfrey to Laurier, 17 Nov. 1916, Laurier Papers, Public Archives of Canada [PAC], 193817–21 [hereafter LP]

2. The use of the term 'middle class' is an impressionistic one, based on variables such as occupation, income, and educational status. It includes persons engaged in business, industry, manufacturing, finance, and commerce, at both the ownership and managerial levels, as well as those in professions such as law, medicine, engineering, education, and journalism.

3. As far as can be determined, no major Canadian daily newspaper dissented from this decision, while a whole range of groups and organizations like the Association of Canadian Clubs applauded it. See R. M. Bray, 'The Canadian Patriotic Response to the Great War' (unpublished Ph D dissertation, York University, 1976), 14–17.

4. See, for example, *Le Devoir*, editorial by Henri Bourassa, 'Le Devoir National,' 8 Sept. 1914, which tentatively endorsed Canadian entrance into the war. Similarly, even though the 1914 annual meeting of the Trades and Labor Congress of Canada reiterated its condemnation of capitalistic wars, it added the rider that the present conflict was not of Great Britain's choosing.

5. Castell Hopkins, *Canadian Annual Review, 1914* (Toronto 1915), 142–3.

6. For the reaction of the Conservative press in Toronto see the following editorials: *Toronto World*, 4 Aug. 1914; *Toronto Mail and Empire*, 1 Aug. 1914; *Toronto News*, 6 Aug. 1914; *Toronto Telegram*, 5 Aug. 1914; The views of the Liberal journals were to be found in editorials in the *Globe*, 12 Aug. 1914, and the *Toronto Star*, 4 Aug. 1914.

7. *Grain Growers' Guide*, editorial, 12 Aug. 1914; *Manitoba Free Press*, 8 Aug. 1914.

8. Newspapers expressing this editorial viewpoint included *Regina Leader*, 1 Aug. 1914; *Edmonton Bulletin*, 4 Aug. 1914; *Montreal Star*, 31 July 1914; *Ottawa Journal*, 1 Aug. 1914; *Saint John Telegraph*, 1 Aug. 1914; *Winnipeg Tribune*, 1 Aug. 1914; *Winnipeg Telegram*, 1 Aug. 1914; *Halifax Herald*, 1 Aug. 1914; *Halifax Chronicle*, 1 Aug. 1914; *London Advertiser*, 1 Aug. 1914; *London Free Press*, 5 Aug. 1914; *Victoria Times*, 4 Aug. 1914; *Brockville Recorder*, 4 Aug. 1914; *Hamilton Herald*, 5 Aug. 1914; *Hamilton Times*, 3 Aug. 1914; *Hamilton Spectator*, 4 Aug. 1914; *Weekly Sun* (Toronto), 5 Aug. 1914; *Saint John*

Globe, 4 Aug. 1914; *Montreal Gazette,* 5 Aug. 1914; *Calgary Herald,* 5 Aug. 1914; *Financial Post* (Toronto), 15 Aug. 1914; *Charlottetown Examiner,* 8 Aug. 1914; *Saskatoon Star,* 5 Aug. 1914; *Orange Sentinel* (Toronto), 6 Aug. 1914; *Canadian Baptist* (Toronto), 6 Aug. 1914; *Canadian Churchman* (Toronto), 6 Aug. 1914; *L'Evénement* (Quebec), 31 July 1914; *La Presse* (Montreal), 3 Aug. 1914; *La Patrie* (Montreal), 6 Aug. 1914; *Le Droit* (Ottawa), 5 Aug. 1914; *L'Evangéline* (Moncton), 26 Aug. 1914; *Guelph Herald,* 17 Aug. 1914; *Montreal Mail,* 3 Aug. 1914; *Vancouver News-Advertiser,* 7 Aug. 1914; *Quebec Chronicle,* 5 Aug. 1914.

9. One of those rare exceptions was free-lance journalist Arthur Hawkes, who advocated the creation of a Canadian Patriotic League to acquaint Canadians with what was at stake for them in the war. See the *Globe* article, 'Mr. Hawkes Suggests Patriotic League,' 14 Aug. 1914.

10. *Toronto Mail and Empire,* editorial, 'The Second Contingent,' 16 Oct. 1914.

11. For examples, see the editorials cited in note 8 above.

12. Sir Thomas White, *The Story of Canada's War Finance* (Montreal 1921), 13–14.

13. *Saint John Telegraph,* article, 'Shortest War On Record Says U.S. Military Expert,' 5 Aug. 1914.

14. *Globe,* editorial note, 10 Nov. 1914.

15. Hughes even bragged that it was necessary to dampen Canadian patriotic enthusiasm because too many men were volunteering. See Hughes to Borden, 10 Sept. 1914, Borden Papers, PAC, 12469 [hereafter BP].

16. Address by Sir Robert Borden to the Halifax Canadian Club, 18 Dec. 1914, BP, 34672.

17. For a detailed account of these activities see Castell Hopkins, *Canada at War* (Toronto 1919), 246–67.

18. Ibid.

19. Cited in Phillip H. Morris, ed., *The Canadian Patriotic Fund* (Toronto nd), 10.

20. In *The Canadian Patriotic Fund* Morris lists all the local affiliates and their executives. A good example of the middle-class domination of those branches was the case of Hamilton where the executive consisted of Sir John Hendrie as honorary president, Cyrus A. Birge, president of the Mercantile Trust Company of Canada, as president, George C. Coppley, president of Coppley, Noyes and Randall Ltd., as vice-president, Robert Hobson, president of the Steel Company of Canada, as chairman of the finance committee, J. P. Bell, general manager of the Bank of Hamilton, as honorary treasurer, and Norman Slater, president of Slater and Barnard Ltd, as honorary secretary, Ibid. 220.

21. *Calgary Herald,* editorial note, 7 Sept. 1914; *Edmonton Bulletin,* editorial note, 22 Aug. 1914.

22. Borden was petitioned by such individuals as Mayor T. R. Deacon of Winnipeg and the Manitoba minister of education, George Coldwell, to augment the CEF. See Deacon to Borden, 27 Aug. 1914, BP, 104215, and Coldwell to Borden, 8 Oct. 1914, BP, 104264–6. Newspapers which editorially did likewise included *Montreal Star,* 11 Sept. 1914; *Charlottetown Examiner,* 12 Sept. 1914; *Ottawa Journal,* 10 Sept. 1914; *Hamilton Herald,* 19 Sept. 1914; *Montreal Gazette,* 23 Sept. 1914; *London Free Press,* 23 Sept. 1914; *Vancouver News-Advertiser,* 5 Oct. 1914; *Winnipeg Tribune,* 26 Sept. 1914; *London Advertiser,* 5 Oct. 1914; *Halifax Chronicle,* 2 Oct. 1914.

23. Borden to Perley, 7 Oct. 1914, BP, 104249.

24. *Montreal Star,* editorial, 'A Second Contingent,' 7 Oct. 1914.

25. This concern was to be found in the following editorials: *Financial Post,* 17 Oct. 1914; *Toronto Star,* 17 Oct. 1914; *Halifax Chronicle,* 19 Oct. 1914; *Manitoba Free Press,* 13 Oct. 1914; *Victoria Times,* 17 Oct. 1914.

26. *Saturday Night* (Toronto), editorial, 'The Front Page,' 6 Feb. 1915; *Globe,* editorial, 'Call To Young Canada,' 23 Jan. 1915.

27. These Honor Rolls, which became a regular feature in the *Montreal Star* commencing on 22 February 1915, were widely commented upon by the press in other parts of Canada.

28. Bray, 'The Canadian Patriotic Response', 68–75.

29. Davidson to Ames, 9 Feb. 1915, BP, 108444–5.

30. *Speakers' Patriotic League, Central Ontario Branch, Report Of the Executive Committee covering operations from the date of organization to May 31st, 1916* (Toronto nd), 5.

31. Ibid.

32. Ames to Borden, 26 Feb. 1915, BP, 108480–1.

33. The Montreal branch of the Speaker's Patriotic League gave way to the Citizens' Recruiting Association of Montreal on 17 September 1915 because, according to one of its executive, J. S. Brierley, it failed to measure up to the demands made of it. *Montreal Gazette,* article, 'Leading Citizens To Aid Recruiting,' 18 Sept. 1915.

34. *Speakers' Patriotic League, Central Ontario Branch, Final Report of the Executive Committee, January, 1919* (np, nd), 16.

35. John Swettenham, *To Seize the Victory* (Toronto 1965), 77–8.

36. Borden to Norman Ruse, secretary, Regina Canadian Club, 7 June 1915, BP, 31556–7.

37. Morris, *The Canadian Patriotic Fund,* 21.

38. Acting high commissioner to prime minister, 29 May 1915, *Documents on Canadian External Relations,* 1 (Ottawa 1967), Document 125, 73–4.

39. Castell Hopkins, *Canadian Annual Review, 1915* (Toronto 1916), 216.
40. Such a nationalistic perspective was expressed in the following editorials: *Saint John Telegraph,* 2 July 1915; *Hamilton Times,* 12 July 1915; *Edmonton Bulletin,* 14 Oct. 1915; *Montreal Herald,* 4 Aug. 1915; *London Advertiser,* 2 Dec. 1915; *Montreal Star,* 28 Aug. 1915; *Ottawa Journal,* 29 Oct. 1915; *Winnipeg Telegram,* 18 Oct. 1915; *Saturday Night,* 28 Aug. 1915.
41. Foster Diary, PAC, 3 July 1915.
42. J. M. McConnell to Foster, 27 July 1915, BP, 108650–1, and J. J. Gibbons to Foster, 27 July 1915, BP, 108645–9.
43. Hughes to Borden, 24 Sept. 1915, BP, 108704.
44. Hopkins, *Canadian Annual Review, 1915,* 208.
45. Ibid., 211.
46. Cited in the *Montreal Gazette,* article, 'Sir Robert Greeted at Saint John,' 20 Oct. 1915.
47. *Canada and National Service* (Toronto nd), 7.
48. J. L. Granatstein and J. M. Hitsman, *Broken Promises: A History of Conscription in Canada* (Toronto 1977), 34.
49. *The Recruiting League of Hamilton* (Hamilton nd), 3.
50. See, for example, acting Adjutant-General W. E. Hodgins to GOC 6th Division, Halifax, 27 Sept. 1915, Records of the Department of National Defence, PAC, HQ125–1–6.
51. Major-General G. W. Wilson to Sir Edward Kemp, 3 May 1917, Kemp Papers, PAC, Wilson, GOC of Military District #4 based in Montreal, reported that the French-speaking wing of the association had been unable even to raise minimal recruiting expenses and therefore had been inactive.
52. Accounts of the formation of these various recruiting leagues may be found in the following articles: *Halifax Chronicle,* 'Nova Scotia Recruiting Association,' 4 Oct. 1915; *Saint John Telegraph,* 'Recruiting Call Comes To This Province,' 31 Aug. 1915; *Saint John Telegraph,* 'Stream of Recruits Given Encouragement,' 17 Sept. 1915; *Ottawa Journal,* 'Ward Campaign Inaugurated To Get More Recruits For 107th Battalion,' 3 May 1916; *Toronto Mail and Empire,* 'Citizens' League Is Now Organized,' 5 Aug. 1915; *The Recruiting League of Hamilton, 3; London Advertiser,* 'Citizens To Help Recruiting Officers,' 17 Aug. 1915; *Winnipeg Tribune,* 'League Is Formed for Recruiting,' 11 Feb. 1916; *Regina Leader,* 'Citizens' Recruiting League To Be Formed Here Next Friday,' 1 March 1916; *Vancouver News-Advertiser,* 'Recruiting League Formed By Meeting,' 16 May 1916; *Victoria Times,* 'Civilian Committee Will Aid Recruiting,' 24 July 1916; *Quebec Chronicle,* 'Recruiting Association Is Formed By Citizens,' 28 Jan. 1916. An analysis of the spread of the civilian recruiting movement across Canada is to be found in Bray, 'The Canadian Patriotic Response,' 98–119.
53. *Winnipeg Tribune,* article, 'League Is Formed For Recruiting,' 11 Feb. 1916.
54. In the case of the Toronto and York County Patriotic Association, for example, at least half of the executive members were active in some capacity in the Central Ontario branch of the Speakers' Patriotic League and/or the Toronto Citizens' Recruiting League. In smaller communities the overlap between the two was often much greater. In Brantford the Peel County War Auxiliary served both as a branch of the Canadian Patriotic Fund Association and as a recruiting agency.
55. *Edmonton Bulletin,* editorial note, 14 Oct. 1915.
56. Bray, 'The Canadian Patriotic Response,' 153.
57. In the first quarter of 1916 Borden received a series of letters from business men all across Canada complaining about the dislocation caused by recruiting. For example see the following: G. W. Stockton to Borden, 26 Jan. 1916, BP, 108845–7; J. W. Flavelle to Borden, 17 Feb. 1916, BP, 108925–7; Frank Stanfield to Borden, 25 Feb. 1916, BP 108952; Lloyd Harris to Borden, 29 Feb. 1916, BP, 108956–7; D. H. McDougall to Mark Workman, 10 March 1916, BP, 108983; H. Bertram to Borden, 5 April 1916, BP, 109063. The most controversial speech on this issue was made by Lord Shaughnessy, who informed the Montreal Board of Trade on 9 March that Canada could not possibly supply the half million volunteers that Borden had promised. See the *Ottawa Citizen,* article, 'Thinks Canada Cannot Raise Half Million,' 10 March 1916.
58. The call for a national registration of manpower was not a partisan one, as newspapers of both political persuasions articulated it. Some of these were: *Montreal Herald,* 23 Nov. 1915; *Canadian Courier,* Editorial reprinted in the *Hamilton Times,* 16 Dec. 1915; *Regina Leader,* 29 Dec. 1915; *Industrial Canada,* Jan. 1916; *Toronto Star,* 6 Jan. 1916; *Winnipeg Tribune,* 6 Jan. 1916; *Victoria Times,* 5 Jan. 1916; *Ottawa Free Press,* 13 Jan. 1916; *Toronto News,* 26 Jan. 1916; *Stratford Herald,* editorial reprinted in the *Regina Leader,* 7 Feb. 1916; *Toronto Mail and Empire,* 9 Feb. 1916; *Ottawa Journal,* 15 Feb. 1916; *Hamilton Herald,* 23 Feb. 1916; *London Advertiser,* 13 March 1916; *Kingston Whig* and *Brantford Expositor,* editorials reprinted in the *London Advertiser,* 14 March 1916; *Montreal Gazette,* 15 March 1916; *Grain Growers' Guide,* 22 March 1916; *Quebec Chronicle,* 21 March 1916; *Simcoe Reformer,* editorial reprinted in the *Toronto Star,* 28 March 1916; *Halifax Chronicle,* 29 March 1916; *Financial Post,* editorial reprinted in the *Regina Leader,* 29 March 1916. For other examples of this demand see the undated memorandum entitled 'Suggestions Received From Correspondents,' BP, 108902.
59. Details of those surveys may be found in the following sources: *The Recruiting League of Hamilton,* 7–8; *Toronto World,* article, 'Taking Census of Men of Age for Service,' 15 Dec. 1915; *London Advertiser,*

article, 'Personal Canvass To Secure Recruits for London's Own,' 5 Jan. 1916; *Saint John Telegraph*, article, 'Military Census To Be Taken In St. John,' 28 Dec. 1915; *Toronto Mail and Empire*, article, 'Berlin Campaign,' 31 Jan. 1916; *Winnipeg Telegram*, article, 'Exempt Married Men In Present Recruiting Plan,' 3 March 1916.

60. This complaint was registered by recruiting leagues in such places as Hamilton, Toronto, and Saint John. See the *Hamilton Times*, article, 'Amend The Act To Get Full Census Returns,' 8 Jan. 1916, and the *Saint John Telegraph*, article, 'Turning Recruiting Over To Military Authorities,' 16 March 1916.

61. Quoted in *Canada and National Service*, 4.

62. Recruiting Leagues which endorsed the substance of the Hamilton Memorial included those of Stratford, Perth County, Bothwell, Wingham, Windsor, Essex County, Berlin, Clinton, Waterloo, Galt, Sault Ste Marie, Woodstock, Oxford County, Strathroy, Leamington, Toronto, Military Division #2, Port Hope, Renfrew, Collingwood, Brockville, St. Catharines, Kent County, Cobalt, Wentworth County, Trenton, Penetanguishene, Lincoln County, Bowmanville, Grey County, Haldimand County, Peterborough, Norfolk County, Burlington, Chatham, Cayuga, Cobourg, West Flamboro, Georgetown, Goderich, Grimsby, New Hamburg, Parry Sound, St Thomas, Walkerton, North York, Saskatoon, Winnipeg, Brandon, Saint John, New Brunswick, and Nova Scotia. Of other organizations to do likewise, the most notable were the legislative assembly of New Brunswick, the Grand Orange Lodge of Ontario West (Hamilton), a joint meeting of the Liberal and Conservative associations of North Perth, the Windsor and Berlin Boards of Trade, the Stratford Ministerial Association, the municipal councils of St Mary's, Listowel, Stratford, and Milverton, and mass meetings of citizens in Hamilton, London, and Saskatoon. See Bray, 'The Canadian Patriotic Response,' 165–70.

63. Borden diary, PAC, 14 April 1916 [hereafter BD]. A transcript of the presentation of the Hamilton memorial is included in *Canada and National Service*, 29.

64. *Canada and National Service*, 28–9.

65. John M. Godfrey, 'The History of the Bonne Entente including A Narrative of the Events leading up thereto,' unpublished manuscript in the Godfrey Papers, PAC, 5.

66. *Canada and National Service*, 2.

67. Godfrey, 'The History of the Bonne Entente,' 5.

68. Ibid.

69. John M. Godfrey, 'Was Outstanding Figure in Great War — Recruiting — Conscription — Repatriation,' *The Iroquois Post and Mathilda Advocate, Lt. Col. Lorne Winfield Mulloy, D.C.M., B.A., Memorial Supplement* (Iroquois 1932), 2.

70. Ibid.

71. At its annual meeting in June 1916 the Central Ontario branch of the Speakers' Patriotic League passed yet another resolution calling for registration and conscription. See the *Speakers' Patriotic League, Final Report*, 10. Other civilian recruiting leagues followed suit; an example was that of Saint John which threatened to disband unless one or the other of those policies was adopted. See the *Saint John Telegraph*, article, 'Something Needed To Stir Recruiting In Loyalist City,' 21 June 1916.

72. See note 58 above. Other newspapers to take up the cry for a national registration included the *Toronto World*, 20 May 1916, the *Edmonton Bulletin*, 2 June 1916, and *Saturday Night*, 10 June 1916.

73. The Anglican synods of the Dioceses of Quebec City and Winnipeg, the General Assembly of the Presbyterian Church in Canada, and the Methodist conferences of Toronto and Winnipeg called for registration; the Methodist Conference of Peterborough and the Presbyterian Ministers' Association of Montreal demanded conscription; and the annual meeting of the Congregational Union of Canada, the Anglican Clericus Club of Edmonton, and the Anglican synods of the dioceses of Toronto, Huron, and Rupert's Land as well as of the province of Ontario all resolved for both. See Bray, 'The Canadian Patriotic Response,' 182.

74. Reports of these meetings are to be found in the following sources: *Toronto Star*, article, 'Women of Toronto Demand A National Registration,' 13 June 1916; *Hamilton Times*, editorial, 'Women of Hamilton Want Registration,' 27 June 1916; Mrs. Ethel Davidson, secretary, mass meeting of Calgary women, to Borden, 11 July 1916, BP, 116309; *Edmonton Bulletin*, article, 'Edmonton Women Ask Registration For All Men Of Military Age,' 6 July 1916; *London Advertiser*, article, 'Registration Favoured by Emergency Corps,' 4 Aug. 1916; *Montreal Herald*, article, 'Women Would Be In Favour of Registration,' 13 Sept. 1916.

75. *Toronto Mail and Empire*, article, 'Registration Is Advocated,' 15 June 1916; W. F. Heal, secretary, Union of Saskatchewan Municipalities, to Borden, 7 July 1916, BP, 116304; *Montreal Gazette*, article, 'Toronto Feels Enlistment Drain,' 13 July 1916.

76. Bray, 'The Canadian Patriotic Response,' 184–5.

77. White to Borden, 9 June 1916, BP, 116160.

78. BD, 15 June 1916.

79. Granatstein and Hitsman, *Broken Promises*, 43–7.

80. Examples of the Conservative press reaction are to be found in the *Ottawa Journal*, editorial, 'A Wise Move,' 16 Aug. 1916, in the *Toronto Mail and Empire*, editorial, 'New Recruiting Methods,'

17 Aug. 1916, and in the *Halifax Herald*, editorial, 'Canada's New Recruiting Methods,' 23 Aug. 1916. The more pessimistic Liberal viewpoint was to be seen in the *Hamilton Times*, editorial, 'Military Registration,' 19 Aug. 1916, and the *Saint John Telegraph*, editorial, 'Registration In Canada,' 19 Aug. 1916.

81. John Godfrey to Borden, 18 Aug. 1916, BP, 34695–6; Lt-Col. Lorne W. Mulloy to Borden, 18 Aug. 1916, BP, 34692–4.

82. G. W. L. Nicholson, *The Canadian Expeditionary Force, 1914–1919* (Ottawa 1962), 218.

83. D. J. Hunden, 'Manpower Mobilization in the First World War' (unpublished MA dissertation, University of Toronto, 1959), 67.

84. These statistics were cited in the *Toronto Mail and Empire*, editorial, 'The Recruiting Decline,' 11 Nov. 1916, and correspond closely to those given by Nicholson in *The Canadian Expeditionary Force*, 218.

85. Castell Hopkins, *Canadian Annual Review, 1917* (Toronto 1918), 307.

86. *Toronto World*, editorial, 'Useful or Ornamental,' 16 Dec. 1916. Other newspapers to follow the *World*'s editorial example were *Globe*, 24 Jan. 1917; *Toronto Mail and Empire*, 30 Jan. 1917; *Hamilton Herald*, 25 Jan. 1917; *Hamilton Times*, 25 Jan. 1917; *Brandon Sun*, 9 Feb. 1917; *Regina Leader*, 14 Feb. 1917; *Quebec Chronicle*, 17 Feb. 1917; *Toronto Star*, 15 March 1917; *Saint John Telegraph*, 16 March 1917; *Ottawa Journal*, 20 March 1917; *Edmonton Journal*, *Calgary Herald*, and *Halifax Herald*, cited the *Ottawa Journal*, 20 March 1917.

87. See newspapers listed in note 86 above.

88. *Regina Leader*, editorial, 'The Recruiting Problem,' 16 Oct. 1916; *London Advertiser*, editorial, 'A Vote On Conscription,' 31 Oct. 1916; *Toronto Telegram*, editorial, 'Conscription Is The Only Cure For Slow Recruiting,' 18 Aug. 1916; *Ottawa Journal*, editorial, 'The Real Democracy,' 15 Dec. 1916.

89. Granatstein and Hitsman, *Broken Promises*, 50–3.

90. Additional papers to call for conscription for overseas military service included *Toronto News*, 1 Nov. 1916; *Saint John Globe*, 4 Dec. 1916; *Toronto World*, 27 Dec. 1916; *Industrial Canada*, Jan. 1917; *Vancouver News-Adviser*, 5 Jan. 1917; *Edmonton Bulletin*, 5 Jan. 1917; *Journal of Commerce* (Montreal) cited by the *Ottawa Journal-Press*, 9 Jan. 1917; *St. Catharines Standard*, 18 Jan. 1917; *Winnipeg Telegram*, 7 March 1917; *Canadian Churchman*, 26 April 1917; *Brandon Sun*, 30 April 1917; *London Free Press*, 2 May 1917; *Victoria Colonist*, 6 May 1917; *Windsor Record*, cited by the *London Free Press*, 7 May 1917; *Toronto Mail and Empire*, 8 May 1917; *Toronto Star*, 8 May 1917; *Montreal Gazette*, 10 May 1917; *Victoria Times*, 10 May 1917; *Brockville Recorder*, 10 May 1917.

91. *Vancouver News-Advertiser*, article, 'League For War and National Service,' 25 Jan. 1917.

92. The lengthy list included the Boards of Trade of Montreal, Kitchener, Halifax, Ottawa, Orillia, and Chatham; municipal councils of St Catharines, Port Arthur, Simcoe, Welland, Thorald, Walkerville, Chatham, Goderich, North Bay, London, Guelph, Stratford, Parkhill, and Toronto; religious bodies such as the Montreal, Chatham, and Westminister Presbyteries of the Presbyterian Church in Canada, the Clerical Patriotic Association of Toronto, the Chatham Methodist church, the Montreal Methodist Ministerial Association, and the Anglican Synod of the Diocese of Fredericton; women's organizations such as the Women's Canadian Clubs of Montreal, Fort William, Winnipeg, Hamilton, and Belleville, the National Council of Women, and the Montreal branch of that association; and other miscellaneous groups as the Army and Navy Veterans of Canada, the Canadian Military Institute, the Great War Veterans' Association (Ontario Section), the Grand Orange Lodges of British Columbia, Toronto, Alberta, and New Brunswick, the national executive of the Independent Order of the Daughters of the Empire, and the annual convention of the Manitoba Agricultural Societies. Bray, 'The Canadian Patriotic Response,' 330–9.

93. These factors are discussed in depth in John English, *The Decline of Politics: The Conservatives and the Party System, 1901–1920* (Toronto 1977), 136–60, and in Margaret Prang, *N. W. Rowell; Ontario Nationalist* (Toronto 1975), 174–210.

94. *Toronto Star*, editorial, 'A National Government: Can It Be Had In Canada?' 24 Nov. 1916.

95. John W. Dafoe, *Clifford Sifton in Relation to his Times* (Toronto 1931), 405–6.

96. *Manitoba Free Press*, editorial, 'Changed Views,' 29 Nov. 1916; *Toronto Star*, editorial, 'National Government,' 27 Dec. 1916; *Grain Growers' Guide*, editorial, 'The National Service Campaign,' 27 Dec. 1917; *Toronto World*, editorial, 'A National Government For Canada,' 9 Dec. 1917; *Vancouver News-Advertiser*, editorial, 'What Is A National Government?' 25 Feb. 1917. Other Liberal newspapers to support editorially the national government idea were *Ottawa Free Press*, 4 Dec. 1916; *London Advertiser*, 7 Dec. 1916; *Regina Leader*, 4 Dec. 1916; *Saint John Telegraph*, 13 Dec. 1916; *Hamilton Times*, 29 Dec. 1916; *Winnipeg Tribune*, 9 Jan. 1917; *Halifax Chronicle*, 25 Jan. 1917; *Victoria Times*, 23 Feb. 1917. Other independent journals to do likewise were the *Christian Guardian*, editorial cited in the *Toronto World*, 9 Dec. 1917, and the *Financial Post*, 17 Feb. 1917. Additional Conservative papers to embrace the proposal were the *Hamilton Herald*, 22 Jan. 1917, the *Montreal Mail*, editorial cited in the *Globe*, 30 Jan. 1917, and the *Ottawa Citizen*, 16 May 1917.

97. Organizational support for a national government was forthcoming from the Winnipeg Presbytery of

the Presbyterian Church in Canada, the annual (1917) convention of the Manitoba Grain Growers' Association, the Winnipeg local of the National Council of Women, the Winnipeg Ministerial Association, the Winnipeg Canadian Club, the Winnipeg Rotary Club, the Winnipeg Board of Trade, and the Brandon Canadian Club. Outside of Manitoba only the annual (1917) convention of the Baptist Union of Western Canada, the Calgary Canadian Club, the Victoria Returned Soldiers' Association, the Vancouver Board of Trade, the British Columbia Methodist Conference, and the Toronto Canadian Club followed suit. See Bray, 'The Canadian Patriotic Response,' 431–4.

98. Circular letter signed by John M. Godfrey describing the deliberations of the meeting at the National Club in Toronto on 9 Feb. 1917, dated 16 Feb. 1917, BP, 91928.

99. Godfrey to T. G. Mathers of Winnipeg, 1 Aug. 1916, Godfrey Papers.

100. For a recent account of the Bonne Entente see Brian Cameron, 'The Bonne Entente Movement, 1916–1917,' *Journal of Canadian Studies*, XIII, 2, summer 1978, 42–55. Unfortunately, this article is somewhat hazy with respect to the origin of the Bonne Entente, and consequently it underestimates the importance of the idea for the English-Canadian patriotic movement.

101. See R. M. Bray, 'A Conflict of Nationalisms: The Win the War and National Unity Convention, 1917,' to be published in a forthcoming issue of the *Journal of Canadian Studies*.

102. Godfrey to Laurier, 2 Feb. 1917, LP, 194716–20.

103. Dafoe to Sir Clifford Sifton, 27 Feb. 1917, Dafoe Papers, University of Manitoba Library.

104. Frank Fetherstonhaugh to Borden, 15 May 1917, BP, 116994–5. See also Bray, 'The Canadian Patriotic Response,' 279–80.

105. English, *The Decline of Politics*, 129–35.

106. *La Presse*, article, 'L'Enthousiasme De La "Victoire,"' 10 March 1917.

107. This resolution was passed by a meeting of the Ontario branch of the Win the War League held in Toronto on 14 June. See *Globe*, article, 'Win-The-War Party In Election Arena,' 15 June 1917. These sentiments were reaffirmed by the mass (800 delegates) Ontario Win the War Convention which met in Toronto on 2 August, and were endorsed too by local Win the War associations in such major western cities as Winnipeg, Regina, Calgary, Edmonton, Vancouver, and Victoria, as well as by a series of smaller towns and villages. See Bray, 'The Canadian Patriotic Response,' 464–84.

108. When it became apparent at the end of May that Prime Minister Borden was in deadly earnest in seeking a coalition with the conscriptionist Liberals, partisan Conservative newspapers such as the *Montreal Star*, the *Toronto Mail and Empire*, *L'Evénement*, and the *Toronto Telegram* suddenly discovered the virtues of the national government idea. For the English-Canadian press in Ontario a similar turning-point came with the decision of the Ontario Liberal members of parliament and nominated candidates on 20 July to continue supporting the Laurier position on the Military Service Act. As a result of that decision twenty-one Ontario Liberal newspapers supported a resolution for the creation of a non-partisan war government. Other Liberal newspapers outside of Ontario soon followed this example, so that by the time of the formation of Borden's Union government on 12 October only two major Canadian daily newspapers, the *London Advertiser* and the *Edmonton Bulletin*, opposed the development. See Bray, 'The Canadian Patriotic Response,' 448–97.

An Open Letter from Capt. Talbot Papineau to Mr. Henri Bourassa*

(A copy of this letter was sent to Mr. Bourassa by Mr. Andrew-R. McMaster, K.C., on the 18th of July, 1916. It was published, on the 28th of July, in most of Montreal, Quebec, Ottawa and Toronto papers, English and French).

In the Field,
France, March 21, 1916.

To Monsieur Henri Bourassa,
    Editor of Le Devoir,
        Montreal.

345

My dear Cousin Henri, —
    I was sorry before leaving Quebec in 1914 not to have had an opportunity of discussing with you the momentous issues which were raised in Canada by the outbreak of this war.

You and I have had some discussions in the past, and although we have not agreed upon all points, yet I am happy to think that our pleasant friendship, which indeed dates from the time of my birth, has hitherto continued uninjured by our differences of opinion. Nor would I be the first to make it otherwise, for however I may deplore the character of your views, I have always considered that you held them honestly and sincerely and that you were singularly free from purely selfish or personal ambitions.

Very possibly nothing that I could have said in August 1914 would have caused you to change your opinions, but I did hope that as events developed and as the great national opportunity of Canada became clearer to all her citizens, you would have been influenced to modify your views and to adopt a different attitude. In that hope I have been disappointed. Deeply involved as the honour and the very national existence of Canada has become, beautiful but terrible as her sacrifices have been, you and you alone of the leaders of Canadian thought appear to have remained unmoved, and your unhappy views unchanged.

Too occupied by immediate events in this country to formulate a protest or to frame a reasoned argument, I have nevertheless followed with intense feeling and deep regret the course of action which you have pursued. Consolation of course I have had in the fact that far from sharing in your views, the vast majority of Canadians, and even many of those who had formerly agreed with you, were now strongly and bitterly opposed to you. With this fact in mind, I would not take the time from my duties here to write you this letter did I not fear that the influence to which your talent, energy and sincerity of purpose formerly entitled you, might still

* From *Canadian Nationalism and the War*. Published in Montreal, 1916.

be exercised upon a small minority of your fellow countrymen, and that your attitude might still be considered by some as representative of the race to which we belong.

Nor can I altogether abandon the hope — presumptuous no doubt but friendly and well-intentioned — that I may so express myself here as to give you a new outlook and a different purpose, and perhaps even win you to the support of a principle which has been proved to be dearer to many Canadians than life itself.

I shall not consider the grounds upon which you base your opposition to Canadian participation in this more than European — in this World War. Rather I wish to begin by pointing out some reasons why on the contrary your whole-hearted support might have been expected.

And the first reason is this. By the declaration of war by Great Britain upon Germany, Canada became "ipso facto" a belligerent, subject to invasion and conquest, her property at sea subject to capture, her coasts subject to bombardment or attack, her citizens in enemy territory subject to imprisonment or detention. This is not a matter of opinion — it is a matter of fact — a question of international law. No arguments of yours at least could have persuaded the Kaiser to the contrary. Whatever your views or theories may be as to future constitutional development of Canada, and in those views I believe I coincide to a large extent, the fact remains that at the time of the outbreak of war Canada was a possession of the British Empire, and as such as much involved in the war as any country in England, and from the German point of view and the point of view of International Law equally subject to all its pains and penalties. Indeed proof may no doubt be made that one of the very purposes of Germany's aggression and German military preparedness was the ambition to secure a part if not the whole of the English possessions in North America.

That being so, surely it was idle and pernicious to continue an academic discussion as to whether the situation was a just one or not, as to whether Canada should or should not have had a voice in ante bellum English diplomacy or in the actual declaration of war. Such a discussion may very properly arise upon a successful conclusion of the war, but so long as national issues are being decided in Prussian fashion, that is, by an appeal to the Power of Might, the liberties of discussion which you enjoyed by virtue of British citizenship were necessarily curtailed and any resulting decisions utterly valueless. If ever there was a time for action and not for theories it was to be found in Canada upon the outbreak of war.

Let us presume for the sake of argument that your attitude had also been adopted by the Government and people of Canada and that we had declared our intention to abstain from active participation in the war until Canada herself was actually attacked. What would have resulted? One of two things. Either the Allies would have been defeated or they would not have been defeated. In the former case Canada would have been called upon either to surrender unconditionally to German domination or to have attempted a resistance against German arms.

You, I feel sure, would have preferred resistance, but as a proper corrective to such a preference I would prescribe a moderate dose of trench bombardment. I have known my own dogmas to be seriously disturbed in the midst of a German artillery concentration. I can assure you that the further you travel from Canada and the nearer you approach the great military power of Germany, the less do you value the unaided strength of Canada. By the time you are within fifteen yards of a German army and know yourself to be holding about one yard out of a line of five hundred miles or more, you are liable to be enquiring very anxiously about the presence and power of British and French forces. Your ideas about charging to Berlin or of ending the war would also have undergone some slight moderation.

No, my dear Cousin, I think you would shortly after the defeat of the Allies have been more worried over the mastery of the German consonants than you are even now over a conflict with the Ontario Anti-bi-linguists. Or I can imagine you an unhappy exile in Terra del Fuego eloquently comparing the wrongs of Quebec and Alsace.

But you will doubtless say we would have had the assistance of the Great American Republic! It is quite possible. I will admit that by the time the American fleet had been sunk and the principal buildings in New York destroyed the United States would have declared war upon Europe, but in the meantime Canada might very well have been paying tribute and learning to decline German verbs, probably the only thing German she *could* have declined.

I am, as you know, by descent even more American than I am French, and I am a sincere believer in the future of that magnificent Republic. I cannot forget that more than any other nation in the world's history — England not excepted — she has suffered war solely for the sake of some fine principle of nationality. In 1776 for the principle of national existence. In 1812 for the principle of the inviolability of American citizenship. In 1860 for the preservation of National unity and the suppression of slavery. In 1896 for the protection of her National pride and in sympathy for the wrongs of a neighbouring people.

Nor disappointed as I am at the present inactivity of the States will I ever waiver in my loyal belief that in time to come, perhaps less distant than we realise, her actions will correspond with the lofty expression of her national and international ideals.

I shall continue to anticipate the day when with a clear understanding and a mutual trust we shall by virtue of our united strength and our common purposes be prepared to defend the rights of humanity not only upon the American Continent but throughout the civilised world.

Nevertheless we are not dealing with what may occur in the future but with the actual facts of yesterday and to-day, and I would feign know if

347

you still think that a power which without protest witnesses the ruthless spoliation of Belgium and Servia, and without effective action the murder of her own citizens, would have interfered to protect the property or the liberties of Canadians. Surely you must at least admit an element of doubt, and even if such interference had been attempted, have we not the admission of the Americans themselves that it could not have been successful against the great naval and military organisations of the Central Powers?

May I be permitted to conclude that had the Allies been defeated Canada must afterwards necessarily have suffered a similar fate.

But there was the other alternative, namely, that the Allies even without the assistance of Canada would *not* have been defeated. What then? Presumably French and English would still have been the official languages of Canada. You might still have edited untrammeled your version of Duty, and Colonel Lavergne might still, publicly and without the restraining fear of death or imprisonment, have spoken seditiously (I mean from the Prussian point of view of course). In fact Canada might still have retained her liberties and might with the same freedom from external influences have continued her progress to material and political strength.

But would you have been satisfied — you who have arrogated to yourself the high term of Nationalist? What of the Soul of Canada? Can a nation's pride or patriotism be built upon the blood and suffering of others or upon the wealth garnered from the coffers of those who in anguish and with blood-sweat are fighting the battles of freedom? If we accept our liberties, our national life, from the hands of the English soldiers, if without sacrifices of our own we profit by the sacrifices of the English citizen, can we hope to ever become a nation ourselves? How could we ever acquire that Soul or create that Pride without which a nation is a dead thing and doomed to speedy decay and disappearance.

If you were truly a Nationalist — if you loved our great country and without smallness longed to see her become the home of a good and united people — surely you would have recognised this as her moment of travail and tribulation. You would have felt that in the agony of her losses in Belgium and France, Canada was suffering the birth pains of her national life. There even more than in Canada herself, her citizens are being knit together into a new existence because when men stand side by side and endure a soldier's life and face together a soldier's death, they are united in bonds almost as strong as the closest of blood-ties.

There was the great opportunity for the true Nationalist! There was the great issue, the great sacrifice, which should have appealed equally to all true citizens of Canada, and should have served to cement them with indissoluble strength — Canada was at war! Canada was attacked! What mattered then internal dissentions and questions of home importance? What mattered the why and wherefore of the war, whether we owed anything to England or not, whether we were Imperialists or not, or

348

whether we were French or English? The one simple commending fact to govern our conduct was that Canada was at war, and Canada and Canadian liberties had to be protected.

To you as a "Nationalist" this fact should have appealed more than to any others. Englishmen, as was natural, returned to fight for England, just as Germans and Austrians and Belgians and Italians returned to fight for their native lands.

But we, Canadians, had we no call just as insistent, just as compelling to fight for Canada? Did not the *Leipzig* and the *Gneisnau* possibly menace Victoria and Vancouver, and did you not feel the patriotism to make sacrifices for the protection of British Columbia? How could you otherwise call yourself Canadian? It is true that Canada did not hear the roar of German guns nor were we visited at night by the murderous Zeppelins, but every shot that was fired in Belgium or France was aimed as much at the heart of Canada as at the bodies of our brave Allies. Could we then wait within the temporary safety of our distant shores until either the Central Powers flushed with victory should come to settle their account or until by the glorious death of millions of our fellowmen in Europe, Canada should remain in inglorious security and a shameful liberty?

349

I give thanks that that question has been answered not as you would have had it answered but as those Canadians who have already died or are about to die here in this gallant motherland of France have answered it.

It may have been difficult for you at first to have realised the full significance of the situation. You were steeped in your belief that Canada owed no debt to England, was merely a vassal state and entitled to protection without payment. You were deeply inbued with the principle that we should not partake in a war in the declaration of which we had had no say. You believed very sincerely that Canadian soldiers should not be called upon to fight beyond the frontier of Canada itself, and your vision was further obscured by your indignation at the apparent injustice to a French minority in Ontario.

It is conceivable that at first on account of this long held attitude of mind and because it seemed that Canadian aid was hardly necessary, for even we feared that the war would be over before the first Canadian regiment should land in France, you should have failed to adapt your mind to the new situation and should for a while have continued in your former views; — but now — now that Canada has pledged herself body and soul to the successful prosecution of this war — now that we know that only by the exercice of our full and united strength can we achieve a speedy and lasting victory — now that thousands of your fellow citizens have died, and alas! many more must yet be killed — how in the name of all that you hold most sacred can you still maintain your opposition? How can you refrain from using all your influence and your personal magnetism and eloquence to swell the great army of Canada and make it as representative of all classes of our citizens as possible?

Could you have been here yourself to witness in its horrible detail the cruelty of war — to have seen your comrades suddenly struck down in death and lie mangled at your side, even you could not have failed to wish to visit punishment upon those responsible. You too would now wish to see every ounce of our united strength instantly and relentlessly directed to that end. Afterwards, when that end has been accomplished, then and then only can there be honour or profit in the discussion of our domestic or imperial disputes.

And so my first reason for your support would be that you should assist in the defence of Canadian territory and Canadian liberties.

And my second would be this: —

Whatever criticism may to-day be properly directed against the Constitutional structure of the British Empire, we are compelled to admit that the *spiritual* union of the self governing portions of the Empire is a most necessary and desirable thing. Surely you will concede that the degree of civilisation which they represent and the standards of individual and national liberty for which they stand are the highest and noblest to which the human race has yet attained and jealously to be protected against destruction by less developed powers. All may not be perfection — grave and serious faults no doubt exist — vast progress must still be made — nevertheless that which has been achieved is good and must not be allowed to disappear. The bonds which unite us for certain great purposes and which have proved so powerful in this common struggle must not be loosened. They may indeed be readjusted, but the great communities which the British Empire has joined together must not be broken asunder. If I thought that the development of a national spirit in Canada meant antagonism to the "spirit" which unites the Empire today, I would utterly repudiate the idea of a Canadian nation and would gladly accept the most exacting of imperial organic unions.

Hitherto I have welcomed your nationalism because I thought it would only mean that you wished Canada to assume national responsibilities as well as to enjoy its privileges.

But your attitude in the present crisis will alienate and antagonise the support which you might otherwise have received. Can you not realise that if any worthy nationality is possible for Canada it must be sympathetic to and must co-operate with the fine spirit of imperial unity? That spirit was endangered by the outbreak of European war. It could only be preserved by loyal assistance from all those in whom that spirit dwelt.

And so I would also have had you support Canadian participation in the war, *not* in order to maintain a certain political organism of Empire, but to preserve and perpetuate that invaluable *spirit* which alone makes our union possible.

The third reason is this: You and I are so called French-Canadians. We belong to a race that began the conquest of this country long before the days of Wolfe. That race was in its turn conquered, but their personal liberties were not restricted. They were in fact increased. Ultimately as a minority in a great English speaking community we have preserved our racial identity, and we have had freedom to speak or to worship as we wished. I may not be, like yourself, "un pur sang", for I am by birth even more English than French, but I am proud of my French ancestors, I love the French language, and I am as determined as you are that we shall have full liberty to remain French as long as we like. But if we are to preserve this liberty we must recognise that we do not belong entirely to ourselves, but to a mixed population, we must rather seek to find points of contact and of common interest than points of friction and separation. We must make concessions and certain sacrifices of our distinct individuality if we mean to live on amicable terms with our fellow citizens or if we are to expect them to make similar concessions to us. There, in this moment of crisis, was the greatest opportunity which could ever have presented itself for us to show unity of purpose and to prove to our English fellow citizens that, whatever our respective histories may have been, we were actuated by a common love for our country and a mutual wish that in the future we should unite our distinctive talents and energies to create a proud and happy nation.

351

That was an opportunity which you, my cousin, have failed to grasp, and unfortunately, despite the heroic and able manner in which French Canadian battalions have distinguished themselves here, and despite the whole-hearted support which so many leaders of French Canadian thought have given to the cause, yet the fact remains that the French in Canada have not responded in the same proportion as have other Canadian citizens, and the unhappy impression has been created that French Canadians are not bearing their full share in this great Canadian enterprise. For this fact and this impression you will be held largely responsible. Do you fully realise what such a responsibility will mean, not so much to you personally — for that I believe you would care little — but to the principles which you have advocated, and for many of which I have but the deepest regard. You will have brought them into a disrepute from which they may never recover. Already you have made the fine term of "Nationalist" to stink in the nostrils of our English fellow citizens. Have you caused them to respect your national views? Have you won their admiration or led them to consider with esteem, and toleration your ambitions for the French language? Have you shown yourself worthy of concessions or consideration?

After this war what influence will you enjoy — what good to your country will you be able to accomplish? Wherever you go you will stir up strife and enmity — you will bring disfavour and dishonour upon our race, so that whoever bears a French name in Canada will be an object of suspicion and possibly of hatred.

And so, in the third place, for the honour of French Canada and for the unity of our country, I would have had you favourable to our cause.

I have only two more reasons, and they but need to be mentioned, I think to be appreciated.

Here in this little French town I hear about all me the language I love so well and which recalls so vividly my happy childhood days in Montebello.

I see types and faces that are like old friends. I see farm houses like those at home. I notice that our French Canadian soldiers have easy friendships wherever they go.

Can you make me believe that there must not always be a bond of blood relationship between the Old France and the New?

And France — more glorious than in all her history — is now in agony straining fearlessly and proudly in a struggle for life or death.

For Old France and French civilisation I would have had your support.

And in the last place, all other considerations aside and even supposing Canada had been a neutral country, I would have had you decide that she should enter the struggle for no other reason than that it is a fight for the freedom of the world — a fight in the result of which like every other country she is herself vitally interested. I will not further speak of the causes of this war, but I should like to think that even if Canada had been an independent and neutral nation she of her own accord would have chosen to follow the same path of glory that she is following to-day.

Perhaps, my cousin, I have been overlong and tedious with my reasons, but I shall be shorter with my warning — and in closing I wish to say this to you.

Those of us in this great army, who may be so fortunate as to return to our Canada, will have faced the grimest and sincerest issues of life and death — we will have experienced the unhappy strength of brute force — we will have seen our loved comrades die in blood and suffering. Beware lest we return with revengeful feelings, for I say to you that for those who, while we fought and suffered here, remained in safety and comfort in Canada and failed to give us encouragement and support, as well as for those who grew fat with the wealth dishonourably gained by political graft and by dishonest business methods at our expense — we shall demand a heavy day of reckoning. We shall inflict upon them the punishment they deserve — not by physical violence — for we shall have had enough of that — nor by unconstitutional or illegal means — for we are fighting to protect not to destroy justice and freedom — but by the invincible power of our moral influence.

Can you ask us then for sympathy or concession? Will any listen when you speak of pride and patriotism? I think not.

Remember too that if Canada has become a nation respected and self-respecting she owes it to her citizens who have fought and died in this distant land and not to those self-styled Nationalists who have remained at home.

Can I hope that anything I have said here may influence you to consider the situation in a different light and that it is not yet too late for me to be made proud of our relationship?

At this moment, as I write, French and English-Canadians are fighting and dying side by side. Is their sacrifice to go for nothing or will it not cement a foundation for a true Canadian nation, a Canadian nation inde-

352

pendent in thought, independent in action, independent even in its political organisation — but in spirit united for high international and humane purposes to the two Motherlands of England and France?

I think that is an ideal in which we shall all equally share. Can we not all play an equal part in its realisation?

I am, as long as may be possible,

Your affectionate Cousin,

TALBOT M. PAPINEAU.

Mr. Bourassa's Reply to Capt. Talbot Papineau's Letter*

Montreal, August 2nd, 1916.

Andrew R. McMaster, Esq., K.C.,
    189 St. James St.,
      City.

Dear Sir,

On my return from an absence of several weeks, I found your letter of the 18th ult., and the copy of a letter apparently written to me by your partner, Capt. Talbot Papineau, on the 21st of March.

Capt. Papineau's letter, I am informed, appeared simultaneously, Friday last, in a number of papers, in Montreal, Quebec, Ottawa and elsewhere. You have thus turned it into a kind of political manifesto and constituted yourself its publisher. Allow me therefore to send you my reply, requesting you to have it transmitted to Capt. Papineau, granting that he is the real author of that document. I can hardly believe it. A brave and active officer as he is has seldom the time to prepare and write such long pieces of political eloquence. Then, why should Capt. Papineau, who writes and speaks French elegantly, who claims so highly his French origin and professes with such ardour his love of France, have written in English to his *"dear cousin Henri"*? How is it that a letter written on the 21st of March has reached me but four months later, through your medium? For what purpose did you keep it so long in portfolio? and why do you send me a copy, instead of the letter itself?

It is, you say, an "open letter". It was, nevertheless, meant to reach me. It opens and ends with forms of language bearing the touch of intimate relationship — more so even than could be expected from the rare intercourse which, in spite of our blood connection, had so far existed

* From *Canadian Nationalism and the War.* Published in Montreal, 1916.

between your partner and myself. The whole thing has the appearance of a political manoeuvre executed under the name of a young and gallant officer, who has the advantage or inconvenience of being my cousin. That Capt. Papineau has put his signature at the foot of that document, it is possible; but he would certainly not have written it in cool thought, after due reflexion. It not only expresses opinions radically opposed to those I heard from him before the war; it also contains inaccuracies of fact of which I believe him honourably incapable.

He mentions "some discussions in the past", "differences of opinion", which have left "uninjured" a "pleasant friendship", dating, he says, "from the time of [his] birth." From his childhood to his return from Oxford, I do not think we had ever met, and certainly never to exchange the slightest glimpse of thought or opinion. Of matters of national concern we talked but once in all my life. From that one conversation I gathered the impression that he was still more opposed than myself to any kind of imperial solidarity. He even seemed much disposed to hasten the day of the Independence of Canada. Since, I met him on two or three occasions. We talked of matters indifferent, totally foreign to the numerous questions treated with such eloquent profuseness and so little reasoning in his letter of the 21st of March.

How can he charge me with having expressed "unhappy views" "at the outstart of the war", in August 1914, and held them stubbornly "unchanged" till this day? In August 1914, I was abroad. My first pronouncement on the intervention of Canada in the war is dated September 8th, 1914. In that editorial, while repelling the principles of Imperial solidarity and their consequences, and maintaining the nationalist doctrine in which Capt. Papineau — and you as well — pretends to be still a believer, I pronounced myself in favour of the intervention of Canada, *as a nation*, for the defence of the superior interests uniting Canada with France and Britain. My "unhappy views" were thus analogous to those of your partner. It is but later, long after Capt. Papineau was gone, that my attitude was changed and brought me to condemn the participation of Canada in the war, — or rather the political inspiration of that participation and the many abuses which have resulted therefrom. The reasons of that change are well known to those who have read or heard with attention and good faith all my statements on the matter. To sum them up is now sufficient.

The free and independent participation of Canada — free for the nation and free for the individuals — I had accepted, provided it remained within reasonable bounds, in conformity with the conditions of the country. But the Government, the whole of Parliament, the press and politicians of both parties all applied themselves systematically to obliterate the free character of Canada's intervention. "Free" enlistment is now carried on by means of blackmailing, intimidation and threats of all sorts. Advantage has been taken of the emotion caused by the war to assert, with the utmost intensity and intolerance, the doctrine of Imperial solidarity, triumphantly

354

opposed in the past by our statesmen and the whole Canadian people, up to the days of the infamous South African War, concocted by Chamberlain, Rhodes and the British imperialists with the clear object of drawing the self-governing colonies into "the vortex of European militarism". That phrase of your political leader, Sir Wilfrid Laurier, is undoubtedly fresh in your mind. After having given way to the imperialistic current of 1899, Sir Wilfrid Laurier and the liberal party had come back to the nationalist doctrine. The naval scare of 1909 threw them again under the yoke of imperialism; the war has achieved their enslavement: they united with the tory-jingo-imperialists of all shades to make of the participation of Canada in the war an immense political manoeuvre and thus assure the triumph of British imperialism. You and your partner, like many others, have followed your party through its various evolutions. I have remained firmly attached to the principles I laid down at the time of the South African war and maintained unswervingly ever since.

As early as the month of March 1900, I pointed out the possibility of a conflict between Great Britain and Germany and the danger of laying down in South Africa a precedent, the fatal consequence of which would be to draw Canada in all the wars undertaken by the United Kingdom. Sir Wilfrid Laurier and the liberal leaders laughed at my apprehensions; against my warnings they quoted the childish safeguard of the "no prededent clause" inserted in the Order in Council of the 14th of October 1899. For many years after, till 1912, and 1913, they kept singing the praises of the Kaiser and extolling the peaceful virtues of Germany. They now try to regain time by denouncing vociferously the "barbarity" of the "Huns". To-day, as in 1900, in 1911, and always, I believe that all the nations of Europe are the victims of their own mistakes, of the complacent servility with which they submitted to the dominance of all Imperialists and traders in human flesh, who, in England as in Germany, in France as in Russia, have brought the peoples to slaughter in order to increase their reapings of cursed gold. German Imperialism and British Imperialism, French Militarism and Russian Tsarism, I hate with equal detestation; and I believe as firmly today as in 1899 that Canada, a nation of America, has a nobler mission to fulfil than to bind herself to the fate of the nations of Europe or to any spoliating Empire — whether it be the spoliators of Belgium, Alsace or Poland, or those of Ireland or the Transvaal, of Greece or the Balkans.

Politicians of both parties, your liberal friends as well as their conservative opponents, feign to be much scandalised at my "treasonable disloyalty." I could well afford to look upon them as a pack of knaves and hypocrites. In 1896, your liberal leaders and friends stumped the whole province of Quebec with the cry "WHY SHOULD WE FIGHT FOR ENGLAND?" From 1902 to 1911, Sir Wilfrid Laurier was acclaimed by them as the indomitable champion of Canada's autonomy against British Imperialism. His resisting attitude at the Imperial Conferences of 1902 and 1907 was praised to the skies. His famous phrase on the "vortex of European militarism", and his determination to keep Canada far from

355

it, became the party's by-word — always in the Province of Quebec, of course. His Canadian Navy scheme was presented as a step towards the independence of Canada.

Then came the turn of the Conservatives to tread in the footsteps of the Nationalists; they soon outstripped us. A future member of the conservative Cabinet, Mr. Blondin, brought back to life an old saying of Sir Adolphe Chapleau, and suggested to pierce the Union Jack with bullets in order to let pass the breeze of liberty. The tory leaders, Sir Robert Borden, Sir George Foster, the virtuous Bob Rogers, and even our national superKitchener, Sir Sam Hughes, while trumpeting the purity of their Imperialism, greeted with undisguised joy the anti-imperialist victory of Drummond-Arthabaska, and used it for all it was worth to win the general elections in 1911.

By what right should those people hold me as a "traitor", because I remain consequent with the principles that I have never ceased to uphold and which both parties have exploited alternately, as long as it suited their purpose and kept them in power or brought them to office?

Let it not be pretended that those principles are out of place, pending the war. To prevent Canada from participating in the war, then foreseen and predicted, was their very object and *raison d'être*. To throw them aside and deny them when the time of test came, would have required a lack of courage and sincerity, of which I feel totally incapable. If this is what they mean by "British loyalty" and "superior civilisation", they had better hang me at once. I will never obey such dictates and will ever hold in deepest contempt the acrobats who lend themselves to all currents of blind popular passion in order to serve their personal or political ends.

This, let it be well understood, does not apply to your partner. His deeds have shown the sincerity of his political turn. Without agreeing with his new opinions, I admired his silent courage in running to the front at the first call. His verbose political manifesto — supposing he is really responsible for it — adds nothing to his merits. Still less does it enhance the dignity and moral worth of the politicians and pressmen of all kinds, who, after having denounced war and imperialism, and while taking great care not to risk their precious body, have become the apostles of war and the upholders of imperialism.

I will not undertake to answer every point of the dithyrambic plea of my gallant cousin. When he says that I am too far away from the trenches to judge of the real meaning of this war, he may be right. On the other hand, his long and diffuse piece of eloquence proves that the excitement of warfare and the distance from home have obliterated in his mind the fundamental realities of his native country. I content myself with touching upon one point, on which he unhappily lends credit to the most mischievous of the many antinational opinions circulated by the jingo press. He takes the French-Canadians to task and challenges their patriotism, because they enlist in lesser number than the other elements of the population of Canada. Much could be said upon that. It is sufficient to signalise one patent fact: the number of recruits for the European war, in the various Provinces of Canada and from each component element of the population, is in inverse ratio of the enrootment in the soil and the traditional patriotism arising therefrom. The newcomers from the British Isles have enlisted in much larger proportion than English-speaking Canadians born in this country, while these have enlisted more than the French-Canadians. The Western Provinces have given more recruits than Ontario, and Ontario more than Quebec. In each Province, the floating population of the cities, the students, the labourers and clerks, either unemployed or threatened with dismissal, have supplied more soldiers than the farmers. Does it mean that the city dwellers are more patriotic than the country people? or that the newcomers from England are better Canadians than their fellow-citizens of British origin, born in Canada? No; it simply means that in Canada, as in every other country, at all times, the citizens of the oldest origin are the least disposed to be stampeded into distant ventures of no direct concern to their native land. It proves also that military service is more repugnant to the rural than the urban populations.

357

There is among the French-Canadians a larger proportion of farmers, fathers of large families, than among any other ethnical element in Canada. Above all, the French-Canadians are the only group exclusively Canadian, in its whole and by each of the individuals of which it is composed. They look upon the perturbations of Europe, even those of England or France, as foreign events. Their sympathies naturally go to France against Germany; but they do not think they have an obligation to fight for France, no more than the French of Europe would hold themselves bound to fight for Canada against the United States or Japan, or even against Germany, in case Germany should attack Canada without threatening France.

English Canada, not counting the *blokes*, contains a considerable proportion of people still in the first period of national incubation. Under the sway of imperialism, a fair number have not yet decided whether their allegiance is to Canada or to the Empire, whether the United Kingdom or the Canadian Confederacy is their country.

As to the newcomers from the United Kingdom, they are not Canadian in any sense. England or Scotland is their sole fatherland. They have enlisted for the European war as naturally as Canadians, either French or English, would take arms to defend Canada against an aggression on the American continent.

Thus it is rigourously correct to say that recruiting has gone in inverse ratio of the development of Canadian patriotism. If English-speaking Canadians have a right to blame the French Canadians for the small number of their recruits, the newcomers from the United Kingdom, who have supplied a much larger proportion of recruits than any other element of the population, would be equally justified in branding the Anglo-Canadians with disloyalty and treason. Enlistment for the European war is supposed to be absolutely free and voluntary. This has been stated right and left from beginning to end. If that statement is honest and sincere, all provocations from one part of the population against the other, and exclusive attacks against the French-Canadians, should cease. Instead of reviling unjustly one-third of the Canadian people — a population so remarkably characterised by its constant loyalty to national institutions and its respect for public order, — those men who claim a right to enlighten and lead public opinion should have enough good faith and intelligence to see facts as they are and to respect the motives of those who persist in their determination to remain more Canadian than English or French.

In short, English-speaking Canadians enlist in much smaller number than the newcomers from England, because they are more Canadian; French-Canadians enlist less than English-Canadians because they are totally and exclusively Canadian. To claim that their abstention is due to the "baneful" influence of the Nationalists is a pure nonsense. Should I give way to the suggestion of my gallant cousin, I would be just as powerless as Sir Wilfrid Laurier to induce the French-Canadians to enlist. This is implicitly acknowledged in Capt. Papineau's letter: on the one hand, he asserts that my views on the participation of Canada in the war is denied by my own friends; on the other he charges the mass of the French-Canadian population with a refusal to answer the call of duty. The simple truth is, that the abstention of the French-Canadians is no more the result of the present attitude of the Nationalists than the consequence of the liberal campaign of 1896, or of the conservative appeals of 1911. It relates to deeper causes: hereditary instincts, social and economic conditions, a national tradition of three centuries. It is equally true, however, that those deep and far distant causes have been strengthened by the constant teaching of all our political and social leaders, from Lafontaine, Cartier, Macdonald, Mackenzie, to Laurier inclusively. The only virtue, or crime, of the Nationalists is to persist in believing and practising what they were taught by the men of the past, and even those of to-day. This is precisely what infuriates the politicians, either *blue* or *red*. To please the Imperialists, they have renounced all their traditions and undertaken to bring the French-Canadians under imperial command. Unable to succeed, they try to conceal their fruitless apostasy by denouncing to the hatred of the jingos the obtrusive witnesses of their past professions of faith.

The jingo press and politicians have also undertaken to persuade their gullible followers that the Nationalists hinder the work of recruiters *because* of the persecution meted out to the French minorities in Ontario and Manitoba. This is but another nonsense. My excellent cousin, I am sorry to say, — or his inspirer — has picked it up.

The two questions are essentially distinct, this we have never ceased to assert. One is purely internal; the other affects the international status of Canada and her relations with Great Britain. To the problem of the teaching of languages we ask for a solution in conformity with the spirit of the Federal agreement, the best interests of Confederation, and the principles of pedagogy as applied in civilised countries. Our attitude on the participation of Canada in the war is inspired exclusively by the constant tradition of the country and the agreements concluded half a century ago between Canada and Great Britain. Even if the irritating bilingual question was non existent, our views on the war would be what they are. The most that can be said is, that the backward and essentially Prussian policy of the rulers of Ontario and Manitoba gives us an additional argument against the intervention of Canada in the European conflict. To speak of fighting for the preservation of French civilisation in Europe while endeavouring to destroy it in America, appears to us as an absurd piece of inconsistency. To preach Holy War for the liberties of the peoples overseas, and to oppress the national minorities in Canada, is, in our opinion, nothing but odious hypocrisy.

Is it necessary to add that, in spite of his name, Capt. Papineau is utterly unqualified to judge of the feelings of the French-Canadians? For most part American, he has inherited, with a few drops of French blood, the most *denationalised* instincts of his French origin. From those he calls his compatriots he is separated by his religious belief and his maternal language. Of their traditions, he knows but what he has read in a few books. He was brought up far away from close contact with French-Canadians. His higher studies he pursued in England. His elements of French culture he acquired in France. The complexity of his origin and the diversity of his training would be sufficient to explain his mental hesitations and the contradictions which appear in his letter. Under the sway of his American origin, he glories in the Revolution of 1776; he calls it a war "for the principle of national existence". In good logic, he should approve highly of the tentative rebellion of the Sinn Feiners, and suggest that Canada should rise in arms to break the yoke of Great Britain. His American forefathers, whom he admires so much, fought against England and called upon France and Spain to help them against their mother-country, for lighter motives than those of the Dublin rebels. The Imperial burden they refused to bear was infinitely less ponderous than that which weighs today upon the people of Canada.

With the threat contained in the conclusion of his letter, I need not be concerned. Supposing always that he is truly responsible for that document, I make broad allowance for the excitement and perturbation resulting from his strenuous life. He and many of his comrades will have enough to do in order to help Canada to counteract the disastrous consequences of the war venture in which she has thrown herself headlong. To propagate systematically national discord by quarreling with all Canadians, either French or English, who hold different views as to the theory and practice of their national duty, would be a misuse of time. Moreover, it would be a singular denial of their professions of faith in favour of liberty and civilisation.

As to the scoundrels and bloodsuckers "who have grown fat with the wealth dishonourably gained" in war contracts, I give them up quite willingly to their just indignation. But those worthies are not to be found

359

in nationalist ranks: they are all recruited among the noisiest preachers of the Holy War waged for "civilisation" against "barbarity", for the "protection of small nations", for the "honour" of England and the "salvation" of France.

Yours truly,

Henri BOURASSA

P.S. — I hope this will reach you before you leave for the front: no doubt, you have been the first to respond to the pressing call of your partner. H.B.

Topic Ten
Hinterland Revolts: The West and the Maritimes

In the midst of the postwar euphoria, protest movements emerged in two regions of the country: the West and the Maritimes. Both were indicators that some Canadians did not feel that they were benefiting equitably from the nation's growth. The national policy had helped build a transcontinental nation that by the 1920s had become highly industrialized. But in the process it had alienated many in the hinterland regions.

The Progressive Movement was the continuation of western protest that dated back to the time of the region's inclusion in the Canadian Confederation and the resulting Riel rebellions. The target of discontent was the hated National Policy of 1879, which western farmers believed put them at a disadvantageous position with respect to Eastern manufacturers and industrialists. In an effort to fight back, they formed co-operatives. These became not only effective economic organizations but also powerful political entities and focal points around which to organize protest. Western dissatisfaction grew in the prosperity at the turn of the century, during the war years, and in the immediate postwar depression until it emerged as a full-scale political protest movement and a powerful third party in the early 1920s. W. L. Morton in "The Western Progressive Movement 1919–1921" chronicles the origins of the Progressive Movement, analyses its nature, and explains its decline.

The Maritimes also had a history of protest dating back to Confederation. Dissatisfaction had erupted at various times, usually during periods of economic dislocation and social unrest. The postwar years were a particularly disquieting period during which Maritimers reexamined their position in Confederation and compared their region's rate of growth to that of Central Canada and the West. The focal point of their protest was the system of freight rates. At its height, the Maritime Rights agitation was an effective regional protest movement. In "The Origins of the Maritime Rights Movement," E. R. Forbes analyses the motives of the different groups that participated in it.

Together these two studies provide students with an opportunity to compare regional protest and development.

Walter Young's *Democracy and Discontent* (Toronto: Ryerson, 1969) de-
votes several chapters to a general overview of the Progressive Movement.
W. L. Morton's *The Progressive Party in Canada* (Toronto: University of
Toronto Press, 1950) is still the definite study. The link between the
progressive Movement and the social gospel movement is shown in R.
Allen's "The Social Gospel as the Religion of the Agrarian Revolt," in *The
West and the Nation: Essays in Honour of W. L. Morton*, edited by C. Berger
and R. Cook (Toronto: McClelland and Stewart, 1976) pp. 174–186.

Students will find the essays on the Maritimes in *Canada and the Burden
of Unity*, edited by D. Bercuson (Toronto: Macmillan, 1977), of value in
placing the Maritime Rights movement in a wider perspective.

362

The Western Progressive Movement, 1919–1921 *

W. L. MORTON

The Progressive Movement in the West was dual in origin and nature. In
one aspect it was an economic protest; in another it was a political revolt.
A phase of agrarian resistance to the National Policy of 1878, it was also,
and equally, an attempt to destroy the old national parties. The two
aspects unite in the belief of all Progressives, both moderate and extreme,
that the old parties were equally committed to maintaining the National
Policy and indifferent to the ways in which the "big interests" of protection and monopoly used government for their own ends.

At the root of the sectional conflict, from which the Progressive Movement in part sprang, was the National Policy of 1878. Such conflict is
partly the result of the hardships and imperfect adaptations of the frontier,
but it also arises from the incidence of national policies.[1] The sectional
corn develops where the national shoe pinches. The National Policy, that
brilliant improvisation of Sir John A. Macdonald, had grown under the
master politician's hand, under the stimulus of depression and under the
promptings of political appetite, until it had become a veritable Canadian
System Henry Clay might have envied. Explicit in it was the promise that
everybody should have something from its operation; implicit in it — its
inarticulate major premise indeed — was the promise that when the infant
industries it fostered had reached maturity, protection would be needed
no more.

This, however, was but a graceful tribute to the laissez-faire doctrine of
the day. This same doctrine it was which prevented the western wheat

* From *Canadian Historical Association Report*, 1946, 41–55. Copyright by Canadian Historical
Association. Reprinted by permission.

grower from demanding that he, too, should benefit directly from the operation of the National Policy. That he did benefit from the system as a whole, a complex of land settlement, railway construction, and moderate tariff protection, is not to be denied. But the wheat grower, building the wheat economy from homestead to terminal elevator in a few swift years, was caught in a complex of production and marketing costs, land values, railway rates, elevator charges, and interest rates. He fought to lower all these costs by economic organization and by political pressure. He saw them all as parts of a system which exploited him. He was prevented, by his direct experience of it, and by the prevailing doctrine of laissez-faire, from perceiving that the system might confer reciprocal benefits on him. Accordingly, he hated and fought it as a whole. Of the National Policy, however, the tariff was politically the most conspicuous element. Hence, the political battle was fought around the tariff; it became the symbol of the wheat growers' exploitation and frustration, alleged and actual. Like all symbols, it over-simplified the complexities it symbolized.

363

This clash of interest had, of course, to be taken into account by the national political parties. The Liberal-Conservatives, as creators of the National Policy, had little choice but to extol its merits even in regions where they seemed somewhat dim. They could stress its promise that a good time was coming for all, they could add that meanwhile the Yankees must be held at bay. When the Liberals quietly appropriated the National Policy after attaining national power in 1896, the task of the Conservatives became much easier. Not only could the Liberals be accused of having abandoned their principles; they could even be accused of unduly prolonging the adolescence of infant industries. A western Conservative, Mr. Arthur Meighen, could indict the Laurier administration on the charge of being maintained in power "behind ramparts of gold"[2] erected by the "interests." This echo of the "cross of gold" was not ineffective in the West, where the charge that there was no real difference between the parties on the tariff not only promoted the growth of third party sentiment, but also prolonged the life of western conservatism.

The Liberals, for their part, had not only abandoned "continentalism" in the Convention of 1893, but with the possession of power had developed that moderation without which a nation-wide majority may not be won or kept in a country of sectional interests.[3] Liberal speakers might proclaim that the party was the low tariff party; Fielding might make the master stroke of the British preferential tariff; certain items might be put on the free list here, the rates might be lowered on certain others there; but the Liberal party had become a national party, with all the powers and responsibilities of government, among them the maintenance and elaboration of the now historic National Policy. In consequence each national party began to appear more and more in the eyes of the wheat grower as an "organized hypocrisy dedicated to getting and holding office,"[4] and the conditions were created for a third party movement in the West.

The tariff, then, was a major predisposing cause of a third party movement in the West. Down to 1906 the British preference and other concessions of the Fielding tariff, together with reiterated promises of further reductions, kept the western Liberals within the fold. The completion in that year, however, of the three-decker tariff marked the beginning of more serious discontent. It grew with the offer of reciprocity in the Payne-Aldrich tariff of 1909. With the increase of agricultural indebtedness, concomitant with the settlement of the West, and the disappearance of the advantageous price differential between agricultural prices and those of manufactured goods, on which the wheat boom had taken its rise, the discontent deepened. It found expression through the grain growers' organizations, those "impressive foci of progressive ideas."[5] In 1909 came the organization of the Canadian Council of Agriculture, in 1910 Laurier's tour of the West,[6] and the Siege of Ottawa by the organized farmers. Plainly, the West was demanding its due at last. The Liberal party, which had lost support in Ontario in every election since 1896, which saw its hold in Quebec threatened by the Nationalists under Bourassa, could not afford to lose the support of a new and rapidly growing section. In 1911 the helm was put hard over for reciprocity, and Liberal prospects brightened in the West.[7] But this partial return to continentalism in economic policy was too severe a strain for a party which had become committed as deeply as its rival to the National Policy. The "Eighteen Liberals" of Toronto, among them Sir Clifford Sifton, broke with the party, and it went down to defeat under a Nationalist and a National Policy cross-fire. At the same time the Conservative party in the West, particularly in Saskatchewan and Alberta, suffered strains and defections which were to show in a lowered vitality in succeeding elections. But the offer of reciprocity remained on the statute books of the United States for another decade, and year by year the grain growers in convention demanded that the offer be taken up.

The demand of the western agrarians for the lowering of the tariff, however, was by no means an only factor in the rise of the third party. Into the West after 1896 poured immigrants from the United States and Great Britain. Most of the Americans came from the Middle West and the trans-Mississippi region. Many brought with them the experience and the political philosophy of the farmers' organizations and the third parties of those regions. Perhaps the clearest manifestation of their influence on the political development of the West was the demand for direct legislation which found expression in those forums of agrarian opinions, the grain growers' conventions, and which also found its way to the statute books of the three Western Provinces. From the British Isles came labour and socialist influences, felt rather in labour and urban circles, but not without effect among the farmers. These populist and socialist influences were mild; their exponents were in a minority. Nonetheless, they did much to give western discontent a vocabulary of grievance. Above all, they combined to repudiate the politics of expediency practised by the national parties, to denounce those parties as indifferently the tools of the "big interests," and to demand that the farmer free himself from the toils of the old parties and set up a third party, democratic, doctrinaire, and occupational.[8]

In the Canadian West this teaching fell on a soil made favourable not only by a growing disbelief in the likelihood of either of the national parties lowering the tariff, but also by a political temper different from that of Eastern Canada. (One exception must be made to this statement, namely, the old Canadian West in peninsular Ontario, from which, indeed, the original settlement of the West had been largely drawn.) This difference may be broadly expressed by saying that the political temper of the eastern provinces, both French and English, is whiggish. Government there rests on compact, the vested and legal rights of provinces, of minorities, of corporations.[9] The political temper of the West, on the other hand, is democratic; government there rests on the will of the sovereign people, a will direct, simple, and no respector of rights except those demonstrably and momentarily popular. Of this Jacksonian, Clear Grit democracy, reinforced by American populism and English radicalism, the Progressive Movement was an authentic expression.

No better example of this difference of temper exists, of course, than the Manitoba school question. Manitoba was founded on a balance of French and English elements; this balance was expressed in the compact of the original Manitoba Act, the essential point in which was the guarantee of the educational privileges of the two language and religious groups. The balance was destroyed by the Ontario immigration of the eighteen-seventies and eighties; in 1890 Manitoba liberalism swept away the educational privileges of the French minority and introduced the "national" school, the chief agency of equalitarian democracy. This set in train a series of repercussions which, through the struggle over the Autonomy Bills in 1905, the introduction of compulsory education by the Liberal party in Manitoba in 1916, and the friction caused by Regulation 17 in Ontario, led up to the split in the Liberal party between the western and the Quebec Liberals on the Lapointe resolution in the federal Parliament in 1916. This split not only foreshadowed and prepared the way for that on conscription; it also contributed to the break-up of the old parties which opened the way to the rise of the Progressive party after 1919.[10] The western Liberals, that is to say, were turning against Laurier because they feared Nationalist domination of the party.

Thus it was that the ground was prepared for the West to throw its weight behind Union Government, first suggested as a war measure, then persisted in to prevent a Liberal victory under Laurier. Western Liberals and radicals did so with much reluctance and many misgivings. An independent movement was already taking root.[11] For the Liberal party, an electoral victory was in sight, following a succession of provincial victories and the discontent with the Borden Government's conduct of the war.[12]

This probable Liberal victory, to be based on anti-conscription sentiment in Quebec and low tariff sentiment in the West, was averted by the formation of the Union Government. The issue in that political transformation was whether the three western Liberal governments could be detached from the federal party. But the attempt made at the Winnipeg convention in August, 1917, to prepare the way for this change was defeated by the official Liberals.[13] The insurgents refused to accept the verdict of the convention; and by negotiations, the course of which is by no means clear, the support of the three western administrations and of the farmers' organizations was won for Union Government. Thus the leadership of the West was captured, and assurance was made doubly sure by the Wartime Elections Act. At the same time, the nascent third party movement was absorbed by the Union Government, and the Liberal party in the West was wrecked by the issue of conscription, as the Conservative party had been mortally wounded by reciprocity.

Though the Union Government was constituted as a "win the war" administration, which should still partisan and sectional strife, other hopes had gone to its making. It was thought that a non-partisan administration might also be an opportunity to carry certain reforms, such as that of civil service recruitment, that it would be difficult, if not impossible, for a partisan government to carry. There was also, and inevitably, the tariff. The Union Government was not publicly pledged to tariff reform, but there can be no doubt that western sentiment had forced Unionist candidates to declare themselves on the tariff; indeed many western Unionists were low tariff Liberals, or even outright independents. The eastern industrialists, on the other hand, were alert to see that the weighty western wing of the Cabinet should not induce the government to make concessions to the West. Thus there was an uneasy truce on the tariff question during the remainder of the war, the issue lying dormant but menacing the unity of the Government and its majority once the pressure of war should be removed. The test was to come with the first peace budget, that of 1919.

These, then, were the underlying causes of the rise of the western Progressive Movement. In 1919 they came to the surface, unchanged in themselves but now operating in a heated and surcharged atmosphere. That there would have been a Progressive Movement in any event is not to be doubted; the war and the events of the post-war years served to give it explosive force.

Certain elements in this surcharged atmosphere were general, others peculiar to the farmer, in effect. Chief of the general elements was the fact that the War of 1914–18 had been fought without economic controls of any significance. The result was inflation with all the stresses and strains inflation sets up in the body economic and social. The high cost of living, as it was called, was an invariable theme of speakers of the day, particularly of spokesmen of labour and the farmer. The farmer was quite prepared to believe that he, as usual, was especially the victim of these circumstances, and would point to the "pork profiteers," to clinch his contention. Inflation was at the root of the general unrest of the day, and the influence of the Russian Revolution, the radical tone of many organizations and individuals, the Winnipeg strike, and the growth of the labour movement are to be ascribed to inflation than to any native predisposition to radical courses.

Among the farmers' special grievances was the conscription of farmers' sons in 1918. The farming population of English Canada, on the whole had supported conscription, but with two qualifications. One was that there should also be "conscription of wealth," by which a progressive income tax was meant. The other was that the farms should not be stripped of their supply of labour, a not unreasonable condition in view of the urgent need of producing food. But the military situation in the spring of 1918 led to the revocation of the order-in-council exempting farmers' sons from military service. The result was a bitter outcry from the farmers, the great delegation to Ottawa in May, 1918, and an abiding resentment against the Union Government and all its works, especially in Ontario.

In the West itself, drouth, especially in southern Alberta, had come to harass a farm population already sorely tried. Suffice it to indicate that in the Lethbridge area of southern Alberta, the average yield of wheat between 1908 and 1921 ranged from sixty-three bushels to the acre in 1915 to two in 1918, and eight in 1921.[14] This was the extreme, but the whole West in varying degrees suffered a similar fluctuation in yield. It was a rehearsal of the disaster of the nineteen-thirties.

To the hazards of nature were to be added the hazards of the market. In 1917 the government had fixed the price of wheat to keep it from going higher, and had established a Wheat Board to market the crops of the war years. Now that peace had come, was wheat once more to be sold on the open market, or would the government fix the price and continue to market the crops through the Wheat Board, at least until the transition from war to peace was accomplished? Here was a chance to make the National Policy a matter of immediate benefit and concern to the western farmer, a chance not undiscerned by shrewd defenders of the National Policy.[15] Here also, under the stimulus of war, was the beginning of the transition from the old Jeffersonian and laissez-faire tradition of the frontier West, to the new West of wheat pools, floor prices, and the Cooperative Commonwealth Federation. The point of principle was clearly grasped by the farmers, but their response was confused. The Manitoba Grain Growers and the United Farmers of Alberta declined in annual convention to ask the government to continue the Wheat Board, but this decision was severely criticized, one might almost say, was repudiated, by the rank and file of the membership. The Saskatchewan Grain Growers, who met later, emphatically demanded that the Wheat Board be continued. In the upshot it was, but only for the crop yield of 1919, and in 1920 it was liquidated. From this action came much of the drive, indeed the final impetus, of the Progressive Movement.[16] Thereafter the western farmer was caught between fixed debt charges and high costs on one hand and falling prices on the other; his position seemed to him desperate. From his despair came

367

drouth

first, the Progressive electoral sweep in the West, and then the economic action which created the wheat pools.

Finally, there was the question of tariff revision. It was, however, no longer the simple clash of sectional interests it had been. The customs tariff had been increased to help finance the war. Any revision now would affect governmental financing of the war debt, and also the financial resources of private individuals and corporations in the post-war period. In short, the question had now become, what place should tariff revision have in reconstruction?

It was to this question that the Union Government had to address itself, while preparing the budget of 1919 under the vigilant eyes of the farmers' organizations on the one side and of the Canadian Manufacturers' Association on the other. The decision was, in effect, to postpone the issue, on the ground that 1919 was, to all intents and purposes, a war year and that only a very moderate revision should be attempted. The decision was not unreasonable, and was clearly intended to be a compromise between eastern and western views on the tariff.[17] But western supporters of the Union Government were in a very vulnerable position, as the McMaster amendment to the motion to go into Committee of Supply was to show.[18] The pressure from the West for a major lowering of the tariff was mounting and becoming intense. In the outcome, the Honourable Thomas A. Crerar, Minister of Agriculture, resigned on the ground that the revision undertaken in the budget was insufficient. In the vote on the budget he was joined by nine western Unionists. This was the beginning of the parliamentary Progressive party.

The position of the remaining western Unionists became increasingly difficult, though also their pressure contributed to the moderate revision of 1919.[19] The fate of R. C. Henders is very much in point. Henders had been, as President of the Manitoba Grain Growers, an ardent and outspoken agrarian. In 1916 he had been nominated as an independent candidate for Macdonald. In 1917 he accepted nomination as Unionist candidate and was elected. In 1919 he voted with the Government on the budget on the ground that this was in effect a war budget, and the time premature for a revision of the tariff. In 1920 the United Farmers of Manitoba, following the action of their executive, "repudiated his stand, accepted his resignation, and reaffirmed [their] confidence in the principles of the Farmers' Platform."[20] In 1921 he vanished from political ken. An honest man had taken a politically mistaken line and was mercilessly held to account. Such was the fate of western Unionists who did not cross the floor or find refuge in the Senate. Western low tariff sentiment would admit of no equivocation.

The third party movement, stirring in the West before 1917 but absorbed and over-ridden by the Unionist Government, was now free to resume its course with a favourable wind fanned by inflation, short crops, and post-war discontent. A chart had already been provided. The Canadian Council of Agriculture had in 1916 taken cognizance of the mounting demand that political action be taken by the farmers. Without committing the Council itself, it prepared the Farmers' Platform as a programme which the farmers' organizations might endorse and which they might press upon the government. The events of 1917 diverted attention from it, but in 1918 it was revised and enlarged, and in 1919 was adopted by the farmers' organizations. In substance, the platform called for a League of Nations, dominion autonomy, free trade with Great Britain, reciprocity with the United States, a lowering of the general tariff, graduated income, inheritance, and corporation taxes, public ownership of a wide range of utilities, and certain reforms designed to bring about a greater measure of democracy, such as reform of the Senate, abolition of titles, and the institution of direct legislation and proportional representation.[21] The platform gave the incoherent western discontent a rallying point and a programme, and was the occasion for the organized farmers entering federal politics. Its title, "The New National Policy," was a gage of battle thrown down before the defenders of the old National Policy, a challenge, direct and explicit, to make that policy national indeed.

This decision to enter federal politics was opportune beyond the dream of seasoned politicians. The prairie was afire in a rising wind, and soon the flames were flaring from one end of the country to the other. In October, 1919, the United Farmers of Ontario carried forty-six seats in a house of 111, and formed an administration. Later in the same month O. R. Gould, farmers' candidate in the federal seat of Assiniboia, defeated W. R. Motherwell, Liberal stalwart and a founder of the Grain Growers' Association, by a majority of 5224.[22] A few days later Alex Moore carried Cochrane in a provincial by-election for the United Farmers of Alberta. In 1920 the organized farmers carried nine seats in Manitoba, seven in Nova Scotia, and ten in New Brunswick.[23] By-election after by-election went against the Government, usually to farmer candidates, until the smashing climax of the Medicine Hat by-election of June, 1921, when Robert Gardiner of the UFA defeated a popular Unionist candidate by a majority of 9764.[24] Even the Liberals' tariff plank of 1919 did little to check the sweep of the flames. The political prophets were estimating that of the forty-three seats west of the lakes, the Progressives would carry from thirty-five to forty.[25]

All was propitious, then, for the entry of the Progressives into federal politics. There they might hope to hold the balance of power, or even emerge as the largest group. The work of organization was pushed steadily. In December, 1920, the Canadian Council of Agriculture recognized the third party in the House of Commons as the exponent of the new national policy and endorsed the members' choice of the Honourable T. A. Crerar as leader.[26] During 1920 and 1921 Progressive candidates were nominated by local conventions in all federal constituencies in the West.

Two major difficulties, however, were arising to embarrass the Progressives in their bid for national power. The first was the charge that they were a class party. The second was the demand that political action be taken in the provincial as well as the federal field.[27] These embarrassments

369

were eventually to split the Movement, defeat its bid for national power, and reduce it to the status of a sectional party.

The origin of these divisions in the Movement may best be examined by turning to provincial politics in the West. That the entrance into federal politics could not be kept separate from a demand that political action be taken in the provinces, arose in part from the federal composition of national parties. Any federal political movement is driven to attempt the capture of provincial governments, in order to acquire the means, that is to say, the patronage, whereby to build an effective political organization. It is not to be supposed that this political maxim was unknown to the leaders of the Progressive Movement. They hoped, however, that national success would be followed by a voluntary adherence of the western governments, which would render capture by storm unnecessary.

The Progressive Movement, at the same time, was a genuine attempt to destroy machine politics, and there was in its leadership a sincere reluctance to accept the facts of political life. They hoped to lead a popular movement, to which the farmers' economic organizations would furnish whatever direction was necessary. It was the zeal of their followers, eager to destroy the old parties wherever they existed, that carried the Progressive Movement into provincial politics.

370

Province by province, the leaders were compelled to bow to the pressure of the rank and file, and allow the organized farmers to enter the provincial arenas. The methods and the results, however, were by no means identical, for they were conditioned by the different political histories of the three provinces.

In Manitoba the dominating fact was that from 1899 until 1915 the province had been governed by the Conservative Roblin administration. The sheer power and efficiency of the Roblin-Rogers organization, perhaps the classic example of the political machine in Canadian history, accounts in great part for the victory of the anti-reciprocity campaign in Manitoba in 1911. Its spectacular demise in the odour of scandal in 1915 left the provincial Conservative party badly shattered. Henceforth there were many loose Conservative votes in the most conservative of the Prairie Provinces, a province a whole generation older than the other two, and during that generation the very image and transcript of Ontario. But the succeeding Liberal Government, that of the Honourable T. C. Norris, was reformist and progressive. There was little the Grain Growers could ask of the provincial administration that it was not prepared to grant. Why then should the organized farmers oppose the Norris Government? The answer was that the Progressive Movement was, for many Progressives, a revolt against the old party system, and the provincial Liberal organization had been affiliated with the federal Liberals. It might, indeed, become a major buttress of Liberalism as the breach between the Laurier and the Unionist Liberal closed. If the old parties were to be defeated at Ottawa, they must be rooted out at the source of their strength in the provinces. Out of this conflict, largely one between leaders and rank and file, came the decision of the new United Farmers of Manitoba in 1920 that the organization as such should not enter provincial politics, but that in the constituencies the locals might hold conventions, nominate candidates, and organize. If a majority of constituencies should prove to be in favour of political action, then the executive of the United Farmers would call a provincial convention to draft a platform.[28] As a result, political action was taken locally, and nine farmer representatives were elected to the Manitoba legislature in 1920.[29] As a result of this success, the UFM placed the resources of the organization behind the farmers' political action,[30] and in the election of 1922 the farmers won a plurality of seats in the legislature. The suspected *rapprochement* of the Norris Government with the federal Liberals may have contributed to its defeat.[31]

In Saskatchewan and Alberta the dominating factor was that at the creation of the two provinces in 1905 the federal Liberal government used its influence to establish Liberal administrations. In Canada the possession of power is all but decisive. Governments fall not so much by the assaults of their enemies as through their own internal decay. From 1905 until 1921 the Liberals ruled in Alberta; from 1905 until 1929 they were in power in Saskatchewan. Moreover, in both, the Conservative party was cut off from patronage and unnaturally compelled to be a party of provincial rights. Both provincial Conservative parties declined from 1911 on, and rapidly after the provincial elections of 1917. In these provinces too, the administrations were careful to govern in harmony with the wishes of the organized farmers. Why then should the farmers enter provincial politics against the Liberal government? Again the answer is that the provincial Liberal parties were affiliated with the federal party, and were examples of the machine politics which Progressives hoped to destroy, politics rendered noisome by the corruption arising from the scramble for the resources of the West, and the political ruthlessness of the professional politicians of the day.

Down to 1917 the political developments of the two provinces were alike, but a remarkable diversion occurs thereafter. In Saskatchewan the Liberal party enjoyed shrewd leadership, considerable administrative ability, and a fine political organization. Threatened by scandal in 1917, it made a remarkable recovery under Premier William Martin. In that almost wholly rural province, the Liberal government was a government of the grain growers. Leadership, as in the instance of the Honourable Charles A. Dunning, graduated from the Association to the government. The slightest wish of the Saskatchewan Grain Growers became law with as much dispatch as the conventions of government allow.[32] When the demand for provincial political action arose, Premier Martin met it, in the Preeceville speech of May, 1920, by dissociating the provincial from the federal party. At the same time the weight of the executive of the Grain Growers was thrown against intervention as a separate party in provincial politics. As in Manitoba, when the demand, partly under pressure from the Non-Partisan League, became irresistible, it was referred to the locals.[33] The locals gave little response during 1920–1, and an attempt of third party men in 1921 to commit the central organization to political action was foiled.[34] As a result, the provincial Progressive Movement in Saskatchewan became largely an attempt at organization by independents, under the leadership of Harris Turner of Saskatoon.[35] Before organization could be well begun, Premier Martin dissolved the legislature and headed off the movement by a snap election. This was decisive. Only thirteen independents were returned, to a great extent, it would seem, by Conservative votes, for the provincial Conservative party simply did not contest the election. Thus the Liberal administration in Saskatchewan survived the Progressive rising, but at the price of severing temporarily its ties with the federal party.

In Alberta the same story was to have a very different outcome. Not only was the Liberal party of that province less fortunate in its leadership, though no less realistic in its tactics, not only did it suffer division by the quarrel over the Alberta Great Waterways Railway scandal, which created a weakness in the party that the division into Laurier and Unionist Liberals did nothing to mend,[36] but the farmer organization of that province was separate in its leadership from the government, and the leadership was from 1915 the leadership of Henry Wise Wood. In Alberta, the forceful personalities were outside the government; in Saskatchewan, they were, on the whole, in the government or close to it. Alberta lost the brilliant A. L. Sifton to the Union Government in 1917, and Alberta alone possessed a Henry Wise Wood. Wood and the executive of the United Farmers of Alberta were no more anxious than other leaders of the farm organizations to go into provincial politics. He, indeed, was on principle opposed to going into politics at all. The drive for a third, independent, farmer party, however, developed much greater force in Alberta than elsewhere. This was partly because the decline of the Conservative party was even more pronounced in Alberta than in Saskatchewan. It was also because the Non-Partisan League became more powerful in that province than in Saskatchewan. American populism and British radicalism had freer play in frontier Alberta than in older Saskatchewan. The Non-Partisan League, for example, captured two provincial seats in Alberta in 1917, whereas it had captured only one in Saskatchewan in the same year, and that by a fluke. The League went on to threaten to capture the locals of the UFA by conversion and infiltration. This was a threat that could not be ignored, because it was in and through the locals that the farmers' organizations lived. Wood and the UFA leaderships were therefore caught on the horns of a dilemma. They knew that political action had invariably ruined farm organizations in the past, as the Farmers' Alliance in the United States had gone to wreck in the Populist party. They knew also that they might lose control of the UFA if the Non-Partisan League obtained control of a majority of locals and assumed leadership of the drive for political action. Wood solved the dilemma by his concept of "group government", and in doing so crystallized the strong tendency of the Progressive Movement, a tendency which owed much to the Non-Partisan League, to become a class movement, deeply averse to lawyers, bankers, and politicians. The UFA would take political action, but it would take it as an organization. It would admit only farmers to its ranks; it would nominate only farmers for election; its representation in the legislature would constitute a separate group, co-operating with other groups but not combining with any to constitute a political party. Guided by this concept, the UFA in 1919 entered politics, both federal and provincial.[37] In 1921 it won a majority of the seats in the Alberta legislature.

These varying fortunes of the Progressive Movement in the three provinces were significant for the character of the federal Progressive party. Broadly speaking, two concepts of the character and future of the party prevailed among its members. One, which may be termed the Manitoba view, was that the Progressive Movement was one of insurgent liberalism, which might have the happy result of recapturing the federal Liberal party from the control of the conservative and protectionist Liberals of the East. This was the view, for example, of J. W. Dafoe, a mentor of Progressivism. It aimed at building up a national popular movement by "broadening out," by "opening the door" to all sympathizers. The Saskatchewan federal Progressives also accepted this view, the more so as the provincial movement had been headed off for a decade. The other concept may be called the Alberta concept. It was that the Progressive Movement was an occupational or class movement, capable of extension by group organization to other economic classes, but not itself concerned with bringing about such extension. Farmer must represent farmer, the group must act as a group.

It may be noted in passing that neither view of the Progressive Movement demands an explicit farmer-labour alliance. Why Progressivism did not develop this characteristic of the earlier Populist party and the later Cooperative Commonwealth Federation cannot be explained here, but it may be said that the leadership of both wings of the Movement was averse to an open alliance with labour.

Here again is the two-fold character of the Progressive Movement postulated in the opening paragraph. Progressivism which was an economic protest, seeking a natural remedy by political action little more unconventional than a revolt from caucus rule, is here termed Manitoban. Progressivism which was doctrinaire, class conscious, and heterodox, is here called Albertan. The former assumed that exploitation would cease in a society made competitive by the abolition of protection; the latter proposed to produce a harmony of interests by putting an end to competition by means of the co-operation of organized groups. Both tendencies, of course, existed all across the Movement. Each was personified and had as respective protagonists the Honourable T. A. Crerar and Henry Wise Wood.

The extremes, however, were fundamental and irreconcilable. Manitoban Progressivism sought economic ends through conventional political means and admitted of compromise with the old parties. Albertan Progressivism sought much the same economic ends, but also sought to transform the conditions of politics. In this it was closer to the essential nature of Progressivism, with its innate distrust of elected representatives and of party organization.[38] Its pledging of candidates, its frequent use of the signed recall, its levy on members for campaign funds, its predilection for direct legislation and for proportional representation, establish its fundamental character. That in so conducting itself it was to give rise to forms of political organization which old line politicians were to envy, is one of those little ironies which delight the sardonic observer.

An examination of the course of the general election of 1921 adds little to the exposition of the theme. As revealed in the campaign literature, it turned on the issues of protection and of the class doctrines of Henry Wise Wood. Prime Minister Meighen, first of those western men with eastern principles to be called to head the Conservative party, put on the full armour of protection, and fought the western revolt in defence of the National Policy. It was courageous, it was magnificent, but it was not successful. His party attacked the Progressives as free traders seeking to destroy the National Policy for selfish class advantage. Mr. W. L. Mackenzie King stood firmly on the Liberal platform of 1919, which, marvelously contrived, faced squarely all points of the political compass at once. Liberal strategy was to avoid a sharp stand, to pose as the farmers' friend — "There never was a Farmers' Party while the Liberals were in power"[39] — and to denounce the class character of Progressivism. Mr. Crerar was in the embarrassing position of a leader whose followers persist in treading on his heels, but he fought the good fight with dignity and moderation, protesting that his was not a class movement.

In the upshot, the Progressives carried sixty-five seats, and emerged as the second largest group in the House. Coalition with the Liberals was seriously considered and was rejected only at the last moment, presumably because Messrs. Crerar and Drury could not obtain from Mr. King those pledges which would have ensured the identity of the group and the curbing of the protectionist elements in the Liberal Cabinet. This decision marked the beginning of the disintegration of the Movement, for the Progressives neither imposed their policies on the Liberals nor definitely became a parliamentary party seeking office. With that fatal tendency of third parties to avoid responsibility, of which George Langley had warned a decade before,[40] they declined to become even the official opposition.

Thereafter Manitoban Progressivism lost its bright speed amid the sands and shallows of official Liberalism. Albertan Progressivism, represented by the Ginger Group, the federal UFA members and a few others, alone survived the decay of Progressive zeal, and remained for fourteen years to lend distinction to the national councils, and to bear in its organization the seeds at once of Social Credit and the Cooperative Commonwealth Federation.

Notes

1. *Cf.* Frederick Jackson Turner, *The Significance of Sections in American History* (New York, 1932), 314.

2. *Hansard*, 1910–11, I, 1918.

3. Wilfred E. Binkley, *American Political Parties* (New York, 1944) — ". . . Madison's principle that a nation wide majority can agree only on a moderate program," 87; also 17–18.

4. Dafoe Library of the *Winnipeg Free Press*, Dafoe Papers, Dafoe to Sir Clifford Sifton, July 21, 1919; on the prospects of re-organizing the Liberal party.

5. *Manitoba Free Press*, April 10, 1917, 9.

6. *Grain Growers' Guide*, September 14, 1910, 13. Fred Kirkham, advocate of a third party, wrote to the editor from Saltcoats, Saskatchewan: "If the memorials presented to Sir Wilfrid Laurier have failed to imbue him with the determination to battle with the vested interests of the East to grant our just requests, we have no alternative but to become democratic insurgents, and form a new party and find a new general to fight under. We must be courageous in politics before Laurier will treat with us as a big community of votes to be reckoned with."

7. Public Archives of Canada, Laurier Papers, 3089, J. W. Dafoe to Laurier, April 28, 1911. "In my judgment reciprocity has changed the whole political situation in the West. Until it was announced the drift out West was undoubtedly against the government; but now it is just other way about."

8. *United Farmers of Alberta, Annual Report*, 1910, 43. "Moved by the Vermilion Union: Resolved, that ten farmers, as members of Parliament with votes would have more weight in shaping the laws and influencing government than one thousand delegates as petitioners:
   Therefore be it further resolved that the farmers, to secure this end, should vote for farmers only to represent them in Parliament and vote as a unit and cease dividing their voting power. Carried."

9. I am indebted to Professor J. R. Mallory of Brandon College, now of McGill, for a discussion clarifying this point.

10. *Manitoba Free Press*, May 13, 1916. Editorial, "Consequences." "Whatever may be the political consequences of this blunder to Liberalism in Canada at large, Western Liberalism will not suffer if it adheres to the independence which its representatives have displayed at Ottawa this week. These developments at the capital must tend to strengthen the feeling which has been growing steadily for years that Western Liberals need not look to the East, at present, for effective and progressive leadership. . . . Canadian public life will thus be given what it sorely needs, . . . a group of convinced radicals. . . . To your tents. O Israel!"

11. *Ibid.*, June 28, 1917, 9. "The Saskatchewan Victory." "The Canadian West is in the mood to break away from past affiliations and traditions and inaugurate a new political era of sturdy support for an advanced and radical programme. The break-up of parties has given the West its opportunity: and there is no doubt it will take advantage of it." At least four independent candidates had been nominated in the West before June, 1917, in provincial and federal seats. In December, 1916, the Canadian Council of Agriculture had issued the first Farmers' Platform.

12. Henry Borden (ed.), *Robert Laird Borden: His Memoirs* (Toronto, 1938) II, 749–50, J. W. Dafoe to Borden, September 29, 1917.

13. Dafoe Papers, Dafoe to Augustus Bridle, June 14, 1921. "The Western Liberal Convention was a bomb which went off in the hands of its makers. It was decided upon at Ottawa by a group of conscription Liberals; the intention was to bring into existence a Western Liberal group free from Laurier's control who would be prepared to consider coalition with Borden on its merits, but the Liberal machine in the West went out and captured the delegates with the result that the convention was strongly pro-Laurier."

14. *Report of the Survey Board for Southern Alberta*, January, 1922.

15. *Hansard*, 1919, I, 558. Colonel J. A. Currie (Simcoe) "I am quite in agreement with the hon. member for Maple Creek (J. A. Maharg) when he says we should fix a price for the wheat of the West. That is in line with the National Policy," See also the Right Honourable Arthur Meighen's proposal for a modified Wheat Board in his speech at Portage la Prairie during the campaign of 1921. *Canadian Annual Review*, 1921, 449–50.

16. *Cf.* Vernon C. Fowke, *Canadian Agricultural Policy* (Toronto, 1946), 268.

17. The changes were as follows: the $7^1/_2$ per cent increase for war purposes was removed from agricultural implements and certain necessities of life; the 5 per cent war duty was modified; an income tax was levied.

18. Fourteen western Unionists voted for the amendment. *Hansard*, 1919, IV, 3678.

19. *Hansard*, 1919, IV, 3475. W. D. Cowan, Unionist (Regina). "I believe that the changes which have been made in the tariff have been made entirely because of the agitation which has been carried on by the West. We have had, for the first time, I fancy, in the history of Parliament, a western caucus and in that we have been united. Old time Liberals united with old time Conservatives. On the one point that they should try to get substantial reductions in the tariffs. . . ."

20. *Canadian Annual Review*, 1920, 741.

21. See *ibid.*, 1919, for text. 365–8.

22. *Parliamentary Companion*, 1921, 196.

23. *Manitoba Free Press*, February 25, 1921; *Grain Growers' Guide*, August 4, 1920, 4, and October 27, 1920, 5.

24. *Parliamentary Companion,* 1922, 247.

25. Dafoe Papers, Dafoe to Sir Clifford Sifton, January 20, 1920.

26. *Grain Growers' Guide,* December 15, 1920, 3. Resolution of executive of the Canadian Council of Agriculture in meeting of December 7–9, 1920.

27. Dafoe Papers, Dafoe to Sir Clifford Sifton, January 26, 1921. "Crerar's only troubles out here arise from the ardor with which certain elements in his following insist upon organizing a purely class movement against the three local governments, thereby tending to antagonize the very elements which Crerar is trying, by broadening its basis, to add to his party."

28. *United Farmers of Manitoba Year Book,* 1920, 67.

29. *Grain Growers' Guide,* July 7, 1920, 6. Editorial, "The Manitoba Election." "The United Farmers of Manitoba, as an organization, took no part in the election, and each constituency where farmer candidates were nominated and elected acted entirely on its own initiative."

30. *Ibid.,* January 19, 1921, 3.

31. *Manitoba Free Press,* April 28, 1922. Dafoe Papers, Dafoe to Sir Clifford Sifton, July 7, 1922.

32. *Minutes of the Annual Convention of the Saskatchewan Grain Growers' Association,* February 18–21, 1919, 4. Report of Premier Wm. Martin's address. "There are questions now coming before you affecting the welfare of the whole community of the Province. It is the policy of the present government and will continue to be the policy of the present government to carry out these suggestions."

33. *Ibid.,* February 9–13, 1920, 114–19.

34. *Ibid.,* January 31–February 4, 1921. The debate on provincial political action was involved: a motion to enter provincial politics as an organization was defeated (118) and a motion to support action by constituencies was, it would seem, shelved (93).

35. *Saskatoon Daily Star,* June 1, 1921. Report of the convention of independents at Saskatoon, May 31, 1921.

36. John Blue, *Alberta Past and Present* (Chicago, 1924), 125. "The session of 1910 witnessed a perturbation and upheaval that split the Liberal party into two factions, which more than a decade afterwards regarded each other with some jealousy and distrust."

37. *United Farmers of Alberta, Annual Report,* 1919, 52–3.

38. *Grain Growers' Guide,* March 5, 1919, 26. Article by Roderick McKenzie on "Political Action." "The purpose of the movement inaugurated by the farmers is that whenever the time comes to make a choice of representation to parliament, the electors get together to make their selection."

39. P.A.C., Pamphlet no. 5081, *Group Government Compared with Responsible Government.*

40. *Grain Growers' Guide,* September 21, 1910, 13–14. "It may be urged that a separate farmers' party might influence the government even if it did not become strong enough to take on itself the actual work of governing. The answer to that is this. The legitimate objective of a political party is to control the legislative and administrative functions. Without [that] objective it cannot exist for any length of time. . . ."

The Origins of the Maritime Rights Movement *

E. R. FORBES

Canadian historians have devoted considerable attention to post-war agitation on the Prairies: they have virtually ignored similar agitation in the Maritimes, the regional protest movement which became known by the slogan "Maritime Rights." The few comments it has received, in biographical literature or in sweeping analyses of long periods of history, have been largely concerned with its political manifestations.[1] Such a preoccupation is not surprising. Both Liberals and Conservatives were vociferous in their efforts to portray themselves as the champions of the movement. Shortly before the Antigonish-Guysborough by-election of 1927 a Protestant clergyman set out to review the issues of the campaign

* From *Acadiensis,* 5 (1975): 54–66. Copyright by University of New Brunswick Department of History. Reprinted by permission.

from the pulpit. Both candidates, he noted, were clamouring for attention as the defenders of "Maritime Rights." This aspect of their campaign, he said, reminded him of the behaviour of his own young children one evening when he and his wife were getting ready to go visiting. The little girl set up an awful howl from the moment the babysitter arrived. She bawled and bawled. Finally, just as her parents were going out the door, her brother turned, slapped her sharply, and declared, "Shut up, I wanna cry."

There was much more to "Maritime Rights" than the conspicuous wail of the politicians. One cannot begin to tell here the story of the movement — the intensive organizational campaign with its delegations to Ottawa, economic conferences, and country-wide speaking tours; the erratic swings in the popular vote from one party to another as Maritimers searched desperately for solutions to their problems; and the inevitable royal commissions sent in to defuse the agitation[2] — but one can at least attempt a more basic introduction through the analysis of the motives of the different social groups which participated in it. Their behaviour suggests that the issues involved went much deeper than mere political manoeuvering or even, as professor G. A. Rawlyk has suggested, the attempt by the local "Establishment" to undercut other forms of social protest.[3] All classes in the region, although often in conflict on other issues, were united in their support of Maritime Rights. Each was aware that its own particular aspirations were incapable of realization until the region's declining influence was checked or reversed.

The social categories employed here will be those used by the people themselves. Maritimers spoke frequently in this period of their "classes." They were not referring to any clear Marxian structure nor did they imply the status-based stratification of the modern sociologist. Essentially they were talking about broad occupational interest groups. Such divisions were partly theoretical: the members of each group or "class" were assumed to have interests in common of which not all might be conscious. But they also had an empirical basis through such exclusively occupational organizations as the Maritime Division of the Canadian Manufacturers Association, retail merchants associations, the United Farmers, federations of labour and, by the end of the decade, the Maritime Fishermen's Union. These were the kinds of groupings to which New Brunswick Premier P. J. Veniot referred early in 1923 when he reported to Mackenzie King that, after looking "carefully into the [Maritime Rights] movement," he had found it was "purely non-political and embraces [the] efforts of all classes to obtain what is sincerely considered fair play for [the] Maritime Provinces."[4]

The development of Maritime regionalism, of which the Maritime Rights movement formed the climax, took place largely in the first two decades of the century. Previously, popular loyalties had been focused upon larger imperial or national entities or upon smaller political, cultural or geographical units. The shift was dictated by a growing realization of the need for co-operation. Co-operation was essential if the three Atlantic

Cook^{?)}

Provinces were to counteract the eclipse of their influence which resulted from the rise of the West and the growing metropolitan dominance of Central Canada. Another factor contributing to the growth of regionalism was the progressive ideology of the period, which increased the pressure upon the small governments for expensive reforms while at the same time suggesting the possibility of limitless achievement through a strategy of unity, organization and agitation. Consequently, regional awareness increased sharply in the three provinces. Their leaders joined forces to fight losses in representation, which followed every census after 1891; to increase their subsidies, which had fallen far behind those of the Prairies; and to defend the Intercolonial Railway, whose pro-Maritime policies came under attack from both the Prairies and Central Canada.[5]

378   The manufacturers' stake in the regionalization of the Maritimes was most obvious, particularly for the defense of the Intercolonial Railway. By the end of the 19th Century that railway had become an important agent of industrialization in the region. Its management had accepted the principle that half a loaf was better than none and had reduced rates to develop traffic. It created a basic freight rate structure which was between 20 and 50 percent lower than that in force in Ontario and offered in addition special rate concessions based upon "what the traffic would bear."[6] Built into the structure was a system of "arbitraries" or especially low rates between the Maritimes and Montreal on goods destined for points further west. These rates enabled the secondary manufacturers in the Maritimes to penetrate markets in Western and Central Canada to obtain the sales volume necessary for competitive production.[7] With such encouragement, capital investment in manufacturing in the Maritimes quadrupled between 1900 and 1920.[8] The old dream of some Nova Scotian entrepreneurs that their province would play the role of a great industrial metropolis to a Canadian hinterland was far from realization. But the Maritimers' optimism for their manufacturing potential persisted. The Halifax *Morning Chronicle* in 1906 explicitly touted Nova Scotia's pioneer programme in technical education as encouraging the industrialization which would reverse the region's declining status in Confederation. The Saint John *Standard* in 1916 enthused about a hydro-electric project to harness the Bay of Fundy tides, which, by providing cheaper energy for manufacturing, would raise the Maritimes "to a position of commercial supremacy as compared with any other part of the Dominion."[9]

Such aspirations received a severe check with the integration of the Inter-colonial into a national system. The happy partnership between the Inter-colonial management and the local producers had come under attack both from competing Central Canadian manufacturers and Prairie farmers preoccupied with their demand for the equalization of freight rates.[10] The Borden Government apparently decided to get rid of the anomaly of a Maritime-oriented railway once and for all. In November, 1918, it shifted the Intercolonial's headquarters to Toronto, transferred its senior officials to other lines and replaced them with appointees from the Canadian

Northern. The following year, the Intercolonial was placed under the *de facto* jurisdiction of the Board of Railway Commissioners which raised the rates to the Ontario level.[11] The process was completed in time to provide an inflated base for the 40 per cent general rate increase of 1920. In Ontario and Quebec freight rates increased 111% between 1916 and September 1920; in the Maritimes basic rates rose between 140 and 216% and the simultaneous cancellation of special rates, such as the special commodity rate on sugar, led to still greater increases.[12]

The rate changes not only threatened the local entrepreneurs' dreams of industrial grandeur, but left them seriously exposed to the pressure for metropolitan consolidation. For many, the campaign for Maritime Rights became a struggle for survival. In 1919 a group of manufacturers mounted a delegation to Ottawa, demanded the restoration of the Intercolonial to independent management and revived the Maritime Board of Trade as a channel for their agitation.[13] They continued to play a prominent role in the leadership of the movement through such representatives as W. S. Fisher of Saint John, a former Canadian Manufacturers' Association president, who served as a spokesman for another delegation to Ottawa in 1921, and D. R. Turnbull, managing-director of the Acadia Sugar Corporation, who, in 1925, became Nova Scotia's representative on the newly-formed Maritime Rights Transportation Committee.[14]

379

Maritime merchants were also seriously affected by the integration of the Intercolonial into a national system. The wholesalers were injured by the shift in supply purchasing for the railway from the Maritimes to Toronto.[15] They were weakened further, in relation to their metropolitan competitors, by the sharp increase in "town distributing rates" — especially low rates which had enabled them to import quantities of goods from Central Canada, break them up and send them out to individual towns and villages at little more than the cost of direct shipment. Similarly higher rates on the Intercolonial accelerated the shift away from Maritime ports as distributing points for products entering from abroad. H. R. Silver, a commission merchant, reported a decline in molasses shipments out of Halifax from 130 carloads in 1916 to 17 in 1921.[16] Retailers were also adversely affected. They had to pay more for their goods and had difficulty in passing the full charge on to their customers. The Halifax *Maritime Merchant* commented tersely in 1920 upon the general effect of the increase: "Added to the handicap already suffered by firms seeking western business, the new rate will be hard on the merchants and add materially to the cost the local consumer must pay."[17]

The issue which generated the greatest heat from the merchant and commercial interests of Halifax and Saint John was the development of their ports as entrepôts for Canada's winter trade. The two cities were engaged in a Darwinian struggle with the American seaports and with each other. The key to victory was volume and variety of traffic. The more traffic, the lower the port charges and ocean rates; the lower the rates, the greater the traffic. The Maritime ports were most conscious of their rivalry with Portland, Maine, which had traditionally enjoyed the advantage of a very active canvass for trade from the Grand Trunk Railway.[18] The Maritime ports' aspirations for Canadian trade, aroused initially by Confederation, had blossomed under the "national policy" of the Laurier Government. Laurier had promised that the National Transcontinental Railway would channel exports, particularly grain, through national ports. In 1903, he appointed a Royal Commission to investigate other means of routing trade through "all-Canadian channels," and in 1911, he pledged that his government would restrict the Imperial preference to goods entering through Canadian ports.[19]

Such expectations were rudely shaken by the federal take-over of the Grand Trunk. With it, the Canadian Government inherited a strong vested interest in the commercial success of Portland. At Halifax, prominent Liberals urged the return of a Conservative cabinet minister in the by-election of 1920 to give the Maritimes at least a voice in defending their port's interest.[20] Early in 1922 the Halifax and Saint John boards of trade appointed a joint committee, consisting largely of merchants and manufacturers, to co-ordinate their agitation on such issues as the restoration of the Intercolonial and the routing of trade through Maritime Ports.[21] The merchant's position in the Maritime Rights movement continued to be a prominent one through the organized activities of boards of trade and the role of individuals such as W. A. Black, of the leading merchant-shipping firm of Pickford and Black. At seventy-six years of age, against "his physicians' advice, his wife's fears and his family's opposition," Black came out of retirement to fight the Halifax by-election of 1923 on a platform of Maritime Rights.[22]

Another business group, the lumbermen, also jointed the agitation. For them, the impact of the increased freight charges was compounded in 1921 by increased American duty on timber products under the Fordney tariff. Angus MacLean of The Bathurst Company, later president of the New Brunswick Lumberman's Association, appealed to Mackenzie King for relief on both issues.[23] When none was forthcoming he and other so-called "Lumber lords" of New Brunswick such as Archie and Donald Fraser, owners of the second largest lumber company in the Maritimes, threw their very considerable support behind the Conservative "Maritime Rights" candidates in the federal election of 1925.[24] In that year, MacLean became the titular leader of the protest movement as president of the Maritime Board of Trade.

Although labour in the Maritimes was at the peak of its "class" consciousness in 1919, it joined with the business groups in the agitation. Between 1916 and 1920, reported union membership in the Maritimes had quadrupled to about 40 000.[25] Spurred by the anticipation of a "new era" to follow the War[26] and beset by the grim reality of galloping inflation,[27] the workers attempted new techniques in organization and challenged their employers in a series of strikes in 1919 and 1920. At the same time they were conscious that their aspirations for a greater share of the fruits of

380

their labour could not be achieved if their industries were destroyed from other causes. Early in 1919 the *Eastern Federationist*, published by the Trades and Labour Council of Pictou County, argued that the freight rate increases violated the "rights of the Maritime Provinces' people under the terms of Confederation."[28] After the Amherst "General Strike" in May and June of 1919, the *Federationist* was particularly incensed by reports that the Canada Car Company was planning to transfer its Amherst operation to Montreal. The thrust of the editor's bitterness was directed at both the capitalists involved and the trend towards metropolitan consolidation which posed a continual threat to Maritime industry and jobs.[29] Similarly the Halifax *Citizen*, the organ of the local Trades and Labour Council, severely criticized the removal of the railway headquarters from Moncton and commended the activities of the Maritime Board of Trade president, Hance J. Logan, in seeking Maritime union as a counterweight to the declining political influence of the region. Bemoaning the unfair treatment accorded the Maritimes by the rest of the country, the *Citizen* concluded that there was "very little hope of any justice for us under present conditions."[30] The journal periodically returned to this theme and remained a consistent supporter of Maritime Rights.

The Railway Brotherhoods, which, after the United Mineworkers, constituted the largest bloc of organized labour in the region, were directly involved in the Maritime Rights campaign. During the first decade of the century the brotherhoods had won the acceptance of the principle of seniority in promotions and lay-offs on the Intercolonial.[31] In theory at least, the humblest employee could aspire to the highest office on the road. Under the new regime after 1918, that principle went by the board. According to one estimate, 400 employees were transferred out of the Moncton headquarters and any replacements came from other government roads. In addition, the repair shops declined and staff was reduced all along the line. To some workers it seemed the principle of seniority had been replaced by the principle that no Maritimer need apply.[32]

Labour did not need to be coaxed into the Maritime Rights movement by the Halifax *Herald* or other politically-oriented journals in the 1920's; large segments were already there, drawn by a consideration of their own immediate interest. The railway centres provided the most consistent voting support for Maritime Rights candidates throughout the 1920's. F. B. McCurdy attributed his victory in the important Colchester by-election of 1920 to the railway workers' belief that in the cabinet he would "be strong enough to afford some relief in the railway grievance." He blamed his defeat in the general election of 1921 on his inability to do so.[33] Labour also threw its support behind W. A. Black in the Halifax by-election of 1923.[34] Neil Herman, Labour-organizer, Social Gospel clergyman and sometime editor of the Halifax *Citizen* was a founder and executive member of the Halifax Maritime Club.[35] He later accompanied its president, H. S. Congdon, in a tour of Central Canada to drum up newspaper support for the movement. When the so-called "Great" Maritime

Rights delegation went to Ottawa in February 1925, J. E. Tighe, president of the Saint John local of the International Longshoreman's Association, was one of four speakers who addressed the Members of Parliament on Maritime problems.[36]

The farmers were only slightly behind labour in their support for Maritime Rights. They too had expected to play a greater role in the new society which was supposed to follow the war; instead they were confronted by the realities of rural depopulation and community disintegration.[37] They challenged the business groups with new or intensified, political, occupational and economic organization. But their problems were in part those of the region. The new freight rates hit them, both as producers and consumers. Some were also angered by federal policies which seemed not only to encourage new immigrants to by-pass their region but also to promote westward migration at their expense. As much as they might resent the growth of industrial towns and their own relative loss in status, the farmers were conscious of their dependence on these towns for their markets. Even those who sold their apples or potatoes in Great Britain or the West Indies usually earned a significant proportion of their income in local markets — an important hedge against the sometimes widely fluctuating international prices.[38]

For a brief period the farmers' regional concern was obscured by their participation in what they believed was a national "class" movement. But their organizations, such as the Canadian Council of Agriculture, were dominated by the Prairies. Manitobans, T. A. Crerar and George Chipman, also sought to direct the movement in the Maritimes through the *United Farmers' Guide*. The *Guide*, theoretically the organ of the New Brunswick and Nova Scotia United Farmers Associations, was in fact a subsidiary of the *Grain Growers' Guide*.[39] The two regionalisms were soon in conflict. Western organizers tried in vain to get unequivocal statements against the tariff from the United Farmers of Nova Scotia and were cool to suggestions that "necessary" protection for local industries should be retained.[40] At the same time they offered no support for the Maritime positions on such issues as the Intercolonial, freight rates and subsidies. Most Maritime farmers realized they could not achieve their regional goals through a movement which was, in federal politics at least, "an agrarian and sectional bloc from the continental West, the representation of the monolithic wheat economy.[41] In 1921 support for the western-affiliated United Farmers Associations rapidly dwindled. By mid-summer "a majority" in the Maritime Co-operative Companies was reported anxious to dispose of the *United Farmers Guide* in which they had initially invested but were unable to control.[42]

The agricultural interests of Prince Edward Island had been involved in the Maritime Rights movement from the outset. At the Maritime Board of Trade meeting in 1919 they were happy to associate with the broader issues of the movement their own special problems. These were two: the need for a second car ferry and the completion of the widening of their

382

narrow gauge railways to permit a more rapid, reliable and cheaper delivery of their products to mainland markets.[43] In 1921 the Mainland farmers met in conference with representatives of manufacturing, merchant and shipping groups to launch a delegation to Ottawa to demand the return of the Intercolonial to independent management.[44] Thereafter, farm leaders assumed an increasingly important role in the Maritime Rights agitation. In 1923, for example, A. E. McMahon, president of the United Fruit Companies and a former vice-president of the United Farmers of Nova Scotia, became president of the Maritime Board of Trade, and, a year later, of the Maritime Development Association. One of the primary purposes of the latter organization was the rehabilitation of the rural areas through immigration and colonization.[45]

The fishermen's contribution to the Maritime Rights movement was largely restricted to the intensification of the discontent which underlay it. Their aspirations had been relatively moderate. The victims of a declining salt fish trade with the West Indies, they hoped to restore their industry through the expansion of their sales of fresh fish in Central Canada and New England. The former had been encouraged by a federal subsidy of one third of the express rate to Montreal on less than carload lots, the latter by a *modus vivendi* with the United States which had permitted them to land and sell their catches directly at American ports.[46] In 1919, the federal subsidies on fresh fish were terminated just as the trade was hit by the higher freight rates.[47] Needless to say, the fish merchants passed on their losses to the largely unorganized fishermen. Meanwhile, the door to the New England market was slammed shut by the American cancellation of the *modus vivendi* and the introduction of the Fordney tariff.

In the election of 1921, some fishermen seem to have accepted the Liberal promises of reciprocity to restore the American markets.[48] When this failed to materialize, their desperate plight led many (for example, the Yarmouth halibut fleet) to pack up and move to the United States.[49] Those who remained formed one group in Maritime society which seemed genuinely prepared to contemplate secession in their frantic search for markets. It was surely no coincidence that both Howard Corning, who proposed the famous secession resolution of 1923, and the lawyer Robert Blauveldt, self-proclaimed secessionist and Maritime Rights publicist[50] were both residents of Yarmouth county.

The role of professional classes in the Maritime Rights movement was prominent, but their motivation ambiguous. It is often difficult to discern whether lawyers, doctors, clergymen, academics and journalists were speaking for themselves or for the other groups in society by whom they were directly or indirectly employed. Certainly they played an important function in articulating and rationalizing the aspirations of the other groups. This role was explicit in some cases. The Nova Scotia government retained H. F. Munro of Dalhousie University to aid in the preparation of its submission to the Duncan Commission. The boards of trade hired freight rate experts, professional organizers and lawyers to prepare, publicize and help present their cases before the federal government and its various commissions. Significant also was the relationship between Maritime Rights journalists and the interests who paid their salaries, or patronized their newspapers through advertising and subscriptions. The lumberman-industrialist, Angus MacLean, for example, was reportedly "the principal owner" of the Saint John *Telegraph Journal*.[51] That paper in 1925 promoted the cross-country speaking-tours of president J. D. McKenna and editor A. B. Belding as part of its campaign for Maritime Rights. Similarly C. W. Lunn, who was credited with the initial popularization of the defence of the Intercolonial as guaranteed under the "compact of confederation," aspired to a labour readership and was even hired for a brief period to write for the *Eastern Federationist*.[52] More tenuous but still significant was the relationship between clergymen and the congregations which they represented. It is clear, for example, that the priests who protested the Duncan Commission's failure to help the fishermen were acting as agents for the fishermen in their parishes. Their intervention resulted in the Royal Commission investigation of the fisheries in 1928.[53]

384

In articulating the progressive reform ideology, which provided an important element in the developing Maritime regionalism, the professionals' motivation was also ambiguous. As various American scholars have pointed out, "progressivism" with its optimism, social criticism and focus on government as an agent of reform might be inspired by many and mixed motives.[54] To farmers, labour and their representatives, "progressivism" could be the desire to improve the lot of the weak and exploited, namely themselves. On the part of the business-oriented it might be concern for efficiency, the replacement of old-fashioned party structures, and the development of a more dynamic role by government which might more effectively serve the interests of the entrepreneur. To the professionals, besides any humanitarian concern, "progressivism" might mean an improved status or an expansion of their role in society in social work, health services or the government bureaucracy.

In the Maritimes, the clergy and academics were most prominent in articulating the various strains of an amorphous progressive ideology. The clergy, imbued with the social gospel, promoted a variety of reforms ranging from prohibition to widows' pensions and occasionally engaged in wholesale attacks on the capitalist system.[55] Academics used a more secular terminology but they too championed a wide range of reforms for the welfare of the community. Dr. F. H. Sexton hailed Nova Scotia's programme of technical education — he happened to be its superintendent — as a valuable means of "social service" in improving the lot of the miners and industrial workers.[56] That it was also a service for local industry went without saying. Dr. Melville Cummings, of the Truro Agricultural College and Rev. Hugh MacPherson of Saint Francis Xavier University displayed a similar zeal for agricultural education and farmers' co-operatives as the means of rural regeneration. President George B. Cutten of Acadia University, having failed to persuade governments to undertake the hydro-electric development of the Bay of Fundy, organized the Cape Split Development Company in an attempt to interest private capital in the scheme.[57]

All these progressive proposals placed strong pressure upon provincial governments to inaugurate or expand programmes for which revenue was not readily available. This fact led progressive elements into an ephemeral campaign for Maritime union, which was expected to provide a more efficient use of available resources[58]; and into a more substantive campaign for Maritime unity, one object of which was to wrest from the Federal Government a "fair" share of Dominion revenues.

Increased federal subsidies were sought, for example, by professionals concerned about the declining quality of instruction in the schools as higher salaries drew experienced teachers westward. But, since fiscal need had never been accepted as a justification for higher subsidies, Maritime governments developed the claim that they were entitled to monetary compensation for grants of land from the public domain — grants such as had been given to Ontario, Manitoba and Quebec in the boundary settlements of 1912. They also demanded subsidies in lieu of the increasingly lucrative "school lands" funds held in trust by the federal government for the Prairie Provinces. The Maritime Educational Convention at Moncton in 1918 and a Catholic educational conference at Antigonish a year later both discussed the subsidy claims as a matter vital to educational reform.[59] In the latter year the Conservative Halifax *Herald* enthusiastically endorsed a Liberal resolution which outlined the Maritime claims in the Nova Scotian Legislature. The "serious material injustice" inflicted upon the Maritimes through "the unfair distribution which has been made of federal assets by successive governments" had, according to the *Herald*, starved local government services or supplied them" in such a niggardly manner that progress is almost impossible." The *Herald* advocated the launching of "a concerted movement and (sic) properly directed activity. *We suggest that a maritime popular league should be forthwith organized, with provincial and county and town and village branches in all parts of the Maritime provinces, until the whole country has been enlightened, aroused and arrayed in a support of the resolution unanimously adopted by the Nova Scotia legislature.*" Although as their problems increased, Maritimers sought more fundamental solutions, the subsidy claims remained one of the basic components of the campaign for Maritime rights.

The Maritime Rights agitation which had emerged by 1919 was a regional protest movement which saw all classes united in their demands upon the rest of the country. This did not mean that different classes did not have distinct aspirations of their own; on the contrary, they were probably more conscious of them in 1919 than in any other period before or since. Each held a dream of progressive development in which its own collective interests were directly involved: for the manufacturers, their growth as the major industrial suppliers of the country; for the urban merchants, the final attainment of their communities' status as the entrepots

385

of Canada's trade; for labour and farmers, the emergence of a new more democratic society in which they would break the economic and political dominance of the business classes; for the fishermen, the chance to rehabilitate their industry through the new fresh fish trade; and for the professionals, the elevation of Maritime society through education. But none of these aspirations was capable of realization with the continued decline of the economic and political status of the Maritimes in the Dominion. Just as electricity might channel the usually conflicting molecular energies of an iron bar to produce a magnetic force, so the federal government's adverse policies served to re-align the various "classes" in the Maritimes to produce a powerful social force — regionalism. This force, dressed up in a variety of complex rationalizations, became the Maritime Rights movement of the 1920's.

386 Notes

1. See J. M. Beck, *The Government of Nova Scotia* (Toronto, 1957), pp. 338–40; W. R. Graham, *Arthur Meighen Vol. II; And Fortune Fled* (Toronto, 1963), ch. 11; H.B.Neatby, *William Lyon Mackenzie King: 1924–1932; The Lonely Heights* (Toronto, 1963), pp. 67 and 220–24; K. A. MacKirdy, "Regionalism: Canada and Australia" (Ph.D. thesis, University of Toronto, 1959), pp. 245–50; and G. A. Rawlyk, "The Maritimes and the Canadian Community" in M. Wade, ed., *Regionalism in the Canadian Community*, 1867–1967 (Toronto, 1969) pp. 113–5. The only previous study which focused directly on Maritime Rights was Michael Hatfield, "J. B. Baxter and the Maritime Rights Movement" (B.A. honours essay, Mount Allison University, 1969).
2. E. R. Forbes, "The Maritime Rights Movement, 1919–1927: A Study in Canadian Regionalism," (Ph.D. thesis, Queens University, 1975).
3. G. A. Rawlyk "The Farmer-Labour Movement and the Failure of Socialism in Nova Scotia," Laurier LaPierre *et al* eds., *Essays on the Left* (Toronto, 1971), pp. 37–8.
4. P. J. Veniot to W. L. M. King, 27 February 1923, W. L. M. King Papers, Public Archives of Canada (hereafter PAC).
5. See Canada, *Sessional Papers* (1910), No. 100; Halifax *Wesleyan*, 12 May 1909; Saint John *Standard*, 30 October 1913; W. Eggleston and C. T. Kraft, *Dominion Provincial Subsidies and Grants* (Ottawa, 1939) pp. 188-9; and the "Presentation to His Royal Highness in Council of the claims of the Provinces of New Brunswick, Nova Scotia and Prince Edward Island, for Compensation in Respect of the Public Lands of Canada, transferred to Certain Provinces of Canada or held in trust for their Benefit, January 29, 1913," R. L. Borden Papers, p. 5249, PAC.
6. R. A. C. Henry and Associates, *Railway Freight Rates in Canada* (Ottawa, 1939), pp. 266 and 268 and Transcripts of the hearings of the Royal Commission on Maritime Claims, pp. 462–5, Atlantic Provinces Transportation Commission (hereafter APTC).
7. See S. A. Saunders *The Economic History of the Maritime Provinces* (Ottawa, 1939), p. 27.
8. *Canada Year Book* (1922–3), pp. 220, 415–6.
9. Halifax *Morning Chronicle*, 17 August 1906 and Saint John *Standard*, 25 March 1916.
10. Judgement of the Board of Railway Commissioners, 15 March 1919, R. L. Borden Papers, pp. 131069–9, PAC; Canada, Debates (1917), pp. 787, 4339–77.
11. Transcript of hearings of the Board of Railway Commissioners, 1920, p. 11703, PAC.
12. Calculated from percentages in B.R.C. transcripts 1926, p. 6602, and from "standard mileage rates" in R. A. C. Henry, *op cit.*
13. Sackville, *The Busy East of Canada*, September, 1919.
14. "Report of Meeting with the Prime Minister and the members of the Government, Delegation from the Maritime Province," 1 June 1921, R. B. Bennett Papers, p. 10142, P.A.C. and F. C. Cornell to H. D. Cartwright, 12 October 1925, Maritime Provinces Freight Rate Commission Papers, APTC.
15. E. M. Macdonald to Mackenzie King, 8 December 1922, W. L. M. King Papers, PAC.
16. F. C. Cornell "Memorandum re the Transportation Problems and Freight Rate Structure of the Province of Nova Scotia," 1926, p. 10 and Transcripts, B.R.C., 1926, pp. 6765-7, PAC.
17. *Maritime Merchant*, 16 September 1920, p. 104.
18. Transcripts, Royal Commission on Maritime Claims, p. 2173, APTC.

19. "Report of the Royal Commission on Transportation . . . 1903," Canada, *Sessional Papers* (1906), No. 19a; Canada, *Debates* (1922), pp. 708–10.
20. Halifax *Herald*, 18 September 1920.
21. Minutes of the Council of the Saint John Board of Trade, 13 July 1922, New Brunswick Museum.
22. Hector McInnes to Arthur Meighen, November 1923, Arthur Meighen Papers, p. 051956, PAC.
23. A. MacLean to W. L. M. King, 25 April 1922 and 8 October 1924, W. L. M. King Papers, PAC.
24. J. C. Webster to Arthur Meighen, 26 September 1925, and R. O'Leary to Meighen, 3 September 1925, Arthur Meighen Papers, PAC.
25. *The Fifth Annual Report on Labour Organization in Canada 1916* (Ottawa, 1917) pp. 206–7 and the *Tenth Annual Report on Labour Organization in Canada 1920* (Ottawa, 1921), p. 279.
26. For examples of their optimistic rhetoric see the Sydney *Canadian Labour Leader*, 8 February 1918; the new Glasgow *Eastern Federationist*, 19, 26 April 1919; and the Moncton *Union Worker*, February, 1920.
27. *The Labour Gazette*, January 1921, p. 117.
28. *Eastern Federationist*, 8 March 1919.
29. *Ibid.*, 7 June 1919.
30. The Halifax *Citizen*, 21 May and 10 September 1920.
31. "Being an address by Mr. Geo. W. Yates, Assistant Deputy Minister of Railways, Before the History and Political Science Club of Western Ontario, Feb. 16, 1923", Arthur Meighen Papers, pp. 157485–9, PAC.
32. *The Busy East*, June and July 1923.
33. F. B. McCurdy to Robert Borden, 21 December 1921, Robert Meighen Papers, PAC.
34. H. L. Stewart to M. W. L. King, 9 December 1923, W. L. M. King Papers, PAC.
35. "Minutes of the Maritime Club of Halifax," 11 February 1924, H. S. Congdon Papers (courtesy of Mr. H. H. Congdon, Huntsville, Ontario).
36. Saint John *Telegraph Journal*, 27 February 1925.
37. See A. A. Mackenzie, "The Rise and Fall of the Farmer-Labour Party in Nova Scotia" (M.A. thesis, Dalhousie University, 1969), and L. A. Wood, *A History of Farmer Movements in Canada* (Toronto, 1924).
38. *Proceedings of the Select Special Committee of the House of Commons to inquire into Agricultural Conditions* (Ottawa, 1924), p. 475.
39. Three of the five members of the directorate were Manitobans. C. F. Chipman to "The Editor" *Maritime Farmer*, 13 March 1920, T. A. Crerar Papers, The Douglas Library, Queens University.
40. J. M. Pratt to T. A. Crerar, 9 November 1920, and G. G. Archibald to T. A. Crerar, 4 October 1920, *ibid*.
41. W. L. Morton, *The Progressive Party in Canada* (Toronto, 1950), p. 129.
42. S. H. Hagerman to G. F. Chipman, 18 June 1921, T. A. Crerar Papers, Douglas Library, Queens University.
43. *The Busy East*, September 1919. See also M. K. Cullen. "The Transportation Issue, 1873–1973" in F. W. P. Bolger, ed., *Canada's Smallest Province: a History of Prince Edward Island* (Charlottetown, 1973), pp. 255–7.
44. *Ibid.*, May 1921.
45. Charlottetown *Evening Patriot*, 23 January 1925.
46. *Report of the Royal Commission Investigating the Fisheries of the Maritime Provinces and the Magdalen Islands* (Ottawa, 1928), pp. 32, 61–5.
47. "Fifty-third Annual Report of the Fisheries Branch . . . 1919," *Sessional Papers* (1919), No. 44, p. 11.
48. G. B. Kenny reported to Hector MacInnes after a trip along the Eastern Shore that the Liberal candidates had "actually got many people to believe that real free trade with the U.S., is in sight." 21 November 1921, Hector MacInnes Papers, (courtesy of Donald MacInnes, Halifax, N.S.).
49. Transcripts of the hearings of the Royal Commission Investigating the Fisheries . . . 1928, p. 3476, APTC.
50. R. Blauveldt to H. S. Congdon, 30 September 1924, H. S. Congdon Papers.
51. J. H. McGaffigan to Arthur Meighen, 28 February 1924, Arthur Meighen Papers, PAC.
52. See Halifax *Morning Chronicle*, 16 November 1921; C. W. Lunn to H. S. Congdon, 13 April 1929, H. S. Congdon Papers.
53. Transcripts, Royal Commission to investigate the Fisheries . . . 1927, p. 6.
54. See for example R. H. Wiebe, *The Search For Order*, 1877–1920 (New York, 1967); Gabriel Kolko, *The Triumph of Conservatism* (New York, 1963) and D. W. Noble, *The Progressive Mind 1890–1917* (Chicago, 1970).
55. See E. R. Forbes "Prohibition and the Social Gospel in Nova Scotia," *Acadiensis* Vol. 1, No. 1 (Autumn 1971), pp. 15–19 and his review of Richard Allen, *The Social Passion* in *Acadiensis* Vol. II No. 1 (Autumn, 1972), p. 98.

387

56. Halifax, *Daily Echo*, 24 May 1913.
57. *Industrial Canada*, August 1918.
58. See J. M. Beck, *The History of Maritime Union: A Study in Frustration*, pp. 31–44.
59. O. T. Daniels, *The Claims of the Maritime Provinces for Federal Subsidies in Lieu of Western Lands* (Halifax, 1918) and *Proceedings of the Second Annual Educational Conference, Antigonish*, (1919).

Topic Eleven
Depression Politics

In the 1930s economic dislocation, social unrest, and international tension
all contributed to the state of anxiety that affected every Canadian. As an
economic phenomenon, the Depression hit Canada very severely because
of the overextension of the Canadian economy during the previous decade
and because of the nation's reliance on foreign trade in an intensely
nationalistic and protectionist era. Hardest hit were primary commodities.
Wheat prices for example, fell from $2.00 a bushel for some years in the
1920s to 34¢ a bushel in 1932. The resulting downswing in the economy
quickly affected secondary and service industries. Between 1929 and 1933
the gross national expenditure declined by 29%. Unemployment reached
an all-time high of 20% across the country and as high as 35% in some
regions. Thousands were forced to endure the humiliation of going on
relief — a last, desperate solution to their critical situation.

At first Canadians tried to wait out the Depression, expecting it to be a
temporary phenomenon that would end as quickly as it began. But, as the
Depression continued, many looked to politicians for solutions. The two
traditional parties, the Conservatives and the Liberals, appeared unable
to deal with the unprecedented situation. Lacking any overall plan of
action, they seemed prepared only to implement stop-gap measures. New
parties emerged at the national and provincial level with grandiose schemes,
charismatic leaders, and radical solutions.

In "The Evolution of the Social Credit Movement," John Irving outlines
the historical development of that party in Alberta in the 1930s, looking at
its appeal as a phenomenon of mass psychology. In the excerpt from *The
Anatomy of Party: The National CCF*, Walter Young examines the roots of
the Co-operative Commonwealth Federation and the various components
of the party. Herbert Quinn analyses political events in Quebec in the
Depression era in "The Formation and Rise to Power of the Union
Nationale."

A good overview of Depression politics through biographical sketches of the leaders is H. B. Neatby's *The Politics of Chaos: Canada in the Thirties* (Toronto: Macmillan, 1972). It also contains a biographical essay on sources published to that date. *The Dirty Thirties: Canadians in the Great Depression*, edited by M. Horn (Toronto: Copp Clark, 1972), is a valuable collection of primary and secondary sources on the economic, social, personal, and political repercussions of the Depression. For more detail on the national CCF, students should consult W. Young's *The Anatomy of a Party: The National CCF* (Toronto: University of Toronto Press, 1969), from which the reading is taken, and I. Avakumovic's *Socialism in Canada: A Study of the CCF–NDP in Federal and Provincial Politics* (Toronto: McClelland and Stewart, 1978). A series of studies of the Social Credit Movement in Alberta published by the University of Toronto Press should be examined, particularly John Irving's *The Social Credit Movement in Alberta* (1959) and C. B. Macpherson's *Democracy in Alberta: Social Credit and the Party System (1953)*. Equally enlightening is John Barr's *The Dynasty: The Rise and Fall of Social Credit in Alberta* (Toronto: McClelland and Stewart, 1974). Herbert Quinn's article is an excerpt from his book, *The Union Nationale: A Study in Quebec Nationalism* (Toronto: University of Toronto Press, 1963).

The Evolution of the Social Credit Movement *
JOHN A. IRVING

Although the doctrines of Social Credit have been systematically and extensively promoted throughout many parts of the British Commonwealth and the United States for nearly thirty years, it is only in Alberta that there has emerged a Social Credit movement sufficiently strong to win and maintain political power. It is proposed, in the present paper, to trace the historical development of this movement with specific reference to those data that are essential for its interpretation as a phenomenon of mass psychology. Such an approach must be restrictive and selective: data of primary importance to the economist, the political scientist, and even the sociologist must necessarily be omitted.

The Social Credit upsurge in Alberta was essentially a people's movement which sought to reform, but not to revolutionize, the existing social order by changing the pattern of certain existing institutions. It has passed through the four stages which constitute the natural history of a social movement — social unrest, popular excitement, formalization, and institutionalization; and it has exhibited, in the course of its evolution, the five mechanisms of reform movements — agitation, *esprit de corps*, morale, ideology, and operating tactics. From the perspective of social psychology,

* From *Canadian Journal of Economics and Political Science*, 14 (1948): 321–341. Copyright by University of Toronto Press. Reprinted by permission.

the movement may best be understood if, taking its more general sociological aspects for granted, we consider its appeal to the people of Alberta in terms of its leadership, its philosophy, and its techniques of organization and promotion. In analysing this particular social movement, the social psychologist is faced with two serious methodological difficulties; he must be careful not to confuse the evolution of the movement with the political history of Alberta, especially after 1935; and he must, as far as possible, present the movement as a dynamic rather than a static social phenomenon.

Social movements tend to appear during periods of widespread social unrest, when profound dissatisfaction with the existing social order arises. No conditions could have been more favourable for the development of such unrest than those which existed in Alberta in the autumn of 1932. The farmers of the province had experienced every possible agricultural ordeal; they had been made the playthings of the high tariff manipulators; they had built up markets in the United States only to have them ruthlessly cut off; they had suffered drought and every agricultural pestilence from root-rot to grasshoppers; they had seen prices drop to such incredibly low levels that sometimes it did not pay to haul their produce to market. Under such circumstances, it is not surprising that a large percentage of the farms of Alberta had been heavily mortgaged. The utterly discouraged farmers, looking for some tangible cause for all their miseries, focussed their resentment and hate upon the banks and loan companies. In the cities, towns, and villages the masses of the people were no better off. Unemployment was general: thousands were living on relief; still other thousands lacked the elementary provision of food, clothing, and shelter. Psychologically, hundreds of thousands of people were experiencing a profound personality disintegration: they were caught in a steel web from which there seemed no escape; their social environment, their feeling for the process of life, their hope for the future, all became meaningless. Amid such desperate social and economic conditions, William Aberhart appeared as the prophet of a new social order.

Born at Egmondville, Ontario, in 1878, he was educated at the Seaforth Collegiate Institute, the Hamilton Normal School, the Chatham Business College, and Queen's University, from which he obtained extra-murally the degree of B.A. After teaching in Ontario for several years, he settled in Calgary in 1910. Five years later he became principal of the Calgary Crescent Heights High School, one of the largest and best organized institutions in Western Canada. In addition to his heavy administrative duties, Aberhart was an efficient and successful teacher of arithmetic, transplanting to the West the nineteenth-century techniques of instruction he had acquired in Ontario. He first became prominent in Alberta, outside educational circles, as a religious leader. In his youth he had fallen under the influence of a great Bible teacher, and had hoped to enter the Presbyterian ministry. Almost as soon as he arrived in Calgary he organized a large Bible Class, which met in a succession of Presbyterian and Methodist churches, later in a Baptist church. By the early nineteen-twenties his following had become so large that he organized the Calgary Prophetic Bible Conference which assembled on Sunday afternoons in the largest theatre of the city to hear him give two-hour interpretations of Christian fundamentalism and Bible Prophecy to audiences that numbered 2200. Owing to the enthusiasm of his followers he was persuaded, in 1924, to broadcast his Sunday services over CFCN, known as "The Voice of the Prairies" and, until recent years, the most powerful radio station in Canada. In addition to his Bible Conference, he organized a Radio Sunday School which continued to function throughout the worst years of the depression. By his use of radio, he built up a personal following that, according to certain estimates, numbered between two and three hundred thousand persons. In 1927 his organization was put on a more permanent basis when he and his followers constructed in the heart of Calgary, at a cost of $65 000, the large Prophetic Bible Institute, which thenceforth became the centre of all his religious activities.

392

Until 1932, although Aberhart personally favoured the Conservative party, he had never taken part in civic or political activities at any level, nor had he engaged in public discussion of economic questions. But like most people, as the depression wore on, he gradually became acutely aware of the plight of unemployed youth, and more especially of the plight of the graduates of his own school. There is evidence that, in the autumn of 1931, certain young men who knew him well, both as high-school teacher and as religious leader, urged him to tackle the problem of the depression, but they elicited no apparent response. In the summer of 1932, when he was living in an Edmonton college during the period of marking matriculation examination papers, he was introduced by another teacher to the highly popularized version of the doctrines of Social Credit contained in Maurice Colbourne's *Unemployment or War*. After reading the book, Aberhart decided that Social Credit offered the hope of redeeming his province from the depths into which the politicians and bankers had plunged it. Without that fateful decision it is doubtful if there could have been a successful Social Credit movement in Alberta.

In its most developed and complex form, the philosophy of Social Credit includes a monetary theory which both "explains" the inner workings of the capitalistic financial system and offers a remedy for its unsatisfactory functioning in periods of depression and inflation, a political theory which reinterprets the role of the individual in the democratic state, and an interpretation of history in terms of a long-existing Judaic plot or conspiracy to secure control of and dominate the world. Underlying these three basic doctrines of Social Credit is a moral-religious theory of the fundamental rights of man, which has been variously expressed in terms of elusive conceptions such as Cultural Heritage, Political Liberty with Economic Security, and the Struggle of the Powers of Light against the occult Powers of Darkness in the world. At no time has Social Credit advocated the overthrow of the capitalistic system or of private enterprise.

Social Credit owes its origin to a Scottish engineer, Major C. H. Douglas, who was impressed by the fact that many developments, *physically* possible from the engineer's point of view, are *financially* impossible. As assistant director in England of the Royal Aircraft Works during the First World War, he made comprehensive studies of cost accounting which led him to the conclusion that, in over 100 industrial establishments, the weekly sum total of wages and salaries was continually less than the weekly collective price of the goods produced. It was upon this conclusion that he formulated his now famous "A + B Theorem." In this theorem, A = the flow of purchasing power to the masses (as represented by wages, salaries, and dividends), and B = bank charges, overhead costs, taxes, and the cost of raw materials. If A + B represents the cost of production under the financial system, the rate of flow of purchasing power to the masses will be less than the rate of flow of prices in the same period of time. There will thus be a discrepancy, which Douglas maintains must be permanent, between A (the purchasing power of consumers) and A + B (the total cost of production). The "A + B Theorem" became the key conception of Douglas's economic theories, and provided him and his followers with one of their principal slogans, "Poverty in the Midst of Plenty," a paradox which clearly has very great propaganda value in a period of widespread social unrest fostered by an economic depression.

On its negative or critical side Social Credit maintains that a permanent deficiency of purchasing power is inherent in the capitalistic financial system in the Machine Age; on its positive or constructive side it seeks to solve the problem of distributing the abundance of goods produced, as well as to increase production. It is maintained that other proposals for social reconstruction suffer from three fallacies: that there is a limit to production; that work is the only just prior condition of individual income; and that there is magic in state ownership. Further, other reformers have not realized the significance of the distinction between financial credit, which is based upon gold, and real credit, which is based upon such factors as raw materials, power, and labour. Under the existing system, financial credit has fallen into the control of bankers who, through its manipulation, exploit the community for purposes of private profit. A functional financial system should be concerned with the issue of credit to the consumer up to the limit of the productive capacity of the producer, so that both the consumer's real demands may be satisfied, and the productive capacity of the industrial system may be utilized and developed to the fullest extent.

The present political system of democracy has led to the development of economic slaves: money has become the master rather than the servant of man. The people, as the sovereign authority, have lost their control over the monetary system; their sovereign authority has been usurped by bankers who have set up a financial dictatorship, and who use their control of credit to render ineffectual the voting power of the people. The economic system no longer fulfils a moral purpose: instead of economic security and freedom from want, the individual is faced with "poverty in the midst of plenty," misery, and unhappiness.

If the economic system is to function successfully, the state must make at least three fundamental changes: it must recover its control over the monetary system; it must issue social credit in the form of a *national dividend* (based upon a survey of the real wealth of the nation) to every person; and, to prevent the possibility of inflation, it must establish a *just price* for all goods. The evils in the existing economic system can be remedied by supplying the people with credit based upon the potential goods and services of society. This is the people's right, their *cultural heritage*. Only in this way will the individual be freed from wage slavery, be able to choose the work he likes best, be in a position to claim those goods which are rightfully his so that he can enjoy more leisure time. There was, from the beginning, a moral foundation for the changes in the monetary system proposed by Social Credit — the financial system must be reformed to enable the individual to achieve the fullest measure of self-realization.

As a political theory, Social Credit is presented as a "Way of Life": human nature is essentially good, and the individual, as the most important fact of society, is an end in himself, not a means to an end. Personal freedom is the most precious possession of life, and every individual should therefore have political freedom, at the same time that he enjoys economic security. The state exists solely to promote the individual's welfare, freedom, and security. The Social Credit Way of Life is compatible with both Christianity and democracy, but its philosophers are extremely critical of the existing form of political democracy as well as being opposed to socialism and communism. It is asserted that there exists today only constitutional democracy, not functioning democracy. Parliament should be under the direct and continuous control of the electors; in actual practice, the people's representatives are controlled by the party machine. In place of the present system of limited state dictatorship, it is proposed to restore sovereign authority to the people: they must be organized in a "Union of Electors" through which the individual can directly express his aims and desires to his representatives in parliament.

It is as an interpretation of history that the theories of Social Credit are curiously familiar and at the same time most elusive. As the constant criticism of "Finance" wore somewhat threadbare, there gradually evolved the colourful doctrine that national and international events can only be understood in terms of the machinations of a select group of bankers (most of whom bear Jewish names) who are indissolubly linked with a long-standing Judaic conspiracy to dominate the world, working through the Masonic Order, and both international capitalism and international communism. The wars, depressions, and revolutions of our time can only be understood if one realizes that they are one and all the result of the activities of world conspirators or world plotters who will stop at nothing in their efforts to destroy both democracy and the system of free enter-

394

prise, and who are especially malicious in their attempts to ruin the British Empire. The emphasis that has been given in Alberta to each of these aspects of the philosophy of Social Credit has varied with the time, the occasion, and the person; but there can be no doubt that, for Aberhart, Social Credit was essentially a theory of monetary reform which had its moral foundation in the conception of the cultural heritage and its religious foundation in his own interpretation of Christian fundamentalism and Bible prophecy.

For a variety of reasons, monetary reform had long been advocated in Alberta as a solution of the shortage of money or "purchasing power" from which the province, like most frontier rural economies, has chronically suffered. As far as can be discovered, Social Credit literature was introduced into Western Canada by a magazine editor who, through his writings and personal friendships, brought the doctrines of Major Douglas to the attention of certain leaders of the United Farmers of Alberta in the House of Commons. Major Douglas himself came to Ottawa in 1923, at the suggestion of a U.F.A. member, and testified before the Standing Committee of the House on Banking and Commerce. During the next ten years, the Social Credit theories, along with other proposals for monetary reform, were much discussed in the U.F.A. locals. Monetary reform took on the psychological characteristic of a "preferred group tendency" in Alberta, and there can be no doubt that the long period of preparatory work by the U.F.A. was one of the most powerful psychological factors in the rapid development of the Social Credit movement in the middle thirties. In addition certain intellectual leaders in Calgary, who had formed the Open Mind Club, were vigorously engaged in discussing the theories of Social Credit at the very time that Aberhart became a convert; and the Edmonton teacher who introduced Aberhart to the doctrine was himself a member of a group of Social Crediters who had long been looking for a likely leader.

395

In the autumn of 1932, Aberhart gradually, and with cautious reservations, began to introduce Social Credit ideas into his Sunday afternoon religious broadcasts. In January, 1933, he prepared a series of mimeographed lessons, which in the main were incisive summaries of Douglas's earlier books, for use as the basis of discussion in a study group he organized in the Bible Institute. In the spring he held a number of meetings in various halls and schools in the suburbs of Calgary; and he published and sold extensively a pamphlet, *The Douglas System of Economics.* Leaving the study group in the Bible Institute during the summer months in the hands of several ardent followers whom he had instructed during the winter, Aberhart and the secretary of the Bible Institute, Mr. Ernest C. Manning, made a speaking tour of southern Alberta. Almost 95 per cent of their audiences during that summer consisted of persons who had long been listening to Aberhart's religious broadcasts, but enthusiasm rapidly began to spread beyond the religious following.

By September, 1933, hundreds of people were coming to the Institute to discuss Social Credit, and new techniques of organization had to be developed. Aberhart and his followers now began a systematic propagation of Social Credit theories throughout the city of Calgary and adjoining rural areas. As these early efforts were entirely educational, and in no sense political, he received many invitations to lecture to various Calgary groups and organizations and to many U.F.A. locals in rural districts surrounding the city. The natural outcome of all this activity was the formation of local study groups in Calgary, in the towns and cities nearby, and ultimately throughout the whole of Alberta.

Public enthusiasm for Social Credit was apparent at the annual convention of the U.F.A. held at Edmonton in January, 1934, and the delegates engaged in a hot debate on the advisability of forcing their government in Edmonton to introduce Social Credit legislation immediately. But there was grave dissension within the U.F.A. organization owing to the presence in its ranks of many supporters of the Cooperative Commonwealth Federation which had been founded at Calgary in 1932. During the winter of 1934, Aberhart and his followers held so many meetings, and the movement developed such strength, that the U.F.A. government very reluctantly invited him, along with others, to give evidence before the Agricultural Committee of the Legislature on the feasibility of introducing Social Credit legislation in Alberta. A petition signed by 12 000 people was offered as testimony of the wide appeal of Social Credit; many U.F.A. locals, Social Credit groups, and various clubs forwarded resolutions to members of the legislature.* At the height of the investigation, Major Douglas himself came to Alberta, addressed a vast and memorable meeting in Calgary, and expounded Social Credit at length before the Agricultural Committee.

In the midst of the popular excitement over the Social Credit theories of monetary reform, there occurred the first of three serious schisms within the movement. Many of the members of the New Age Club, the most intellectual of all the Social Credit study groups had contended for several months that Aberhart was not a strict disciple of Douglas, and that the Social Credit monetary theories could not be applied in the provincial sphere under the British North America Act. The Social Credit Secretariat in London seems to have shared in this view, and in February, 1934, Aberhart relinquished to his chief critic in the New Age Club, Gilbert McGregor, the presidency of the Central Council, the executive group which at that time controlled the movement. This schism, although it had many of the marks of a struggle for power, was nevertheless of very great importance, for its outcome determined that Aberhart, and not Douglas, was to be the chief inspiration of the Alberta movement. Within two

*For an analysis of the response of the people during the period from 1932 to April, 1935, see John A. Irving, "Psychological Aspects of the Social Credit Movement in Alberta" (*Canadian Journal of Psychology*, vol. 1, 1947, pp. 17–27, 75–86, 127–40). Acknowledgment is made to the editor of the above journal, Dr. John A. Long, for permission to incorporate into the preceding pages certain material describing the early phases of the movement.

months, the new president realized that he could accomplish little without the remarkable propaganda facilities of the Bible Institute and Aberhart's large, enthusiastic personal following. In April, public demand forced Aberhart's return as president of the Central Council and leader of the Social Credit movement. McGregor and most of the New Age Club members then formed an opposing organization known as the Douglas Social Credit League, which established its own newspaper, the *Douglas Social Credit Advocate*. In referring to this controversy, Aberhart's followers always insist that they merely "brushed aside" an insignificant minority group within the movement; but the idea of "Douglas Social Credit" as distinguished from "Aberhart Social Credit" could not, as we shall see, be so easily dismissed.

The bitter controversy within the inner circle of the movement, and the expected favourable report of the legislative investigation produced a temporary lull in the mounting popular excitement during the spring of 1934. Early in the summer of 1934 two important moves were made by the hardpressed U.F.A. administration in Edmonton: the report of the legislative investigation, which was definitely hostile to the Social Credit proposals, was published and widely circulated; and, upon a reorganization of the Cabinet, the premier and his minister of public works (both of whom had been involved in law-suits touching their personal conduct) resigned. Amid the public outcry over the moral *débâcle* within the U.F.A. Cabinet, and the public disapproval of the negative results of the legislative enquiry, Aberhart returned to the leadership of the Social Credit movement with redoubled vigour. He and Manning spent the whole summer of 1934 on a second speaking tour which took them into almost every inhabited part of the province south of Edmonton: disciples who were prepared to engage in equally strenuous speaking tours appeared on all sides. The movement was consolidated further by the founding of a weekly newspaper, the *Social Credit Chronicle*, and by the development in the autumn of the famous "Man from Mars" series of week-night radio discussions of economic problems. Throughout all this intense educational activity there was still no hint of the formation of a political organization, and Aberhart constantly stated that he had no personal political ambitions. But during the autumn of 1934 there was an increasingly urgent demand from the masses of the people that a Social Credit political party should be organized to contest the provincial election which had to be held by the following August at the latest. In spite of pressure from his followers, Aberhart was so reluctant to take the extreme step of forming a new political party that he urged the leaders of the three existing political parties to include the Social Credit monetary theories in their platforms. The Conservatives were unequivocal in their opposition to Social Credit; the Liberals promised to give the theories careful study but would make no further commitments; at their annual convention in January, 1935, the U.F.A. leaders debated with Aberhart for hours, and finally voted almost unanimously against the Social Credit proposals. The pressure from the people to transform the Social Credit movement into a political party now became so great that Aberhart realized it could not much longer be resisted. But he still hesitated to take the final step. To meet what he considered to be the moral needs of the hour he sent out clarion calls over the radio for "One Hundred Honest Men"; to determine more accurately the extent of Social Credit support he organized a straw vote. The results were beyond his most optimistic expectations: honest men, who were prepared to fight to the utmost for Social Credit, were named by the score; the results of the straw vote indicated that in many communities 93 per cent of the people were prepared to vote for the adoption of the Social Credit monetary theories. Aberhart was now convinced that a Social Credit party would be victorious in the forthcoming provincial election and in April, 1935, the Southern and Northern Alberta Social Credit Leagues met in Calgary and Edmonton. These enthusiastic conventions, which were made up largely of delegates from Social Credit study groups, voted to go into politics and gave almost supreme power to Aberhart to develop the tactics for the election. What had been a social movement now became a political party, but behind the party there remained always the inspiration of the social movement.

The decision to take the movement into politics produced a surging response from the people, and within a few weeks scarcely anyone in Alberta remained unaffected by the Social Credit propaganda. The number of secondary leaders who came forward to spread the doctrine was one of the most astonishing features of the movement. Between three and four hundred "Honest Men," who had been carefully selected from the names sent in earlier to Aberhart, now emerged as the principal organizers of the provincial constituency conventions, and many of them were subsequently nominated as candidates. But the secondary leaders were by no means confined to Aberhart's religious following: they were drawn from town and country alike, and included farmers, small business men, teachers, clergy, and a few physicians, dentists, and lawyers. Their critics asserted that the average local leader in the movement was a man who had previously taken no part in politics and who was "sub-standard" in his thinking about economics. Aberhart had realized that the entrance of the movement into politics would attract the type of opportunist who is always waiting to climb on a new bandwagon, and he made a rule that no one who had been associated as a leader with any of the other political parties could be a Social Credit candidate in the election. The rigid application of this principle naturally brought to the front a new group of men, most of whom were entirely inexperienced in politics.

One of Aberhart's most successful devices, which was calculated to keep everybody working enthusiastically for the movement until at least official nomination day, was his method of selecting candidates. Douglas has always maintained that the people should be primarily concerned with *results* rather than with the *method* of attaining results. Aberhart argued that the people in a constituency were not electing a man but voting for a set of principles. In accordance with this doctrine, each constituency convention was asked to nominate four or five possible candidates, each of whom was subsequently interviewed by an advisory committee composed of representatives from the constituency and the province at large. Critics of the movement claimed that Aberhart personally made the final choice in a dictatorial manner, but his eager followers considered that such an accusation was merely comic. In spite of violent criticism from the opposition parties, this method of selecting candidates persisted until after Aberhart's death, but it was dropped by Manning in the election of 1944.

Faced with an overwhelming social movement, the opponents of Social Credit were guilty of serious tactical blunders. The Liberals, who were making their greatest effort to return to power since the disastrous collapse of 1921, remained evasive: their leaders, hoping for support if group government should be necessary, hesitated to alienate the Social Crediters, and in general directed their attack almost entirely against the greatly weakened U.F.A.; in fact, the Liberals finally went so far in their efforts to win support from the new movement that, in their appeal to the people, they pledged themselves, when returned to power, to employ three expert Social Credit advocates to carry out a complete investigation of the schemes proposed by Aberhart, and to evolve and submit a plan to the new legislature for the application of Social Credit to Alberta.

Coerced by the people's enthusiasm for Social Credit, the U.F.A. government summoned the Agricultural Committee of the Legislature, for the second year in succession, to hear the evidence of experts in law and economics on the constitutionality and economic aspects of Social Credit. But the subsequent publication of another legislative report hostile to Social Credit merely seemed to increase the momentum of the movement. The desperate U.F.A. leaders, in spite of the negative vote of their annual convention only a few months previously, now proceeded to bring back Douglas himself under contract as their technical adviser. By this manoeuvre they hoped to secure from Douglas a repudiation of Aberhart's interpretation of Social Credit and a definite statement that his monetary theories could not be applied in the provincial sphere. Coincident with Douglas's arrival in Edmonton, both the constitutional issue and Aberhart's understanding — or lack of understanding — of Social Credit were being hotly debated by all sides over the radio and on public platforms. If the U.F.A. believed that Douglas would resolve this great debate in their favour, they were greatly mistaken. Far from denouncing Aberhart's position, the shrewd Douglas merely dramatized anew for an ever-increasing following the basic theories of Social Credit; and before leaving for England in June he published in the *Social Credit Chronicle* an unequivocal statement that there were no essential differences between Aberhart and himself.

Realizing, unlike the Liberals, that the Social Crediters were the real challengers in the election, the U.F.A. campaigners, in spite of Douglas's announcement, continued to insist, tediously and tirelessly, that Aberhart had no genuine understanding of the principles of Social Credit and that,

399

in any event, the attempt to apply Douglas's monetary theories in Alberta would immediately be invalidated by the courts under the existing Canadian constitution. Their position was considerably weakened in the eyes of the people by the known adherence of certain of the U.F.A. federal members to Social Credit principles, and by the failure of most of their speakers to condemn Aberhart's proposals outright. When challenged by the U.F.A. to state precisely how he would apply Social Credit in Alberta, Aberhart invariably argued that the people wanted Social Credit as a "result"; the method of its application would be left to experts. But in spite of his evasive attitude regarding methods, tens of thousands of people came to believe, as a result of his speeches and their reading of the *Social Credit Manual*, which he issued shortly before the election, that each adult would receive as his share of the national dividend at least $25.00 monthly for the rest of his life. A month before the election, his followers had become so convinced of the essential rightness of their beliefs that they developed closed minds, and further discussion of the merits or otherwise of Social Credit was no longer possible. At this point a group of business and financial leaders realizing, for the first time, the possibility of a Social Credit victory, formed the Economic Safety League and threw its weight against the movement. Aberhart immediately dubbed it the Comic Safety League, and characterized it as the last desperate act of the financiers, the "Fifty Big Shots," to save themselves from the wrath of a people's movement.

400

The new party did not need to depend upon the weaknesses of its opponents for victory in the tumultuous election campaign of 1935. With charismatic leadership, a positive philosophy, and superb techniques of organization and promotion, the Social Credit movement developed into an avalanche that swept everything before it. The massive strength of the movement, apart from Aberhart and the Douglas theories, was based upon the study groups. When public enthusiasm for Social Credit was approaching the stage of mass hysteria a few weeks before the election, there were sixty-three groups in Calgary alone, and some 1600 in the whole province. In addition to their functions as dynamic nuclei of propaganda in almost every city block or rural district, they were the principal media through which funds were raised for the movement. Aberhart often said in later years that the groups won the election of 1935.

The struggle of the Social Credit movement for political power was successful beyond reasonable expectations: the U.F.A. was permanently eliminated as a political force in the province; the Liberal party was so crushed that it remained disorganized for the next twelve years; the Conservatives remained, as usual, a negligible factor. Of the 163 700 people who had voted for Social Credit, thousands now confidently expected that, with fifty-six supporters in a legislature of sixty-three, Aberhart would immediately introduce the necessary legislation to create in Alberta an economic paradise. It is said that the morning after the great victory several persons of central and eastern European origin were already "lined-up" at the city hall in Calgary to collect their basic dividend. Thousands of others, not quite so optimistic, interpreted Aberhart's statements to mean that the $25.00 a month would be forthcoming within at least a year and a half.

For several years after the election there was little diminution of the popular enthusiasm which the movement had evoked. The members of the legislature were in such demand as speakers that many of them found it impossible to resume their normal occupations, so insatiable was the public desire for further information concerning Social Credit. Aberhart himself, although now premier and minister of education, was constantly addressing such tremendous crowds throughout the province that no buildings large enough could be found to accommodate the people who wanted to hear him: in the smaller towns and villages he frequently had to force his way to his hotel or the place of meeting through crowd-jammed streets. To the year of his death he continued to ask his vast audiences for approval or disapproval of his government's actions and the thunderous roar of favourable applause would often shake the building. As time went on, he deliberately encouraged great mass meetings by the celebration of anniversaries, by bitter and dramatic attacks on his political opponents, and by the development of such devices as the registration for dividends and the dated stamp money experiment, which were calculated to keep the people agitated and working for the movement. Events like the great insurgency of 1937 within the ranks of the movement, the disallowance of the Social Credit legislation some months afterwards, the establishment of treasury branches, the fierce controversy over the "Accurate News and Information Act," and the "bankers' toadies" incident, were all grist for Aberhart's mill: he was invariably "big" news, and until the outbreak of the Second World War his ingenious tactics kept Alberta in an almost constant state of tension if not of actual tumult. In the legislative press gallery, which had had representatives from only two Edmonton daily newspapers during the last years of the U.F.A. régime, there were, during the hectic years from 1935–9, twenty regular and several special reporters sitting in every day. Aberhart himself was frequently interviewed by newspaper representatives of international reputation, including John MacCormac of the *New York Times*. Telegraph companies were kept working overtime to clear copy, and, on one day in 1937, 35 000 words were sent out over the wires.

During nearly eight years as premier, Aberhart carried on most of his former religious activities in the Calgary Prophetic Bible Institute and continued, in a manner that infuriated his political opponents, to link the philosophy of Social Credit with the basic principles of Christianity. In addition to the familiar expositions of Bible prophecy and pre-millenial fundamentalism, his Sunday afternoon radio addresses now contained announcements and defences of government policy, as well as mocking, satirical attacks on all who in any way opposed Social Credit. His use of divine sanctions coupled with his new prestige as premier of the province assisted immeasurably in the transition of the Social Credit movement from the stage of popular excitement to the stage of formalization and still later to the stage of institutionalization.

In 1936 the Southern and Northern Conventions of the movement were formally consolidated into the Alberta Social Credit League which thereafter met annually, usually in the late autumn, as the people's arm of the political party. The League's constitution indicates the continued importance of the Social Credit study groups: throughout the years they have remained as the nucleus of the movement, and to them its leaders still direct appeals for support in time of need. Propaganda facilities were strengthened in 1936, by the transformation of the *Social Credit Chronicle* into a new paper, *Today and Tomorrow*, which somewhat later, as *The Canadian Social Crediter*, became the organ of the national movement. Imitating the pattern of the old U.F.A. organization, the Social Credit Women's Auxiliary was organized in 1938 and has remained among the most active agencies in the propagation of Social Credit theories.

402

One of the most important factors in the institutionalization of the movement was the violent opposition that developed with the passage of the Social Credit legislation of 1937 and the Mortgage and Debt legislation of the following years. Although thirteen acts passed by the Alberta legislature were declared *ultra vires* by courts or disallowed by the Dominion government, the business and financial leaders of the province now became thoroughly convinced that the Social Credit movement represented a dangerous threat to their interests, and it was not long before they began to organize a united front to defeat the Aberhart Government at the next election. The most scornful opponent of the movement was unquestionably the *Calgary Herald* which, in a series of incredibly brilliant cartoons, applied the whip-lash to Aberhart almost daily and more than once drove him to the breaking point. He retaliated by calling on his loyal supporters to boycott the paper, a strategy which seriously affected its circulation and even threatened it for a time with loss of advertising. The tactics of both Aberhart and the *Herald* in this great battle are indicative of the state of mind which developed in Alberta at the height of the movement. Lesser and more ephemeral publications, of which *The Rebel* may be selected as an example, did not hesitate to sink to the lower depths in their vilification of Aberhart personally and of the movement in general.

The most serious threat to the future of the movement, however, came not from the turbulent, external opposition but from within the ranks of the Social Crediters themselves. Shortly after the election Aberhart had attempted, in a somewhat perfunctory manner, to persuade Douglas to return and fulfil the two-year contract he had made with the U.F.A. as reconstruction adviser to the government. For months the two men, as Douglas has revealed in *The Alberta Experiment*, carried on an equivocal correspondence, alternating cablegrams of miraculous compression with letters of miraculous length. The gap between Aberhart's conception of Social Credit and that of its originator now proved wider than expected;

and, in any case, *Premier* Aberhart did not relish the idea of *Major* Douglas as an active collaborator. Far from engaging an expert on Social Credit as his adviser on financial policy and business administration, the premier shocked many of his supporters by bringing to Alberta an entirely ortho- dox financier, R. J. Magor, who had previously put Newfoundland's gov- ernment on a better financial and administrative basis.

Faced with an empty treasury on their accession to power, the Social Credit members of the legislature readily accepted an orthodox budget during the session of 1936. They were encouraged regarding Aberhart's ultimate intentions when he defied the Money Power by defaulting on a large bond issue and when, several months later, he reduced by 50 per cent the coupon-rate of interest on all Alberta's bonds and debentures, including the bonds in default. The introduction of the so-called "prosperity certifi- cates" later in the summer, although in no sense a part of Douglas's Social Credit plan, also appealed to thousands of people as evidence that drastic action was imminent. During the early winter, however, criticism of the Government for its delay in introducing Social Credit legislation increased among the less fanatical followers of Aberhart: the mounting tension was not eased by the arrival and sudden departure of John Hargrave, a colour- ful leader of the London Greenshirts, a group affiliated with the Douglas movement in England.

Criticism reached the boiling point only after eighteen months had passed and Social Credit was yet non-existent in Alberta. The province was still in the midst of the depression; although thousands of hungry people continued to exhibit a blind loyalty to Aberhart they began urging their representatives to insist on immediate Social Credit legislation. Dur- ing the debate on the speech from the throne on the opening of the legislature in 1937, about twenty Social Credit members began holding closed meetings nearly every night in Edmonton hotel rooms. When the budget was presented by the Honourable Solon E. Low, the new provin- cial treasurer, the subject of the secret meetings was revealed. An insur- gency had broken out. The insurgent Social Crediters charged that the Government had brought down merely a second orthodox budget, rather than one based on the credit of the province that would provide for the payment of the basic monthly dividend of $25.00. One after another of the insurgents arose in the House and demanded that Aberhart implement his promise to put Social Credit into effect within eighteen months after his election. The Government was narrowly sustained in several recorded votes, but the insurgency was strong enough to prevent the passage of the budget and to force an adjournment of the legislature until June.

Aberhart's attempts to pacify the insurgents by insisting that he was giving good adminstration were unsuccessful: they were in deadly earnest and demanded that qualified economic assistants be obtained at once so that Social Credit reforms could be instituted. Although a resolute, deter- mined leader, Aberhart was forced, after considerable personal bitterness had developed on both sides, to agree to the appointment of a Social Credit

403

Board, composed of five members of the legislature, the object of which would be the achievement of Social Credit in Alberta. The Chairman of the Board, Glen L. MacLachlan, then made a pilgrimage to England to try to induce Douglas to come to Alberta and assist in working out a plan for the institution of Social Credit. Douglas declined, but recommended two of his associates, G. F. Powell and L. D. Byrne, both of whom arrived in Edmonton for the re-convening of the legislature in June.

When the Social Credit Board was set up, both the insurgents and loyalists agreed to a truce until its chairman should return from England. But it was not long before both sides had taken their case to the people: the insurgents have always claimed that Aberhart was the first to break the truce by denouncing them in one of his Sunday afternoon religious broadcasts. Great mass meetings were held once again throughout the province: loyalist speakers frequently sought to state their position immediately after the insurgents had spoken, or if that privilege was refused they would hold another meeting in the same town the following night. The insurgents tried to put Aberhart at a disadvantage by outdoing him at his own techniques of mass appeal, but his position as prophet of the movement generally gave him the better of the bitter controversy. The loyalists charged that the insurgents were merely ambitious men, who were either seeking Cabinet posts if Aberhart's administration should fall or had been bribed by the Money Power to destroy the movement. The insurgents retaliated by questioning Aberhart's understanding of Douglas's theories and suggesting that he had truckled to the Money Power in taking advice from Magor, the Money Power's nominee.

The people, on the whole, were shocked and mystified by the disloyal attitude (as they supposed) of the members who challenged Aberhart's leadership: they refused to believe that he was merely marking time, and on at least one occasion resorted to stoning the insurgent speakers as an indication of their disapproval. As the months went by both insurgents and loyalists, having grown tired of endless stormy meetings, found the necessary pretext for healing the schism in MacLachlan's return from England with Powell (followed shortly thereafter by the arrival of Byrne), as well as in Aberhart's solemn promise that a special session of the legislature would be held in August to implement the recommendations of the Social Credit experts. As a formal indication to the people that the family quarrel was over Powell arranged for the Social Credit members of the legislature to sign a pledge that they would uphold the Social Credit Board and its technicians, and would work thereafter in harmony for the attainment of their common objectives. Magor and two cabinet ministers, who had never really been disciples of Aberhart, proved to be convenient scapegoats, and the public uproar created by the insurgency slowly subsided, although the essential differences between the followers of Douglas and the followers of Aberhart remained unresolved. The insurgency was the driving force behind the celebrated Social Credit legislation of 1937, the disallowance of which has formed the subject of so much controversy.

404

If the Social Credit, and Mortgage and Debt, legislation pacified the insurgents, it terrified the financial and business interests of Alberta whose representatives, infuriated by what they considered was a thoroughly high-handed attitude in Aberhart's dealings with them, now proceeded to give wide currency to the view that he was the leader of a Canadian form of fascism. His attempt to change the status of the Royal Canadian Mounted Police in the province, coupled with the "press gag" legislation, lent further strong support to this accusation, and also caused the newspapers to redouble their attacks on him. Organized opposition to the Social Credit movement crystallized around the People's League, which developed into the Unity movement and finally emerged as the Independent party. Within the Independent party, as the bitter election of March, 1940, drew near, were included Liberals, Conservatives, and all others who were opposed to the Social Credit movement except the supporters of the Cooperative Commonwealth Federation, which was slowly and painfully developing from an alliance of labour groups with the socialistically minded members of the U.F.A.

405

During his second election campaign, Aberhart attributed his failure to introduce Social Credit to the Dominion government: under the influence of the Money Power it had sabotaged his constructive legislation. As the depression had not yet lifted, he was able to use again the shop-worn slogans of 1935 and make an issue of debt: he promised that, with more time, he could yet effectively destroy the power of the embattled Money Barons and pay the long over-due basic dividend. The Independents had no constructive programme to offer the people. Their one cry was, *"Throw out Aberhart!"* The very violence of the *Calgary Herald's* personal attacks on the premier caused many wavering Social Crediters to rally behind their old leader, and thousands of members of the League gave him the same unquestioning loyalty and enthusiastic support as in 1935. Apart from their lack of any positive policy, the greatest weakness of the Independents consisted in their association with the more prosperous classes of Edmonton and Calgary: although this connexion gave them a fairly large following in most of the urban centres, it proved an insuperable handicap in the rural, and especially the dried out, areas. Yet for all the weaknesses of the Independents, the Social Credit party almost lost the election. The issue was so close that a shift of only 1000 votes, properly distributed in ten constituencies, would have led to Aberhart's fall. As it was, the Social Crediters won thirty-six of the fifty-seven seats in the new legislature.

Shortly after the election, the German Army began its great *blitzkrieg* in Western Europe. Aberhart, severely shaken by the insurgency, as well as by his near electoral defeat, realized that the people had become weary of the long years of political turmoil. He shrewdly suggested that the energies of all should now be devoted to Canada's war effort; and it would appear that some sort of agreement was reached that no further controversial Social Credit legislation would be attempted until the war was over.

Certain tendencies that were developing in the Social Credit movement had been clearly revealed as a result of the campaign of 1940. Many people who were interested only in the economic theories of Social Credit were beginning to object strongly to Aberhart's constant mixture of religion and politics, especially in his Sunday afternoon broadcasts. The halo that had formerly surrounded the leader had been somewhat dimmed by his fierce quarrel with the insurgents and his failure to cope successfully with the Money Power. Many of the Social Credit study groups had begun to lose their enthusiasm: people were growing tired of constantly attending meetings merely to hear the same doctrines expounded over and over again. The formalization of the media of propaganda served to enchannel the earlier popular enthusiasm into more determinate patterns of response. The rise of the C.C.F. movement was slowly draining away from Social Credit its genuine left-wing supporters: immediately after the election of 1940, a defeated Social Credit candidate who had been one of Aberhart's most tireless supporters joined the C.C.F. and began to work enthusiastically for socialism; still others deserted Social Credit through disillusionment with its doctrines or because of personal disappointment in not receiving satisfactory governmental appointments for long years of loyal effort. Finally, politically power was tending more and more to turn a popular movement into a highly institutionalized political party: it was not only the Independents and socialists who asserted, at the height of the campaign of 1940, that the Social Credit movement had become "just another political party." The process of institutionalizing a remarkable social movement was completed, for all practical purposes, when Aberhart's death, in May, 1943, led to the selection, not by a representative convention but by the Social Credit members of the legislature, of his chief lieutenant, the Honourable Ernest C. Manning, as leader of the party and the movement. In his initial address, the new premier gave a pledge to his followers that the fight for Social Credit would never be given up and that the effective control of the monetary system would eventually be taken from private, monopolistic interests and restored to the people's democratically elected representatives. He also promised, while carrying on the fight for permanent social justice and economic security, to give the best possible administration in every department of government.

Aberhart's death gave the waning Social Credit movement a new impetus in that it attracted supporters from unexpected quarters. The more prosperous classes of the province, headed by the business and financial interests, had developed over the years such embittered attitudes toward the late leader that they could never have joined hands with him to oppose the rising C.C.F. movement. But they entertained no such personal hostility to Mr. Manning, although they knew full well that he had long been Aberhart's ardent disciple in both religion and politics. The invalidation of Social Credit legislation by the courts and the attitude of the Dominion government had convinced them also that they no longer had anything to fear from Manning's Government, whereas the accession of the C.C.F. to power might become a real threat to the continuance of the present economic system. The new premier was enthusiastically received by service clubs and other business men's organizations: his friendly manner and his persuasive defence of Social Credit against socialism led to an entirely new alignment in the provincial election of 1944.

No sooner had the election been called than Mr. Manning, taking his cue from certain large city newspapers, announced that the only significant issue was socialism. In the campaign that followed, the philosophy of Social Credit was thoroughly unmasked for the first time in Alberta: Douglas, its originator, turned out to be in reality no radical at all but the most rugged individualist, an arch conservative; for him, capitalism was the ideal form of economic organization, provided only that its monetary system could be changed. Accepting literally Mr. Manning's rightist interpretation of Social Credit and his frequently repeated statement that he sincerely wanted "to make Capitalism work," and convinced also that they could depend on him to give good government, thousands of people who feared socialism deserted the Independents and voted for the party which they had opposed so energetically only four years before. When the election was over the Independent party had been well-nigh destroyed, and the Social Crediters were returned to power with an even more overwhelming majority than that of 1935.

Three important trends in the Social Credit movement were revealed by the third election: its philosophy, which had hitherto been masked by seemingly radical monetary theories, no longer appealed to a considerable number of leftists who now turned to socialism; the support which it had drawn from the propertied classes more than made up for defections to the C.C.F.; the undimmed enthusiasm of thousands of its original members, although the movement had become strongly conservative, seemed to indicate that Social Credit would long remain a powerful factor in Alberta politics. During the campaign, the C.C.F. had suffered from poor organization and inadequate funds, but it had become the second strongest party in Alberta and was recognized as the only effective opposition to the Social Credit movement. Mr. Manning and his associates realized clearly that, if their movement was to survive, they must in the future shatter the Socialists as they had previously shattered the United Farmers and the Independents. Confronted with the challenge of another people's movement, the propaganda for Social Credit has, since 1944, taken on almost entirely the character of a crusade against socialism.

In the struggle with socialism during the campaign of 1944, Social Credit leaders had said little about basic dividends and the just price, partly because of the general understanding that such controversial issues would remain dormant for the duration of the war, partly because these doctrines would have disturbed those whom they hoped to attract from the Independent party. But over the years many of the original members of the movement had cherished the hope of basic dividends and, as soon as possible after the war ended, they revived at the annual meeting of the Social Credit League in December, 1945, the whole question of the legislative implementation of Douglas's monetary theories. There is reason to believe that the lively, almost revolutionary, statements made at the convention were inspired by certain cabinet ministers as a technique for retaining control of the discussion. At the same time, there can be no doubt whatever that the demand for the Government to keep Aberhart's promises of 1935, by paying the basic dividend, had a genuine source in the growing unrest and agitation among the people themselves. The League, in no uncertain terms, gave the Government instructions to carry out its long promised programme and also made clear that its members wanted most especially the basic dividend, now ten years overdue. Responding immediately to the popular demand, the Government presented the people with the Bill of Rights.

408

The new Charter of Freedom gave both a statutory declaration of the just rights and responsibilities of the citizens of Alberta and outlined the methods by which those rights could be realized in actual experience: it promised social and economic security with individual freedom to everybody. Its most spectacular feature was the offer of a social security pension and medical benefits to everyone between the age of nineteen and sixty who was unable to obtain employment or who was disabled; at the age of sixty every citizen would be entitled to retire and receive similar benefits. By an adequate "Social Security Pension" was meant, in terms of the price level of 1945, a payment to the individual concerned of an annual income of not less than $600 a year, or a minimum income of $1200 for a married couple. The second part of the Bill contained an elaborate description of the Social Credit techniques by means of which money would be made available to the government to pay the pensions and medical benefits. An unusual feature of the Bill, which created considerable cynicism among non-Social Crediters concerning the good faith of the Government, was the provision that before being proclaimed it should be tested by the courts.

Printed copies of the Bill of Rights were widely distributed by members of the legislature and by the Social Credit Board. Its contents were thoroughly discussed at meetings of groups and constituency organizations but, unlike the earlier Social Credit legislation, it aroused neither great enthusiasm from within the movement nor violent antagonism from without. An informal straw vote conducted by the members of the legislature indicated that over 95 per cent of the people interviewed favoured the Bill, although to a certain number of pure Douglasites it seemed to bear the taint of socialism. The Bill was presented to the annual meeting of the Social Credit League in 1946 as evidence of the strong intentions of the government to overthrow the "Financiers," but the delegates exhibited little excitement. There was a widespread feeling that the Bill would be declared *ultra vires,* and when the expected adverse judgment of the Supreme Court of Alberta was confirmed by the Privy Council in mid-summer, 1947, the decision was received apathetically by most Social Crediters. Certain of them felt that the post-war prosperity had, in any case, made basic dividends unnecessary: Social Credit was not primarily a monetary theory but a way of life. The majority still felt, however, that there must surely be some way by which Douglas's monetary theories could be implemented, and much speculation arose concerning the future course of the movement.

As they faced the future in the late summer of 1947, the Social Credit leaders could no longer ignore, as they had tried to do for several years, the fact that deep within the structure of the movement there had developed another dangerous schism. The serious internal dissension with which they were confronted can best be understood in terms of an analysis of the media and the content of Social Credit propaganda which existed at that time.

In addition to the provincial and national leaders and members of the Alberta legislature and the House of Commons, the principal media of propaganda were the Social Credit League, the *Canadian Social Crediter,* and the Social Credit Board. The leaders of the movement, as well as the M.L.A.'s and M.P.'s, were tireless in their efforts to promote Social Credit ideas, missing no opportunity of addressing any available group either in Alberta or elsewhere in Canada. The Social Credit League, on the other hand, appeared moribund: although it still met annually and passed resolutions for governmental consideration, its deliberations and actions (apart from the upsurge in 1945) had not for years inspired much enthusiasm among its membership, which had decreased considerably since 1940. In the early years of the movement the study groups had been its dynamic foundation, but they had also declined both in numbers and importance. For many Social Crediters the old group life had been replaced by the more institutionalized constituency organization which was taking on more and more the appearance of an old line party machine. The weekly newspaper, the *Canadian Social Crediter,* now had a national circulation, and was in the hands of John Patrick Gillese, a young and energetic editor who lost no opportunity of presenting to his readers the latest developments in Douglas's theories and their significance for the interpretation of provincial, national, and especially international events. Among its organs of propaganda, a unique feature of the movement was the Social Credit Board which had been set up by legislative action after the great insurgency of 1937.

Technically a committee of the whole legislature, financed by public funds, and theoretically non-partisan, the Board had become in actual practice the philosophical arm of the Social Credit movement. It was the principal and, apart from the newspaper, the only agency through which Douglas's developing ideas were systematically filtered through to the people. The four or five members of the Board, who were members of the legislature, gave numerous public addresses and exhibited pictures and films illustrating the basic principles of Social Credit; they also wrote occasional pamphlets and served as a centre for giving wide distribution to Douglas's books and articles. The activities of the Board, so obviously associated with the interests of one political party only, inevitably gave rise to the criticism that such an identification of the party with the state was fascism in its purest form. Douglas had originally sent out two associates to serve as technical advisers of the Board: after a stormy career ending with a term in prison for his part in the "bankers' toadies" incident, Powell returned to England. Byrne, a strict disciple of Douglas, then became and remained for ten years the principal intellectual force behind the Board's activities, a hidden hand, but a *recognized* hidden hand. Probably his most important task was to give some genuine understanding of Social Credit to the M.L.A.'s and M.P.'s and subsequently to the people in general. He inspired, if he did not actually write, the reports which were presented annually to the legislature by the Social Credit Board. It was the submission of the tenth report in the spring of 1947 that precipitated the most recent crisis within the movement.

As we have already pointed out, there are three aspects to Douglas's philosophy: a monetary theory, a political theory, and an interpretation of history. During the middle and late thirties the second and third aspects began to appear more prominently in Douglas's writings than the monetary theories. He had apparently concluded, even before Aberhart came into power, that the grip of international finance was so unshakable that nothing short of a transformation of democracy and of the organization of the world in general would make it possible to put his monetary theories into practice. The changed emphasis in Douglas's position had already begun to appear in *Today and Tomorrow* as early as 1939, and it was reflected in the report of the Social Credit Board for the following year. Although the Board's reports were supposed to give a review of the progress made in the realization of the Social Credit monetary theories in Alberta and to explore possibilities for the future, from 1941 on more and more space was devoted to criticism of the functioning of the democratic process and to an analysis of the international situation. It is noteworthy that the Board viewed every proposed form of international co-operation, including Dumbarton Oaks, Bretton Woods, the United Nations, UNRRA, and UNESCO as indisputable evidence of the existence of the international Masonic-Judaic conspiracy, in league with high finance and communism, to secure control of the world by destroying nationalism, private enterprise, capitalism, and Christianity.

Inspired by Douglas's latest writings, the Board's analysis of problems in these terms reached a climax in its sensational report of 1947. After calling attention once again to the existence of the conspiracy, the report reviewed and analysed the various techniques by which the World Plotters had developed and extended their monopolistic control in both the financial and political spheres with world dictatorship as their ultimate goal. Realizing that freedom of the individual was their greatest obstacle, the Plotters had launched a planned attack against such freedom by encouraging socialism, communism, atheism, materialism, totalitarianism, and the weakening of the British Empire. The report asserted that any "programme for action" must begin with a criticism of democracy *as it func-*

tions at present: majority rule, the secret ballot, and the political party system must all be abolished for they have become instruments, not of genuine democracy, but of the World Plotters. Political parties should be replaced by a union of electors with three objectives: "to state the results wanted from the management of the affairs of the country in all spheres affecting the lives of the People; to control the elected representatives of the people *at all times* [not merely on the day of an election] and through them, all of the People's governing bodies, — local, provincial, and national; to insist on and enforce obedience to the will of the People on all matters of Policy [results]." Only in this way, the report concluded, could a genuine Christian democracy be established and security with freedom be enjoyed by everyone.

The report produced an uproar in the Social Credit caucus, which had been given no knowledge of its contents prior to its submission to the legislature; and it caused a critical re-evaluation of Douglas's theories throughout the movement and the country at large. Immediately after the close of the session, the party caucus issued a statement in which it reaffirmed its unswerving allegiance to the principles of Social Credit as enunciated by Aberhart, while at the same time it dissociated both itself and the movement in Alberta "from any statements or publications which were incompatible with the established British ideals of democratic freedom or which endorsed, excused, or incited anti-Semitism or racial or religious intolerance in any form." In the repudiation and condemnation of the world conspiracy theory of Douglas, the lead was given by Premier Manning.

But the storm would not blow over so easily, and it soon became evident that two sharply opposed factions, known as the realists and the Douglasites, had been developing within the movement during the past few years. The realists thought of Social Credit essentially in terms of Douglas's earlier monetary theories as propounded by Aberhart, and considered it suicidal to attack majority rule, the secret ballot, and the party system. The Douglasites, on the other hand, thought of Social Credit primarily in terms of the Jewish world conspiracy and insisted that it was essential to establish a union of electors without delay — for many of them, the monetary theories were no longer of immediate importance. Wherever one looked at the movement the conflict between the two factions was unmistakably evident — within the Cabinet, among the members of the legislature and the House of Commons, among the members of the Social Credit Board, among the staff of the official newspaper, and finally, among the members of the Social Credit League.

During the summer of 1947 the leaders of both groups, while they glared at each other across an ideological chasm, still entertained the hope that they might continue to work together in harmony for the movement in its crusade against socialism. But the differences in their interpretation of Social Credit ultimately proved irreconcilable. In the early autumn the premier and his associates skilfully began a carefully planned purge which

411

has resulted in the removal from power or office of most of the Douglasites and their replacement in the cabinet, on the staff of the newspaper, and elsewhere by realists. The Social Credit Board itself was liquidated in March of this year; and even Byrne, whom many Social Crediters thought of as Douglas's personal representative, was dropped both as technical adviser and as deputy minister of economic affairs. The dismissal of Byrne and the "resignation" of the editor of the *Canadian Social Crediter* broke the last links (which had been growing steadily weaker since Aberhart's death) of the official Alberta movement with Douglas. The author of the Social Credit theories now proceeded to belabour the realists in his Liverpool weekly, the *Social Crediter*; and his strict disciples in Alberta, although deprived of their official positions, continued the propagation of their doctrines by organizing the Edmonton Council of the Douglas Social Credit Movement of Canada. In their new journal, the *Social Credit Challenge*, the Douglasites leave one with the impression that they believe the World Plotters are directly responsible for separating the premier of Alberta from Douglas as well as for dividing the movement.

It is too early to assess the impact of the third schism within the movement upon its future. But it is safe to say that Douglas's proposals for monetary reform mark the limits to which his teachings can hope to obtain general acceptance in Alberta. Such a limitation is not surprising if one remembers that monetary reform had become a preferred group tendency in the province long before the rise of the Social Credit movement; and, apart from obvious considerations such as the economic and political situation in Alberta and the remarkable leadership of Aberhart, this has been the determining tendency both in the origin and the evolution of the movement, when one examines it in historical and social psychological perspective.

This paper was presented at the annual meeting of the Canadian Political Science Association in Vancouver, June 18, 1948; it grows out of an investigation by the author of the philosophy and psychology of the Social Credit movement in Alberta which will constitute one of a series of studies being sponsored by the Canadian Social Science Research Council under the direction of Professor S. D. Clark. As the paper forms part of a larger study, which it is hoped to publish eventually in book form, footnotes and references have been omitted.

412

The Radical Background of the CCF*
WALTER D. YOUNG

As all traced their particular grievances to the same cause, the capitalist system, so all saw
in a socialist society the one and only remedy for those grievances.

SAMUEL BEER
British Politics in a Collective Age

The CFF has generally been seen by students of Canadian politics as an
agrarian protest movement, in some ways the successor to the Progressive
party, with much in common with the Social Credit party and similar
movements of agrarian radicalism in the American middle west.[1] In
general, this view is misleading. For, although the CCF first formed a
government in Saskatchewan, won more rural than urban seats, had as its
statement of principles the Regina Manifesto, and owed a great deal to the
tradition of agrarian radicalism that flourished in the Canadian wheat belt,
it would be foolish to ignore the vital role played in the establishment and
growth of the party by labour and urban socialist elements. The distribution of its votes in national elections is a further indication of the strong
urban strain in the CCF. Although the votes were infrequently translated
into seats, the CCF had more supporters in the urban areas of Ontario,
Manitoba, and British Columbia than it had among the wheat farmers.
Professor McNaught has pointed out that "the movement of the 'Thirties
sprang from urban labour, the Christian social gospel of the Protestant
churches and . . . the radical urban intellectuals — as well as from the soil
of the wheat belt."[2]

The party's founders recognized these roots at the Calgary conference in
1932. They insisted on appending the words "farmer, labour, socialist" to
the full name of the party.[3] Among its supporters the CCF was often
referred to as a "farmer-labour" party,[4] but since not all farmers were
socialists, and the Fabian intellectuals of the League for Social Reconstruction were neither farmers nor labour, the Calgary appendage makes
more sense. Clause three of the Calgary resolution was quite explicit: "The
general viewpoint and program involved in the socialization of our economic life, has already been outlined and accepted by the Labour, Farmer,
Socialist and other groups affiliating."[5] Why these forces should have
come together in the Canadian West at the time they did was the result of a
combination of factors, the roots of which extend back beyond the period
of the First World War. It is enough to say for the moment that given the
nature of rural society, the political traditions of the prairie provinces, and
the effect of the depression on the western economy, the West offered the

413

*Chapter 2 from *The Anatomy of a Party: The National CCF*, by Walter D. Young. © University of
Toronto Press 1969. Reprinted by permission.

most fertile soil for the establishment of a party like the CCF. But without the presence of the urban labour parties, it is likely that the CCF would have suffered the same fate as the Progressives.

The background of agrarian protest in Canada has been carefully and exhaustively studied elsewhere.[6] Only brief mention needs to be made here of the growth and development of the agrarian movements and labour parties in order to provide a background for the events immediate to the formation of the CCF. Simplicity would seem to require that the CCF be seen as the lineal descendant of the Progressive party. This proposition, however attractive, does not sustain close scrutiny because the Progressive party was never in any sense a socialist party, and it clearly showed its dislike of radical labour politics on several occasions. The *Grain Growers' Guide*, organ of the Progressives and usually in the van of Progressive and political thought,[7] vigorously opposed the Winnipeg General Strike. During the 1921 election campaign no effort was made to solicit labour support and those elements of the Progressive platform shared by the labour parties were deliberately understated. The Progressives were radicals in that they advocated change, but the change they favoured was not socialism. They were, in Morton's apt phrase, "crypto-Liberals,"[8] particularly in the Manitoba wing of the party though less so in the Alberta movement. Agrarian politics in Alberta were more radical and more class-conscious, a result of the activities of the United Farmers of Alberta and the Non-Partisan League. The "Ginger Group" of Progressive MPs who bolted their party and made common cause with J. S. Woodsworth's Labour group in Parliament were largely Albertans.

Progressivism was more a product of the same forces that subsequently gave rise to and sustained both the CCF and Social Credit parties than it was their progenitor. The Progressive party was not class-oriented; it supported reform within the established system, not fundamental change of the system itself. The fleeting success which the Progressives enjoyed did demonstrate that such movements could succeed, just as their failure demonstrated that such movements would also collapse unless they were prepared to enter the political arena as an organized, disciplined party, competing with the others. The Progressive movement was a product of the same feelings of economic and political isolation, of "quasi-colonial" exploitation,[9] and of frustrated ambitions that led to the establishment of the CCF and Social Credit parties.

Many who later played an active part in the formation of the CCF were members of the Progressive party, since it was at that time a logical vehicle of protest against the studied refusal of the political establishment in the East to recognize the special problems of the rural and urban inhabitants west of the Lakehead. M. J. Coldwell, who succeeded J. S. Woodsworth as leader of the CCF, remained a member of the Saskatchewan Progressive party until it was superseded by the Farmers' Political Association in the rural areas by the Independent Labour party in the cities and towns. The Progressive party was equally a home for those in all three provinces who

moved into the Conservative party — although in Manitoba most Progressives entered happily into formal union with the Liberals in 1932.[10] In
Saskatchewan the decline in Progressive strength was matched by a parallel growth in Conservative support. Between 1921 and 1930 the Progressive share of the vote fell from 61 to 12 per cent and the Conservative's
share rose from 16 to 38 per cent.[11]

The Progressive party was, in fact, something different in each province. Its legacy to the CCF was a heightened awareness of the feasibility of
political action and of the importance of a distinctly radical platform to
discourage the cannibalistic enthusiasms of Mackenzie King. In Alberta,
Progressivism can best be equated with American populism for the reasons
advanced by Sharp, chief of which was the predominance of American
settlers in the province, many of whom had some experience of agrarian
politics in their own country.[12] The predominance in Manitoba of settlers
from eastern Canada provided the basis in that province for agrarian
liberalism in the Grit tradition of rural Ontario. In Saskatchewan a stronger
concentration of British and European immigrants means a population to
whom protest meant socialism.[13] The pedigree of the CCF bears traces of
all three strains from urban as well as rural antecedents. Much of the
struggle over doctrine within the party was caused by the mingling of
these strains. To this day there are oldtimers in the CCF/NDP for whom
socialism is a fascinating blend of American populism and Social Credit
monetary reform. Most of these oldtimers are from Alberta.

Two of the early antecedents of the CCF deserve some comment. The
Non-Partisan League and the United Farmers of Alberta represented the
purely North American strain in the CCF's pedigree. Both had something
in common with British socialism, which helped attract support from
those immigrants familiar with that body of doctrine, but American ideas
were more dominant. Henry Wise Wood, leader of the UFA, for example,
was born in Missouri, and came to Canada in his forties. Like many of his
compatriots who had emigrated to Alberta, he had been a member of the
Populist party and put an emphasis on active non-partisan citizenship that
was clearly more an American than a British concept.

The Non-Partisan League was a direct import from the United States,
fresh from its triumphant capture of the government of North Dakota.
Although it was an agrarian movement, the outright socialism of much of
its platform attracted a number of urban radicals to its ranks when it first
appeared in Canada in 1916.[14] J. S. Woodsworth likened its program to
that of the British Labour party, and along with Salem Bland, William
Irvine, and Fred Dixon, worked as an organizer for the League.[15]

Unlike the UFA, the League had little success. Its forthright opposition
to conscription in the 1917 election appeared to do more harm than good,
despite the feeling of many farmers that it was another instance of the
government's refusal to appreciate their needs. But despite its failure, the
League provided considerable impetus to the reform movement: it sharpened
class consciousness and put a more vigorous and radical language on the

415

tongues of many farmers.[16] Woodsworth's brief spell as organizer provided him with contracts with the rural community that served him well fourteen years later when he filled the role of catalyst in bringing the farm and labour groups together in a single party. More specifically, the League had a profound influence on the development of the UFA, laying the foundation for its subsequent success in Alberta politics.

Although not as socialistic as the League, the UFA was both more radical and more class conscious than the Progressives. Its repudiation of the competitive system in economics and politics and its willingness to co-operate with other economic groups made it an easy companion for labour and socialists alike. The spokesmen of the UFA were not blind to the traditional antagonism between farm and labour, but they were sufficiently realistic to see the necessity for closer ties. In any case the size of the labour "group" in Alberta was too small to be a problem. As Wood put it in 1921, the year the UFA became the government of the province,

416

If we turn away from Labour, who are we to turn to? The salvation of the world depends upon the mobilization of a democratic strength sufficient to work social redemption and social salvation. The mobilization of this force depends upon the co-operation of democratic elements. It may be a difficult road to travel but there is no other.[17]

Characteristically, the first minister of labour in the UFA government was Vernon Smith, elected on the Labour ticket.

The UFA philosophy was similar in some respects to guild socialism. Co-operation with labour was simply a case of one economic group working with another in the effort to establish group government and thereby "fundamental democracy," in which the economic groups making up society are represented.[18] Wood believed that democracy was citizens in action organized around their economic interests. Parties had no place in this system; they not only belonged to the past but were demonstrably corrupt.[19] Farmers and workers entered politics to preserve — or establish — their group identity and to exercise their rights as participants in the economic and political processes. Government was the process of arriving at decisions that were in the interest of all groups through non-partisan discussion of the issues. The activities of the UFA helped generate a class consciousness among the rural population and paved the way to co-operation with the labour parties by emphasizing the common grievances and common interests of farmers and worker.

The road to co-operation was not a difficult one in Alberta. Nor was it difficult in Saskatchewan, but in Manitoba the situation was different. There the working-class population was much larger, less Anglo-Saxon, and generally more militant and radical. The memory of the General Strike lingered to sour relations. Co-operation was never fully achieved. Even in Alberta and Saskatchewan there were many workers who saw farmers as proprietors and employers, and many farmers who viewed labour's agitation for the eight-hour day as some kind of sick joke. But when the mills of the Depression ground out destitution and misery on the farm and in the cities alike, there was no real difficulty in bringing the farmers' groups into close liaison with the labour parties in the cities.

One serious obstacle, as far as the UFA was concerned, was the persistent opposition of Wood to party activity as such. Engagement in politics as an economic group was one thing; emerging as a united political party was another again. The understandably strong anti-party sentiment in the UFA and the persuasive advocacy of Henry Wise Wood made co-operation with labour *parties* virtually impossible while Wood was in command.

Wood retired in 1931 and was succeeded by Robert Gardiner, an MP and a member of the Ginger Group who had been working closely with Woodsworth's two-man labour party in the House of Commons since 1924. The 1932 convention of the UFA passed a resolution offering close co-operation with other political groups and pledged its support for the establishment of a co-operative commonwealth which was defined as:

A community freed from the domination of irresponsible financial and economic power, in which all social means of production and distribution, including land, are socially owned and controlled either by voluntarily organized groups of producers and consumers, or — in the case of the major public services and utilities and such productive and distributive enterprises as can be conducted most efficiently when owned in common — by public corporations responsible to the people's elected representatives.[20]

417

The definition is a socialist one, more so in fact than the Regina Manifesto turned out to be, at any rate with respect to land ownership. At the end of June 1932, the UFA executive, MPs, and the provincial Legislature endorsed the convention resolution and drafted a ten-point manifesto outlining the aims of the UFA. They reiterated the invitation to other groups, "urban and rural, whose aims are fundamentally the same as those of the UFA," to co-operate with them in order to realize these aims.[21] Specifically, they invited all such groups to attend a conference in Calgary in August to discuss action in their common cause. There is little doubt that the specific invitation was instigated by Robert Gardiner in his capacity as co-chairman of the parliamentary group which that May had decided to begin the process of bringing the radical movements together. For this reason the third conference of the Western Labor Political Parties, originally scheduled for Regina, was held in Calgary.[22]

The moment was propitious. By 1932 the Depression had stalked across the plains and the good times of the post-war period had totally disappeared. There had been crop failures before, in Alberta in the years 1917-20, and a disastrous fall in the price of wheat between 1920 and 1923, but the boom which followed 1923 had restored confidence and injected optimism into the prairie economy. The price of wheat was nevertheless exceptionally vulnerable, whereas the fixed costs of the farmers were not. The post-war slump demonstrated the interdependence of farmer and worker, for, as the farmers' incomes declined, fewer manufactured goods were purchased and unemployment resulted, most noticeably in those industries directly related to farm purchases. Both were adversely affected by the steadily rising cost of living.

The fat years that followed the 1920-3 slump brought the National Policy to full fruition. The western plains were occupied; 3000 miles of track were added to the railways in the West; virtually all the arable land was within easy reach of the railhead. Saskatchewan and Alberta enjoyed a 20 per cent increase in population and their economies flourished, but there was little diversification, as there had been in Manitoba. The growth was almost all in agriculture and most of that in wheat farming. British Columbia experienced economic expansion as well. The opening of the Panama Canal and the general health of the overseas market for lumber and minerals contributed to a growth rate that was the highest in Canada, but dependence on overseas markets and primary production meant that its economy was vulnerable. The growth rate attracted to the province a host of unskilled labourers who accentuated the unemployment problem in Vancouver when the Depression came.

418

In the twelve months from January to December of 1930, the price of wheat fell by 57 per cent. By December 1932 farm prices generally had fallen 70 per cent from the levels of July 1929. The expansion during the boom had been financed extensively with borrowed capital and the farmer was quickly crushed between the upper and nether millstones of declining income and fixed costs. Drought exacerbated the situation in Saskatchewan. By 1932 two-thirds of the farm population in that province were destitute.[23] The greatest decrease in income occurred in Saskatchewan, then Alberta, Manitoba, and British Columbia, in that order. Winnipeg and Vancouver were centres of severe unemployment. Farm yields were higher in Alberta, where the drought was less severe, but higher fixed debt charges offset what advantage this brought the farmers in that province. Across the country from Port Arthur westwards, the Depression was a time of impossible debt, high unemployment, and utter destitution.

It deepened the conviction of those already committed to the radical point of view and made new recruits among those whose farms were repossessed or who were living on the dole or spoiling in a labour camp. The traditional western distrust of the established political parties was not diminished by the countless stories of privilege and influence peddling in the distribution of jobs and relief to party hacks and hangers-on.

By 1931 the militant and politically oriented Saskatchewan section of the United Farmers of Canada had begun to work closely with the Farmers' Political Association and the Saskatchewan Independent Labour party. The United Farmers had been formed in 1926 through the fusion of the Grain Growers Association and the Farmers Union. The Farmers' Political Association was formed two years earlier in the federal constituency of Last Mountain by a group of politically conscious farmers led by George Williams. Its objectives were more radical and its leaders more militant than those of the Saskatchewan Section (SS) of the UFC, but both organizations were a product of widespread disappointment with the failure of the Progressives. Initially, the UFC(SS) was more reluctant than the Political Association to become directly involved in politics. The two groups developed separately and gradually came together in 1929 and 1930.

Political activity on the urban front in Saskatchewan intensified as economic conditions worsened. The Independent Labour party was organized by M. J. Coldwell following his success in the 1926 Regina civic elections when he topped the aldermanic poll on a labour ticket. The ILP was distinctly Fabian in outlook and drew heavily on traditional British socialist material. Mimeographed pamphlets from the National Labour College and old copies of Robert Blatchford's *Clarion* were circulated among the membership.[24] Sections of the party were established in Melville and Saskatoon. It was not long before contact was made with the more militant of the farmers.

In 1929 the Farmers' Political Association and the ILP nominated three candidates under the joint banner of the Farmer-Labour party. The same year, the Saskatchewan group was in touch with the Manitoba ILP. Woodsworth spoke at the July convention of the Saskatchewan ILP and John Queen and Arthur Heaps spoke at a general meeting in Regina that fall. Links with other similar groups were established by exchanging speakers and by the contacts provided through the conferences of the Western Labour Political Parties which had begun in 1929. In 1932 the Weyburn Labor Association was formed by the Rev. T. C. Douglas to provide assistance to the unemployed in Weyburn. He had written to Woodsworth about his activities and was asked to get in touch with M. J. Coldwell. The result was the formation of the Weyburn branch of the ILP.[25] By this time Coldwell was very active in politics in the province; his regular Monday evening radio broadcasts on socialism and economics had made him a well-known figure in the Regina district. At this juncture the aim of the ILP was to set up locals throughout the province and then work to amalgamate at that level with the local UFC(SS) lodge.

The Farmers' Political Association became a province-wide organization in March of 1930. The following month a joint conference with the ILP was held in Regina at which the three hundred delegates approved a joint constitution and statement of objectives. Coldwell was elected a vice-chairman of the Farmers' Political Association, linking the urban and rural movements together. The meeting did not merge the two groups; it demonstrated their decision to pool resources in what was increasingly referred to as the common struggle.

The two groups nominated 13 candidates in the federal election of 1930 and succeeded in electing 2 of them. More impressive were the 40 000 votes cast in favour of the radical candidates. The enthusiasm was reflected in the decision of the UFC(SS) to endorse political action by farmers as such. A resolution calling for the UFC itself to engage in political action failed by only 9 votes. The following year a similar resolution passed with a good majority.

G. H. Williams, founder of the Farmers' Political Association, was elected president of the UFC(SS) in 1930, bringing the three radical political groups in Saskachewan still closer together. At that convention the delegates adopted a thirteen-point program prepared by Williams which declared that: "the present economic crisis is due to inherent unsoundness in the capitalistic system which is based on private ownership of resources and capitalistic control of production and distribution and involves payment of rent, interest and profit."[26] In July 1932, the ILP and the UFC(SS) held their conventions in Saskatoon. At a joint meeting they decided that fusion was undesirable but that a joint program and joint action were essential. Although executive positions were shared by people in all three organizations — the Farmers' Political Association had been virtually absorbed by the UFC at this point — and the separation was in reality only nominal, years of struggle to achieve class consciousness and a sense of identity precluded any submerging of farm and labour movements into a single inclusive movement.

420

The two movements decided to contest the provincial elections under the old Farmer-Labour banner. M. J. Coldwell was elected president and leader of the joint venture. G. H. Williams had intended to stand for this post, but he was advised that his impromptu visit to Russia after the world wheat conference in 1930 had lowered his political stock. There were obvious limits to the radicalism of the farmers and the Regina Fabians. The two groups did, however, instruct their delegates to the UFA-sponsored Calgary conference later that month that the new party to be built should be called "The Socialist Party of Canada."[27] And the emphasis in Coldwell's provincial party was to be "fundamentally socialistic."[28] The ideological raiment of the Farmer-Labour party was provided largely by the urban socialists, while the reformist energy and the "troops" were supplied by the farmers, who outnumbered the five hundred members of the Saskatchewan ILP.

Sask

The urban and rural wings of the Farmer-Labour party came together with little rancour. The labour wing was relatively young and the nature of the provincial economy ensured that there was a clear appreciation of the farmers' problems. In other provinces there was less understanding and consequently less co-operation, particularly of a formal kind, prior to the formation of the CCF. Some of the labour parties, however, had been active in politics before any of the rural movements had begun to consider political action.

For the most part the urban labour parties that participated in the formation of the CCF had a long history, one of division and, consequently, impotence. However, labour candidates did manage to win seats in Parliament. A. W. Puttee and Ralph Smith were the first and were followed by J. S. Woodsworth, William Irvine, and A. A. Heaps. It is uncertain whether more concerted action would have produced better results; what is clear is that a good deal of time and energy were expended in waging internecine war and in establishing "new" branches of the old parties to hold the true doctrine. The Winnipeg ILP was formed in 1921 when Fred Dixon, S. J. Farmer, and William Ivens, among others, left the

Dominion Labour party which, in their view, was too conservative.[29] The Canadian Labour party was founded in the same year under the aegis of the Trades and Labor Congress although the TLC was not affiliated with it.

By 1921 there was a host of various labour parties in Canada, most with branches — some with headquarters — in the western cities.[30] In addition to those already mentioned, there was a Labour Representation League, a Federal Labour party, a Federated Labour party, a Workers' party, and the Socialist Party of Canada, to mention a few. In the 1917 Dominion election, the labour parties contested 25 seats; in 1921 there were 29 labour/socialist candidates — at least one in every province. That year, in which two candidates were elected, Woodsworth and Irvine, was the pinnacle of activity and the number of candidates declined from then until the CCF was formed.

The results of the effort and debate that went into left-wing politics were, from an electoral point of view, rather dismal. But the enthusiasm of the labour parties and their prodigious feats of publication and propagandizing through public meetings and such left-wing newspapers as *Citizen and Country*, *The Federationist*, *Western Labour News*, and *The Clarion* made them particularly effective in popularizing the radical point of view. Within the subculture of working-class politics in the cities and in the logging and mining camps, these papers were widely read and the current topics eagerly discussed.

Woodsworth made an abortive attempt to knit together the disparate socialist groups in 1926. At a meeting in the Vancouver home of Robert Skinner with Angus MacInnis, John Sidaway, and John Price — all active in the Vancouver branch of the Canadian Labour party — the formation of a national socialist party was discussed. Woodsworth provided Skinner with the names of 22 people whom he considered to be key contacts. Skinner wrote to them but the response was disappointing and served to confirm a suspicion the five men shared that the labour and socialist parties were "all mixed up like a dog's breakfast."[31] Yet Woodsworth and the others recognized the inevitability of failure if the elements of the urban left were unable to make common cause in their opposition to capitalism.

Three years later the move toward unity began in Regina with the first convention of the western labour parties. The meeting took place as a result of the initiative of the Brandon local of the Manitoba Independent Labour party. Invitations were sent to all elected labour representatives and all labour and socialist parties west of the Lakehead. The purpose of the gathering was to "correlate the activities of the several labour political parties in Western Canada."[32] The *Manitoba Free Press* saw more to it than that: "From the flux of individual labour groups existent in Western Canada, a skeleton framework of a Western Canada Labour Party was built Saturday and today at a conference of labour representatives from points from Winnipeg to the Pacific Coast."[33] The significance of the

421

conferences of the western labour parties has generally been overlooked by students of CCF origins. The conferences helped knit together the urban left and eventually provided a point of contact for the farmers' organizations. The possibility of forming a united party from among the diverse protest movements became real when order began to appear among what had previously been the most chaotic element in the complex of western radicalism. M. J. Coldwell remarked some years later that the conferences of the labour parties deserve "much of the credit for the formation of the CCF."[34]

The program adopted by the first conference was not so much radical as it was practical, containing nothing of an ideological nature that would either deter other groups from affiliating or lead to dissension at the conference itself. As old practitioners of left-wing politics, the leaders of the conference knew when to leave well enough alone. The program called for pensions for the blind, relief for the unemployed, and a minimum wage standard. Like so many agrarian manifestos, it also demanded public ownership and development of natural resources. In any case, the main point of the gathering was not to put together a workers' platform — there was no shortage of them in any case — but to "unify the activities of the affiliated parties, to arrange common action, and to bring about the unification of the entire labour and socialist movement throughout Western Canada."[35]

J. S. Woodsworth was among the delegates at Regina that year, along with representatives of the branches of the Canadian Labour party in Calgary and Edmonton; the Vancouver, Edmonton, and Regina Trades and Labour councils; the Dominion Labour party of Lethbridge; and locals of the Manitoba Independent Labour party. Eight of the nineteen delegates were from Saskatchewan, six from Alberta, four from Manitoba, and one from British Columbia. M. J. Coldwell, Clarence Fines, and Fred White, all destined to play important roles in the CCF, were delegates. At Woodsworth's request each delegate reported on the state of labour political organization in his particular region. It was useful for Woodsworth to have some notion of the degree of support each party had so that he could arrange speaking tours for his colleagues in the House of Commons to best advantage and, of perhaps greater importance, through his good offices, pool the resources of the farm and labour groups where such pooling seemed feasible.

The second Western Conference of the Labor Political Parties met in Medicine Hat in September 1930. A more detailed program was adopted, one which demanded improved old age pensions, consumer co-operatives, and social control of credit and currency, in addition to the points made in the first program. Among the additions was a call for immigration restrictions limiting entry to those "who willingly come and who are financially equipped to be self-supporting."[36] The tone of the resolutions was more radical: the unemployment resolution emphatically declared that "The problem of unemployment cannot be solved under the capitalistic competitive system of production." W. J. Bartlett of the Vancouver and District Trades and Labour Council and the Vancouver Independent Labour party was elected president of the conference.

The third and most significant gathering of the labour parties was held in Winnipeg in 1931. The *Manitoba Free Press* again observed that the conference was likely to result in the formation of a Canadian party "corresponding to the British Labour Party."[37] Invitations to attend had been sent to labour groups in Montreal, Hamilton, Toronto, and "other centres." Woodsworth had personally invited those members of labour parties in the East that he knew. Conference secretary W. E. Small reported that the replies received indicated that the groups in the East, while unable to send delegates, "favoured the formation of a Dominion political body."[38] A major obstacle for all delegates outside the immediate vicinity was the cost of travel. Vancouver was a vigorous centre of socialist activity but only W. J. Bartlett could attend the conference. He worked for the CPR and had a railroad pass. The conference had also invited the United Farmers of Canada (SS) and other farm groups to send delegates and a number did so. A. J. MacAuley of the United Farmers addressed the meeting. According to the *Labour Statesman* "it was as if a radical Labour man were setting forth the aims and ideals of the workers."[39]

This was the most radical of the three conferences, "resolutions galore were offered to the effect that capitalism must go and socialism be established,"[40] The decision to set up a committee of five farm representatives and five labour representatives to "work out a plan for the effective education of the workers and farmers looking to the establishment of the co-operative commonwealth" was the first formal exercise in farmer-labour co-operation at other than the local level.[41] During the discussion of this proposal it was pointed out that the Independent Labour party had been working with farmers and farm groups in British Columbia as well as in Brandon, Souris, and Melville.The problems of the Depression occupied much of the time of the delegates and resolutions were passed dealing with the situation in relief camps and with the handling of relief funds. At the conclusion of the conference, the delegates called upon "workers throughout the world to organize politically and industrially for the abolition of capitalism and the establishment of a co-operative common-wealth."[42] Rejecting a suggestion that the labour parties "get together" with the Communist party, the conference agreed that the representatives of the labour parties in the East should again be invited to the fourth conference to be held in Regina the following year (1932).

The location of the fourth meeting was subsequently changed on the advice of Woodsworth in response to the UFA invitation to hold a joint meeting in Calgary.[43] The Calgary meeting was the culmination of the gradual intermingling of the radical farm and labour movements in western Canada. The labour parties' conferences gave radical leaders like Coldwell and Woodsworth an insight into the extent of radical thought and feeling in western Canada. And latterly they provided those whose experience had been limited to purely labour activities with contact with the farmers' political groups and *vice versa*. The consolidation of the forces of the socialist, labour, and farm groups had begun in the West under the aegis of these conferences before the co-operating groups in the House of Commons had decided to form a Dominion-wide party based on farmer-labour co-operation. That the MPs could see the need for action and the possibility of unity was to some extent due to the meetings of the labour parties, for these at least demonstrated the viability of a broadly-based political organization. They provided both a framework for the future party as well as a solid core of members. There were, for example, approximately four hundred members of the Independent Labour party in Regina alone.[44]

Woodsworth and his colleagues in the House were also aware of the feverish though disparate activity of the labour parties in Ontario. This activity, and the evidence of the three conferences in the West, provided what would appear to be reasonably conclusive proof of the viability of a Dominion-wide socialist party. The Labour MPs had sent letters to all trade unions in Canada urging political action and the general support the replies indicated led Grace Woodsworth, caucus secretary, to conclude with some optimism that the unions were "almost ready for political organization on a large scale."[45]

When the urban and agrarian radicals did combine their forces under the spur of the Depression, the ease with which the combination — for it was never a union — took place was due in large measure to the presence of men who were *persona grata* with farmer and worker alike. The key figure was Woodsworth. As spokesman in the House of Commons for the radical group, he was the institutional leader. He was also the inspirational leader, a position derived from his religious background and close association with the struggles of the persecuted and the alienated in the West almost since the turn of the century. Countless people in the halls and school houses of the western provinces had heard him speak and witnessed his honesty and conviction. For some he was the dedicated evangelist of the Social Gospel, for others one of the martyrs of the Winnipeg General Strike.

The message of the Social Gospel was relevant for the urban worker as much as for the wheat farmer. Although more closely associated with labour politics, his association with the Non-Partisan League and his own travels through the prairies gave Woodsworth a clear understanding of the farmers' problems. Because he was the parliamentary leader of a mixed urban-agrarian alliance, if only in an informal sense, and because his obvious sincerity and conviction removed him from any suspicion by either side, Woodsworth became the linchpin between the urban labour groups and the farm groups, providing a central figure around whom the parties could unite.

His own political views were more radical than those of many of the farmers and less radical than those of many of the labour party figures. His "middle of the road" position made him more acceptable to both sides. He was, in a sense, above politics. He was not a politician in the way that his successor, M. J. Coldwell, was. For Woodsworth, party politics were anathema and throughout his career his vision was of a great movement, not of a great party. The CCF was to be a movement of men and women motivated by Christian ideals, volunteering their services and determined upon the reformation of society to achieve the co-operative common-wealth. It should be pointed out that these ideals were shared by Coldwell who was, nevertheless, more pragmatic. Although he was no fonder of the two-party system than Henry Wise Wood, Woodsworth had serious reser-vations on the subject of group movement.[46] Apart from opposing cabinet dictatorship and supporting "true representation" of the constituencies, Woodsworth displayed whole-hearted support for the institutions of par-liamentary democracy. Like his colleagues and those who came after him in the CCF, he had great skill in the techniques of Parliament and was prepared to use the available machinery to achieve the goals of his move-ment, as he did in 1926 to force Mackenzie King to establish old age pensions.

425

Although he could on occasion demonstrate the skills of management and the thrust and determination of a political leader — notably in the remaking of the Ontario CCF in 1934[47] — his leadership of the co-operating groups and later the CCF was as much a tribute to his vision and the devotion he aroused as to his skill as a politician. As a symbolic leader he represented the ideals of the farmer and the working man. The compara-tive ease with which the federation of the farm and city parties and movements was completed was in no small way due to Woodsworth's personality and the image it fostered in his followers.

His parliamentary ability was instrumental in separating the "Ginger Group" from the Progressive party in 1924. Following their election to the House of Commons in 1921 in the Progressive landslide, Woodsworth and William Irvine made a point of meeting frequently with "certain Progres-sives who recognize their responsibility to the labour section of their constituencies."[48] By 1923 Woodsworth had established his right in the Commons to speak after Robert Forke (who had succeeded T. A. Crerar as leader of the Progressives) as the leader of a party, even though there were only two in his party, that is, Irvine and himself.

By 1924 Forke was experiencing some difficulty in holding the Progres-sives together. During the debate on the budget that year Woodsworth moved an amendment which was essentially the same as one moved by Forke the year before. Woodsworth's amendment placed the Progressives in an awkward position. Support it and they defeated Mackenzie King's government, which had been wooing them assiduously. If they voted against it they were repudiating their own principles. The bulk of the Progressives followed their leader and supported the government. A small number, known subsequently as the Ginger Group,[49] voted with Woodsworth and Irvine. All the members of the original Ginger Group became members of the CCF, most of them for the remainder of their political careers: W. C.

Good withdrew when the doctrine became too much for him, and Agnes Macphail was more in than out although she carried her own label.

After the separation of the Ginger Group from the decaying hulk of the Progressive party, the way was clear for more formal co-operation. A document was drawn up in 1930 providing for regular consultation, something which had, in fact, taken place since the break in 1924. The preamble of the document stated:

Whereas, we the Farmer and Labour groups in the House of Commons, Ottawa, in conference assembled, find that we have much in common and recognize that we are engaged in the common fight against a strongly entrenched system of special privilege, which is functioning through the party system, recognize the advisability of each Group retaining its identity in Parliament, thus enabling the groups to give voice to the distinctive viewpoint held by the electorate represented by them, and also that in working together, we may assist in the development of a cooperative system of administration.[50]

Despite the tentative tone of the preamble, the co-operation proposed was fairly close and involved the appointment of a steering committee and a secretary. Most significantly, it included a statement of intent to find a common stand on major issues and to choose a spokesman who would represent the whole group. A chairman was to be elected with power to act on behalf of the co-operating groups in the event that there was insufficient time for a conference.

From this close and formal co-operation came the parliamentary impetus for the establishment of the CCF. On May 26, 1932, the members of the group met in William Irvine's office, which served as a group caucus room, and agreed to extend their parliamentary organization into the country at large. They decided to set up a federation of groups to promote co-operation between the constituent organizations in the provinces. The new organization was to be called the "Commonwealth Party."[51] Woodsworth and Robert Gardiner of the UFA were appointed co-chairmen. Agnes Macphail was to organize Ontario; Coldwell was invited to organize in Saskatchewan; the Socialist Party of Canada and the ILP were to undertake similar duties in British Columbia and Manitoba; and Gardiner was put in charge of the Alberta organization, where his position as president of the UFA had enabled him to lay the foundation for the Calgary conference.

A final fillip was given to their growing enthusiasm by the organization of the League for Social Reconstruction in January 1932. A Canadian version of the Fabian Society, the League provided intellectual leadership for the CCF for the better part of its history, and at the beginning demonstrated to Woodsworth and his colleagues that there was support for their new party outside farm and labour circles.

The League for Social Reconstruction, or LSR as it was usually called — initials seem to be a characteristic of left-wing politics in Canada — was the direct result of a conversation Frank Underhill and Frank Scott had while on a hiking trip in the Berkshire hills of Massachusetts. They agreed that Canadian politics needed a third party, one which would not be readily absorbed by the Liberals as the Progressives had been. They decided to

426

establish an organization in Canada that would be similar to the British Fabian Society or its American equivalent, the League for Industrial Democracy. This body would work out a program for the new party that would clearly distinguish it from the Liberal party.

The first meeting of the LSR was held in Toronto in January 1932. It was attended largely by Underhill's colleagues from the University of Toronto and Scott's from McGill. A link with the established left was provided by Woodsworth, who was made honorary president. The LSR described itself in its inaugural manifesto as ". . . an association of men and women who are working for the establishment in Canada of a social order in which the basic principle regulating production, distribution and service will be the common good rather than private profit."[52] The task the LSR set itself was "to work for the realization of its ideal by organizing groups to study and report on particular problems and by issuing to the public in the form of pamphlets, articles, lectures, etc., the most accurate information obtainable about the nation's affairs in order to create that informed public opinion which is necessary for effective political action."[53] It did not affiliate with the party it helped create, but it became increasingly involved in the affairs of the CCF; members of the LSR were frequently officers in the CCF and often candidates for election under the party banner. For this reason, among others, it was gradually absorbed by the party and never did achieve the status of the Fabian Society.

The existence of the LSR had an undeniable effect on the CCF not merely in the initial stages of its development, when the first draft of what was to become the Regina Manifesto was prepared by a committee of the LSR, but throughout the first half of the party's life when the books and pamphlets published by the LSR shaped the party's doctrines. Its influence was also exerted through the pages of the *Canadian Forum* which was, for the most part, the organ of the left in Canada and for a time the journal of the LSR.[54] The League also provided the new party with at least a patina of eastern sophistication. It was a little more difficult for the opposition to stereotype the party as readily as it had stereotyped the Progressives. In this way the LSR assisted the CCF in creating a slightly more palatable image of itself for the urban radical who had cause to suspect the purity and consistency of the socialism of many agrarian members.

The League grew fairly rapidly in the first year or two of its existence. In 1933, the Toronto branch of the LSR held a series of public lectures given by some of its leading figures, Underhill, Scott, and King Gordon. The average attendance at these meetings was 135. The Toronto branch had a membership of 145 by 1933.[55]

Support in academic circles in Montreal and Toronto with the promise of expansion was undoubtedly of value to Woodsworth, who was at this point in the process of determining what should be done with the radical farm and labour groups in the West. The knowledge would be doubly encouraging for, apart from the fact that there was a natural desire on

427

Woodsworth's part for intellectual support, the aims of the League were entirely consistent with his own. Woodsworth was an educator and evangelist in the cause of reform. The aims of the LSR were similar. It was an organization of educators with no personal political ambitions.

By 1932 it was clear to the leaders of the co-operating groups that there was almost a national base of popular support for a new radical political movement. The election of Angus MacInnis of the ILP ticket in Vancouver South in 1930 underlined the growing strength of socialism in British Columbia, and added a vigorous spokesman to the "group" in the House of Commons. The arrival on the scene of the LSR merely added to the proof and extended the support of the party eastward into the universities and the urban middle class.

At this point there was reason for believing that a national urban-agrarian socialist movement could be established with good prospects for success. The formation of the LSR meant that the new movement would have its "brains trust." The willingness of the labour parties and farm groups to co-operate and the apparent similarity of their aims pointed to success. The old antagonism between farm and labour appeared to have been submerged by their common plight. The farm and labour groups took advantage of the UFA invitation, and the farm, labour, and intellectual groups gathered in Calgary in 1932 to create the Co-operative Commonwealth Federation.

The Depression made the union possible but could not guarantee its success. The return of prosperity in the forties opened the old wounds of farm-labour antagonism. In Saskatchewan, where labour was a relatively minor element, the CCF succeeded. In Manitoba, where the two elements were more closely balanced and the major impetus for the movement came from the ILP in Winnipeg and Brandon, union between the two was never fully achieved and the CCF had only limited success. The United Farmers of Manitoba never did affiliate, although they did give the CCF access to their lodges and district organizations for the purpose of spreading propaganda. In Alberta the UFA found no difficulty in co-operating with labour; indeed in some respects the Dominion Labour party, as one member put it, was merely "the city side of the UFA."[56] But the defeat of the UFA government in the 1935 election, which the CCF naturally did not contest, put the Social Credit party into office. In Ontario and eastern Canada generally, the CCF never did find an agrarian base. It remained an urban labour movement, "finding its greatest strength in those districts where old country Britishers predominate."[57] British Columbia was similar to Ontario, for there the party remained a socialist labour movement with insignificant rural support. The CCF was, in the East and far West, an urban labour party but, paradoxically, with relatively little support from organized labour until it was almost too late.

The existence of all the groups examined above spelled success for the CCF's organization, although there was really no fundamental compatibility in the doctrines the various groups espoused. There were, on the one hand, the doctrinaire socialists from British Columbia who viewed the farmers with suspicion and distrust, seeing them for what they really were — frustrated *petit bourgeois*.[58] The members of the Dominion Labour party, the Canadian Labour party, and the Independent Labour party in Alberta and Saskatchewan were either Fabians or trade unionists, schooled in the socialism of Bellamy and Blatchford and the Social Gospel. Along with their compatriots in Winnipeg they were familiar with the literature of democratic socialism and for the most part clear on their doctrine. The members of the LSR were socialist intellectuals who saw the new party as the vehicle for an ideology, and to this they lent their energies. The farm groups were seeking reform. For the most part they were led by men who were acquainted with socialism and had, in many instances, urban backgrounds. The farmers who supported them were less familiar with the doctrines of democratic socialism. Their interest was in reform, not social revolution. Thus William Irvine and Henry Spencer could, as "socialists," frequently advocate what was essentially Social Credit monetary reform.[59]

429

What brought the groups together was a shared belief in the need for a co-operative commonwealth, though this meant different things to the different groups; and a common recognition of the inadequacy of the existing system to provide even the necessities of life. The urban socialists made the protest coherent and gave it specific content. They provided, in men like Woodsworth, Coldwell, MacInnis, and Irvine, the cement to bind the groups together. But the fundamental differences that existed could not be eradicated, and for this reason the party started its career as a federation of rural and urban protest movements. The federal structure was to be one of the stumbling blocks in the development of the party, yet it was necessary if the party was to get off the ground.

The ideological disagreement that existed between the various elements could not have been easily reconciled within the framework of a single party. The federal structure meant that each constituent group could retain to a large degree its original doctrine under the broad umbrella of the Regina Manifesto. As well, and perhaps most important, all the elements which formed the new organization were, to some extent, the result of sectional and occupational discontent. They represented those regions and occupations which were on the economic periphery and largely in the control of the vested interests in the East. The anti-centralism and individualism of the prairies that had typified the Progressive groups had not disappeared and was reasserted in the Depression. It would hardly have been consistent with a protest that was to some extent the result of an inability to establish a local identity and status to create as a vehicle for this protest a party which required members and groups to submerge the identity they had succeeded in building for themselves in that larger whole. There was, in addition, the anti-party bias of the agrarian radical.

Membership in a radical political movement is usually the result of a moral and an intellectual conviction about the fundamental iniquity of some aspect of the existing social and economic system. It is also, for some, the result of a need to establish an identity in an alien society. In societies that are clearly class-structured, the need for identity is less pressing because membership in a class is in itself an identity. In so-called classless or open societies the need is more pressing, particularly so when the economic and social systems leave the individual free of social ties and place him in a state of competition with actual and supposed equals.[60] Lacking the reference points of a clearly defined class structure, involved in a competitive struggle which he feels — and usually rightly — he is losing, the individual searches for some locus of his existence and for some satisfactory explanation of his apparent failure.

Only those with a fanatical devotion to the existing system or incredible psychological stamina could undertake to explain, in terms of their own shortcomings, their failure to get a job, raise a crop, or get fair prices for their produce. For the underpaid, unemployed, or hailed-out, there had to be another reason for failure, for they had done all that they could. Beaten by the system, the soil, or the climate, they were themselves blameless; the fault lay elsewhere. Once the fault was found and remedied, they could receive the just returns for their labour.

Alienated by a system in which the cards were stacked against them, the farmers and urban workers found in the protest movements an identity and an explanation. They were united with others who shared the disabilities of poverty and political impotence. In a purportedly classless society, they created a kind of class. This class was provided with a doctrine by the protest movements that explained the causes of the common affliction, allocated responsibility for the condition, and offered a cure that did not do too much violence to the prevailing value system — particularly those aspects related to the ownership of real property; to this day the "family farm" is a sacred prairie concept. Capitalism was the cause, but capitalists were the enemy. The co-operative commonwealth was the cure, for it promised a society in which labour received its due reward and the institutions of liberal democracy operated as they were supposed to operate, free from the perversions of the old party system.

The intellectuals in the LSR and the Marxians in British Columbia saw more in the situation and favoured root-and-branch reform, but even they, for the most part, accepted the framework of liberal democracy and parliamentary institutions. As a result it was a moderate socialism with a wide variety of interpretation that triumphed in the CCF. In the light of the history of the several strands that made up the CCF fabric, it is in no way surprising that consistency of view where the party doctrine was concerned was not easily found. Farmers and workers responded to the doctrines of the movements that federated in 1932 as the CCF because they made sense of a chaotic situation. In Alberta three years later, farmers responded to a different doctrine for essentially the same reasons. Social Credit proposed to repair and modify the free enterprise system to make it work as it should; the CCF groups proposed to substitute a better system. Both agreed that the members of the social and economic establishment were the villains in the piece and both offered the farmer what he wanted; the opportunity for an honest man to make an honest dollar.

The men who met in Calgary in 1932 in the winter of their discontent were not revolutionaries in the ordinary sense. They did not want to overturn the system entirely; they wanted to reform it along the lines dictated by the social gospel and the doctrines of Fabian socialism. To achieve their goals they had decided to become a political party, competing with the "old-line parties" only as a painful necessity. From the beginning they showed a determination to resist the forces that would destroy the individual groups they had built up by submerging them in a larger party. Their eyes were firmly fixed on the establishment of the co-operative commonwealth because they had learned that the existing system could guarantee them nothing. When it is dark, the light on the distant shore always appears nearer than it is.

Notes

1. See, for example, S. M. Lipset, *Agrarian Socialism* (Berkeley 1950), *passim*, and F. H. Underhill, who casually states, "Progressivism was reborn in the Cooperative Commonwealth Federation," in his "Political Parties and Ideas," in G. Brown, ed., *Canada* (Berkeley 1950), 341. See also G. Carter in S. Neuman, ed., *Modern Political Parties* (Chicago 1956). John Irving, "Prairie Ideals and Realities," *Queen's Quarterly*, LXIII (Summer 1956), sees the CCF "as a development from the more radical wing of the UFA," 194.
2. K. W. McNaught, "CCF Town and Country," *Queen's Quarterly*, LXI (Summer 1954), 213. See also his *A Prophet in Politics* (Toronto 1959), 225–6, n. 1. And see Appendix III.
3. Minutes, "Conference Resulting in Formation of the Co-Operative Commonwealth Federation," CCF Minute Books, Aug. 1, 1932, CCF Papers, Public Archives of Canada (hereafter CCFP and PAC).
4. See, for example, David Lewis and F. R. Scott, *Make This Your Canada* (Toronto 1943), 118–19, and M. J. Coldwell, *Left Turn Canada* (Toronto 1945), 20.
5. Minutes, "Conference Resulting in the Formation of the CCF," CCFP.
6. Lipset, *Agrarian Socialism*; C. B. Macpherson, *Democracy in Alberta* (Toronto 1953); W. L. Morton, *The Progressive Party in Canada* (Toronto 1950); P. F. Sharp, *Agrarian Revolt in Western Canada* (Minneapolis 1948); John Irving, *The Social Credit Movement in Alberta* (Toronto 1959).
7. Morton, *Progressive Party*, 117–18.
8. *Ibid.*, 200–1.
9. Macpherson, *Democracy in Alberta*, 6 ff.
10. See M. S. Donnelly, *The Government of Manitoba* (Toronto 1963), 63–4.
11. Election statistics are from the *Reports* of the Chief Electoral Officer (Ottawa, Queen's Printer) and Howard Scarrow, *Canada Votes* (New Orleans 1963).
12. See Sharp, *Agrarian Revolt*, ch. 1.
13. See R. England, *The Colonization of Western Canada* (London 1936), 86, 310–11, and *Report on the Seventh Census of Canada* (1931), "Population of Canada by Racial Origins" (Ottawa 1933).
14. The best discussions of the League are in Sharp, *Agrarian Revolt*, and Macpherson, *Democracy in Alberta*.
15. Salem Bland, Methodist clergyman and professor at Wesley College in Winnipeg, a notable preacher of the Social Gospel, was dismissed from the College in 1917 for his radical views. He remained a social gospeller and later wrote a column for the Toronto *Star*. Fred Dixon, a close friend of Woodsworth, ran as Social Democratic candidate in the 1910 Manitoba provincial election, was elected in 1914, and edited the *Western Labour News* with Woodsworth during the Winnipeg Strike and was arrested with him. William Irvine, at various times in his career Labour and UFA MP, CCF MP, pamphleteer, journalist, and preacher, was, in one way or another, always in the van of western radicalism.
16. Macpherson, *Democracy in Alberta*, 39, n. 26; Sharp, *Agrarian Revolt*, 102–3.
17. Reprinted in *Alberta Labour News*, Sept. 26, 1925.
18. See Macpherson, *Democracy in Alberta*, ch. 2; Morton, "The Social Philosophy of Henry Wise Wood," *Agricultural History*, XXII (April 1948), 114–23; and W. K. Rolph, *Henry Wise Wood of Alberta* (Toronto 1950).
19. William Irvine, *The Farmers in Politics* (Toronto 1920), 56–7.

20. *Declaration of Ultimate Objectives* (n.p., n.d., [c. Feb. 1933]), CCFP.
21. *The Co-operative Commonwealth Federation (Farmer, Labour, Socialist), An Outline of its Origins, Organization and Objectives* . . . (Calgary, n.d. [c. 1932]), CCFP.
22. *How the CCF Got Started* (Regina, n.d., mimeo), CCFP.
23. *Report of the Royal Commission on Dominion-Provincial Relations* (Ottawa 1954), Bk. I, 169.
24. Interview with M. J. Coldwell, July 1962.
25. Transcript of interviews with T. C. Douglas by C. Higginbotham, 1958–60.
26. *Canadian Annual Review, 1930–31* (Toronto 1931), 258.
27. Lipset, *Agrarian Socialism*, 104.
28. Morton, *Progressive Party*, 280; Coldwell, *Left Turn*, 3.
29. See McNaught, *A Prophet*, 147–8.
30. The rise and fall of the many labour parties and the Labour Representation League is catalogued in the annual reports of the Department of Labour, *Labour Organization in Canada* (Ottawa 1910–59).
31. Interview with Robert Skinner, July 1966. See also the unpublished MA thesis by R. Grantham, "Some Aspects of the Socialist Movement in British Columbia, 1898–1933" (University of British Columbia 1942), Appendix 15.
32. *Alberta Labour News*, Nov. 2, 1929.
33. *Manitoba Free Press*, Oct. 28, 1929, Regina *Leader-Post*, Oct. 26, 1929.
34. Interview with Coldwell, July 1962.
35. "Minutes of the Western Conference of Labour Political Parties," 26–7, Oct. 1929, CCFP.
36. *Ibid.*, 1930.
37. *Ibid.*, July 6, 1931.
38. *Ibid.*, July 17, 1931.
39. *Ibid.*, July 31, 1931.
40. *Ibid.*
41. *Ibid.*, and see also *Manitoba Free Press*, July 18, 1931, and "Minutes of the Western Conference," 1931, CCFP.
42. "Minutes of the Western Conference," 1931. For the first time, delegates are referred to as "comrade."
43. Morton, *Progressive Party*, 279–81, and see below.
44. *Alberta Labour News*, July 18, 1931.
45. G. Woodsworth, "Trade Unions and Political Action," *Labour Statesman*, Sept. 18, 1931.
46. McNaught, *A Prophet*, 168.
47. J. S. Woodsworth in *The Independent*, March 24, 1922, cited in McNaught, *A Prophet*, 164.
48. See the unpublished MA thesis (Toronto 1961) of Gerald Caplan, "Socialism and Anti-Socialism in Ontario, 1932–45," *passim*.
49. The group consisted of Robert Gardiner (who became leader of the UFA in 1931), E. J. Garland, H. E. Spencer, G. G. Coote, D. M. Kennedy, J. T. Shaw, all of the UFA; M. N. Campbell of Saskatchewan; W. J. Ward of Manitoba; Preston Elliot, W. C. Good, and Agnes Macphail of the United Farmers of Ontario.
50. CCFP and Henry Spencer Papers, PAC. According to W. Eggleston, "Groups and the Election," *Toronto Star*, June 6, 1930, the document was drawn up following the budget debate of that year.
51. McNaught, *A Prophet*, 259–60; Woodsworth Papers, scrapbook, v. 1932–7, PAC; and see also *How the CCF Got Started*.
52. LSR *Manifesto*, papers in the possession of Professor G. M. A. Grube. See also F. R. Scott, "A Decade of the League for Social Reconstruction," *Saturday Night*, Jan. 24, 1942.
53. LSR *Manifesto*.
54. See the unpublished MA thesis (Toronto 1953) by Margaret Prang, "Some Opinions of Political Radicalism between Two World Wars."
55. LSR "Minutes," 1935, Grube Papers.
56. Transcript of an interview with Fred White in the possession of Professor Paul Fox. White was a member of the Dominion Labour party in Alberta.
57. *Ibid.*
58. See Dorothy Steeves, *The Compassionate Rebel* (Vancouver 1960), ch. 7.
59. See *Hansard*, 1935, 446 ff. In an interview with the author Frank Underhill described Irvine's address at Toronto's Hygeia Hall in 1932 as "pure social credit."
60. See W. Kornhauser, *The Politics of Mass Society* (London 1960), ch. 4; Wendell King, *Social Movements in the United States* (New York 1956), ch. 1; and Erich Fromm, *The Fear of Freedom* (London 1942), ch. 4, esp. 114–16. Ostrogorski commented on the isolation of the individual in America in 1902. See M. Ostrogorski, *Democracy and the Organization of Political Parties*, S. M. Lipset, ed. (New York 1964), II, 307–9. John Porter points out that "it is indisputable that some form of group affiliation lying between the extremes of the mass and the individual is a prerequisite for mutual health." *The Vertical Mosaic* (Toronto 1964), 73.

The Formation and Rise to Power
of the Union Nationale*
HERBERT F. QUINN

The Union Nationale had its origin in a revolt which took place within the ranks of the Liberal party in the early 1930's. This revolt began when a group of young left-wing Liberals, who called themselves L'Action Libérale Nationale (ALN), became dissatisfied with the party's conservative economic policies and the tight control exercised over the party organization by Taschereau and a few close colleagues. The leader of the ALN was Paul Gouin, the son of a former Liberal Prime Minister of Quebec and grandson of Honoré Mercier. Gouin and his associates, like most of the younger generation, had been influenced greatly by the nationalistic ideas of Bourassa, Groulx, and members of L'Action Nationale (formerly L'Action Française). As a consequence, they were alarmed at the threat which industrialism presented to the survival of the traditional French-Canadian culture and were critical of the close ties which existed between the Taschereau administration and the foreign capitalists.[1]

433

The original plan of the ALN was to reform the Liberal party from within by forcing it to shift to the left in its economic and social policies and by persuading it to adopt a more nationalistic philosophy. However, within a short time the Gouin group became convinced of the futility of trying to reform the party or break the control of the ruling oligarchy. As a result, the ALN severed all connections with the Liberals shortly before the provincial election of 1935 and set itself up as a separate political party. Aside from Gouin, other key figures in the ALN at that time were Oscar Drouin, who was to become chief organizer of the new party, J. E. Grégoire, mayor of Quebec City, and Dr. Philippe Hamel, a dentist by profession, also from Quebec City. Both Grégoire and Hamel were bitter enemies of what they termed "the electricity trust" and for some years had been campaigning for the nationalization of the power companies.

When the ALN was launched it met with a favourable response from many sections of the population since its ideas conformed with the nationalist ideology then sweeping the province. It was endorsed by the influential L'Action Nationale,[2] and was looked upon favourably by the Union Catholique des Cultivateurs[3] and other Catholic Action groups. The new party had one handicap, however: most of its key figures had had little practical experience in politics. Very few of them had ever been candidates in either provincial or federal elections or played any kind of active

*From *The Union Nationale: A Study in Quebec Nationalism,* by Herbert F. Quinn. © University of Toronto Press 1963. Abridged for *Prophecy and Protest,* edited by Clark et al. Copyright 1975 by Gage Publishing Limited. Reprinted by permission.

political role before. In contrast, their Liberal opponents were skilled politicians, strongly entrenched in office, and with a powerful and well-financed political machine. Moreover, in a province where traditional habits of voting were an important factor in politics, the Liberals had been looked upon as the party of the French Canadian ever since 1897. In many families, particularly in the rural areas, political affiliation was inherited with the family farm, and a large number of people were Liberal for no better reason than the fact that their fathers had always voted that way. It was only too apparent that Taschereau's administration was not going to be easily dislodged by a new and untried party, led by a group of young men who, however idealistic and enthusiastic, had little knowledge of the "know how" of the political game. For all these reasons there were obvious advantages for the ALN in making an alliance with some other group equally opposed to the Liberal administration, but with more political experience and with a better electoral organization. The only group which could meet these requirements was the provincial Conservative party. A brief look at the political history of that party will indicate why it might be receptive to such an alliance.

434

The Conservative party had been the official opposition in the Quebec Legislature ever since its defeat at the polls in the election of 1897. From that time onward it was only on a few occasions that the party had been able to capture sufficient seats to present the Liberals with any kind of challenge. It suffered from its close association with the federal Conservative party which was, of course, looked upon by the average voter as the party of "British Imperialism," and, above all, as the party which had imposed conscription in 1917.

The leader of the Quebec Conservative party during the greater part of the 1920's was Arthur Sauvé, member of the Legislative Assembly for the electoral district of Deux Montagnes, who had become party leader in 1916. Acutely aware of the disadvantageous position in which his party was placed by its close connections with the federal Conservatives, Sauvé was determined to make every effort to dissociate the Quebec Conservative party from its federal counterpart. When the nationalist movement of Abbé Groulx and L'Action Française began to gain ground following the brief postwar depression of 1921 Sauvé adopted most of its ideas and slogans. He also gave his party a new orientation in matters of economic and social policy. Although the Conservatives, like the Liberals, had been staunch supporters of laissez-faire capitalism during most of their history, the party now took a turn to the left. Sauvé began to criticize the role of foreign capital in the industrial development of the province and to attack the Liberals for their generous concessions to the business interests. In one election speech he made this statement: "Our natural resources must serve not only the ends of speculators, but the welfare of contemporary classes and of the generations to come. . . . The government . . . has sold our wealth to foreigners who shared with ministers and politicians, while our own people emigrated from the province." Sauvé proposed "that we develop, as far as possible, our natural resources by our own people and for our people."[4]

Sauvé's attempt to dissociate his party from the federal Conservatives was only partly successful. It is true that the new orientation which he gave the Quebec Conservative party won it the editorial support of *Le Devoir* and *L'Action Catholique*,[5] and that it was soon on friendly terms with such groups as the UCC whose agitation for a government-sponsored scheme of low-cost rural credit had been turned down by the Liberals. Sauvé was not able, however, to convince the vast majority of voters that the Quebec Conservatives were completely independent of the federal organization.[6] The reason for this failure is not hard to find. Sauvé's party still contained a strong right wing which was closely associated with the business interests and had strong ties with the federal Conservatives. This right wing had always been critical of his policies. In giving up the leadership shortly after the defeat suffered by his party in the 1927 election Sauvé attacked this group for its hostile attitude:

435

Une fraction du parti conservateur fédéral a toujours été hostile à ma direction. On m'accuse de nationalisme. Le nationalisme que j'ai prêché et pratiqué est celui de Cartier, c'est le conservatisme intégral et foncièrement national . . . Mes efforts n'ont pas été couronnés de succès. Il convient donc que je laisse le commandement du parti . . . .[7]

In 1929 Camillien Houde, mayor of Montreal and member of the provincial legislature for Montreal-Ste Marie, succeeded Sauvé as party leader. Houde was a colourful politician who was to play an important role in municipal and provincial politics for the next twenty years. In the eastern and working class section of Montreal where he had been brought up Houde was affectionately known as "le petit gars de Ste Marie." Like Sauvé, Houde was a nationalist with radical ideas but he showed a greater readiness to compromise on policy if the situation demanded it. Moreover, he was a much more dynamic and hard-hitting politician than his predecessor.

In the election campaign of 1931 Houde followed the same line of attack as Sauvé. His main accusation against the Liberals was that they had turned over the natural resources and wealth of the province to foreign capitalists, and he referred to them as "a nest of traitors to their race and their province."[8] His platform consisted of a number of social reforms which trade unions, the farmers' organizations, and other groups had been demanding for a long time: government pensions for widows and the aged, a reduction in electricity rates, an intensified programme of colonization, the establishment of a Ministry of Labour, and a government-sponsored scheme of low-cost rural credit.[9] Houde waged a vigorous campaign in all parts of the province and hopes were high in the ranks of the party that it would be able to defeat the Liberals. However, the latter emerged victorious once more and Houde himself lost his seat in the Assembly. When he resigned from the leadership a year later the party decided to call a convention made up of delegates from all parts of the province for the purpose of selecting a successor.

The Quebec Conservative party's convention of 1933 was one of the most famous in the history of the province. Before the convention met, the name most prominently mentioned for the leadership was Maurice Duplessis. The son of a judge and a lawyer by profession, Duplessis had started his career in politics when he was elected as Conservative member to the Legislative Assembly from the electoral district of Three Rivers in 1927. (He was to be returned to the legislature by the constituency in every election from that time until his sudden death in 1959.) Duplessis soon built up a reputation in the Assembly as a clever debater and able parliamentarian. He was also adept at those skilful manoeuvres which are an asset in rising to the top in the field of politics. A short while after Houde lost his seat in the Legislative Assembly in the election of 1931, Duplessis was chosen as temporary leader of the party in that House.

When the Conservative convention started its proceedings in the city of Sherbrooke on October 3, 1933, the delegates were divided into two factions.[10] One of them supported Duplessis as leader, and the other supported Onésime Gagnon, a Conservative member of the federal Parliament. The Gagnon faction had been organized by Camillien Houde, who was determined to block Duplessis' bid for the leadership. Houde's antagonism towards Duplessis arose out of a disagreement which had developed between these two forceful personalities shortly after the 1931 election over matters of party strategy. But Houde was not successful in his attempt to prevent Duplessis from capturing the leadership. While the latter had been temporary leader of the party in the Assembly he had built up a considerable following within the party ranks, and as a result, he had control of the party machine by the time the convention was called. The chairman of that convention was one of his supporters. Moreover, he had the influential backing of most of the Conservative members of the federal Parliament from Quebec, and these federal Conservatives participated in the convention as voting delegates. When the time came for the balloting Duplessis was elected leader by 334 votes to 214 for his opponent.

Although it was not apparent at the time, the political ideas of the new Conservative leader differed from those of Sauvé and Houde in one very important respect. Duplessis was certainly a nationalist, but he was by no means a radical. As subsequent events were to show, he was a "practical politician" whose main objective was to defeat the Taschereau government and put the Conservative party in its place rather than to bring about sweeping economic and social reforms. However, it was only after the Union Nationale's victory over the Liberals in 1936 that the economic conservatism of Duplessis was to be fully revealed.[11]

When Duplessis took over the Conservative leadership he inherited a party which had won only fourteen out of ninety seats in the previous election,[12] a party whose chances of defeating the Liberals did not appear to be any brighter than they had been at any other time during the preceding thirty-five years. There were obvious advantages, with little to lose, in making an alliance with another group, such as L'Action Libérale

Nationale, which was equally opposed to the Liberals. If the Conservative party could supply the practical knowledge of the techniques of politics and some of the financial backing, the ALN could provide new men, new ideas, and considerable popular support.

Thus, a short while before the provincial election of November 25, 1935, Duplessis and Gouin entered into negotiations with a view to forming a united front against the Taschereau administration. These negotiations were successful and on November 8 the two leaders issued a joint statement announcing that their respective parties had joined forces against the Liberals. This statement read in part, "Répondant au désir de l'électorat du Québec, le parti conservateur provincial et L'Action Libérale Nationale déclarent par leurs représentants attirés qu'aux élections du 25 novembre, ils présenteront un front uni contre l'ennemi commun du peuple de la province de Québec: le régime Taschereau."[13] The new coalition was to be known as the Union Nationale Duplessis-Gouin.

The Duplessis-Gouin combination was soon joined by a number of independent nationalists who had hitherto taken little or no active part in politics, although many of them were leaders of various Catholic Action and patriotic organizations. The outstanding figures among these independents were Albert Rioux, a former president of the UCC, and René Chaloult, a Quebec City lawyer who was one of the directors of L'Action Nationale.

Undoubtedly one of the most important aspects of the Union Nationale was the nature of the programme which it presented to the electorate. This programme was significant in two respects: for the first time in the history of the province a political movement presented to the electorate a clear-cut and comprehensive set of proposals for economic, social, and political reform; secondly, this programme was to lay down the basic principles which were to be followed by all reform movements in the province for the next decade or so. It is essential, therefore, to understand just how this programme originated, and the particular proposals for reform it put forward.

The nationalist intellectuals of the twenties, in spite of their campaign against the industrial system, had never formulated any concrete and coherent programme of social reform and had not been in agreement as to how the industrialists were to be curbed. In other words, their critique of the economic system was stronger than their positive suggestions for its transformation. With the spread of nationalistic sentiments to the masses of the people in the early thirties it soon became apparent that such a constructive programme was urgently needed. It was the Roman Catholic hierarchy which provided the nationalists with the positive proposals for which they had been looking, proposals which were the result of a new orientation taking place in the social thinking of the Church after 1930. . . .

In the early thirties a change took place in the social thinking of the Quebec hierarchy and it was prompted to put forward a programme of reform which would come to grips with the problems of an urban and

437

industrial society. An immediate reason was that the breakdown of the capitalist system in the depression focussed attention on certain social problems arising out of that system which could no longer be ignored. Even more persuasive was the appearance in 1931 of the encyclical, *Quadragesimo Anno*, of Pope Pius XI. This encyclical was the most important papal pronouncement on social questions since *Rerum Novarum*, and had a tremendous influence on Catholic thought in all parts of the world, including Quebec. Its purpose was to reaffirm the basic principles laid down in the early encyclical and to clarify and re-interpret those principles in the light of the changes which had taken place in industrial capitalism since the 1890's. Like his predecessor, Pius rejected both laissez-faire capitalism and socialism, although recognizing that one wing of the latter movement, democratic socialism, had moved away from the more extreme position of the Marxists. The Pope's critique of capitalism was expressed in statements such as this: " . . . the immense number of propertyless wage earners on the one hand, and the superabundant riches of the fortunate few on the other, is an unanswerable argument that the earthly goods so abundantly produced in this age of industrialism are far from rightly distributed and equitably shared among the various classes of men."[14] As a remedy for this situation, he called for a redistribution of private property.

A related consideration, nearer to home, also prompted the Quebec hierarchy to take a particular stand on the problems arising from the industrialization of that province. The depression had resulted in widespread dissatisfaction with the capitalist system, and unless the Church put forward a programme of reform within the framework of Catholic social philosophy it was quite conceivable that it would be faced by the growth of a socialist or communist movement which might very well be not only secularistic but even militantly atheistic. The need to take some positive action seemed all the more imperative to the hierarchy when the Co-operative Commonwealth Federation (CCF), an avowedly socialist party, was formed in western Canada in 1932 and announced its intention of spreading its doctrines to all provinces. An eminent theologian who had been assigned the task of making a careful study of the social philosophy of the new party came to the conclusion that the CCF "did not merit the support of Catholics" because of its promotion of the class war, its extensive programme of socialization, and "its materialistic conception of the social order."[15] A different solution to the problems of the day was imperative.

The responsibility for the formulation of the Church's programme of reform was entrusted by the hierarchy to an organization sponsored by the Jesuit Order in Montreal called the Ecole Sociale Populaire. This was not actually a school in the ordinary sense but an organization which had been set up before the First World War for the purpose of studying and propagating the teachings of the Church on a wide range of moral, educational, and social problems.

The Montreal Jesuits did not themselves draw up the proposed programme. Instead they called together a group of prominent Catholic laymen and gave them the assignment of outlining a set of proposals which would be a concrete application of the principles put forward in *Quadragesimo Anno* to the specific conditions and problems peculiar to Quebec. This group of laymen was composed of individuals playing a leading role in all phases of French-Canadian life: the Catholic trade unions, the farmers' organizations, the co-operatives and credit unions, the patriotic and professional societies, the universities. The most prominent members of the group were Albert Rioux, president of the Union Catholique des Cultivateurs; Alfred Charpentier, one of the leaders of the Catholic unions; Wilfrid Guérin, secretary of the Caisses Populaires, or credit unions, in the Montreal area; Esdras Minville, a professor at the Ecole des Hautes Etudes Commerciales in Montreal; and Dr. Philippe Hamel and René Chaloult of Quebec City. Most of these people were also directors of L'Action Nationale.

439

The Ecole Sociale Populaire published the conclusions arrived at by this study group in a pamphlet entitled *Le Programme de restauration sociale* which appeared in the fall of 1933.[16] This pamphlet contained proposals for reform in four different areas. "Rural Reconstruction" suggested the steps which should be taken to strengthen and even extend the agrarian sector of the economy; "The Labour Question" put forward an extensive scheme of labour and social legislation which would raise the incomes and provide greater economic security for the working class; "Trusts and Finance" dealt with measures which should be taken to curb the power of the public utilities and other large business enterprises; and, "Political Reforms" called for legislation which would eliminate patronage politics and electoral and administrative corruption.

We come now to the immediate background of the programme of the Union Nationale. The relationship of this programme to the proposals of the Ecole Sociale Populaire can be traced back to the formation of L'Action Libérale Nationale. Paul Gouin, its leader, had not been a member of the group of Catholic laymen who had drawn up and formally affixed their signatures to *Le Programme de restauration sociale*, but he was in general sympathy with the ideas put forward for he had participated in some of the discussions leading up to the final proposals. It was not too surprising, therefore, that when he launched the ALN a short while later he adopted the Ecole Sociale Populaire document as the basis for his own programme.[17] He did, however, make some minor changes, and included a few additional proposals of his own. When the alliance with Duplessis was arranged the following year one of the basic conditions which Gouin insisted upon was that the Conservative leader accept the complete ALN programme. In the light of later developments it is important to make it quite clear that Duplessis agreed to this condition at the time.[18] One of the clauses in the joint statement issued by the two leaders announcing the formation of the Union Nationale states this firmly:

Après la défaite du régime anti-national et trustard de M. Taschereau, le parti conservateur provincial et L'Action Libérale Nationale formeront un gouvernement national dont le programme sera celui de l'Action Libérale Nationale, programme qui s'inspire des mêmes principes que celui du parti conservateur provincial.[19]

One other significant aspect of the Duplessis-Gouin programme should be mentioned here. The fact that the reforms proposed by the two leaders were based on *Le Programme de restauration sociale* was a decisive factor in winning the support of such influential figures as Rioux, Hamel, and Chaloult, all of whom had participated in the drawing-up of the Jesuit-inspired programme. . . .

The formation of the Union Nationale meant that for the first time since the days of Honoré Mercier in the 1880's a powerful nationalist movement had arisen to play an important role in provincial politics. Like Mercier's party, the Union Nationale was determined to maintain all those traditional values and rights which had always been considered essential for cultural survival. It differed, however, in that it was also concerned with a problem which, in the nature of things, Mercier did not have to contend with. This was the Union Nationale's determination to raise the economic status of the French Canadian by bringing about extensive reforms in the system of industrial capitalism. For this reason the Duplessis-Gouin coalition must be described, not merely as a nationalist movement, but as a radical nationalist movement.[20]

Perhaps the greatest source of strength of the Union Nationale was the fact that it had the unofficial, but nevertheless effective support of all the various Catholic Action and patriotic organizations across the province: the Catholic trade unions, the farmers' organizations, the co-operative and the credit unions, the youth organizations, the associations of French-Canadian businessmen and merchants. All of these organizations were supposed to be neutral in politics, but as pointed out earlier, they were all strongly nationalistic and therefore opposed to the Liberal party's policy towards the industrialists.[21] Moreover, many of the leaders of these organizations had participated in drawing up the programme of the Ecole Sociale Populaire which the Union Nationale had adopted. Needless to say, the new movement also had the enthusiastic backing of such nationalist publications as *L'Action Nationale* and the Montreal daily, *Le Devoir*. There was little doubt too that, although the hierarchy was careful that the Church as such should not become directly involved on one side or the other in the political struggle, most of the clergy were sympathetic towards the political movement which had adopted its programme of social reform.

As a result of the wide support behind the Union Nationale the Liberals, for the first time in nearly forty years, were presented with a real challenge to their continued control over the provincial administration. The seriousness of this threat was to become apparent in the election of 1935, the first test of strength of the Duplessis-Gouin combination.

The Union Nationale Comes to Power

When Paul Gouin and a few other young Liberals formed L'Action Libérale Nationale in 1934 and began to attack the policies of the Liberal "old guard," neither Taschereau nor any of his colleagues took the new movement very seriously. It was only when the Gouin group began to win wider support, and then joined forces with the Liberals' traditional enemy, the Conservative party, that Taschereau slowly began to recognize the serious nature of the challenge with which he was faced. He was still confident, however, that his party would be able to weather the storm and retain control over the provincial adminstration as it had done so often in the past. . . .

When the election of 1935 was called, Taschereau toured the province denouncing the Union Nationale coalition as "un mariage qui va se terminer par un désastreux divorce."[22] He accused Duplessis of abandoning the principles for which the Conservative party stood and attacked Gouin for betraying the ideals of his father, Sir Lomer Gouin, who had preceded Taschereau as leader of the Liberal party. Taschereau also defended the policies which his administration had pursued in the past and contended that these policies had been of immeasurable benefit to the farmer, the worker, and other sections of the population. Although the Liberals had never shown much enthusiasm for the Ecole Sociale Populaire programme,[23] Taschereau promised to introduce some of the reforms which it put forward, such as old age pensions and a government-sponsored scheme of low-cost farm credit.

441

However, the Liberals did not rely on the introduction of a few reforms to win the support of the electorate. They had even more tangible benefits to offer. As in the past the government embarked on an extensive programme of public works several months before the election. New roads, public buildings, and bridges were built, or at least started, in all parts of the province. Some of these projects were discontinued the day after the election. The public works programme provided additional, if temporary employment, and meant sizable government orders for local hardware merchants and shopkeepers in various towns and villages. Whenever the government provided a community with some badly needed public facility it was able to present itself as a "benefactor" which had "done something" for that particular town or district. This was an important consideration for the average Quebec voter when he was trying to decide which party to vote for. Government candidates in most electoral districts also spent fairly large sums of money on the distribution of drinks of "whisky blanc" and handed out other gifts and favours which might help to convince the voters that the Liberals were "des bons garçons." . . .

The well-entrenched position of the Liberals, and their readiness to use all kinds of questionable tactics, obviously placed the Union Nationale in a disadvantageous position in the election campaign of 1935. However, shortly after the date of the election had been announced, the new coalition entered candidates in every electoral district and proceeded to wage a vigorous campaign in all parts of the province. Its appeal to the electorate was for the most part based on the comprehensive programme of economic and social reform summarized above. The Union Nationale leaders also made strong attacks on the administrative and electoral abuses of the Taschereau government. In spite of the many handicaps under which it fought the election, the Duplessis-Gouin combination succeeded in capturing a total of forty-two seats, almost four times the number of seats held by the Conservative opposition in the previous legislature.[24] Although the Liberals, with forty-eight members elected, still maintained control over the administration, they had only a narrow margin of six seats — five after the Speaker had been elected.

The results of the election were a serious setback for the Taschereau régime. The gains made by the Union Nationale coalition completely changed the situation in the legislature where the Liberals had always had an overwhelming majority and had thus been able to put their legislative programme through with a minimum of obstruction. After the 1935 election the government was not only faced by a large and vigorous opposition, but one of the leaders of that opposition, Maurice Duplessis, was an astute politician who knew all the tricks of the parliamentary game.

When the 1936 session of the legislature was called, Duplessis used the many delaying tactics of the experienced parliamentarian to hold up the passing of the budget until such time as the government agreed to enact some of the proposals outlined in the Union Nationale programme. The result was that as time went on the government found itself in increasing financial difficulties. The most telling blow struck by Duplessis, however, and the one which was to sound the death knell of the Taschereau régime, was the information he was able to bring to light concerning the administration's handling of public funds.

Ever since the early 1920's, the Conservative party had been accusing the Liberals of graft, corruption, and inefficiency in the administration of government departments. Owing to the weakness of the party in the legislature, however, it had never been able to coerce the government into setting up a parliamentary inquiry to investigate these alleged irregularities. The Public Accounts Committee, which was supposed to maintain a close check on how public money was being spent, had not met for a long time. Even if it had been called into session at any time before the election of 1935, the huge Liberal majority would have been able to dominate proceedings and prevent any serious investigation from taking place. In the legislature of 1936, however, the Liberals no longer enjoyed this strategic advantage. The opposition was not only successful in bringing the Public Accounts Committee back to life, but the strength of its forces in that Committee made it difficult for the Liberals to control the inquiry.

The Public Accounts Committee was in session from May 5 to June 11, and under the skilful probing of Duplessis it quickly brought to light a picture of patronage, nepotism, and the squandering of public funds which involved most government departments.[25] It was discovered that members of the administration, from cabinet ministers down to the lowest level of the civil service, were using the contacts and influence which they had as government officials to increase their private incomes and those of their friends and relatives. Certain officials made a substantial income by selling materials of all kinds to various government departments at very high prices. One such case involved the director of the government-run School of Fine Arts who made sizable profits from the sale of automobile license plates to the government.[26] The Treasury lost many thousands of dollars every year through the inflated travelling expenses of ministers and other individuals; this was especially true of the expenditures of the Department of Colonization.[27] One of the most startling discoveries was that a brother of the Prime Minister, who was the accountant of the Legislative Assembly, had been putting the interest on bank deposits of government money into his own personal account. His only defence was that all his predecessors in the position of Assembly accountant had done the same thing.[28] . . .

443

The revelations of the Public Accounts Committee created a sensation throughout the province and completely discredited the Taschereau administration. Around the beginning of June, when the committee was still in the midst of its deliberations, Taschereau suddenly announced his resignation as Prime Minister and recommended to the Lieutenant Governor that Adelard Godbout, Minister of Agriculture, be appointed in his place. At the same time the Legislative Assembly was dissolved and a new election was called for the following August. . . .

Godbout appeared determined to set up a government, not only of new men, but also of new policies, for he recognized the extent of the dissatisfaction throughout the province with the economic system and the widespread desire for social reform. When the election campaign of 1936 got under way he put forward a programme which was similar in many respects to that of the Union Nationale. The main proposals in that programme were: an extension of rural credit facilities, a programme of rural electrification, and the provision of subsidies on certain farm products; an intensified colonization programme; a sweeping reduction of electricity rates throughout the province; a public works programme to solve the problem of unemployment; a minimum wage scale for industrial workers not covered by collective labour agreements, and the introduction of certain amendments to the Workmen's Compensation Act requested by the trade unions; the establishment of a system of needy mothers' allowances; and the elimination of the practice of cabinet ministers accepting directorships from companies doing business with the government.[29] . . .

The election of 1936 was to demonstrate that the deathbed conversion of the Liberal party to social reform and honest administration had come too late. All through the election the opposition forces attacked the Liberals for the administrative and political corruption of the Taschereau régime and refused to absolve the Godbout government from the sins of the previous administration. They strongly denied that it was "a government of new men." As stated by Duplessis, "M. Godbout est l'héritier de M. Taschereau. . . . En politique comme ailleurs, l'héritier d'un régime assume la responsabilité des dettes et des méfaits de son auteur. . . ."[30] In another speech later in the campaign he repeated the charge that there had been no real change of direction: "Le gouvernement Godbout est une nouvelle pousse des branches décrépites du gouvernement Taschereau. . . . Pouvez-vous avoir confiance en un régime qui refuse de punir les voleurs d'élections en favorisant des lois électorales malhonnêtes? Lorsqu'un régime refuse de protéger la source même de la démocratie, on ne peut avoir confiance en lui."[31] Duplessis promised that if the Union Nationale was elected to office it would continue the investigations begun by the Public Accounts Committee into the administrative practices of the Taschereau régime, and all those found guilty of misusing public funds would be punished. A clean sweep would be made of the whole administration, graft and corruption would be eliminated, and an end would be put to the squandering of government money. . . .

444

Perhaps one of the most telling aspects of the Union Nationale's campaign was its appeal to the nationalistic and anti-English sentiments of the French-Canadian population. Antagonism towards the English reached a peak as Union Nationale orators, in meeting after meeting, warned the people of Quebec that their cultural values and their traditional way of life were threatened by the dominant role played by the British, American, and English-Canadian industrialists in the economic life of the province. The strong feelings of the nationalists towards "les étrangers" were forcibly expressed in a speech delivered at a mass meeting in Montreal by Dr. Phillippe Hamel, the outstanding opponent of the large corporations, and particularly of "le trust de l'électricité":

Or notre patrie, notre foi, nos traditions, nos libertés, tout cela est menacé. Nos ressources naturelles, elles ont été vendues par le régime pour un plat de lentilles aux étrangers. Vos foyers, ouvriers, on est en train de vous les arracher et déjà la lutte s'organise contre votre clocher par de sourdes menées anticléricales qui se font plus audacieuses et violentes.[32]

At another meeting Hamel's close associate, J. E. Grégoire of Quebec City, spoke in similar vein of the usurpations of "les étrangers":

. . . . une calamité nous étreint de toutes parts. Chacun est exploité, l'épicier canadien-français, le bûcheron, le petit propriétaire. Les meilleures places sont prises par des étrangers. . . . Les usines sont fermées, parce que notre province a été vendue aux étrangers. Les produits agricoles ne se vendent pas, parce que l'on a fermé nos débouchés.[33]

. . . .

The Union Nationale's appeal to the nationalistic sentiments of the French Canadian, and its promises of economic, social, and administrative reform, met with an unequivocal response from the electorate. When the time came for the balloting the people of Quebec turned the Liberal party out of office and elected the nationalist movement led by Maurice Duplessis. The Union Nationale won seventy-six out of the ninety seats in the legislature, while the Liberals with only fourteen seats were now in the novel position of being the official opposition.[34]

The chain of events leading to the Union Nationale victory of 1936 shows two things. First of all, the Quebec voter seemed to be convinced that the time had come for a government housecleaning, the elimination of graft and corruption, and the introduction of extensive reforms in administrative and electoral practices. Even more important, the success of this new nationalist movement was a clear indication of the strong opposition which had developed to the Liberal party's policy of promoting the industrialization of the province through the intervention of foreign capital. The defeat of the Liberals was a protest, not only against an economic system which had changed the traditional way of life and brought economic insecurity in its wake, but also against the dominant role played by English-speaking industrialists in the system. This protest was accompanied by a demand that the new capitalist economy be reformed and modified and that positive steps be taken to enable the French Canadian to regain control over the wealth and natural resources of his province. The direction these reforms were to take was to be determined by the principles of social Catholicism as laid down in the encyclicals of Pope Leo XIII and Pope Pius XI.

445

Notes

1. Many of Gouin's ideas are to be found in a number of speeches which he delivered to various groups in the 1930s and which are collected in his *Servir, I, La Cause nationale* (Montreal, 1938).
2. Mason Wade, *The French Canadians*, 1760–1945 (Toronto, 1955), p. 906.
3. See statement of A. Rioux, president of UCC, *Le Devoir*, 7 août 1934.
4. *Montreal Star*, May 10, 1927.
5. Robert Rumilly, *Histoire de la Province de Québec, xxvi, Rayonnement de Québec* (Montreal, 1953), p. 157.
6. This was an important factor in the Liberal victory over the Conservatives in the provincial election of 1927. See Jean Hamelin, Jacques Letarte, and Marcel Hamelin, "Les Elections provinciales dans le Québec," *Cahiers de Géographie de Québec*, 7 (oct. 1959–mars 1960), 39. See also, "L'Election provinciale de 1927: les conservateurs de Québec battus par les conservateurs d'Ottawa," *Le Devoir*, 11 fév. 1950.
7. Robert Rumilly, *Histoire de la Province de Québec, xxix, Vers l'âge d'or* (Montreal, 1956), p. 98.
8. *Montreal Star*, July 6, 1931.
9. *Canadian Annual Review*, 1932, p. 165.
10. A detailed description of the organization proceedings of the convention is to be found in *La Presse*, 30 sept. -5 oct. 1933. See also Pierre Laporte, "Il y a 25 ans, la convention de Sherbrooke," *Le Devoir*, 1–3 oct. 1958.
11. See H. Quinn, *The Union Nationale*, pp. 73–5.
12. *Ibid.*, Appendix A, Table IV.
13. *Le Devoir*, 8 nov. 1935.
14. Pope Pius XI, *Quadragesimo Anno* (London, 1931), 29.
15. R. P. Georges Levesque, O.P., "La Co-operative Commonwealth Federation," *Pour la restauration sociale au Canada* (Montreal, 1933). An even stronger condemnation of the CCF was made a year later by Archbishop Georges Gauthier of Montreal. See *Montreal Gazette*, Feb. 26, 1934. This ban on the party was not to be lifted until the bishops of Canada, both English and French, issued a joint statement in

1943 declaring that Catholics were free to support any Canadian party except the Communists. See *Canadian Register* (Kingston), Oct. 23, 1943.

16. A. Rioux, *et al.*, *Le Programme de restauration sociale* (Montreal, 1933).

17. Gouin acknowledged his debt to the Ecole Sociale Populaire in a speech which he delivered in August, 1934: "Nous avons pris comme base d'étude et de discussion, pour préparer notre manifeste, le programme de Restauration sociale public sous les auspices de l'Ecole sociale populaire . . . . ce document reflétait de façon assez juste non seulement l'opinion de nos esprits les plus avertis mais aussi les sentiments, les aspirations et les besoins populaires." *Le Devoir*, 13 août 1934.

18. H. Quinn *op. cit.*, chap. v.

19. *Le Devoir*, 8 nov. 1935.

20. In applying the term "radical" to the Union Nationale I mean only, of course, that its approach to economic policy was considered to be radical at the time. Many of its proposals for reform would not be considered very radical today.

21. The leaders of the UCC had always been close to the old provincial Conservative party. Albert Rioux, president of the association until 1936, resigned his post to run as Union Nationale candidate in the election of that year. Several leaders of the Catholic unions supported Union Nationale candidates on the platform in the same election.

22. *Le Devoir*, 11 nov. 1935.

23. When the programme appeared Olivar Asselin, a prominent Liberal, stated, "It bears a greater resemblance to a 'bleu' [Conservative party] pamphlet than to a work of social apostolacy." *Montreal Gazette*, Nov. 21, 1933.

24. See H. Quinn, *The Union Nationale*, Appendix A, Table IV.

25. Although a stenographic report was made of the proceedings of the Public Accounts Committee, this report was never published. Consequently the discussion here of the evidence presented before the committee has had to be based on newspaper reports. For each case at least two sources have been referred to in order to make sure of the accuracy of the reporting. One of the main sources has been Montreal's *La Presse*, a newspaper which has usually been a strong supporter of the Liberal party. Another important source has been a series of articles published in *Le Devoir* shortly after the sessions of the committee had ended and entitled, "M. Godbout était ministre au temps des scandales révélés au comité des comptes publics." *Le Devoir* was anything but friendly towards the Liberals at the time, but these articles are well documented and contain verbatim reports of many of the sessions.

26. See reports in *La Presse*, 13 mai 1936; *Le Devoir*, 23 juillet 1936; *Canadian Annual Review*, 1935-6, p. 283.

27. See *La Presse*, 9, 14, 29 mai and 2, 3, 4 juin 1936; *Canadian Annual Review*, 1935-6, pp. 282-3.

28. See *La Presse*, 5, 6, 9, 10 juin 1936; *Le Devoir*, 6 août 1936; *Sherbrooke Daily Record*, June 12, 1936.

29. These proposals were put forward by Godbout in a radio address. See *La Tribune* (Sherbrooke), 6 juillet 1936.

30. *Le Devoir*, 24 juin 1936.

31. *La Tribune*, 6 août 1936.

32. *Le Devoir*, 13 août 1936.

33. *La Tribune*, 5 août 1936.

34. H. Quinn, *The Union Nationale*, Appendix A, Table IV.

Topic Twelve
World War II and Foreign Affairs

On 10 September 1939 Canada declared war on Germany. For the second time within a quarter of a century, Canadians were involved in a world war. This time, however, Canada entered as an independent nation rather than a colony of Britain as she had at the beginning of the First World War. The Canadian government waited one week after Britain before obtaining parliamentary approval to declare war on Germany. Yet the spirit of independence was short-lived. During the war, and particularly in the formulation of foreign policy in the immediate postwar era, Canada became dependent on the United States.

Canada's notable contribution to the war effort during World War I had provided the initial enthusiasm to achieve greater autonomy during the interwar years. It had not, however, encouraged Canada to build up her military might. In fact, Canadian politicians were committed to keeping the nation out of further European entanglements. Thus Canada was unprepared for war in September 1939. Her initial contribution was mainly economic — the provision of war supplies — although she did participate in the British Commonwealth Air Training Plan and sent a respectable contingent of men overseas. This commitment, however, soon proved inadequate. After the German offensive in the spring of 1940 swept through the Low Countries, conquered France, and threatened to invade Britain itself, Canada was forced into the role of a major participant. This involvement eventually led to the resurrection of the bitter issue of conscription. Despite a pledge not to bring in conscription, the Mackenzie King government was pressured into holding a plebiscite on the issue in 1942 and implementing it in 1944. Once again, as in 1917, the country was divided into its English- and French-speaking sections.

In external relations, Canada was drawing closer to the United States during the war years. In August 1940 the two nations signed the Ogdensburg agreement, which provided for the mutual defence of North America. In 1941 the Hyde Park agreement integrated Canadian and American war production to avoid duplication and to encourage specialized production.

These joint endeavours were followed by others in the war and postwar eras. Canada had passed from the British to the American sphere of influence.

C. P. Stacey outlines Canada's effort in World War II in this abridged version of his introduction to *Arms, Men and Governments: The War Policies of Canada: 1939–1945*. John Holmes provides a synopsis of Canada's external policies in the critical postwar decade in "Canada's External Policies Since 1945."

The best primary source on World War II is J. W. Pickersgill's *The Mackenzie King Record* (Toronto: University of Toronto Press, 1960–70), a four-volume collection of excerpts from the Mackenzie King diaries. Stacey's views are also presented in his recent book, *Canada and the Age of Conflict: A History of Canadian External Policies*, Volume II: *1921–1948: The Mackenzie King Era* (Toronto: University of Toronto Press, 1981). For an understanding of the conscription crisis in World War II, see J. L. Granatstein's *Conscription in the Second World War: 1939–1945* (Toronto: Ryerson, 1969). On foreign policy, see J. Eayrs's *In Defence of Canada*, Vol. III: *Peacemaking and Deterrence* (Toronto: University of Toronto Press, 1972). In addition see the relevant sections of R. Bothwell, I. Drummond, and J. English's *Canada since 1945: Power, Politics and Provincialism* (Toronto: University of Toronto Press, 1981).

448

The Canadian Effort, 1939–1945: A General Survey*

C. P. STACEY

The Approach to War, 1933–1939

The First World War of 1914–18 was in many respects the most important event in Canadian history. In the course of it the Dominion made an unparalleled effort, an effort so great that in 1914 few people would have ventured to forecast its proportions.

Some 425 000 Canadians served overseas, and some 60 000 lost their lives. The record of the Canadian Corps in the bitter fighting on the Western Front was one of sustained distinction. There was a remarkable expansion of Canadian industrial production, and the country proved to have reserves of financial strength hitherto largely unsuspected. The ultimate result was a fundamental change in Canada's status within the

* Abridged from *Arms, Men and Governments: The War Policies of Canada: 1939–1945*, by C. P. Stacey. Copyright 1970 by the Ministry of National Defence. Reprinted by permission of the Minister of Supply and Services Canada.

THE CANADIAN EFFORT, 1939-1945

British community which was evolving from Empire into Commonwealth. The Statute of Westminster of 1931 registered the transformation of the "self-governing colony" of 1914 into a nation which, in law at least, was co-equal with the United Kingdom.

In one respect, however, the hard experience of 1914-18 worked no change in Canada. The country's defence policy remained very much as it had been, founded upon an apparently deep-rooted reluctance to spend money on military preparation in time of peace. As in so many other nations, the years after 1918 witnessed in Canada a revulsion of feeling against war and "militarism". What we can now see as wishful thinking was the order of the day. Because Canadians wished and hoped for peace, they seemed to believe that peace would endure; and they showed no realization of the probable consequences if war did come and found their country unprepared.

This attitude became even more pronounced during the world economic depression which set in in 1929. Canada found herself grappling with ever-increasing problems of unemployment and relief. In spite of the Briand-Kellogg Pact of 1928 renouncing war (which Canada had signed), the international situation continued to be threatening; but public attention was focussed on the sombre aspect of affairs at home. In the four-year period beginning with the fiscal year 1928-29, the national revenue fell from $460 000 000 to $311 000 000. The government of Mr. R. B. Bennett (1930-35) attempted to deal with the situation in the first instance by a policy of drastic retrenchment; and it instituted a sharp reduction in the already small expenditure on national defence. In the fiscal year 1930-31 expenditure on militia, naval, air and associated services was $23 732 000; in 1932-33 it fell to $14 145 000. Even this figure included some provision for unemployment relief and public works construction.[1]

Canada drew out of the depression only slowly. Not until 1938 did the national revenue, rising to $516 000 000, exceed the figure for 1929. The population was growing; but the census of 1931 (the last before the Second World War) showed a total of only 10 376 786 persons, of whom fully 60 per cent lived in the provinces of Quebec and Ontario. The estimated population at 1 September 1939 is 11 295 000.[2]

While the state of the Canadian economy gradually improved, the international outlook grew darker. The clash of arms was heard in both the Far East and Africa. In 1931 Japanese aggression in Manchuria had provided the first major challenge to peace; four years later, when Italy made its unprovoked attack on Ethiopia, and the League of Nations failed to halt it, the League's shaky prestige collapsed.[3] It was, however, in Europe, and more particularly in Germany, that the greatest threat emerged. Adolf Hitler's assumption of power as Chancellor of the Third Reich on 30 January 1933 marked the beginning of another tragic period in German history. Under Hitler's dictatorship the Germans rearmed rapidly, reoccupied the Rhineland (1936), established the Rome-Berlin Axis, and flouted world opinion by seizing Austria in March 1938 and the Sudetenland of

Czechoslovakia later the same year. As if these things were not enough, civil war had broken out in Spain in 1936, raising new problems of intervention by Communist and Fascist sympathizers. The horizon was ringed with conflagrations, and the democratically-minded nations had not yet learned the importance of strength and unity.

The reaction in Canada to these developments was, to put it mildly, cautious. In the general election of 1935, held in the midst of the Ethiopian war, the contending parties showed no disposition whatever to run risks on behalf of collective security or the League of Nations; and the incoming government of Mr. W. L. Mackenzie King, who now formed his third administration, adopted a policy of "no commitments" in advance of an actual serious crisis, using the formula that when the final moment came "Parliament would decide" the country's course. The paramount object was to maintain the unity of the nation. As late as 1936 Mr. King declared in Parliament, "Our country is being drawn into international situations to a degree that I myself think is alarming."[4]

The Canadian defence policy, or lack of one, received a degree of support from the nature of official opinion in the United Kingdom on the imminence of a major war and the need for an expeditionary force. Immediately following the First World War the British government adopted the so-called "Ten Years Rule" — an assumption that the Empire would not be involved in a large-scale conflict for at least ten years, and that defence policies could be planned accordingly. This rule was never formally adopted in Canada, but it became in effect the basis for the annual estimates of the Department of National Defence; and although it seems to have been abandoned in England as early as March 1932, the abandonment had no immediate effect in Canada.[5] The British example influenced Canadian political thinking in another important respect. For a long period British public and official opinion was loath to consider dispatching an expeditionary force to the Continent again in the event of another war; the comfortable view was taken that Britain would do her fighting at sea and in the air. It was not until the spring of 1938 that the British government authorized discussions with French representatives which envisaged the possibility of sending a body of troops to France and, even at this late stage, the result was no more than "a tentative plan for the despatch of two infantry divisions."[6] Only in the spring of 1939, after the German seizure of Czechoslovakia, did Britain begin to contemplate sending a larger force; and again this change of policy found for the moment no echo in Canada.

The impoverished state of Canadian defence in 1935 was revealed in a confidential memorandum prepared for the government by Major-General A. G. L. McNaughton, Chief of the General Staff.[7] He pointed out that there was "not a single modern anti-aircraft gun of any sort in Canada"; that available stocks of ammunition for field artillery represented only "90 minutes' fire at normal rates"; that coast defence armament was obsolescent, when not defective; and that there was not one service aircraft "of a type fit to employ in active operations", nor one service air bomb. Mr.

King's government took steps to repair the gaps in the nation's defences, but its measures were very modest and its action deliberate. The estimates for the fiscal year 1936–37 totalled $29 986 749; this figure was actually slightly less than the equivalent amount ($30 112 589) for the previous year, but a reallocation of appropriations benefitted the services. The estimates for the Militia rose by $1 367 926 to $12 018 926; those for the naval service doubled, to reach $4 853 000, and the appropriation for the air service (including, however, civil air operations) jumped by $2 500 000 to reach $6 809 215.[8] . . .

The policy of "no commitments", adopted to protect the unity of a potentially seriously divided country, was a limiting factor in defence planning which had to be accepted. It led to the programme being represented, to an unrealistic extent, as primarily if not exclusively a scheme of home defence. Thus the Joint Staff Committee, in its basic paper of 5 September 1936,[9] felt it necessary to define the tasks of the Canadian forces in these terms:

451

(a) The direct defence of Canada is the major responsibility of its armed forces.
(b) The indirect defence of Canada by co-operation with other Empire forces in a war overseas is a secondary responsibility of this country, though possibly one requiring much greater ultimate effort.

The last eight words, it is now evident, were the most important part of the definition. The same political factors resulted in much talk — highly theoretical it now appears — of the need for readiness to defend Canada's neutrality in case of a war between the United States and Japan, and in more attention being paid to the defences of the Pacific than to those of the Atlantic coast; though for the latter measure there was the justification that the main strength of the British Fleet lay between Canada and potential aggressors in Europe.

The "Munich Crisis" of September 1938, when Britain and France purchased a brief respite at the cost of sacrificing Czechoslovakia, administered a severe shock to Canadians generally and probably produced among them a more practical appreciation of the situation. At any rate, the defence appropriations provided before the outbreak of war for the fiscal year 1939–40 leaped up to $64 666 874, an impressive figure by the low standards of the time and place.[10] At the same time there was a considerable change in the balance of proposed expenditure as between the three services.

The government had laid down, as early as 1936, certain priorities between the services and between tasks. As stated to the House of Commons in 1939, they were "Fortification of Pacific coast prior to Atlantic coast"; "Development of the air force in priority to navy and, so far as possible, the navy in priority to the militia"; and, finally, "Reorganizing and re-equipping the militia as soon as our resources permit us to do so." There is some reason to believe that these priorities may have been suggested by the Prime Minister. They dictated the tendencies of the programme from 1937 to 1939; but it was only in the latter year that appropriations for the Royal Canadian Air Force actually moved ahead of those for the

Militia, the pre-war round figures being $29 733 000 and $21 397 000 respectively; the Navy got only $8 800 000.[11]

Surveying the individual services' progress towards rearmament in the years immediately before the outbreak of war,[12] we find that the Royal Canadian Navy, long the Cinderella of the nation's defence services, may be said to have remained so in spite of the official priority. Yet though its estimates were still small, they quadrupled during the five-year period beginning in 1934–35; and strength and efficiency grew accordingly, the more so as Canada was able to purchase ships on favourable terms from the British Admiralty. Increased financial provision, however, was in itself only a partial solution, since it was considered that five years were required to train personnel for new vessels.[13] . . .

Because of the higher priorities given the other services, the Militia received proportionately less money than in previous years; in absolute terms, however, there was a considerable increase. Few changes were made in the structure of the regular force, the Permanent Active Militia, and its strength rose only slightly from 3509 all ranks at 31 March 1935 to 4169 four years later. . . . The situation as regards equipment was much less satisfactory. Canada had almost no munition industry of her own, and the circumstances of the time made it difficult to obtain equipment rapidly from her traditional source of supply, the United Kingdom. In 1939, in consequence, the Canadian Militia was still largely armed with the weapons of 1918.

A special aspect of Canadian rearmament was the coast-defence programme. As already mentioned, the Pacific coast had been given priority; but comprehensive plans were prepared in 1936–37 for both coasts. The estimated cost of the programme (not including armament for the works) was about $4 000 000. The focal points were the naval bases of Halifax and Esquimalt.[14] . . .

The Royal Canadian Air Force expanded rapidly in the pre-war years, in keeping with the official recognition of its increased importance. During the four years ending on 31 March 1939 the combined strength of the Permanent and Non-Permanent (after 1 December 1938 the Auxiliary) Active Air Force rose from 157 officers and 945 airmen (of whom 118 and 676 were in the Permanent force) to 360 officers and 2797 airmen; the Permanent strength at the end of the period being 261 and 1930.[15] Three Air Commands (Western, Training and Eastern) were organized; new air stations were established and old ones improved. . . .

As Canada moved reluctantly towards her second major war of the century, public and political opinion were tortured by memories of the conscription controversy of 1917–18. There is no need to describe in detail here this disruptive legacy of the First World War. It is enough to recall the deep rift between French-speaking Canada and the rest of the country which resulted from the enforcement of the Military Service Act of 1917; in particular, the near-isolation of the province of Quebec after the general election in December of that year, and the post-war political consequences in Quebec for the party that was in power when the Military Service Act was passed. These things were enough to make any party leader regard the prospect of another such crisis with extreme alarm, and they certainly provide much of the background for the policy of "no commitments" and for the reluctance of the major parties to identify themselves with any line of action that might seem to involve assuming responsibilities abroad.

Nevertheless, as Hitler's aggression marched on from stage to stage, Canadian public opinion gradually began to show signs of hardening. It became more and more evident, particularly after Munich, that the democratic nations might be forced to fight to halt the advance, and that in that event Canada would not stand aside. In the spring of 1939, after the final German extinguishment of Czechoslovakia laid Mr. Neville Chamberlain's policy of "appeasement" in ruins and made war virtually inevitable, the Canadian political parties may be said to have found a formula to meet this situation — a formula which it was clearly hoped might combine support of Canada's friends abroad with avoidance of the domestic perils of 1917. It was first enunciated by the leader of the Conservative Opposition, Dr. R. J. Manion, in a newspaper interview on 27 March. While recommending that Canada should stand beside Britain, he declared, "I do not believe that Canadian youth should be conscripted to fight outside the borders of Canada." Three days later, in the House of Commons, Mr. King gave a pledge against "conscription of men for service overseas".[16]

The Manion formula, as we may call it, was fateful. It doubtless helped to enable Canada to go to war as a united country. It also prepared the way for the most bitter and prolonged Canadian controversy of the war period.

The Canadian defence programme of 1936–39 was effective as far as it went. It was, of course, utterly inadequate to the scale of the coming emergency. In 1939 the country was better prepared for war, on balance, than it had been in 1914; though that is not saying a great deal. Its domestic defences, while not strong, were in better condition than they had been, and a better basis existed for expansion of its forces. But it was in no condition to intervene abroad with any effect; and many months would pass before forces adequate to such intervention could be raised, trained and equipped. Such delay could have been obviated only by the expenditure before the war of sums far greater than the government and parliament of Canada were prepared to lay out, and by a defence programme undertaken long before 1937.

At the same time, it is evident that the political conditions of the time militated against a completely effective and practical programme. The emphasis on home defence rather than on expeditionary action; the emphasis on the defence of the Pacific rather than the Atlantic coast; the fact that (as will appear in its place) there was virtually no consultation or joint planning with those countries — notably the United Kingdom — with which Canada would be cooperating from the outbreak of war: all these were aspects or products of the no-commitments policy. . . . But strictly military interests were inevitably, and perhaps properly, subordinated to the political necessity for avoiding measures that might divide the country. The justification for Mr. King's policies — and it is a powerful justification — must be sought in the fact that, after all the uncertainty and debate of the pre-war years, Canada entered the conflict in September 1939 a united nation. Yet it should be said that military policies such as she pursued in those years were luxuries which could not have been afforded by any country which did not, like her, enjoy the double advantage of having both great physical obstacles and powerful friends between her and the potential enemy. During the early months of the war Great Britain and France held the front line. Secure behind their strength and the barrier of the Atlantic, Canada made the preparations which she ought to have made long before.

454 The Period of Mobilization, 1939–1940:
The Reign of the Dollar

Canada entered the Second World War in a solemn and sombre mood very different from that of 1914. But the country, contrary to many expectations, was essentially united.

On 26 August 1939 Mackenzie King visited the Governor General (Lord Tweedsmuir) and recorded in his diary the report he made to him:

I told him I thought the King's visit had helped immensely re uniting Canada for this crisis, that last Sept. I wd. not have had a united Cabinet, that Lapointe Cardin & Power (I might have added Rinfret) wd. probably have resigned, & there wd. have been difficulty besides in fighting for Czecho-Slovakia. Today I had all united on our participation if there were an act of aggression which brought England & France into a war with Germany.

This report (which may have somewhat exaggerated the dangers of Cabinet disunity in 1938) reflected the decisions of a vitally important Cabinet meeting held two days before.

Mr. King himself, there is ample evidence, had never had any doubt as to the action Canada would have to take in a world crisis, though he carefully refrained from making any statement on this in public. . . . King never seems to have changed this view, and in the crisis of 1938 he explained his own position very clearly to at least some of his colleagues. In his diary for 31 August of that year he wrote:

I made it clear to both Mackenzie and Power that I would stand for Canada doing all she possibly could do to destroy those Powers which are basing their action on *might* and not on *right*, and that I would not consider being neutral in this situation for a moment. They both agreed that this would be the Cabinet's view, Power saying that a coalition might be necessary, with some of the Quebec men leaving the party. I told him that the Cabinet Ministers should realize that it would be the end of Quebec if any attitude of that kind were adopted by the French Canadians in a world conflict such as this one would be. They, as members of the Government, ought to lead the Province in seeing its obligation to participate, and making clear the real issue and what it involves. Power thought Lapointe would become no [so] nervous and upset that he would be good for nothing,* which I fear is only too true, though what he learns at the League and in France may cause him to feel differently ere his return.

Skelton,† who is for Canada keeping out of European conflicts as much as anyone, agrees that the Government could not, without suffering immediate defeat, adopt any such policy; that the country's sentiment would be strong for intervention and even for participation by a possible expeditionary force. . . .

Now, on 24 August 1939, with war evidently about to break out in Europe, King polled the Cabinet. It was advisable, he said, according to his diary, "while we were all in a calm frame of mind," that policy should be decided; he had a clear idea in his own mind, but would like his colleagues to express their views before he stated it. He turned first to Ernest Lapointe, but the Minister of Justice also preferred to hear others' opinions. J. E. Michaud, the Minister of Fisheries, favoured no "participation outside of Canada". Rogers (Labour) recommended full support for Britain, and an immediate announcement of policy. Power (Pensions and National Health) said that Canada would have to go into the war, but the government should not state this before Parliament met. P. J. A. Cardin (Public Works) agreed with him. J. L. Ilsley (National Revenue) spoke for issuing a statement at once. Lapointe now broke in to oppose this idea. Mackenzie (National Defence) supported Ilsley and made a specific remark on behalf of his department, "vulnerable points" should be guarded at once. Some English-speaking ministers (Norman McLarty, Postmaster General, and C. D. Howe, Transport) favoured participation, but no immediate statement. W. D. Euler (Trade and Commerce) was not far from Michaud's position, and against a statement. Finally, King took a position which he defined as between the extremes:

455

I got general agreement and unanimity on this position. In the event of war we had now decided that Canada would participate. We had further decided that we would summon Parliament at the moment war was declared, or that it appeared that efforts for peace were certain to fail. At the same time, we would announce our policy with respect to Canada being at war. . . . Parliament would decide details.

In fact, however, the government's decision to support Britain and France was announced in less firm terms than this statement indicated, and Parliament was allowed to go through the form of deciding, not just "details", but the main issue.

It will be observed that no minister advocated neutrality. The main disagreement was merely upon a point of timing. The "Quebec men" did not leave the party, though they tended to favour a cautious and limited participation in the coming war. The student of the history of this administration may see in the events of 24 August some vague prefiguring of future divisions.

*A premonition which the events of 1939 were far from bearing out.
†Under-Secretary of State for External Affairs.

On 1 September the guns opened fire in Poland; and the Canadian Cabinet, meeting at nine a.m., decided to summon Parliament for the 7th, a date which the superstitious Prime Minister confided to his diary he liked. It met that day, accordingly, to make the decision which the government had so often asserted would be left to it. Virtually everyone now knew what the decision would be. On the 9th it was made, in the form of approval of the Address in reply to the Speech from the Throne. There was not enough opposition to divide the House of Commons though a French-speaking member from Quebec moved an adverse amendment. King's diary records that after a Cabinet discussion with the Speaker, Clerk and Deputy Clerk the words "On division" were written into Hansard; some ministers had heard them. Only four members, three of them Quebec nationalists, the other a convinced English-speaking pacifist, spoke against Canadian participation.[17] On 10 September, after a week of formal neutrality, Canada declared war on Germany.

456   This unity had been purchased, in some degree at least, by the prospect that Canada would be able to fight a war of limited liability. One French-speaking member (who however spoke in English on this occasion) said in the Commons, "I have consulted my conscience, and I know that in casting my vote in favour of co-operation, but against the sending of an expeditionary force and against conscription, in this critical hour, I am really and truly serving my compatriots."[18] The commitment against overseas conscription was itself of course a formidable prospective trammel on the war effort; but it seems certain that it was widely, and accurately, believed that the government envisaged a limited war effort in other respects as well, and certain too that this policy was acceptable in many areas of the country besides Quebec. It is true that warfare conducted on a "limited" basis is essentially a contradiction in terms; it is true that in the end "moderate" war proved a delusion; but it cannot be doubted that these ideas had much to do with the maintenance of national unity in Canada in the first phase of the Second World War. . . .

[The war programme's] very modest proportions are indicated by the smallness of the financial provision made for it. The short session of Parliament ending on 13 September 1939 appropriated $100 million (including over $16 million of emergency expenditure already authorized by Governor-General's Warrants) for the prosecution of the war to 31 March 1940. Less than $13 million of the pre-war defence appropriation of over $60 million had been spent at the end of August,[19] and the balance of this was available in addition. The total appropriation for the Department of National Defence for the whole fiscal year ending on 31 March 1940 was $144 409 674; the actual expenditure was $125 679 888, of which $74 799 380 went to the Army. Even within the limits of the appropriation, all concerned were enjoined to spend as little money as possible. . . .

A relatively large military force was mobilized on 1 September, the day on which hostilities began in Europe. Defence Scheme No. 3 provided for a mobile force of two divisions and ancillary troops, to be available either for home defence or for action abroad as circumstances might dictate. The General Staff had contemplated the possibility that the government might decide in a crisis to organize only part of this force; nevertheless, although the order in council passed on 1 September merely authorized vaguely "the organization forthwith of a Canadian Active Service Force", it was the entire Mobile Force that was ordered mobilized that day. In addition, many units were authorized for coast defence and similar purposes. However, within a few days the process began of postponing or suspending the mobilization of various miscellaneous units. (The $292 million Army programme of 17 September was based on one division and ancillary troops overseas and a corps of two divisions plus numerous miscellaneous units at home; however, as we have seen, the government would have none of this.) At the end of September the actual strength of the Canadian Active Service Force was 61 497 all ranks; if all the units authorized at the beginning of the month had been fully recruited, it would have been close to 80 000. It is evident that these deferments were the result partly of equipment shortages, partly of the need for financial economy.[20] . . . .

457

After, undoubtedly, considerable thought and discussion, of which no official record seems to exist, the government decided, and informed the Chiefs of Staff on 16 September, that while no "large expeditionary force" would be dispatched at present, one division would be sent overseas. It must be said that the Canadian ministers, interpreted the word "unit" in the British communication rather generously. The 1st Canadian Division, commanded by Major-General A. G. L. McNaughton, reached the United Kingdom in two convoys during December 1939.[21] At this stage it had only begun its training and was very incompletely equipped. . . .

Army officers, with 1914–18 precedents in their minds, inevitably thought in terms of further expansion of the overseas force and the creation of a Canadian Corps; but the government was unwilling to make such commitments at this time. It is true that on 25 January 1940, during the one-day session of Parliament at which the dissolution was announced, the intention to send the 2nd Division overseas was made known; but the Cabinet War Committee was told on 12 February that this had been done merely to prevent the question from becoming a political issue during the coming election campaign. When General McNaughton explored the implications of the expected arrival of the 2nd Division with the British War Office, tentative arrangements were made to constitute the 1st Division and the Canadian ancillary units (those provided as a result of the British request for technical troops) as a self-contained formation under G.H.Q. British Expeditionary Force, pending the organization of a Canadian Corps. The government, doubtless with its eye on the 8000 additional ancillary troops that would be required for a Corps, disapproved this initiative; the 1st Division, it ruled, should be employed, on its arrival at the front, in the manner previously planned — as part of a British Corps. This was on 27 February 1940; five days earlier a message from Ottawa to the Canadian High Commissioner in London had emphasized the extent of Canadian war expenditures and remarked, "Obviously it would be nothing but a disservice to the task we have in mind and to our Allies for us to attempt something beyond our capacity." McNaughton and Mr. Vincent Massey, the High Commissioner, continued to urge the plan for a self-contained formation. On 17 March King assured them the matter would be taken up when the political campaign was over. After the election, the government accepted the plan.[22]

With respect to the Navy, the United Kingdom memorandum of 6 September asked for a considerable number of detailed measures, among them placing the naval bases at Halifax and Esquimalt in complete readiness, including anti-submarine booms, and making them available to the Royal Navy; and taking up and fitting out a total of 14 minesweeping vessels and three anti-submarine vessels at Sydney, N.S., and St. John's, Nfld. The Royal Canadian Navy worked along the lines suggested. Its share of the $314 million allotted for the first year of war was $35 888 000. By the last week of 1939 the personnel strength of the naval forces was up to 5042 all ranks and ratings. The strength in ships gradually increased, small vessels suitable for patrol duty being acquired from other government departments and private owners. After considerable discussion and negotiation the three coastal liners *Prince David, Prince Robert* and *Prince Henry* (the last was sailing in 1939 under the name *North Star*) were purchased in 1940 and converted into armed merchant cruisers.[23]...

On 16 September 1939 the first convoy of a very long series sailed from Halifax, escorted by two British cruisers and two Canadian destroyers. The convoys were organized under the direction of a Canadian officer, the Commanding Officer Atlantic Coast; the ocean escort forces were under an officer of the Royal Navy, the Rear Admiral Third Battle Squadron, who in turn was under the Royal Navy's Commander-in-Chief, America and West Indies Station. It may be mentioned that under the policy of priority for the Pacific which we have noted, four of Canada's six destroyers were on the west coast at the outbreak of war. Two of them sailed for Halifax as early as 31 August 1939, and all of them were on duty in the Atlantic before the end of the year.[24]...

The Inception of the British Commonwealth Air Training Plan

The story of the origins of the British Commonwealth Air Training Plan must be told here in some detail. For this there are three reasons: the fact that the Plan was so important an element in the Canadian effort; the fact that the circumstances of its inception go far to reveal the springs of Canadian policy in 1939; and the fact that in the absence so far of an official history of the Royal Canadian Air Force the story has never been fully told.

The Royal Canadian Air Force was allotted in the first instance $77 158 000 of the funds made available to the Department of National Defence for the first twelve months of the war. Its modest expansion in the autumn of 1939 paralleled the Navy's; by the end of the year its personnel strength was 8287 officers and airmen. Fourteen squadrons were then "operational", all in Canada and six of them on the east coast. Thanks to the pre-war measures, a few new aircraft of service type were available when war broke out; among them 19 Hurricane fighters, 10 Battle bombers and eight Stranraer flying boats. A fairly ambitious programme of construction in Canada of airframes of British type had been undertaken from 1937 onward. The immediate responsibility of the R.C.A.F. after the outbreak was cooperation with the navies to ensure the security of Canadian coasts and waters and the protection of convoys.[25] Almost at once, however, its energies began to be directed primarily into the training of aircrew personnel in Canada.

In the spring of 1939 a new training scheme intended to provide pilots who would hold short-service commissions had been introduced for the R.C.A.F. One feature of it, the result of long confidential negotiations with the United Kingdom, was that 50 pilots would be trained annually for the Royal Air Force. Before the scheme got under way, war came; and the British government at once asked for what was in effect a large expansion of it. . . .

459

As early as 12 September 1939 the Canadian Prime Minister wrote to the British High Commissioner in Ottawa concerning arrangements for R.C.A.F. co-operation.[26] The expansion of R.C.A.F. training facilities, he said, was being put in hand immediately: a number of Canadian officer pilots (experienced only in the handling of civil aircraft), and some newly enlisted airmen of various trades, could be dispatched to Britain within six weeks for loan to the R.A.F. Mr. King added:

It is the desire of this Government that Canadian Air Force units be formed as soon as sufficient trained personnel are available overseas for this purpose, such squadrons to be manned by and maintained with Canadian personnel at the expense of the Canadian Government. Owing to the shortage of service equipment in Canada, Canadian squadrons overseas would require to be completely equipped by the United Kingdom authorities at Canada's expense.

The Prime Minister specified that personnel lent to the R.A.F. under the proposed arrangement would be available for transfer to R.C.A.F. units "if the Canadian Government should later decide upon the organization of distinctive Canadian air units for service overseas."

Mr. King emphasized that these suggestions were very tentative and might be superseded "after the situation becomes clearer". In fact, they were immediately "overtaken by events.". . .

The war was still in its first days when it was reported that the air training suggestions made by the United Kingdom on 6 September would soon be supplanted by something still larger. On 15 September the Chief of the Air Staff, Air Vice-Marshal G. M. Croil, told the first meeting of the Emergency Council (the Cabinet's Committee on General Policy, which was later replaced by the War Committee) that he understood that the British request for 2000 pilots annually would shortly be increased to 8000. He presented in the meantime a tentative Canadian scheme under which, as a long-term objective, 12 000 men a year might be trained (8000 apparently being ground staff). This was evidently intended to meet the first British request and the R.C.A.F.'s own requirements as well. He estimated the cost at $92 million for the first year, and the training staff required at 600 officers and 6500 men. With such an effort in prospect, he did not favour sending any R.C.A.F. personnel overseas in the near future. The scheme of 12 September was already a thing of the past.

The germ of the still larger conception which came to be called the British Commonwealth Air Training Plan* is presumably to be found in the very modest pre-war scheme for training British pilots in Canada, and in the expanded plan proposed by the United Kingdom on 6 September. It seems evident that a large project for training in Canada was a basic part of the war plans of the British Air Ministry. There had also, however, been an initiative on the part of certain Dominion High Commissioners in London. On 13 September Mr. Vincent Massey discussed air training with Mr. Stanley Bruce, the Australian High Commissioner, and Canadian and Australian air force officers; and on 16 September Massey and Bruce suggested at a High Commissioners' meeting at the Dominions Office a scheme whereby Canadian, Australian and New Zealand airmen would be trained in Canada. It is important to note that the Dominions Office record states that after training the men should be "sent to the front as distinctive Canadian, Australian and New Zealand air forces."[27] No record of these discussions is to be found in the Department of External Affairs at Ottawa, and it seems evident that Mr. Massey took the considerable responsibility of sponsoring a plan which was likely to have a major effect upon the structure and balance of the Canadian war effort without telling his government what he was doing.

Mr. Eden, the Dominions Secretary, "undertook to look into" the High Commissioners' proposal. He apparently discussed it with the Air Minister, Sir Kingsley Wood. At any rate, on 26 September the British Prime Minister (Mr. Neville Chamberlain) sent communications to the Commonwealth governments proposing the Air Training Plan.

The British War Cabinet, he said, had lately sanctioned immediate measures designed to produce "a greatly enlarged air force". It was calculated that the maintenance of this force would require "not less than 20 000 pilots and 30 000 personnel of air crews annually". Such a feat of production required "more than twice the entire training capacity available in the United Kingdom, having regard to limited space, operational restrictions and vulnerability to air attack". Nor did Britain have the man-

*This designation was officially adopted by the R.C.A.F. in 1939, with "Joint Air Training Plan" as an alternative for use in certain official correspondence. In Australia the usual term was "Empire Air Training Scheme".

power required. The solution appeared to be to use the resources of the Dominions, and particularly those of Canada. Chamberlain put forward a detailed scheme for some fifty flying training schools overseas, with advanced training concentrated in Canada, and suggested a conference in Canada to discuss details.

The British Prime Minister called his message to Mr. King "a special personal appeal", and it evidently struck a responsive chord. On 28 September the Canadian government considered it at a meeting of the Emergency Council at which certain additional ministers and the Chiefs of Staff were present. It was pointed out that undertaking so large a project might involve considerable modification of the Canadian war programme so lately approved. The Chief of the General Staff (Major-General T. V. Anderson) expressed the view that the Canadian public would not be satisfied with a participation confined to air activity; they thought in terms of ground troops, and it was important that the army programme should not be interrupted. But the Ministers seem to have been impressed by the possibilities of the air plan; and on the same day Mr. King cabled back to Mr. Chamberlain,

461

I can say at once that our Government fully agree that Canadian cooperation in this field would be particularly appropriate and probably the most effective in the military sphere which Canada could furnish. We would therefore be prepared to accept the scheme in principle.[28]

. . . .

In the light of what we now know about Mr. King's thinking, as revealed in his diary, it is pretty evident that one reason why an air effort had more political appeal than "great expeditionary forces of infantry" was the fact that it seemed to hold out the hope of smaller forces, fewer casualties, less pressure on manpower and a reduction of the danger of conscription. The Air Training Plan project was particularly attractive, presumably, in that it would be largely carried on within Canada and held out the prospect of a considerable portion of the R.C.A.F. being employed on training at home instead of in operations abroad. At the same time, no thinking person could possibly deny the vast importance of air power in this new war, and no one could doubt that the production of trained aircrew on a great scale would be a tremendous contribution to victory. And the project came with the very highest recommendations: an urgent appeal from the British Prime Minister. Mr. Chamberlain may not have realized it, but it is scarcely too much to say that in 1939 the Air Training Plan must have seemed the answer to any Canadian politician's prayer; and Mr. King embraced it accordingly. . . .

It would seem that Lord Riverdale [head of the United Kingdom Air Mission], arrived without any detailed estimate of the cost of the scheme, and that he spent the fortnight after reaching Ottawa in attempting to draw an estimate with the assistance of the R.C.A.F. The formal discussions between the United Kingdom and Canada began on 31 October, on which day Riverdale and Balfour met both the Cabinet committee and the Emergency Council. The negotiations immediately ran hard aground on the rocks of finance. Chamberlain's original proposals had not dealt with this matter. Now Riverdale indicated that the total cost of the scheme over the proposed period of its duration, to 31 March 1943, might be $888 500 000. The United Kingdom would make its contribution in kind, chiefly in the form of aircraft, to the extent of $140 million of this in capital and $51 500 000 in maintenance equipment. Of the balance of $697 000 000, Riverdale seems to have suggested, half would be paid by Canada and the other half by Australia and New Zealand. He pointed out that the whole force created as a result of the scheme (some 100 new squadrons) would be maintained in the field by the United Kingdom, at an estimated cost of $1 500 000 000 per year.[29]

It is clear that the scale of the proposed contribution by Canada took the Canadian ministers by surprise. The situation was not improved when the visitors indicated that they were not worrying about where the money which the United Kingdom would have to spend was coming from — finding it was up to the Chancellor of the Exchequer. The United Kingdom had abandoned "limited liability" (so far as finance was concerned) in the spring of 1939. Not so Canada. The Canadian Prime Minister indicated to the visitors that his government could not afford so cavalier an attitude: they would proceed under the advice of the Minister of Finance. The same calculations as to national income and national capacity which had been given to Mr. Crerar were laid before Riverdale and his colleagues. Evidently the meetings of 31 October were a shock to both parties. The British were taken aback when told that Canada could not come "within shooting distance" of the figures that had been suggested, and the day's sessions (Sir Gerald Campbell told Dr. Skelton) left them "blue and depressed". Later discussions of the exchanges suggest that Riverdale, making his presentation, had been thrown "off his base" by an interjection from Ralston expressing surprise at the size of his estimated costs; that this led Riverdale to refer to the British contribution in kind as "a free gift to you"; that this in turn nettled King, who said, "This is not our war" — meaning that it was a contribution not to Canada but to the common cause. The phrase nevertheless shocked the British, and Campbell was unwise enough to mention that it had been cabled to London — which led King, in one of his fits of childishness, to ask the Governor General, as the King's representative, to reprove the High Commissioner for allowing such a report to go through his office![30] The negotiation had begun badly.

On 3 November the Canadian Cabinet considered the problem and approved the terms of a Prime-Minister-to-Prime-Minister cable to Mr. Chamberlain. The British proposal, it said, appeared to imply "that a United Kingdom project for reinforcing the Royal Air Force had become a Canadian plan, with corresponding assumption by Canada of the major provision of recruits and major proportion of the cost which detailed study now indicates would be of huge magnitude". The Canadian share pro-

462

posed was quite beyond Canada's financial resources as reflected in the recent computation of national income. The cable went on to emphasize the relationship between the Canadian military programme and British purchases in Canada:

I may instance the fact that while the British Air Mission are pressing us in regard to their air training proposals which would involve a substantial increase in Canada's direct military expenditures, we on our part have for many weeks been pressing without satisfactory result for a decision in regard to wheat purchases which is the biggest single item in our whole economic program and the most far-reaching in its public consequences. In our opinion the questions of military and economic participation in the war effort are inextricably intertwined and cannot be dealt with separately. Until some understanding evolves from the discussions either here or in London, I frankly cannot see how a decision can be arrived at in regard to the proposals for the special air training program. . . .[31]

Chamberlain's reply, sent on 7 November, promised "urgent consideration" and was hopeful that further discussions with Mr. Crerar would make a useful contribution.[32]

463

Meanwhile, the air training discussions in Ottawa went on; and about 10 November it began to be evident that Australia and New Zealand also were not happy about the scheme as presented by Lord Riverdale. They too had financial scruples, and in particular they were short of Canadian dollars (though it may be noted that ultimately the United Kingdom promised to find the Canadian exchange they needed for the Air Training Plan if difficulties arose and they so requested).[33] Mr. Fairbairn said later that he was impressed by the discovery that the aircraft to be used in advanced training were either to come from Britain or were of a U.S. type which was being manufactured in Australia, whereas he had supposed the main reason for concentrating advanced training in Canada was that country's proximity to U.S. aircraft plants. At any rate, he proposed that Australia, in addition to undertaking all her own elementary training, should give advanced training to seven-ninths of her own aircrew at home, sending only two-ninths instead of all of them to Canada.[34] He also objected to the original British proposal under which Australia would produce 40 per cent of the Dominion aircrew required by the scheme, and Canada 48 per cent; Australia, he said, could produce men only in proportion to her population. New Zealand felt obliged to ask for changes in the same direction. On 22 November, after consulting the Australian Prime Minister (Mr. Menzies) by telephone, Mr. Fairbairn put his final proposal before the Canadian Cabinet committee and the visiting missions; the only alternative, he said, was for Australia to "attempt the whole of its population proportion of the training in Australia."[35] This "ultimatum", as the Canadians called it, was perforce accepted. The change resulted in reducing the planned number of advanced schools in Canada from 55 to 36; on the other hand, Canada paid for 29 of these schools instead of 26 as originally planned, and the increase in expense to her over the whole initial duration of the Plan was estimated in August 1940 at $34 or $35 million.[36]

In the meantime, the discussions between Canada and the United Kingdom had proceeded, still turning mainly on financial questions. By 14 November they had advanced to the point where (the United Kingdom having agreed to undertake certain addition financial responsibilities relating to equipment, which raised its estimated contribution to $220 million) the Canadian committee were prepared to recommend to their Cabinet colleagues an arrangement whereby Canada would pay 72^1/$_2$ per cent of the balance, leaving 27^1/$_2$ per cent for Australia and New Zealand. As a result of those two countries' amendments, the balance was now estimated at $432 000 000 for the duration of the Plan. The committee also recommended two conditions: *first*, the British War Cabinet must be prepared to allow the Canadian government to state publicly that the air training scheme should have priority over other measures as being in the opinion of the War Cabinet the most important contribution that Canada could make to the war; and *secondly*, the agreement was contingent upon a reasonably and mutually satisfactory agreement being reached in the discussions on general financial and economic relations being carried on in London, where Mr. Crerar was now to be reinforced by Mr. Graham Towers, Governor of the Bank of Canada.* These recommendations were approved by the Cabinet on 14 November, and were communicated to Riverdale and Balfour at a meeting of the Emergency Council the same afternoon.[37] . . .

Another basic issue that might have given infinite trouble was disposed of relatively easily. This was the question of the system of command and administration for the Plan. It was discussed in detail between Rogers and Balfour; and when the latter left for England on 28 November he carried with him a letter from Rogers making proposals. The first and basic proposition was, "The air training plan in Canada will be administered through the organization of the R.C.A.F. and the executive command shall be in the hands of the R.C.A.F." The general supervision of the Plan should be entrusted to a Supervisory Board with the Canadian Minister of National Defence as Chairman and the other participating countries represented upon it. Those countries might appoint liaison officers who might visit stations or units involved in the Plan at any time, might offer criticisms or suggestions to the Board, and would be free to report on progress to their own governments. In due course the British government accepted these proposals as written.[38] . . .

The four-party air training agreement envisaged an organization which would ultimately produce every four weeks 520 pilots with elementary flying training (all Canadians), 544 pilots with service (advanced) flying training, 340 observers and 580 wireless operator-air gunners. Of greatest interest are the provisions concerning the graduates of the Plan. It will be noted that (except for R.C.A.F. aircrew retained for home defence squad-

---

*It is perhaps a commentary upon the degree of the sense of emergency entertained in Canadian official circles at this period that the Governor, undertaking this urgent wartime journey, was accompanied by his wife. The general public, needless to say, was at least equally unaware of the emergency. Many Canadian officers' wives went to England, in these early months, to be with their husbands.

rons) pupils who had completed their training were to be placed at the "disposal" of the British government. During their time in Canada all the pupils from other countries were "attached" to the R.C.A.F. and paid at R.C.A.F. rates; upon embarkation for the United Kingdom all became charges upon the British government at R.A.F. rates of pay, except that the Dominion governments could supplement these rates of pay if they so desired. Canada did in fact pay the difference between R.A.F. and R.C.A.F. rates for all Canadian graduates of the Plan. As for the results of Article 15, and the interpretation of it so painfully arrived at between Canada and the United Kingdom, much more would be heard of these things in due course.

A word of comment on the negotiations may be in order. On the Canadian side they were obviously dominated by financial considerations, and by the fact that the project bore (as at least two Canadian ministers remarked during the Ottawa discussions) the appearance of being a recruiting scheme for the R.A.F. The Canadians looked at the figures of what they would pay to create and maintain the training organization in Canada, and thought them staggering. They were not impressed by the much larger sums which Britain would have to lay out to maintain the trainees when formed into squadrons in the field; the remark was made that "she would have to do so no matter where they came from".[39] There were in fact strong arguments on both sides. The British "compromise" scheme was hastily and tactlessly presented at a moment of pressure; but although it was so ill received by Mr. King the idea of relating the number of Canadian squadrons in the field to the amount spent by Canada on the training organization was not without merit. It was not very different in effect from the arrangement finally adopted in 1941, although the number of squadrons then agreed on as an initial figure was 25, whereas the British in 1939 were very tentatively thinking of something like 15.

A post-war commentator in Canada described this agreement as in some ways "a colonial document". The description is apt, not least with respect to the payment of Canadian graduates of the Plan serving with the R.A.F. The system by which Canada paid merely the difference between their R.A.F. pay and Canadian rates was precisely that followed with the Canadian contingents in the South African War of 1899-1902. The explanation, of course, is to be found largely in the determined regard for economy which dominated Canadian war policy at this early period. The British government came forward with an imaginative plan on a war-winning scale; but that scale was disproportioned to the Canadian government's financial thinking in 1939. The result was permanent damage to the R.C.A.F.'s status in the field. Had Mr. King and his colleagues felt equal in 1939 to producing Canadian ground crews as well as aircrew, and to paying the full cost, or a large part of the cost, of Canadian squadrons overseas, in addition to the large training expenditure, the force's status would have been assured. . . . Because they thought such action impracticable on the scale indicated by the Air Training Plan, the R.C.A.F. over

KCAF

a period of years had to fight its way slowly back from a position of dispersion and subordination; and it never fully achieved an overseas status parallel to that of the Canadian Army. . . .

Meanwhile, the Canadian war effort on the industrial front developed slowly. The spirit of limited liability, and the small appropriations for the armed forces, which we have noted, were not favourable to rapid growth. The Canadian supply organization moved into a new phase; the War Supply Board succeeded the Defence Purchasing Board (15 September 1939) and was itself succeeded by the Department of Munitions and Supply (9 April 1940). The manufacture of clothing and similar personal requirements for the forces went forward with praiseworthy rapidity.[40] But equipment and weapons were necessarily a different matter. As we have seen, large orders for naval vessels were placed early in 1940; considerable orders for airframes were authorized at the same period; but very few weapons were ordered, and the first really big order for motor transport ($4 440 294) was placed with General Motors of Canada only on 20 March 1940.[41] It is a rather remarkable fact that large orders for weapons for the Canadian land forces were not placed until concurrent orders for the British forces became available in the following summer.

industrial front

466

Mr. King confided to his diary on 3 June that at the War Committee that day he had advocated a great increase in the Canadian production effort; he had apparently recommended that this be done even if British orders were not forthcoming. He recalled that "Howe and Ralston" had opposed him earlier when he asked for larger war production, and that he had held a special meeting of the Committee on the subject.[42] This was apparently the meeting of 8 December 1939 — the first the War Committee held under that name — during which reference was made to reports that the Deputy Minister of Finance was putting barriers in the way of the War Supply Board's desire to provide for supplies beyond the current fiscal year, and the possibility that the Board's Chairman might resign was mentioned. The Committee was told that the Minister of Finance had made it clear in a letter that his department would permit commitments for future years so far as the Navy and Air Force were concerned. The Minister (Mr. Ralston) reported that he took full responsibility for what had been done, and his Deputy should not be blamed; and further, that he felt that he would be derelict in his duty as Minister of Finance if he failed to keep the matter of cost constantly in mind. King's diary shows that he had returned to the subject of manufacturing arms "for our own armies" in Cabinet on 29 January, urging that there should be no waiting for British orders.

Canadians, expecting a flood of war orders from the United Kingdom to make use of their idle industrial capacity, were disappointed when these did not come. Mr. Howe reported to the Cabinet War Committee at the meeting on 8 December 1939 that, apart from an order for Lysander aircraft, British orders so far amounted only to $5 000 000. A certain number of others had of course been placed before the outbreak. A British Purchasing Mission reached Ottawa in September 1939, and in November a British Purchasing Commission, headed by the Scots-Canadian Arthur B. Purvis, was set up in New York to coordinate purchases in Canada and the United States.[43] It must be remembered that there were special and powerful reasons operating to limit British orders. One was the factor of time. Canada had developed virtually no military industrial capacity in peacetime, and developing it would be the work of years rather than months. In the words of a British official writer, "Requisitions from Canada were confined in the main therefore to such minor projects as could be expected to bear fruit within the first year or so of war." At the same time, the barrier of dollar exchange was an extremely serious one for the United Kingdom, the more so as that country would have to buy vast quantities of foodstuffs and other raw materials from Canada. Canadians were over-captious in their complaints against British purchasing policy. Express instructions from London gave Canada precedence over the United States as a source of supply. "In all, the value of Ministry of Supply orders placed or pending in Canada at the end of April 1940, excluding orders for machinery or raw materials, was approximately $81 million; the corresponding figure for the United States was only $33 million."[44] Though the figures were beginning to be respectable, the surface was hardly scratched yet. The whole aspect of affairs, however, was shortly to be altered by cataclysmic events in Europe.

467

The Expansion of the Effort, 1940:
The Dollar Dethroned

European events

The "phony war" which had lasted since the Germans overran Poland in September 1939 ended suddenly when they invaded Denmark and Norway on 9 April 1940. The humiliating defeat of the Allies in the brief Norwegian campaign that followed brought down the Chamberlain government in Britain. Winston Churchill became Prime Minister on 10 May, the actual day on which the German offensive against France, Belgium and the Netherlands initiated a new series of disasters. By 4 June the Allied armies had been split in two and the British Expeditionary Force and a large number of French soldiers had been evacuated through Dunkirk. The next day the Germans struck the surviving French forces holding the line of the Somme and Aisne; and by 17 June those forces had been hopelessly routed, the French government had fallen and the new Prime Minister, Marshal Pétain, had asked the enemy for an armistice. In this phase a few thousand Canadian troops had reached France, as part of the attempt to build up a new B.E.F. and keep France in the war; fortunately they were withdrawn almost without loss.[45] On 10 June Benito Mussolini's Italy, hastening to join what now seemed clearly the winning side, announced its entrance into the war as an ally of Germany.

Against these powerful and triumphant enemies the British Commonwealth now "stood alone", and its peoples, shaken out of the easy confidence
of the opening months, suddenly found themselves confronting the possibility
of defeat. In Canada as in Britain, the response was an outburst of effort
and energy greater than anything that had preceded it. A magazine writer
described the national capital as he saw it about the time of Dunkirk:[46]

> To tell that Ottawa, as this is written, is in the midst of a crisis is to put it mildly. The
> "quietest war capital in Christendom" has become a cauldron of excitement; disillusioned,
> shocked from its complacency. Day by day, as the shadow of the Swastika lengthens across
> the English Channel, old shibboleths, old comfortable delusions, go overboard. Where once
> reigned smugness, self-satisfaction, there is now a wholesome fear; with it, fortunately,
> more of war stir and vigor.

The new situation was reflected in the activity of the government. The
Cabinet War Committee had held only six meetings during the four
months following its inception on 5 December 1939. The Norwegian crisis
468   produced no meetings. But from the moment the *Blitzkrieg* was loosed in
the West on 10 May it met frequently; there were eight meetings, beginning on that date, before the end of the month. The meeting on 10 May
decided to offer to accelerate the dispatch of the 2nd Division to the
United Kingdom, and to invite the British government to make suggestions concerning additional measures which Canada might usefully take.
On 17 May the Committee heard the Minister of National Defence, Mr.
Rogers, who had just returned from overseas, report on Britain's inadequate
preparation for mechanized warfare, and on what he called the incompetence
and lack of imagination of some British officials. This meeting decided
both to form a Canadian Corps overseas and to mobilize a 3rd Division. It
anticipated by only a day a message from the British government suggesting
the formation of a Corps with the necessary Corps, Army and G.H.Q.
troops, and of a third division, which "would prove of great military
assistance and encouragement in prosecuting our common task".

The official record indicates that these large measures were taken without
any anxiety whatever being expressed over their cost; though the King
diary for 24 and 27 May still speaks of difficulty with Ralston over his
financial scruples. Of King himself, it records on 17 May, "I insisted
strongly, so long as we could make a useful contribution at all, of [on] not
considering the expenditure." The atmosphere had changed remarkably
since the discussions with the British Air Mission in the early winter and
those in February concerning the possibility of forming a Corps. The fact
is that the dollar sign had suddenly come off the Canadian war effort.
Financially speaking, at least, the days of limited liability were over. The
actual appropriations for the Department of National Defence for the
fiscal year ending 30 March 1941, the first complete year of war, were
$681 438 416, as compared with the $125 679 888 of the previous year.[47]

Such immediate help as unprepared Canada could offer was being
rushed across the Atlantic in answer to British calls. On 22 May the
Cabinet War Committee heard with satisfaction that the R.C.A.F.'s one
fully-equipped fighter squadron was to go to Britain. The same day it

approved providing a brigade to garrison Iceland. The next it authorized the dispatch overseas of four destroyers — the country's whole disposable naval force at that moment. The 2nd Division had already been offered and accepted, and a Canadian battalion was preparing to sail for Bermuda and Jamaica.

Bad news — appalling news — continued to arrive. On 26 May Ottawa received a highly secret telegram from London reporting the decision to withdraw the British Expeditionary Force to the United Kingdom and mentioning the possibility, which would have seemed inconceivable a few months earlier, that the French "are not going to carry on". The next day brought another telegram informing the Canadian government of the results of "preliminary consideration" of this possibility by the British War Cabinet: namely, that in such a case there could be no question of Britain giving up the contest.[48] By 13 June it was evident that, so far as France was concerned, the worst was likely. That day the Canadian War Committee met with Opposition leaders and all agreed that Canada must continue the fight for freedom as long as Britain and France together, or Britain alone, remained in it.[49] On 14 June Paris fell to the enemy; on the 17th came Pétain's request for an armistice; and on the 18th Mr. Churchill, in words that rang around the world, announced the British intention to fight on.

Under the impulsion of the new circumstances, Canadian public opinion was ready for measures which it would not have tolerated earlier; indeed, it was demanding such measures. At the meeting of the Cabinet War Committee on 14 June it was stated that there was a growing feeling throughout the country that provision should be made for every able-bodied man to be used in some phase of the war effort; and at the next meeting, on 17 June, there was general agreement that compulsory military service for the domestic defence of Canada was desirable. (It is relevant that two leaders of the Opposition had called on Mr. King that morning and demanded, among other things, that the government take authority to mobilize all manpower and material resources for aid to Britain and the defence of Canada.)[50] The Secretary was directed to draft a bill in consultation with Mr. Ernest Lapointe and Mr. C. G. Power (who incidentally were the senior French-speaking and English-speaking representatives of the Province of Quebec in the Cabinet). The result was the National Resources Mobilization Act.[51] Though not passed quite as expeditiously as the Prime Minister had hoped (he had suggested that, like the United Kingdom's very similar Emergency Powers Act, 1940, it might be put through all its stages in a single day), it became law on 21 June after three days' discussion in the House of Commons. It was short and general, authorizing the Governor in Council to make orders or regulations "requiring persons to place themselves, their services and their property at the disposal of His Majesty in the right of Canada, as may be deemed necessary or expedient for securing the public safety, the defence of Canada, the maintenance of public order, or the efficient prosecution of the war, or for maintaining supplies or services essential to the life of the community". There was one reservation; these powers might not be exercised "for the purpose of requiring persons to serve in the military, naval or air forces outside of Canada and the territorial waters thereof". The government's repeated pledges were thus duly honoured. Conscription for overseas service was impossible so long as this section of the act remained on the statute book.

To administer the act, a new department of government, that of National War Services, was set up by statute; its first Minister was Mr. J. G. Gardiner.* The act was implemented by regulations setting up a scheme of compulsory military training under which the first trainees reported in October 1940. At first only thirty days' training was given; but this was shortly extended to four months, and in April 1941 the decision was made to keep men trained under the National Resources Mobilization Act on duty indefinitely for home defence. At the end of 1941 over 16 000 N.R.M.A. soldiers were on such duty or in training; and the number rose steadily thereafter. The dualism thus created in the Army, between the men freely enlisted for general service and the men called up for compulsory service in Canada, was to pose a continuing and increasing problem as time passed. It should be noted, however, that the N.R.M.A. provided an important by-product: large numbers of general service recruits. Many men called up for home defence preferred to volunteer for general service; there were 18 274 such volunteers in the peak year, 1942, and the total for the whole period was 58 434.[52]

Though the feverish summer of 1940, while Britain prepared against what seemed the imminent threat of German invasion, the Canadian forces expanded steadily. The most important units of a 4th Division — its nine rifle battalions — were authorized late in May, and many miscellaneous units were formed as the weeks passed. On 22 July Major-General H. D. G. Crerar, lately Senior Officer at Canadian Military Headquarters, London, succeeded General Anderson as Chief of the General Staff. He proceeded to draw up an army programme for 1941 based upon the creation overseas of a Canadian Corps of three divisions plus an armoured brigade. The armoured brigade was formed in Canada that autumn. While Crerar refrained from sketching specifically a long-term programme for the Army, his memoranda foreshadowed an overseas force of six or seven divisions, two of them armoured, plus two divisions for home defence in Canada mainly composed of N.R.M.A. soldiers.[53] By the end of the calendar year 1940, the authorized expansion and the manner in which the young manhood of Canada pressed forward to volunteer during that tremendous summer had increased the general-service strength of the Canadian Army to 177 810 all ranks.†

470

---

*The administration of the N.R.M.A. was transferred to the Department of Labour late in 1942.
†Several unfortunate typographical errors occurred in Appendix "A" of *Six Years of War* in the early printings. In three columns opposite the date 29 Dec (1940) the figure 117 302 should read 177 302 and the figure 117 810 should read 177 810. In the Remarks column the date on which the CA(A) reached its peak strength should be 22 Mar 44, not 22 Mar 45.

The summer crisis of 1940 appeared to throw the British Common-wealth Air Training Plan into the melting-pot. The immediate need was air defence for Britain; the Cabinet War Committee was told on 24 May that she could not now undertake to send to Canada the aircraft she had promised. For a moment the future of the Plan seemed to hang in the balance; but the R.C.A.F. stepped into the breach with substitute proposals,[54] and in the event the Plan went forward fully and rapidly, with Canadian-built air-frames and American engines taking the place of the British-built aircraft originally intended.* The first school under the Plan, No. 1 Initial Training School at Toronto, had opened in April, and others began work as the summer advanced. The first overseas draft of B.C.A.T.P. trainees, 37 strong, landed in the United Kingdom on 24 November. In the meantime, however, No. 1 Fighter Squadron, R.C.A.F. had reached England on 20 June. Ready for operations by mid-August, it helped to win the famous victory over the *Luftwaffe* in the Battle of Britain.[55] . . .

The Royal Canadian Navy continued to expand, in ships and in personnel, and it now extended its activities across the Atlantic and took its share of the naval encounters and losses which accompanied the German offensives in the West. No enemy submarines had yet appeared in North American waters (on 23 February 1940 Hitler had negatived a proposal of Admiral Raeder for operations by two submarines off Halifax; though they might well have had a field-day, the Führer wisely decided that it was more important to avoid alarming the United States).[56] But on 23 May, an urgent request from the British government led the Cabinet War Committee to order the four available Canadian destroyers to England at once.† . . . One of the destroyers (H.M.C.S. *Fraser*) was lost by collision on 25 June off St. Jean de Luz, during the last stages of the evacuation of France. She was replaced by another taken over from the Royal Navy under the name *Margaree,* who unluckily was herself sunk in a collision while on convoy escort duty on 22 October. But when fifty over-age destroyers were transferred from the U.S. Navy to the Royal Navy late in the year, the R.C.N. got seven of them.[57] There were plenty of Canadians willing to man them, though trained men were few and training took time. By 31 March 1941 the Royal Canadian navy had 2080 officers and 17 036 ratings on war duty.[58] . . .

Such material help as a country so ill-prepared as Canada could give was sent to Britain as soon as the desperate nature of the crisis began to be apparent; 75 000 Ross rifles and 60 million rounds of small arms ammunition were dispatched before the beginning of June. When Britain, and France, then made further requests, they had to be told that the Canadian cupboard was bare. At the same moment, however, the situation with

---

*The Anson aircraft was redesigned to take the Jacobs engine and American instruments and accessories.
†The R.C.N. now had seven destroyers, having acquired one from the Royal Navy in the autumn of 1939; but two were under repair and a third (also by British request) was serving in the West Indies.

respect to Canadian war industry was being transformed. The Minister of Munitions and Supply reported to the War Committee on 5 June that he had been informed that the British government proposed to place in Canada orders for the equipment for 10 divisions; and in fact during the last seven months of 1940 the United Kingdom placed, or had under negotiation, new contracts in Canada for 300 tanks, 1000 universal carriers, 72 434 vehicles, 3450 artillery equipments and naval guns and 100 000 rifles; while its pre-war order for Bren light machine-guns had been increased from 5000 to 42 600. British orders for ships and aircraft had likewise greatly increased. Britain, under the stress of the crisis, had defied the dollar exchange problem and the considerations of time that had deterred her from placing such orders earlier. The great influx of orders from the United Kingdom encouraged the Department of Munitions and Supply to contract in Canada for equipment for Canada's own expanding forces, and large concurrent orders were placed in these months.[59] But since the manufacture of weapons was an almost completely new activity in Canada, the fact had to be faced that much time would elapse before the material now ordered actually became available.

472

The Canadian forces had expanded greatly during 1940. It seems clear also that there had been some change in the balance of emphasis between them. The government's previously evident policy of concentration upon the air, and particularly upon the Air Training Plan, had undergone a degree of alteration as the result of the summer crisis. The French Army — the one really large land force on the Allied side — had suddenly vanished from the chessboard of the war; the British government's desire for a considerable Canadian army effort, obvious in the discussions on the priority of the Air Training Plan, had been made apparent again; the danger to the United Kingdom, and the British requests for help in specific areas, underlined the need for large disposable forces; and in the shadow of the emergency the War Committee, apparently without any doubt or hesitation, authorized a succession of major increases in the army. The Prime Minister himself, usually the chief opponent of a large army, refrained from opposing these measures.[60] Indeed, if one can take his diary literally, he momentarily took the lead in them. He wrote on 17 May concerning that day's War Committee meeting,

I . . . discussed with my colleagues at length the situation from our point of view. Got their agreement to send a 3rd division; establish a Canadian Corps of Ancillary troops [sic] in England; advance the time of the departure of the 2nd division; and arrange for a reserve division in Canada.

The Air Training Plan continued to be of fundamental importance in the eyes of the government; but, while there had been specific discussion of or decision on the point, it clearly no longer enjoyed quite the overriding priority indicated in the discussions of November and December 1939.

The expansion of the forces necessitated changes in the machinery for controlling them. A single Minister, a single Department, had been adequate for the tiny services of peacetime; now something more was needed. Accordingly in May 1940 new legislation provided for a Minister of National Defence for Air, and in July for a Minister of National Defence for Naval Services. Mr. C. G. Power (formerly Postmaster General), who also became Associate Minister of National Defence, and Mr. Angus L. Macdonald (formerly Premier of Nova Scotia) were respectively appointed to these portfolios. Although in law separate departments were not set up, in practice this is what took place. On 10 June 1940 Mr. Norman Rogers, who had been a competent if colourless* Minister of National Defence since September 1939, was killed in an air crash. After a short interregnum, the Minister of Finance, Colonel J. L. Ralston, a Nova Scotian who had been a famous battalion commander in the Canadian Corps of 1915-18, was transferred to National Defence (a portfolio he had already held in 1926-30) on 5 July; he was to hold it now for fifty-two eventful months. Ralston, we have seen, had so far been chiefly notable as the watchdog of the Treasury who constantly emphasized the need for economy during the "phony" or "twilight" war; he now moved to the great spending department and was to preside over the expenditure of sums that would have appalled him and his advisers in 1939-40.† The new Minister of Finance was another rugged Nova Scotian, J. L. Ilsley, who was promoted from the Department of National Revenue; though never liked by the Prime Minister, he was to be a pillar of the state through the years of war, and to be remembered as the man who taxed Canadians as they had never been taxed before, and almost made them like it.

The summer crisis of 1940 changed many things and many men. The Canadian Prime Minister had always claimed to be a staunch Commonwealth man, yet the note struck in his diary for 24 May, as he commented grimly on the decision the day before to throw Canada's little naval force into the European battle, was strange for him:

One wonders if Canadian destroyers will come back. We may find our own coasts left bare in giving our last possible aid to the Mother country. That, however, to my mind, is right. We owe to her such freedom as we have. It is right we should strike with her the last blow for the preservation of freedom.

On the same date he recorded a stage in what may be called the education of O. D. Skelton:

It amuses me a little to see how completely some men swing to opposite extremes. No one could have been more strongly for everything being done for Canada, as against Britain, than Skelton was up to a very short time ago. Yesterday, in our discussion, he naturally [? actually] did not want me to suggest any help for Canada, but rather the need for Britain. He now sees that the real place to defend our land is from across the seas. He

---

*Mackenzie King recorded in his diary on 19 September 1939 that the Governor General, Lord Tweedsmuir, referred to Rogers' lack of colour. King says, "I said I thought that was perhaps all to the good at this time."
†Unfortunately the Ralston papers preserved in the Public Archives of Canada include none relating to his tenure of the Department of Finance.

did not want the Americans to undertake the protection of our coasts, lest they might not do as much for Britain.

For perhaps the first time in his career, the Under-Secretary of State for External Affairs was in full agreement with the Chiefs of Staff.

The Effort Moves towards its Peak, 1941–1943

The strategic situation at the beginning of 1941 was painful. The Commonwealth, supported only by the exile government of the countries which Hitler had overrun, and living under the constant threat of an attack by Japan, still confronted Germany and Italy alone. Canada, her war effort now steadily expanding on a wide front, was for the moment the United Kingdom's most powerful ally, and her growing military force in Britain had been an important factor in British defensive calculations when invasion seemed imminently threatened in the autumn.

474

Early in 1941 it was difficult for the British government and Chiefs of Staff to devise a strategy that offered a genuine hope of victory. Publicly, victory was never despaired of; but there seems to have been, not surprisingly, some pessimism in confidential official circles. The Commonwealth's manpower resources were quite unequal to providing an army that could land on the Continent and challenge Germany's 200 or so divisions. Some British military economists were doubtful of being able to do this even if the United States should play an active part. In June 1941 the Future Operations Section of the Joint Planning Staff in London wrote, "The effort involved in shipping modern armies with the ground staff of Air Forces is so great that even with American help we can never hope to build up a very large force on the Continent."[61] A lucid summary was given to the Canadian Cabinet War Committee on 27 January 1941 by Mr. C. D. Howe, who had that day returned from the United Kingdom (his trip had nearly cost him his life, for the ship in which he made his eastward passage, the *Western Prince*, was torpedoed and sunk). It was difficult, he reported, to say how the actual defeat of Germany could be accomplished. Germany would continue to command a vast superiority in army divisions. The numbers of aircraft at the Germans' disposal, and the shorter distances over which they had to operate, gave them distinct advantages. Everyone felt that an attempt at invasion of the United Kingdom, which was still considered probable, could be beaten off; but the difficulties in the way of achieving positive victory, without internal trouble in Germany, were very serious. And there were no real signs as yet of serious economic deterioration or weakness in the enemy's country.

The only offensive weapons immediately available to Britain were economic pressure and a mounting air campaign, plus subversion in the occupied countries, and these were accordingly made the basis of policy. In July 1940 Winston Churchill wrote, " . . . when I look round to see how we can win the war, I see that there is only one sure path. . . . that is an absolutely devastating attack by very heavy bombers from this country upon the Nazi homeland."[62] It was hopefully felt, however, that when Germany had been worn down, a relatively small land striking force sent to the Continent might clinch the matter. The British Prime Minister emphasized the importance of armour. "We cannot hope to compete with the enemy in numbers of men, and must therefore rely upon an exceptional proportion of armoured fighting vehicles."[63] He wanted ten armoured divisions; but the War Office preferred to think in terms of organizing its tank brigades. If more of the former were organized, it would simply mean fewer of the latter. The War Office in September 1940 was planning for 1942 a possible field force of 55 divisions, though it seemed likely that the actual practicable total would be only 50. It should be noted that of the 55, only 34 would come from the United Kingdom; India was expected to provide nine, and Canada and Australia three each. Other countries of the Commonwealth and Empire would find the rest. An appreciation by the British Chiefs of Staff dated 4 September 1940 spoke optimistically of passing "to the general offensive in all spheres and in all theatres with the utmost possible strength in the spring of 1942". In discussions with U.S. officers a few days earlier, the Chiefs of Staff had emphasized the elimination of Italy from the war as a strategic aim of the first importance.[64]

475

The course of 1941, however, saw the whole war situation transformed. On 22 June Germany attacked Soviet Russia. Hitler failed to achieve his aim of crushing Russia in a single brief campaign; and thereafter the bulk of the German Army was tied down by the vast and exhausting struggle on the Eastern Front. This fact dominates the strategic situation in Europe from that moment. On 7 December Japan attacked territories of the United States, Britain and the Netherlands. The immediate result was catastrophic defeats and appalling embarrassments in the Far East; but the involvement of the United States, with its vast war potential, in fact sounded the knell of Japan and Germany alike. The British and American leaders at once confirmed a tentative decision made some months before — that in the event of the United States coming into the war alongside Britain, and against Japan and Germany the basic Allied strategy would be to *beat Germany first*. The result of all these developments was that at the end of 1941 major land operations against the Germans bade fair to be practicable in the not remote future. In the meantime, however, the only theatre where the Western Allies were engaging Germany on land was the Mediterranean basin. Early in 1941 Hitler had sent a small German force under General Erwin Rommel to North Africa to rescue his Italian ally, who had been sorely smitten by General Wavell. For many months thereafter a doubtful and dramatic battle raged back and fourth across the desert.

Against this background we can consider briefly the question of the employment of the Canadian services at this period. For the moment this was not a particularly serious problem with respect to either the Navy or

Canada the Air Force. The expanding Navy had slipped naturally and as though inevitably into the task of convoy escort. It was fully employed in cooperation with British naval forces in the battle to protect the all-important trans-Atlantic lifeline from North America to Britain against the attacks of German submarines. As for the Air Force, its squadrons based on Canada's east coast were sharing in this vital task; while the R.C.A.F. units gradually formed overseas from graduates of the Air Training Plan (there were 21 squadrons in the United Kingdom by the end of 1941) were absorbed, as they became operational, into the pattern of Royal Air Force operations in defence of Britain and in the offensive against the Germans on the Continent.[65]

The employment of the Army was the issue of which the government and the public were most aware, chiefly because circumstances resulted in the Canadian overseas force being denied active employment for a very long period. The Allied *débâcle* of 1940 ruined the plan by which the 1st

476 Canadian Division was to serve with the British Expeditionary Force in France, and it, and the 2nd Division when it arrived, found themselves committed to the defence of Britain against what seemed imminent invasion. But the invasion did not come; and by December 1940 a Canadian Press correspondent was speculating, "The Canadians may be thrown into Britain's increasingly important campaign in the Near East".[66] It was doubtless this report that led General Crerar (then in England with Colonel Ralston) to mention the matter on 4 December to the Chief of the Imperial General Staff. Sir John Dill replied that there were British divisions available for the Middle East, and there would be employment for the Canadians "nearer home". Crerar told him that he knew of no desire on the part of the Canadian government to discourage the use of its forces in any operations in which they could usefully play a part, "no matter where the theatre might be".[67] But although it had not told its Chief of the General Staff, the government (and the Prime Minister most particularly) were on the whole hostile at this time to having Canadian troops sent to the Mediterranean. Mr. King had raised the question briefly in the Cabinet War Committee on 1 October, none of the Chiefs of Staff being present; and the opinion was expressed that the Canadian public, while not questioning the importance of defending the British Isles, would not be enthusiastic about sending Canadian soldiers to new and distant scenes of operations.

On 14 November 1940 Colonel Ralston had asked the War Committee whether there would be any objection to his mentioning in the House of Commons the possibility of Canadian troops serving in Egypt, or in overseas theatres other than the United Kingdom. The Committee's decision was that this would be "inadvisable". "It had not been decided whether or not Canadian forces would be sent upon active service elsewhere than to Great Britain (apart from Iceland), and no proposal to that effect had come from the U.K. government. The question involved a most important one of policy, upon which no decision had yet been taken."

Now, on the same day on which Crerar discussed the question with Dill, the Prime Minister, in Ralston's absence, again brought the matter before the War Committee, doubtless on the basis of the same press report.* There was a long discussion, and some variety of opinion. Mr. Power, King sadly recorded in his diary, argued that the morale of the forces was suffering because of lack of opportunity for fighting.[68] Mr. J. G. Gardiner, who had lately returned from England, reported that Mr. Eden had raised the question with him and had inquired whether the Canadian government would object to Canadian troops going to Egypt. General McNaughton had also mentioned the matter, Gardiner said, but was inclined to oppose any such course.

The committee agreed unanimously "that no decision with regard to the despatch of Canadian troops for service outside of the United Kingdom should be made until there had been full consideration of the question by the Canadian government". It was also agreed that a telegram should be sent to Colonel Ralston in England, "stating that it was understood that a proposal to transfer Canadian troops to the Near East might be raised, or might already have been discussed, [and] that, while it was recognized that there might be strong arguments in favour of such a course, there were also strong arguments against it and that, in any event, full opportunity for preliminary consideration by the Canadian government was essential". The telegram, drafted by Dr. Skelton, was dispatched on 6 December. It went somewhat beyond the mere terms of the Committee's resolutions. "It is pretty certain to be felt", it remarked, "that if troops are being sent to the Near East they should be sent from the parts of the Commonwealth which control policy in the Near East or which are more geographically concerned with the Near East. It is one thing for Canada to raise additional forces to assist Britain in the British Isles or in Western Europe, it might become a very different thing to get the support necessary for Canadian forces to be sent to other parts of the world."[69]

477

Ralston replied on 9 December. He had found, he said, that the press report had no authoritative foundation, and Crerar (as we have already seen) had received from the British staff the impression that there was little likelihood of such a proposal being made. McNaughton and Crerar would be against "such a disposition", except in the event of new strategic developments arising. Ralston concluded, "Will be meeting the Minister† this week and will have views and considerations mentioned in your telegram fully in mind."[70] Ralston's record of a conference between himself and Churchill on 17 December[71] says:

I mentioned that in Canada already there had been newspaper reports already [sic], intimating that it was proposed to send Canadians to the Middle East. I had advised the Government that such a proposal had never even been put forward and I intimated that we would assume that employment of our troops, outside of the United Kingdom, be left for our suggestions. His reply was "of course."

*The statement in J. W. Pickersgill, The Mackenzie King Record, I, 156, that this was "a suggestion emanating from the Canadian Army authorities", is mistaken.
†This was obviously garbled in transmission. Ralston probably wrote "the Prime Minister".

After his return to Ottawa Ralston reported to the War Committee on 24 January that there had been no suggestion that Canadians be employed in North Africa. Mr. Churchill, he said, had confirmed that there had been no thought of so doing.

Two things seem to emerge from these exchanges with the British authorities. First, those authorities appear to have had little disposition to send Canadians to the Mediterranean (and criticisms that circulated during 1941 of an alleged British tendency to fight battles with "other people's troops and blood" can only have stiffened this attitude).[72] Secondly, Ralston's communication to Churchill after receiving King's telegram of 6 December was certainly likely to leave in British minds, for the moment, the impression that the Canadian government preferred not to have its forces transferred to the Middle East. Mr. King's diary reinforces the official records and leaves no doubt of his own views. He had no objection whatever to the army's remaining inactive in England; he was anxious to avoid casualties (and, undoubtedly, the manpower problem which long casualty lists would bring in their train). Of the War Committee discussion on 4 December 1940 he wrote, "I strongly stated my view that we owed it to our men to seek to protect their lives."[73]

In May 1941 the Department of National Defence, increasingly conscious of the problems arising from the Canadians' static role, including the fact that "absence of active participation of Canadians in recent operations is having a frustrating effect on public outlook" in Canada,[74] made an attempt at authorizing General McNaughton to seek opportunities for raiding operations for his troops. There was another difference of opinion in the War Committee when the proposal was discussed on 20 May. Mr. Power suggested that Canada offer a brigade for service in Egypt. King recorded, "I said at once that I would not countenance anything of the kind: that it might be my Scotch conscience, or it might be common sense, but I do not feel that any Government has the right to take the lives of any men for spectacular purposes. Moreover, I do not think we should interfere with the disposition of troops, when our policy was that of allowing the High Command to make whatever disposition was thought most effective."[75]

Next day the Committee considered a revised draft, prepared by General Crerar for Colonel Ralston in the form of a telegram to the British Secretary of State for War, which suggested that while it had been indicated to Ralston during his visit that the British authorities desired to keep the Canadians in England, the Canadian government would be glad to consider any proposals which the Secretary of State might forward for more active employment if this now seemed desirable "in the view of your military advisers".[76] The Committee agreed "that a telegram be sent to the U.K. Prime Minister along the lines proposed by Mr. Ralston", containing a reference to a recent conversation on the subject which Mr. King had had with the British High Commissioner. No such telegram has been found; but the draft is in the King Papers with a note by the Prime

Minister to one of his secretaries, "not sent — hold", and in the following September the file containing the draft which Ralston had placed before the Committee was returned to his secretary by the Privy Council Office with a note indicating that it "was not used and is now out of date".[77] It seems probable that Mr. King put off dispatching the telegram and ultimately simply did not send it. Nevertheless, the War Committee's decision, even if King circumvented it for the moment, was apparently not without effect. On the following 6 November Ralston, reporting to the Committee on his latest visit to Britain, said that he had discussed the question with the Secretary of State for War and had "again" emphasized the Canadian government's position: Canadian troops were to be regarded as available for service anywhere and at any time they might be needed: the government would gladly consider any suggestion that might be made. Mr. Margesson had, however, made it quite clear that for the present the Canadians' job was in Britain. . . .

On 21 October 1942 Colonel Ralston, just returned from another visit to Britain, reported to the War Committee that he had made it clear both to Mr. Churchill and the political and military chiefs of the War Office that the Canadian Army was available for service anywhere it could be most effectively employed. He told them that no condition that the Army must be employed as a whole was being imposed; the sole consideration was how and where it could serve best. The Canadian government were willing to consider any project, though they would of course wish to have the advice of their own military advisers upon any operations which were proposed. There is no evidence that King took any exception to this report.[78] It was after all only a reinforced version of that of the previous 6 November; and it was probably conceived by Ralston as authorized by the decision of 21 May 1941, which the Prime Minister, even if he had omitted to act upon it, had doubtless not forgotten.

From this time the Canadian government brought increasing pressure upon the British cabinet to find active employment for the Canadian troops. A climax came on 17 March 1943, when it was reported to the War Committee that there was still no prospect of early action and that Mr. Churchill had proposed moving additional United States airmen to the United Kingdom at the expense of the movement of Canadian Army personnel. The Committee decided to tell Churchill "that his proposal had come as a serious shock". That night King sent to Churchill a strong personal cable urging "earnest re-examination"* of the desirability of sending Canadians to North Africa.[79] It is clear from King's diary that he was doubtful about this action, but his protests seem to have been limited to private conversations with Ralston. His great interest was still "the conservation of our men";[80] but he was finding it necessary to swim with

*There appears in fact to have been no formal request earlier that Canadians be employed in North Africa. But the War Committee on 21 October 1942 had approved (without mentioning the objective) participation in a proposed operation against the Canary Islands, which in the event was never required; and King seems to have remembered this as a North African project.

the tide. Moreover, his concern with manpower itself worked to influence him in favour of Mediterranean operations.[81] Both Ralston and the Chief of the General Staff (Lieut.-General Kenneth Stuart) were strongly in favour of early action for the Army. The ultimate results of insistence by them and others were the participation of the 1st Canadian Infantry Division and the 1st Canadian Army Tank Brigade in the invasion of Sicily on 10 July 1943, and the movement of additional units sufficient to form a complete Canadian Corps to the Mediterranean in the following autumn.[82]

All this had, essentially, been arranged between the Canadian and British governments over the head of General McNaughton, the Canadian Army Commander in Britain; and he was not in sympathy with the policy of dividing the Army. He was thus in difficulties with his own government at the time when the British military authorities decided to represent to Canada that he was not the best person to command the First Canadian Army in the field; and in spite of the fact that the Prime Minister had recorded on 21 March 1943 that he felt it his duty "to back up McNaughton rather than Ralston",[83] it was McNaughton who lost the fight — for the moment.

The question of the employment of the Army was closely linked with another difficult problem which likewise tended to divide the government: that of the proper balance between the armed services in the Canadian war effort. The publication of portions of Mr. King's diary has served to establish beyond question a fact which indeed was already evident — the fact that from the beginning the Prime Minister envisioned the proper orientation of Canadian military policy in terms of concentration upon air and (to a somewhat lesser degree) naval forces, and upon industrial production, in preference to the creation of a large army. It is also very clear that the basic reason for this preferred policy was the hope which it held out of avoiding the infinitely dangerous question of overseas conscription. We have already seen that this policy, so important in King's eyes, received a severe setback in the summer of 1940. A large increase in the Canadian Army was rapidly authorized in circumstances — notably the tremendous impact of the French collapse — that prevented the Prime Minister from offering the opposition that might normally have been expected from him. The active strength of the Army rose from about 63 500 all ranks at the end of 1939 to about 178 000 at the end of 1940.[84] But subsequent further increases were usually made only in the face of resistance from the Prime Minister, who may be said to have fought a consistent rearguard action against a large army and in favour of an effort concentrated primarily upon the air force and war industry. Sometimes his attitude verged on the comic, as when he said of the butter famine of 1942, "It all comes down again on too large an army. They have been buying up most of the butter."[85]

The stages by which the Army expanded have all been described elsewhere.[86] General Crerar's original Army Programme for 1941 envisaged building the Canadian force overseas up to three divisions and an army tank brigade; in addition the 4th Division might go overseas late in the year. But while in England at the end of 1940 Ralston and Crerar were strongly pressed by the British authorities to provide and send overseas during 1941 a complete armoured division, for which the War Office would find the tanks. (The armoured division had already been authorized in principle on 13 August 1940.) The programme was amended accordingly, with the dispatch of the 4th Division (likewise in accordance with British advice) postponed until 1942. The War Committee approved its essential features on 28 January 1941. A few weeks later General Crerar, writing to McNaughton, remarked that Colonel Ralston had "backed the Programme 100% and needed to use fairly strong arguments with some of his colleagues".[87]

The Army Programme for 1942-43 encountered stronger opposition and was approved only after prolonged discussion. In the summer of 1941 the Chief of the General Staff, General Crerar, was considering, very tentatively, the possibility, as an ultimate objective, of an overseas Canadian Army "comprising 2 Corps each of 2 Divisions and an Armoured Division". The programme for 1942 gradually developed after conversations overseas in which the United Kingdom authorities emphasized the desirability of another armoured division from Canada. It comprised the formation of an Army Headquarters, an armoured division to be obtained by converting the 4th Infantry Division, a second army tank brigade, and a large number of miscellaneous Corps and Army units. The picture thus emerged of an overseas Army of five divisions, which was to be organized in two Corps.[88]

Increasing governmental worry over manpower supply had been reflected in a decision of 29 July 1941, when the Cabinet War Committee approved the mobilization for home defence purposes of a 6th Division. During this meeting there was specific discussion of the possibilities of conscription latent in a large army. It was agreed that Canada should maintain abroad four divisions and an army tank brigade; at home, two divisions; beyond this, there were no commitments.[89] In these circumstances, the new programme, which was formally placed before the Committee on 2 December, occasioned a controversy which was not resolved for over a month. The issue opened on 29 July immediately arose again. There was what may be termed a head-on collision between the Prime Minister and the Minister of National Defence. King inquired whether the programme could be implemented without recourse to overseas conscription, and said that he could not lead a government that resorted to that expedient. Ralston on his side said that he could not guarantee that conscription might not be necessary. He always kept himself free to advocate it, though he would do his utmost to get the men without it.[90] On 3 December General Stuart, who had now become Chief of the General Staff, was specifically asked whether the programme could be carried out by the voluntary method; and whether it was being presented as a maximum contribution or would be subject to increase later. He replied that in his

481

opinion the programme could be carried out by volunteering, and that it represented the visible ceiling of army expansion. Mr. King was delighted with this reply and with the new C.G.S.[91]

On 4 December the Navy and Air Force Programmes for 1942–3 were presented to the War Committee. The Navy required 13 000 additional men by 31 March 1943, bringing the total strength to some 40 000 all ranks and ratings. The Naval Minister (Mr. McDonald) explained that under the present building programme Canada would have by then some 15 destroyers and 48 minesweepers, and about 100 corvettes. The Air Force required 96 818 men between 1 December 1941 and 31 March 1943, including 56 692 by 31 July 1942. The Chief of the Air Staff, Air Vice-Marshal L. S. Breadner, explained that by 31 March 1943 it was expected that in addition to 28 "all-Canadian" R.C.A.F. squadrons overseas and certain Canadian station and group headquarters, there would be more than 100 squadrons in the field* whose aircrews would be completely Canadian. By that date R.C.A.F. personnel would total approximately 196 000 (less wastage); by the beginning of "next year" (presumably 1 April 1942) 15 000 would be overseas; while some 90 000 would be required to remain in Canada for operation of the British Commonwealth Air Training Plan at full capacity. Neither the navy nor the air force had had any difficulty in obtaining the men they needed by voluntary enlistment. Since the army programme required 104 000 additional men by 31 March 1943, the total needs for the three services for the period amounted to about 214 000.

The problem was remitted to the full Cabinet, which began studying it on 9 December. By this time the war situation had been fundamentally altered by the Japanese attack and the consequent involvement of the United States in the war. (Canada's declaration of war on Japan was authorized by the Cabinet on the evening of the 7th, anticipating those by the United Kingdom and the United States which followed on the 8th.)[92] This, combined with Mr. Churchill's visit to Ottawa on 29–31 December, and Mr. King's to Washington (26–28 December), no doubt had some effect on the outcome. Churchill made it clear at this time that another armoured division was very desirable. Nevertheless the Cabinet discussions were long and serious, and again there was a collision between Ralston and King on the still theoretical question of conscription. On 5 January the Prime Minister recorded that he felt that the Cabinet was largely in favour of granting the additional armoured division provided it did not involve overseas conscription. He added, "I have felt strongly that Ralston would resign if he did not get the extra armoured division and that Angus Macdonald would follow his example." King now gave his support to the armoured division accordingly.[93] On 6 January the Cabinet approved the Navy, Army and Air Force programmes as they had been presented, the only reservation being financial; officials of the Department

*He may have said "the equivalent of more than 100 squadrons".

482

of Finance had expressed the view that economic facts might compel some revision of the R.C.A.F. plans, which they considered impossible of accomplishment within the period.

These discussions, in which manpower had been so prominent, left no doubt that in essentials the Army had reached its furthest expansion. General Crerar's six-division army would never eventuate. Only minor increases were authorized after January 1942. A number of such measures were included in the Army Programme for 1943, approved by the War Committee on 6 January of that year. At this time a "manpower ceiling" was approved for the army overseas. Including the base units in England and three months' reinforcements calculated at the "intense" rate of activity, it amounted to about 226 000 all ranks. A final adjustment in August 1944 fixed it at 234 500 all ranks.[94]

The controversy over the Army Programme did not lay the manpower difficulty to rest. On the contrary, it shaded off into the "first conscription crisis" which nearly blew the King government apart early in 1942. Within ten days of the attacks on Pearl Harbor and Hong Kong, Mackenzie King was beginning to think in terms of the possibility of a direct appeal to the public to release the government from its commitments against overseas conscription. This might, he thought, serve to counteract the growing agitation in the country for such conscription, which found expression on 17 December 1941 in a resolution of the legislature of Manitoba. He certainly did not intend to use the proposed release to introduce overseas conscription; on the contrary, he proposed to continue to pursue a policy of avoiding it unless and until compelled to adopt it. He saw a plebiscite as a means of avoiding a split in his party and in the country over the issue.[95]

The plebiscite was duly held on 27 April 1942; Quebec, holding to its traditional attitude, voted strongly against release, but every other province voted "Yes". The next step was to introduce legislation amending the National Resources Mobilization Act to remove the prohibition against overseas conscription. The result was the resignation on 9 May of the senior French-speaking Minister from Quebec, P. J. A. Cardin, the Minister of Public Works. This was not the end of the difficulty. Before the amending bill ("Bill 80") became law, King was assailed from the opposite side. J. L. Ralston, supported by Angus L. Macdonald, had already taken exception to King's proposition that before using its new powers to send conscripts to Europe, the government should go again to Parliament and "ask for an expression of confidence". Over this issue there was conflict in the Cabinet until 7 July, when Ralston offered his resignation. King did not accept it, and within a few days the cracks in the two men's relationship were temporarily papered over by an exchange of conciliatory letters.[96]

French Canada was, of course, the centre of the government's anxieties over the manpower question; and the ministry had been weakened there by the death on 26 November 1941 of King's great lieutenant, Ernest Lapointe, the Minister of Justice, who had shown such high resolution in the Quebec crisis of 1939. Replacing him was not easy; but on 10 December King brought into the Cabinet in the same portfolio Louis S. St. Laurent, a Quebec lawyer of high reputation though of little political experience. This appointment was to prove one of King's most successful strokes.

The outbreak of war with Japan in December 1941 was the beginning of a period in which the needs — real or supposed — of home defence received increased attention from government. No informed and competent officer ever suggested that the Japanese were in a position to undertake anything more than nuisance raids against the coast of North America. On 11 December the Chiefs of Staff Committee submitted to the Ministers of National Defence a memorandum[97] forecasting that "considerable pressure" might be brought to bear on the government to increase the military strength on the Pacific Coast. The Chiefs recommended that "this pressure should be resisted". They pointed out that in certain respects the Canadian situation on the Coast was actually better than before Pearl Harbor, since the powerful forces and installations of the United States, formerly neutral, were now cooperating in the defence effort. The cooperation of the U.S. coast defences meant that the sea approaches to Victoria, Vancouver and Seattle were effectively blocked. "The defence of the West Coast of Canada", the Chiefs pointed out, "is primarily a matter for the Navy and the Air Force. The Army acts as 'goalkeeper' of the team. It is there for the purpose of resisting any attacks that have eluded the forces of the other two Services." The memorandum concluded:

> We must not allow ourselves to be stampeded by public opinion on the West Coast. The decisive theatre in this war is to the East and not to the West. If we forget this truth and divert an unnecessary proportion of our strength to the West, then we are merely playing into the hands of our enemies.

On 17 December the Cabinet War Committee "took note" of this advice. But it was without effect. The people of British Columbia and the Pacific Coast States were frightened; they duly brought pressure to bear upon their governments; and in Canada, at least, the pressure was not very seriously resisted. Although on 7 December there were already the equivalent of two brigades of infantry in British Columbia, and some additional units were moved thither at once, panic feeling grew in the province as the Japanese swept across South-East Asia and the islands early in 1942. On 16 March the Chief of the General Staff was moved to recommend that units be mobilized to complete the order of battle of the 6th Division (which as we have seen was authorized for home defence on July 1941) and that authority be given to mobilize the three brigade groups of a 7th Division, also for home defence. This was authorized in 18 March by the War Committee, which simultaneously approved a great increase in the Home War Establishment of the Royal Canadian Air Force — the record says, an addition of 49 squadrons, to cost some $206 million. This was still not considered enough. Two days later General Stuart recommended the completion of the 7th Division and the mobilization of the brigade groups of an 8th*. The War Committee approved this action the same evening.[98] The contrast between the ease with which authority was obtained for these unnecessary home defence formations, and the difficulty of obtaining that for divisions to fight overseas, is very marked. The whole series of events is a striking example of the extent to which Canadian military policy was sometimes governed by political considerations to the exclusion of genuine military considerations and professional military advice. . . .

Those aspects of the Canadian war effort lying outside the direct purview of the Department of National Defence can be dealt with only briefly but a word may be said here concerning the further development of war production.

We have seen that the summer of 1940 witnessed great activity in Canadian production planning, as under the impulsion of the defeats on the Continent orders were placed for a great variety of equipment on British or Canadian account. The harvest then sown began to be reaped on a large scale only in 1942. The exceptions were chiefly those items of equipment for which some foundation for manufacture had existed in 1939. Thus 1941 saw the production of over 383 million rounds of small arm ammunition, some 17 800 Bren guns, more than 1300 field guns and, above all — for Canada had a well-developed peacetime automotive industry — over 189 000 mechanical transport vehicles. But in all these fields, even the last-named, production was higher — as to all except vehicles, very much higher — in 1942. And in many other fields — artillery ammunition, naval and anti-aircraft guns, rifles and pistols, aircrafts and shipbuilding — 1942 was a great year of achievement. Although by the summer of 1942 "the phase of expansion was virtually complete" and the requirements of the British Army, Canada's most important overseas "customer" actually began to decline that year, 1943 witnessed still greater total production.[99]

485

New arrangements had been made to overcome the exchange barrier which made it difficult for Britain and other Allied countries to pay for Canadian supplies. The passage of the Lend-Lease Act by the United States Congress in March 1941 inevitably affected Canadian policy. The Cabinet War Committee discussed the question a number of times early in 1941 (11 and 26 February, and 12, 13 and 21 March). Apprehension was expressed that the new U.S. policy would result in large diversions of British orders from Canada to the United States. It was evident that Canada must provide credit in some form to match the American action, and on 27 March the Committee approved an offer to finance the whole United Kingdom deficit in Canada, on certain conditions. The result was an agreement under which no British orders were diverted from Canada to the United States, and Canada met British requirements for Canadian

---

*The writer has been assured that General Stuart told officers about him that he made this recommendation under political pressure, feeling that he would not retain his appointment unless he did so.

dollars. By the end of 1941 Canada had accumulated large "sterling balances" in London. On 27 January 1942 Mr. King announced that these funds were being converted into an interest-free loan to Britain, to the amount of $700 million, for the duration of the war; and that as from December 1941 all war supplies, including food, produced in Canada for Britain would constitute an outright gift to the amount of one billion dollars. This "billion-dollar gift" was superseded in 1943 by "Mutual Aid" instituted under acts passed by the Canadian parliament[100] and administered by a Canadian Mutual Aid Board consisting of five (later six) members of the Cabinet under the chairmanship of the Minister of Munitions and Supply. Mutual Aid was available to any Allied country.[101]

Proper pride in Canada's production achievement, and in the direction of it by the Department of Munitions and Supply headed by Mr. C. D. Howe, should not blind us to the fact that weaknesses in Canada's economy as compared with that of the greater industrial powers had certain inevitable results. A notable example is thus described in the British official history, which dwells with reason on the facts that Canadian industry "was dominated to an undue extent by automobile production" and that the Canadian automobile industry was so dependent upon American components: ". . . no engines were built in Canada either for tanks or for aircraft. As a result, these forms of production occupied a relatively small place in the Canadian war effort; for there was clearly little advantage to Britain in encouraging the creation of a really large capacity which would have had to be fed with supplies of the most crucial limiting components from the United States."[102] With respect to tanks, it may be doubted whether the production of these vehicles in Canada really made economic sense, the more so as the Canadian cruiser tank, the Ram, never actually saw battlefield service as a fighting tank. The Ram contained very important components from the United States.* It appears that the original "mock-up" model of the Ram, said to have been influenced by the British Tank Mission in the United States, may have considerably influenced in its turn the designers of the American Sherman;[103] but the Sherman when it emerged was undoubtedly a better operational tank, and it was the Sherman that Canadian armoured formations used in the field. . . .

By the end of the year 1943, the Canadian effort, built up gradually through four years, was almost at its peak. War production had reached its greatest expansion. Over 1 100 000 Canadians were working in the war industries.[104] There were some 790 000 in the armed forces. The recession of the small direct threat to Canada's shores (especially the expulsion of the Japanese from the Aleutians during the summer of 1943) had resulted in the disbandment of the 7th and 8th Divisions and a reduction in the Home War Establishment of the R.C.A.F. The Royal Canadian Navy, still expanding, was deep in the war in many sectors, but above all in the Battle

*Cast steel hull tops; cast steel turrets; engines; transmissions; Browning machine-guns.

of the Atlantic; in the spring of 1943 its contribution had finally been adequately recognized when it took over the control of convoy work in the North-West Atlantic. The Royal Canadian Air Force, with the British Commonwealth Air Training Plan producing aircrew at capacity (the number of "graduates" in the second half of 1943 averaged over 3700 per month),[105] was now fighting on a large scale overseas. Since the beginning of 1943 it had had a Group of its own operational in the R.A.F. Bomber Command. As for the Canadian Army, its long period of frustration was at last drawing to a close. Since July 1943 it had had one division in action in the Mediterranean theatre, and now there was a full Corps there. But the supreme moment for all three Canadian services, and for the nation as a whole, still lay ahead. It came with the invasion of North-West Europe on 6 June 1944. The campaign launched on the Normandy D Day was to bring Canada her greatest military triumphs and also her most acute political crisis of the war.

487

Crisis and Victory, 1944-1945

The strategic picture was bright for the Allies when 1944 dawned. The tide of war had turned during 1942, as the great resources of the United States and the latent strength of Russia began to tell. The Axis had now been expelled from North Africa, Italy had been driven out of the war and Allied forces were on European soil halfway up the Italian peninsula. In the vast campaign in Eastern Europe the Russian armies were rolling forward, approaching the Polish frontier of 1939. In the Pacific the Americans and their allies were advancing through the Japanese-held islands, and the British were shortly to smash a last Japanese offensive on India's eastern borders. But for the moment public attention in the Western countries was centred on North-West Europe and the expected Allied invasion there. Plans for this had in fact been discussed at the conferences at Quebec in August 1943 and at Cairo and Teheran late in the year. The great air offensive to clear the way for it was already in progress. On 6 June 1944 the landings in Normandy inaugurated the final phase of the war against Germany.

In this phase the Canadian Army's whole field force was engaged for the first time in the war. The toll in blood was very heavy; two Canadian infantry divisions had heavier losses than any others in Field-Marshal Montgomery's army group in the summer campaign, and by the end of the Falaise battle the Canadian Army's casualties in Normandy since D Day exceeded 18 000. There were likewise very severe losses in Italy in the late summer and autumn. All told, the army had just over 50 000 casualties in 1944, of which nearly 13 000 were fatal; and only 1300 of the grand total were not sustained in battle.[106]

In these circumstances, the manpower question, which had haunted the minds of Canadian politicians so long, assumed the critical form which the Prime Minister in particular had always feared. The "second conscription crisis", which arose in the autumn of 1944, was caused by the sudden shortage of infantry reinforcements. The long contention between Ralston and King over overseas conscription, the lines of which had been drawn in the Cabinet War Committee as early as the spring of 1941,[107] now issued in the "acceptance" by the Prime Minister of the resignation offered by Ralston in 1942 and the appointment of General McNaughton, the former commander of the First Canadian Army, to the portfolio of National Defence. McNaughton, ever an optimist, hoped and believed that men in sufficient numbers could still be obtained under the voluntary system; but they were not forthcoming. On 22 November, after McNaughton had received a strong recommendation from his military advisers, the Prime Minister accepted what he now recognized as the condition of his government's continuance; for the demands for compulsion heard from the country were being strongly echoed in the Cabinet. An order-in-council was passed providing for sending overseas 16 000 soldiers enlisted under the National Resources Mobilization Act. This measure caused the resignation of an anti-conscriptionist Minister, Mr. C. G. Power, but it nevertheless saved the government by averting the mass withdrawal of six conscriptionists. Quebec may be said to have accepted it, though with great and obvious reluctance. Mr. King's position, which for a moment had been seriously threatened, was restored as strong as ever. Angus L. Macdonald took over Mr. Power's Air Portfolio, in an acting capacity, until 10 January 1945, when Mr. Colin Gibson was appointed. On 17 April 1945 Mr. Macdonald relinquished the appointment of Minister of National Defence for Naval Services to return to his own kingdom in Nova Scotia; he was succeeded by Mr. D. C. Abbott. Simultaneously King got rid of another of the conscriptionists who had plagued him when Mr. T. A. Crerar left the Cabinet to go to the Senate. General McNaughton, the neophyte in politics, was the chief political victim of the crisis. He failed of election to the House of Commons both in a by-election and in the general election of 11 June 1945, but he remained Minister of National Defence until 20 August 1945, by which time the Second World War was over.

Of the operations of the fighting services during these months we need say little here. All three were heavily engaged on the Normandy D Day, and all continued to bear heavy burdens until the end of that campaign and of the war with Germany. The Navy, in addition to playing a considerable part in European waters, remained hard at work on the Atlantic convoy routes which it protected in cooperation with the air forces. The crisis of the submarine war was long past, but there was still danger and there were still losses; as late as 16 April 1945 the Canadian minesweeper *Esquimalt* was sunk in the approaches to Halifax.[108] The convoys were larger now, and the Royal Canadian Navy was furnishing a larger proportion of the escorts. Many British vessels were withdrawn for the invasion operations, and Canadian ones with them; but by June 1944 "Canadian ships were providing all the close escort for trade convoys from North America to the United Kingdom and were also furnishing several of the support group."[109] In July-August 1944 the largest North Atlantic trade convoy of the war, HXS-300, consisting of 167 vessels, crossed the ocean without casualty under the escort of one frigate and six corvettes of the R.C.N.[110]

The Royal Canadian Air Force had 46 squadrons overseas at the end of 1944, including 14 in No. 6 Bomber Group, 17 in North-West Europe, one in Italy, and two in Burma. It was also continuing to play its part in the anti-submarine war in the Atlantic; one Coastal Command squadron had sunk four U-boats and shared in the destruction of a fifth in the single month of June. In these various intense operations the R.C.A.F. was suffering heavy casualties, particularly as usual in the bomber group. One example may illustrate the scale of the effort. On 14 October No. 6 Group put up a total of 501 bombers for two attacks on Duisburg within 16 hours; its loss was four aircraft, fortunately much less than in some earlier attacks.[111]

The curtain was now falling on the great British Commonwealth Air Training Plan. The original agreement had been for three years; on 5 June 1942 its duration was extended to 31 March 1945 and at the same time its scope was somewhat enlarged. The Plan was wound up on schedule, having fully achieved its purpose. It had produced 131 553 trained aircrew — 72 835 for the R.C.A.F., 42 110 for the R.A.F., 9606 for the R.A.A.F., and 7002 for the R.N.Z.A.F. Recruiting of both air and ground personnel for the R.C.A.F. had been suspended as early as May and June 1944.[112]

489

As for the Army, it was at last doing the job for which it was created. General Crerar's First Canadian Army, serving in Field-Marshal Montgomery's 21st Army Group, fought on the left of the Allied line throughout the eleventh-month campaign that led to victory. One Canadian division and an armoured brigade took part in the D Day landing. Thereafter came the bitter and bloody fighting, lasting two and a half months, that ended in the destruction of the greater part of two German armies in and around the Falaise Gap. The next task was the hard one of capturing the fortresses of the Channel Coast, followed in the autumn by the even nastier assignment of clearing the Germans from the Scheldt Estuary to enable the Allied armies to use the port of Antwerp. February and March saw the costly battle in the Rhineland, the object of which was to evict the enemy from the corridor between Rhine and Maas and drive him across the Rhine. The losses inflicted on the Germans in this desperate struggle served to prevent them from offering equally formidable resistance to our advance beyond the great river. When the fighting ended early in May the Canadians were still driving on towards the coast of the North Sea. The campaign cost the Canadian Army 44 339 casualties, of which 11 336 were fatal.[113]

Before the end, General Crerar's command had been joined by the 1st Canadian Corps from Italy. It is a notable fact that, although as we have seen the creation of that corps in that distant theatre in 1943 was the result of the strong insistence of the Canadian government, the same government was urging the British authorities, even before the 1st Corps had been in full action, to arrange for its return. This can only be called a silly chapter in Canadian war policy.[114] But before the Corps returned, Canadian regiments had earned many battle honours and left many of their dead on the famous fields of Italy. They had broken the Hitler Line and helped to break the Gothic Line. From Sicily to the Senio the whole campaign resulted in 26 254 Canadian Army casualties; 5764 men lost their lives.[115]

. . .

The Cost

For Canada as for other countries, the war had been a painfully costly business. In terms of money — the least important form of wartime expense — "war" expenditures during the eleven fiscal years ending on 31 March 1950 amounted to $21 786 077 519. This does not include the costs of dependents' and disability pensions and medical expenses for ex-service men and women. At 31 March 1966 there were 122 077 Second World War pensions in force, and the total amount paid had been $1 613 468 269. The cost in blood, though happily less than in 1914–18, was still tragic. Of the 1 086 343 men and women who performed full-time duty in the three fighting services, 96 456 were killed or wounded or died on service; 2343 in the Royal Canadian Navy. 75 596 in the Canadian Army, 18 517 in the Royal Canadian Air Force. Those who lost their lives numbered 2024 in the Navy, 22 917 in the Army, and 17 101 in the Air Force (the last a particularly high figure in relation to total strength).[116] Such was the ultimate price paid by Canada for the victory of the good cause for which she had drawn her sword, so grimly and reluctantly, far back in September 1939.

490

Notes

(Files cited are normally Army files of the Department of National Defence, Ottawa, unless otherwise specified.)

1. *Canada Year Book, 1933*, 827; *ibid., 1934–35*, 889; *Report of the Department of National Defence, Canada, for the Fiscal Year ending March 31, 1938*, 13.
2. *Canada Year Book, 1940*, 70–71. Information from Dominion Bureau of Statistics, 27 May 1960.
3. G. M. Gathorne-Hardy, *A Short History of International Affairs 1920 to 1939* (London, 1947), 383.
4. Statement by the Prime Minister, House of Commons, 28 Feb 36; F. H. Soward, J. F. Parkinson, N. A. M. MacKenzie and T. W. L. MacDermot, *Canada in World Affairs: The Pre-War Years* (Toronto, 1941), 21, 28–30, 56–7.
5. Memorandum, "The Defence of Canada" (revised) by Maj.-Gen. A. G. L. McNaughton, 28 May 35, in McNaughton Papers, Historical Section, Canadian Forces Headquarters, Ottawa. Cf. C. P. Stacey, *Six Years of War* (Ottawa, 1955), 7.
6. Basil Collier, *The Defence of the United Kingdom* ("History of the Second World War, United Kingdom Military Series") (London, 1957), 71. Cf. W. K. Hancock and M. M. Gowing, *British War Economy* ("History of the Second World War, United Kingdom Civil Series") (London, 1949), 67–8.
7. "The Defence of Canada" by Maj.-Gen. A. G. L. McNaughton, 28 May 35. Cf. *Six Years of War*, 6–7, and Hancock and Gowing, 62–3.
8. *Reports* of D.N.D., 1936, 10; 1937, 10. *Six Years of War*, 9.
9. "An appreciation of the Defence Problems Confronting Canada . . .", 5 Sep 36, Privy Council Office. The greater part of this paper is published as Document 1 in James Eayrs, *In Defence of Canada: Appeasement and Rearmament* (Toronto, 1965).

10. *Report* of D.N.D., 1940, 11–12.
11. Speech of Hon. Ian A. Mackenzie, House of Commons, 26 Apr 39.
12. A contemporary survey is C. P. Stacey, *The Military Problems of Canada* (Toronto, 1940). A more recent book, based largely on official records, is Eayrs, note 9 above.
13. G. N. Tucker, *The Naval Service of Canada: Its Official History* (Ottawa, 1952), I, 348, 358.
14. *Six Years of War*, 26–9.
15. *Reports* of D.N.D., 1934, 82–83; 1939, 109.
16. *Evening Telegram* (Toronto), 27 Mar 39. Debates, House of Commons, 30 Mar 39.
17. Debates, House of Commons, 9 Sep 39, speeches of Messrs. Lacombe, Lacroix, Raymond, and Woodsworth.
18. *Ibid.*, speech of Mr. Héon.
19. *Report* of D.N.D., 1940, 12.
20. *Six Years of War*, 42–4, 55, 58. Appx. "B" to Chiefs of Staff to the Minister, 17 Sep 39, note 32.
21. *Six Years of War*, 60–61, 72.
22. *Six Years of War*,73–5. Tel. from Prime Minister for Massey, 17 Mar 40, King Papers, binder "Military Co-Operation with United Kingdom — Expeditionary Forces".
23. *Six Years of War*, 69: Tucker, II, 7–12, 34–41. Appx. "A" to Chiefs of Staff to the Minister, 39.
24. Tucker, II, 12, 7–8.
25. *RCAF Logbook*, 58-62.
26. King to Campbell, 12 Sep 39, King Papers, binder "Military Co-Operation with United Kingdom — Air Force".
27. *What's Past Is Prologue: The Memoirs of the Right Honourable Vincent Massey, C.H.* (Toronto, 1963), 303–6. Cf. John Herington, *Air War Against Germany and Italy, 1939–1943* ("Australia in the War of 1939–1945, Series 3 (Air)") (Canberra, 1954), 2.
28. Exchange of cables, Chamberlain-King, 26–28 Sep 39, H.Q.S. 5199-S, vol. 1.
29. Mr. Mackenzie's notes, 31 Oct 39. "Cost of Proposed Training Scheme" (Privy Council Office).
30. "Memorandum for the Prime Minister", ODS/ET, 1 Nov 39, Dept. of External Affairs file II-B-84 Pt. 2. Further memo ODS/ET, 2 Nov 39, recording conversation with the Prime Minister, *ibid.* Pickersgill, I, 43–5.
31. Unnumbered telegram, 3 Nov 39, Dept. of External Affairs file 72-T-38c Part One. Cf. memo ODS/ET, 3 Nov 39, "Air Training Telegram", External file II-B-84 Pt. 2.
32. External file 72-T-38c Part One.
33. Riverdale to Ralston, "Strictly confidential", 3 Dec 39, External file II-B-84 Pt. 2.
34. Speech in Australian House of Representatives, 10 May 40.
35. Mr. Mackenzie's notes. "Memorandum for United Kingdom Mission presented on behalf of Australian Mission and submitted to Canadian Sub-Committee on November 22, 1939".
36. Acting D.M. (Air), D.N.D., to Under-Sec. of State for External Affairs, 6 Jul 40, and B. J. Roberts, Financial Adviser, B.C.A.T.P., to same, 30 Aug 40, Dept. of External Affairs file 72-T-38c Part Two.
37. Mr. Mackenzie's notes.
38. Rogers to Balfour, 27 Nov 39, and Balfour to Rogers, same date, External file 72-T-38c Part One; Brooke-Popham to Rogers, 19 Dec 39, External file II-B-84 Pt. 2.
39. Mr. Mackenzie's notes.
40. See e.g., *Six Years of War*, 56–7.
41. *Record of Contracts awarded for the month of April, 1940, with Amendments to previous Record* (Ottawa, 1940), 334.
42. Pickersgill, I, 85–6.
43. H. Duncan Hall, *North American Supply* ("History of the Second World War, United Kingdom Civil Series") (London, 1955), 68–71, 74.
44. *Ibid.*, 16, 14–15, 17.
45. *Six Years of War*, 257–83.
46. *Maclean's*, 1 Jul 40.
47. *Six Years of War*, 77–9, Appx. "C".
48. King Papers, binder "War Strategy".
49. Pickersgill, I, 92.
50. *Ibid.*, 94–5. R. B. Hanson to R. B. Bennett, 4 Jul 40, Bennett Papers, Notable Persons File, P.A.C.
51. 4 George VI, Chap. 13.
52. Department of National War Services Act, 4 George VI, Chap. 22 (12 Jul 40). *Six Years of War*, 118–22 and Appx. "A".
53. *Six Years of War*, 76–81, 87–9.
54. Secretary of State for External Affairs to Secretary of State for Dominion Affairs, London, Tel. No. 103, 13 Jun 40, Dept. of External Affairs air training files, II-B-84.
55. *RCAF Logbook*, 62–4.

56. *Führer Conferences on Naval Affairs* (see *Brassey's Naval Annual,* 1948, 81).
57. J. Schull, *The Far Distant Ships* (Ottawa, 1950), 32–7, 49, 56.
58. *Report* of D.N.D., 1941, 12.
59. *Ibid.,* 83, H. Duncan Hall and C. C. Wrigley, *Studies of Overseas Supply* ("History of the Second World War, United Kingdom Civil Series") (London, 1956), 58.
60. Pickersgill, I, Chap. V.
61. J. R. M. Butler, *Grand Strategy*, II, *September 1939–June 1941* ("History of the Second World War, United Kingdom Military Series") (London, 1957), 549.
62. Winston S. Churchill, *Their Finest Hour* [Toronto], (1949), 643 (8 Jul 40). Cf. Denis Richards, *Royal Air Force 1939–1945*, I (London, 1953), 229.
63. *Their Finest Hour*, 462, (15 Oct 40).
64. Butler, *Grand Strategy*, II, 341–7.
65. *R.C.A.F. Logbook*, 67.
66. Ottawa *Evening Journal*, 2 Dec 40.
67. *Six Years of War*, 323n.
68. Pickersgill, I, 156.
69. Tel. No. [1910], P.M. for Ralston, 6 Dec 40, King Papers.
70. Tel. No. 2040, Ralston to P.M., 9 Dec 40, *Ibid.*
71 "Notes on Mr. Churchill's Conversation of Tuesday 17th December 1940 (as corrected by Mr. Churchill)", Ralston Papers, P.A.C.
72. *Six Years of War*, 323; cf. Churchill, *The Grand Alliance* [Toronto], (1950), 413–14, 495–7.
73. Pickersgill, I, 156.
74. Draft telegram to Lt.-Gen. McNaughton, submitted to M.N.D. by Maj.-Gen. Crerar, 19 May 41, H.Q.S. 8809, vol. 1.
75. Pickersgill, I, 220–21.
76. Submitted to M.N.D. by Crerar, 21 May 41, H.Q.S. 8809, vol. 1.
77. *Ibid.*, note of 27 Sep 41. Copy of draft with minute, King Papers (loose papers).
78. Cf. Pickersgill, I, 423, and *The Canadians in Italy*, 22.
79. *The Canadians in Italy*, 24.
80. Pickersgill, I, 495–9.
81. *Ibid.*, 607.
82. *The Canadians in Italy*, 24–6, 340–44.
83. Pickersgill, I, 500.
84. *Six Years of War*, Appx. "A".
85. Pickersgill, I, 464.
86. *Six Years of War*, Chap III.
87. *Ibid.* 87–92.
88. *Ibid.*, 93–96.
89. *Ibid.*, 94.
90. Pickersgill, I, 302–3.
91. *Ibid.*, 303–4. *Six Years of War*, 97.
92. Pickersgill, I, 297–300.
93. *Ibid.*, 334.
94. *Six Years of War*, 103.
95. Pickersgill, I, 313–15.
96. *Ibid.*, I, 370–1, 367, 394–402.
97. Memorandum "Defence of West Coast", 11 Dec 41.
98. *Six Years of War*, 168–71.
99. J. de N. Kennedy, *History of the Department of Munitions and Supply* (2 vols., Ottawa, 1950), I, 33, 88, 102, 205, 247. Hall and Wrigley, *Studies of Overseas Supply*, 62–3.
100. The War Appropriation (United Nations Mutual Aid) Acts, 1943 and 1944, 7 George VI, Chap. 17 (20 May 43) and 8 George VI, Chap. 15 (23 Jun 44).
101. Hall, *North American Supply*, 235–42.
102. Hall and Wrigley, 49.
103. *Six Years of War*, 546; Hall and Wrigley, 103; Kennedy, I, 98–9.
104. Kennedy, II, 355.
105. *Final Report of the Chief of the Air Staff to the Members of the Supervisory Board, British Commonwealth Air Training Plan* (16 Apr 45), 50.
106. *Six Years of War*, Appx. "A", Table 2. The Victory Campaign, 271.
107. Pickersgill, I, 219–20.
108. Schull, *The Far Distant Ships*, 397–8.
109. *Ibid.*, 216.
110. Tucker, II, 394.

492

111. *RCAF Logbook,*76–7, 81.
112. *Ibid.*, 83, 76. *Final Report of the Chief of the Air Staff to the Members of the Supervisory Board, British Commonwealth Air Training Plan,* 53.
113. *The Victory Campaign,* 611.
114. *Ibid.*, 33–4, 43–4.
115. *The Canadians in Italy,* 681.
116. Information from War Service Records, D.V.A., June 1967.

Canadian External Policies since 1945 *

JOHN W. HOLMES

Until the Second World War, Canada's external relations were tentative and circumscribed, limited in later years not so much by colonial status as by a lingering colonial mentality — a mentality even more characteristic of Liberal nationalists like Mackenzie King than of the traditionally imperialist Conservative Party. Mr. King, having secured with disconcerting ease recognition of Canada's right to an independent role in the world, was left with undeveloped convictions about what to do next. He cherished the view that Canada was a remote and uniquely peace-loving area, too much burdened with domestic problems to be drawn into the struggles of an obstreperous world. Because his primary impulse was to keep out of trouble, he preferred that Canada's role in the world be a modest one. To satisfy a modest sense of mission the illusion was nourished that Canada was a linchpin which kept the United States and Britain in harmony, and Canadians lectured the League of Nations without pain or cost on the virtuous example of North America.

493

This attitude was swept away at the end of the War. Self-doubt, an innate suspicion of great powers, and a quality of self-righteousness lingered. Nevertheless, Canada went through a remarkably swift transition from the status of a wartime junior partner in 1945 to that of a sure-footed middle power with an acknowledged and applauded role in world affairs ten years later. The change was accentuated by the passing from the political scene of Mr. King in 1948 and his replacement by Mr. Louis St. Laurent, a Prime Minister less inhibited by the phobias which had prevented both nationalists and imperialists in the past from seeing Canada's place in the world clearly and confidently. Mr. St. Laurent, furthermore, worked in close harmony with his new Secretary of State for External Affairs, Mr. Pearson, who had been trained as a professional diplomat. Mr. Pearson became a major architect of the United Nations and of NATO, and the rapid growth of Canada's stature was inextricably associated with his position as one of the most respected foreign ministers of the post-war era. The new approach was encouraged also by the national pride of a country

* From *International Journal*, XVIII (1963): 137–147. Copyright by Macmillan of Canada. Reprinted by permission of Gage Publishing Limited.

in the course of unparalled economic expansion, capable even of assisting the ruined great powers of the pre-war world. The rise of the United Nations, which acknowledged the formal equality of states regardless of size, set the stage for accomplishments by lesser powers with will and skill to play the new kind of diplomatic game.

It can be said of Canadians as of Americans, however, that their new international activity was the result more of responding to a need than of thrusting themselves forward as world salvationists in accordance with preconceived notions of national mission. The precarious state of the world after 1945 required the forceful intervention in far corners of a benevolent great power like the United States. It turned out also that the preservation of order often enough required the services of middle powers whose principal value was their very incapacity to threaten or command. Canada was no longer reluctant to be useful. Canadians coveted responsibilities, and Canadian diplomatic missions multiplied from seven in 1939 to sixty-five in 1962.

At the conclusion of the War, Canada was faced with the problem of finding for itself, along with Australia, Sweden, Brazil and other countries of middle stature, a place in international councils appropriate to their position as something less than major and something more than minor powers. In the case of Canada and Australia, this was a continuation of the frustrated struggle to acquire some influence on the direction of the Allied war effort. It was not surprising, therefore, that at San Francisco in 1945 it was directed most often towards reducing the pretensions of the great powers and prescribing as much international 'democracy' as possible in the United Nations. Canadian demands were, however, tempered by some understanding of the relation between function and power, and the more rabid campaign against the great powers was left to the Australians and New Zealanders. Canada did accept the special position of the great powers and the inevitability of the veto, even while seeking to place restraints on it.

Contrary to habit, Canadian officials even evolved a theory which determined their attitude on the composition of the new international bodies being established in the late 1940s. They called it the "functional theory", and although the term has dropped out of use, it is perhaps worth mentioning to illustrate the nature of Canadian pragmatism in foreign policy — a characteristic endeavour to find theories to fit the facts of international life and at the same time justify a Canadian role rather than to impose moral abstractions on an untidy world. The essence of the "functional theory" was that each nation should have responsibility appropriate to its particular capacities. Great powers, by reason of their extraordinary military capacity, were entitled to special positions in matters of security. For the non-permanent seats of the Security Council, however, preference would be given to middle powers able to make some military contribution, over smaller powers which might act irresponsibly because they had no forces of their own. Important trading nations would be accorded special influence in international commercial organizations whether or not they happened to be great military powers. Those concerned with colonial questions would have places on the Trusteeship Council, and the privileged places in bodies dealing with health or communications or immigration would go to those countries which had special interests or special qualifications in those specific subjects. To each according to his capacities seemed to be the best rule of thumb to encourage a maximum sense of responsibility in world councils, and also to avoid a permanent hegemony of the great powers on all subjects and see that middle and lesser powers had reasonable parts to play.

On the whole, this conception of function and responsibility in international organization was subdued by the pressure of regional and group representation, although it still conditions the attitudes of member states, especially middle powers, on such matters as disarmament negotiations and the direction of U.N. operations in the Middle East or Congo. The theory was, of course, never intended to be applied rigidly — rigid theories are very un-Canadian. Its application did at the beginning provide one triumph for Canada when, as one of the three powers which had worked to create nuclear energy, it became a permanent member, along with the great powers, of the U.N. Atomic Energy Commission. This priority position for Canada on an important security organ was maintained in successor bodies dealing with disarmament until 1957, and contributed considerably to Canada's prestige as a middle power which kept influential company. Canada's anxiety to limit the functions and privileges of great powers were replaced by a conception of special functions for great powers and special functions for middle powers — and even for small powers as well. Each nation was seen as unique, its history and geography as well as its size giving it some special part to play ad hoc in world affairs. The world did not consist merely of great powers on the one hand and small powers on the other. Nor should it be divided arbitrarily into blocs, Western, Communist, and Uncommitted. Or into good guys and bad guys, black and white. The international scene would be more manageable if relationships remained flexible, if we were not driven into rigid blocs and regions. Canada became the persistent advocate of flexibility in international associations, constantly worried about what seemed a too categorical approach in Washington.

Having staked out a claim for the powers of middle strength, Canada worked throughout the 1950s to put meaning into the concept — along with other comparable countries, nations of the Commonwealth and Scandinavia in particular. If the San Francisco concept of world order maintained by the great powers in unity had been maintained, the middle powers would probably have continued to see their mission in banding together to mitigate the rule of the great. When the great powers fell apart, however, their smaller associates soberly recognized that the first priority was to maintain the strength of their large friends. The polarization of the blocs produced a situation in which middle powers found themselves with

495

functions unlike those they had conceived for themselves in 1945. When crises developed in the Middle East, in Indo-China or the Congo, for instance, middle powers were required to fill diplomatic and even para-military roles from which the great powers excluded each other. Whereas Canada in the past had kept free of entanglements in Asia because it had no direct interests there, now it found that its very lack of interests was the reason it was involved. For this reason and because Canadians had developed a reputation for objectivity and independence, if not neutrality, in interna-tional affairs, Canada was chosen in 1954, along with India and Poland, to man the International Supervisory Commissions to patrol the truces in Indo-China. In 1956 Canada took the lead in proposing and also in staffing the first United Nations Emergency Force. Canadians participated in similar operations in Kashmir and Palestine, Lebanon and Congo. The performance of these essential tasks gave a certain style to Canadian diplomacy. The reputation for independence and objectivity had to be reflected in endeav-ours to establish bridges between the blocs, to find compromise solutions. Because this independence was more natural in colonial questions than in cold war questions, the mediatory role was, of course, more assiduously cultivated in relations with the uncommitted than with the Communists.

There were those in Canada who began to argue that Canada would be a more useful force in the world if it could move to a position of neutrality in the Cold War and concentrate on mediatory functions. This was not necessarily a rejection of nuclear diplomacy for the great powers but rather a pushing to extremes of the theory of a functional distinction between the roles in the world of great and middle powers. For Canada, however, it was not possible because Canadians felt too directly committed in the struggle against communism.

Canada played an active and strategic part in the creation of NATO in 1949. Canadian spokesmen were, in fact, among the first to enunciate the North Atlantic idea. In doing so they were moved by fear of the Soviet threat to Western Europe and also by the opportunity perceived to end their historic schizophrenia. For a generation Canadian external policy had been wracked by a conflict between the advocates of continental and trans-Atlantic attachments. Now leaders of all parties, having cast off the tradition of Canadian helplessness, saw in the military alliance of Britain and France with the United States the opportunity to be part of a team in which Canada's international interests and its domestic emotions could both be satisfied.

Although differences between the major allies were by no means extinguished in NATO, Canada's mutual alliance with them all did have a soothing effect on the considerations which determine external relations. The Canadian hand in diplomacy was strengthened by an unprecedented unity among parties and races within the country on the basic directions of foreign policy. Within NATO, however, Canada found itself aligned not with one large friend against another so much as with the other smaller members against the domination of the great powers. A persistent but not very successful campaign was waged to persuade the larger powers to consult their allies. Another Canadian prejudice, a traditional uneasiness about the morality of military alliances, was reflected in the continuing effort to emphasize the economic, cultural and spiritual aspects of the North Atlantic association. Whatever success this worthy endeavour achieved was largely rhetorical. Canada contributed forces to NATO in Europe and never doubted the need to resist the Soviet Union with military power, but Canada usually joined the Scandinavians in NATO to oppose the rigidities of the great powers in their attitudes both to the Communist states and the neutralists. This approach was attributable not to neutralism or to softness on communism but, rightly or wrongly, to a somewhat less ideological concept of the forces in conflict. It frequently brought Canadians into sharp difference with Americans and French but less often with the British with whose intellectual traditions of foreign policy they had more in common.

One way in which Canada maintained its independence was by keeping *497* its feet in two camps. To balance its close continental and Atlantic associations with the major Western powers were the unique associations through the Commonwealth with the leading states of Asia and Africa. The footwork was tricky; Washington often thought Canadian policy too much swayed by Mr. Nehru; and Paris and Lisbon were offended by Canadian association with the anti-colonialists. These ambivalent loyalties did, however, encourage the Canadian inclination for compromise and trouble-shooting and fortify its diplomatic strength for this purpose.

The Commonwealth played a significant role in shaping Canadian external policy after 1945. Although the impact of the Commonwealth on Canadians was more diffuse than in imperial days, the institution roused a new and in some ways more positive kind of enthusiasm, and enthusiasms which reflected the new self-confidence of a nation which saw in the ancient ties not a limitation upon but an instrument for Canadian policy. As it was transformed from an unfashionable empire into a more fashionable association among peoples of different races, the Commonwealth caught the imagination of young and progressive elements in the country, the very elements which traditionally had looked askance on the imperial tie as nostalgic, reactionary, and racialist. Canadian nationalists, no longer afraid the British were restricting their freedom, saw in the Commonwealth a counterforce to the threat to Canadian independence posed by the increasing dominance of the United States in world affairs.

The Commonwealth, furthermore, was being reshaped in the Canadian image. The British and the Australians until the late 1940s had hankered *agst* after a more unified Commonwealth, speaking in unison in international councils. Canada had insisted that the effort to impose a rigid framework on scattered peoples would induce friction rather than harmony. India, Pakistan, and the other new countries were disposed to continue membership only if the Canadian concept prevailed, and Canada's obvious preference for the new over the old Commonwealth inspired a special bond with the non-European members. In the United Nations especially, Canada found that the Commonwealth association, including as it did the major nations of Asia and Africa, extended its own diplomatic resources. Canada was canny, nevertheless, about sharing Britain's responsibilities for dependent territories. It did participate wholeheartedly, although with restrained generosity, in the Colombo Plan, a scheme for mutual economic aid of Commonwealth origin. The British proceeded to transform their empire into the kind of Commonwealth Canada preferred, and the end product, not surprisingly, now seems to appeal more to Canada than to Britain itself. It is by no means for commercial reasons only that the Canadian Government has sought of late to rally other Commonwealth countries to question the advisability of Britain's inclination to align itself with the Europeans.

498   Canada strove after 1945 to play an active role in the United Nations for sound and conscientious reasons. In the foreign policies of democracies, however, there is always an element of calculation as well as conscience, and neither the cynic nor the idealist is ever right in an absolute judgement on motives. Trust in the possibilities of the United Nations is more necessary to a weak power than a strong power. The United Nations, furthermore, provides a middle power with a stage on which to perform, and an arena in which skill counts for more than muscle. Thanks to its racial homogeneity and brief history, Canada escaped censure in the United Nations and was inevitably disposed, therefore, to look upon its activities with more enthusiasm than were, say, France or South Africa. The Commonwealth, NATO, GATT, and dozens of other international associations likewise gave Canada scope to exercise its national capability. The zeal with which a distinct and forceful foreign policy was pursued was not unrelated to the constant compulsion Canadians felt to preserve and assert their identity.

It is significant that the international associations which Canada favoured were trans-oceanic rather than regional. The very existence of Canada is a defiance against regionalism, and Canadians instinctively have clung to overseas associations for balance. An international association for which they were presumably eligible but which they did not embrace was the Organization of American States. The practical reason for this aloofness was that a country, one-tenth the size of the United States, had limited diplomatic resources for playing a responsible hand in international bodies. This was compounded by wariness about extending the areas of trouble in which to become involved. The "Western Hemisphere", furthermore, is not a geographical reality but a historical tradition. Canadians, never having shared the Washington-Bolivar mystique and the revolutionary republican tradition, have not taken very seriously the idea that they have special links with peoples of vastly different political traditions merely because they happen to be linked by an almost untraversible neck of land. History has bound Canada across traversible oceans to the Northern Hemisphere.

In recent years, however, there has been increasing interest in the O.A.S. The continuous brain-washing from the United States to which Canadians are subjected has led many to accept the assumption that the Western Hemisphere is a region. More significant perhaps has been the escalation of Latin America from the status of backwater to that of crisis zone, and some Canadians have sniffed another useful role to play in the world. They have been brain-washed also by the new dogma of regionalism inspired by the Western Europeans. Goaded by economists crying doom, many Canadians, against all their political instincts, have been troubled that they too will have to find a region to cling to. The fear that their traditional associates across the Atlantic will draw in on themselves, taking Britain along, threatens, although it has by no means triumphed over, the deep historical instinct to brace against a southward pull. In any regional reorientation that might take place, however, the Continent is likely to be taken more seriously than the Hemisphere.

Relations with the United States since 1945 illustrated the validity of the statement in 1950 of the Secretary of State for External Affairs, Mr. Pearson, that the days of easy and automatic relations were over. Relations were more complex and more irritable not because the two nations were drifting apart but because they were impinging more. Bilateral disputes, the problems of water power and canals and tariffs, continued as they presumably always will continue between neighbours. Although they inspire regional passions, they have come to be taken for granted, and in the past decade and a half they disturbed official harmony less than in earlier years when there were fewer world issues to think about. However, since the United States and Canada moved actively into the international arena, their policies on international issues clashed more frequently. Harmonious relations were threatened more by differences over defence or disarmament, over Cuba or trade with China, than over the St. Lawrence Seaway or the Columbia River. The distinct identities of the two countries have been more readily discernible in their approaches to international problems than their common social and economic habits would suggest — differences reflecting diverse political institutions, histories, overseas associations, temperament, and the inevitable variations between the approach of a nation of decisive power and that of a nation of modest influence in the world. Canada was, in fact, less docile than more distant allies, Australia and Turkey, for example. These differences reflected on the Canadian side honest convictions, tempered with a strain of perversity perhaps and the assurance of a country which was never dependent on economic aid from the United States and which, unlike overseas friends and clients, knew that the United States could not disinterest itself from its defence. In its defence policy, however, Canada was stimulated at all times by sober recognition of the fact that Canadian defences must not fall below a certain minimum lest the United States be tempted in its own interest to intervene.

These strains, however, should not obscure the profound change that

499

took place in the formal relationship between the two countries in the period under consideration. The United States and Canada became peacetime military allies, a fact so taken for granted now that its revolutionary nature is perhaps grasped only by historians. Contrary to the view recently repeated in the highest circles, history did not make the United States and Canada friends; it made them natural antagonists — and they remained antagonists from the eighteenth to the twentieth centuries. It took the Germans and then the Russians to make them allies. And even at that, Canada was prepared in 1949 to enter into such an alliance only in partnership with others, including its two mother countries. Having grown accustomed to the association and having grown more conscious of present perils than past anxieties, Canada was ready in 1957 to enter into a more specific bilateral commitment in the North Atlantic Air Defence Command, NORAD. The surrender of independent action involved in this agreement continued to disturb many people in Canada, even though few doubted the practicality of integrated continental defence. Canadians have shown an inclination, therefore, to see NORAD not as an isolated bilateral arrangement but as a regional but integral part of the NATO Alliance — thereby, as is their custom, seeking to bring in the Old World to redress the overwhelming imbalance of the New.

The process of rise and decline which affects good and evil states alike is normally spread over centuries, or at least generations. Canada, however, experienced a cycle of unnatural expansion and subsequent diminution of its international influence in considerably less than one generation. The phenomenon has been disconcerting. At the end of the Second War, Canada emerged as the third strongest of the Western powers and assumed in international organizations a position of influence not far behind that of the minor great powers. During the decade and a half since that time Canada's population and resources continued to grow, but its relative position in the world fell off considerably. The reasons were natural and not discreditable. Canada's position in 1945 had been temporarily inflated because of the exhaustion of countries such as France, Germany and Japan. Then, the appearance of new independent states and the multiplication of the membership of the United Nations gradually reduced the relative importance of the founding members. Canada, for instance, had two active terms on the Security Council in the first fifteen years, but is unlikely to have another for decades. Canada in no time at all became one of the older nations of the world, and the appeal of youth and chastity which a new country enjoys is a waning asset. As it lurches through a decade of active diplomacy, even a lesser power steps on toes and injures feelings.

Many people are inclined to attribute the decline of the Canadian position in the world to the end of the long period of Liberal government in the election of 1957. There was, however, little detectable difference in the basic external policies of the Liberal and Conservative régimes. It was inevitable, of course, that a new government whose members had had little experience of diplomacy would find difficulty sustaining a position of influence which, in the case of middle powers, is peculiarly dependent upon the authority of personality and experience. The change of government did, however, tend to obscure certain inexorable factors.

Others would say that the influence of all powers other than the two largest declined because the role of nuclear weapons throughout the 1950s became more and more decisive. There is force in this argument. Paradoxically, however, it was the nuclear stalemate that paralyzed the initiatives of great powers in fear of each other's intervention and enabled militarily weak but diplomatically influential lesser states to act effectively, particularly in those areas where there was no direct confrontation of the major powers.

During this swift period the theory of Canadian foreign policy never caught up with the reality. By the time theorists had begun to define a middle power role for Canada, based on a record of diplomatic honest brokerage culminating in a leading role in the Suez Crisis of 1956, the continuing effectiveness of this role was already being challenged by new alignments of the powers and shifting patterns in the United Nations. The patterns of middle power diplomacy can never be set for long periods if it is to retain its vitality and its relevance. Finding themselves a role appropriate to the circumstances of the 1960s is the present preoccupation of Canadians, and it is complex. The foreign policies of middle powers are inevitably directed not only at the substance of an issue but also at the means by which they can affect the resolution of that issue. The machinery of world politics is their special concern. The more responsible of them want to be of some serious consequence in the world. Since Canada first recognized its power to influence events, Canadians have been groping for a justification of their existence. What might have been a sordid pursuit of international recognition was redeemed by a puritan conscience. It was not enough to possess sovereignty, Canada must justify its independence by being somehow good for humanity. In the record since 1945 there are some grounds at least for satisfaction and encouragement for those who believe that powers of middle size have the capacity, if they wish to use it wisely, to contribute to the international community as sovereign entities.

501

See p 447

Topic Thirteen
Economic and Cultural Nationalism

502 Since the Second World War Canadians have enjoyed a higher standard of living than the citizens of almost any other country in the world. Initially, few Canadians seemed worried by or even aware of the fact that American capital was largely supporting this economic expansion. Similarly most Canadians seemed unconcerned that the country's cultural identity was more North American than uniquely Canadian. The issues of foreign ownership of Canadian industries and the Americanization of Canadian culture reached the stage of heated debate only in the 1960s and 1970s.

The Second World War was followed by a decade of tremendous growth in the Canadian economy. The large expansion of population by natural increase (Canada had the highest birth rate of any industrial country in the world in the immediate postwar era) and immigration led to an increased demand for housing projects and consumer goods. The country's growing industrial sector and increased government spending on public services also contributed to the economic expansion. But the investment capital came largely in the form of American control of Canadian natural resources and direct investment in Canadian industries. By the mid-fifties the situation was critical, with an estimated foreign investment of $17.4 billion. Walter Gordon, a concerned Canadian businessman, convinced the Liberal government in 1955 to establish a Royal Commission on Canada's Economic Prospects as a preliminary step to study the question. In the 1960s and early '70s, the debate intensified. The two excerpts from Kari Levitt's *Silent Surrender* presents one side of this complex issue.

The Americanization of Canadian culture was more difficult to detect, although no less alarming to some Canadians. In 1949 the Canadian government established the Royal Commission on National Development in the Arts, Letters and Sciences, better known as the Massey Commission, to study the problem. Their findings and recommendations have influenced the federal government's cultural policies since that time. The excerpt from the commission's report outlines their mandate, their major findings, and their recommendations.

Students wishing to pursue further the subject of economic and cultural nationalism should consult some of the publications of the University League for Social Reform: *Nationalism in Canada*, edited by P. Russell (Toronto: McGraw-Hill, 1966); *Close the 49th Parallel etc.: The Americanization of Canada*, edited by I. Lumsden (Toronto: University of Toronto Press, 1970); *The Prospect of Change: Proposals for Canada's Future*, edited by A. Rotstein (Toronto: McGraw-Hill, 1965). In addition see A. Rotstein's *The Precarious Homestead: Essays on Economics, Technology and Nationalism* (Toronto: New Press, 1973); S. M. Crean's *Who's Afraid of Canadian Culture?* (Toronto: General Publishing, 1976); and George Grant's *Empire and Technology* (Toronto: Anansi, 1969).

Regression to Dependence*
KARI LEVITT

503

Some sixty years ago Sir Wilfrid Laurier declared that the twentieth century belongs to Canada. By the middle of the century it had become clear that Canada belongs to the United States. Indeed Canada provides a dramatic illustration of the stultification of an indigenous entrepreneurial class and the regression to a condition of underdevelopment in spite of continuous income growth.

Until recently the change in Canada's status has largely gone unnoticed. Most Americans are barely aware of the existence of Canada; if they were, it would not be necessary for our political leaders to remind them so often and so politely that Canada is not the fifty-first state of the Union, nor the thirteenth district of the Federal Reserve System. Canadians tend to be more impressed by their relative wealth than by their neo-colonial satellitic relationship to the United States. As for the rest of the world, it is not really interested.

The instrument by which the Canadian economy has been recolonized since the days of Sir John A. Macdonald and Sir Wilfrid Laurier is that of direct investment — more specifically U.S. direct investment. The distinction between the import of foreign capital by the sale of bonds or debentures or non-controlling equity stock, and the intake of direct investment in the form of subsidiaries and branch plants controlled by externally-based parent corporations is crucial. In the former case control remains with the borrower; in the latter it rests unequivocally with the lender. Liabilities incurred by debt borrowing can be liquidated by the repayment of the loan. Direct investment creates a liability which is, in most cases, permanent. The following description of the difference between direct and portfolio investment is taken from a study prepared by an organization

* Chapter 4 from *Silent Surrender: The Multinational Corporation in Canada*, by Kari Levitt. Copyright 1970 by Macmillan of Canada. Reprinted by permission of Gage Publishing Limited.

representing American corporations with interests in scores of foreign countries.[1]

Direct investment refers to an investment made to create some kind of permanent organization abroad — plants, refineries, sales offices, warehouses — to make, process and market goods for local consumption and, in some instances, for sale in third areas. Such operations typically combine U.S. personnel, technology, knowhow, machinery and equipment, to expand the productive capacity of the countries in which the investment is made and to open important markets for the products of the investing country. Venture capital engaged in the location, extraction and refining of mineral resources; in developing agricultural resources; in establishing manufacturing, trade and banking enterprises; and in building and operating public utilities that serve foreign areas — all these represent direct investments.

It is important to distinguish between direct investments and the other forms of private investments abroad — banking and portfolio. A bank loan or credit to a foreigner is strictly a financial transaction between the lender and the borrower with a fixed maturity; . . . the bank may require the borrower to deposit some collateral. A portfolio investment may take two forms — purchase of foreign bonds and debentures or purchase of foreign stocks by a U.S. resident. Purchases of bonds and debentures are, like bank credits, at fixed terms with no equity interest; purchases of stocks involve equity interest, but generally not controlling interest. Only when 25 per cent or more control is attained is the investment considered a direct investment. This assumes some measure of managerial influence.

This exposition stresses the acquisition of markets for the investing country as a prime motive for direct foreign investment. The literature of under-development, including that written on Canada, has emphasized the expectation that the host country will acquire markets when it takes in direct investment. The contradiction is more apparent than real; in general the host country acquires a market for its raw materials and becomes a market for the manufactured goods of the investing country. Direct American investment in Europe has concentrated on producing and selling manufactures in these markets; in the underdeveloped countries of Latin America and the Middle East it has concentrated on extracting raw materials. In Canada we are in the unique situation of playing host to large American investments both in the resource and in the manufacturing sectors. As a result Canada has acquired markets for its industrial raw materials and has become a market for manufactured goods produced by American corporations located both here and in the United States.

Prior to the First World War Canada was the prototype of a borrowing country, old style. It contained the highest concentration of British portfolio investments to be found in any major area of the world; 14 per cent of all British foreign capital was invested in Canada, compared with 20 per cent in the United States and 20 per cent in all of Latin America.

Within fifty years Canada had become the prototype of a borrowing country, new style. By 1964, 80 per cent of long-term foreign investment in Canada was American, $12.9 billion in the form of U.S. direct investments in branch plants and subsidiaries. Canada, a relatively small country, accounted for 31 per cent of all U.S. direct investment abroad, more than the total U.S. investment in Europe, more than in all of Latin America.

As a result of the penetration of the Canadian economy by direct investment some 60 per cent of Canada's manufacturing industry, 75 per

TABLE I – **Foreign direct investment in Canada, 1945 and 1965**

	U.S. direct investment (millions of dollars)		All other foreign direct investment (millions of dollars)	
	1945	1965	1945	1965
Wood and paper products	316	1 164	32	195
Iron and ore products	272	1 769	5	244
Non-ferrous metals	203	1 021	8	91
Vegetable and animal products	184	798	63	181
Chemical and allied products	118	947	26	224
Non-metallic minerals	39	160	4	102
Textiles	28	97	28	44
Miscellaneous manufactures	31	142	2	6
TOTAL MANUFACTURING (*Excluding petroleum refining*)	*1 191*	*6 098*	*168*	*1 087*
Petroleum and natural gas	141	3 600	—	930
Mining and smelting	215	1 875	22	143
Utilities (excl. pipelines)	358	286	17	20
Merchandising	147	695	55	362
Financial	198	1 041	141	644
Other enterprise	54	345	6	82
TOTAL	*2 304*	*13 940*	*409*	*3 268*

Source: Dominion Bureau of Statistics: *Canadian Balance of International Payments, Third Quarter 1968*, p. 25, December 1968.

505

cent of her petroleum and natural gas industry and 60 per cent of her mining and smelting industry are now in the control of foreign corporations. This contrasts with the situation only twenty-five years ago when 38 per cent of manufacturing and 42 per cent of mining and smelting were under foreign control (see Tables I and II).[2]

The switch from portfolio to direct investment and the associated displacement of Canadian by American entrepreneurship has taken place against a relatively diminishing need for foreign capital. It has been estimated that the book value of all foreign assets in Canada in 1926 amounted to 117 per cent of Canada's annual output (G.N.P.). By 1948 the corresponding figure has declined to 50 per cent. Since then it has risen to 61 per cent.[3] A similar picture emerges from the trend in the cost of servicing foreign borrowing. These diminished from 3 per cent of G.N.P. in the late twenties, rose to 6 per cent in the depressed thirties and fell to a mere 2 per cent over the period 1957 to 1964. Interest and dividend payments abroad as a percentage of export earnings declined from 16 per cent in the twenties and 25 per cent in the thirties to 9 per cent in the recent period.

The use of the value of foreign assets in Canada as a measure of the contribution of foreign capital to Canadian productive capacity invites two

TABLE II – **Non-resident control as a percentage of selected Canadian industries 1926 — 1963**

Percentage of total controlled by all non-residents	1926	1939	1948	1963
Manufacturing	35	38	43	60
Petroleum and natural gas	—	—	—	74
Mining and smelting	38	42	40	59
Railways	3	3	3	2
Other utilities	20	26	24	4
TOTAL	17	21	25	34
Percentage of total controlled by US residents				
Manufacturing	30	32	39	46
Petroleum and natural gas	—	—	—	62
Mining and smelting	32	38	37	52
Railways	3	3	3	2
Other utilities	20	26	24	4
TOTAL	15	19	22	27

Source: Dominion Bureau of Statistics, *Canadian Balance of International Payments, 1963, 1964 and 1965,* August 1967, p. 127.

words of caution. First, this measure of "capital inflow", includes the appreciation in the book value of direct investment due to the ploughing back of retained earnings. This reflects the fact that a significant portion of foreign assets in Canada have been financed from Canadian savings. Second, the measure is a gross figure; in order to obtain an estimate of Canada's net indebtedness it is necessary to subtract the value of Canadian assets abroad. For both these reasons the value of foreign assets in Canada exceed significantly the sums of the net inflow of capital as shown in Canada's balance of payments.

Prior to the First World War Canada, like the United States, was unquestionably short of capital. She borrowed heavily, lent almost nothing abroad. At the time of the wheat boom in the early years of the twentieth century net capital imports reached a peak of $42 per person during the five years 1909–1913.

In the 27-year period spanning the Depression and the Second World War (1930 to 1947) there was no increase in the value of foreign assets in Canada. Indeed during the Second World War and the immediate postwar period Canada had attained a level of economic strength and maturity of fiscal and monetary institutions which enabled her to export capital on a large scale, and to contribute to the financing of the British war effort and post-war reconstruction. In the ten years 1940 to 1950 Canada's surplus on current account totalled $6.5 billion. Between 1946 and 1950 the *net export* of capital averaged $8 per head.[4]

The acceleration in the loss of control over the manufacturing and mining industries commenced with the decade of the 1950s. Since 1950 there has been a deficit on current account on the balance of payments in every year except one, and during the boom of the 1950s net capital imports averaged $12 per head. After the recession of 1957–58 capital continued to flow into Canada despite rising rates of unemployment and a slowing down of the growth of output. During the ten-year period 1957 to 1967 Canada's net indebtedness more than doubled from $11.8 billion to $24 billion.

Those who believe that all the fuss about foreign ownership and control is misguided nationalism, have taken comfort in the diminishing dependence of Canada on external sources of finance. The figures, however, lend themselves to a different interpretation; it is simply not true that Canada is short of capital. The expensive infra-structure required by her peculiar geography has long been put in place and paid for. Levels of per capita income are second only to the United States and the rate of personal savings is higher. The brutal fact is that the acquisition of control by U.S. companies over the commodity-producing sectors of the Canadian economy has largely been financed from corporate savings deriving from the sale of Canadian resources, extracted and processed by Canadian labour, or from the sale of branch-plant manufacturing businesses to Canadian consumers at tariff-protected prices. Thus, over the period 1957 to 1964 U.S. direct investment in manufacturing, mining and petroleum secured 73 per cent of their funds from retained earnings and depreciation reserves, a further 12 per cent from Canadian banks and other intermediaries and only 15 per cent in the form of new funds from the United States. Furthermore, throughout the period payout of dividends, interest, royalties and management fees exceeded the inflow of new capital.

Pattern of Investment from Confederation to Centennial

The chart on the next page illustrates the stages by which the British-financed east-west national economy has yielded to the new mercantilism of direct foreign investment of American corporations. (See also Tables III and IV.)

In 1867, there was little foreign capital in Canada. Of $200 million, $185 million was in the form of U.K. bonds; the remaining $15 million was American direct investment.

In the formative years (1867–1900) of the Canadian nation-state, there was an inflow of $815 million of U.K. bond capital and $160 million of U.S. direct investment.

In the period of the wheat boom (1900–1913), there was a total increase in indebtedness of $2545 million, in the form of portfolio investments, predominantly British, and $530 million in the form of direct investment, mainly American. By 1913 foreign capital in Canada was $3850 million of

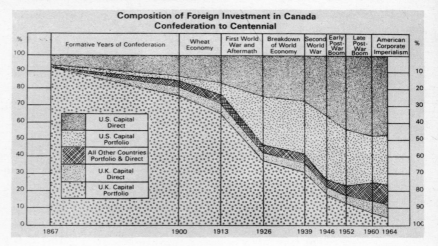

which $3080 million was portfolio debt, almost all of it British. Significantly, of the remaining $770 million of direct investment, $520 million was American. As in Australia, India, Latin America and the United States, British portfolio capital was used primarily to finance the construction of a transcontinental system of communication geared to the growing markets for foodstuffs and agricultural raw material required by metropolitan industrialization in Europe. The borrowers were Canadian entrepreneurs, both public and private. Canada was indeed short of capital — but not of entrepreneurship. Control over commodity-producing sectors remained in Canadian hands. The number of well-known Canadian businesses established before the First World War bears testimony.

TABLE III – Foreign Capital Invested in Canada, Selected Year Ends
(book value of assets in millions of Canadian dollars)

	1867	1900	1913	1926	1939	1946	1952	1960	1964	1965
U.K. direct		65	200	336	366	335	544	1 535	1 944	2 013
portfolio	185	1 000	2 618	2 301	2 110	1 333	1 340	1 824	1 519	1 485
Total	*185*	*1 065*	*2 818*	*2 637*	*2 476*	*1 668*	*1 884*	*3 359*	*3 463*	*3 498*
U.S. direct	15	175	520	1 403	1 881	2 428	4 532	10 549	12 901	13 940
portfolio		30	315	1 793	2 270	2 729	3 466	6 169	8 542	9 365
Total	*15*	*205*	*835*	*3 196*	*4 151*	*5 157*	*7 998*	*16 718*	*21 443*	*23 305*
Other direct			50	43	49	63	144	788	1 044	1 255
portfolio		35	147	127	237	290	358	1 349	1 404	1 449
Total		*35*	*197*	*170*	*286*	*353*	*502*	*2 137*	*2 448*	*2 704*
All direct	15	240	770	1 782	2 296	2 826	5 220	12 872	15 889	17 208
All portfolio	185	1 065	3 080	4 221	4 617	4 352	5 164	9 342	11 465	12 299
GRAND TOTAL	200	1 305	3 850	6 003	6 913	7 178	10 384	22 214	27 354	29 507
Direct as percentage of total foreign investment	7.5	18.5	20.0	30.0	33.5	39.0	50.0	58.0	58.0	58.3
U.S. as percentage of total foreign investment	7.5	15.5	21.5	53.0	60.0	72.0	77.0	75.0	78.5	79.0

Source: Dominion Bureau of Statistics, *The Canadian Balance of International Payments, 1963, 1964 and 1965* and *International Investment Position,* p. 126, and *Quarterly Estimates of the Canadian Balance of International Payments, Third Quarter 1968,* p. 17.

TABLE IV – Changes in Canadian Long-Term Indebtedness, Select Periods
(in millions of Canadian dollars)

	U.K.	U.S. (Direct)	U.S. (Portfolio)	Other	Total
Formative years					
1867–1900 (33 years)	+880	+160	+30	+35	+1 105
Wheat economy					
1900–1913 (13 years)	+1 753	+345	+285	+162	+2 545
First World War					
1913–1926 (13 years)	−181	+883	+1 478	−27	+2 153
Breakdown of world economy					
1926–1939 (13 years)	−161	+478	+477	+116	+910
Second World War					
1939–1946 (7 years)	−808	+547	+459	+67	+265
Early postwar boom					
1946–1952 (6 years)	+216	+2 104	+737	+149	+3 208
Late postwar boom					
1952–1960 (8 years)	+1 475	+6 017	+2 703	+1 635	+11 830
The Sixties					
1960–1965 (5 years)	+139	+3 391	+3 196	+567	+7 293
TOTAL INFLOW (1867–1964)	*+3 498*	*+13 940*	*+9 365*	*+2 704*	*+29 507*
INFLOW 1952–1965 (13 years)	*+1 614*	*+9 408*	*+5 899*	*+2 202*	*+19 123*

Source: Derived from Table III

During the First World War and its aftermath, there was large-scale liquidation of British investments and a corresponding increase in American portfolio investment. As a result of British financial weakness and some acceleration of U.S. direct investment, American ownership of total foreign assets in Canada has topped the halfway mark at 53 per cent by 1926. Direct investment as a percentage of all foreign investment stood at 30 percent.

In the breakdown of world economy (1926–1939), the rate of foreign capital inflow slowed down in Canada, as everywhere else in the world. During these thirteen years the value of foreign assets increased by only $910 million, compared with the increase of $2153 million in the previous thirteen years or indeed the increase of $2545 million during the years of the wheat boom. British assets declined, while the book value of American direct investment continued to increase by $478 million, in spite of the Depression.

During the Second World War when Canada became a heavy net exporter of capital, foreign indebtedness increased by only $265 million, but American direct investment increased by $547 million, reflecting heavy liquidation of $808 million of British assets. By 1946 the American share of Canada's foreign liabilities had climbed to 72 per cent and direct investment liabilities accounted for close to 40 per cent of all Canada's external indebtedness.

The early stage of the postwar boom (1946–1952) was dominated by the Korean War and the stock-piling of raw materials by the United States. Canada's foreign indebtedness rose by $3208 million in six years. Of these investments, two-thirds were in the form of U.S. direct investment, mainly in resource industries. By 1952, direct had exceeded portfolio investment, and the American share of Canada's foreign debt had reached 77 per cent.

The later stage of the postwar boom (1952–1960) witnessed the largest inflow of capital in Canada's history. Over half of the total increase in foreign liabilities of $11 830 million came in the form of U.S. direct investment ($6017 million), much of it in manufacturing. Portfolio borrowing also increased because the boom caused a severe shortage of capital in the public as well as the private sectors. Tight monetary conditions drove regional and local governments as well as corporations to New York to borrow funds. By 1960, 58 per cent of Canada's long-term indebtedness was in the form of direct investments. Forty-eight per cent of all foreign capital in Canada was directly controlled by American corporations.

In the sixties, there are indications of a change in the pattern of investment. Although half of the increased indebtedness of $7293 million in the five years 1960–1965 was U.S. direct investment, the share of Canada's debt represented by such investments had levelled off at 58 per cent. In part this is to be explained by the relative shift of U.S. direct investment toward Europe in the 1960s, and in part by the unusually heavy portfolio borrowings on the American capital market by provincial governments and corporations.

These briefly are the trends. Total reliance by Canada on foreign capital has declined. Yet the degree of dependence and the degree of control by metropolitan enterprise have increased. The key to this apparent paradox lies in the misleading practice of treating direct investments as capital inflows, presumed to be similar to portfolio borrowings. In fact, the element of capital transfer is only incidental to the process of direct investment, which involves a transfer of market organization, technology, and marketing channels. There is no explicit borrower, as in the case of portfolio capital. Direct investment comes for reasons of its own. Loans floated in foreign countries can, in due course, be redeemed, leaving no trace of foreign ownership. Direct investments have no necessary termination. Lenders of portfolio capital are attracted by a market rate of return. Direct investment capital comes for reasons which are quite different. Aitken has perceptively described the impact of direct investment on the Canadian economy:

Direct investments typically involve the extension into Canada of organizations based in other countries; these organizations establish themselves in Canada for purposes of their own and bring with them their own business practices, their own methods of production, their own skilled personnel, and very often their own market outlets. If all Canadian borrowings from other countries were to cease tomorrow, these direct investment organizations would continue to exist and function. Many of them, indeed, would continue to expand, financing their growth from retained earnings. And the corporate linkages which integrate them — and the sectors of the Canadian economy that they control — with organizations in other countries will survive.[5]

Notes

1. *The United States Balance of Payments,* An Appraisal of U.S. Economic Strategy, International Economic Policy Association (Washington, D.C., 1966), pp. 24, 25.
2. These figures exclude the estimated book value of foreign branch plants of Canadian enterprises

which themselves are controlled abroad. The inclusion of these branch plants of branch plants would raise the value of direct investments in Canada from $17.2 billion in 1965 to $22.9 billion.
3. A. E. Safarian, *Foreign Ownership of Canadian Industry* (Toronto, 1966), p. 10.
4. Calculated by P. Hartland, and quoted in Aitken, *American Capital and Canadian Resources* (Cambridge: Harvard University Press, 1961), p. 60.
5. Aitken, pp. 66–67.

Metropolis and Hinterland *
KARI LEVITT

The intrusion of the metropolitan-based corporation into the world economy is proceeding at an explosive rate. According to the most recent estimates the production of all multinational corporations, outside their home countries, in 1968 exceeded $300 billion, a figure considerably larger than the whole of non-communist trade in that year. The foreign production of these companies alone now forms in aggregate the third largest economy in the world following only the domestic economies of the United States and the Soviet Union.[1]

511

Addressing the Couchiching Conference of 1968, Professor J. D. Behrman, former U.S. Undersecretary of Commerce, estimated that the output of American industry and its foreign affiliates accounted for some 55 per cent of total non-communist world production in the mid-sixties. As American multinational corporations are growing roughly at twice the rate of domestic ones, the share of total world production under American control is expected to rise to 64 per cent by 1980 and 80 per cent by 1990.[2] In a more recent projection Professor Behrman predicted that the multinational corporations alone will control one-third of the output of the non-communist world by 1987.[3] The concentration of private economic power on such a scale is unprecedented, particularly if we take into account the fact that the multinational corporations are gaining almost exclusive control over new technologies.

American business enterprise enjoys an evident advantage in the new commercial and industrial mercantilism which is reflected in the fact that two hundred of the largest multinational corporations in the world operate out of the United States, but only some twenty to thirty out of other countries.

American enterprise has been extending itself into the neighbouring areas of Canada and Mexico, the Caribbean and Latin America since the Civil War. The next five paragraphs summarize some of the statistical material.

The rate of American corporate expansion by means of foreign direct investment did not attain its current momentum until the post-Second

World War era. In 1950 the book value of U.S. direct investment assets abroad was a mere $11 billion; by 1960 it had grown to $32 billion and in 1966 had reached $55 billion. The value of assets of U.S.-controlled manufacturing facilities abroad increased from $3.8 billion in 1950 to $22.1 billion in 1966. Thirty-five per cent of all U.S. manufacturing assets and 31 per cent of total direct investment assets are located in Canada. The book value of U.S. subsidiaries in Canada exceeds the amount of total U.S. direct investment in Europe, and total U.S. investments in Central and South America.

Some indication of the rate of expansion of the American-based multi-national corporations may be gleaned from the fact that, despite balance of payments crises and restrictions, new U.S. capital outflows for foreign direct investment in the *eight* years 1960 to 1967 ($19.4 billion) exceeded the sum of all U.S. direct investment undertaken in the previous *sixty* years ($17.2 billion).

512   These investments are so profitable that annual remittances of dividends, royalties, licence fees, rentals and management charges exceeded the value of new capital outflows in every year since 1900, with the exception of the depression years of 1928–31. The flow into the U.S. of profits and royalties during the eight-year period 1960–67 amounted to $33.3 billion — slightly more than total U.S. income from foreign direct investments over the previous sixty years ($31.7 billion). Currently remittances from U.S. subsidiaries to the metropolis are running at the level of $5.5 billion per annum, with a further $1.5 billion of non-remitted, reinvested profit. The net contribution of foreign direct investments to the U.S. balance of payments in terms of the surplus of remitted income over new capital outflows was $13.8 billion over the eight-year period 1960–67, almost as much as the net contribution of $14.5 billion over the previous sixty years.

These "capital-income" balances underestimate the total effect of foreign subsidiaries on the metropolitan economy. To the remitted profits and royalties must be added the increase in the book value of foreign assets by the ploughing back of retained earnings in hinterland countries, and the boost to the profitability of domestic industry by the generation of new markets for commodity exports and the availability of new raw materials on favourable terms.

A regional breakdown reveals the fact that the "Development Decade" of the 1960s has witnessed a substantial transfer of income from poorer to richer areas through the system of multinational corporations. In the period 1960–67, U.S. subsidiaries took $8.8 billion out of Latin America in remitted profits while investing only $1.7 billion; from the Middle East, Africa, Asia and the Far East they extracted $11.3 billion in profits while investing $3.9 billion. The funds extracted from the poorer areas of the world were, in effect, transferred to the rich and growing markets of Europe, where U.S. direct investment inflows of $9.6 billion exceeded the remittance of profits of $7.3 billion. Canada, which in the 1950s was a net gainer in the sense that U.S. direct investment inflows exceeded remitted profits by $1.2 billion, became a net loser in the 1960s. In the period 1960–67 remitted profits of American subsidiaries in Canada ($5.9 billion) exceeded new capital inflows ($4.1 billion) by $1.8 billion.

The New Mercantilism

Within the new mercantile nexus, direct investment complements and stimulates metropolitan exports. Indeed, insofar as "international investment has become the major channel of international economic relations" and "the international corporation the main expression of this unprecedented phenomenon,"[4] the distinction between international trade and the "domestic" sales of foreign subsidiaries is becoming increasingly irrelevant to the calculations of the multinational corporation.

The dynamics of competition are creating a new world economy. If there were no barriers to trade in the form of tariff and currency restrictions the corporations would still locate their manufacturing facilities abroad, and the operations of these facilities would still be complementary to economic activity in the metropolis.[5]

513

Direct investment complements and stimulates metropolitan exports. Expansion by American corporations has contributed to the favourable balance of payments of the United States and to the profits and further expansion of the companies which undertake these investments. We may list seven ways in which direct investments abroad promote U.S. exports and contribute to the American balance of payments:

1. Where the high-cost structure of domestic production, tariffs in foreign markets, or transportation costs make it impossible for firms to export from the U.S., overseas subsidiaries generate a flow of dividends and branch profits back to the United States. Incomes created in hinterland countries by the payment of wages and taxes and by local purchases increase the demand for imported goods in these countries, including imports from the United States.

2. If investments in foreign markets were not made by American firms they would sooner or later be made either by local or by other foreign firms. In this way direct investment blocks potential competition from rival producers, and assures a continuing return from profits.

3. As "local residents" in the host countries, subsidiaries are in a position to aggressively promote and sell abroad goods produced in the United States by their parents, which could otherwise not be exported.

4. Investment abroad leads to the export of capital goods and provides a continuing market for replacement equipment from the United States.

5. When finished goods cannot be exported from the United States, foreign subsidiaries facilitate an outflow of goods for further processing and assembly.

6. Direct investment in the extraction of raw materials ensures a constant and cheap supply of inputs to the processing industries of the United States, and a very considerable inflow of profit and dividend income.

7. The presence abroad of some four thousand subsidiaries and branch plants contributes to the cultural homogenization of the countries in which these branch plants are located, and thus expands the market for the output of the American economy at a rate faster than that at which income grows.

Hinterland countries which borrow on the U.S. capital market, the American taxpayer who finances U.S. aid programs and the many subsidies granted to U.S. corporations are assisting in the expansion of American export sales. The growth of the world market is assisted by the funds made available to the rest of the world by U.S. government lending, private portfolio lending and the aid programs of national and international agencies.

In this regard there exists a similarity with conditions in the old world economy by which long-term fixed interest loans supplied the funds to purchase the exports of the metropolitan countries. The difference lies in the fact that, by means of direct investment, American corporations supply the expanding world market from facilities located abroad, as well as those located in the United States. In this way they gain a competitive advantage over enterprises in the countries in which they establish themselves. The incomes they generate expand the markets for their sales and provide the profits from which they can finance further expansion. The logic of competition drives them to make the world their domain.

American companies long ago developed the techniques of internal self-financing. When they go "international" they finance the major part of expenditures on continued foreign expansion from the domestic savings of the hinterland countries. The capital consumption allowances and retained earnings of foreign subsidiaries are at one and the same time the internal savings of the corporations and the domestic savings of the host countries. The resources they mobilize in the hinterlands are not confined to financial capital in the sense of command over purchasing power. To an increasing degree, the international corporations are drawing the technical and managerial resources of hinterland countries into their private domain. This they achieve principally by the acquisition of existing firms in hinterland countries. The personnel of these firms then become, in effect, citizens of private corporate empires.

The International Corporation and National Sovereignty

It is becoming clear that the international corporations would find it profitable to impose on the world an "internationalism" which would break down all possible cultural, institutional and political barriers to their unlimited expansion. It is evidently in their pecuniary interests to wash away all resistance to "modernization" in a sea of detergent. To this end, President Nixon's Secretary of Commerce proclaimed a new charter of four economic freedoms: the freedom to travel, the freedom to trade, the freedom to invest and the freedom to exchange technology. The counterpart of these freedoms — which sound innocuous enough — is the suggested adoption of "rules of good behaviour" to outlaw "discrimination by host countries inconsistent with a reasonable exercise of sovereignty."

It has been said that the old colonialism brought the bible and took the land. It imposed Christianity and carried off the wealth of the Indies, the Americas and Africa. The new colonialism is carried by the ideology of materialism, liberalism — and anti-nationalism. By means of these values they seek to disarm the resistance of national communities to alien consumption patterns and the presence of alien power.

Their spokesmen proudly tell us that the large globe-circling corporations are, in fact, immensely powerful political states; they are "the colonizers of the twentieth century, and the chief colonizers because of their vast wealth and technological superiority will be the large American companies. Their armies consist not of men bearing arms but of engineers and executives equipped with vast amounts of capital and organizational know-how. Their embassies are their factories and their sales offices. The only thing they usually lack is a flag."[6]

If the nation state is a barrier to the efficient production of material goods by international corporations then, in this liberal view, the nation state is regressive, reactionary and obsolete. It should be food for thought to the liberal that this view coincides so snugly with that of the great corporations. We draw attention to the well-known statement of the former United States Under-secretary of State, Mr. George Ball:

The multinational corporation is ahead of, and in conflict with existing political organizations represented by the nation states. Major obstacles to the multinational corporation are evident in Western Europe and Canada, and a good part of the developing world.

Resistance to the assumption that the quality of life is undoubtedly improved by the mass consumption of American-type consumer goods, and to the consequent conclusion that national and cultural barriers which act to reduce the efficiency with which these goods can be supplied should be swept away, arouses the deepest indignation of American liberals.

How can American corporate capitalism be assured that the values which serve their interests can be made to prevail all over the "free" world? To ask the question is to answer it — it cannot. The attempt to do so, however, has been great and costly. In this effort lies the basis of co-operation between big business and the government of the United States.

Corporations and Metropolitan Government

The contribution by the international corporations to surpluses on current account forms one basis for their co-operation with metropolitan government in international relations; part of the surplus of foreign exchange

515

created by the operations of the corporations is made available to government for economic, political or military expenditures abroad. The point is made succinctly by the authors of a book published by the International Economic Policy Association, on the U.S. balance of payments. "Without the income from U.S. direct investments abroad, it is doubtful that the U.S. would be able to meet its world-wide military, political and economic commitments."[7] In return, the investments of the citizen of the metropolitan country are protected by the political and military strength of their government.

In this respect, also, the new mercantilism resembles the old. Economists have created the impression that the European states of the seventeenth and eighteenth centuries wished to accumulate gold because their statesmen were not sufficiently schooled in the wisdoms of political economy to understand the difference between real wealth and a bag of gold. Is it not more likely that these governments and the mercantile ventures which they promoted and protected required access to a universally acceptable means of payment to finance both their international expenditures on navies, on armies and foreign supplies, and their domestic expenditures on law and order?

In discussing some areas of common purpose from the standpoint of the United States and its multinational corporations, the government assured the corporation that it was well aware of the magnitude of American investments and of their contribution to increased employment, assets and earnings of profit.

In referring to the increasingly important role in the expansion of world trade of these "mighty engines of enlightened capitalism," Mr. Henry Fowler, U.S Secretary of the Treasury, declared that: "For this nation, therefore, they have not only a commercial importance — but a highly significant role in the United States foreign policy that has met with general approval by the Atlantic countries."[8] He elaborated on the reasons why the corporations should, in their own self-interest, assist the government of the United States in maintaining military expenditures abroad, without running down reserves to a dangerously low level.

. . . for let us understand that the United States government has consistently sought, and will continue to seek to expand and extend the role of the multinational corporation as an essential instrument of strong and healthy economic progress through the Free World.

Mr. Fowler then explained that the American firms abroad could not long continue to operate without the American political presence:

Indeed, while it is most difficult to quantify, it is also impossible to overestimate the extent to which the efforts and opportunities for American firms abroad depend upon the vast presence and influence and prestige that America holds in the world. It is impossible to overestimate the extent to which private American ventures of overseas benefit from our commitments, tangible and intangible, to furnish economic assistance to those in need and to defend the frontiers of freedom . . . in fact if we were to contemplate abandoning those frontiers and withholding our assistance . . . *I wonder not whether the opportunities for private American enterprise would wither — I wonder only how long it would take.* [Our emphasis.]

He went on to warn the corporations that the rising tide of nationalism in both developed and less developed countries was generating public attitudes that could obstruct their growth and expansion.

There are signs in quite a few developed countries that their political leaders believe they have a diminished need for foreign capital, technology and management. In a number of less developed countries, new political leaders manifest a distinct preference for government-to-government grants and loans for local or state-owned enterprises over the entry of foreign direct investment.

While acknowledging that the multinational corporation is subject to the laws of the country in which it operates, Mr. Fowler suggested that the United States would assist the corporation by bringing pressure to bear on these governments to "forego voluntarily as a matter of national policy the exercise of extremes of nationalism, even though within the bounds of sovereignty."

The areas in which countries may expect to experience pressure to "forego voluntarily" the exercise of their national sovereignty were clearly defined by American government in the same speech. There will be pressure to create or enlarge regional marketing areas. These, it was specifically pointed out, "are conducive to the infusion of capital, initiative and technology from external, as well as internal sources." We have already referred to the remarks of Mr. George Ball to the effect that the interests of the multinational corporation are in conflict with the political sovereignty of the nation state.

The corporations were warned by Mr. Fowler that failure in the efforts to reduce trade barriers "will bring the multinational corporation hard up against national or larger regional interests seeking self-containment and self-sufficiency and turning away from the post-war movement toward increasing interdependence." These remarks appeared to be addressed as much, if not more, to the countries of Western Europe and Canada, as to the so-called developing countries.

Pressure will be placed on the less developed countries to understand "by word and by deed" that "an institutional environment which accepts state confiscation or state operation of competitive units on an unrestricted basis as a national policy" is incompatible with the interests of the multinational corporation. A few years earlier Dean Rusk was less oblique in spelling out the possible consequences to aid-receiving countries of exercising their national sovereignty in a manner detrimental to the multinational operation: "We don't challenge in the strictest constitutional sense the right of a sovereign government to dispose of properties and people within its sovereign territory. We do think as a matter of policy it would be wise and prudent on their side to create conditions which would be attractive to the international investor, the private investor."[9]

Whereas commercial capital outflows from the United States generate, after a period, inflows of dividends, interest, and similar income as well as commodity exports, government expenditures on military purchases abroad

517

do not produce any compensating inflows. These foreign military expenditures have been rising rapidly. Between 1946 and 1950 the U.S. spent an average of $589 million per year; between 1951 and 1955 foreign military spending rose to an average of $2300 million. Since 1956 these expenditures have been running at $3100 million per year. If we add the net effect on the U.S. balance of payments of foreign aid the deficit is raised to at least $3500 million per year.

The cost of protecting the "enlightened engines of capitalism" is increasing. The message of the various "guidelines" programs is that Americans must increase their contribution to the financing of the empire. The demands on the corporations to cut back the outflow of direct capital means they must slow the rate of capital accumulation, and in fact liquidate assets. The request by the government brought the charge that the restriction of U.S. investment abroad "will not only kill the goose that lays the golden eggs but will serve to deplete our store of golden eggs as well."

518   America's closest friends have been harnessed in the effort to finance the rising costs of empire. Canada, which has contributed more than any other country to the overseas expansion of U.S. corporations, and whose share in world trade of manufactured goods has declined in the past decade, agreed to restrict its official exchange reserves no matter what the cost in terms of inflationary pressures. Heavily geared to the continuing inflow of American capital, Canada is highly vulnerable to a reversal in the established patterns of capital investments in the service of protection of the U.S. balance of payments and the U.S. dollar.

Hinterland Economy

While we have seen the close relation between government and the economic aim of the multinational corporation, an entirely different set of effects and relationships prevails in the hinterland or host country where the multinational companies operate. We now have a system of corporate empires, most of them centred in the United States. They extend into hinterland countries through branch plants and subsidiaries. Where the subsidiaries and affiliates are located in countries which are not themselves in a relation of metropolis to other countries, there is extreme technological, financial and organizational dependence. But there exists a range of intermediate situations where a country stands, at one and the same time, in a metropolitan relation to some countries and in a hinterland relation to others. Canada falls into this category. Both her resource and her manufacturing industries are dominated by foreign-controlled concerns. At the same time her financial institutions, which have always been highly concentrated and powerful, have extended to the Caribbean and other countries, through affiliated branches. So have some of her resource industries, such as the aluminum industry.

It is widely believed that countries benefit from metropolitan direct investment because they thereby acquire entrepreneurship as well as funds. This, so the argument runs, compensates for the weakness of the local entrepreneurial class and introduces the necessary "know-how" of modern industrial techniques into the hinterland economy. In the course of time, it is argued, the presence of modern enterprise will impart managerial and technical skills to the population and local entrepreneurship will be stimulated.

Branch-plant development, however, results in the erosion of local enterprise, as local firms are bought out and potential local entrepreneurs become the salaried employees of the multinational corporation. Enterprises which remain locally-owned tend to be marginal in the sense that they are small, or inefficient, or operate in industries which do not lend themselves to corporate organization. Exceptions to this pattern include publicly-owned or controlled enterprises or firms which have established an early technological lead over the metropolitan concerns.

The entrepreneur, operating in a well-developed branch-plant economy, is increasingly confronted with an organizational and institutional complex which presents him with a choice either of joining his resources with those of the international corporation, as a salaried employee or contenting himself with a very limited role. *519*

In the mineral resource industries, independent enterprises face a situation where the large established corporations control the terms of sale of raw materials. For independents, markets are uncertain, prices too low to cover costs, and for these reasons their capacity to borrow funds is limited. Their activities tend, therefore, to be of the riskier kind — drilling, prospecting, exploration, operation of marginal mines in abnormal market conditions and sub-contracting for work where large companies enjoy the stronger bargaining position. Ironically, success increases the risk. At the point where a venture succeeds in reaching the threshold beyond which it could become really profitable, it discovers that the doors to entry are opened only by coming to terms with those already inside.

The nature of manufacturing industry makes entry very much easier, but independent entrepreneurs have less security against loss than do branch plants. The latter can charge back losses against parent companies, which can offset them against profits earned on their exports to subsidiaries and against royalties and fees received. The existence of the branch-plant firm is thus justified even where its profits are small or negative. The disadvantage of the local firm is even greater where incentive programs are biased in favour of foreign concerns.

It is to be noted that entrepreneurship does not bear any simple relationship to high levels of income, or to high levels of education. Canada, as well as some countries of Latin America and some Caribbean countries today, has higher levels of per capita income than prevailed in the metropolitan countries during the heyday of private accumulation. They have far higher levels of per capita income than contemporary Japan, where private and public entrepreneurship is highly developed.

The lack of entrepreneurship in countries where branch-plant economy has taken root has sometimes been explained in terms of religious or ethnic factors. The superficial nature of all these explanations is best illustrated by the case of Canada. The relative decline in local entrepreneurship in contemporary English-speaking Canada as compared with the late nineteenth and early twentieth century has occurred in a period of rising income, rising educational attainment and within a framework of "modern" culture and institutions.

One of the few economists who has suggested that branch-plant economy may be as much the cause as the result of a lack of indigenous entrepreneurship is Dr. Stephen Hymer. Although addressed to the Canadian case, the following observation may well have general validity:

> The large volume of foreign investment in Canada seems to suggest a shortage of Canadian entrepreneurs. But which is cause and which is effect? We usually think of foreign investment as a consequence of a shortage of domestic entrepreneurs, but perhaps the former has helped to create the latter.
>
> Suppose, in the extreme case, Canada forbade all foreign direct investment. This would certainly slow down the flow of technology and create a gap between techniques used in Canada and the best available technique elsewhere. What would happen then? Through time the gap would grow and there would be an increasing incentive for Canadians to learn how to breach it. Might not this stimulate a growth of Canadian entrepreneurship? Once over their initial learning period, might not Canadian entrepreneurs be able to stand on their own feet? The shortage of entrepreneurs in Canada might disappear and with it the need for so much foreign investment.[10]

A branch-plant economy dependent on imported technology is assured of a perpetual technological backwardness *vis-à-vis* the metropolis. Furthermore, dependence is addictive and the dynamics of dependence are cumulative. Countries with indigenous entrepreneurship and with consumption and behavioural patterns differing from those of the metropolis relinquish a potential advantage in production for domestic and foreign markets, when they permit branch-plant economy to take over indiscriminately and on a large scale.

These tendencies become more pronounced to the degree that product and technological innovation play an increasingly important role in international competition. The advantages of temporary monopoly acquired by manufacturers in some nations by producing new products or differentiating old ones have been offered as explanations for the pattern of trade in manufactured goods. This "technology-gap" theory coincides with the argument we have been presenting, that advantages accrue to countries to the extent that they are innovators and not takers of technology. The importance of maintaining distinctive consumption and cultural patterns in encouraging the development of indigenous innovation has received less attention. It is noted in the literature, however, that there is a tendency for exporters of manufactured goods to find markets in countries where income levels are similar. Resistance to the importation of metropolitan values and consumption patterns, and barriers to the absorption of a country's intellectual, scientific and managerial resources into the world of the multinational corporation, force the country to develop its own resources of entrepreneurship.

Obviously products developed on the basis of particular climatic, geographical and cultural factors, or traditional skills and crafts, have an advantage similar to that accruing to the "temporary monopoly" acquired by producing new products or differentiating old ones. Obvious examples are small aircraft developed for use in the Canadian north, the small-scale automobiles of Europe, the glassware of Czechoslovakia, the woodworking industries of Scandinavia, or the many Italian industries developed on the basis of excellence of artistry in design.

Indigenous entrepreneurship can "learn by doing." It has been pointed out that the dynamic economies resulting from indigenous technological innovation are of particular importance for countries of limited size, and further that they are irreversible in that a nation, having acquired them, will not lose them. The importance of these factors is best illustrated in countries which are relatively poor in resources but, perhaps for that reason, rich in resourcefulness. Examples include Japan, Switzerland, Israel, the Scandinavian countries. Branch-plant economy destroys the mobilizational basis of indigenous entrepreneurship. Direct investment produces growth, but not development:

521

> The main weakness of direct investment as a development agent is a consequence of the complete character of its contribution. As it brings enterprise, management and technology to the country, it may inhibit the emergence and formation of local personnel and local institutions to perform these essential functions. Insofar as this happens foreign investment does not help the country to advance itself towards self-sustaining development. . . . Direct investment increases production and income, expands employment, creates jobs of higher productivity, augments tax revenues and raises foreign exchange receipts or reduces foreign exchange payments. The country receives benefits but not as a result of its own initiative and effort; and the production facilities created do not belong to the country nor are they run by it. . . . For the above-mentioned reasons, direct foreign investment can be depended on to play an important role in development but not a decisive one; that must be played by local entrepreneurs.[11]

The most direct expression of technological dependence in branch-plant economies is found in the relative absence of research facilities in these countries. Technological and innovational activity is concentrated in the research laboratories, boardrooms and academic centres of the metropolitan countries. Where research is carried out in hinterland countries, it tends to be limited to the modification of products developed in the metropolitan country to special conditions in particular hinterland countries.

Professor Chandler has suggested that a country's investment in research and the development of the technical skills and equipment that can handle a range of products is a far more meaningful indicator of economic strength than is the output of steel, or meat, or automobiles.[12] Skilled personnel are attracted to the metropolitan industrial and academic centres by high salaries, superior facilities and the fact that the professionals involved have internationalized the values of the metropolitan society. By means of the "brain drain," the brightest and ablest people from lower-income countries swell the technological resources of private international business empires.

Similar processes are at work with respect to managerial skill. The following account of company policy, provided by the Procter and Gamble Company, illustrates the point:

When Procter and Gamble moves into a country for the first time, it has to bring in a skilled top-management team, already developed. The initial cadre goes about building an organization in depth. Just as soon as local talent can be developed, it is. Of the American group in Canada Procter and Gamble in 1947, only two of us are left. The others have gone to Geneva, to Venezuela, to Cincinnati, and elsewhere. More important, from the organization they built, we have taken cuttings. Today the General Manager of Procter and Gamble in France is a Canadian; the General Manager in Morocco is a Canadian, the General Manager in Mexico is a Canadian; and the man responsible for all our business in the "outer Seven," including Britain is a Canadian. The important thing is that in the total organization they were neither helped nor hampered by their nationality.

These Canadians have become citizens of an international corporate empire. Their professional and management skills have been harnessed to the service of some particular international company. Meanwhile there is much wailing that Canada is short of managerial talent.

522   Although the total savings generated by the activities of branch plants are considerable, the access to these savings by local enterprise is limited. The major part of the contribution which the branch-plant sector makes to national income comes in the form of wages and salaries and government revenue. The overwhelming part of profit income, whether distributed or retained, accrues as factor income to shareholders of the parent corporation or to the corporation itself and makes no direct contribution to national income. The branch-plant economy thus chokes the development of local capitalists and inhibits the development of a local capital market. Mr. Kierans once complained that international corporate "free enterprise" discriminates against capitalism in the hinterland.

The advantage of a capitalist system is that it provides income from savings and investment, as well as from labour. To deny local participation abroad is to confine the benefits of capitalism to the United States. We need capitalists in all parts of the world.[13]

The savings out of employment income, even when the latter are high, come in the form of contributions to insurance and pension plans and are channelled through financial intermediaries whose placements tend to flow into less risky investments or the blue chip stocks of the multinational corporations. This is in contrast to the classical mechanism by which high personal income accrued to men of property, who were in fact the transactors on both sides of the capital market and could match savings with investment opportunities.

In a branch-plant economy, the reinvested profits of the subsidiaries form a significant portion of private domestic savings. The decision to dispose of these domestic savings in order to increase the assets of the branch plants is not however taken in the hinterland countries. In this case the domestic savings of the hinterland country are really part of the national economy of the metropolitan country.

The increase in foreign investment which occurs in the hinterland when subsidiaries finance expansion from retained earnings can have a serious impact on the current balance of payments situation in the event that the corporations decide to transfer capital out of the country. Such transfers may take the form of heavy payments of dividends to parent companies, repayment of loans to parents, a halt to reinvestment, or even a liquidation of reserves held by subsidiaries. The distinction between the payment of dividends and the withdrawal of capital, and between the retention of earnings and the inflow of capital are not really meaningful in transactions between parents and foreign subsidiaries. According to a study of remittance policies of U.S. subsidiaries in Europe decisions to remit dividends from subsidiaries are made solely by the parent:

> The international headquarters reserve the right to make the final decisions on almost all matters concerning the timing and size of the flow of corporate-controlled funds across national borders. The centralization of authority is often explained in terms of headquarter's "unique, world-wide point of view" — which apparently refers to top management's ability to identify *all* of the alternatives open to the international company, and to make decisions which are in the best interest of the entire organization.[14]

523

Evidently remittances are not determined only by the past and future profit position of the subsidiary, as would be the case for an independent national company. They are, we are told, made with respect to *all* alternative options open to the parent company. It may suit the parent company to step up remittances (as they were, in effect, asked to do by the U.S. government) even where earnings are not particularly high; or again it may pay the parent company to expand by borrowing local funds in the host country, even though the cost of borrowing there is raised in efforts to cut back aggregate investment expenditures and relieve inflationary pressures.

Clearly funds flow more freely within the multinational corporation than they do between sectors of the national economy of hinterland countries. Canada is an excellent example. The underdeveloped state of her capital market is not due to low income, nor to a low rate of personal savings, nor to the proverbial "conservatism" of the Canadian investor. It is the result of a colonial past and the proximity of the United States.[15]

It has been widely noted in recent years that the growing importance of U.S. foreign direct investment and the related financial and commercial flows between American firms at home and abroad has transformed "foreign" economic relations:

> The traditional balance-of-payments identification of these flows as taking place between Americans and foreigners is increasingly inadequate as a description of exports and imports of goods and capital. Some executives and economists alike now ask whether the relation between exports and foreign investment has not gone beyond the realm of traditional balance-of-payments analysis, requiring a global (not national) orientation as the pre-requisite for understanding trade among nations and national balance of payments itself.[16]

As national economies are increasingly penetrated by the operations of private corporate empires it may indeed become necessary to redefine the conventions of national accounting; it may become appropriate to draw up a "balance of payments account" of the large multinational corporations.[17]

The international corporations have evidently declared ideological war on the "antiquated" nation state. George Grant's charge that materialism, modernization and internationalism is the new liberal creed of corporate capitalism is a valid one. The implication is clear: the nation state as a political unit of democratic decision-making must, in the interest of "progress," yield control to the new mercantile mini-powers.

Although the new mercantilism of the multinational corporations is to be distinguished from the older territorial imperialism of annexation and political subjugation by colonial and quasi-colonial political administrations, cultural colonization is undeniable and undenied. *Patronat français*, the publication of the French management association, has expressed concern that the American economy is stamping its own character on industrial society the world over. This character consists of a set of values, a way of life, a philosophy, and a social structure. There is, they suggest, increasing recognition of the fact that the American corporation has a deep sociological effect on the United States. Its impact on a foreign society, which did not generate the structure in the first place, may be far greater and less understood.[18]

When corporations plan their operations to reduce or eliminate uncertainties, these are not so much removed as shifted to all those who stand outside the protection of the corporate system: small entrepreneurs, unorganized workers, inhabitants of urban ghettos and decaying rural areas, and the entire populations of peripheral or hinterland countries. As technology is harnessed to the requirements of the corporate system an unknown amount of risk is incurred in upsetting the ecological balance of the planet. Concern over the consequences of alienating man from his natural and human environment range all the way from the "normal" daily pollution of air and water to the destructive possibilities inherent in the existence of vast stockpiles of chemical and biological killing-power; all the way from the "normal" incidence of violent crime, suicide and personal insanity to the irrationalities of organized genocide and the rise of racial conflict and confrontation the world over. Mr. Fowler's "enlightened engines of capitalism" may, if they are not brought under control, literally pollute the world with the "fall-out" from unrestrained technological "progress."

Canada's Minister of Justice, the Hon. John Turner, expressed similar fears although no solutions were offered:

> Next to the nation state, the international corporation is today's most influential institution. It commands vast resources, stretches across countless boundaries, directs the fate of millions of world's citizens and carries a common culture which has been labelled "Cocacolonization." We have no international institutions to control the power of the multinational corporation. Can't we readily see a world of economic behemoths, in fierce competition, owing some loose allegiance to some nation state, but really having the power of a private government? The implications are serious. They will largely determine the quality and standard of life — not just in the western world but in Asia, Africa and Latin America.[19]

Even economists are finally expressing concern, although it is a sad commentary on the timid-minded colonial attitudes of the profession in Canada that the articulation of concern has largely come from Americans and Europeans. Sweden's Goran Ohlin, speaking in Montreal in October 1968 conceded the "power and flexibility of multinational corporations to thwart designs of national policy,"[20] while Professor Charles Kindleberger called for international regulation: "The corporations are too large and too powerful to turn them loose."[21] Professor Rosenstein-Rodan recently advised underdeveloped countries to announce which are the more and the less desirable sectors for foreign direct investment, and to close certain sectors altogether to foreign equity investment for political reasons.[22]

The suggestion that countries might negotiate international agreements for the control of multinational corporations has come from a number of sources.[23] The difficulties experienced by the U.S. government in imposing voluntary restraint on their own U.S.-based corporations for balance of payments reasons indicates that, as Professor Mikesell has said, "a rational solution achieved through international arrangements will not readily be welcomed either by international business or by most sovereign states."[24] Meanwhile, there is no escaping the fact that the defence of each nation's interest remains the responsibility of the nation itself. In no country is the matter more urgent than in Canada.

Notes

1. Abraham Rotstein: Statement Before the Standing Committee on External Affairs and National Defence, January 20, 1970.
2. See also J. N. Behrman, "An Essay on Some Critical Aspects of the International Corporation," Economic Council of Canada. Special Study (January 1970). p. 7.
3. *Interim Report on Competition Policy*, Economic Council of Canada (Ottawa, 1969), p. 180.
4. Mr. Neil McElroy, chairman of the Procter and Gamble Corporation.
5. "The political boundaries between markets . . . have no inherent economic significance for producers in their role of responding to demand. Expansion to serve foreign markets is, in principle, not different from expansion to meet domestic, regional, or national demand possibilities, and may actually present itself to producers as a necessity of maintaining their existing competitive position. . . . Were there no obstacles to their exports competitive considerations leading to expanding marketing would in time require greater production and therefore more investment abroad." Polk, Meister and Veit, *U.S. Production Abroad and the Balance of Payments*, p. 134.
6. Richard J. Barber, "The Political Dimensions of Corporate Supernationalism," in *Worldwide Projects and Installations Planning*, Sept. Oct., 1969, pp. 77–90.
7. Polk *et al., op. cit.* See also Walter Salant, *The United States Balance of Payments in 1968* (The Brookings Institution, Washington, D.C., 1963), p. 22.
8. Remarks by the Hon. Henry H. Fowler, Secretary of the Treasury, before the U.S. Council of the International Chamber of Commerce, December 8, 1965. *U.S. Information Service*, Press Release. And subsequently quoted statement by Mr. Fowler derived from the same source.
9. Dean Rusk addressing a Senate Committee in 1962. Quoted by Melville Watkins, *Toronto Daily Star*, March 22, 1969.
10. Stephen Hymer, "Direct Foreign Investment and the National Economic Interest," p. 198, in *Nationalism in Canada* by the University League for Social Reform, ed. Peter Russell. Copyright ©McGraw-Hill Company of Canada Limited, 1966.
11. Dr. Felipe Pazos, "Organization of American States," in J. H. Adler (ed.), *Capital Movements, Proceedings of a Conference held by the International Economic Association* (Macmillan, Toronto, 1967), pp. 196–197.
12. Chandler, *Strategy and Structure*, p. 395.
13. Mr. Eric Kierans, "Economics Effects of the Guidelines," *op. cit.*
14. David B. Zenoff, "Remittance Policies of U.S. Subsidiaries in Europe," *The Banker*, May 1967.

15. G. R. Conway, *The Supply of, and the Demand for, Canadian Equities*, A conspectus of the study commissioned from the Faculty of Administrative Studies, York University, by the Toronto Stock Exchange (Toronto, September 1968), (mimeo).

16. Polk *et al.*, *op. cit.*, p. 127.

17. Dr. Rolfe recently commented that "the system of national accounting is becoming anachronistic." *Globe and Mail*, May 13, 1969.

18. "U.S. Investment in France: The Case of the Hesitant Host," in the *Conference Board Record*, January 1967.

19. *Toronto Daily Star*, October 3, 1968.

20. *Toronto Daily Star*, September 17, 1968.

21. C. Kindleberger, *American Business Abroad, Selective or Direct Investment* (McGill University Press, 1969).

22. P. N. Rosenstein-Rodan, "Philosophy of International Investment in the Second Half of the Twentieth Century," in J. H. Adler (ed.), *Capital Movements*, pp. 179, 180.

23. See for example Raymond Vernon, "Multinational Enterprise and National Sovereignty," *Harvard Business Revue*, March-April, 1967, pp. 156–72.

24. R. Mikesell, *op. cit.*, p. 452.

National Development in the Arts, Letters and Sciences*
THE MASSEY REPORT

The Mandate

Our task has been neither modest in scope nor simple in character. The subjects with which we have dealt cover the entire field of letters, the arts and sciences within the jurisdiction of the federal state. But although numerous and varied they are all parts of one whole. Our concern throughout was with the needs and desires of the citizen in relation to science, literature, art, music, the drama, films, broadcasting. In accordance with our instructions we examined also research as related to the national welfare, and considered what the Federal Government might do in the development of the individual through scholarships and bursaries. Such an inquiry as we have been asked to make is probably unique; it is certainly unprecedented in Canada.

2. Our primary duty was precisely defined in our Terms of Reference. We were equipped to examine certain national institutions and functions and to make recommendations regarding their organization and the policies which should govern them. These subjects are listed in the Order in Council which established the Royal Commission. They were extended by a letter from the Prime Minister which appears with our Terms of Reference. Our recommendations will be found in Part II of our Report.

3. This major task involved a further undertaking. The agencies and functions with which we were required to deal are only certain threads in a

vast fabric. To appreciate their meaning and importance we had to view the pattern into which they are woven; to understand them we had to study their context. We found it necessary therefore to attempt a general survey of the arts, letters and sciences in Canada, to appraise present accomplishments and to forecast future progress. This stock-taking appears as Part I of our Report.

4. In the preamble to our Terms of Reference appears the following passage:

"That it is desirable that the Canadian people should know as much as possible about their country, its history and traditions; and about their national life and common achievements; that it is in the national interest to give encouragement to institutions which express national feeling, promote common understanding and add to the variety and richness of Canadian life, rural as well as urban."

There have been in the past many attempts to appraise our physical resources. Our study, however, is concerned with human assets, with what might be called in a broad sense spiritual resources, which are less tangible but whose importance needs no emphasis.

527

5. The introductory passage quoted above suggests two basic assumptions which underlie our task. First, it clearly implies that there are important things in the life of a nation which cannot be weighed or measured. These intangible elements are not only essential in themselves; they may serve to inspire a nation's devotion and to prompt a people's action. When Mr. Churchill in 1940 called the British people to their supreme effort, he invoked the traditions of his country, and based his appeal on the common background from which had grown the character and the way of life of his fellow countrymen. In the spiritual heritage of Great Britain was found the quickening force to meet the menacing facts of that perilous hour. Nothing could have been more "practical" than that appeal to thought and emotion. We have had examples of this truth in our own history. The vitality of life in French-speaking Canada and its effective coherence as a living community have come of a loyalty to unseen factors, above all of fidelity to an historic tradition. When the United Empire Loyalists came to British North America they were carried as communities through the years of danger and hardship by their faithful adherence to a common set of beliefs. Canada became a national entity because of certain habits of mind and convictions which its people shared and would not surrender. Our country was sustained through difficult times by the power of this spiritual legacy. It will flourish in the future in proportion as we believe in ourselves. It is the intangibles which give a nation not only its essential character but its vitality as well. What may seem unimportant or even irrelevant under the pressure of daily life may well be the thing which endures, which may give a community its power to survive.

6. But tradition is always in the making and from this fact we draw a second assumption: the innumerable institutions, movements and individuals interested in the arts, letters and sciences throughout our country

are now forming the national tradition of the future. Through all the complexities and diversities of race, religion, language and geography, the forces which have made Canada a nation and which alone can keep her one are being shaped. These are not to be found in the material sphere alone. Physical links are essential to the unifying process but true unity belongs to the realm of ideas. It is a matter for men's minds and hearts. Canadians realize this and are conscious of the importance of national tradition in the making.

7. Our task was opportune by reason of certain characteristics of modern life. One of these is the increase in leisure. The work of artists, writers and musicians is now of importance to a far larger number of people than ever before. Most persons today have more leisure than had their parents; and this development, along with compulsory education and modern communications, enables them to enjoy those things which had previously been available only to a small minority. But leisure is something more than just spare time. Its activities can often bring the inner satisfaction which is denied by dull or routine work. This lends added import to an inquiry concerned with such matters as books, pictures, plays, films and the radio.

528

8. At the outset of the inquiry we were asked whether it was our purpose to try to "educate" the public in literature, music and the arts in the sense of declaring what was good for them to see or hear. We answered that nothing was further from our minds than the thought of suggesting standards in taste from some cultural stratosphere. A correspondent quoted by one witness complained that he was confronted by too much "cultural tripe" on the air. If his grievance was that he had no alternative to the serious programmes he found unpalatable he was a legitimate object of sympathy. Our hope is that there will be a widening opportunity for the Canadian public to enjoy works of genuine merit in all fields, but this must be a matter of their own free choice. We believe, however, that the appetite grows by eating. The best must be made available to those who wish it. The inquiry will have served one important purpose if it contributes to this end.

9. Today governments play a part not foreseen a generation ago, in the matters which we are required to review. In most modern states there are ministries of "fine arts" or of "cultural affairs". Some measure of official responsibility in this field is now accepted in all civilized countries whatever political philosophy may prevail. In Great Britain, to avoid the danger of bureaucratic control or of political interference, semi-independent bodies, referred to later in this Report, have been set up for the promotion of the arts and letters. We have given careful consideration to this experience as it may apply to Canada.

10. In this country we have two problems. One is common to all states, the other is peculiar to ourselves. First, how can government aid be given to projects in the field of the arts and letters without stifling efforts which must spring from the desires of the people themselves? Second, how can

this aid be given consistently with our federal structure and in harmony with our diversities? On these matters we have received many and varying views. The response of the general public reflects an acceptance of the usefulness of the inquiry and the assumption underlying it, that the Federal Government has some measure of responsibility in this field.

The Question of Education

11. There is, however, one problem which has troubled a number of those presenting briefs to us. We feel it to be of sufficient importance to warrant attention at the beginning of this Report. Although the word culture does not appear in our Terms of Reference, the public with a natural desire to express in some general way the essential character of our inquiry immediately and instinctively called us the "Culture Commission". We have listened to many interesting discussions on the significance of culture: "The greatest wealth of the nation," says a French-speaking group; of "equal importance" with bathtubs and automobiles observes a more cautious English-speaking counterpart.[1] Some witnesses have welcomed an investigation into our cultural life and its possibilities. Others, however, have shown some concern lest in occupying ourselves with our national cultures, we should encroach on the field of education obviously so closely related.

529

12. We feel that on the delicate and much disputed question of education there is a good deal of unnecessary confusion which can and should be cleared away. A more precise understanding of the word in its several implications may help to remove the atmosphere of tension which unnecessarily worries many serious people, including some who have presented briefs to us. "Education belongs exclusively to the provinces", say some. "But that", is the retort, "does not affect the right of the Federal Government to make such contributions to the cause of education as lie within its means." The conflict can be resolved very simply by a clarification of the issue. The whole misunderstanding arises from an imperfect grasp of the nature and the end, the kinds and the methods of education.

13. Education is the progressive development of the individual in all his faculties, physical and intellectual, aesthetic and moral. As a result of the disciplined growth of the entire personality, the educated man shows a balanced development of all his powers; he has fully realized his human possibilities. Modern society recognizes, apart from the common experience of life, two means of achieving this end: formal education in schools and universities, and general non-academic education through books, periodicals, radio, films, museums, art galleries, lectures and study groups. These are instruments of education; when, as often happens, they are used by the school, they are a part of formal education. They are, however, more generally the means by which every individual benefits outside school hours, and much more after his school days are over.

14. This point brings us to the relation of culture to education. Culture is that part of education which enriches the mind and refines the taste. It is the development of the intelligence through the arts, letters and sciences. This development, of course, occurs in formal education. It is continued and it bears fruit during adult life largely through the instruments of general education; and general or adult education we are called upon to investigate.

15. The essential distinction between formal education and general non-academic education has been reflected in submissions made to us and in our public sessions. For example, the Canadian Catholic Conference, in its brief, says:

"We feel it appropriate to observe that we could not properly deal here with the specific problems of formal education at its various levels. This is a matter which belongs entirely within the competence of the provinces. . . . It is our wish to speak in particular of this kind of education which is ordinarily referred to as 'adult education'."[2]

530

The delegation of the *Comité Permanent de la Survivance Française en Amérique* made the following further observation in giving evidence in Quebec City:

". . . The domain of formal education belongs to the provinces, but beside the domain of formal education is that of culture or general education; and this you have been instructed to review. In our view, culture should be a matter for federal and even for international interest."[3]

16. In a country which boasts of freedom based on law and inspired by Christian principles, it is perhaps unnecessary to say that education is not primarily a responsibility of the state at all, whether provincial or federal. Education is primarily a personal responsibility, as well as a fundamental right of the individual considered as a free and rational being. Naturally, however, the individual becomes entirely himself only as a member of society; and for his education he must depend first on his parents and then on various more or less formal social groups, including those controlled by Municipal, Provincial and Federal Governments. To maintain that education must always be primarily a personal and family responsibility is not to deny the supplementary but essential functions of these groups and their governments, nor their natural and permanent interest in the education of the individual. These functions in each country are determined by law.

17. There is no general prohibition in Canadian law against any group, governmental or voluntary, contributing to the education of the individual in its broadest sense. Thus, the activities of the Federal Government and of other bodies in broadcasting, films, museums, libraries, research institutions and similar fields are not in conflict with any existing law. All civilized societies strive for a common good, including not only material but intellectual and moral elements. If the Federal Government is to renounce its right to associate itself with other social groups, public and private, in the general education of Canadian citizens, it denies its intellectual and

moral purpose, the complete conception of the common good is lost, and Canada, as such, becomes a materialistic society.

18. In accordance with the principles just explained, we are convinced that our activities have in no way invaded the rights of the provinces but may rather have been helpful in suggesting means of co-operation. We are happy to have been confirmed in this belief by several provincial departments of education which, by presenting briefs and discussing freely with us those general aspects of education in which they and we have a common concern, have given us most valuable help and encouragement in our work.

The Conduct of the Inquiry

19. In the pursuance of our task we have held public hearings in sixteen cities in the ten provinces. We have travelled nearly 10 000 miles, over 1800 of these by air. In all, the Commission has held 224 meetings, 114 of these in public session. We have received 462 briefs, in the presentation of which over 1200 witnesses appeared before us. The briefs included submissions from 13 Federal Government institutions, 7 Provincial Governments, 87 national organizations, 262 local bodies and 35 private commercial radio stations. We were aided in our work by four advisory committees, one on scholarships and research, another on museums, a third on a national library and the public archives and a fourth on historical sites and monuments. We also commissioned a number of eminent Canadians, each an authority in his own field, to prepare critical studies on a variety of subjects to provide a background for our work.[4] Certain of these studies have been published in a companion volume to this Report.

531

20. On our journey across Canada we made an effort, in so far as a heavy programme of public hearings would permit, to get in touch at first hand with activities in our field. It is useful to see things as well as to hear about them. Thus we profited from the opportunity to visit universities, local museums, provincial archives, historical monuments, local art centres, exhibitions of handicrafts, private collections of Canadian pictures; to visit broadcasting stations, privately and publicly-owned; to witness television programmes; to attend a typical showing of National Film Board films in a prairie village, the rehearsal of an opera under the auspices of the Canadian Broadcasting Corporation, a programme of local talent at a private radio station, a performance by a Canadian ballet group, a play by a representative amateur company and concerts by two symphony orchestras. We wish that our schedule had made it possible for us to do more.

21. We should like to record our deep appreciation of the warm co-operation we received from Provincial Governments; we greatly valued their interest in our task and the collaboration and hospitality they so kindly offered us. Municipalities and universities also were our generous hosts. Through the kindness of many persons we had the advantage of

meeting groups of representative citizens whose views and opinions were of the greatest use to us. We would like to record our appreciation of the frankness with which witnesses appearing before us met our requests for information. We much appreciated the friendly co-operation of the Press. The active interest of the public generally throughout the period of the inquiry encouraged us greatly and emphasized the importance of the task with which we had the honour to be entrusted.[5]

22. We have had before us a complete cross section of the Canadian population. In fact our agenda has been created by the public at large. The response to our efforts has been even greater than we had expected. The interest in our inquiry has grown as the work proceeded and this was reflected by the friendly help we received wherever we went. We were conscious of a prevailing hunger existing throughout the country for a fuller measure of what the writer, the artist and the musician could give. There appears to have been a widespread recognition of the fact that the inquiry was timely, that Canada was ripe for such a study. It was clearly realized that our economic stature and political maturity are not in themselves enough; that these must be matched by progress in another field.

23. We have been concerned with both producers and consumers, and the briefs presented have been nicely balanced between the two groups. We have been impressed throughout with the need to provide in Canada wider opportunities for our own workers in the arts, letters and sciences. In this respect we have arrears to make up. The delegations of professional groups of painters, authors, musicians, artists, architects, teachers have been fully representative of their respective fields of work, but everywhere we have sat we have heard also from the average citizen. Indeed by the briefs which have come from the three largest religious bodies in Canada, trade unions, chambers of commerce, universities, agricultural organizations, associations of women, and numerous national societies of various kinds, a large proportion of the public of Canada has been directly represented.

24. An impression has apparently been created in the minds of some observers that in the submissions from most voluntary organizations appearing before us were requests for financial aid. That was not so. With few exceptions these bodies fully realized that the Commission was not authorized by its instructions to recommend grants of public funds for such purposes. If the financial difficulties of various organizations were mentioned in their briefs, and seldom could they claim affluence, this naturally followed from an effort on their part to tell the Royal Commission about their affairs. Without a reference to finance the picture would have been incomplete. What we were impressed with was the disinterested effort which lay behind these briefs. The persons appearing asked nothing for themselves. In each case they represented a cause in which they believed and often the delegates had come to our sessions from great distances and at personal inconvenience and expense. A Nootka Indian travelled 125

miles to tell us about the vanishing art of his race and how in his view it might be saved.

25. This long and searching inquiry and the generous co-operation we have received have enabled us to see in a new perspective the various national institutions and services which we were called upon to examine. We have gained a new conception of their value in Canadian life and of their possibilities of growth and development. In Part I of this Report we describe the activities and the needs of these institutions. In Part II we offer recommendations which seem to us to arise naturally from what we have observed.

The Forces of Geography

Canadians, with their customary optimism, may think that the fate of their civilization is in their own hands. So it is. But this young nation, struggling to be itself, must shape its course with an eye to three conditions so familiar that their significance can too easily be ignored. Canada has a small and scattered population in a vast area; this population is clustered along the rim of another country many times more populous and of far greater economic strength; a majority of Canadians share their mother tongue with that neighbour, which leads to peculiarly close and intimate relations. One or two of these conditions will be found in many modern countries. But Canada alone possesses all three. What is their effect, good or bad, on what we call Canadianism?

2. The vast resources of our country are obviously a material advantage although a somewhat perilous one in this age. The intangible qualities of our sprawling mass of territory also have their consequences. Canada's scattered regions are dominated by the mysterious expanses of the Canadian Shield, with the still more mysterious Arctic beyond, pressing down and hemming in the areas of civilized life. No feeling person could be unaffected by the stark beauty of our hinterland. It has moved the artist as well as the prospector. Through the painters and poets who have interpreted their country with force and originality, Canadians have a quiet pride in what even in this overcrowded twentieth century world is still "the great lone land".

3. Along with attachment to the whole of the country with its receding distances goes the sturdy self-reliance of local communities. These are separated by both geography and history. In all our travels we were impressed by differences of tradition and atmosphere in regions such as the Atlantic Provinces, the Prairies and British Columbia. The very existence of these differences contributes vastly to "the variety and richness of Canadian life" and promises a healthy resistance to the standardization which is so great a peril of modern civilization. There is nothing in this antagonistic to a Canadian spirit. On the contrary, it has been as essential in the inspiration of artist and poet as has been the massive Canadian

533

landscape. Canadian civilization is all the stronger for its sincere and unaffected regionalism.

4. On the other hand, the isolations of this vast country exact their price. "Art is a communication." Even in acknowledging what the artist has done to create a Canadian spirit, we are reminded that he must be able to reach his community, and that he must have some intercourse with colleagues and critics if he is to do good work. Moreover, he must have the material support which as a rule only a concentrated community can give. Canada has bound herself together with expensive links of physical communication, but these exact a tax which the artist can bear even less easily than can trade and industry. This problem was discussed before us at length especially by some representative groups on the Pacific Coast; there, as in the Maritimes, people understand the cost of isolation.

5. Even the everyday activities of civilized life suffer. In a country small in area and compact in population, national organizations of painting, letters, music, architecture, drama and of other such activities are relatively simple to create and maintain. In Canada all national gatherings for whatever purpose, are costly in time and money; yet our regionalism makes them doubly necessary. It would be easy to give many concrete instances of worthy organizations whose activities lack energy and coherence merely because they want the resources for a permanent secretary and for regular, well attended meetings. Commercial organizations realize the problem and pay the price. Voluntary societies realize the problem too, but without adequate resources they must resign themselves to a limited effectiveness.

6. This isolation imposed by the conditions of our life affects the work of government institutions also. In a country such as ours where many people are remote from the national capital and from other large centres of population, it is of obvious importance to extend to them as far as may be possible the services of the national institutions in Ottawa. This was a point freely admitted by all except a few metropolitan groups with strong urban preoccupations. Our national institutions operating on a restricted budget and preoccupied with their immediate task are sometimes in danger of confusing Canada with Ottawa. This danger, those who live at a distance and who know the need of national services, are quick to notice. "It was with considerable amusement", said a group from the Prairies, "that we read under the heading National Museum . . . that 'It is centrally located and readily reached by bus and street car' . . . We ask if we can be expected to take this statement seriously?"[6] The good-natured joke was preliminary to a helpful discussion of what such a national institution could do for the rest of Canada. The responsibility is obvious and is fully accepted. The difficulty is a measure of the cost of our size and shape.

7. But apart from these problems of dispersal we face, for the most part without any physical barriers, a vast and wealthy country to which we are linked not only by language but by many common traditions. Language and tradition link us also with two mother countries. But from these we

534

are geographically isolated. On this continent, as we have observed, our population stretches in a narrow and not even continuous ribbon along our frontier — fourteen millions along a five thousand mile front. In meeting influences from across the border as pervasive as they are friendly, we have not even the advantages of what soldiers call defence in depth.

8. From these influences, pervasive and friendly as they are, much that is valuable has come to us, as we shall have occasion to observe repeatedly in this chapter and indeed throughout this entire survey: gifts of money spent in Canada, grants offered to Canadians for study abroad, the free enjoyment of all the facilities of many institutions which we cannot afford, and the importation of many valuable things which we could not easily produce for ourselves. We have gained much. In this preliminary stock-taking of Canadian cultural life it may be fair to inquire whether we have gained a little too much.

9. We are thus deeply indebted to American generosity. Money has flowed across the border from such groups as the Carnegie Corporation, which has spent $7 346 188 in Canada since 1911 and the Rockefeller Foundation, to which we are indebted for the sum of $11 817 707 since 1914.[7] There are other institutions from whose operations we benefit such as the Guggenheim Foundation and the American Association for the Advancement of Science. Through their generosity countless individuals have enjoyed opportunities for creative work or for further cultivation of their particular field of study. Applied with wisdom and imagination, these gifts have helped Canadians to live their own life and to develop a better Canadianism. Libraries given to remote rural areas or to poorly endowed educational institutions are another example of the great diversity of our neighbour's broad benevolence. Many institutions in Canada essential to the equipment of a modern nation could not have been established or maintained without money provided from the United States. In addition, the scholarships and fellowships awarded to Canadian students in American universities without any discrimination, represent an impressive contribution to the advanced training of our young men and women of promise.

535

10. Of American institutions we make the freest use, and we are encouraged to do so by the similarities in our ways of life and by the close and friendly personal relations between scholars as individuals and in groups. Not only American universities and graduate schools but specialized schools of all sorts (library schools, schools of art, of music and dramatics) great national institutions (libraries, museums, archives, centres of science and learning) — all are freely placed at our disposal.[8] We use various American information services as if they were our own, and there are few Canadian scholars who do not belong to one or more American learned societies.

11. Finally, we benefit from vast importations of what might be familiarly called the American cultural output. We import newspapers, periodicals, books, maps and endless educational equipment. We also import artistic talent, either personally in the travelling artist or company, or on the

screen, in recordings and over the air. Every Sunday, tens of thousands tacitly acknowledge their cultural indebtedness as they turn off the radio at the close of the Sunday symphony from New York and settled down to the latest American Book of the Month.

12. Granted that most of these American donations are good in themselves, it does not follow that they have always been good for Canadians. We have not much right to be proud of our record as patrons of the arts. Is it possible that, beside the munificence of a Carnegie or a Rockefeller, Canadian contributions look so small that it seems hardly worth while making them? Or have we learned, wrongly, from our neighbour an unnecessary dependence on the contributions of the rich? A similar unworthy reliance on others appears in another field. Canada sends a number of students abroad, many of them on fellowships provided by other countries; Canada offers very few of her own fellowships to non-Canadians, none at all until very recently. Perhaps we have been tempted by a too easy benevolence, but this leaves us in an undignified position, unworthy of our real power and prestige.

13. Canada has, moreover, paid a heavy price for this easy dependence on charity and especially on American charity. First, many of our best students, on completing their studies at American institutions, accept positions there and do not return. The United States wisely relaxes its rigid immigration laws for all members of "learned professions" and profits accordingly. Our neighbours, able to take their choice of the foreign students attracted to their universities by far-seeing generosity, naturally choose many Canadians, partly because they are there in such numbers, partly because they fit in more readily with American ways than do others.

14. In consideration of American generosity in educating her citizens Canada "sells down south" as many as 2500 professional men and women in a year.[9] Moreover, Canada by her too great dependence on American fellowships for advanced study, particularly in the humanities and social studies, has starved her own universities which lack not only money but the community of scholarship essential to the best work. ". . . American generosity has blinded our eyes to our own necessities. Culturally we have feasted on the bounty of our neighbours, and then we ask plaintively what is wrong with our progress in the arts." So runs a comment in the brief of the National Conference of Canadian Universities.[10]

15. This impoverishment of Canadian universities for want of effort to keep our scholars at home, brings us to the whole question of our dependence on the United States for the satisfaction of so many non-material needs. Few Canadians realize the extent of this dependence. We know that if some disaster were to cut off our ready access to our neighbours, our whole economic life would be dislocated; but do we realize our lack of self-reliance in other matters?

536

16. Such a catastrophe for instance would no doubt hasten the establishment of the National Library so long overdue, but without many bibliographical aids now coming to us from the United States this would be very difficult, and the library would be deprived of countless invaluable Canadian books now available only in the United States. Moreover, it would be difficult to staff it properly without the facilities for advanced library training not found in Canada. The National Conference of Canadian Universities would no doubt make hasty plans for developing and expanding the few adequate schools of graduate studies which we now possess in view of the expense of sending large numbers of students to England or France. The development of many various specialized schools in the arts would be essential. Extensive provision would have to be made also for advanced study, research, and publication in the humanities and social studies as these are now almost wholly supported by American bounty. One Canadian body in this field indeed derives its entire support from the United States.

17. In this general picture of American influence on our cultural life it is *537* perhaps permissible to mention that it extends to an extraordinary degree into an area beyond the limits of our inquiry, but closely related to it. Teachers from English-speaking Canada who wish to improve their talents or raise their professional status almost automatically make their pilgrimage to Teachers' College at Columbia University or to one of half a dozen similar institutions. They return to occupy senior positions in elementary and high schools and to staff our normal schools and colleges of education. How many Canadians realize that over a large part of Canada the schools are accepting tacit direction from New York that they would not think of taking from Ottawa? On the quality of this direction it is not our place to pronounce, but we may make two general observations: first, Americans themselves are becoming restive under the regime; second, our use of American institutions, or our lazy, even abject, imitation of them has caused an uncritical acceptance of ideas and assumptions which are alien to our tradition. But for American hospitality we might, in Canada, have been led to develop educational ideas and practices more in keeping with our own way of life.

18. It may be added that we should also have been forced to produce our own educational materials — books, maps, pictures and so forth. As it is, the dependence of English-speaking Canada on the United States for these publications is excessive. In the elementary schools and high schools the actual texts may be produced in Canada, but teachers complain that far too much of the supplementary material is American with an emphasis and direction appropriate for American children but unsuitable for Canadian. As an illustration of the unsuitability of even the best American material, the statement was made in one of our briefs that out of thirty-four children in a Grade VIII class in a Canadian school, nineteen knew all about the significance of July 4 and only seven could explain that of July 1.

19. In our universities the situation is very much more serious. The

comparative smallness of the Canadian university population, and the accessibility of American publishing houses with their huge markets has resulted in an almost universal dependence on the American product. It is interesting that a vigorous complaint of American text books should come from a scientist:

"Where personalities and priorities are in question, American writings are very much biased in favour of the American. This is not to suggest that the facts will be distorted, but by mentioning the American names and industries and omitting mention of any others, a very unbalanced picture can be given. To subject Canadian students year in and year out to these influences are not particularly good for the growth of a wholesome Canadianism."[11]

20. In other fields, the complaint may be not so much one of bias as of emphasis. In history, for example, dependence on the United States for source books and text books makes it difficult for history departments to plan any courses not generally taught in American universities. Junior courses in Canadian history present particular problems because American publishers do not find an adequate market for books and maps in that field. It must be emphasized that we have benefited greatly from many American productions; but because we have left the whole field to our neighbour our own special needs are not supplied.

21. Although in French-speaking Canada the difference in language offers some measure of protection, elsewhere in Canada the uncritical use of American training institutions, and therefore of American educational philosophy and what are referred to as teaching aids, has certainly tended to make our educational systems less Canadian, less suited to our traditions, less appreciative of the resources of our two cultures. It has also meant — and this is a matter with which we have a direct concern — that a large number of our leading teachers who are not only teachers but community leaders have received the final and often the most influential part of their training in the United States. This training may be excellent in itself, but it is surely permissible to wish that men and women who are going to exercise such a powerful influence on Canadian life should meet and work in some institution which, however international its staff may be, could put Canadian interests and problems in the first place.

22. The problem of text books just mentioned shows how American imports may harm as well as help us. But this is only part of the larger problem of vast cultural importations. Elsewhere in this Report we refer to concert tours in Canada organized beyond our borders. These are good in so far as they enable Canadians to hear artists eminent in the musical world. But, to hear the recognized artists, subscribers must also support many who are unknown and who, we are told, could not compete with Canadian talent if they were not supported by these powerful organizations. The unfortunate Canadian artist to get placed must go across the line, not the most happy solution for him or for his community.

23. Every intelligent Canadian acknowledges his debt to the United States

538

for excellent films, radio programmes and periodicals. But the price may be excessive. Of films and radio we shall speak in more detail later, but it may be noted in passing that our national radio which carries the Sunday symphony from New York also carries the soap-opera. In the periodical press we receive indeed many admirable American journals but also a flood of others much less admirable which, as we have been clearly told, is threatening to submerge completely our national product:

"A Canadian culture with an English-French background,"so runs the brief of the *Société des Ecrivains Canadiens*, "will never reach the level which we desire so long as suitable measures are not taken against the invasion of the Canadian press by one of the most detestable products of the American press, so long as thousands of pages *Made in the United States* are slavishly reproduced by English language papers or translated for French-speaking readers, so long as pulp magazines and other works of the same nature enter or are distributed in Canada without any restriction, as is now the case."[12]

24. The Canadian Periodical Press Association tells the same tale. Although during the last generation our periodicals have maintained and greatly strengthened their position, the competition they face has been almost overwhelming. Canadian magazines with much difficulty have achieved a circulation of nearly forty-two millions a year as against an American circulation in Canada of over eighty-six millions. "Canada . . . . is the only country of any size in the world," one of their members has observed, "whose people read more foreign periodicals than they do periodicals published in their own land, local newspapers excluded."[13] The Canadian periodical cannot in its turn invade the American market; for Americans, it seems, simply do not know enough about Canada to appreciate Canadian material. Our periodicals cannot hold their own except in their limited and unprotected market, nine million English-speaking readers. These must be set against the one hundred and sixty millions served by their competitors in the whole North American continent.[14]

539

25. The American invasion by film, radio and periodical is formidable. Much of what comes to us is good and of this we shall be speaking presently. It has, however, been represented to us that many of the radio programmes have in fact no particular application to Canada or to Canadian conditions and that some of them, including certain children's programmes of the "crime" and "horror" type, are positively harmful. News commentaries too, and even live broadcasts from American sources, are designed for American ears and are almost certain to have an American slant and emphasis by reason of that they include or omit, as well as because of the opinions expressed. We think it permissible to record these comments on American radio since we observe that in the United States many radio programmes and American broadcasting in general have recently been severely criticized. It will, we think, be readily agreed that we in Canada should take measures to avoid in our radio, and in our television, at least those aspects of American broadcasting which have provoked in the United States the most out-spoken and the sharpest opposition.[15]

26. American influences on Canadian life to say the least are impressive. There should be no thought of interfering with the liberty of all Canadians to enjoy them. Cultural exchanges are excellent in themselves. They widen the choice of the consumer and provide stimulating competition for the producer. It cannot be denied, however, that a vast and disproportionate amount of material coming from a single alien source may stifle rather than stimulate our own creative effort; and, passively accepted without any standard of comparison, this may weaken critical faculties. We are now spending millions to maintain a national independence which would be nothing but an empty shell without a vigorous and distinctive cultural life. We have seen that we have its elements in our traditions and in our history; we have made important progress, often aided by American generosity. We must not be blind, however, to the very present danger of permanent dependence.

540 Mass Media

Introduction

Before proceeding to the problems of broadcasting, of moving pictures and of the other "mass media" in Canada, we think it worth while to point out that about one half of the Canadian population was born earlier than 1923 and that most of these older members of our population spent their formative years in a society where radio was unknown, where the moving picture was an exceptional curiosity rather than a national habit, and where as a consequence the cultural life of most communities centred about the church, the school, the local library and the local newspaper.

2. It is probably true, for example, that most Canadians now in their thirties or older will recall that the church organist and the church choir provided much of the music of their earlier years. More often than not the organist in English-speaking Canada was from the old country, trained in the English tradition of organ and choral music. He not infrequently was at odds with the church authorities on matters of musical taste and propriety. The great musical events of the year were usually the concerts given by the local church choirs, aided by a visiting celebrity. Although the radio has vastly increased the size of listening audiences, we must not forget that long before its day there flourished in the towns and cities of Canada a vigorous musical life, or that the musical tastes of a considerable part of our population were in large measure formed by the well-trained musicians who came to us, bringing with them a tradition of fine music. We might suggest that the work of English organists in Canada from about 1880 to 1920 would form the subject of a valuable historical and social study. The names of a few of these in Toronto and Montreal and in some other cities came to be nationally known and are still remembered; but the work of the scholarly musicians who brought to so many of our smaller towns an important part of the world's great music should not pass unrecorded.

3. Not only in music but in letters did the church make important contributions to the life of the community. The rector or the pastor of the church lectured on Dante or on Browning, on Victor Hugo or on Lewis Carroll; he was in wide demand with his lantern slides of London or the Holy Land, and in many of the smaller places his was the only library for many miles. He produced and directed the annual sacred pageant of his Sunday School, the first intimation of the theatre to his unruly small actors, and he usually both chose and contributed the prizes of books which rewarded the less undisciplined of his young flock.

4. The School of thirty or forty years ago occupied a central place even in the larger communities which now it has perhaps retained only in our rural areas. Who could forget the weeks of preparation and the mounting excitement, reaching a climax in the school concert and the school play? The great night arrives, the curtains part — rather shakily and half an hour late — but the play with its lights and colour, its tears and laughter, its triumphs and disasters — the play is on! Or can we recall the final number of the concert with the entire school assembled on the rising tiers, charging into *The Maple Leaf*, a semi-tone too high and half a beat too soon, but with the easy skill of born musicians redressing the balance in the first few bars, to the astounded relief of the indignant conductor? But it was our play and our concert, and beyond doubt it was our audience.

541

5. We imagine, too, that many Canadians will remember with grateful affection the librarians of the little towns and cities where they grew up who did so much both to create and to satisfy a taste for good books. There must be many of us who came to know the pure delight of reading because of a quiet suggestion from the rather aloof and amused lady, who seemed to us of great age, hardly visible behind the piles of books. We had no comics, so went home to read *Treasure Island* or the *White Company*, or began the long series of Henty which we hoped would never run out. Nor must we forget the editor of the local paper with his strong views on politics and on cigars, who in his young days had met Mark Twain and who, long before the day of the syndicated columnist, recorded and commented upon the life of his community, respecting nothing so much as pungent English prose. He did not publish a mass medium of communication; he edited a newspaper.

6. The radio, the film, the weekly periodical have brought pleasure and instruction to remote and lonely places in this country, and undoubtedly have added greatly to the variety of our enjoyment. In the great plenty that now is ours, there is some danger that we may forget that music and drama and letters call for more than passive pleasure on our part; in this new world of television, of radio and of documentary films, it will be unfortunate if we hear no more our choir and our organist in valiant and diligent practice of the Messiah, making together a gracious music that reaches us faintly but with great sweetness across the quiet of an early winter night.

7. If we turn to the Province of Quebec in the same period toward the

beginning of this century, we could write that there too were happy towns and villages which, from their own resources, produced almost everything they needed for their own amusement and instruction, apart from books and illustrated papers.

8. This was the era when the telephone was in its infancy. Our grandparents had some exciting times with these instruments experimentally built in a period when the refinements of industrial design were still far in the future. At first they hesitated to trust real human words to a machine which could hear and could speak to you without seeing you. Then, suddenly aware that by some miracle their voices could be heard even three or four miles away, they began to shout into the mouthpiece under the natural illusion that you must speak louder to be heard a long way off than if you were chatting to your neighbour over the fence.

9. The telephone was the first step; the gramophone and the radio followed closely; before that, communication was on a voluntary and personal basis; it became automatic, easy and impersonal. Culture, too, came to lean heavily on the machine.

10. In the early years of this century, we still counted for our music upon skilled or amateur performers whom we saw every day. In the little towns and villages of Quebec, music was the domain of the precentor, of the curé, of the organist, and of the wife of the doctor or the notary. The precentor, though equipped with a voice to rival in power the organ itself, was particularly good at plain-chant. The organist, though fully occupied with both hands and with both feet, was still able to maintain contact with her fast moving choir. On Sunday, the singing of the curé, endowed with a hearty farmer's voice that easily carried over two or three fields, must have echoed pleasantly through the courts of Heaven.

11. In the towns, the band of the seminary or of the college was responsible for music on special occasions, and, in that era, anniversaries rolled round often enough. The band leader used to lay aside his baton a few months before the occasion to compose a cantata or an overture in accordance with the needs of the celebration or, more likely, to suit himself. He took great care to place a solo at a suitable point in his work to be performed by the trombonist. The chosen artist would rise in his place, and gathering his resources of breath and of courage, would brandish his instrument with a gesture which alone would have brought down the walls of Jericho.

12. But in the cities, in the larger churches, one could hear music which has not yet been surpassed. The renowned organists of the time had learned the true qualities of church music in Europe, and on Sunday during the hush of the offertory they remembered in playing great pieces of classical music the fine lessons learned abroad. One might be as brilliant on the keyboard as Liszt, another as classical and correct as Saint-Saëns.

13. This was a period, too, when there was plenty of time and plenty of quiet for reading. In the country, the parish library of three or four

hundred books was quite large enough for the needs of the readers. It was generally kept on the shelves of the sacristy, and little by little over the years these harmless novels or lives of the saints, some of them filled with an astonishing erudition, took on the gentle aroma of old incense. The curé kept an eye on the library, but it was the school mistress who was usually in charge. She had never heard of the decimal system of classifying books; it would not have occurred to her that there could be so curious an expression as "library science"; but nonetheless she did her duty devotedly and with good sense. Without being at all aware of it, she was a leader in the adult education movement, and a good leader.

14. In the cities, the tall, quiet houses all sheltered fine libraries as, of course, in the country did the houses of the advocate and the notary. As late as 1900, the legal profession still preserved in the original bindings complete collections of those customary laws of France which for so long had had authority in Canada. These books, unopened for half a century, were still handed on from one generation to the next. The library of the wealthy merchant in Quebec or Montreal was rather more modern; but there could be found on the shelves handsome volumes of all our first historians, and a few diminutive books of the seventeen hundreds. Side by side with the book shelves usually stood a cupboard filled with china and family treasures, platters and silver serving-dishes with the hallmark of Laurent Amyot, or some other famous Canadian craftsman of long ago.

543

15. The hollow voice of a loudspeaker would have echoed strangely in these surroundings, and the clicking of a television set would have dismayed a family accustomed to look only at the family portraits with their tranquil expressions. Nowadays, opera has a rival in "soap opera", and perhaps a "pin-up girl" grins from the exact place on the wall where used to hang the portrait of a shy young woman of twenty, of whom they used to say: *"Qui est-ce? Mais vous savez bien que c'est le portrait de grand'mère."*

Conclusion

The task assigned to this Royal Commission was conceived by its authors in the Government with imagination and boldness, and this throughout our work we have found stimulating. We have been more and more impressed by the timeliness, indeed by the urgency, of our inquiry. If, at the outset, we were convinced of the importance of what we were to do, as we proceeded this conviction deepened. The work with which we have been entrusted is concerned with nothing less than the spiritual foundations of our national life. Canadian achievement in every field depends mainly on the quality of the Canadian mind and spirit. This quality is determined by what Canadians think, and think about; by the books they read, the pictures they see and the programmes they hear. These things, whether we call them arts and letters or use other words to describe them, we believe to lie at the roots of our life as a nation.

2. They are also the foundations of national unity. We thought it deeply significant to hear repeatedly from representatives of the two Canadian cultures expressions of hope and of confidence that in our common cultivation of the things of the mind, Canadians — French and English-speaking — can find true "Canadianism". Through this shared confidence we can nurture what we have in common and resist those influences which could impair, and even destroy, our integrity. In our search we have thus been made aware of what can serve our country in a double sense: what can make it great, and what can make it one.

3. In the preceding pages, we sought to present a view of our cultural landscape. We cannot claim that this is a close appraisal; such a subject does not lend itself to statistics even had there been time for such exhaustive methods. The stock-taking, therefore, reveals the brush strokes of an impressionistic painting rather than the precise lines of a blueprint. The subject matter did not lack volume or variety. The materials for this study have been derived from a close examination during a year and a half of the hundreds of briefs and the many volumes of oral evidence heard at our sessions, and of the numerous studies commissioned from authorities in various fields. The survey covers a wide territory: from the ballet to philosophy, from totem poles to medical research. For all its diversity, however, it will be found to disclose a unity of pattern. In our Terms of Reference appear some words which we have often invoked, and which serve as a *leit-motif* for our Report. Our attention was directed to: ". . . institutions which express national feeling, promote common understanding and add to the variety and richness of Canadian life . . ." Nothing can so well achieve these high purposes as the subjects which we have had under review.

4. But the institutions, the movements, the activities we have examined share something more than a purpose; they suffer in common from lack of nourishment. No appraisal of our intellectual or cultural life can leave one complacent or even content. If modern nations were marshalled in the order of the importance which they assign to those things with which this inquiry is concerned, Canada would be found far from the vanguard; she would even be near the end of the procession. Some of the reasons are suggested in an earlier chapter: vast distances, a scattered population, our youth as a nation, easy dependence on a huge and generous neighbour. But while engaged in these material matters we were confronted with new problems which we share with all modern states. "Unfortunately", says the author of one of our special studies,

"just as in the western world, we are beginning to understand how deeply our spiritual traditions need guarding, just as we are ready to divert some of our energy from technology for that purpose, our society is being challenged to defend itself against a barbaric empire which puts its faith in salvation by the machine. We are tempted to forget the spiritual necessity in the face of the more present danger."[16]

The tidal wave of technology can be more damaging to us than to countries with older cultural traditions possessing firmer bulwarks against these contemporary perils.

5. It seems to us that two things are essential to restore in Canada the balance between the attention we pay to material achievements and to the other less tangible but more enduring parts of our civilization. The first must be of course the will of our people to enrich and to quicken their cultural and intellectual life; our inquiry has made clear that this will is earnest and widespread among our fellow-citizens. The second essential is money. If we in Canada are to have a more plentiful and better cultural fare, we must pay for it. Good will alone can do little for a starving plant; if the cultural life of Canada is anaemic, it must be nourished, and this will cost money. This is a task for shared effort in all fields of government, federal, provincial and local. We, however, are concerned with the federal field alone; in the rest of this volume we shall give our views on how the national government may appropriately advance our cultural and intellectual life.

545

6. If, in Canada, the state is to assume an increasing measure of responsibility in these matters, we shall find ourselves in step with most modern nations. Governmental support of the arts and letters has long been a reality in most countries of the world. Even in Great Britain, so loyal to the voluntary principle, where cultural life was for so long the beneficiary of private wealth, the state has steadily intervened as funds from traditional sources have diminished. But state intervention in Great Britain, as we have pointed out, has left the artist and the writer free and unhampered. British Governments have paid heed to Lord Melbourne's dictum, "God help the minister who meddles in art".

7. The United States remains the one conspicuous exception to the general rule that modern governments are increasingly becoming the principal patrons of the arts. The reason for this is not far to seek. In no other country in the world are there still vast reservoirs of private wealth from which cultural and intellectual life is nourished. The great trusts and foundations existing for these purposes control massive sums in capital and in annual expenditure.[17] The Americans can, therefore, still afford to leave such matters largely in their hands. Other countries cannot afford to follow their example.

8. It has been our task not only to examine the state of the arts, letters and sciences in Canada, but to give our views on how the Federal Government may aid them. In many countries throughout the world, government assistance has been necessary both in economic and in cultural matters because of the inequalities imposed upon the population by geographical factors; in Canada, a variety of such geographical factors has made government aid in a wide range of matters of particular importance. Much has been done in this country, and much more has been frequently advocated, to ensure that the harsh accidents of distance do not impose inequitable hardships on the shippers or the consumers of certain commodities. It

seems to us that the logic and the communal justice which underlie these accepted practices might properly be extended to include the movement throughout Canada of companies of players, or orchestras or of concert artists whose regular and frequent appearances in the great and small communities of Canada are of importance to our well-being as a civilized community.

9. In the following pages will be found a series of recommendations proposing federal action in certain of the matters which we have had under review. These, if accepted, will involve administrative or legislative action, and the use of public funds, both in capital grants and in annual outlay. If all our recommendations were accepted, the total figure might in isolation appear substantial; but in comparison with the costs of other activities of Government, it would be modest, almost insignificant.

10. The most striking items in governmental budgets today are related to defence. This is a subject rightly high in the thoughts and responsibilities of statesmen. As our task reaches its conclusion and our Report goes to press, we find ourselves working against a darkening horizon in the international world. This may suggest to the citizen that the objects of our recommendations are at the moment irrelevant. Are not tanks more needed than Titian, bombs more important than Bach? It has been said more than once that however important our suggestions may be, their acceptance might well be delayed until the sky is clearer. To answer this, we must ask another question. If we as a nation are concerned with the problem of defence, what, we may ask ourselves, are we defending? We are defending civilization, our share of it, our contribution to it. The things with which our inquiry deals are the elements which give civilization its character and its meaning. It would be paradoxical to defend something which we are unwilling to strengthen and enrich, and which we even allow to decline.

11. It was during the war years in Great Britain that a hunger for the finer things of life had to be appeased by special measures which later became permanent. The Council for the Encouragement of Music and the Arts came into being along with the Home Guard. C.E.M.A., as it was called, was founded to quicken and maintained to satisfy interest in music and drama and pictures. These things were not cherished for their own sake alone; they became in time of war a spiritual weapon. In such times, national morale is of paramount importance. This could perhaps be left to the superficial short-term methods of propaganda, but spiritual strength can be built only on foundations which are laid in time of peace. For this further reason we must strengthen those permanent instruments which give meaning to our unity and make us conscious of the best in our national life. Posters and pep-talks are not enough.

12. The circumstances in which our Report has been finished and presented have given point and urgency to our recommendations. We have, of course, been keenly aware of the practical problems of the moment, and have had them constantly in mind in the preparation of this document. We

have reduced our recommendations to the minimum. If we felt obliged to propose a new activity or function, we have urged the establishment of no new body to perform it if one in being could be made to serve the purpose. We have not suggested the erection of a new building if existing premises could possibly be made to provide quarters. Therefore, when we ask for the expenditure of money it is only because we are convinced that nothing less would achieve the end which we assume the Government had in mind when this Royal Commission was appointed. We might properly have gone much further. In this present crisis we have tried to propose the necessary measures through the simplest and least costly methods; but we have not for a moment lost sight of the paramount importance of strengthening those institutions on which our national morale and our national integrity depend.

13. Our military defences must be made secure; but our cultural defences equally demand national attention; the two cannot be separated. Our recommendations are the least we can suggest in conformity with our duty; more, indeed, should be done. We now proceed to these recommendations.

547

The recommendations of the Royal Commission on the National Development in the Arts, Letters and Sciences were many and varied, affecting Broadcasting; the National Film Board; other Federal Institutions such as the National Gallery, National Museum, Federal Libraries, Public Records and Archives, Historic Sites and Museums; Aid to Universities; National Scholarships; Information Abroad; and a Council for the Arts, Letters, Humanities and Social Sciences.

Three recommendations were of special importance: first, the grant of federal aid to Canadian universities on the basis of student enrolment; secondly, the creation of a Canada Council for the encouragement of the Arts, Letters, Humanities and Social Sciences, and to stimulate and to help voluntary organizations within these fields to foster Canada's cultural relations abroad; and thirdly, the establishment of national scholarships by the Federal Government in the Natural Sciences, Humanities, Social Sciences, Law and the Creative Arts.

Notes

1. Association Canadienne des Educateurs de Langue Française, Brief, page 3 (original in French); Division of Adult Education, Department of Education, Province of Nova Scotia, Brief, page 3.
2. Conférence Catholique Canadienne, Brief, pages 3 and 4 (original in French).
3. Comité Permanent de la Survivance Française en Amérique, Transcript of Evidence, page 77 (original in French).
4. For detailed information concerning Briefs, Sessions, Committees and Special Studies see Appendices I–IV, pages 423–435 of the report.
5. As a Royal Commission of the Federal Government we both needed and secured the fullest co-operation of Government Departments and Agencies. To the many officers and officials of the Federal Government and its various Agencies we should like to express our gratitude for their never failing courtesy and help.
6. Saskatoon Archaeological Society, Brief, page 1.
7. For details of Carnegie and Rockefeller grants in Canada see Appendix V, pages 436–422 of the report.

8. We are informed that there is in Canada no adequate advanced training in a number of important studies including: Town Planning, Industrial Design, Library Science, Dramatic Art, Ballet, Pictorial Arts, Journalism.
9. Private report from Dominion Bureau of Statistics based on figures supplied by United States Immigration Service.
10. National Conference of Canadian Universities, Brief, page 12.
11. Professor J. W. T. Spinks, Dean of Graduate Studies, University of Saskatchewan, Special Study, *Scientific Research in Canada*, page 48.
12. Société des Ecrivains Canadiens, Brief, page 10 (original in French).
13. B. K. Sandwell, Special Study, *Present Day Influences on Canadian Society,* page 16.
14. Ibid., page 17.
15. Cf. John Crosby, *Seven Deadly Sins of the Air*, published in *Life*, New York, November 6, 1950, pp. 147 ff.
16. Professor G. P. Grant, Special Study, pp. 28–9.
17. The resources at the disposal of certain American foundations are illustrated by the following tables for which we are indebted to F. Emerson Andrews, *Philanthropic Giving*, Russell Sage Foundation, pages 70 and 92 (reprinted by permission of the copyright holder).

ESTIMATED VALUE OF PHILANTHROPIC PROPERTY AND
ENDOWMENT IN THE UNITED STATES, 1949

Category	Property and endowment
Religion	$10 000 000 000
Higher education, private	4 005 000 000
Foundations	2 574 000 000
Hospitals, private	5 369 000 000
Other welfare organizations	1 000 000 000
Total	$22 948 000 000

The largest five foundations and the assets they report are these:

Ford Foundation	$238 000 000
Carnegie Corporation of New York	173 013 520
Rockefeller Foundation	153 000 000
Duke Endowment	135 000 000
Kresge Foundation	75 041 237

Topic Fourteen
The North

The North is an important region of Canada. Symbolically, it has been the source of inspiration for the image of Canadians as a "northern people." Physically, it contains nearly half of Canada's land mass and much of the country's natural resources. Yet until recently, the Canadian North has received little scholarly attention. Only as the North has been discovered to be of economic benefit to southern Canada has its own history become better known and appreciated.

One of the difficulties in studying the North is defining the term. It takes on different meanings and a different shape according to the definition used. In "Images of the North" Louis-Edmond Hamelin gives perspective to the subject by pointing out that many of the "images" that have been common through European and Canadian history were myths perpetuated by individuals or groups who had never visited or seen the North that they described.

In recent years Canadians have tended to look at the North from the perspective of its value to the prosperity and expansion of the southern sections of the country. Many have been unconscious of or unsympathetic to the native peoples who have inhabited the region for thousands of years. As their way of life has been threatened, these peoples have protested the invasion of their territory. The issue has focussed on the controversial question of native land claims that have not yet been settled in much of the North. The excerpt from the Berger Report, *Northern Frontier, Northern Homeland*, outlines the history of native claims in Canada, presents the native peoples' case for self-determination, and raises implications for the rest of Canada of an economic policy that recognizes the legitimate claims of the native peoples.

The Dene are one of the groups of Indians in the North. Their determination to maintain themselves as a distinct "nation" is evident in the Dene Declaration that was issued in 1975.

Morris Zaslow has completed a history of the early North, *The Opening of the Canadian North: 1870–1914* (Toronto: McClelland and Stewart, 1971) that includes a comprehensive bibliography. He is writing a second volume on the years 1914–1967. On the question of defining the North, see W. L. Morton's "The 'North' in Canadian Historiography," Royal Society of Canada, *Transactions*, Series IV Vol. VIII (1970): 31–40. A useful collection of essays is *Canada's Changing North*, edited by William Wonders (Toronto: McClelland and Stewart, 1971). K. J. Rea's *The Political Economy of the Canadian North: An Interpretation of the Course of Development in the Northern Territories of Canada to the Early 1960s* (Toronto: University of Toronto Press, 1968) reviews economic developments in the Northwest Territories and the Yukon. H. V. Nelles in *The Politics of Development* (Toronto: Macmillan, 1974) examines aspects of the economic development of Northern Ontario between 1849 and 1941. An interesting study of Vilhjalmur Stefansson (1879–1962), one of the Canadian North's greatest publicists, is Richard J. Diubaldo's *Stefansson and the Canadian Arctic* (Montreal: McGill-Queen's University Press, 1978).

550

Images of the North *
LOUIS-EDMOND HAMELIN

Several types of documents relate to assorted over-all, or specific images of the North. Among them is the oral literature of the indigenous peoples, with a delightful and enigmatic body of stories and legends;[1] the writings of researchers, non-specialized, but widely disseminated; literature such as newspapers; and finally, results of specific objective tests. In spite of the need for the latter, we should not decry images of the North that have emerged from texts based on more traditional approaches. Indeed, these documents may exercise an enormous influence on the thoughts of the northern inhabitant. Thus, Voltaire, speaking to the French of France, referred to the miserable Canadian settler, squatting "in the snow between the bear and the beaver." Present-day tests might still reveal a distant echo of that writer's opinion.[2] The same thing happened around 1900; those who produced the overly enthusiastic bulletins on the Klondike were largely responsible for the paradoxical image of the gold-fields that became current. A critical and complete survey of all visions of the North would have to consider northern literature in all its forms, and that in itself would result in a major work. I shall touch on only a very small part of that encyclopedic total.

Among Whites, the popular imagination has rarely perceived the North

* Chapter 1 from *Canadian Nordicity: It's Your North, Too*, by Louis-Edmond Hamelin. Copyright 1979 by Harvest House, Montreal. Reprinted by permission.

as a whole; it has, rather, regarded only particular and very localized northern situations. The current perceptive totality would include a host of little sectoral tableaux relating, for example, to the Northwest Passage, a particular polar expedition, the Inuit, the RCMP, the cold, and to the Klondike. Moreover, many of these topics would be characterized by inadequate information. Ten centuries after the arrival of the Vikings in North America, we still have not been able to interpret the deceptive appellation of "Vinland." For several centuries, a persistent confusion has prevailed between Hudson Bay and "the frozen sea of the North." Cartier's expression, "the land God gave to Cain," still appeared to have its echo in the scientific literature in 1935.[3] Captain J. Elzéar Bernier is considered to be an explorer, but in reality he mainly played a political role in territories that were already discovered. Biologist M. J. Dunbar has spoken about the reputation of Hudson Bay for infertility. This kind of reappraisal would be desirable for the great majority of particular northern situations. It is at the level of specific conditions, rather than at that of the total area, that we find true or erroneous images of the Canadian North. Nonetheless some overviews have been presented.[4]

551

From what may be established from an incomplete inventory of mirages about the North, two extreme opinions frequently emerge:[5] an over-idealized vision and an excessively pessimistic vision. Whereas these two illusions have usually operated alternately, they have also undergone parallel development — and that has made them even more confused.

The Double Illusion among Non-Indigenous People

The majority of informative or interpretive documents have given rise to two types of conflicting and mutually regulating emotions: mirages and disappointments. Attractive mirages, particularly those fired with the pioneer spirit, are contrasted with disappointments, which have disabused, in particular, those seeking massive, quick profits. These two sentiments have not affected members of the various social classes proportionately; the executives have been, on the whole, more unconsolable over their blighted hopes, and the little man has been more intoxicated by the prospect of intense, if short-lived, illusions of good fortune. Because the misfortunes have become better known than the successes, this mechanism has nourished a generally negative perception of the North.

The list of northern adventures that did not give rise to further development, such as Martin Frobisher's gold rush to Baffin four centuries ago, would be a very long one. Much later, miners had been talking about the copper at Chibougamau for fifty years before they began to exploit it. Few of the Klondikers grew rich during the three months that they had judged *a priori* to be long enough to make a pile of gold nuggets. And how many fortunes have disappeared in ill-justified ventures of financing and prospecting?

We can see the same result in the realm of exploration. We remember more readily disasters, such as that of Franklin in the mid-nineteenth century, than successful journeys such as that of Mackenzie in the late eighteenth. And, even in the latter case, the great river Mackenzie discovered did not lead to the Pacific as he had hoped. Polar toponymy reflects the difficulties and disappointments of a host of adventurers.

The North has certainly been the victim of myths based on indifference, if not of repulsion. Explorers and missionaries, who worked during periods that might be described as pretechnical, have left the idea of a harsh land and climate, a view that was not at all unfavourable to the success of their book sales and the gathering of alms. The anticipated harshness combined to accentuate the physical harshness. It is easy to concur with Vilhjalmur Stefansson's apt comment that in the North, "imaginary problems are more important than real problems."[6] It was, in large measure, natural and historic conditions that created the heroism of the sailors, "men of iron in wooden ships." In our generation, we might consider the reverse!

Settlement also produced an overwhelming amount of negative evidence, although northern settlement has been neither abundant nor always permanent. The great majority of centres in the Northwest Territories have less than 500 inhabitants; a similar situation prevails in both the Yukon and Nouveau-Québec. Even in the Near North, which is more fully integrated with the communications networks of the South, the population is very scanty. This sparseness would be even greater if the inhabitants had not learned to fulfill a great diversity of functions. In Abitibi (Quebec), most of the settlers who came to practise agriculture in the tradition of North American pioneering now earn their living by totally different means.

Further, human achievements have been difficult and limited. In a nation where yield and profit are the usual measure of things, it is not surprising that an acute feeling of repulsion and disinterest arises and is nourished.

Parallel to this, but working in the opposite direction, there are the prophets, men who are more optimistic than realistic. They have been touched by the magic of the North. They have come from every walk of life and, in their ardent promotions, they have turned their attention to every last little scrap of the immensity of northern Canada. To Curé Labelle, the North[7] was to become the "main highway for French-Canadian nationalism." To cite another case, a certain influential man of politics predicted thirty-one million inhabitants on the two shores of James Bay by the end of this century.[8] Before preliminary operations began for harnessing the Quebec rivers that debouch into James Bay, there were not even 5000 inhabitants in this area.

The enforced opening up of the North associated with the Second World War created a climate of enthusiasm regarding the North. In 1946 Maurice Duplessis, commenting on his own laws on mining development, stated that in Ungava "Providence had already gone three-quarters of the way"; one only had to bend over to pick up the iron scattered on the surface.

After the re-discovery of oil at Prudhoe Bay in 1968, United States

552

capitalists shipped to Alaska all the materials necessary for the imminent construction of pipelines; but several years passed before the first line was built. A similar euphoria presided over the organization of the conferences on *Mid-Canada Development* between 1968 and 1971; up until now, few concrete results have emerged from this project.

What must be clearly recognized is this duality between appeal and disappointment, between means to development and the natural propensity to avoid difficulties. These twin tendencies constantly recur: "There seem to be many visions of the North. . . . The southern vision (the North is a hinterland to be exploited for the benefit of southern Canada). . . . The romanticized vision (wilderness must never be touched). . . . The pessimistic vision (which sees only the problems) and the developmental vision (with natural gas opportunities.)"[9] The entire history of the North revolves around this confrontation, at the same time both clear and confused. Idealists are incessantly attempting to involve southerners in northern adventures; incessantly, people lacking the pioneer spirit, or disappointed investors, put the brake on northern projects. Apart from the war years, when the northern surge was unnatural, development has coincided with periods when mirages of feasibility dominated. Thus, at any given moment, concepts of good or bad exercise a profound impact on life, financial activity, mobility of the labour force, presence of political forces, and on awareness of certain problems. These mechanisms should not be surprising. Is a country not the fruit of the mind?

553

In the minds of the Whites, a comparable oscillation applies equally with respect to the Amerindians. As far as the Euro-Canadian is concerned, the twin images of the good Indian and the bad Indian have existed side by side. In 1972, responses to a test still gave the Eskimo the status of the "noble savage," with a pure ideology threatened by southern civilization. On the other hand, disagreeable prejudices are more common. The fact that Whites are surprised at the technical skill of adults, the intelligence of children, the ease of childbearing on the part of the mothers, constitutes so many manifestations of the preconceived image of the indigenous people.[10] Others have noted that the "learning materials" of the Department of Education of the Northwest Territories had included numerous uncharitable, incorrect, or incomplete allusions to the indigenous peoples, who comprised 54% of the school population.

There Are so many Norths within the North

Although the input is imposing, it does not form a compact mass or an organized whole; it consists rather of a whole series of disparate and poorly connected interpretations. This divergence is initially apparent at the individual level. Jim Lotz distinguished among White northerners: "The Developers, the Maintainers, the Innovators, the Old Northern Whites, the Transients, the Outsiders, the outside Insiders."[11] Each perceives the North differently. In a community in the Eastern Arctic, a study on the perception of ethnic identity revealed three type-portraits of people: "the priest, the Anglican missionary's wife, and the trader." Moreover, it was found that behaviour and gestures were adjusted according to perception of things and individuals. Thus, by custom, only the Eskimo language was used when asking people to wipe their feet before coming in.[12] Administrators coming from the towns of Southern Canada tend to have a distorted view of the North with regard to the environment in which northern residents live. This perceptive dissonance, this distortion, is very obvious particularly with regard to housing and education policies.

On the spatial level, the North is again perceived differently. The majority of inhabitants, even northerners, have great difficulty picturing the North in its geographic immensity; theirs is still a fragmented North. This Balkanization tendency is not at all surprising, given, on the other hand, the lack of one natural polar unity and, on the other hand, the lack of any old, strong, unified political structure. Thus the images, on the level of the perceptible North, those to which the individual can develop his own behaviour, have multiplied. There is not one single mental image of the North; a host of partial and often contradictory assessments are found. On the spatial level, they are over-lapping or discontinuous; on the chronological level, they display prolongations, adaptations, and even reversals of opinion.

Mentally, a Canada that is only slightly Northern

Despite the importance of the mental aspect in the definition of the North, and the polymorphic nature of that perception, the North has still not penetrated deeply into the comfortable society of southern Canada. Even while resident northerners are on the increase in absolute numbers, the small proportion they represent in the total population is growing slowly. This demographic situation has its equivalent on the level of thought and everyday life. Evidence of this is widespread. Only 7% of Canadian stamps carry a northern message and, even then, they often do so in a deceptive manner — for example, by amputating Canada's Far North. At Dorval Airport in Montreal, the large mural devoted to Canada seems to represent only southern Canada. In 1970, W. L. Morton recognized that "no scheme of Canadian historiography yet advanced is wholly satisfactory because none as yet takes account of the occurrence of the North."[13] The Canadian historian most intimate with northern archives is M. Zaslow, and his testimony is just as clear: "Canadians fail to recognize that they are essentially a northern people."[14] The same assertion has been expressed differently by F. K. Hare: "Canadians have not, as a nation, put the North anywhere near the centre of their mythology."[15] Henri Dorion concluded his comments on a text devoted to boundaries (including those of Labrador) by speaking of political ignorance, and by affirming that, "our territorial awareness is not very rigorous."[16] To give another example, some Laval students, when asked to enumerate Canada's major problems, mentioned the North in only 9% of cases, and even then it was bracketed along with

554

the cold climate.[17] Finally, to mark the occasion of the Olympic Games in Montreal in 1976, Canada issued a $5 coin displaying a map of the country: part of the High Arctic does not appear on the map.

The limited interest Canadians seem to evince regarding their North does not contradict the fact of a large number of characterizations of the North, as such. On the contrary, this apathy expresses rather the determining effect that excessively severe and painful images have produced on people's minds. An inadequacy of accurate knowledge has certainly not favoured the process of perception based on reliable stimuli, and conversely, it has tended to develop images full of distortions. A North that was poorly known at the outset could not avoid becoming the target of illusions and prejudices.

The North — A State of Mind

In a White mining community in Alberta's Middle North, a test has shown that the most significant local factor was neither the cold nor the snow, but the friendly atmosphere; moreover, the principal desire of the inhabitants was a relative decrease in isolation. It was primarily by means of these two psychological terms that these residents defined their own situation most clearly. A traditional monograph on this locality would not have allowed one to pinpoint the deeper thoughts of the local population.[18]

555

The North is more than an area, it is a passion. The mental configuration which it inspires constitutes a trait as deeply anchored as a European's attachment to the site of his hamlet or his valley. Félix-Antoine Savard's Gildore[19] is more than just a simple canoeman from Rabasca; like other northerners, his route to the North lay through the "pays d'en haut" and the West. Other adventurers have served their northern apprenticeship in the "King's Posts" of the Quebec North Shore. Throughout history, certain types of men, coming into contact with the various zones of the North, have developed very characteristic attitudes. Could anybody have expressed or embodied better the virtues of liberty and vitality than the *coureur des bois* of the Middle North? For him, as with the logger of yesteryear, and even the moose hunter, the North is like an irresistible itch, which implacably drives the man to mobility. In certain cases, nothing succeeds in stifling the call of the North. Equally, one finds cases of escape into the North, where distance from the daily, monotonous round serves as nourishment, cure, and even renaissance. The North is not simply a thing of wonder, however. Fear, tragedy and bravery all emerge from one of the first novels written by an Eskimo.[20] Northern themes have fed part of Canada's literature.[21]

Perceptions Differ between North and South

To analyse the northern setting by means of tests is to discover, in most instances, a difference between the views expressed by southerners and northerners.

A study of the regions preferred by forty-three second year geography honours students[22] established that the mainland Arctic coast was the least desirable area of Canada; but yet, the design of the mental map did not include the northern part of the Arctic archipelago.[23] Conversely, the two preferred regions were southern Ontario, and southwestern British Columbia. This kind of differential appreciation of places could have very important consequences on the future development of the nation. The author concludes, "The preferred areas may well plan for sizeable increases in population and pollution; conversely, places which are particularly disliked may well plan on development being even more difficult than usual." If this trend is realized, intra-Canadian disparities are not likely to decrease. In Quebec, the North is again perceived differently from the South; a questionnaire distributed in the spring of 1971 included, among others, two sections relevant to the present topic: "As compared to the Montreal Plain, does the Quebec shore of Hudson Strait appear to you to be a region isolated from the minds of and misunderstood by the people of southern Quebec?" The percentage of positive responses to the two parts of this question were 77% and 80% respectively.

556

Clearly, resident northerners are strongly aware of the uniqueness of their region, as one of the members of the Northwest Territories Council declared, "Our laws must harmonize with the land and its people. Unfortunately, Mr. Chairman, the laws that are continuously brought before this Council for enactment have been determined by, and patterned after, the laws which exist in the ten provinces of Canada. They are generally a carbon copy of provincial acts. The people who are in a policy-making capacity and drafting legislation, are people whose experience, primarily, has been in the South. Their understanding of people and their life style and society is of the South. This is what they understand. The life styles of the people are vastly different. Housing is a good example. The southern Caucasian society is concerned about good houses, they are concerned about security, they are concerned about worldly possessions, and there is nothing wrong with that, but the northern society is not concerned about these things.

". . . the very differences that exist between the North and the South are climatic conditions and the vast distances that we are confronted with. Also we have a great many problems associated with liquor, different concepts of justice, health, work habits, and the skills of the people."[24] This extract from the official minutes of the Territories demonstrates the rift, which in the minds of northerners, separates the Canadian North from the Canadian South. It is not my intention here to discuss the value of the opinions expressed nor to consider whether they apply only to Amerindians.

On another occasion, fifty school children with twelve years of education, and living in Frobisher Bay, Inuvik, and Yellowknife were asked what, according to their understanding, the problems of the North were (Table I). In the interpretation, the reader should be made aware of two

TABLE I – **Percentage distribution of northern problems as seen by northern students**

Order	Problem perceived	Frequency of mention (per cent)
1	Impact of development	18.2
2	Alcoholism	15.2
3	High cost of living	13.7
4	Isolation	12.1
5	Pollution	10.6
6	Cultural changes	9.1
7	Education	9.1
8	Housing	4.5
9	Abuses in welfare allocations	4.5
10	Amerindian land claims	3.0
Total		100.0[25]

points. First, there is the originality of the northern implications of certain 557 words in current usage. The problems of the North associated with housing, alcoholism, and pollution assume a form and characteristics very different from those of the South. The same is true of cultural changes and development. Seen in their true dimensions, the school children's responses express greater nordicity than is apparent from the terms alone. Moreover, items 4 and 10 are manifestly northern. In the second place, this view of the North is not the back-country view; it reflects, rather, the urban location of the educational institutions, and the articulation of a sophisticated system of education. Regionally, it applies particularly to the Mackenzie District, which is waiting for its pipeline, and to the acute social problems of Frobisher Bay.

Northerners, both Whites and Amerindians, have a clear awareness of their difficult, misunderstood situation. Consequently, many have been moved to bitterness. "A large proportion of people interviewed express considerable dissatisfaction with their present life."[26] This attitude is translated into a desire to move (also among the Indians), into a pessimism with regard to the future, and into a high incidence of suicide. Attitudes of despair are so widespread that the concepts southern planners have applied to northern Canada must be questioned.

This attitude has been clearly exposed by researchers.[27] A test of perception on the economic development of the Northwest Territories sought to find out the degree of causal relations of "big business" with regard to certain parameters. According to Table II, the judgement made by "enlightened" southerners with regard to major economic developments in the North is both significant and harsh. The North is not respected. Amerindians are almost totally ignored; northern public opinion is scarcely listened to at all; the territorial government wields only a limited influence; and ecology, whether cultural or natural, is not a matter of concern. Without any doubt, the South leads the North, flaunting a colonial, centralized, and purely capitalist form.

TABLE II – **In the Territorial North, to what extent is large-scale economic development influenced or determined by**

Item	Level of Influence	
	To a greater extent	To a lesser extent
Resident Northerners		x
Northern Native People		x
Federal Politics	x	
Territorial Politics		x
Northern Public Opinion		x
Large Companies	x	
Smaller Economic Activities in the North		x
Non-Economic (cultural)		x
Ecological Considerations		x
Concern for the Post-Developmental Era		x
Southern Canada as a Whole	x	
Northern Regional Disparities		x

SOURCE: Based on a perception test, LEH, Toronto, 1974

In conclusion, I believe that I have established the existence of images, especially their multifaceted nature. Hence, a cold region does not consist solely of measurable natural elements, capable of becoming the object of so-called natural and objective knowledge. All the polar components are analysed on their merits or not, by the mind; even the idea of cold becomes an identifying element. The North does not lend itself to a study of "realities"; tests and historical documents allow us to grasp partially the fruits of the cognitive processes themselves. One of the least known northern fields concerns the different images evoked by each ethnic group regarding the same theme; for example, territoriality.

A simple concern with the liberal expansion of knowledge prompts some reflection on the attitudes that should be taken regarding the North. Official policy, for example, is a source of much anxiety. If it is true that southerners are not mentally northern-oriented,[28] and that their orientation is erroneous, or at least is different from that of northerners themselves, or that they are constantly torn between aspects of a double illusion, is it not therefore dangerous to permit southern Canadians to make major decisions concerning the country's North and to impose a form of government on northern areas? Moreover, do not the perceptions that the main northern groups hold of their own cultural differences beg that they rise up against the excesses of "homogeneous Canadianization?" Present policies stress legal niceties and engineers' designs, but perception of a "true" reality must also enter the current preoccupations. Knowledge of psychology and the possession of some fellow-feeling may be of great help in understanding the northern people, native and otherwise.[29] Mental images can be found for each of the themes of the North, whether a person is dealing with territoriality, the environment, settlement, politics, peoples, or development.

Notes

1. Three references to illustrate this developing literature: Maurice Métayer, *Tales from the Igloo*. Edmonton, Hurtig, 1972; Marie-Jeanne Basile and G. McNulty, *Atanukana: Légendes montagnaises*. Quebec, CEN, 1971; R. Savard, *Carcajou et le sens du monde: Récits Montagnais-Naskapi*. Quebec, 1971.
2. M. Trudel, *L'influence de Voltaire au Canada*. Montreal, Fides, 1945.
3. M. Jefferson, "The Problem of Ecumene: The Case of Canada." *Geografiska Annaler*, 16, 1934, pp. 146–159.
4. W. C. Wonders, "Our Northward Course." *The Canadian Geographer*, 6, 3–4, 1962, pp. 96–105; J. W. Watson, "The Role of Illusion in North American Geography." *The Canadian Geographer*, 13, 1, 1969, pp. 10–27; H. L. Sawatsky and W. H. Lehn, *The Cultural Geography of the Arctic Mirage*. CAG '75, Vancouver, 1975, pp. 29–36.
5. The opposition between these two attitudes is expressed even at the level of journalistic literature. See Blair Fraser, ed., "Our Double Image of the North." *MacLean's*, 77, October 17, 1964. (The double image: the vision, the reality.) This special issue contains 118 pages on the North. Among the collaborators of this report are Pierre Berton, Doug Wilkinson, G. Hunter, and R. Harrington.
6. V. Stefansson, *The Arctic in Fact and Fable*. New York, Headline Series, 51, 1945.
7. He was referring to the Near North in the western Laurentians; second half of the nineteenth century.
8. J. C. Langelier, *Le bassin méridional de la baie d'Hudson*. Quebec, Dussault, 1887.
9. W. P. Wilder, [text of conference], Yellowknife, NWT Council, June 12, 1973, p. 1.
10. Pierrette Désy, "Les Indiens du Nouveau-Québec," In *De l'Ethnocide* 10/18, Plon, Paris, 1972; Markoosie, *Harpoon of the Hunter*, Montreal, McGill-Queen's Press, 1970.
11. J. Lotz, *Northern Realities*, Toronto, New Press, 1970.
12. J. Briggs. In R. Paine, ed., *Patrons and Brokers in the Eastern Arctic*. St. John's, 1971, pp. 55–73.
13. W. L. Morton, "The 'North' in Canadian Historiography." *Transactions of the RSC*, 4, 8, 1970, pp. 31–40.
14. M. Zaslow, *The Opening of the Canadian North*, 1870–1914. Toronto, McClelland and Stewart, 1971, p. xi.
15. F. K. Hare. In J. B. Bird, *The Natural Landscapes of Canada*. Toronto, Wiley, 1972, Introduction, p. 1.
16. Henri Dorion, "Connaissances des frontières canadiennes." *Cahiers de Géographie de Québec*, 11, 1962, pp. 147–148.
17. L.-E. Hamelin, P. Beaubien, and G. Poulin, "Perception du Canada au premier cycle de géographie." *Didactique Géographie*, 1, 3, 1972, pp. 1–9.
18. This is not an isolated example; psychologists have noted a comparable order of priorities among workers wintering in Antarctica. "It may come as a surprise that the bitter temperature, the long polar night and other physical problems of antarctic living are not the most significant causing human adjustment problems. The physical deprivations and dangers are remarkably well tolerated by almost everyone. The three basic stresses to which members must adjust are: 1) intimacy of an isolated group; 2) sameness of environment; 3) absence of customary sources of satisfaction and gratification." R. E. Strange, "Emotional Aspects of Wintering Over." *Antarctica*, 6, 6, 1971, p. 255.
19. Hero of *La Dalle-des-Morts*. Montreal, Fides, 1965.
20. Markoosie, *The Harpoon of the Hunter*. Montreal, 1970.
21. Jack Warwick, *The Long Journey*. Toronto, University of Toronto Press, 1968.
22. H. A. Whitney, G. W. Brown, and R. Elliott, "The View from Southern Ontario: Preferred Locations in North America." CAG, *Preconference Publication of Papers*, Waterloo, 1971, pp. 25–32. See also CAG 1975, Vancouver, Simon Fraser University, 1975, pp. 191–195.
23. The frequency with which the High Arctic is expunged from United States maps representing Canada seems to surpass the exigencies of scale and to prolong a certain tradition of contesting geopolitically Canadian ownership of the Arctic Islands. Canadian teaching materials, inspired by the USA, do not even prepare students for the existence of a Canadian Extreme North.
24. L. Trimble, *Official Report of the Council of the Northwest Territories Debates*, 46th Session, Yellowknife, January 27, 1972, pp. 780 — 781.
25. Gemini North, *Man and Resources: A Survey of Northern Priorities*. Yellowknife, 1972.
26. A. A. Mackinnon and A. H. Neufeld, *Project Mental Health: A Study of Opinion North of 60°*. Saskatoon, 1973.
27. During the Canadian Association of Geographers Conference in Toronto, May 1974, within the framework of a special session on the development of the Canadian North. The question was: "In the Territorial North, up to what extent large-scale development is influenced or determined by . . .?"
28. To the question: "What do you think Southerners know about the NWT?" addressed to northern men in the street, 77% replied "nothing," and 23% "very little," *Yellowknifer*, Yellowknife, February, 1974.
29. AINA, "Psychiatric Problems of Man in the Arctic." In J. E. Sater, *The Arctic Basin*, Centreville, 1969, pp. 215–224.

Northern Frontier, Northern Homeland*
THE BERGER REPORT

The paramount cry of the native people of the North is that their claims must be settled before a pipeline is built across their land. In this chapter, I shall outline the history of native claims in Canada. This history is important because the concept of native claims has evolved greatly in recent years: they have their origin in native use and occupancy of the land, but today they involve much more than land.

When treaties were signed during the 19th century, the settlement of the native people's claims was regarded primarily as surrender of their land so that settlement could proceed. The payment of money, the provision of goods and services, and the establishment of reserves — all of which accompanied such a surrender — were conceived in part as compensation and in part as the means of change. The government's expectation was that a backward people would, in the fullness of time, abandon their semi-nomadic ways and, with the benefit of the white man's religion, education and agriculture, take their place in the mainstream of the economic and political life of Canada.

560

The governments of the day did not regard the treaties as anything like a social contract in which different ways of life were accommodated within mutually acceptable limits; they gave little consideration to anything beyond the extinguishment of native claims to the land, once and for all. The native people, by and large, understood the spirit of the treaties differently; they regarded the treaties as the means by which they would be able to retain their own customs and to govern themselves in the future. But they lacked the power to enforce their view.

The native peoples of the North now insist that the settlement of native claims must be seen as a fundamental re-ordering of their relationship with the rest of us. Their claims must be seen as the means to the establishment of a social contract based on a clear understanding that they are distinct peoples in history. They insist upon the right to determine their own future, to ensure their place, but not assimilation, in Canadian life. And the Government of Canada has now accepted the principle of comprehensive claims; it recognizes that any settlement of claims today must embrace the whole range of questions that is outstanding between the Government of Canada and the native peoples.

The settlement of native claims is not a mere transaction. It would be wrong, therefore, to think that signing a piece of paper would put the whole question behind us. One of the mistakes of the past has been to see such settlements as final solutions. The definition and redefinition of the

*From *Report of the Mackenzie Valley Pipeline Inquiry*. Crown copyright 1977. Reprinted by permission of the Minister of Supply and Services Canada.

relationship with the native people and their place in Confederation will go on for a generation or more. This is because the relationship has never been properly worked out. Now, for the first time, the federal government is prepared to negotiate with the native people on a comprehensive basis, and the native people of the North are prepared to articulate their interests over a broad range of concerns. Their concerns begin with the land, but are not limited to it: they extend to renewable and non-renewable resources, education, health and social services, public order and, overarching all of these considerations, the future shape and composition of political institutions in the North.

Perhaps a redefinition of the relationship between the Government of Canada and the native people can be worked out in the North better than elsewhere: the native people are a larger proportion of the population there than anywhere else in Canada, and no provincial authority stands in the way of the Government of Canada's fulfilment of its constitutional obligations.

In considering the claims of the native people, I am guided primarily by the testimony that the Inquiry heard at the community hearings in the North. No doubt the native organizations will, in due course, elaborate these claims in their negotiations with the government but, for my own purposes, I have, in assessing these claims, relied upon the evidence of almost a thousand native persons who gave evidence in the Mackenzie Valley and the Western Arctic. Finally, I shall indicate what impact construction of the pipeline would have on the settlement of native claims and the goals that the native people seek through the settlement of these claims.

561

History of Native Claims
The Issue: No Pipeline before Native Claims Are Settled

All the native organizations that appeared at the hearings insisted that this Inquiry should recommend to the Minister of Indian Affairs and Northern Development that no right-of-way be granted to build a pipeline until native claims along the route, both in the Yukon and the Northwest Territories, have been settled. The spokesmen for the native organizations and the people themselves insisted upon this point with virtual unanimity.

The claims of the Dene and the Inuit of the North derive from their rights as aboriginal peoples and from their use and occupation of northern lands since time immemorial. They want to live on their land, govern themselves on their land and determine for themselves what use is to be made of it. They are asking us to settle their land claims in quite a different way from the way that government settled native land claims in the past; government's past practice, they say, is inconsistent with its newly declared intention to achieve a comprehensive settlement of native claims.

Arctic Gas suggested that the native people should not be permitted to advance such an argument before the Inquiry because it did not fall within my terms of reference. The Order-in-Council stated that I am "to inquire into and report upon the terms and conditions that should be imposed in respect of any right-of-way that might be granted across Crown lands for the purposes of the proposed Mackenzie Valley pipeline." Those words, they argued, limit the Inquiry to the consideration of only the terms and conditions that must be performed or carried out by whichever pipeline company is granted a right-of-way.

It is true that, according to the Pipeline Guidelines, any terms and conditions that the Minister decides to impose upon any right-of-way must be included in a signed agreement to be made between the Crown and the pipeline company. But the Order-in-Council does not confine this Inquiry to a review of the Pipeline Guidelines nor to the measures that the pipeline companies may be prepared to take to meet them. The Order-in-Council calls upon the Inquiry to consider the social, economic and environmental impact of the construction of a pipeline in the North. The effect of these impacts cannot be disentangled from the whole question of native claims. Indeed, the native organizations argue that no effective terms and conditions could be imposed on a pipeline right-of-way, with a view to ameliorating its social and economic impact, before native claims have been settled. It was essential therefore, if the Inquiry was to fulfil its mandate, to hear evidence on the native organizations' principal contention: that the settlement of native claims ought to precede any grant of a right-of-way.

Only the Government of Canada and the native people can negotiate a settlement of native claims in the North: only they can be parties to such negotiation, and nothing said in the report can bind either side. Evidence of native claims was heard at the Inquiry to permit me to consider fairly the native organizations' principal contention regarding the pipeline, and to consider the answer of the pipeline companies to that contention.

Native Lands and Treaties in North America

When the first European settlers arrived in North America, independent native societies, diverse in culture and language, already occupied the continent. The European nations asserted dominion over the New World by right of their "discovery." But what of the native peoples who inhabited North America? By what right did Europeans claim jurisdiction over them? Chief Justice John Marshall of the Supreme Court of the United States, in a series of judgments in the 1820s and 1830s, described the Europeans' claim in these words:

America, separated from Europe by a wide ocean, was inhabited by a distinct people, divided into separate nations, independent of each other and of the rest of the world, having institutions of their own, and governing themselves by their own laws.

It is difficult to comprehend the proposition that the inhabitants of either quarter of the globe could have rightful original claims of dominion over the inhabitants of the other, or over the lands they occupied; or that the discovery of either by the other should give the discoverer rights in the country discovered which annulled the existing rights of its ancient possessors.

Did these adventurers, by sailing along the coast and occasionally landing on it, acquire for the several governments to whom they belonged, or by whom they were commissioned, a rightful property in the soil from the Atlantic to the Pacific: or rightful dominion over the numerous people who occupied it? Or has nature, or the great Creator of all things, conferred these rights over hunters and fishermen, on agriculturists and manufacturers?

To avoid bloody conficts, which might terminate disastrously to all, it was necessary for the nations of Europe to establish some principle which all would acknowledge and which should decide their respective rights as between themselves. This principle, suggested by the actual state of things, was "that discovery gave title to the government by whose subjects or by whose authority it was made, against all other European governments, which title might be consummated by possession."

This principle, acknowledge by all Europeans, because it was the interest of all to acknowledge it, gave to the nation making the discovery, as its inevitable consequence, the sole right of acquiring the soil and making settlements upon it. [*Worcester* v. *Georgia* (1832) 31 U.S. 350 at 369]

The Europeans' assumption of power over the Indians was founded on a supposed moral and economic superiority of European culture and civilization over that of the native people. But it was, nevertheless, acknowledged that the native people retained certain rights. Chief Justice Marshall said:

[the native people] were admitted to be the rightful occupants of the soil, with a legal as well as just claim to retain possession of it, and to use it according to their own discretion; but their rights to complete sovereignty, as independent nations, were necessarily diminished and their power to dispose of the soil at their own will, to whomsoever they pleased, was denied by the original fundamental principle that discovery gave exclusive title to those who made it. [*Johnson* v. *McIntosh* (1823) 21 U.S. 543]

563

The concept of aboriginal rights has a firm basis in international law, and we subscribe to it in Canada. During the last century, the Supreme Court of Canada in the St. Catherines Milling case and this century in the Nishga case affirmed the proposition that the original peoples of our country had a legal right to the use and occupation of their ancestral lands. The courts have had to consider whether, in given cases, the native right has been taken away by competent authority, and sometimes the courts have decided it has been. But original use and occupation of the land is the legal foundation for the assertion of native claims in Northern Canada today.

From the beginning, Great Britain recognized the rights of native people to their traditional lands, and acquired by negotiation and purchase the lands the colonists required for settlement and cultivation. That recognition was based not only on international law, but also upon the realities of the times, for in those early days the native people greatly outnumbered the settlers.

The necessity to maintain good relations with the native people led the British to formulate a more clearly defined colonial policy towards Indian land rights in the mid-18th century. The westward expansion of settlers from New England during this period had given rise to discontent among the Indian tribes and during the Seven Years War (1756-1763), the British were at pains to ensure the continued friendship of the Iroquois Confederacy lest they defect to the French. When the war ended, the British controlled the whole of the Atlantic seaboard, from Newfoundland to Florida, and the government promulgated the Royal Proclamation of 1763. This document reserved to the Indians, as their hunting grounds, all the land west of the Allegheny Mountains, excluding Rupert's Land, the territory granted in

1670 to the Hudson's Bay Company. The Proclamation stated that, when land was required for further settlement, it should be purchased for the Crown in a public meeting held for that purpose by the governor or commander-in-chief of the several colonies. This procedure for the purchase of Indian land was the basis for the treaties of the nineteenth and twentieth centuries.

The Treaties

Following the Proclamation of 1763, the British made a series of treaties with the Indians living in what is now Southern Ontario. Many of these treaties were with small groups of Indians for limited areas of land, but, as settlement moved westward in the mid-19th century, there was a dramatic increase in geographical scale. The Robinson treaties, made in Ontario in 1850, and the "numbered treaties," made following Canada's acquisition from Great Britain in 1870 of Rupert's Land and the Northwestern Territory, covered much larger tracts of land.

564

The treaties concluded after 1870 on the prairies cleared the way for the settlement of Western Canada and the construction of the Canadian Pacific Railway. The government's instructions to the Lieutenant-Governor of the Northwest Territories in 1870, after the cession of Rupert's Land, were explicit:

> You will also turn your attention promptly to the condition of the country outside the Province of Manitoba, on the North and West; and while assuring the Indians of your desire to establish friendly relations with them, you will ascertain and report to His Excellency the course you may think the most advisable to pursue, whether by Treaty or otherwise, for the removal of any obstructions that might be presented to the flow of population into the fertile lands that lie between Manitoba and the Rocky Mountains. (Canada, Sessional Papers, 1871, no. 20, p. 8)

Treaties 1 to 7, made between 1870 and 1877, covered the territory between the watershed west of Lake Superior and the Rocky Mountains. In 1899, Treaty 8 covered territory northward to Great Slave Lake. Then, in 1921, Treaty 11 dealt with the land from Great Slave Lake down the Mackenzie River to the Mackenzie Delta. Treaties 8 and 11 together cover the whole of Northern Alberta and the western part of the Northwest Territories, including the Mackenzie Valley.

The treaties conform to a distinct pattern: in exchange for the surrender of their aboriginal rights, the Indians received annual cash payments. The amount varied with the treaty: under Treaties 1 and 2, each man, woman and child received $3 a year; under Treaty 4, the chiefs received $25, headmen $15, and other members of the tribe $12. In addition, the government established reserves for the use of the Indian bands: the area in some cases was apportioned on the basis of 160 acres of land for a family of five; in other cases, it was one square mile of land for each family. The treaties also recognized the continued right of the native people to hunt and fish over all the unsettled parts of the territories they had surrendered. Beginning with Treaty 3, the government agreed to supply the Indian

bands with farm and agricultural implements, as well as with ammunition
and twine for use in hunting and fishing.

The spirit of these clauses, together with the guarantee of hunting and
fishing rights and the establishment of reserves was, according to the
understanding of the Indians, to support their traditional hunting and
fishing economy and to help them to develop a new agricultural economy
to supplement the traditional one when it was no longer viable.

White settlers soon occupied the nonreserve land that the Indians had
surrendered, and their traditional hunting and fishing economy was un-
determined. Legislation and game regulations limited traditional activities
yet further. The land allocated for reserves was often quite unsuitable for
agriculture, and the reserves were often whittled away to provide additional land for white settlement. The government never advanced the
capital necessary to develop an agricultural base for the Indians, and when
the native population began to expand, the whole concept of developing
agriculture on reserve lands became impractical.

These prairie treaties were negotiated in periods of near desperation for
the Indian tribes. The decimation of the buffalo herds had ruined their
economy, and they suffered from epidemic diseases and periodic starva-
tion. Often they had no alternative to accepting the treaty commissioner's
offers.

The recent settlement of native claims in Alaska and the James Bay
Agreement follow the tradition of the treaties. The object of the earlier
surrenders was to permit agricultural settlement by another race. The
objects of the Alaska Native Claims Settlement Act and of the James Bay
Agreement are to facilitate resource development by another race. The
negotiators for the Province of Quebec stated that, if the native people
refused to approve the James Bay Agreement, the project would go ahead
anyway, and they would simply lose the benefits offered by the Province.
This attitude parallels the position of the treaty commissioners a century
ago; they said that if the Indians did not sign the treaties offered them,
their lands would be colonized anyway.

Treaties in the Northwest Territories

Throughout the British Empire, the Crown, not the local legislature, was
always responsible for the welfare of the aboriginal people. In 1867,
therefore, the British North America Act gave the Parliament of Canada
jurisdiction over Indian affairs and Indian lands throughout the new
country. This jurisdiction encompasses the Inuit, and the Métis, as well,
at least to the extent that they are pressing claims based on their Indian
ancestry. With Canada's acquisition of Rupert's Land and the Northwestern
Territory, and the entry of British Columbia into Confederation, that
jurisdiction extended from the Atlantic to the Pacific, from the 49th
Parallel to the Arctic Ocean.

The constitutional documents that effected the transfer to Canada of
Rupert's Land and the Northwestern Territory all refer to "aboriginal

rights." The Imperial Order-in-Council, signed by Queen Victoria, that assigned Rupert's Land to Canada provided that:

Any claims of Indians to compensation for lands required for purposes of settlement shall be disposed of by the Canadian Government in communication with the Imperial Government; and the [Hudson's Bay] Company shall be relieved of all responsibility in respect of them. (Exhibit F569, p. 42)*

It was upon these conditions that Canada achieved sovereignty over the lands that comprise the Northwest Territories and Yukon Territory, including the lands claimed today by the Dene, Inuit and Metis. After the transfer of these territories, the federal government enacted the Dominion Lands Act of 1872, the first statute to deal with the sale and disposition of federal crown lands. It stated:

42. None of the provisions of this Act respecting the settlement of agricultural lands, or the lease of timber lands, or the purchase and sale of mineral lands, shall be held to apply to territory the Indian title to which shall not at the time have been extinguished. (Exhibit F569, p. 43)

All of these instruments acknowledge the rights of the native people. They illustrate that the recognition of aboriginal title was deeply embedded in both the policy and the law of the new nation.

Treaties 8 and 11, made with the Indians of Northern Alberta and the Northwest Territories, continue both the philosophy and the form of earlier treaties. These two treaties are the subject of a recent book by Father René Fumoleau, *As Long as this Land Shall Last*. I cite his text for many official and historical documents related to these treaties.

In 1888, government surveyors reported that there was oil in the Mackenzie Valley, and that the oil-bearing formations were "almost co-extensive with the [Mackenzie] valley itself." The report of a Select Committee of the Senate on the resources of the Mackenzie Basin, in March 1888, has a familiar ring today:

. . . the petroleum area is so extensive as to justify the belief that eventually it will supply the larger part of this continent and be shipped from Churchill or some more northern Hudson's Bay port to England. . . . The evidence . . . points to the existence . . . of the most extensive petroleum field in America, if not in the World. The uses of petroleum and consequently the demand for it by all Nations are increasing at such a rapid ratio, that it is probable this great petroleum field will assume an enormous value in the near future and will rank among the chief assets comprised in the Crown Domain of the Dominion. (cited in Fumoleau, *Land Shall Last,* p. 40)

A Privy Council Report of 1891 set forth the government's intentions:

. . . the discovery [of] immense quantities of petroleum . . . renders it advisable that a treaty or treaties should be made with the Indians who claim those regions as their hunting grounds, with a view to the extinguishment of the Indian title in such portions of the same, as it may be considered in the interest of the public to open up for settlement. (cited in Fumoleau, *Land Shall Last,* p. 41)

* Exhibits and transcripts of the Inquiry hearings are identified by the page number preceded by F (formal hearings) and C (community hearings).

No treaty was made, however, until the Klondike gold rush of 1898. It was
the entry of large numbers of white prospectors into the Mackenzie Valley
on their way to the Yukon gold fields and the desire of the government to
ensure peaceful occupation of the land that led to the making of Treaty 8.
The boundaries of Treaty 8 were drawn to include the area in which
geologists thought oil or gold might be found; they did not include the
area inhabited by the Indians north of Great Slave Lake because, in the
words of the Indian Commissioner, Amédée Forget:

. . . their territory so far as it is at present known is of no particular value and they very
rarely come into contact with Whites. (cited in Fumoleau, *Land Shall Last*, p. 59)

Treaty 8 was signed at various points including Fort Smith in 1899 and
Fort Resolution in 1900. While the treaty commissioners negotiated with
the Indians, a Half-Breed Commission negotiated with the Metis. Following
the procedure established on the prairies, the government gave the Metis
the option of coming under the treaty with the Indians or of accepting
scrip, which entitled the bearer either to $240 or to 240 acres of land.
Many Metis chose to come under the treaty.

567

Treaty 8, like the prairie treaties, provided for an annual payment of $5
per head, the recognition of hunting and fishing rights, and the allocation
of reserve lands. But these lands were not allocated then, and, with the
sole exception of a small reserve at Hay River in 1974, none have been
allocated to this day.

The Indian people did not see Treaty 8 as a surrender of their aboriginal
rights: they considered it to be a treaty of peace and friendship. Native
witnesses at the Inquiry recalled the prophetic words that Chief Drygeese
spoke when Treaty 8 was signed at Fort Resolution:

If it is going to change, if you want to change our lives, then it is no use taking treaty,
because without treaty we are making a living for ourselves and our families . . . I would
like a written promise from you to prove you are not taking our land away from us. . . .
There will be no closed season on our land. There will be nothing said about the land. . . .
My people will continue to live as they were before and no White man will change
that. . . . You will in the future want us to live like White man does and we do not want
that. . . . The people are happy as they are. If you try to change their ways of life by treaty,
you will destroy their happiness. There will be bitter struggle between your people and my
people. (cited in Fumoleau, *Land Shall Last*, pp. 91 ff.)

In the years that followed, legislation was enacted restricting native hunting
and trapping. In 1917, closed seasons were established on moose, caribou,
and certain other animals essential to the economy of the native people,
and in 1918 the Migratory Birds Convention Act further restricted their
hunting. The Indians regarded these regulations as breaches of the promise that they would be free to hunt, fish and trap, and because of them they
boycotted the payment of treaty money in 1920 at Fort Resolution.

In 1907, and repeatedly thereafter, Henry Conroy, who accompanied
the original treaty party in 1899 and who had charge of the annual

payment of treaty money, recommended that Treaty 8 should be extended farther north. But, in 1910, the official position was still that:

. . . at present there is no necessity for taking that action. The influx of miners and prospectors into that country is very small, and at present there [are] no settlers. (cited in Fumoleau, *Land Shall Last*, p. 136)

The official position remained unchanged until 1920, when the Imperial Oil Company struck oil on the Mackenzie River below Fort Norman. The government quickly moved to ensure that these oil-rich lands should be legally open for industrial development and free of any Indian interest. F. H. Kitto, Dominion Land Surveyor, wrote:

The recent discoveries of oil at Norman [Wells] have been made on lands virtually belonging to those tribes [of non-treaty Indians]. Until treaty has been made with them, the right of the Mining Lands and Yukon Branch [of the federal government] to dispose of these oil resources is open to debate. (cited in Fumoleau, *Land Shall Last*, p. 159)

568

Treaty 11 was soon signed. During the summer of 1921, the Treaty Commission travelled down the Mackenzie River from Fort Providence to Fort McPherson, then returned to visit Fort Rae. In 1922, the treaty was made with the Dene at Fort Liard. As with Treaty 8, the Metis were given the option of taking treaty or accepting scrip. However, the parliamentary approval necessary to pay the scrip was delayed, and the Metis were not paid until 1924, when 172 Metis took scrip. The payments of $240 to each Metis represent the only settlement made with the Metis of the Northwest Territories who did not take treaty. Rick Hardy, President of the Metis Association, told the Inquiry that the Metis do not consider that these payments extinguished their aboriginal rights.

The Dene do not regard Treaty 11, which followed the pattern of Treaty 8, as a surrender of their land, but consider it to be a treaty of peace and friendship. Father Fumoleau writes of Treaty 11:

A few basic facts emerge from the evidence of documents and testimonies. These are: treaty negotiations were brief, initial opposition was overcome, specific demands were made by the Indians, promises were given, and agreement was reached. . . .
They saw the white man's treaty as his way of offering them his help and friendship. They were willing to share their land with him in the manner prescribed by their tradition and culture. The two races would live side by side in the North, embarking on a common future. (cited in Fumoleau, *Land Shall Last*, pp. 210 ff.)

In 1921, as in 1899, the Dene wanted to retain their traditional way of life and to obtain guarantees against the encroachment of white settlers on their land. In fact Commissioner Conroy did guarantee the Dene full freedom to hunt, trap, and fish, because many Dene negotiators were adamant that, unless the guarantee was given, they would not sign the treaty. To the Dene, this guarantee that the government would not interfere with their traditional life on the land was an affirmation, not an extinguishment, of their rights to their homeland.

It is important to understand the Dene's view of the treaty, because it explains the vehemence with which native witnesses told the Inquiry that the land is still theirs, that they have never sold it, and that it is not for sale.

Father Fumoleau has written an account of the Treaty negotiations at Fort Norman, based on the evidence of witnesses to the event:

Commissioner Conroy promised the people that this was their land. "You can do whatever you want," he said. "We are not going to stop you. . . ." This was the promise he made to the people . . . that we could go hunting and fishing. . . .

Then the Treaty party, Commissioner Conroy . . . said, "As long as the Mackenzie River flows, and as long as the sun always comes around the same direction every day, we will never break our promise." The people and the Bishop said the same thing, so the people thought that it was impossible that this would happen — the river would never reverse and go back upriver, and the sun would never go reverse. This was impossible, so they must be true. That is why we took the Treaty. (cited in Fumoleau, *Land Shall Last*, pp. 180 ff.)

Joe Naedzo told the Inquiry at Fort Franklin that, according to the native people's interpretation of the treaty, the government made "a law for themselves that as long as the Mackenzie River flows in one direction, the sun rises and sets, we will not bother you about your land or the animals." (C606)

When the treaty commissioners reached Fort Rae in 1921, the Dogrib people there were well aware that the promises the government had made to the Dogribs and Chipewyans, who had signed the treaty at Fort Resolution in 1900, had not been kept. The native people would not sign Treaty 11 unless the government guaranteed hunting and trapping rights over the whole of their traditional territory. This is Harry Black's account of the negotiations with the Dogribs:

Chief Monfwi stated that if his terms were met and agreed upon, then there will be a treaty, but if his terms were not met, then "there will be no treaty since you [Treaty Officials] are on my land." . . . The Indian agent asked Chief Monfwi . . . what size of land he wanted for the band. Monfwi stated . . . "The size of land has to be large enough for all of my people." . . . Chief Monfwi asked for a land boundary starting from Fort Providence, all along the Mackenzie River, right up to Great Bear Lake, then across to Contwoyto Lake . . . Snowdrift, along the Great Slave Lake, back to Fort Providence.

The next day we crowded into the meeting tent again and began the big discussion about the land boundary again. Finally they came to an agreement and a land boundary was drawn up. Chief Monfwi said that within this land boundary there will be no closed season on game so long as the sun rises and the great river flows and only upon these terms I will accept the treaty money. (cited in Fumoleau, *Land Shall Last*, pp. 192 ff.)

The Government of the Northwest Territories had, by this time, begun to take shape. The first territorial government headquarters opened in Fort Smith in 1921, and its first session was the same year, with oil the main item on the agenda. The duties of the new administration included inspection of the oil well and of the country to see if it was suitable for a pipeline.

The Dene had signed Treaties 8 and 11 on the understanding that they would be free to hunt and fish over their traditional territory, and that the government would protect them from the competition and intrusion of white trappers. Yet, contrary to treaty promises, an influx of white trappers and traders into the country was permitted to exploit the game resources almost at will, and soon strict game laws were necessary to save certain animal populations from extinction. The enforcement of these game laws caused hardship to the native people who depended on the animals for survival.

The encroachment of white trappers on lands that the native people regarded as their own led them to demand the establishment of game preserves in which only they would be permitted to hunt and trap. Frank T'Seleie told of such a request made by Father Antoine Binamé on behalf of the people of Fort Good Hope in 1928:

At the present time the Indians are in fear of too many outside trappers getting into the districts outlined . . . and should these preserves be granted . . . the Indians would be more likely to endeavour to preserve the game in their own way. They at present are afraid of leaving the beaver colonies to breed up as the white man would in all likelihood come in and hunt them. (C1773)

The request was never granted, although some game preserves were established in other areas.

570

Wood Buffalo National Park was established in 1922 and enlarged in 1926. Shooting buffalo was strictly forbidden, although Treaty Indians were allowed to hunt other game and to trap furbearing animals in the park. These regulations were strictly enforced, and the protection of buffalo took precedence over the protection of Indian hunting rights.

In 1928, the government imposed a three-year closed season on beaver in the Mackenzie District. This regulation came at the worst possible time for the Dene, for that year they were decimated by an influenza epidemic. Other furbearing animals were scarce, and without beaver they were short of meat. The Dene at Fort Rae protested and refused to accept treaty payment until they had been assured that they could kill beaver. Bishop Breynat had appealed to the government on their behalf, and some modifications to the closed season were made. Despite continuing protests about the activities of white trappers, they received no protection from this threat. In 1937, the Indians of Fort Resolution again refused, as they had in 1920, to accept treaty payment in protest against their treatment by the government.

Finally, in 1938, legislation was passed to regulate the activity of white trappers and to restrict hunting and trapping licences only to those white persons who already held them. But, as Father Fumoleau told us, by this time most of the white trappers had turned from trapping to mining. At the same time that the native people had been restricted in their traditional activities, oil and mineral exploration and development had proceeded apace. In 1932, the richest uranium mine in the world began operation at Port Radium on Great Bear Lake. Gold was discovered in Yellowknife in 1933. In 1938, Norman Wells produced 22 000 barrels of oil, and in 1938-1939 the value of gold mined in the Northwest Territories exceeded for the first time the total value of raw furs produced.

The Dene insist the history of broken promises continues today. Jim Sittichinli, at the very first community hearing, held in Aklavik, related the recent experience of the native people.

Now, at the time of the treaty . . . 55 years ago . . . they said, "As long as the river runs, as long as the sun goes up and down, as long as you see that black mountain up there, well, you are entitled to your land."

The river is still running. The sun still goes up and down and the black mountain is still up there, but today it seems that, the way our people understand, the government is giving up our land. It is giving [it up] to the seismic people and the other people coming up here, selling . . . our land. The government is not keeping its word, at least as some of us see it.

Now, there has been lots of damage done already to this part of the northland, and if we don't say anything, it will get worse. . . .

The other day I was taking a walk in Yellowknife . . . and I passed a house there with a dog tied outside. I didn't notice it and all of a sudden this dog jumped up and gave me a big bark, and then, after I passed through there, I was saying to myself, "Well, that dog taught me a lesson." You know, so often you [don't] see the native people they are tied down too much, I think, by the government. We never go and bark, therefore nobody takes notice of us, and it is about time that we the people of this northland should get up sometime and bark and then we would be noticed. (C87ff.)

So far I have been describing treaties made with the Indians and Metis. No treaties were ever made with the Inuit, although the boundaries of Treaty 11 include part of the Mackenzie Delta that was occupied and used by the Inuit. They were not asked to sign the treaty in 1921 and, when they were invited to do so in 1929, they refused.

571

The absence of a treaty has made very little difference to the Inuit, although they have been spared the invidious legal distinctions introduced among the Dene by treaty and non-treaty status. The Inuit witnesses who spoke to the Inquiry made clear that they, no less than the Dene, regard their traditional lands as their homeland. They also demand recognition of their rights to the land and their right to self-determination as a people. At Tuktoyaktuk, Vince Steen summarized the historical experience of the Inuit:

A lot of people seem to wonder why the Eskimos don't take the white man's word at face value any more. . . . Well, from my point of view, it goes way back, right back to when the Eskimos first saw the white man.

Most of them were whalers, and the whaler wasn't very nice to the Eskimo. He just took all the whales he could get and never mind the results. Who is paying for it now? The Eskimo. There is a quota on how many whales he can kill now.

Then next, following the whalers, the white traders and the white trappers. The white traders took them for every cent they could get. You know the stories in every history book where they had a pile of fur as high as your gun. Those things were not fair. The natives lived with it — damn well had to — to get that gun, to make life easier for himself.

Then there was the white trapper. He came along and he showed the Eskimo how to use the traps, steel-jawed traps, leg-hold traps. They used them, well they're still using them today, but for the first 70 years when they were being used, there were no complaints down south about how cruel those traps are — as long as there was white trappers using them. Now for the last five years they are even thinking of cutting us off, but they haven't showed us a new way of how to catch those foxes for their wives though.

After them, after the white trappers and the fur traders, we have all the settlements, all the government people coming in and making settlements all over, and telling the people what to do, what is best for them. Live here. Live there. That place is no good for you. Right here is your school. So they did — they all moved into settlements, and for the 1950s and 1960s they damn near starved. Most of them were on rations because they were not going out into the country any more. Their kids had to go to school.

Then came the oil companies. First the seismographic outfits, and like the Eskimo did for the last 50 or 60 years, he sat back and watched them. Couldn't do anything about it anyway, and he watched them plough up their land in the summertime, plough up their traps in the wintertime. What are you going to do about it? A cat [caterpillar tractor] is bigger than your skidoo or your dog team.

Then the oil companies. Well, the oil companies, I must say, of all of them so far that I have mentioned, seem to . . . have the most respect for the people and their ways; but it is too late. The people won't take a white man's word at face value any more because you fooled them too many times. You took everything they had and you gave them nothing. You took all the fur, took all the whales, killed all the polar bear with aircraft and everything, and put a quota on top of that, so we can't have polar bear when we feel like it any more. All that we pay for. Same thing with the seismic outfits. . . .

Now they want to drill out there. Now they want to build a pipeline and they say they're not going to hurt the country while they do it. They're going to let the Eskimo live his way, but he can't because . . . the white man has not only gotten so that he's taken over, taken everything out of the country . . . but he's also taken the culture, half of it anyway. . . .

For the Eskimo to believe now that the white man is not going to do any damage out there . . . is just about impossible, because he hasn't proven himself. As far as I'm concerned he hasn't proven himself worthy of being believed any more. . . .

The Eskimo is asking for a land settlement because he doesn't trust the white man any more to handle the land that he owns, and he figures he's owned for years and years. (C4199 ff.)

572   Because the native people of the North believe the pipeline and the developments that will follow it will undermine their use of the land and indelibly shape the future of their lives in a way that is not of their choosing, they insist that, before any such development takes place, their right to their land and their right to self-determination as a people must be recognized. They have always held these beliefs, but their articulation of them has seldom been heard or understood.

Entrenchment, Not Extinguishment

Canadian policy has always contemplated the eventual extinguishment of native title to the land. The native people had to make way for the settlement of agricultural lands in the West, and now they are told they must make way for the industrial development of the North. But the native people of the North do not want to repeat the history of the native peoples of the West. They say that, in the North, Canadian policy should take a new direction.

Throughout Canada, we have assumed that the advance of western civilization would lead the native people to join the mainstream of Canadian life. On this assumption, the treaties promised the Indians education and agricultural training. On this assumption, the federal government has introduced programs for education, housing, job training and welfare to both treaty and non-treaty Indians. Historical experience has clearly shown that the assumption is ill-founded, and that such programs do not work. The statistics for unemployment, school drop-outs, inadequate housing, prison inmates, infant mortality and violent death bespeak the failure of these programs. George Manuel, President of the National Indian Brotherhood, told the Inquiry that the programs failed because the native people were never given the political and constitutional authority to enforce the treaty commitments or to implement the programs. Every program has assumed, and eventually has produced, greater dependency on the government. Manuel told the Inquiry:

We, the aboriginal peoples of Southern Canada, have already experienced our Mackenzie

Valley pipeline. Such projects have occurred time and time again in our history. They were, and are, the beginnings of the type of developments which destroy the way of life of aboriginal peoples and rob us of our economic, cultural and political independence. . . .

Developments of this kind can only be supported on the condition that the [native] people must first be assured economic, political and cultural self-reliance. (F21761)

Manuel argued that the settlement of native claims in the North must recognize the native people's rights to land and to political authority over the land, as opposed to cash compensation for the purchase of their land. The object of negotiations, he said, should be the enhancement of aboriginal rights, not their extinguishment. Only through transfer to them of real economic and political power can the native people of the North play a major role in determining the course of events in their homeland and avoid the demoralization that has overtaken so many Indian communities in the South. The determination to arrest this historical process, which is already underway in some northern communities, explains the native people's insistence on a settlement that entrenches their right to the land and offers them self-determination.

The demand for entrenchment of native rights is not unique to the native people of the North. Indians in Southern Canada, and aboriginal peoples in many other parts of the world, are urging upon the dominant society their own right to self-determination. As Manuel said:

Aboriginal people everywhere share a common attachment to the land, a common experience and a common struggle. (F21760)

James Wah-Shee, voicing a sentiment shared by virtually all of the native people in the North, said:

The general public has been misinformed on the question of land settlement in the North. What is at issue is land not money.

A land settlement in the Northwest Territories requires a new approach, a break in a historical pattern. A "once-and-for-all" settlement in the tradition of the treaties and Alaska will not work in the Northwest Territories. What we are seriously considering is not the surrender of our rights "once and for all" but the formalization of our rights and ongoing negotiation and dialogue. We are investigating a solution which could be a source of pride to all Canadians and not an expensive tax burden, for ours is a truly "developmental" model in the widest and most human sense of the word. It allows for the preservation of our people and our culture and secures our participation as equals in the economy and society of Canada. (*Delta Gas: Now or Later*, speech presented in Ottawa, May 24, 1974, p. 14)

The treaties already made with the Dene do not stand in the way of a new settlement. The Dene maintain that Treaties 8 and 11 did not extinguish their aboriginal rights, and the government, for its part, has agreed to negotiate settlement of native claims without insisting on whatever rights it may claim under the treaties. Since no reserves were ever set aside under the treaties (except one at Hay River), federal policy, therefore, is not impeded by the Indian Act, the provisions of which relate primarily to the administration of reserve lands.

In the case of the non-status Indians — treaty Indians who for one reason or another have lost their treaty status — the Indian Act has no

573

application, and the federal government has agreed to negotiate with them on the footing that they are entitled to participate in a settlement in the same way as treaty Indians. The government has made the same undertaking to the Metis. The government is not, therefore, arguing that the payment of scrip by the Half-Breed Commissions in the past extinguished the aboriginal rights of the Metis. In the case of the Inuit, there are neither treaties nor reserves, and the provisions of the Indian Act have never been applied to them.

There is, therefore, no legal or constitutional impediment to the adoption of a new policy in the settlement of native claims. The federal government, in dealing with the claims of the northern people, has recognized both that there are new opportunities for the settlement of claims and that such claims must be treated as comprehensive claims. The Honourable Judd Buchanan, in addressing the Territorial Council of the Northwest Territories on February 13, 1976, described the claims, as the government saw them:

574

First, the claims involved are regarded as comprehensive in the sense that they relate to all native claimants residing in the area concerned, and the proposals for settlement . . . could include the following elements: categories of land, hunting, trapping and fishing, resource management, cultural identity, and native involvement in governmental evolution (pp. 7 ff.)

The native people of the North, for their part, also wish the settlement of their claims to be a comprehensive settlement. They, like the federal government, see their claims as the means of opening up new possibilities. Robert Andre, at Arctic Red River, articulated for the Inquiry the native people's view of the objectives of their claims:

We are saying we have the right to determine our own lives. This right derives from the fact that we were here first. We are saying we are a distinct people, a nation of people, and we must have a special right within Canada. We are distinct in that it will not be an easy matter for us to be brought into your system because we are different. We have our own system, our own way of life, our own cultures and traditions. We have our own languages, our own laws, and a system of justice. . . .

Land claims . . . [mean] our survival as a distinct people. We are a people with a long history and a whole culture, a culture which has survived. . . . We want to survive as a people, [hence] our stand for maximum independence within your society. We want to develop our own economy. We want to acquire political independence for our people, within the Canadian constitution. We want to govern our own lives and our own lands and its resources. We want to have our own system of government, by which we can control and develop our land for our benefit. We want to have the exclusive right to hunt, to fish and to trap. (C4536 ff.)

We are saying that on the basis of our [aboriginal] land rights, we have an ownership and the right to participate directly in resource development. (C4536)

We want, as the original owners of this land, to receive royalties from [past] developments and for future developments, which we are prepared to allow. These royalties will be used to fund local economic development, which we are sure will last long after the companies have exhausted the non-renewable resources of our land. The present system attempts to put us into a wage economy as employees of companies and governments over which we have no control. We want to strengthen the economy at the community level, under the collective control of our people. In this way many of our young people will be able to participate directly in the community and not have to move elsewhere to find employment.

We want to become involved in the education of our children in the communities where we are in the majority. We want to be able to control the local schools. We want to start our own schools in the larger centres in the North where we are in the minority. . . .

Where the governments have a continuing role after the land settlement, we want to have a clear recognition as a distinct people, especially at the community level. Also at the community level, powers and control should lie with the chief and band council. To achieve all this is not easy. Much work lies ahead of us. . . .

We must again become a people making our own history. To be able to make our own history is to be able to mould our own future, to build our society that preserves the best of our past and our traditions, while enabling us to grow and develop as a whole people.

We want a society where all are equal, where people do not exploit others. We are not against change, but it must be under our terms and under our control. . . . We ask that our rights as a people for self-determination be respected. (C4539 ff.)

Robert Andre was speaking only of the Dene land claims, but the evidence I have heard indicates that the claims of the Inuit coincide in principle with those of the Dene. The Metis Association of the Northwest Territories originally indicated its agreement with the Dene position, but they are now developing a claim of their own. I am satisfied that the position Andre articulated represents the concept of native claims held by the majority of the people of Indian ancestry in the Mackenzie Valley.

575

Self-Determination and Confederation

The Claim to Self-Determination

Why do the native people in the North insist upon their right to self-determination? Why cannot they be governed by the same political institutions as other Canadians? Many white people in the North raised these questions at the Inquiry. Ross Laycock at Norman Wells put it this way:

I don't see why . . . we say Dene nation, why not a Canadian nation? The Americans in coping with racial prejudice have a melting pot where all races become Americans. We have a patchwork quilt, so let us sew it together and become Canadians, not white and Indians. (C2149)

But all of our experience has shown that the native people are not prepared to assimilate into our society. The fact is, they are distinct from the mass of the Canadian people racially, culturally and linguistically. The people living in the far-flung villages of the Canadian North may be remote from the metropolis, but they are not ignorant. They sense that their determination to be themselves is the only foundation on which they can rebuild their society. They are seeking — and discovering — insights of their own into the nature of the dominant white society and into the relationship between that society and their own. They believe they must formulate their claims for the future on that basis.

Native leadership can come only from the native people, and the reasons for this lie deep within man's soul. We all sense that people must do what they can for themselves. No one else, no matter how well-meaning, can do it for them. The native people are, therefore, seeking a fundamental reordering of the relations between themselves and the rest of Canada. They are seeking a new Confederation in the North.

The concept of native self-determination must be understood in the context of native claims. When the Dene people refer to themselves as a nation, as many of them have, they are not renouncing Canada or Confederation. Rather they are proclaiming that they are a distinct people, who share a common historical experience, a common set of values, and a common world view. They want their children and their children's children to be secure in that same knowledge of who they are and where they come from. They want their own experience, traditions and values to occupy an honourable place in the contemporary life of our country. Seen in this light, they say their claims will lead to the enhancement of Confederation — not to its renunciation.

It is a disservice to the Dene to suggest that they — or, for that matter, the Inuit or the Metis — are separatists. They see their future as lying with and within Canada, and they look to the Government of Canada, to the Parliament of Canada, and to the Crown itself to safeguard their rights and their future. Indeed it is this Inquiry, established by the Government of Canada under the Territorial Lands Act, a statute enacted by the Parliament of Canada, which they have chosen to be a forum for the presentation of their case before the people of Southern Canada.

Self-Determination and the Canadian Constitution

Can a settlement that embraces the native people's claim to self-determination be accommodated within our constitutional tradition and framework?

The roots of most Canadians lie in Europe, but the cultures of the native peoples have a different origin: they are indigenous to North America. The Fathers of Confederation provided in the constitution that the Parliament of Canada should protect the native people of our country. There is no such provision in the constitution for any other people.

Parliament has exclusive legislative jurisdiction in relation to the native peoples of Canada, but the British North America Act does not prescribe any particular legislative arrangements for them. There is nothing in the constitution that would preclude the kind of settlement the native people of the North are seeking.

Under the constitutional authority of Parliament to legislate for the peace, order and good government of Canada, there has been a wide range of administrative arrangements in the Northwest Territories, beginning with the Act of 1869 (S.C. 32-33 Victoria, chap. 3), which established a temporary system of administrative control for Rupert's Land and the Northwestern Territory, right up to 1970 with the establishment of the contemporary Territorial Council under the Northwest Territories Act (R.S.C. 1970, Ch. N-22). It is certainly within Parliament's power to reorganize the territorial government to permit a devolution of self-government to Dene and Inuit institutions. Parliament is competent, in the exercise of its jurisdiction under Section 91(24) of the British North America Act, to restrict participation in such institutions to persons of a certain racial heritage.

Could the native people's claims to self-determination, to the land, and to self-governing institutions be accommodated constitutionally within any future legislation that might establish a province in the Territories? Under our constitution, specific limitations and conditions could be attached to the powers of a new province. Constitutionally, there is no bar to the native ownership of land nor to a guarantee of native institutions of self-government in a new province.

I think such special guarantees would be in keeping with the Canadian tradition. Lord Durham, in his report of 1839, looked toward the assimilation of all Canadians into the British culture. The Act of Union in 1840 established a framework of government designed to promote this solution: one province and one legislature for both the French-speaking people of Lower Canada and the English-speaking people of Upper Canada. But the people of Quebec would not be assimilated. Thus, in 1867, as Dr. Peter Russell wrote, "it was Cartier's ideal of a pluralistic nation, not Durham's ideal of a British nation in North America, that prevailed." The Dene, the Inuit and the Metis call for the extension to Canada's native people of the original spirit of Confederation.

577

Canada has not been an easy nation to govern, but over the years we have tried to remain true to the ideal that underlies Confederation, an ideal that Canada and Canadians have had to affirm again and again in the face of continuing challenges to their tolerance and sense of diversity. Why should the native people of Canada be given special consideration? No such consideration has been offered to the Ukrainians, the Swedes, the Italians, or any other race, ethnic group or nationality since Confederation. Why should the native people be allowed political institutions of their own under the Constitution of Canada, when other groups are not?

The answer is simple enough: the native people of the North did not immigrate to Canada as individuals or families expecting to assimilate. Immigrants chose to come and to submit to the Canadian polity; their choices were individual choices. The Dene and the Inuit were already here, and were forced to submit to the polity imposed upon them. They were here and had their own languages, cultures and histories before the arrival of the French or English. They are the original peoples of Northern Canada. The North was — and is — their homeland.

Special Status

Experience has shown that our concept of universal assimilation cannot be applied to the native people. Dr. Lloyd Barber, Commissioner of Indian Claims in Canada, has said:

> . . . native people are seriously talking about a distinctly different place within Canadian society, an opportunity for greater self-determination and a fair share of resources, based on their original rights. No doubt this will require new and special forms of institutions which will need to be recognized as part of our political framework. (Speech to the Rotary Club in Yellowknife, 1974)

The idea of new political institutions that give meaning to native self-determination should not frighten us. Special status for the native people is, and has been since Confederation, an integral part of our constitutional tradition. Their special status has, however, often led them into a state of enforced dependency. The self-determination that the native people of the North are now seeking is an extension of the special status they have always had under the constitution. In working out the nature and scope of that special status and of the political institutions that it will have, the native people of the North see an opportunity to break the cycle of dependency and to regain their sense of integrity and self-reliance. Barber had this to say about the importance of native self-determination:

> The old approaches are out. We've been allowed to delude ourselves about the situation for a long time because of a basic lack of political power in native communities. This is no longer the case, and it is out of the question that the newly emerging political and legal power of native people is likely to diminish. We must face the situation squarely as a political fact of life but more importantly, as a fundamental point of honour and fairness. We do, indeed, have a significant piece of unfinished business that lies at the foundations of this country. (ibid.)

578

I have used the expression "special status," and I do so advisedly. A special status for the native people is embodied in the constitution and reflected in the Indian Act and the treaties. In 1969, the Government of Canada proposed to end special status for the native peoples, and the native peoples throughout Canada opposed that idea so vigorously that the government abandoned it.

The Honourable Judd Buchanan, then Minister of Indian Affairs and Northern Development, in a statement of policy issued on July 26, 1976 — a statement of policy approved by the Cabinet and described as "the foundation for future policy" — reaffirmed the idea of special status. The statement of policy foresees "that there would continue to be recognition for Indian status, treaty rights and special privileges resulting from land claims settlements." This, of course, would apply to the treaty Indians in the Mackenzie Valley and the Western Arctic. But it must, in the Northwest Territories, entail also some form of special status for non-treaty Indians, Metis and Inuit because their aboriginal rights have been also recognized. The government cannot admit special status for treaty Indians, yet deny it to those living in the same village, even in the same houses. Special status for the native people has always been federal policy in Canada: the time has now come to make it work.

Local, regional, or territorial political entities may evolve that have a predominantly native electorate, an electorate in which a native majority might be entrenched by a suitable residency clause. Or political instruments may be developed by which the native people can, under an ethnic franchise and within a larger political entity, control matters that are, by tradition and right, theirs to determine. One approach would be geographical, the other functional. I am not attempting here to list all of the political possibilities. The native people and the Government of Canada must explore them together. I am saying that the Constitution of Canada does not necessarily require the imposition of existing political forms on the native people. The constitution offers an opportunity to deal comprehensively with native claims in the North, unfettered by real or imagined constitutional constraints. I express no opinion on the various options: I simply want it understood that all of them are open.

The claim by native people for institutions of their own is not going to be abandoned. In the North — indeed, all over Canada — it is gaining strength. It may seem odd — and out of keeping with liberal notions of integration and assimilation — but it is an ethnic strand in our constitutional fabric going back to 1867 and before. The European settlement of this country was an heroic achievement, but that history should not be celebrated in a way that fails to recognize the presence and history of the original inhabitants. We may take pride in the achievements of ancestors who settled the Atlantic coast, the St. Lawrence Valley, and then pushed on to the West and to the Pacific, but we should never forget that there were already people living in those lands. These peoples are now insisting that we recognize their right to develop political institutions in the North that will enable them to build on their own traditions and on their own past so they can share more fully in our country's future.

579

Evolution of Government in the Northwest Territories

The concept of native self-determination is antithetical to the vision of the future held by many white people in the Northwest Territories, who believe that, in due course, the Territories should become a province like the other provinces. They see no place for native self-determination in such a future. It is not surprising they should feel this way, because their vision of the future is a reflection of what occurred during the settlement of the West. Agricultural settlers moved into Indian country, and when they were well enough established, they sought admittance to Confederation as a province. In 1870 Manitoba was carved out of the Northwestern Territory; in 1880 a large area of the Northwestern Territory was transferred to Ontario; in 1905 Alberta and Saskatchewan were created; and in 1912 a large area was added to the Province of Quebec. Many white northerners expected the Northwest Territories, following this process, to become a province like the others; a province in which white men govern a land that once belonged to others. Some witnesses have urged me to recommend to the federal government the granting of additional powers to the Territorial Council in order to bring the Northwest Territories closer to provincial status.

In fact, the evolution of political institutions in the Northwest Territories since 1905 has followed the pattern of the provinces. The Territorial Council is modelled after the provincial legislatures, although because it is the creation of Parliament, it has no standing under the constitution.

In 1966, the Carrothers Commission recommended that local municipal bodies should be the basis for the development of self-government in the Northwest Territories. As a result, institutions of local government were established following the model of municipal institutions as they exist in

Southern Canada. In the larger centres, local government has a tax base founded on private property. The same system, whereby increased responsibility for local affairs is tied to the evolution of a tax base, was established in native communities. Even though there is virtually no private property in these communities, the assumption seems to have been that they would progress in time from settlements and hamlets — the most limited forms of local government — to the status of villages, towns and cities, like Fort Simpson, Inuvik and Yellowknife.

Settlements and hamlets, the highest levels of local government that the native communities have so far achieved, have very limited authority. In practice, this authority relates only to the day-to-day operations of the community, such as roads, water, sewage and garbage. In the native communities, most members of the local council are natives, but the native people made it quite clear to me that these councils have no power to deal with their vital concerns, such as the protection of their land and the education of their children. These important decisions are still made in Yellowknife and Ottawa. The native people regard local government, as it exists at present, as an extension of the territorial government, not a political institution of the community itself. Paul Andrew, Chief of the Fort Norman Band, had formerly worked as settlement secretary at Fort Norman. He described local government in this way:

580

It was quite obvious that this whole Settlement Council system have never worked and never will work because it is a form of tokenism to the territorial government. . . . [It is] an Advisory Board whose advice [is] not usually taken. . . .
The frustrations that I found for the position was that I was told that I was working for the people. But I was continuously getting orders from the regional office. They were the ones that finally decided what would happen and what would not happen. (C875 ff.)

Though there is a majority of native people on the Territorial Council, it is not regarded as a native institution. The bureaucracy of the territorial government, concentrated in Yellowknife and the other large centres, plays a far more important part than the Territorial Council in shaping the lives of the native people and their communities. The native people see the Government of the Northwest Territories as a white institution; indeed, of the persons who hold the position of director in the Government of the Northwest Territories, all are white. For the most part, native employees hold clerical and janitorial positions. Noel Kakfwi expressed to the Inquiry at Fort Good Hope the native people's sense of nonparticipation in the existing government:

In Yellowknife last week I spent about eight days. Out of curiosity I went into the offices and I was exploring the building in different places. All I seen was those white people with the brown hair, white collar, neckties, sitting on the desk. I looked around if I could see one native fellow, one Dene. Nothing doing. (C1923 ff.)

In developing institutions of government in the North, we have sought to impose our own system, to persuade the native people to conform to our political models. We have not tried to fashion a system of government based on the Dene and Inuit models of consensus, or to build on their traditional forms of local decision-making. So long as the native people are obliged to participate in political institutions that are not of their making or of their choosing, it seems to me their participation will be half-hearted. Indeed, two Dene members withdrew from the Territorial Council last year on the ground that such membership was inconsistent with the furtherance of the claims of the Dene.

To understand why Dene and Inuit models have not been used to develop local and regional government in the North, we have to look closely at our own assumptions about the native people. During the past few years, the native people have challenged the validity of these assumptions.

We have assumed that native culture is static and unchanging, and we have not seriously considered the possibility that the native people could adapt their traditional social, economic and political organization to deal with present realities. The native people are seen as a people locked into the past. Such an assumption becomes self-fulfilling. By not allowing them the means to deal with their present problems on their own terms, their culture does, in fact, tend to become degraded and static. Their challenges to our assumptions and their assertion of their rights have made many white people in the Northwest Territories uneasy. Native organizations are resented, and the federal government is criticized for providing funds to them. A world in which the native people could not assert their rights is changing into a world in which they can insist and are insisting upon them.

581

Many white people in the North are convinced that it is wrong to concede that differences based on racial identity, cultural values and economic opportunities even exist. But it is better to articulate and understand these differences than it is to ignore them. The differences are real. They have always existed, but they have been suppressed. Now the native people are proclaiming their right to shape their world in their own image and not in the shadow of ours. As a result, some white people now resent what they regard as an attempt to alter the political, economic and social order of the Northwest Territories. They are right to regard this as an attempt to change the existing order. But they should not resent it, because a growing native consciousness is a fact of life in the North. It was bound to come. It is not going to go away, even if we impose political institutions in which it has no place.

But the white and the native people in the North realize that the government's decision on the pipeline and on the way in which native claims are settled, will determine whether the political evolution of the North will follow the pattern of the history of the West or whether it will find a place for native ideas of self-determination. The settlement of native claims must be the point of departure for any political reorganization in the Northwest Territories. That is why the decision on the pipeline is really a decision about the political future of the Northwest Territories. It is the highest obligation of the Government of Canada, now as it was a century ago in the West, to settle the native people's claims to their northern homeland.

The pipeline project represents a far greater advance of the industrial system into the North than anything that has gone before it. The native people throughout the Mackenzie Valley and the Western Arctic sense that the decision on the pipeline is the turning point in their history. For them the time of decision has arrived. . . .

The Claims to Renewable Resources

Some Implications for Canada

There are lessons to be learned from these experiences. On the one hand, development must be under the control of the people whose lives and economies are being changed: the strengthening of the renewable resource sector of the native economy must go forward under the direction of the native people themselves. If development proceeds in a manner and at a scale that is out of keeping with local needs and wishes, it will tend to be counterproductive at the local level — whether it is renewable or non-renewable resources that are being developed.

The contrast between Thule-Qanak and the new towns of Greenland is instructive. Greenlandic economic development was imposed from the outside, and we should likely learn as much about its economic and technical aspects in Copenhagen as in Godthaab. In essence, the problem of the Greenland fishery is that the Danes have done the thinking and planning and have provided the capital, whereas the Greenlanders have provided only the labour.

Thule-Qanak offers a much better example of the direction that small native communities may wish to take — development on a scale compatible with the traditions of the people whose economy is being developed. It corresponds with Dene and Inuit ideas of how their native economy should be developed. And, although we are uncertain about the details of the native economies in the Soviet Union, we have learned enough to urge that a closer examination be made of their scheme for professionalization of hunting. The contrast between the Lummi aquaculture project and other instances of economic development on Indian reservations in the United States also shows that the development of economic programs for native people must be firmly based upon the structures of native society and their pattern of land use.

If renewable resources are to be the basis of an economy, perhaps the native people will have to be subsidized. We already subsidize wheat farmers by price supports because we regard the production of wheat and the stability of farm families as an important goal. We subsidize fishermen on the Atlantic and Pacific coasts by the payment of extended unemployment insurance benefits in the off-season. But, until now, we have never regarded hunting and trapping in the same light. In the North, hunters and trap-

582

pers have been subsidized — and stigmatized — by welfare. It should now be recognized that people who hunt and trap for a living are self-employed in the same way that commercial fishermen or farmers are.

There should be a reassessment of the goals of educational and social policy as they relate to the traditional sector and to wage employment. There are many young people today who want to participate in the renewable resource sector, not necessarily to the exclusion of other employment, and not necessarily as a lifetime career. They wish to choose and, perhaps, to alternate choices. The teaching of skills that are necessary to participate in a modernized renewable resource economy must therefore be integrated into the educational program, and the importance of these skills must be properly recognized in economic and social policies.

The native economy of the Western Arctic and the Mackenzie Valley is unfamiliar to urban southerners, and policy-makers are generally uncomfortable in thinking about it. They may regard the native economy as unspecialized, inefficient and unproductive. It is true that such economies have not historically generated much surplus, nor have they produced a labour force that is easily adaptable to large-scale industrial enterprise. They can provide, however, for the needs of those who participate in them. The ways in which we measure economic performance in a modern industrial setting do not necessarily apply in other settings. Nevertheless, other economies can change and modernize in their own way, just as an industrial economy does.

583

It is increasingly recognized that the economic development of the Third World hinges on agrarian reform, on the modernization of existing agriculture to serve domestic needs; in the same way, and to a greater extent than we have been prepared to concede, the economic development of the north hinges on the modernization of the existing native economy, based as it is on the ability of the native people to use renewable resources to serve their own needs. Productivity must be improved and the native economy must be expanded so that more people can be gainfully employed in it. In my judgment, therefore, the renewable resource sector must have priority in the economic development of the North.

Native Management of Renewable Resources

The idea of modernizing the native economy is not new. It has been adumbrated in many reports bearing the imprimatur of the Department of Indian Affairs and Northern Development. But nothing has been done about it. Why? Because it was not important to us, whereas large-scale industrial development was. Indeed, such large-scale projects hold great attraction for policy-makers and planners in Ottawa and Yellowknife. Small-scale projects, amenable to local control, do not.

The remarkable thing is that, despite two decades of almost missionary zeal by government and industry, the native people of the North still wish to see their economic future based on renewable resource development. They have argued that the renewable resource sector must take priority over the non-renewable resource sector. This was said in every native village, in every native settlement.

The native people claim the right to the renewable resources of the North. This claim implies that all hunting, trapping, and fishing rights throughout the Mackenzie Valley and the Western Arctic, along with the control of licensing and other functions of game management, should be given to the native communities, and that, for matters affecting all native communities, the control should be vested in larger native institutions at the regional or territorial level. The native people seek the means to manage, harvest, process and market the fur, fish and game of the Northwest Territories.

It is worth bearing in mind that modernization of the renewable resource sector can be achieved with a comparatively small capital outlay. A reasonable share of the royalties from existing industries based on nonrenewable sources in the Mackenzie Valley and the Western Arctic would suffice. Huge subsidies of the magnitude provided to the non-renewable resource industries would not be necessary. And the possibilities for native management and control would be greater.

The question of scale, however, suggests that we may consider some resources that, although they are not renewable, are nonetheless amenable to the kind of development that is consistent with the local interest and local control. I have in mind here certain accessible surface resources, such as gravel. These and other resources will no doubt be of importance in the claims negotiations and in land selection. The native people will, in time, judge this matter for themselves, but they should not be constrained or limited by any narrow meaning of the word "renewable."

I do not mean to say that industrial development should not take place. It has taken place, and it is taking place. But unless we decide that, as a matter of priority, a firmly strengthened renewable resource sector must be established in the Mackenzie Valley and the Western Arctic, we shall not see a diversified economy in the North.

Native Claims and the Pipeline

We must now address the central question, can we build the pipeline and, at the same time, do justice to native claims?

The case made by the native people is that the pipeline will bring an influx of construction workers from the South, that it will bring large-scale in-migration, that it will entail a commitment by the Governments of Canada and of the Northwest Territories to a program of large-scale frontier development that, once begun, cannot be diverted in its course. They say it will mean enhanced oil and gas exploration and development throughout the Mackenzie Valley and the Western Arctic. They say that, to the extent that there is a substantial in-migration of white people to the North, there will be a still greater tendency to persist with southern patterns of political, social and industrial development, and it will become

584

less and less likely that the native people will gain any measure of self-determination.

The native people say that the construction of a pipeline and the establishment of an energy corridor will lead to greater demand for industrial sites, roads and seismic lines, with ever greater loss or fragmentation of productive areas of land. Industrial users of land, urban centres, and a growing non-native population will make ever greater demands on water for hydro-electricity and for other industrial and domestic uses. The threats to the fishery will be increased. And last, but by no means least, the emphasis the Governments of Canada and the Northwest Territories have placed on non-renewable resources will become even greater than it is now, and the two governments will be less and less inclined to support the development of renewable resources.

Others argue that these developments are inevitable, and that there really is no choice. The industrialization of the North has already begun, and it will continue and will force further changes upon the native people. The power of technology to effect such changes cannot be diminished, nor can its impact be arrested. Rather than postponing the pipeline, we should help the native people to make as easy a transition as possible to the industrial system. This is the law of life, and it must prevail in the North, too.

The native people insist that a settlement of their claims must precede any large-scale industrial development. That, they say, is the essential condition of such development. They say that, notwithstanding any undertakings industry may give, and notwithstanding any recommendations this Inquiry may make, they will never have any control over what will happen to them, to their villages and to the land they claim, unless they have some measure of control over the development of the North. The only way they will acquire that measure of control, they say, is through a settlement of their land claims.

The native people do not believe that any recommendations this Inquiry may make for the pipeline project will be carried out, even if the government finds them acceptable, and even if industry says they are acceptable, unless they are in a position to insist upon them. And they will be in that position only if their claims are settled, if their rights to their land are entrenched, and if institutions are established that enable them to enforce the recommendations. They say the experience of the treaties proves this.

Let us consider, then, whether construction of the pipeline and establishment of the energy corridor before native claims are settled, will retard achievement of the goals of the native people or indeed render them impossible of achievement?

Land and Control of Land Use

If the pipeline is built before a settlement of native claims is reached, then the land that is required for the pipeline right-of-way, the energy corridor, and their ancillary facilities will have been selected, and will thereby be excluded from any later selection of land for use by the native people.

585

Under the Alaska Native Claims Settlement Act, the pipeline corridor from Prudhoe Bay to Valdez was excluded from the land selection process, and so was the proposed corridor for the Arctic Gas pipeline from Prudhoe Bay along the Interior Route to the International Boundary between Alaska and the Yukon.

I have recommended in this report that certain areas be withdrawn from industrial development to establish a wilderness park in the northern Yukon and a whale sanctuary in Mackenzie Bay. But all along the route of the proposed pipeline there are areas and places that are of special importance to the native people. If the pipeline is built now, prior to the native people's selection of land, these areas and places may well be lost.

In many villages along the Mackenzie River, the native people expressed great concern over the proximity of the proposed pipeline to their villages. These small villages are the hearth of native life, and the people in them can be expected to seek special protection for the lands near them. Inuit Tapirisat of Canada, in their submission to the federal government, asked for the native communities' right to select any lands within a 25-mile radius, and the Dene may well seek similar protection for their villages. Acceptance by the government of the proposed route and the designation of an energy corridor along that route before native claims are settled would certainly prejudice those claims. The proposed pipeline route at present passes within 25 miles of Fort Good Hope, Fort Norman, Wrigley, Fort Simpson and Jean Marie River.

Of course, the Dene and Inuit claims are not limited to the vicinity of their villages. They seek ownership and control of the use of vast tracts of land to achieve a number of objectives. They seek to strengthen the renewable resource sector of the northern economy. This, they insist, must take place before a pipeline is built. Their reasoning is simple: once the pipeline is underway, the primary flow of capital will be to the non-renewable resource sector. Once the gas pipeline is built and the corridor is established, the gas pipeline will probably be looped, and after that, an oil pipeline may be constructed, and, of course, gas and oil exploration will be intensified all along the corridor. Given the fact that over the past decade, in the pre-pipeline period, there has been a concentration on the non-renewable resource sector of the economy, the shift to that sector, and away from the renewable resource sector, once the construction of the pipeline is begun, will become complete.

A second objective of the claims to land and control of land use relates to non-renewable resources. The native people seek to exercise a measure of control over projects such as the pipeline to protect the renewable resource base and environment upon which they depend. If we build the pipeline now, the federal government will establish a regulatory authority to supervise its construction and enforce, among other matters, environmental protection measures. The authority will employ a large number of inspectors, monitors and other personnel. The public service population in the Northwest Territories, mainly white, will further increase. The necessity,

586

acknowledged on all sides, for a regulatory authority will mean that its staff will have extensive power over land use all along the corridor. There is little likelihood of the native people having any control over land use, whether it be access roads to the pipelines, or seismic exploration, or extensions of the corridor. The machinery for regulating the pipeline will entrench and reinforce the existing federal and territorial bureaucracies.

The native people, through their claims, seek benefits from those industrial developments by which they are prepared to give their consent and which the government deems necessary in the national interest. Would they be in a position to take advantage of any benefits that might accrue from a pipeline, prior to a claims settlement? The native people, with some few exceptions, do not have the necessary capital or the experience to participate effectively in joint ventures on projects such as the pipeline. But a claims settlement would be the means of supplying capital to native development corporations so they could participate in such ventures. The Metis Association of the Northwest Territories told the Inquiry that they are eager to participate in such ventures.

587

Self-Government

The native people believe that, with a new wave of white in-migration in the wake of a pipeline, they will see repeated in the North the experience of native people throughout the rest of North America. An increase in the white population would not only reinforce the existing structure of government; it would reduce the native people to a minority position within that structure, thereby undermining their constitutional claim to self-determination.

We know there was virtually uncontrolled in-migration to Alaska of non-Alaskan residents as a result of the construction of the trans-Alaskan pipeline. Arctic Gas say that measures can be taken to restrict such in-migration to the Northwest Territories. It is also said that stringent measures can be imposed to regulate housing, land use — indeed, the whole of northern life — in a way that was not possible in Alaska. But a proposal to use the power of the state in that way confirms the very fear that the native people have: a large-scale project such as the pipeline would lead to the further entrenchment of the existing, and largely white, bureaucracy in the North, and the chances of achieving a transfer of power to native institutions — one of the major objectives of native claims — would be made so difficult as to be impossible.

Since the Carrothers Commission in 1966, the development of municipal government has been the focus for the evolution of local self government in the Northwest Territories. If this policy is to continue then there is nothing further to be said. If it is to be changed — and the claims of the native people may require change in the existing institutions of local government — the change should be effected before construction of the pipeline is underway and before existing government structures become further entrenched. To the extent that the Dene and Inuit proposals call for the restriction of the franchise in local, regional and territorial political entities to long-term residents of the North, the effect of the construction of the pipeline, swelling the population of white southerners, would render the prospect of agreement on such a limitation that much more unlikely.

The native people seek control over social services so that they themselves can deal with the problems that already exist in the North. It would not be possible to achieve the same objective merely by pursuing a crash program making funds available to support existing local native rehabilitation programs and to establish new ones to deal with the problems associated with the pipeline. The sheer scale of the pipeline's impact on the social fabric of the small communities is likely to overwhelm the capabilities of such native programs as the Koe-Go-Cho Society at Fort Simpson and Peel River Alcoholics Anonymous at Fort McPherson.

At the same time, if the pipeline precedes a settlement of claims, the process of bureaucratic entrenchment will also take place in the social services. The services themselves will have to be expanded to deal with the anticipated increases in alcoholism, crime, family breakdowns, and other forms of social disorganization that experience in the North and elsewhere has shown to be associated with large-scale frontier development. This expansion will mean more social workers, more police, more alcohol rehabilitation workers and a corresponding increase in the size of the bureaucracy.

The idea that new programs, more planning and an increase in social service personnel will solve these problems misconstrues their real nature and cause. The high rates of social and personal breakdown in the North are, in good measure, the responses of individuals and families who have suffered the loss of meaning in their lives and control over their destiny. A pipeline before a settlement would confirm their belief that they have no control over their land or their lives. Whether that conviction is true or not, that will be their perception. These problems are beyond the competence of social workers, priests and psychiatrists. They cannot be counselled away.

Of course, a settlement of native claims will not be a panacea for all of the social ills of the North, but it would permit the native people to begin to solve these problems themselves. That would take time. But it is worth taking the time, because to build a pipeline before native claims are settled would compound existing problems and undermine the possibility of their solution.

I have said that control of education and the preservation of the native languages are central to the issue of cultural survival. The effects that prior construction of a pipeline would have on education and language could be regarded as a litmus test of prejudice to native claims.

The educational system in the North already reflects the demands of white families, who, although they stay only a year or two in the North, insist upon a curriculum similar to that of Ottawa, Edmonton or Vancouver because they intend to return south. They do not want their children to lose a year or to have to adjust to a different school system in the North.

Pipeline construction would bring yet more white families north, and it would therefore entrench the present system and its curriculum. At the same time as the native people find themselves part of an industrial labour force, without having had a chance to build up and develop their own forms of economic development, they would find increasing difficulty in making their case that the curriculum does not meet the needs of their children.

If the native peoples' claim to run their own schools is to be recognized, it must be done now.

The Lessons of History

The native people of the North seek in their claims to fulfil their hope for the future. The settlement of their claims would therefore be an event of both real and symbolic importance in their relationship to the rest of Canada. The native people want to follow a path of their own. To them, a decision that their claims must be settled before the pipeline is built will be an affirmation of their right to choose that path. On the other hand, if the pipeline is built before native claims are settled, that will be a demonstration to the native people of the North that the Government of Canada is not prepared to give them the right to govern their own lives: for if they are not to be granted that right in relation to the decision which more than anything else will affect their lives and the lives of their children, then what is left of that right thereafter?

589

What are the implications of not recognizing that right and proceeding with the pipeline before settlement? Feelings of frustration and disappointment among the native people of the North would be transformed into bitterness and rage. There is a real possibility of civil disobedience and civil disorder.

These things are possibilities. But I can predict with certainty that if the pipeline is built before a settlement is achieved, the communities that are already struggling with the negative effects of industrial development will be still further demoralized. To the extent that the process of marginalization — the sense of being made irrelevant in your own land — is a principal cause of social pathology, the native people will suffer its effects in even greater measure.

Can we learn anything from our own history? I hope we can, if we examine the settlement of the West and the events that led to the Red River Rebellion of 1869 and the Northwest Rebellion of 1885. Let me make it plain that, while I believe there is a real possibility of civil disobedience and civil disorder in the North if we build the pipeline without a settlement of native claims, I do not believe that there is likely to be a rebellion. Nevertheless the events of 1869–1870 and 1885 offer us an insight into the consequences of similar policies today. These events, and their aftermath, make it impossible to reconcile native claims with the demands of white advance to the frontier.

The establishment of a Provisional Government by Louis Riel and his followers in 1869 in the Red River Valley was a consequence of Canada's having acquired Rupert's Land from the Hudson's Bay Company without recognition of the rights of the Metis, Indians and whites living there. The List of Rights drawn up by the Provisional Government called for the settlement of the land claims of the Metis and the signing of treaties with the Indians. In the Manitoba Act of 1870, the claims of the Metis were recognized, and 1.4 million acres were set aside for their benefit. But their claims were processed very slowly, and, with their lands in doubt and their hunting opportunities continually declining, many Metis migrated north and west to the Valley of the Saskatchewan. There they built a prosperous and stable society that was a product of both the old and new ways. In 1873 they established their own government in the unorganized territory of the Northwest with Gabriel Dumont as president. But the advance of white settlement soon reached them even there.

590

Manitoba entered Confederation in 1870, and the following year the Canadian Pacific Railway was incorporated. Between 1871 and 1877, the government signed seven treaties with the Indians to enable rail construction to proceed, and by the mid-1870s railway survey crews reached the Saskatchewan.

The CPR, built across the prairies in 1882 and 1883, with the labour of five thousand men, completed the displacement of Indian society that had begun with the treaty negotiations. The settlers who followed the laying of the track soon spread out across the hunting grounds of the Cree and Blackfoot. The Indians, demoralized and racked by disease, watched from their newly established reserves as their lands were divided.

The construction of the railway was not without serious incident. In 1882, Chief Piapot's Cree pulled up some 40 miles of CPR survey stakes, and camped directly in the path of construction crews. Only the intervention of the Northwest Mounted Police averted violence then. When the railway crossed the Blackfoot reserve, the Indians again confronted the construction crews. Father Lacombe succeeded in persuading them to give up that land for a new reserve elsewhere.

The Northwest Rebellion of 1885 arose from the grievances and frustrations of the Metis and Indians. Dr. Robert Page, an historian from Trent University, told the Inquiry that, although the CPR acted as a catalyst to bring these tensions to a head, it was not the sole issue. In 1884, serious political agitation led the people in Saskatchewan to ask Riel to return. They sent a petition of rights and grievances to Ottawa which cited the government's failure to provide the Metis with patents to the land they already occupied, and the destitution of the Indians.

The government procrastinated in dealing with the claims despite official entreaties of Inspector Crozier of the Northwest Mounted Police urging that the claims should be settled immediately. In March 1885, the Metis rose in rebellion. The Cree, under Poundmaker and Big Bear, also took up arms. A military operation was organized, and the militia was sent to the west on the CPR. The Metis and Indians were defeated.

On November 7, 1885, the last spike was driven at Craigellachie. Nine days later, Louis Riel was hanged at the police barracks in Regina. Eight Indians were also hanged. The Metis were dispersed, and the Indians were confined to their reserves. Some Metis fled to the United States, some to Indian reserves and some to the Mackenzie Valley. In the years after the rebellion, some Metis were granted land or scrip, but the final settlement of their claims dragged on for years. Their scrip was often bought up by white speculators and, under the impact of advancing settlement, some of them retreated to the North.

The historical record shows that if the land claims of the Metis had been settled, there would have been no Northwest Rebellion. It is equally plain that the opening of the West to white settlers made it difficult, if not impossible, for the Government of Canada to recognize the land claims of the native people, who had lived on the plains before the coming of the railway.

There is a direct parallel between what happened on the prairies after 1869 and the situation in the Northwest Territories today. Then, as now, the native people were faced with a vast influx of whites on the frontier. Then, as now, the basic provisions for native land rights had not been agreed. Then, as now, a large-scale frontier development project was in its initial stages, and major reordering of the constitutional status of the area was in the making.

The lesson to be learned from the events of that century is not simply that the failure to recognize native claims may lead to violence, but that the claims of the white settlers, and the railway, once acknowledged, soon made it impossible to carry out the promises made to the native peoples.

The Government of Canada was then and is now committed to settling the claims of the native people. White settlement of the West made it impossible for the government to settle native claims. Today, the Government of Canada is pledged to settle native claims in the North, and the pledge is for a comprehensive settlement. It is my conviction that, if the pipeline is built before a settlement of native claims is made and implemented, that pledge will not and, in the nature of things, cannot be fulfilled.

Postponement of the Pipeline

In my judgment, we must settle native claims before we build a Mackenzie Valley pipeline. Such a settlement will not be simply the signing of an agreement, after which pipeline construction can then immediately proceed. Intrinsic to the settlement of native land claims is the establishment of new institutions and programs that will form the basis for native self-determination.

The native people of the North reject the model of the James Bay Agreement. They seek new institutions of local, regional and indeed territorial government. John Ciaccia, speaking to the Parliamentary Committee convened to examine the James Bay Agreement, said that the

Government of Quebec was "taking the opportunity to extend its administration, its laws, its services, its governmental structures through the
entirety of Quebec" (*The James Bay and Northern Québec Agreement,*
p. xvi). The Dene and the Inuit seek a very different kind of settlement.

They also reject the Alaskan model. The Alaskan settlement was designed to provide the native people with land, capital and corporate
structures to enable them to participate in what has become the dominant
mode of economic development in Alaska, the non-renewable resource
sector. This model is only relevant if we decide against the strengthening
of the renewable resource sector in the Canadian North.

The Alaskan settlement also rejects the idea that there should be any
special status for native people. That is a policy quite different from the
policy formulated by the Government of Canada. In Alaska the settlement
was designed to do away with special status by 1991 and to assimilate
Alaskan natives. The Government of Canada faced that issue between
1969 and 1976 and decided against it.

The issue comes down to this: will native claims be rendered more
difficult or even impossible of achievement if we build a pipeline without
first settling those claims? Must we establish the political, social and
economic institutions and programs embodied in the settlement before
building a pipeline? Unless we do, will the progress of the native people
toward realization of their goals be irremediably retarded? I think the
answer clearly is yes. The progress of events, once a pipeline is under
construction, will place the native people at a grave disadvantage, and will
place the government itself in an increasingly difficult position.

In my opinion a period of ten years will be required in the Mackenzie
Valley and Western Arctic to settle native claims, and to establish the new
institutions and new programs that a settlement will entail. No pipeline
should be built until these things have been achieved.

It might be possible to make a settlement within the year with the
Metis, and perhaps to force a settlement upon the Inuit. It would, however,
be impossible, I think, to coerce the Dene to agree to such a settlement. It
would have to be an imposed settlement.

You can sign an agreement or you can impose one; you can proceed with
land selection; you can promise the native people that no encroachments
will be made upon their lands. Yet you will discover before long that such
encroachments are necessary. You can, in an agreement, promise the
native people the right to rebuild the native economy. The influx of
whites, the divisions created among the native people, the preoccupations
of the federal and territorial governments, faced with the problems of
pipeline construction and the development of the corridor, would make
fulfilment of such a promise impossible. That is why the pipeline should
be postponed for ten years.

A decision to build the pipeline now would imply a decision to bring to
production now the gas and oil resources of the Mackenzie Delta and the
Beaufort Sea. The industrial activity that would follow this decision would

592

be on a scale such as to require the full attention of the government, and entrench its commitment to non-renewable resource development in the North. The drive to bring the native people into the industrial system would intensify, and there would be little likelihood of the native people receiving any support in their desire to expand the renewable resource sector.

If we believe that the industrial system must advance now into the Mackenzie Valley and the Western Arctic, then we must not delude ourselves or the native people about what a settlement of their claims will mean in such circumstances.

It would be dishonest to impose a settlement that we know now — and that the native people will know before the ink is dry on it — will not achieve their goals. They will soon realize — just as the native people on the prairies realized a century ago as the settlers poured in — that the actual course of events on the ground will deny the promises that appear on paper. The advance of the industrial system would determine the course of events, no matter what Parliament, the courts, this Inquiry or anyone else may say.

If we think back to the days when the treaties were signed on the prairies, we can predict what will happen in the North if a settlement is forced upon the native people. We shall soon see that we cannot keep the promises we have made.

Dene Declaration*

Statement of Rights

We the Dene of the Northwest Territories insist on the right to be regarded by ourselves and the world as a nation.

Our struggle is for the recognition of the Dene Nation by the Government and peoples of Canada and the peoples and governments of the world.

As once Europe was the exclusive homeland of the European peoples, Africa the exclusive homeland of the African peoples, the New World, North and South America, was the exclusive homeland of Aboriginal peoples of the New World, the Amerindian and the Inuit.

The New World like other parts of the world has suffered the experience of colonialism and imperialism. Other peoples have occupied the land — often with force — and foreign governments have imposed themselves on our people. Ancient civilizations and ways of life have been destroyed.

*Reprinted in *Dene Nation — The Colony Within*, edited by Mel Watkins for the University League for Social Reform. Copyright 1977 by University of Toronto Press.

Colonialism and imperialism are now dead or dying. Recent years have witnessed the birth of new nations or rebirth of old nations out of the ashes of colonialism.

As Europe is the place where you will find European countries with European governments for European peoples, now also you will find in Africa and Asia the existence of African and Asian countries with African and Asian governments for the African and Asian peoples.

The African and Asian peoples — the peoples of the Third World — have fought for and won the right to self-determination, the right to recognition as distinct peoples and the recognition of themselves as nations.

But in the New World the Native peoples have not fared so well. Even in countries in South America where the Native peoples are the vast majority of the population *there is not one country which has an Amerindian government for the Amerindian peoples.*

594
Nowhere in the New World have the Native peoples won the right to self-determination and the right to recognition by the world as a distinct people and as Nations.

While the Native people of Canada are a minority in their homeland, the Native people of the Northwest Territories, the Dene and the Inuit, are a majority of the population of the Northwest Territories.

The Dene find themselves as part of a country. That country is Canada. But the Government of Canada is not the government of the Dene. The Government of the Northwest Territories is not the government of the Dene. These governments were not the choice of the Dene, they were imposed upon the Dene.

What we the Dene are struggling for is the recognition of the Dene nation by the governments and peoples of the world.

And while there are realities we are forced to submit to, such as the existence of a country called Canada, we insist on the right to self-determination as a distinct people and the recognition of the Dene Nation.

We the Dene are part of the Fourth World. And as the peoples and Nations of the world have come to recognize the existence and rights of those peoples who make up the Third World the day must come and will come when the nations of the Fourth World will come to be recognized and respected. The challenge to the Dene and the world is to find the way for the recognition of the Dene Nation.

Our plea to the world is to help us in our struggle to find a place in the world community where we can exercise our right to self-determination as a distinct people and as a nation.

What we seek then is independence and self-determination within the country of Canada. This is what we mean when we call for a just land settlement for the Dene Nation.

This Declaration was passed at the 2nd Joint General Assembly of the Indian Brotherhood of the NWT and the Metis Association of the NWT on 19 July 1975 at Fort Simpson.

Topic Fifteen

Quebec and Canada

There has long existed tension in Quebec between those who see Quebec as part of Canada and those who favour independence. Until recently the former were clearly in the majority, and Quebec's position within Confederation seemed assured. Since the 1960s, separatist feelings have grown considerably, to the point where the outcome is no longer predictable.

The "Quiet Revolution" of the 1960s inaugurated a number of major changes in Quebec society. The provincial government took a more active role in economic, social, and cultural affairs than it had done previously. The hydroelectric industry was nationalized, the educational system restructured and brought under government control, the civil service reformed and broadened, and a new labour code instituted. Québécois came to grips with the realization that theirs was an urban-industrial society contrary to the popular image of French Canadians as a rural and agricultural people. There arose a new bureaucratic middle class to direct social and economic development. The result was a strong sense of French-Canadian nationalism, which became associated with the province of Quebec. This nationalism heightened Quebec's demand for greater control over fiscal matters and brought the province into further conflict with the federal government on the question of federal-provincial jurisdiction.

Since the sixties, this nationalism has increasingly taken the form of separatism. A substantial group of "indépendantistes" argue that Quebec must separate from the rest of Canada if it is to regain control over its economy and society and maintain the French-Canadian nationality. They point to the weakening position of French Canadians outside the province as evidence of the danger that besets Quebec within Confederation. The separatist groups united in 1968 to form the Parti Québécois under René Lévesque's leadership. They achieved a major breakthrough when the Parti Québécois defeated the Liberal party of Robert Bourassa and achieved power in November 1976. As promised, the Parti Québécois government introduced a referendum on sovereignty-association in May 1980. Their position is outlined in *Quebec-Canada: A New Deal.*

Federalists

Those supporting the federalist position continue to be numerous in Quebec. This group argues that Quebec has consistently won major concessions within Canada as a result of strong political representation in Ottawa; French-Canadian rights are more recognized today than at any other time in the past; French Canadians should continue to fight for a better position, but within Confederation. This view is associated politically with the Quebec Liberal party. *A New Canadian Federation* summarizes the party's position.

Richard Jones presents an overview of Quebec/Canadian developments from 1960 to the summer of 1981 in "French Canada and English Canada: Conflict and Coexistence".

596

For overviews of Quebec in the last half century, Kenneth Postgate and Dale McRobert's *Quebec: Social Change and Political Crisis*, revised edition (Toronto: McClelland and Stewart, 1980), Sheilagh and Henry Milner's *The Decolonization of Quebec* (Toronto: McClelland and Stewart, 1973), and Henry Milner's *Politics in the New Quebec* (Toronto: McClelland and Stewart, 1978) are recommended. René Lévesque's early volume, *Option Québec* (Montreal: Editions de l'Homme, 1968) is available in an English translation by Alan Brown as *An Option for Quebec* (Toronto: McClelland and Stewart, 1968). The opinions of Pierre Elliott Trudeau are presented in his *Le fédéralisme et la société canadienne-française* (Montreal: HMH, 1967), translated by Joanne l'Heureux and Patricia Claxton as *Federalism and the French Canadians* (Toronto: Macmillan, 1968). In *The Rise of the Parti Québécois* (Toronto: University of Toronto Press, 1977), John Saywell has sketched the early history of the party. La Fédération des Francophones hors Québec in 1977 published *Les héritiers de Lord Durham*, a useful study of French-speaking Canadians outside Quebec. It has been translated by Diane Norak as *The Heirs of Lord Durham: Manifesto of a Vanishing People* (Toronto: Burns and MacEachern, 1978). Michel Brunet's "The French Canadians' Search for a Fatherland" in *Nationalism in Canada*, edited by Peter Russell (Toronto: McGraw-Hill, 1966), pp. 47-60, is also helpful. Sheila McLeod Arnopoulos and Dominique Clift review the state of the English-speaking community in Quebec in *The English Fact in Quebec* (Montreal: McGill-Queen's University Press, 1980). For a radical interpretation of Quebec in the mid-twentieth century, see *Nègres blancs d'Amérique* by Pierre Vallières (Montreal: Parti pris, 1968), translated as *White Niggers of America* by Joan Pinkham (Toronto: McClelland and Stewart, 1971).

For two Quebec sociologists' views of Quebec's past, present, and future, consult Marcel Rioux's *La Question du Québec* (Paris: Seghers, 1969), translated as *Quebec in Question* by James Boake (Toronto: James Lewis and Samuel, 1971), and Fernand Dumont's *La Vigile du Québec. Octobre 1970: L'impasse?* (Montreal: HMH, 1971), translated by Sheila Fischman and Richard Howard as *The Vigil of Quebec* (Toronto: University of Toronto Press, 1974). A useful summary of Quebec's aspirations is provided by André Bernard in *What Does Quebec Want?* (Toronto: James Lorimer, 1978).

For an overview of the development of political thought in Quebec, Denis Monière's *Le développement des idéologies au Québec: des origines à nos jours* (Montreal: Editions Québec/Amérique, 1977) has been translated as *Ideologies in Quebec: The Historical Development*, by Richard Howard (Toronto: University of Toronto Press, 1981). Monière's study of the background to the referendum of May 1980 is entitled *Les Enjeux du Referendum* (Montreal: Québec/Amérique, 1979).

Quebec–Canada: A New Deal *

THE PARTI QUÉBÉCOIS

Our ancestors put down their roots in American soil at the beginning of the 17th century, cleared the land of the St. Lawrence Valley and . . . by 1760 they already formed a distinct society which would sooner or later have freed itself of the colonial yoke as did the United States in 1776. But in 1763 they came under British rule.

They chose to remain faithful; they withdrew to the countryside and patiently rebuilt their country. The 60 000 Francophones of the time gradually strengthened their institutions . . . They also made good the numbers they had lacked in 1760; doubling their population every 25 years, they totalled 500 000 by about 1835 . . .

The 1867 Confederation was a federation in name only; the central government, far from being a reflection of the provinces, dominated them in fact, even to the point of deciding on the direction they were to take, thanks to the power it held.

The federal Parliament had exclusive jurisdiction in all the fields deemed essential to the development of a State: transportation, criminal law, money, banking, fisheries, excise and customs duties, interprovincial and international trade; the federal government could also tax and spend as it pleased, make laws on all questions of "national" interest, disallow any provincial statute which appeared to encroach upon its authority, and exercise jurisdiction in any field not covered by the constitution. In other words, it had all the powers it needed to ensure its ascendancy, and that of English Canada.

The provinces had jurisdiction in fields considered at that time to be of purely local interest. And in every respect, Quebec was merely a province like all the others . . .

As a minority within the federal system, Quebecers could no longer make their voices heard, or at any rate heeded; even less were they able to obtain satisfaction. What Quebecers wanted in 1867 was to be able to manage their own affairs and build their own future. Not only were they

597

* From *Quebec–Canada: a New Deal*, a publication of the Parti Québécois, 1979. Abridged by Canadian Press. Reprinted by permission.

unsuccessful, but they even had to submit to interference by the central government in the fields under Quebec's jurisdiction, to look on while its rights and powers were continually eroded. From the outset our federal system has manifested an implacable tendency to centralize . . .

Quebec has, of course, constantly attempted to resist this centralizing trend, particularly in recent years. Duplessis, Sauvé, Lesage, Johnson, Bertrand and Bourassa all struggled to safeguard or even repatriate our powers and fiscal resources. But they were barely able to slow down the centralization, a situation which produced increasingly pronounced overlapping and duplication in almost every area of government activity. The citizen finally loses his bearings; he pays double income tax; he suffers from the administrative confusion resulting from this unacceptable situation, and he must foot the bill for wasted time, energy and money, the total cost of which is difficult to calculate.

In an attempt to settle virtually insoluble problems, committees are set up . . .

598

And while precious time is lost running from committee meeting to conference and back, we men and women of Quebec are becoming an ever-dwindling minority; accounting for 36 per cent of the population in 1851, we made up only 28 per cent in 1971; in 2001, we shall represent only 23 per cent. . . .

It is illusory to believe that under such circumstances Quebecers can play a decisive role within the Government of Canada. On the contrary, they will become a smaller and smaller minority, and it will become increasingly easier for the rest of Canada to govern without them. In this respect the Clark government is far from being an anomaly: it is a sign of the future.

Under the terms of the British North America Act Quebec is not the homeland of a nation, but merely a province among others. Nowhere in the British North America Act is there talk of an alliance between two founding peoples, or of a pact between two nations; on the contrary, there is talk of political and territorial unity, and of a national government which essentially dictates the direction the regional governments are to take. The English provinces know the score since, despite regional differences, they have always considered the central government to be the "senior government," the one that takes precedence over the others — from the point of view of the heart as well as the mind — and the one to which one owes allegiance. It appears certain that in 1867, the Anglophones of Canada saw the British North America Act as simply a British law, not a pact between two nations.

Though federalism is not necessarily synonymous with poverty and political domination, neither is it a guarantee of freedom or a high standard of living; and it is no more the formula of the future than the unitary state is the formula of the past. In fact there are several kinds of federalism: some are found in rich countries, others in poor countries; some in democratic regimes, others in dictatorships . . .

An insurmountable obstacle blocks the way to "renewed federalism." In order to strengthen Quebec, to build it, Quebecers must, as the system now stands, ask English Canadians to undermine and dismantle their national institutions. To respond to Quebec's needs and ensure its development, it would indeed be necessary to transfer to all the provinces so many powers that now belong to Ottawa that it would add up, in the eyes of English Canadians, to the almost total disappearance of the central government.

Logic of the system

Of course English Canadians say they are ready to improve the system. But we must be wary of words: the expression "renewed federalism," very much in fashion these days, can have many meanings.

Certain Quebecers, when they talk of "renewed federalism" because they are dissatisfied with the status quo, think of a serious and substantial transformation of the system, not a cosmetic job.

599

English Canadians, on the other hand, give quite a different meaning to the term: it is a "touched up" federalism that they want, since they feel that any reform must totally respect the role and the prerogatives of the central government, seen as the "national government" of all Canadians . . .

The very balance of the system, as the Canadian majority wants it, requires that Quebec remain a province — or perhaps a territory — among ten others, and forbids the formal and concrete recognition of a Quebec nation. The fact that it is impossible, in the present federal framework, for Quebec to become a nation, constitutes the very basis of the Canada–Quebec political problem.

Special status

Some Quebecers believe in good faith that the answer to the problem is to give Quebec a special status. The idea, fashionable during the sixties . . . seems to have the advantage of answering a good many of Quebec's aspirations without forcing other provinces into constitutional rearrangements they do not want. But this solution is rejected out of hand by English Canada, which has always been opposed to Quebec's possible acquisition of powers denied to the other provinces . . .

One simple conclusion can be drawn from all these observations. If we want both to save the present system and to renew federalism, we will have to resign ourselves to giving up to the central government, in which Quebecers will always be a minority, an impressive number of prerogatives and decision-making centres that to date Quebec has been demanding for itself. For Quebecers that would mean implicitly accepting the fact that control over some of their most vital affairs would go to a government over which they could never exert more than an indirect or passing influence; it would mean entrusting their interests and their future to others. Very few nations in the world would be satisfied with such an arrangement . . .

The recent history of international relations shows that federalism can no longer be regarded as the only formula capable of reconciling the objectives of autonomy and interdependence. Although it was fashionable in the past century, the federal formula must now give way to associations between sovereign countries. While no new federations are being created, economic associations are on the increase on every continent.

Basing itself firmly on the historical trend of Quebec thinking, which has always sought to redefine relations between Quebec and the rest of Canada on a more egalitarian basis, the Government of Quebec proposes this type of modern formula of association between sovereign countries to ensure for Quebecers a better control of their own affairs, without shattering the Canadian economic framework . . . The Quebec government wants to propose to the rest of Canada that the two communities remain in association, not only in a customs union and a common market but in a monetary union as well . . .

600   Through sovereignty, Quebec would acquire, in addition to the political powers it already has, those now exercised by Ottawa.

Sovereign powers

Sovereignty is the power to levy all taxes, to make all laws and to be present on the international scene; it is also the possibility of sharing freely, with one or more states, certain national powers. Sovereignty for Quebec, then, will have a legal impact on the power to make laws and to levy taxes, on territorial integrity, on citizenship and minorities, on the courts and various other institutions, and on the relations of Quebec with other countries.

The only laws applying on Quebec's territory will be those adopted by the National Assembly, and the only taxes levied will be those decreed by Quebec law. In this way, there will be an end to the overlapping of federal and Quebec services . . .

Existing federal laws will continue to apply as Quebec laws, as long as they are not amended, repealed or replaced by the National Assembly.

Quebec has an inalienable right over its territory, recognized even in the present Constitution, which states that the territory of a province cannot be modified without the consent of that province. In becoming sovereign, Quebec, as is the rule in international law, will thus maintain its territorial integrity.

The Quebec government gives its solemn commitment that every Canadian who, at the time sovereignty is achieved, is a resident of Quebec, or any person who was born there, will have an automatic right to Quebec citizenship; the landed immigrant will be able to complete residency requirements and obtain citizenship.

Quebec citizenship will be recognized by a distinct passport, which does not rule out the possibility of an agreement with Canada on a common passport.

The government pledges that Quebec's Anglophone minority will continue to enjoy the rights now accorded it by law, and that other communities in Quebec will be given the means to develop their cultural resources.

The Amerindian and Inuit communities, if they so desire, will be in full possession on their territory of institutions that maintain the integrity of their societies and enable them to develop freely, according to their own culture and spirit.

Interdependence

Quebec has never wanted to live in isolation; from the start it has accepted interdependence. However, it wishes to ensure that it will be directly involved in determining the terms of this interdependence.

To this end, the Quebec government intends to offer to negotiate with the rest of Canada a treaty of community association, whose aim will be, notably, to maintain the present Canadian economic entity by ensuring continuity of exchange and by favouring, in the long run, a more rapid and better balanced development of each of the two partners.

601

This treaty will have an international status and will bind the parties in a manner and for a term to be determined. It will define the partners' areas of common activity and confirm the maintenance of an economic and monetary union between Quebec and the rest of Canada. It will also determine the areas where agreement on goals is considered desirable. Finally, it will establish the rules and institutions to ensure the proper functioning of the Quebec-Canada community, and determine its methods of financing.

Common action

Areas of common action will include:

Free circulation of goods

In order to ensure the free circulation of goods, the present situation in Quebec and Canada will be maintained, and each party will renounce any right to customs barriers at common borders. With regard to foreign countries, the partners will jointly establish the tariff protection they deem necessary, taking into account the short and long-term interests of each of the parties, and multilateral agreements in the areas of trade and customs tariffs.

Monetary Union

The dollar will be maintained as the only currency having legal tender, and real or liquid assets as well as letters of credit will continue to be expressed in dollars. Circulation of capital will be free, but each party will be entitled to proclaim an investment code or to adopt, if need be, particular regulations applicable to certain financial institutions.

Free Movement of People

In order to ensure the free movement of people from one territory to the other, the two States will give up their right to impose a regular police control at their common border. It goes without saying that no passport will be required between Quebec and Canada.

In one of the outstanding documents of our time, the Club of Rome clearly identified the essential conditions for progress in modern societies: according to this prestigious body, the future belongs to countries whose population is young and well educated, which have abundant natural resources and which specialize in international exchanges.

We, in Quebec, have the resources, the talent and the knowledge enabling us to assume, quite calmly, control of our own affairs and to meet the challenges of our general growth, notably in the economic area. For this, we hold trump cards, which might even be called exceptional.

Why then should we be content with an inferior political status?

602

We are already a rich country. In 1978, our per capita Gross Domestic Product ranked Quebec 14th among 150 countries in the world. This is not a matter of chance, the result of some political system or some magnanimous gift from outside; our standard of living is based essentially on our wealth of resources, on our advantageous geographical position, close to rich markets, and on the stimulating effect of the North American environment.

And our country is vast; Quebec ranks 16th in area among the 150-odd countries in the world. It is true that it has only six million inhabitants, but standard of living has nothing to do with the size of a population. Some highly populated countries, such as the United States, France and the Federal Republic of Germany, enjoy high standards of living, but it is striking and noteworthy that five of the six richest countries in the world, Switzerland, Denmark, Sweden, Norway and Belgium, have a population of less than ten million, as does Quebec. On the other hand, countries with the largest populations are often the poorest . . .

Respect for diversity

Sovereignty will not change the policy Quebec has always followed regarding the various cultural communities that make up its people and reflect the cultural riches of our planet. It is in the interest of those communities, as well as of Quebec, that they assert and develop that part of themselves which is essential to their heritage . . .

As for Francophones living outside Quebec, the government promises them the support and solidarity of Quebecers. In an association between equals with the rest of Canada, Quebec will be able to give them the financial and technical help it already provides, and make it easier for those who so wish to settle on its territory. Moreover, reciprocity agreements that would give them the same advantages now enjoyed by Anglophone

Quebecers could preserve many of them from assimilation, which in their present conditions they rightly fear . . .

Quebec will be in a better position to take advantage of its major assets if, as a community, it has new instruments in hand, instruments such as it has never had before. The assumption is that in any society that wants to progress, the impetus must come first and foremost from within — from that society itself. Sweden, Japan, France and Germany, whose performances are remarkable, owe almost nothing to outside help: they owe what they have to the resources and know-how of their own people. Quebec too will follow that fundamental rule: its future rests primarily on Quebecers' increased sense of responsibility and their determination to help themselves.

Mutual areas

To ensure the proper functioning of the monetary and economic community, the two parties will agree on certain goals and types of legislation. This will be the case, notably, in the area of transportation, where it will be possible to make special agreements for railways, air transportation, and inland shipping; such agreements could also provide for joint management of public carriers, Air Canada and Canadian National, for example. Such efforts could be extended to several other areas, in particular defence . . .

In association between two partners, some fundamental subjects must naturally be subjected to parity, otherwise one of the parties would be at the mercy of the other. That does not mean, however, that in everyday practice everything will be subject to a double veto. Certain institutions of the union (the monetary authority, for instance) would, on the contrary, enjoy a large measure of autonomy of management . . .

The Referendum

The Referendum, by directly involving citizens in a debate that has always been the preserve of politicians, will add to the Quebec-Ottawa dispute an element of greater consequence, more decisive than all the files and protest meetings and public statements which so far have brought no results: the democratically expressed will of Quebecers.

This is the main objective of the Referendum. Opponents of the Referendum, aware that a positive answer, democratically expressed under the eyes of the international community, would force Ottawa and the rest of Canada to react in the same democratic way in an attempt to avoid embarrassment, have devoted themselves to convincing Quebecers that a positive answer would be useless since, in their opinion, the rest of Canada would never agree to negotiate the implementation of sovereignty-association.

Many English-Canadian personalities, politicians and others, tell anyone who will listen that they will categorically refuse to negotiate. This is quite fair, though rather crude. We must not be taken in by it but must, on the contrary, stand firm in our conviction that if the majority of Quebecers

603

say YES in the Referendum, Ottawa and the rest of Canada, though they will be disappointed, will have no choice: they will negotiate.

Those Canadian citizens and leaders are realists; they recognize, among other things, the importance of the economic links between Quebec and the rest of Canada, and that it is much better to maintain them than to break and split up markets. Quebec proposes specifically to maintain the existing economic entity rather than break it up.

Economic association, which some English-Canadian spokesmen say will automatically be rejected should there be a YES in the Referendum, already exists insofar as its essentials are concerned, as explained above, and the Quebec government does not challenge it. What it does propose, quite firmly, is to negotiate its structures and its decision-making processes. Under these circumstances, stating that there will be no economic association is tantamount to saying that English Canada is ready to get along without the Quebec market, that it will create its own separate currency to avoid sharing one with Quebec, and that the Maritimes will agree to having a customs barrier put up between them and Ontario! It would then be the rest of Canada that would reject the advantages of economic union . . .

If statements about the possibility of a refusal to negotiate cannot, as we have just seen, justify a negative answer in the Referendum, it is still appropriate to ask what the consequences of such an answer would be for Quebec's future . . .

If they get the NO they want, Ottawa and the rest of Canada, buoyed up by a sense of relief and a bit of simplification, would inevitably conclude that, although somewhat late in the game, Quebecers are resigned and prepared to embrace the present federal system with no special demands, that they have finally chosen the status quo.

The mandate

By giving a positive answer in the Referendum, Quebecers will express their desire to reach a new political agreement with the rest of Canada based, this time, on the legal equality of the two peoples. A YES vote by Quebecers would thus be, in fact, a mandate given the Quebec government to make this new agreement a reality through negotiation. By its vote, the Quebec people will have clearly established the negotiations on the principle of Quebec's accession, in law and in fact, to the status of sovereign state, and association with Canada. Sovereignty is inseparable from association . . .

The Quebec government has always believed that it would take time to achieve the orderly and democratic constitutional change proposed. The transformation of the present federal system into an association between sovereign states can occur only through successive stages. The process proposed thus includes four major phases:

Reflection

Publication of this document is a decisive step in the phase of reflection and consultation to which all citizens are invited, so that they will know the exact content of what they will be asked to decide upon . . .

Referendum

Early in February 1980, the National Assembly should begin the debate on a motion by the Prime Minister proposing the adoption of the text of the question to be submitted to the voters. The text of this question, as the government has pledged, will be revealed before the end of this year, so that no one will be taken by surprise at the time of the debate, at the end of which it will be adopted.

Once the question is approved, the referendum writs will be issued in April or May, so that the vote can be held in May or June 1980.

(Note: The text of the question will be bilingual).

Negotiation

If the result of the Referendum is positive, there will be a period of negotiation with Ottawa and the rest of Canada. Then Quebec will have unprecedented power at its disposal, based for the first time on the clearly expressed will of the Quebec population. These negotiations should bear first on the repatriation to Quebec of those powers exercised by the federal Parliament, and on the transfer of the corresponding resources.

Negotiations will also bear on the nature of the Quebec-Canada association, its content (the powers to be shared), institutions, rules of procedure and financing; other questions to be dealt with include territory, the protection of minorities, citizenship, the transfer of federal civil servants, the armed forces, etc.

All these negotiations will lead to the preparation of a treaty of association creating the Quebec-Canada community.

Implementation

It is necessary to ensure that during the period of transfer of powers the population does not to suffer any decrease in government services. The transition must be planned in the preceding phase so as to avoid upsetting the operation of the administration. That will require agreement on a schedule for the transfers and a gradual establishment of the various services involved.

Acquired Rights

The Government of Quebec, not wanting any individual to be deprived of his or her rights as a result of this constitutional change, pledges to maintain acquired rights — allowances, pensions, services or jobs. The government also promises federal civil servants, if they are residents of Quebec and so wish, that they will be integrated into the Quebec civil service, without financial loss to them, as powers and resources are transferred from Ottawa to Quebec.

Beige Paper?

A New Canadian Federation*
THE LIBERAL PARTY OF QUEBEC

At a moment when Quebecers are preparing to make an historic decision on their collective future, they have every right to ask that the major options competing for their loyalty be presented to them honestly and clearly.

The government of Quebec, led by the Parti Québécois, has already made public the broad outline of its option, sovereignty-association, in the white paper entitled "Quebec-Canada: A New Deal."

One objective emerges clearly from the white paper. The Parti Québécois and the present government, propose to make Quebec a fully sovereign state.

It is true the government's white paper also proposes an economic association between the future sovereign state of Quebec and whatever remains of Canada.

But such an economic association, even in the event of a "yes" vote in the referendum, appears highly improbable. It would depend upon the consent of the other partner, without which it could not come into being.

The Péquiste view of our collective future is new in terms of the radical solution it proposes. However, their resolutely pessimistic view of our past history and our present situation is all too familiar.

In this frame of mind, they perpetuate an attitude which was held by the opponents of Confederation in the last century.

During the years which preceded the proclamation of the BNA Act, the enemies of this new constitution pronounced it to be a suicidal adventure for the people of Quebec. They predicted freely that Quebec and its traditions would be devoured by the Canadian federation, that it would mark the end of our culture and our own institutions.

It is this same theme, with a few variations, which forms the basis of the Péquiste refrain.

But alongside this negative attitude, there has always existed in Quebec another viewpoint, resolutely open to a more optimistic perspective of confidence and co-operation.

Those who hold this vision have always defended the existence in Quebec of a distinct and unique society, with all the attributes of a national community. Far from denigrating the Quebec government's key role in the development of this community, they are its very architects, the ones who have built and strengthened it.

The exponents of this larger vision unhesitatingly affirm the right of the people of Quebec to choose their own future.

*From *A New Canadian Federation*, a publication of the Liberal Party of Quebec, 1980. Abridged by Canadian Press. Reprinted by permission.

606

But today, as in 1867, they believe profoundly that the best future for Quebec lies in a freely-made decision to remain within the Canadian federation.

In their eyes, the Canadian federal framework provides Quebec with two major advantages: the chance to develop freely, in accordance with its own nature, and at the same time to participate, without renouncing its own identity, in the benefits and challenges of a larger and much richer society.

The Quebec Fathers of Confederation did not fear the assimilation of Quebec in 1867. They believed that the federal challenge presented a unique occasion for the disparate colonies of that day to form a great country, one in which Quebec would be called upon to play a major role.

Those who defend the federal tie today are the true inheritors of that vision.

It is certainly necessary to review in depth the constitutional arrangements bequeathed to us in 1867. The venture has become urgent in the light of current tensions which have been generated not only in Quebec but elsewhere, and particularly in Western Canada.

But a realistic and honest evaluation of the Canadian federation can lead to only one conclusion — the assets far outweigh the liabilities.

In the short run, however, the primary and most urgent source of anxiety for the future of Canada comes from a problem as old as the federation itself; the relationship between the two founding peoples. The problem has never been resolved and is today more urgent than ever before.

It is evident that the only reasonably satisfactory relationship is one which is based on equality, an equality accepted by both parties.

However, in the past, francophones, because they were less numerous and much too frequently excluded from important decisions, came to the conclusion that equality worked in only one direction and remained, for them, a platitude, void of content.

For many years the problem presented itself in terms of the linguistic rights of francophones outside Quebec.

In 1867, the French believed that the new constitution guaranteed, at least in principle, the equality of French and English across the new Canadian territory. But the reality was quite different.

Almost everywhere outside of Quebec, the French language was relegated to second-class status.

Since throughout this period the minority language rights of anglophone Quebecers were scrupulously respected, francophones had every right to complain about the disregard in which their rights were held in the federal government, in the other provinces, and indeed, in important sectors of activity within Quebec itself.

It was one hundred years before Parliament began to resolve the situation. The federal Official Languages Act came into effect in 1969. And only in the course of the last twenty years have other provinces begun to redress injustices accumulated over a century.

Yet at a time when new measures have just begun to bear fruit, Quebec has toughened its language policy and oriented it in the direction of French unilingualism.

And at the same time that Quebec has been restricting the rights of the anglophone minority, it has been manifesting a reduced interest in the objective of achieving linguistic equality across the whole country.

So the question of linguistic rights remains critical. Recently some elements of a solution have begun to surface, but a just and durable constitutional resolution remains to be developed.

Before making a start on the project of constitutional reform, agreement should be reached on the objectives which are to be pursued.

We would establish the following as our fundamental goals:

1. We must aim at providing the people of this country with a written constitutional document, modern and Canadian. The document must be solemn and formal in character. It will define the commitment we have made to live together.

2. We must affirm the fundamental equality of the two founding peoples who have given, and still provide, this country its unique place in the family of nations.

3. We must ensure the judicial primacy of the rights and fundamental liberties of individual citizens in the Canadian political system.

4. We must affirm and give faithful recognition to the fundamental rights of the first inhabitants of this country.

5. We must acknowledge the richness of the cultural heritages of the different regions, and affirm Canada's interest in their preservation and development. We must also note the wealth of cultural, economic and social experience contributed by the ethnic groups, and assert their right to preserve their culture and heritage.

6. We must aim to provide equal access to economic, social and cultural development for all individuals, regions and provinces.

Keeping in mind provincial responsibilities in this area, we must, nevertheless, state clearly the federal government's fundamental role in the redistribution of wealth, and see that it is granted the necessary means for the efficient discharge of this responsibility.

7. We must maintain in Canada a federal system of government.

8. We must ensure the existence of a central power strong enough to serve the whole country in the face of whatever new challenges the modern world presents, whether internally or externally. .

9. We must ensure the existence of provincial powers strong enough to take charge, in their respective territories, of the tasks related to the development of their physical and human resources.

This implies, among other things, the management of their natural resources, land use, local and provincial commerce, regional economic development, education and culture, social and sanitary services, the administration of justice, and social insurance schemes.

Strong Prov power

10. We must aim at establishing a clear division of legislative and fiscal responsibilities between the two orders of government. We must also aim at eliminating powers which are too general in nature, which allow almost limitless extension and therefore lead to abuse.

11. We must aim to ensure that the very great disproportion in size among the member-states of the federation can be corrected by the eventual amalgamation of some services, while still respecting the acquired rights of each province.

12. We must establish a system of arbitration for constitutional disputes which recognizes the fundamental dualism of the population and the judicial institutions of this country, and which is above all suspicion.

Fed/prov conference

609

13. We must aim to recognize in the text of the constitution the fact that in almost all fields, any governmental action has international repercussions, a reality which has been magnified by the communications revolution.

We must affirm to need to harmonize provincial initiatives with the broad orientation of federal foreign policy. But we must draft this part of the constitutional text so that the province's role in those international activities relating to its areas of jurisdiction is recognized . . .

Recommendations

1. The constitution should preserve the parliamentary system and responsible government as the form by which the new federation and the provinces will be governed.

2. Constitutional usages and customs basic to the rules of procedure of the House of Commons and of the legislatures should be entrenched in the constitution.

3. The constitution should state that the House of Commons and the legislatures will meet annually, and that the duration of their mandate be no more than four years.

In emergency situations, the mandate could be prolonged for a period not to exceed one year by a two-thirds vote of the members of the House or the legislature.

4. The constitution should oblige the House of Commons and the legislatures to hold at least one session a year.

5. The constitution should recognize the principle of universal suffrage and of free elections to both the House of Commons and the legislatures.

The provinces

The provinces must be sovereign and autonomous in their fields of jurisdiction. This implies that the provinces' exclusive fields of jurisdiction must remain inviolable, except by constitutional amendment or by their approval expressed at the level of the Federal Council.

The provinces are also equal in law to each other. They all have the same powers, the same rights and the same obligations.

The provinces are administered today by legislatures composed of a lieutenant-governor and a legislative assembly. We propose to maintain this regime . . .

The Senate

Under the present constitution, the Canadian Senate has powers comparable to those of the House of Commons. It must approve all federal laws.

However, laws pertaining to taxation and to the use of public funds must first be presented in the House of Commons.

The Senate we have today was conceived at a time when it was deemed necessary to curb the democratic "excesses" of the members of Parliament elected through universal suffrage.

The Pépin-Robarts Report described numerous tasks which could have been carried out by the Senate.

They include the critical evaluation of the central government's bills, and their improvement, the protection of minority rights, the holding of enquiries, the encouragement of federal-provincial consultations in fields of common interest, and representation of the provinces on a basis fairer than that of a House elected through universal suffrage.

In practice, however, principally because of the nomination process which has been employed, the Senate has never been able to use all of the powers entrusted to it by the constitution.

For example, it has never played a significant role in federal-provincial relations.

Because this institution no longer seems to us to be adapted to the needs of a modern federal system, we propose that the Senate be abolished and that, henceforth, the federal Parliament be made up of only one body, the House of Commons. . . .

The Federal Council

It would have been difficult to imagine in 1867 the complex and vast operation which the governing of Canada was to become 100 years later.

It was, at the time, easy to conceive of two levels of government, central and provincial, working more or less independently. Intergovernmental relations involved only a few isolated subjects and except for these special cases, it was unnecessary to establish a formal delineation of federal-provincial relations.

Furthermore, the central government was equipped with extraordinary

610

powers which transcended the division of jurisdictions and which would enable it to ensure the cohesion needed to preserve and unify the federation.

However, particularly in the last thirty years, there has been an uninterrupted and explosive growth in government activity.

Tensions have developed because of the expansion of provincial governments combined with frequent incursions by the federal government into their exclusive jurisdictions.

The imbalance between the responsibilities of each level of government and their fiscal resources has also caused many frustrations. Legislative and administrative overlapping and duplication have multiplied.

It has become more and more evident that federal-provincial relations are not sufficiently defined and are often based on confrontation rather than consultation and cooperation

It has become more evident too, that in a modern federal system it is impossible to grant absolute jurisdiction to one or the other level of government in fields as complex as energy, industrial development, transport and social policy.

611

Constitutional reform will thus be inadequate if it simply improves the existing division of jurisdictions.

It is now imperative to invent an institution which will allow the provinces, which have become senior governments, to participate directly in the government of the federation itself, and to verify or influence, as the case may be, the federal government's actions in matters where consultation between the two levels of government is vital to the health of the federation.

The aim of such an institution is certainly not to prevent the central government from exercising sovereignty in the fields granted to it by the constitution.

Its aim is, rather, to ensure a better cohesion in Canadian policies, by allowing the provinces a say in the development of those federal initiatives which are so far-ranging that they affect the whole country and which, therefore, have implications for provincial jurisdictions.

Composition

This new institution would be known as the "Federal Council", to emphasize the fact that it is conceived as a special intergovernmental institution and not as a legislative assembly controlled by the central government.

The Federal Council would be formed by delegations from the provinces acting on the instructions of their respective governments. These provincial delegates would express the political policies of their governments and the length of their mandate would be determined in accordance with this principle.

The constitution would provide that the provincial premiers or their representatives would be ex officio members of their provinces' delegations.

There would be no delegates of the central government with a right to vote in the Federal Council.

The delegations and their voting procedure

In keeping with the nature of the Federal Council, provincial delegations would vote "en bloc" *according* to the instructions of their respective governments.

For example, a Federal Council of eighty members might be composed of the following delegations:

Prince Edward Island, 2 delegates; Newfoundland, 3 delegates; New Brunswick, 4 delegates; Nova Scotia, 4 delegates; Saskatchewan, 5 delegates; Manitoba, 5 delegates; Alberta, 8 delegates; British Columbia, 9 delegates; Ontario, 20 delegates; Quebec, 20 delegates.

Those territories which do not have the status of provinces, such as the Northwest Territories and the Yukon, nevertheless have important interests and issues which are their own and should enjoy full participation and voting rights at the Federal Council . . .

The Federal Council's jurisdiction should be limited to predetermined subjects and should be exercised in the following way:

a) the council will ratify:
— the use of the federal emergency power;
— the use of federal spending power in fields of provincial jurisdiction;
— any intergovernmental delegation of legislative powers;
— treaties concluded by the federal government in fields of provincial government in fields of provincial jurisdiction;
— international and interprovincial marketing programs of agricultural products;
— the appointment of judges of the Supreme Court and of its chief justice, and their destitution when required;
— the appointment of presidents and chief executive officers of those federal and Crown corporations of major importance;

b) the council will give its advice on the following questions:
— the monetary, budgetary and fiscal policies of the federal government;
— mechanisms and operating formulas used for equalization; and
— in general, on all matters having, in its opinion, substantial regional or provincial impact.

The council should reflect Canada's duality by means of a permanent committee half of which will be made up of francophone delegates, which will be convened whenever this dimension of the Canadian reality is likely to be affected by federal proposals submitted for the council's consideration;

The constitution will contain a provision ensuring the Federal Council the necessary human, physical and financial resources, while protecting its independence from the House of Commons and from the federal government. . .

612

Recommendations

1. The provinces should retain complete jurisdiction in matters of education and development of human resources.

2. The extent of this jurisdiction should be defined so as to cover the following matters:
   a) all levels of education;
   b) matters relating to the language of education, but subject to entrenched language rights;
   c) subsidies and bursaries;
   d) matters relating to social readaptation;
   e) manpower training;
   f) the training and control of trade associations and professional corporations; and
   g) the reception and integration of immigrants.

3. Research should not be considered as a separate head of jurisdiction but as a means of action to achieve objectives under the authority of either order of government.

613

4. The constitution should grant authority to the provinces in cultural matters including the arts, literature, leisure activities, cinema, theatre, plastic arts, radio and television programming, music, libraries, museums, archives, cultural exchanges, publishing and sports.

5. The federal government should be granted the specific powers necessary for the protection and development of the cultural heritage of all Canadians, including the power to create or maintain national institutions such as the Canadian Broadcasting Corporation, the national archives, a national library, the National Gallery and the National Film Board.

6. Aside from these specific jurisdictions, the federal government should be empowered to intervene in cultural matters on the basis of its spending powers. Such interventions should be subject to two-thirds approval by the Federal Council . . .

Other Recommendations

1. The constitution should be repatriated within the framework of an over-all agreement on the content and procedure for adoption of a new constitution.

2. The provincial governments and the federal government should assume the political responsibility for constitutional reform.

3. The mechanism for achieving the reform of the constitution should be a special federal-provincial conference.

4. Such a conference should be preceded by a commitment on the part of all the provincial legislatures and of Parliament to:
   — a) endow Canada with a new constitution and to repatriate the BNA Act;

— b) devote themselves without interruption to the project until it is completed;

— c) agree to increase representation by participating governments so that members of the opposition parties can be included, without voting rights.

5. When the project is completed, the new constitution should be submitted to the provincial legislatures and to Parliament for their approval. . .

French Canada and English Canada: Conflict and Coexistence*

RICHARD JONES

Historically, much has been made of Anglo-French antipathy and it is undoubtedly true that many incidents of an ethnic, linguistic or religious nature have occurred. Racial and religious prejudice and different national objectives, as well as insecurity on both sides, have been at the root of these conflicts. It is easy to understand French-Canadian and Catholic fears at a time when educational "rights" were being trodden upon and "democratically" suppressed by Anglo-Protestant majorities in New Brunswick, Manitoba, Alberta, Saskatchewan and Ontario. It is more difficult, in today's context at least, to believe that Anglophone fears at the turn of the century were equally as genuine. Indeed, many English-speaking Protestants were convinced that Catholic "papist" influence was a real and growing threat to Canada. They felt that a strong French-speaking minority or even a majority was a distinct possibility in Ontario as French Canadians overflowed into the province from neighbouring counties in Quebec, and that French-Canadian "domination" was preventing loyal British Canadians from properly accomplishing their imperial duties.

It was in 1917 during the conscription crisis that Anglo-French relations in Canada ebbed to their lowest point. Unionists were quite rabid in their determination to "make Quebec do her duty." In the course of the 1917 election campaign Sir William Hearst, the Ontario Premier, declared at Georgetown:

The issue today is: Shall Canada have a Union Government of all provinces and parties outside of Quebec, or shall a solid Quebec control the destiny of a divided Canada? Ontario must stand by the Union of the eight provinces, and must do so in a manner so emphatic and conclusive that Quebec domination will never again be attempted."

Pro-Unionist, pro-conscriptionist newspapers joined in the fray. "Men are not volunteering in English-speaking Canada for the express purpose of preserving to French Canadians the freedom to stay at home while

* Revised by the author from an article first published in *The Quarterly of Canadian Studies*, 4 (1976): 105–114. Reprinted by permission of the author.

others brave the dangers of war," editorialized the Toronto *Mail and Empire*. The same newspaper suspected the presence of "the 'hidden hand' of the Kaiser behind Quebec's desire not to reinforce troops overseas" and urged: "English Canada must deny Quebec and Germany's desire." At the time of the disastrous Halifax explosion in December 1917 the *Winnipeg Telegram* bemoaned the fact that the catastrophe had befallen such a patriotic and decent city and suggested that "in Quebec it would have been of inestimable value as an object lesson to those who made so little of the danger . . . of this war to Canada."

Meanwhile, Henri Bourassa, embittered by the virtual abolition of French-language schools in Ontario, his faith shaken in a Confederation that continually denied the rights of French-speaking and Catholic Canadians, drew the conclusion that insofar as the arrival of French Canada was concerned, the "Prussians of Ontario" were a far more dangerous and immediate threat than the Prussians of Germany. Clearly, French-English relations in Canada were at their nadir. It is true that the 1917 experience would be repeated during the Second World War, but this time the political sagacity of a King did much to mollify opinion.

Partisan political interests also contributed to racial bitterness. Throughout the lean years of the twentieth century, many Conservatives blamed Quebec and her Liberal loyalties for their misfortunes, and they not infrequently appealed for Anglo-Saxon unity in the face of what they esteemed to be Quebec's domination over Canada. "It is time to make [French Canadians] understand once and for all that we are English in an English country," proclaimed the Toronto *News* in 1900, for example. Some Anglo-Canadians whose sentiments ran along the same lines listened and undoubtedly voted for Conservative candidates. The theme did not change even when an English-speaking Canadian took over the leadership of the Liberal party after Laurier's death in 1919. During the election campaign of 1921, the Toronto *Telegram* could still advise its readers that W.L.M. King's victory (over the Conservative, Arthur Meighen) would signify that "Quebec, which refused to fight when Canada was in danger, would govern the country whose liberty had been brought by the other provinces at the price of their blood." After the election and King's victory, the weekly *Orange Sentinel* headlined: "French Canadians to govern Canada for five years!"

Liberal propagandists in Quebec were often not satisfied to proclaim simply that their party was the party of national unity; they did not fail to realize that they could turn Conservative denunciations of French Canada to their political advantage. Liberal newspapers in the province printed the defamatory remarks of Conservative dailies in Toronto in order to convince Quebec voters — if this were really necessary! — that there was no home for them in the Tory party.

Intergroup tensions involving French- and English-speaking Canadians are virtually a constant in Canadian history since the early nineteenth century and latent animosities have been quick to flare up given the particular

615

incidents or conditions. Those of an older generation who, today, yearn nostalgically for the good old days of *"bonne entente"* and national unity, thus appear to gloss over much of Canadian history.

II

This paper seeks to explore English-Canadian reactions to the evolution of French Canada since 1960. In Quebec, particularly in nationalist circles, it is easy to gather the impression that a large number of Anglo-Canadians continue to be the dedicated advocates of the cultural assimilation of French Canada, and that they sincerely believe that Canada is, or must be, an English-speaking country. This is scarcely surprising. Throughout the 1970s, the Official Languages Act was the object of vigorous criticism in English Canada, so much so that Francophones became increasingly skeptical of the federal government's promises to work towards equality in its own backyard. Indeed, when the bill was adopted by the House of Commons in 1969, seventeen Conservatives, led by former Prime Minister John Diefenbaker voted against it. During the debate one Tory member even maintained that "the cold hard fact is that Canadians of French origin should be learning English as fast as they can instead of the English learning French," because "English is the easier and more reasonable language to learn." Then in 1972 at the time of the federal election campaign, a backlash against bilingualism seems to have been responsible for the decline of Liberal fortunes in a certain number of constituencies in English Canada. Moreover, a host of other incidents and events have been easily construed in Quebec as evidence of the unextinguished desire of Anglophones to assimilate French Canada. A series of disputes over French-language schools, particularly in Ontario (Cornwall, Sturgeon Falls, Penetanguishene and elsewhere), helped stoke the fires of ethnic conflict. But perhaps no case in recent years aroused as much animosity as the use of French in air-to-air and air-to-ground communications in Quebec. When the Canadian Airline Pilots Association, supported by the English-language controllers, struck Air Canada illegally in June 1976 over the federal government's policy of implanting bilingualism at certain airports in Quebec, Prime Minister Pierre Trudeau termed the conflict "the gravest threat to national unity since the debate over military conscription during the Second World War." In addition, Quebec's language legislation, notably the Bourassa Liberal government's Bill 22 (adopted in 1974) and the Parti Québécois government's Language Charter (voted in 1977), provoked considerable antipathy in English Canada. In regard to these initiatives it has to be said, as any student of French Canada knows, that the fear of assimilation has been a dominant theme in that people's history for at least the past century and a half, and that like any minority, French Canadians are particularly sensitive to real or perceived threats to their existence.

Still, the notion of linguistic equality has made considerable headway in

Canada since the early 1960s. But throughout the period, those Anglo-Canadians accepting the principle of equality of the two communities have generally viewed the problem as being a question of individual free choice. Just as in Quebec, until the adoption of Bill 22 by the Bourassa government in 1974, all parents could choose the language of instruction for their children, so believers in linguistic equality began to admit that French Canadians in other provinces should have the same right. It should be noted that we are talking here of "rights," not "obligations." The fact that many French Canadians outside Quebec opted for an English-language education for their children, even when French-language schools were available, while within Quebec virtually all English-speaking citizens, as well as new Canadians of non-English, non-French origins, enrolled their children in English-language institutions, was irrelevant. The rights of the French speaking outside Quebec could and should be recognized. English Canada should be as generous to her French-speaking minority as Quebec was to her English-speaking minority.

617

To a growing number of Francophones, however, individual freedom of choice was not the solution to the French-speaking community's woes. Statistics demonstrate all too clearly that French Canada outside Quebec was being decimated by assimilation, and demographers were predicting that French Canada, in addition to forming a diminishing proportion of Canada's total population, would be increasingly concentrated within the province of Quebec. The 1971 census showed that fully 54.9% of so-called French Canadians in the English-speaking provinces were using English as the main language of communication at home, that 39.2% had English as their mother tongue — that is, the first language learned and still understood — and that 33.5% — fully a third of French Canadians outside Quebec — were unilingual Anglophones! In the far western provinces, precisely three quarters of French Canadians spoke English at home. Such, then, was the sorry state of the French-Canadian diaspora. Within Quebec, the French-speaking majority of nearly 80% was holding its own but doing very little assimilating. The vast majority of immigrants who arrived in the province in the years after the Second World War learned English as their second tongue and enrolled their children in the English-speaking school system. The "problem" was particularly evident in Montreal where most immigrants settled. So-called "freedom of choice" seemed to be working against French Canada. The attraction of the English language on a continent peopled by 250 million Anglophones was evident, and in the eyes of many French Canadians, the cards seemed to be stacked in advance against French Canada.

While Anglo-Quebeckers and other English-speaking Canadians continued to praise freedom of choice and to demand that it be legislated into law in Quebec, more and more French-speaking Quebeckers came to see legislative action by the Quebec government as a necessity to assure the long-term survival of French Canada. At first, the Quebec government seemed to heed the partisans of free choice: indeed in 1969 Jean-Jacques

Bertrand's Union Nationale government adopted Bill 63, which guaranteed free choice of language in the schools. This law, bitterly described by nationalist groups, was finally abrogated by the Bourassa government and replaced in 1974 by Bill 22 which for the first time curtailed access to English-language schools in Quebec. English Canada reacted bitterly to the new policy and newspapers editorialized that at a time when English Canada was ever more ready to recognize French-language rights, Quebec should not go against the current and revoke rights that it has always recognized for English speakers. The Union Nationale party under its new leader Rodrigue Biron began to advocate a return to free choice and large numbers of English-speaking voters actually deserted Robert Bourassa's Liberals and voted for the Union Nationale in the 1976 election. Their gesture aided the Parti Québécois in winning power on November 15. As it had promised, the Parti Québécois government repealed Bill 22 and replaced it by Bill 101, the French language charter. Bill 101 perhaps clarified the numerous ambiguities of Bill 22 in relation to the language of instruction but it also went further in limiting access to English schools; in addition, it stiffened the clauses relating to the language of work and publicity. English Canada could certainly not respond with enthusiasm to the new law. But it can probably be said that by the end of the decade those most concerned by the law, Anglo-Quebeckers and neo-Quebeckers, became at least resigned to the inevitable. There would be no return to free choice in Quebec in the foreseeable future. Polls show that the great majority of French Canadians support language legislation and specifically Bill 101 (except, perhaps, the clause which requires Canadians from other provinces moving to Quebec to enroll their children in French schools) and all political parties recognize this fact. The relative success of Bill 101 has undoubtedly had a positive effect on French Canada, perhaps diminishing the constant fear of assimilation and thus renders possible a type of coexistence with English Canada.

III

Evolution in Anglophone opinion in regard to French Canada was thus slow — painfully slow — and to a degree at least, it came about as a result of the threat of separatism. Premier Daniel Johnson's slogan, "Equality or Independence," may have been seen by some Anglo-Canadians as a form of blackmail but it undoubtedly made gentle persuasion a little firmer.

Complicating this trend towards greater cultural equality was the constitutional question: what was to be the place of the province of Quebec in the Canadian Confederation? When Quebec Premier Maurice Duplessis died in September 1959 and the Union Nationale government, in power since 1944, was finally ousted by a largely reborn Liberal party under Jean Lesage in the June 1960 elections, English Canada rejoiced. After all, Duplessis had had a bad press outside Quebec and his party's apparent demise brought forth few regrets. The period of reforms instituted over the next few years by the new Liberal government at almost all levels of Quebec society was quickly baptized the "Quiet Revolution." But as long as this remarkable upheaval seemed limited to problems associated with the political, economic and social modernization of Quebec, as long as its apparent aim was to bring the province in step with the rest of Canada and North America, it could only be approved by English Canadians. Nationalizing the hydro-electric system (as Ontario had done decades before), establishing a General Investment Corporation, rebuilding completely educational structures, creating a Minister of Cultural Affairs, reforming labour legislation, and revising the electoral law scarcely affected the rest of Canada nor Quebec's position within Confederation.

Still, throughout the 1960s, greater political and fiscal autonomy was a guideline for both Liberal and Union Nationale governments and a growing segment of Quebec's population leaned towards special status for the province or even independence. Indeed at the first interprovincial conference in more than three decades, held in Quebec City in December 1960, Quebec's new Liberal Premier, Jean Lesage, handed out copies of the Tremblay Report on constitutional problems to the other premiers. This report, submitted four years earlier, was an exposé of classical federalism and a veritable Bible of autonomism.

In the course of his six years in office, Lesage was involved in numerous confrontations with the federal government over such issues as tax-sharing, provincial opting-out of shared-cost projects, the establishment of a Quebec pension plan independent of the federal plan, and federal intervention into certain fields of action (such as loans to municipalities) judged by autonomists to be of provincial responsibility. These recurring incidents, however serious they may have been, were still a far cry from separatism, and it is well known that certain other provincial premiers, such as British Columbia's W.A.C. Bennett, maintained as strident a tone as Lesage.

Towards 1966 and 1967, with the return to power of the Union Nationale, Quebec's political claims began to evolve considerably. Premier Daniel Johnson argued that changed Canadian conditions made a new constitution imperative; a completely revised constitution would modify the separation of powers in favour of the provinces, and notably Quebec, and would offer solid guarantees — this time — that provincial autonomy would be respected.

The *Toronto Star*, discussing Quebec's "demands," linked together very neatly the province's claims to greater autonomy and French Canada's desires for linguistic equality.

If Quebec insists on autonomy, English-speaking Canadians will be less and less inclined to concede to French Canadians a strong influence in the federal government; moreover, in the other nine provinces, they will be less sympathetic in regard to the cultural and linguistic rights of Francophones.

The *Star* was simply admitting what many English Canadians were thinking and continued to think. If Quebec wanted cultural equality for French-speaking Canadians, it would have to be satisfied with political equality as one of the ten provinces, renouncing any claims to "special status." It could not both have its cake and eat it too!

Official English Canada seemed to become much more conciliatory on both the cultural and the constitutional questions for a brief moment at the end of 1967 and at the beginning of 1968. In November the provincial premiers gathered together in Toronto for the Confederation of Tomorrow Conference. Premier John Robarts appeared favourable to the implantation of most of the attributes of official bilingualism in Ontario and Premier Louis Robichaud promised to put both languages on an equal footing in New Brunswick. In a moving speech Premier G. I. Smith of Nova Scotia affirmed that he had a greater attachment for Canada than for a constitution. Even Premier Manning, who on the first day of the conference had taken an uncompromising stand against broader constitutional guarantees for the French language, seemed to join in the new spirit. "I want to see the legitimate interests of Quebec met," he declared. And on the subject of constitutional change he voiced the opinion that the B.N.A. Act had "nothing sacred about it" and that if the Canadian people so desired, it could be altered drastically. Had Daniel Johnson's more or less subtle hint — he promised to do his best to fight separatism by seeking rights for French Canadians outside Quebec — helped to sway certain English-speaking premiers?

This theme of accommodation also dominated the first meeting of the federal-provincial Constitutional Conference, held in Ottawa in February 1968. In a speech described by Daniel Johnson as "unprecedented in the history of Confederation," Premier Robarts stated specifically what Ontario would do in order to fulfil its obligations towards its French-speaking citizens: there would be language courses for civil servants and bilingual public services, members of the Legislative Assembly would have the right to speak either English or French in the House, certain municipalities would function bilingually, and so forth. At the conclusion of the conference the provinces were committed to the acceptance of the recommendations of the Royal Commission on Bilingualism and Biculturalism as well as to a search for means to implement them. In addition, elaborate machinery was set up to consider every aspect of the B.N.A. Act.

IV

This chapter of constitutional revision ended with the failure of the Victoria conference in June 1971. At that meeting, the seventh in the series that had begun in 1968, the federal government put forth an amending formula to the British North America Act that would permit the patriation of the Canadian constitution. In addition the separation of powers between the two levels of government was discussed, with Premier Bourassa insisting on constitutional recognition of provincial legislative primacy in the sphere of social policy. When Ottawa failed to yield to demands formulated by Bourassa and his social affairs minister, Claude Castonguay, Quebec vetoed the proposed charter. Actually, Quebec public opinion was quite divided on the question — but for considerable nationalist agitation, Premier Bourassa might well have signed the Victoria charter. Commenting on Quebec's decision, a somewhat bitter Pierre Trudeau said: "It's not likely that we're going to have other conferences on division of powers." One Liberal member of Parliament went even further, declaring: "We have to take a firm line toward the province of Quebec. We can't keep giving in and vacillating." And the *Globe and Mail*, "Canada's National Newspaper," editorialized: "Mr. Bourassa has proved that Quebec Premiers do not come to the bargaining table to bargain but to demand, to tell the rest of Canada, 'I deliver the pattern of the future and you abide by it.'" And it urged that the rest of Canada cease yielding to Quebec.

In examining the various political options presented in Quebec, English Canada has constantly searched for anti-separatist professions of faith. When Paul Gérin-Lajoie submitted his report on the constitution to the Liberal party in 1967, one Toronto newspaper asked if the ex-education minister were suggesting that his party reject separatism while at the same time accepting it in a slightly modified version and calling it by another name. Another Toronto daily agreed: "Perhaps René Lévesque was right in saying that the minimum demanded by Quebec greatly surpasses the maximum that the most well disposed of English Canadians are ready to concede." In any case it was quite natural that Anglophones welcomed the results of both the 1970 and 1973 provincial elections as proof that Quebec was firmly opposed to separatism and in favour of remaining in Confederation. Robert Bourassa based his sales campaign for federalism on its "profitability" for Quebeckers, in terms of dollars and cents. English Canadians, however, seemed to ignore these unpleasing realities.

The arrival of the Parti Québécois in power in November 1976 seemed to presage important changes on the Canadian constitutional stage. For the first time in Quebec, a separatist party took office pledging to hold a referendum on the province's political future and openly favouring the cause of "sovereignty-association," that is, political sovereignty for Quebec together with an economic association with the rest of Canada. Patriation of the Canadian constitution and even a revision of the current distribution of powers between the governments obviously seemed unimportant in the light of Quebec's new policy. Over the next four years, English Canada announced firmly and nearly unanimously that sovereignty-association was unacceptable and would not be negotiated with Quebec. When the Quebec government published a white paper in the fall of 1979 on the "new entente" proposed between Canada and Quebec, Joe Clark, then prime minister of Canada, judged the suggested treaty of association to be incompatible with the idea of federalism while Premier William Davis of Ontario, supported by the provincial legislature, affirmed that he would not negotiate such an accord with Quebec. The four western premiers also

621

reacted quite negatively, stating that sovereignty-association was in the interest neither of the West nor of the rest of Canada.

Prime Minister Pierre Trudeau intervened in a palpitating referendum campaign in the spring of 1980, declaring that a "yes" vote would lead to an impasse. On the other hand he promised that if Quebec voted "no," he would immediately put into motion the wheels of constitutional reform. On May 20 approximately 59% of Quebeckers did vote "no" to the question submitted by the Lévesque government, but efforts at constitutional renewal during the summer of 1980 again came to nought. The federal government then decided to proceed with the unilateral patriation of the constitution and to incorporate into the document a Charter of Rights. Only the provinces of Ontario and New Brunswick supported the federal measures, and Quebec thus found herself with numerous allies, although evidently the reason for opposition varied from one province to another. Undoubtedly the federal action reinforced the position of the Parti Québécois government and weakened Liberal leader Claude Ryan's chances in the provincial election which took place on April 13, 1981. But the governing party's chances were also strengthened by its decision to soft-pedal its constitutional option and by its pledge not to hold a second referendum in the course of a new mandate. In these circumstances it is not surprising that the wave of fright that swept across English Canada in the wake of the first victory in 1976 was little more than a ripple this time. Has English Canada concluded, in the wake of the referendum result and in the heat of the debate on energy and of the arduous negotiations with the province of Alberta, that the separatist threat from Quebec has been relegated to obscurity? In truth, it appears that Quebec's political clout has diminished and that, taking into account the relative stagnation of the province's population as well as its economic weaknesses, Quebec in the coming years will no longer pose the same threat as over the past twenty years. But then again, prophecy is not the task of the historian.